The Fair Labor Standards Act

2002 Cumulative Supplement

Current through August 2001

BNA Books Authored by the
ABA Section of Labor & Employment Law

Covenants Not to Compete: A State-by-State Survey

The Developing Labor Law

Discipline and Discharge in Arbitration

Elkouri & Elkouri: How Arbitration Works

Employee Benefits Law

Employee Duty of Loyalty: A State-by-State Survey

Employment Discrimination Law

Equal Employment Law Update

The Fair Labor Standards Act

How ADR Works

How to Take a Case Before the NLRB

International Labor and Employment Laws

Labor Arbitration: A Practical Guide for Advocates

Labor Arbitration: Cases and Materials for Advocates

Labor Arbitrator Development: A Handbook

Occupational Safety and Health Law

The Railway Labor Act

Trade Secrets: A State-by-State Survey

The Fair Labor Standards Act

2002 Cumulative Supplement

Current through August 2001

Editor-in-Chief

Monica Gallagher
Attorney-Consultant
Washington, DC

Associate Editors

David Borgen
Saperstein, Goldstein, Demchak & Baller, P.C.
Oakland, CA

Susan Nadler Eisenberg
Akerman Senterfitt
Miami, FL

Senior Editors

Joel M. Cohn
Akin, Gump, Strauss, Hauer & Feld, L.L.P.
Washington, DC

Ellen C. Kearns
Epstein Becker & Green, P.C.
Boston, MA

Sam J. Smith
Burr & Smith, L.L.P.
Tampa, FL

Federal Labor Standards Legislation Committee
Section of Labor and Employment Law
American Bar Association

The Bureau of National Affairs, Inc., Washington, DC

Library of Congress Cataloging-in-Publication Data

The Fair Labor Standards Act / editor-in-chief, Ellen C. Kearns ; senior editor, Monica Gallagher ; board of editors, Michael I. Bernstein... [et al.].
p. cm.
ISBN 1-57018-108-X
1. Wages–Law and legislation–United States. 2. Hours of labor–Law and legislation–United States. 3. Labor laws and legislation–United States. I. Kearns, Ellen C. II. Gallagher, Monica.

KF3484.528 .F35 1999
344.7301–dc21

99-055633

Published by BNA Books
1231 25th St., N.W., Washington, D.C. 20037
http://www.bnabooks.com

International Standard Book Number: 1-57018-338-4
Printed in the United States of America

DAVID F.E. BANKS
Cades, Schutte, Fleming & Wright
Honolulu, HI

FRANK E. BROWN
Zinober & McCrea, P.A.
Tampa, FL

MINDY ROWLAND BUENGER
DeWitt Ross & Stevens, S.C.
Madison, WI

KENNETH R. CARR
Carr Flora, P.C.
El Paso, TX

ROGER K. CRAWFORD
Best Best & Krieger, LLP
Riverside, CA

JEFFREY M. DAITZ
Peckar & Abramson, PC
River Edge, NJ

DAVID H. DIAMOND
Proskauer Rose, LLP
New York, NY

KIM J. DOCKSTADER
Stoel Rives LLP
Boise, ID

JAMES E. ERWIN
Strecker & Associates, P.C.
Tulsa, OK

NOAH FINKEL
Seyfarth Shaw
Chicago, IL

JUDD J. GOLDBERG
Akerman Senterfitt
Miami, FL

WENDY J. HARRISON
Bonnett Fairbourn Friedman & Balint, P.C.
Phoenix, AZ

JOHN S. HO
Rains & Pogrebin
Mineola, NY

HOWARD B. HOFFMAN
Attorney at Law
Baltimore, MD

WAYNE D. LANDSVERK
Newcomb, Sabin, Schwartz & Landsverk, LLP
Portland, OR

JOHAN W. E. MAITLAND
Gravel and Shea, P.C.
Burlington, VT

DENNIS M. MCCLELLAND
Holland & Knight LLP
Tampa, FL

GREGORY K. MCGILLIVARY
Woodley & McGillivary
Washington, DC

TYLER M. PAETKAU
Bingham McCutchen, LLP
Palo Alto, CA

VANESSA SORIANO POWER
Dorsey & Whitney, LLP
Seattle, WA

CHARLES M. POPLSTEIN
Thompson Coburn, LLP
St. Louis, MO

FOREWORD

Since 1945 the ABA Section of Labor and Employment Law has expanded its stated purposes in response to the evolution of the field. Currently, they include the following: (a) to study and report upon continuing developments in the field of labor and employment law; (b) to provide a forum for members of the Association interested in the field of labor and employment law to meet and confer; (c) to assist the professional growth and development of practitioners in the field of labor and employment law; (d) to establish and maintain working liaison with state, federal, and, where applicable, multi-national agencies having jurisdiction over matters affecting labor and employment law toward achieving procedural reform and administrative due process; (e) to study and report upon proposed and necessary legislation and rule making within the field encompassed by the jurisdiction of this Section; (f) to promote justice, human welfare, industrial peace, and the recognition of the supremacy of law in labor-management relations and the employment relationship; and (g) to establish, moderate, and sponsor seminars, workshops, forums, and other programs promoting the advancement of knowledge and practice in the field of labor and employment law.

Through the publication of books such as *The Fair Labor Standards Act* and through annual and committee meeting programs designed to provide a forum for the exchange of ideas, the Section has pursued these stated goals. Gradually, the Section has built a library of comprehensive legal works intended for the use of the Section membership as well as the Bar generally.

The Section of Labor and Employment Law is pleased to provide this 2002 Cumulative Supplement to its treatise on the Fair Labor Standards Act as part of its library of books published by BNA Books, a Division of The Bureau of National Affairs, Inc.

The combined efforts of many individual authors from the Federal Labor Standards Legislation Committee of the Section are reflected in this book.

The Section wishes to express its appreciation to the Committee members, and in particular to the editor-in-chief, Monica Gallagher, and to the associate and senior editors. This group has tried to accomplish two primary objectives: (1) to be equally balanced and nonpartisan in their viewpoints, and (2) to ensure the book is of significant value to the practitioner, student, and sophisticated nonlawyer.

The views expressed herein do not necessarily represent the views of the American Bar Association, or its Section of Labor and Employment Law, or any other organization, but are simply the collective, but not necessarily the individual, views of the authors. Information on the affiliation of government employees who contributed to this work is for informational purposes and does not constitute any official endorsement of the information provided herein.

JANA HOWARD CAREY
Chair

STEPHEN D. GORDON
Chair-Elect

Section of Labor
and Employment Law
American Bar Association

November 2002

PREFACE

This cumulative supplement to the Treatise follows the organization of the main volume, *The Fair Labor Standards Act,* and continues the practice of each previous supplement in adding new sections as indicated by developments.

The Table of Contents entries for this cumulative supplement show, by the use of boldface type, all the sections and subsections to which material has been added since the publication of the main volume. Those subsections which have been added since the publication of the main volume are further identified by use in the text and in the Table of Contents of the bracketed phrase "New Topic." For example, this volume of the supplement includes for the first time in Chapter 5, part IV, Section 7 Exemptions from the Overtime Requirements of the Act, a new subsection D., "Exemptions for Overtime for Employees of a Hospital or Other Establishments Engaged in Care of the Sick," identified in the text and in the Table of Contents as a New Topic. Another subsection not appearing in the main volume of the Treatise, but added to Chapter 18 in a previous cumulative supplement and also identified as a New Topic in the text and in the Table of Contents is subsection D. in part X, Damages, called "Integration with Other Federal Remedies." Yet another subsection not appearing in the main volume of the Treatise, but also added to Chapter 18 in a previous cumulative supplement and also identified as a New Topic in the text and in the Table of Contents, is section I. in part IV, Parties, called "Government Offices."

The Table of Contents does, but the text does not, contain headings where there have been no developments for publication under that heading since publication of the main volume.

This cumulative supplement updates the main volume through August 2001. Because all material included in previous supplements is present here, previous supplements may now be discarded.

The extensive and extremely valuable contributions made to this volume by the Senior Editors are gratefully acknowledged. Material appearing for the first time in this volume was principally brought to our attention by the midwinter 2002 report of the Subcommittee on Fair Labor Standards of the Federal Labor Standards Legislation Committee, Labor and Employment Law Section, under the leadership of David Borgen and Susan Nadler Eisenberg and with contributions made by Michael Aldana, Gavin S. Appleby, David F.E. Banks, Frank E. Brown, Mindy Rowland Buenger, Kenneth R. Carr, Roger K. Crawford, Jeffrey M. Daitz, David H. Diamond, Kim J. Dockstader, James E. Erwin, Noah Finkel, Judd J. Goldberg, Wendy J. Harrison, John S. Ho, Howard B. Hoffman, Wayne D. Landsverk, Johan W.E. Maitland, Dennis M. McClelland, Gregory K. McGillivary, Tyler M. Paetkau, Charles M. Poplstein, Vanessa Soriano Power, Julie L. Pulkrabek, Richard Dean Schramm, Lawrence D. Smith, Kate Tapley, Terry E. Thomason, Pamela J. Walker, Elizabeth S. Washko, and Andrea G. Woods. We would also like to acknowledge the support provided by the staffs of the firms of Mr. Borgen, Ms. Eisenberg, and many other contributors. Many others made valuable contributions without which this project could not have been completed; among these, very special thanks are due the Library and Editorial staff at BNA and BNA Books. We also thank the Section of Labor and Employment Law for its support and encouragement in this endeavor.

MONICA GALLAGHER
Editor-in-Chief

November 2002

ERRATA

The editors and the publisher continue to strive for accuracy and are grateful to users and readers for any errors found and brought to our attention. Any potential errors noted will be checked and subsequently corrected. Please forward information concerning possible errors to the editors by mail to Monica Gallagher, 611 G St. S.W., Washington, DC 20024, or by e-mail to Ikoniclast@aol.com.

Main Volume of Treatise:

1. p. 903, *Drollinger v. Arizona* (9th Cir. 1992) is incorrectly cited as 62 F.3d 956 and **should be cited as** 962 F.2d 956.

2. p. 1151, within footnote 27 in the paragraph beginning *Sixth Circuit,* the text of the final parenthetical, describing *Maloy v. Friedman,* which now reads "remanding to state court under pre-1848 removal provision," **should read** "remanding to state court under pre-1948 removal provision."

SUMMARY TABLE OF CONTENTS

DETAILED TABLE OF CONTENTS

CHAPTER 4. WHITE-COLLAR EXEMPTIONS

CHAPTER 16. RECORD-KEEPING

Chapter 1

BRIEF HISTORY OF THE FAIR LABOR STANDARDS ACT

IV. Significant Amendments to the FLSA

H. Small Business Job Protection Act; Other Developments [New Topic]

As noted in the Treatise,[1] in 1996 Congress amended the Fair Labor Standards Act to increase the minimum wage, effective September 1, 1997, to $5.15 per hour.[2]

---

[1]In this Supplement, "Treatise" refers to the main volume of The Fair Labor Standards Act, Kearns, E., & Gallagher, M., eds., BNA 1999. *See* Chapter 4, "White Collar Exemptions," §I [Overview].

[2]Small Business Job Protection Act, Pub. L. No. 104-188, §2104, 110 Stat. 1755, 1928 (1996).

VI. LATER LEGISLATIVE DEVELOPMENTS [NEW TOPIC]

Under the 1996 Small Business Job Protection Act,[3] employers and employees may agree on the use of employer-provided vehicles to commute to and from work at the beginning and end of the workday, without treating commuting time as hours of work.[4] Section 13(c) of the Act, relating to child labor, was amended in 1996 and in 1998. The 1996 amendments[5] modified the effect of the prohibitions of Child Labor Hazardous Order 12 to permit children 16 and 17 years old to load boxes and other paper products into paper balers and paper box compactors, but not to unload or operate the machines, so long as the machines meet certain design specifications.[6] The 1998 amendments[7] modified the application of Hazardous Order 2, relating to operation of motor vehicles. Employees under 17 years of age are prohibited from driving automobiles or trucks on public roadways, but employees 17 and 18 years of age are permitted to do so under the restrictions and conditions newly set forth.[8]

In August 1998, Congress amended the FLSA definition of "employee" by enacting the Amy Somers Volunteers at Food Banks Act.[9] The amendment excludes from the definition of "employee" individuals who volunteer at food banks for humani-

---

[3] *Id.*

[4] Employee Commuting Flexibility Act of 1996, Pub. L. No. 104-188, §2102, 110 Stat. 1755, 1928 (1996). The Seventh Circuit has held that this provision retroactively reversed a district court judgment in favor of plaintiffs who alleged that use of company trucks to commute to remote sites at the beginning of the day was compensable. Other provisions of the Small Business Job Protection Act of 1996 are covered in the main volume. *See* Treatise at Chapter 4, "White Collar Exemptions," §VII.C.4. [The Computer Occupation Professional].

[5] Compactors and Balers Safety Standards Modernization Act, Pub. L. No. 104-174, 110 Stat. 1553 (1996).

[6] *See* discussion at Chapter 12 of this supplement.

[7] Drive for Teen Employment Act, Pub. L. No. 105-334, 112 Stat. 3137 (1998).

[8] *See* discussion at Chapter 12 of this supplement.

[9] Pub. L. No. 105–221, 112 Stat. 1248 (1998) (codified at 29 U.S.C. §203(e)(5)) provides: "Section 3(e) of the Fair Labor Standards Act of 1938 (29 U.S.C. 203(e)) is amended by adding at the end the following: '(5) The term "employee" does not include individuals who volunteer their services solely for humanitarian purposes to private non-profit food banks and who receive from the food banks' groceries.'" *See* Appendix A.3 in this supplement.

tarian purposes, even if such individuals receive groceries from the food bank, which might otherwise be considered a form of compensation.

The 1998 Labor Department Appropriations Act made relatively minor amendments to the Act, broadening the overtime exemption for irrigation workers.[10]

In 1999 Congress amended the Act in respect to the applicability of the Section 7(k) partial exemption for fire protection and law enforcement employees to various emergency services employees. To "clarify" the application of the Section 7(k) partial exemption it added a new Section 3(y), providing by definition that:

> "Employee in fire protection activities" means an employee, including a firefighter, paramedic, emergency medical technician, rescue worker, ambulance personnel, or hazardous materials worker, who—
>
> (1) is trained in fire suppression, has the legal authority and responsibility to engage in fire suppression, and is employed by a fire department of a municipality, county, fire district, or State; and
>
> (2) is engaged in the prevention, control, and extinguishment of fires or response to emergency situations where life, property, or the environment is at risk.[11]

It went on to provide further guidance in the enactment—namely, Section 2, Construction:

> The amendment made by section 1 shall not be construed to reduce or substitute for compensation standards:

---

[10]Dep't of Labor Appropriations Act, Pub. L. No. 105-78, 111 Stat. 1467 (1998), amending 29 U.S.C. §213 (b)(12). *See* Chapter 6, "Agricultural Exemptions," §IV.B [Section 13(b) Exemptions From the Overtime Requirements of the Act; Agricultural Workers and Those Employed in Operating or Maintaining Irrigation Systems for Agricultural Purposes], in this supplement.

[11]29 U.S.C. §203(y), Pub. L. No. 106-151, 113 Stat. 1731 (1999). The cases construing the application of the special §7(k) provisions to paramedics, emergency medical technicians, and ambulance employees are discussed at Chapter 11, §VI.F.

(1) contained in any existing or future agreement or memorandum of understanding reached through collective bargaining by a bona fide representative of employees in accordance with the laws of a State or political subdivision of a State; and

(2) which result in compensation greater than the compensation available to employees under the overtime exemption under section 7(k) of the Fair Labor Standards Act of 1938.[12]

Effective August 16, 2000, the Fair Labor Standards Act was amended to clarify the circumstances under which value derived from stock options does not have to be included in the compensation of employees for purposes of calculating the regular rate in the course of computing any overtime which may be due to nonexempt workers.[13] The amendment allows any income derived from a stock option, stock appreciation right, or employee stock purchase plan to be excluded from a nonexempt employee's regular rate, as long as:

- the plan requires that employees hold their stock options for at least six months before cashing them in;
- the plan requires that the option price be at least 85 percent of the market price when the option is granted;
- employee participation in the plan is voluntary; and
- the terms of the plan are disclosed to the employees.

The amendment also states that qualifying plans would be permitted to grant stock options based on employees' past performance without overtime consequences if the options are not awarded pursuant to any prior contract. Further, the law allows employers to grant stock options that are without overtime consequences based on the future performance of a facility of any size, or a business unit or group that consisted of at least 10 employees.

---

[12]29 U.S.C. §203(y) Note, Pub. L. No. 106-151, 113 Stat. 1731 (1999).

[13]Pub. L. No. 106-202, 114 Stat. 308 (2000) (codified at 29 U.S.C. §207(e)).

Stock option plans in existence at the time the new law took effect are protected from FLSA overtime liability under the legislation if the stock options:

- were obtained prior to the amendment's August 16, 2000, effective date;
- were issued to employees within a year after the amendment's effective date under plans that must be modified through shareholder approval; or
- are part of a collective bargaining agreement, as of the law's effective date.

Although numerous other bills to amend the Fair Labor Standards Act have been introduced, particularly to provide increases in the minimum wage, no other bills passed during the period of coverage.

CHAPTER 2

OPERATIONS AND FUNCTIONS OF THE DEPARTMENT OF LABOR

II. ORGANIZATION OF THE DEPARTMENT OF LABOR

B. Wage and Hour Administrator

In *Western Illinois Home Health Care, Inc. v. Herman*,[1] the U.S. Court of Appeals for the Seventh Circuit held that a letter from a U.S. Department of Labor (DOL) Wage and Hour Division (Division) Assistant District Director was final and reviewable agency action. Although the court acknowledged that the Assistant District Director's subordinate status "might give one pause," the letter was still final agency action where such an official appeared to have acted within the Wage and Hour Division's chain of command.

IV. REGULATIONS, INTERPRETATIONS, AND OPINIONS

A. Regulations and Interpretations

In *Herman v. Suwannee Swifty Stores, Inc.*,[2] a federal district court in Georgia upheld DOL's interpretation of Section 7(i)'s requirement of a "bona fide commission rate" for a commissioned employee to fall under Section 7(i)'s overtime exemption for commission salespersons. The court held that DOL permissibly construed congressional intent in interpreting the bona fide requirement. DOL's interpretation is that the bona fide requirement is not met if the employee's commission seldom or never equaled the amount of the guarantee.[3]

Following the weight of authority, the court in *Spradling v. City of Tulsa*[4] deferred to the Department of Labor's legislative rules. The tests for determining whether an employee is exempt

---

[1]150 F.3d 659, 661, 663, 4 WH Cases2d 1289 (7th Cir. 1998).

[2]19 F. Supp. 2d 1365 (M.D. Ga. 1998).

[3]29 C.F.R. §779.416(c).

[4]95 F.3d 1492, 1495, 3 WH Cases2d 823 (10th Cir. 1996) (stating that "[g]enerally, DOL regulations are entitled to judicial deference"), *cert. denied,* 117 S. Ct. 1081, 3 WH Cases2d 1376 (1997).

from FLSA's overtime compensation requirements[5] have been repeatedly considered and deferred to by the courts.[6]

Similarly, the Sixth Circuit by a divided panel affirmed in part the decision of the district court finding a funeral director to be an exempt employee. In doing so, the court followed prevailing authority in observing that the Secretary of Labor's white collar exemption regulations[7] "must be given controlling weight unless those regulations are found to be 'arbitrary, capricious or manifestly contrary to the statute.'"[8]

Some courts also have deferred to the interpretations accompanying those regulations.[9] The Supreme Court, for its part, has upheld an interpretation that the Department articulated for the first time in the form of an amicus brief submitted to the

---

[5] *See* 29 C.F.R. §541 subpart A (1997).

[6] *See, e.g.*, Auer v. Robbins, 117 S. Ct. 905, 909–10, 3 WH Cases2d 1249 (1997) (upholding application of the disciplinary deduction element of the salary basis test to public sector employees); *Spradling*, 95 F.3d at 1498 (upholding the salary basis test as applied to public sector employees who are not governed by public accountability pay systems, and stating, at 1495, that DOL regulations are the "primary source of guidance for determining the scope and extent of exemptions to the FLSA"); Stricker v. Eastern Off Rd. Equip., Inc., 935 F. Supp. 650, 654, 3 WH Cases2d 748 (D. Md. 1996) ("[r]egulations promulgated by the Department of Labor establish binding standards for determining whether an employee is employed in a 'bona fide executive, administrative, or professional capacity;'" quoting 29 C.F.R. pt. 541). *See also* Reich v. John Alden Life Ins. Co., 126 F.3d 1, 8, 14, 4 WH Cases2d 129 (1st Cir. 1997) (applying the regulation's "short test" and finding that insurance company's marketing representatives fell within the administrative employee exemption); Haywood v. North Am. Van Lines, Inc., 121 F.3d 1066, 1074, 4 WH Cases2d 59 (7th Cir. 1997) (applying the regulation's "short test" and finding that shipping company's customer service coordinator was an exempt salaried administrative employee).

[7] 29 C.F.R. §541.

[8] Rutlin v. Prime Succession, Inc., 220 F.3d 737, 741, 6 WH Cases2d 359 (6th Cir. 2000) (quoting Freeman v. National Broad. Co., 80 F.3d 78, 82, 3 WH Cases 289 (2d Cir. 1996)).

[9] *See* 29 C.F.R. §541 subpart B (1997). *See, e.g., Stricker*, 935 F. Supp. at 655 n.5 (relying extensively on the interpretations of the regulations and stating that "[t]he Secretary's interpretations of the regulations (and ultimately the statute) are accorded significant deference by the courts"). *But see* Freeman v. National Broad. Co., 80 F.3d 78, 85, 3 WH Cases2d 289 (2d Cir. 1996) (holding that DOL's "Interpretation 302," 29 C.F.R. §541.302(b) (1997), which provides guidelines in determining whether newspaper writers fall under the artistic professional exemption, is "anachronistic, [and] even irrational" when applied to journalists employed by major, modern news organizations).

Court. In *Auer v. Robbins,*[10] the High Court upheld the Secretary's interpretation of the disciplinary deduction element of the salary basis test.[11] Justice Scalia, writing for a unanimous Court, stated: "Because the salary-basis test is a creature of the Secretary's own regulations, his interpretation of it is, under our jurisprudence, controlling unless 'plainly erroneous or inconsistent with the regulation.'"[12] The case will have a wide impact on administrative as well as labor law.[13]

The Fourth Circuit, however, has declined to defer to the Wage and Hour Division's interpretive bulletin defining "loader" under the motor carrier exemption, Section 13(b)(1). The court reasoned that the Interstate Commerce Commission, not the Division, was authorized to define positions under the Motor Carrier Act.[14]

In *Madison v. Resources for Human Development Inc.,*[15] a suit by current and former employees against a nonprofit corporation that provides its clients—mentally ill and mentally retarded adults—with human services programs such as community health centers, transportation services, and community living facilities and assistance, the Third Circuit affirmed the district court's decision that the FLSA applied to the defendant and that the domestic companionship exemption, relied on by the defendants, was not available. However, the district court's decision that the defendant was required to include in the plaintiffs' regular rate the contributions made by the defendant to its cafeteria-type benefit plan which had a cash option was reached,

[10] 117 S. Ct. 905, 137 L. Ed. 2d 79, 65 USLW 4136, 3 WH Cases2d 1249 (1997).

[11] *See id.* at 911. For further discussion of disciplinary deductions and the salary basis test, see Treatise at Chapter 4, "White Collar Exemptions," §IV.B.3 [Impermissible Deductions From an Employee's Salary] (pp. 192–202) and the corresponding section of this supplement.

[12] *Id.* (quoting Robertson v. Methow Valley Citizens Council, 490 U.S. 332, 359 (1989)).

[13] *See, e.g.,* National Wildlife Fed'n v. Browner, 127 F.3d 1126, 1129 (D.C. Cir. 1997) (Clean Water Act case; considering impact of *Auer* on deference issues).

[14] Troutt v. Stavola Bros., Inc., 107 F.3d 1104, 1108 n.1, 3 WH Cases2d 1400 (4th Cir. 1997).

[15] 233 F.3d 175, 187, 6 WH Cases2d 961 (3d Cir. 2000).

according to the appellate court, through reliance on 29 C.F.R. §778.215(a)(5), which the appellate court found the district court had treated as a formal agency regulation, when in fact it is "merely an interpretative guideline of the agency."[16] Accordingly, it remanded for further consideration in light of the Supreme Court's recent deference decision.[17]

In *Wisnewski v. Champion Healthcare Corp.*,[18] the district court set forth the distinction between regulations and interpretations and noted that the provisions of 29 C.F.R. Part 778 with respect to the calculation of overtime are an interpretive bulletin, rather than a regulation.[19]

In *Dufrene v. Browning Ferris, Inc.*,[20] the Fifth Circuit Court of Appeals affirmed a decision of the district court denying a claim for back pay brought by garbage truck drivers who challenged the employer's calculation of overtime for employees paid on a day rate basis as described in 29 C.F.R. §778.112. The court of appeals found that the regulatory interpretation was a permissible one and entitled to *Chevron*[21] deference, rejecting several defense arguments that the employer's practices failed to meet the requirements for day rate payment.[22] Accordingly, the Fifth Circuit upheld the methodology used by the employer.

In *Madison v. Resources for Human Develoopment Inc.*,[23] the Third Circuit affirmed that portion of the district court's judgment which denied summary judgment to the employer on its claim that certain employees were entitled to the companionship exemption, holding that as a matter of law that exemption did not apply to the case made out by the undisputed facts before

---

[16] *Id.*, 6 WH Cases2d at 967.

[17] Christensen v. Harris County, 529 U.S. 576, 5 WH Cases2d 1825 (2000).

[18] 2000 WL 1474414, 141 Lab. Cas. ¶34,095 (D.N.D. 2000).

[19] 2000 WL 1474414 at *4.

[20] 207 F.3d 264 (5th Cir. 2000), decided together with Hartsell v. Dr. Pepper Bottling Co., 207 F.3d 269 (5th Cir. 2000).

[21] Chevron, U.S.A., Inc. v. Natural Res. Defense Council, Inc., 467 U.S. 837 (1984).

[22] 207 F.3d at 268.

[23] 233 F.3d 175, 6 WH Cases2d 961 (3d Cir. 2000), *aff'g* 39 F. Supp. 2d 542 (E.D. Pa. 1999).

the court.[24] The court of appeals observed that the parties did not dispute that Chevron deference was due to the formal regulations issued by the Secretary to implement the statute, but found that the regulation itself was not dispositive of the question whether the employees performed their work in the "private home" of their employers. It eventually agreed with the district court's resolution of this disputed issue.

B. Opinion Letters

As with the Department's interpretive rules, some courts found letter rulings to be persuasive authority.[25]

In *Western Illinois Home Health Care, Inc. v. Herman*,[26] the U.S. Court of Appeals for the Seventh Circuit held that a letter from a U.S. Department of Labor Wage and Hour Division Assistant District Director alerting two health care employers that the Department of Labor would consider them "joint employers" who must calculate overtime based on the aggregate of time worked for both employers was final and reviewable agency action. First, the court noted that the letter was final and "declarative" in form because it concluded that "[a]t a minimum, a joint employment relationship exists in this case." Second, this conclusion, along with the threat of follow-up investigations, established and immediately imposed legal burdens on the employers to accumulate time or be subject to penalties. Finally, although the court acknowledged that the Assistant District Director's subordinate status "might give one pause," the letter was still final agency action where such an

[24] 29 U.S.C. §213(a)(5), as interpreted in 29 C.F.R. §552.3.

[25] *See, e.g.*, Flood v. New Hanover County, 125 F.3d 249, 4 WH Cases2d 139 (4th Cir. 1997) (upholding an employer's fluctuating workweek method of determining overtime compensation and giving substantial weight to a DOL letter ruling). The Fourth Circuit in *Flood* stated: "Although the DOL's letter ruling does not bind the Court, it does 'constitute "a body of experienced and informed judgment,"' and we give it substantial weight." *Id.* at 253 (quoting Schultz v. W.R. Hartin & Sons, Inc., 428 F.2d 186, 191 (4th Cir. 1970) (quoting, in turn, Skidmore v. Swift & Co., 323 U.S. 134, 140 (1944))).

[26] 150 F.3d 659, 661, 663, 4 WH Cases2d 1289 (7th Cir. 1998).

official appeared to have acted within the Wage and Hour Division's chain of command.

In *Christensen v. Harris County,*[27] the Supreme Court addressed the question whether a public employer using a compensation arrangement under which employees accrued comp time in lieu of overtime pay could require employees to use their accumulated comp time involuntarily. This question was presented in the context of the statutory provisions of Section 7(o), the Department's regulations at 29 C.F.R. §553, and a Department of Labor opinion letter[28] to the effect that an employer may compel use of compensatory time only if the employee has agreed in advance to such practice. The Court held that the opinion letter was not entitled to deference, pursuant to *Auer v. Robbins,*[29] as an agency's interpretation of its own regulation, because an *Auer* deference is warranted only when the language of a regulation is ambiguous, and the regulation—providing that an agreement or understanding between an employer and an employee may include other provisions governing preservation, use, or cashing out of compensatory time so long as these provisions are consistent with Section 7(o) of FLSA—is not ambiguous, but is plainly permissive. It stated that "[i]nterpretations such as those in opinion letters . . . do not warrant *Chevron*-style deference. . . . Instead, interpretations contained in formats such as opinion letters are 'entitled to respect' under our decision in *Skidmore v. Swift & Co.*,[30] . . . but only to the extent that those interpretations have the 'power to persuade' . . . ."[31] "Through the five separate opinions filed in the case we are led to the conclusion that a majority of the court was not 'persuaded' and that employer compulsion of the use of accrued comp time is permissible under the FLSA, at least in the absence of a regulation limiting or prohibiting such use."[32]

---

[27]529 U.S. 576, 5 WH Cases2d 1825 (2000).
[28]September 14, 1992, WHM: 99:5274a.
[29]519 U.S. 452, 3 WH Cases2d 1249 (1997).
[30]323 U.S. 134, 140, 4 WH Cases 866 (1944).
[31]529 U.S. at 587, 5 WH Cases2d 1825 (2000).
[32]Opinion of Justice Souter, concurring, 5 WH Cases2d 1825, 1830.

In a decision that illuminates the deference to be given to conflicting Department of Labor opinions offered by different officers of the Department, the Sixth Circuit in *Fazekas v. Cleveland Clinic Foundation Health Care*[33] affirmed the decision of the district court granting summary judgment to the defendants in a case brought by home health care nurses.[34] The question whether the plaintiffs were exempt employees, as claimed by defendants, turned on whether they were compensated on a "fee basis." Deferring to an earlier opinion by the acting Wage and Hour Administrator, rather than to later opinions by counsel and other staff of the Wage and Hour Division, the appellate court ruled that an acting administrator's opinion represented the Department's position. The court found that the Acting Administrator's opinion was controlling, as it was not inconsistent with the regulation or plainly erroneous.

VI. THE DEPARTMENT OF LABOR IN CYBERSPACE [NEW TOPIC]

The U.S. Department of Labor maintains a Web site that in turn links to other sites of interest. Though this description may quickly become out of date as a result of address or technology changes, we note several interesting resources for follow-up:

- the Department's home page,[35] which prompts the viewer through information about its seven major program agencies;
- the Wage and Hour Division home page,[36] which similarly prompts the viewer through numerous interesting choices;

---

[33]204 F.3d 673 (6th Cir. 2000).
[34]*See* text at Chapter 4, note 157, below.
[35]<http://www.dol.gov>.
[36]<http://www.dol.gov/dol/esa/public/whd_org.htm>.

- access to minimum wage compliance posters (available through the Wage and Hour Division home page);[37]
- access to pertinent provisions of the Code of Federal Regulations and rulemaking documents published in the *Federal Register* (available through the Wage and Hour Division home page);[38]
- an address and phone list of district and regional Wage and Hour Division offices (available through the Wage and Hour Division home page);[39] and
- access to compliance reference guides (available through the Wage and Hour Division home page).[40]

Access to Wage and Hour Division Administrator opinion letters is not yet available through these channels. A reasonably complete report of administrative law judge and Administrative Review Board decisions may be found at the U.S. Department of Labor/Administrative Law Judge home page.[41]

On August 30, 2001, the Secretary announced the initiation of toll-free telephone service for compliance assistance in connection with Labor Department programs. The numbers are: General Number 1-866-4-USA-DOL (1-866-487-2365) and Wage-Hour 1-866-4-USWAGE (1-866-487-9243).

[37]<http://www.dol.gov/dol/esa/minwage/poster.htm>.

[38]<http://www.dol.gov/dol/esa/public/regs/whdregs.htm>.

[39]<http://www.dol.gov/dol/esa/public/contacts/whd/america2.htm>.

[40]<http://www.dol.gov/dol/esa/public/regs/compliance/whd/whdcomp.htm>.

[41]<http://204.245.136.2/aljhome2.htm>.

CHAPTER 3

COVERAGE

II. The Employer-Employee Relationship

B. The Economic Reality Test

In *Herman v. RSR Security Services Ltd.*,[1] the Second Circuit affirmed the ruling of the District Court that, under the FLSA's economic reality test, an attorney who helped to incorporate a security guard company, was a 50 percent shareholder and served as chairman of its board of directors, was involved in various aspects of corporate administration, possessed the authority to hire employees, sometimes supervised and controlled employee work schedules and employment conditions, and had the authority to sign employee paychecks, was an "employer," despite the fact that the evidence showed he had little direct control over the work of the guard-employees and no involvement in recordkeeping.

In *Braddock v. Madison County*,[2] court reporters and other court employees brought suit for overtime pay against the county. The county asserted that the judges were the proper defendants in the case, since the county had no authority to prevent the employees from working overtime. A federal court in Indiana ruled that the county was a (joint) employer of the court reporters and other court employees, although the judges

---

[1]172 F.3d 132, 5 WH Cases2d 257 (2d Cir. 1999).

[2]34 F. Supp. 2d 1098, 6 WH Cases2d 207 (S.D. Ind. 1998).

themselves, rather than the county, exercised the power to hire and fire individual employees and supervised and controlled their work schedules and conditions of employment. The county council allocated employee "slots," reviewed budget requests, and appropriated the funds out of which the court employees were compensated. On one occasion the council had rejected a budget request for overtime compensation for court employees. The court held the county liable as an employer. Courts continue to analyze these factors in making their determinations.[3]

Following Ninth Circuit authority, the court in *Bureerong v. Uvawas*[4] noted four factors utilized to guide courts in the analysis of "economic reality." Those factors are whether the alleged employer (1) had the power to hire and fire the employees, (2) supervised and controlled employee work schedules or conditions of employment, (3) determined the rate and method of payment, and (4) maintained employment records.[5] However, the court cautioned that "[a] court must not 'focus[] on selected and isolated control factors . . . [and] lose[] sight of the circumstances of the whole activity."[6] The touchstone of economic reality is the dependency of the employee upon the

---

[3]Preston v. Settle Down Enters., Inc., 90 F. Supp. 2d 1267 (N.D. Ga. 2000) (holding that a consultant was an employer where he is responsible for the day-to-day operations of the company's business); Herman v. Hector I. Nieves Transp., Inc., 91 F. Supp. 2d 435 (D.P.R. 2000); (president and secretary/treasurer who actively controlled and managed the company by regulating its personnel were employers); Derewiecka v. Zlored, Inc., 1999 WL 767203, at *2 (S.D.N.Y. 1999) (president's signature on a waiver-of-lien form not sufficient evidence by itself to show that the president personally liable as employer); Robertson v. Board of County Comm'rs, 78 F. Supp. 2d 1142, 5 WH Cases2d 1149 (D. Colo. 1999); Taylor v. County of Fluvanna, 70 F. Supp. 2d 655, 5 WH Cases2d 1255 (W.D. Va. 1999).

[4]922 F. Supp. 1450, 3 WH Cases2d 383 (C.D. Cal. 1996).

[5]*Id.* at 1467 (citing Bonnette v. California Health & Welfare Agency, 704 F.2d 1465, 1470 (9th Cir. 1983)).

[6]*Id.* at 1468 (quoting court's brackets and ellipsis retained; quoting Castillo v. Givens, 704 F.2d 181, 190, 26 WH Cases 184 (5th Cir.), *cert. denied*, 464 U.S. 850, 26 WH Cases 757 (1983)).

alleged employer.[7] Thus, there may also be more than one employer.[8]

In *Preston v. Settle Down Enterprises, Inc.*,[9] a federal district court in Georgia, citing both Ninth[10] and Eleventh[11] Circuit authority, applied the four-factor economic reality test, and determined that a temporary employment service and its consultant were joint employers of the temporary workers placed to work for the company's clients.[12] The court found that the temporary employment service was the "employer" of the temporary workers because the temporary employment service "recruited, transported, paid, and maintained records" for the temporary workers.[13] More specifically, the court relied on the fact that the temporary employment service "selected workers to send to the job sites, indicating a power to hire and fire"; "told workers when its vans would arrive to take them to the job sites"; and "set the rate of pay [for the workers] and chose to pay its employees by voucher."[14] The court also found that a consultant hired by the temporary employment service was an "employer" of the temporary workers because he was responsible for the day-to-day operations of the business.[15] The court was not persuaded

---

[7] *Id.*

[8] *Id.* (charges that "manufacturer" defendants, who contracted with "operators" to produce garments at prices too low to permit payment of minimum wages and overtime, "directly or indirectly employed" workers and "exercised meaningful control" over the work they performed sufficiently alleged an employment relationship between the "manufacturer" defendants and the garment workers allegedly involuntarily held and employed in the facility, in light of the workers' "economic reality" allegations concerning the garment industry).

[9] 90 F. Supp. 2d 1267 (N.D. Ga. 2000).

[10] *See, e.g.*, Bonnette v. California Health & Welfare Agency, 704 F.2d 1465, 1470 (9th Cir. 1983).

[11] *See, e.g.*, Villarreal v. Woodham, 113 F.3d 202, 205 (11th Cir. 1997).

[12] *Preston*, 90 F. Supp. 2d at 1274. For a discussion of joint employers, see the main volume of the Treatise, Chapter 18, "Litigation Issues," §IV.E. [Parties; Joint Employment] at pp. 1169–84.

[13] *Preston*, 90 F. Supp. 2d at 1274.

[14] *Id.*

[15] *Id.* at 1275.

by the fact that the temporary employment service and the consultant had no control over the workers once they reached the job site, stating "the absence of direct, on-site supervision does not preclude a determination that [a temporary employment service and its principals] are the employers of the temporary workers within the broadest definition of the FLSA."[16]

Two cases involving superficially similar facts came before federal district courts in two different circuits in 2000, *Robertson v. Board of County Commissioners*[17] and *Taylor v. County of Fluvanna*,[18] and produced different results. In *Robertson*, the federal district court in Colorado considered whether certain deputy sheriffs were employees of the Board of County Commissioners for Morgan County (the "Board"). The court applied the four-factor economic reality test and found that the first factor, the authority to hire and fire, weighed in favor of the deputies not being employees of the Board because the Morgan County Sheriff (not the Board) had sole authority to hire and fire deputy sheriffs.[19] However, the court found that the remainder of the factors indicated that the deputies were employees of the Board because (1) though the Sheriff controlled the day-to-day activities of the deputies and other employees, the Board set some conditions of employment (such as the overtime pay and compensatory time policies); (2) the Board approved the rates and frequency of pay fixed by the Sheriff; and (3) though the Sheriff maintained separate pay records of the employees, the Board maintained the "permanent" and "official" records used to calculate pay and compensatory time.[20] Weighing all the factors, and in light of the "expansive" view of the terms "employee" and "employer" under the Act, the court concluded that the Board was an employer of the deputy sheriffs.[21]

---

[16]*Id.* at 1274 (citing Baystate Alternative Staffing, Inc. v. Herman, 163 F.3d 668, 5 WH Cases2d 65 (1st Cir. 1998)).

[17]78 F. Supp. 2d 1142, 5 WH Cases2d 1449 (D. Colo. 1999).

[18]70 F. Supp. 2d 655, 5 WH Cases2d 1255 (W.D. Va. 1999).

[19]*Robertson,* 70 F. Supp 2d at 1151, 5 WH Cases2d at 1456.

[20]*Id.* at 1151–52, 5 WH Cases2d at 1456.

[21]*Id.* at 1152, 5 WH Cases2d at 1456.

In *Taylor v. County of Fluvanna,*[22] the federal district court in Virginia came to the opposite conclusion and held that the County of Fluvanna (the "County") was not the employer of a deputy sheriff who sued the County and the Sheriff for unpaid overtime wages. Applying the same test, the court granted summary judgment for the County on the grounds that the County was not the deputy's employer due to its insufficient control over the deputy sheriff, his working conditions, his work place, and his pay.[23] Specifically, the court found "the county does not (1) hire, fire, supervise, or discipline the deputy sheriffs; (2) supervise or control the deputies' work schedules or conditions of employment; (3) set rates of pay or method of employment; or (4) maintain employment records other than payroll-related records."[24] The court noted that the strongest factor in favor of the County was the fact that it maintained some of the employment records.[25] However, the court opined that "mere maintenance, by itself, of employment records is not sufficient to bestow employer status under the four-part test. . . ."[26] Instead, the court found the Sheriff had exclusive control of the deputy's "day-to-day shift scheduling, job duties, and method of job performance."[27]

In *Derewiecka v. Zlored, Inc.,*[28] a district court in New York applied the four-factor "economic reality" test in determining whether a company was the "employer" of the employees of a subcontractor it had hired to remove asbestos. The company moved for summary judgment on the grounds that it did not have an employment relationship with its subcontractor's employees. The court denied summary judgment, finding that there existed material issues of fact as to whether the company "supervised and controlled employee work schedules or condi-

---

[22]70 F. Supp. 2d 655, 5 WH Cases2d 1255.

[23]*Id.* at 658–59, 5 WH Cases2d at 1258.

[24]*Id.* at 658, 5 WH Cases2d at 1258.

[25]*Id.*

[26]*Id.*

[27]*Id.* Under Virginia law, sheriffs are independent constitutional officers whose power does not derive from the state or the county. *Id.* at 656, 5 WH Cases2d at 1256.

[28]No. 96 Civ. 3382, 1999 WL 767203 (S.D.N.Y. Sept. 28, 1999).

tions of employment" and whether the company "maintained employment records" for its subcontractor's employees.[29]

In 2001, courts in two different circuits applying the same six factor economic reality test to apparently comparable factual situations reached considerably different conclusions in spite of the apparent similarities.

In *Chao v. Mid-Atlantic Installation Services, Inc.*,[30] the Fourth Circuit, in an unpublished decision, affirmed a summary judgment in favor of the employer, holding that, under the FLSA's economic reality test, cable installers were independent contractors rather than employees. Specifically, the court considered: (1) the nature and degree of the alleged employer's control as to the manner in which the work was performed; (2) the alleged employee's opportunity for profit or loss depending upon his managerial skill; (3) the alleged employee's investment in equipment and material required for his task, or his employment of workers; (4) the amount of special skill required to render the service; (5) the degree of permanency and duration of the working relationship; and (6) the extent to which the service rendered is an integral part of the alleged employer's business. In applying the six-factor economic reality test, the court concluded that the bulk of the relevant consideration weighed heavily in favor of independent contractor status, while only the sixth factor favored the conclusion that the installers were employees. The court reasoned that, since no single factor is dispositive, the sixth factor standing alone did not create an employment relationship between the installers and the alleged employer.

In the Fifth Circuit, in *Santelices v. Cable Wiring*,[31] a federal district court in Florida came to a different conclusion. Plaintiff, a cable installer, sued Cable Wiring, Inc. (CWI), a "licensed cable installation vendor for TCI of South Florida" and South Florida Cable Contractors (SFCC), an unaffiliated (with CWI)

---

[29] *Id.* at *1–2.

[30] Herman v. Mid-Atlantic Installation Servs., Inc., 164 F. Supp. 2d 667 (D. Md. 2000), *aff'd mem. sub nom.* Chao v. Mid-Atlantic Installation Servs., Inc., 2001 WL 739243 (4th Cir. 2001, unpublished).

[31] 147 F. Supp. 2d 1313, 6 WH Cases2d 1855 (S.D. Fla. 2001).

business, for overtime violations, alleging that they were joint employers of plaintiff. CWI and SFCC had entered into a contract under which residential installations for TCI were to be done by persons furnished by SFCC. SFCC had made an agreement with plaintiff for performance of the work. Both defendants argued that plaintiff was an independent contractor and not an employee. The court applied the six-factor economic reality test and found that the nature and degree of control exercised by the installation company, SFCC, created a material fact issue which precluded summary judgment, but that there was insufficient evidence to establish that CWI exercised the degree of control necessary under the economic reality test to substantiate an employment relationship between itself and the cable installers. The court noted that some attributes of the plaintiff's work would ordinarily support a conclusion that the plaintiff was an independent contractor, such as the level of skill required to properly install digital cable, the significant amount of money he invested in his work tools and equipment, and his maintenance of general liability insurance and federal employer's identification number, but it concluded that the amount of control which the cable company exerted over installers was sufficient to warrant a trial on the employee issue.

In a case in which the facts made it improbable for this question to be at issue, suit was brought by the wife of a worker receiving workers' compensation payments from an insurance company pursuant to an award under which the wife would provide the disabled worker with all necessary services in exchange for a stipulated hourly payment of $4.25, which amount, under Section 206 of the FLSA, was the minimum hourly wage at the time the agreement was finalized. The wife by her suit attempted to have the amount of her compensation adjusted to reflect the then-current minimum hourly wage, and to obtain overtime for hours worked over 40 in a week. In *Marin v. Travelers Insurance Co.*,[32] a Florida state court, citing Fifth Circuit authority, applied a five-factor economic reality test and determined that there was no employment relationship between the

[32] 771 So. 2d 625 (Fla. Dist. Ct. App. 2000).

workers' compensation recipient's spouse and the workers' compensation carrier. The court held that in reaching an agreement involving compensation for services where compensation was provided for the services by the insurance carrier, the wife did not become an employee of the workers' compensation provider, and that the contractual agreement was not an employment agreement.

C. Employee or Independent Contractor

Some circuits have varied from the five-factor test discussed in the Treatise[33] by using either a smaller (four)[34] or a larger (six)[35] number of factors. A federal district court in Maryland applied the frequently used six-factor test, which adds the factor "whether the service rendered is an 'integral part' of the putative employer's business,"[36] to determine that the economic reality of the relationship between chicken catchers and their putative employer defendant Perdue Farms was that of employees rather than independent contractors.[37]

Furthermore, courts continue to hold that the label that the parties give to their relationship is not controlling.[38] In *Hefferman*

---

[33]Chapter 3, §II.C., pp. 80–82. This test was applied in the Fifth Circuit in *Metzler v. Express 60-Minutes Delivery Servs. Inc.*, 3 WH Cases2d 1737 (N.D. Tex. 1997), and in the Tenth Circuit in *Johns v. Stewart,* 57 F.3d 1544, 1558 (10th Cir. 1995), and *Herr v. Heiman,* 3 WH Cases2d 171, 172 (10th Cir. 1996).

[34]In the Fourth Circuit, Brickey v. County of Smyth, 944 F. Supp. 1310, 3 WH Cases2d 966 (W.D. Va. 1996) (applying four-factor test).

[35]In the Second Circuit, Brock v. Superior Care, 840 F.2d 1054, 28 WH Cases 801 (2d Cir. 1988); in the Third Circuit, Donovan v. Dial Am. Mktg., 757 F.2d 1376, 27 WH Cases 113 (3d Cir.), *cert. denied,* 474 U.S. 919, 27 WH Cases 640 (1985); Cahill v. City of New Brunswick, 99 F. Supp. 2d 464 (D.N.J. 2000); in the Sixth Circuit, Secretary v. Lauritzen, 835 F.2d 1529, 28 WH Cases 654 (7th Cir. 1987); Pfaahler v. Consultants for Architects, Inc., No. 99-C-6700, 2000 WL 198888 (N.D. Ill. Feb. 8, 2000) (recognizing the applicability of the six-factor test); in the Ninth Circuit, Donovan v. Sureway Cleaners, 656 F.2d 1368, 25 WH Cases 105 (9th Cir. 1981); McGuiggan v. CPC Int'l, Inc., 84 F. Supp. 2d 470, 479 (S.D.N.Y. 2000).

[36]Heath v. Perdue Farms, Inc., 87 F. Supp. 2d 452, 457, 5 WH Cases2d 1633 (D. Md. 2000).

[37]*Id.*

[38]*Id.* at 456–57, 5 WH Cases2d at 1636; Hefferman v. Illinois Cmty. Coll. Dist. No. 508, 2000 WL 631309, 6 WH Cases2d 132 (N.D. Ill. 2000).

v. Illinois Community College District No. 508,[39] a coach at a community college alleged that Illinois Community College District No. 508 (the district) violated the FLSA by not paying him for work he performed. The district moved to dismiss the coach's complaint on the grounds that the coach was not an "employee" of the district, relying on a written contract between the parties that the coach attached to his complaint entitled "Independent Contractor."[40] The district court denied the motion to dismiss, noting that "an independent contractor 'label does not necessarily take the worker from the protection of the Act.'"[41]

Passage of the Personal Responsibility and Work Opportunity Reconciliation Act of 1996,[42] which requires work activities by welfare recipients, promises to raise employee, volunteer, and joint employment questions. The Department has generally advised that "[w]elfare recipients would probably be considered employees in many, if not most, of the work activities described in the new welfare law."[43]

In *Morrison v. International Programs Consortium, Inc.* (IPC),[44] plaintiff Morrison had worked as a consultant and performed recruiting and management tasks pursuant to a series of written contracts with defendant. After the last of the contracts expired, Morrison continued to perform services for IPC, and billed for her services on her "Consultant" letterhead. Approximately one year later, Morrison gave notice that she would no longer be offering her services, effective in four weeks' time. During the ensuing weeks she was "fired" by defendant, allegedly for failure to take direction properly. She submitted a statement for her services performed during the last month she had worked, but was not paid. She then submitted a request to the IRS for a

---

[39]2000 WL 631309, 6 WH Cases2d 132 (N.D. Ill. 2000).

[40]*Id.*

[41]*Id.* (quoting Dole v. Amerlink Corp., 729 F. Supp. 73, 76, 29 WH Cases 1019 (E.D. Mo. 1990)).

[42]Pub. L. No. 104-193, 110 Stat. 2105 (1996).

[43]U.S. Dep't of Labor, Office of the Assistant Secretary for Policy, Labor Protections and Welfare Reform (May 26, 1997) (<http://www.dol.gov.oasp> (visited Jan. 14, 1998)).

[44]Morrison v. International Programs Consortium, Inc., 253 F.3d 5, 7 WH Cases2d 74 (D.C. Cir. 2001).

determination whether the employer had properly failed to pay employment taxes for her (if an independent contractor) or improperly done so (if an employee). The IRS determined that she had been an employee and eventually billed the employer for back taxes. Morrison then sued for her wages and overtime for the approximately 4-week period for which she had not been paid at all. Morrison offered no evidence concerning her employment status other than the IRS letter, and sought summary judgment on her employment status. The district court ruled that the IRS letter was not admissible and denied plaintiff's motion for summary judgment. The case then was tried before a jury after admission of the IRS letter was again refused; the court then granted "judgment as a matter of law" to defendant, holding that "there is no legally sufficient evidentiary basis for a reasonable jury to find for the plaintiff."[45]

Plaintiff appealed, challenging both evidentiary rulings and the merits of the decision. The Court of Appeals for the D.C. Circuit affirmed as to the evidentiary rulings, but reversed the judgment. In light of the scanty evidentiary record on both sides, and viewing the available evidence in the light most favorable to Morrison, the Court of Appeals found that a question for trial as to Morrison's employment status remained. Rejecting the district court's heavy reliance on the consultant's description of herself as an independent contractor, it noted that "[F]acile labels and subjective factors are relevant only to the extent they mirror 'economic realities.'"[46] Cataloguing a number of factors which could support a conclusion that plaintiff was in economic reality an employee, the court returned the matter to the district court for further proceedings.

In *Johnson v. Unified Government of Wyandotte County/Kansas City, Kansas,*[47] a federal district court was called on to reconsider a previous ruling that plaintiffs' tax returns should be excluded

---

[45] *Id.* at 10.

[46] *Id.* at 11 (citing Brock v. Mr. W Fireworks, Inc., 814 F.2d 1042, 1044 (5th Cir. 1987)).

[47] 2001 WL 699049 (D. Kan. 2001).

from evidence, and that the defendants were prohibited from soliciting testimony or commenting to the jury on the labeling of plaintiffs' status as independent contractors or employees on those tax returns. The court found those tax returns not relevant to any issue which would be litigated under the six-factor economic reality test adopted by the Tenth Circuit for purposes of deciding whether an individual is an employee or an independent contractor.

In *Ansoumana v. Gristede's Operating Corp.*,[48] a district court in New York determined that it had supplemental jurisdiction over the state law wage claims of unskilled workers who delivered goods from supermarkets to retail customers. In assessing whether the Rule 23(b)(3) criteria for maintenance of a class action were met for the state claims, the court ruled that the common question whether the workers were employees or independent contactors dominated the individual issues; and that accordingly the class action could be maintained.

1. Control

In determining employment status, courts continued to consider, among other factors, the degree of control over the daily work of the individual.[49] Courts have stressed that it is merely the right to control, not whether that right is exercised, that is the key to this inquiry.[50]

---

[48]201 F.R.D. 81 (S.D.N.Y. 2001).

[49]Zelaya v. J.M. Macias Inc., 175 F.R.D. 625, 4 WH Cases2d 89 (E.D.N.C. 1997); Preston v. Settle Down Enters., Inc., 90 F. Supp. 2d 1267 (N.D. Ga. 2000); Heath v. Perdue Farms, Inc., 87 F. Supp. 2d 452, 5 WH Cases2d 1633 (D. Md. 2000).

[50]*Zelaya*, 175 F.R.D. 625, 4 WH Cases2d 89. *See also* Brickey v. County of Smyth, 944 F. Supp. 1310, 3 WH Cases2d 966 (W.D. Va. 1996) (county that did not have power to hire/fire deputy sheriffs or "otherwise control deputies" was not employer); Garcia v. Pace Suburban Bus Serv., 955 F. Supp. 75, 3 WH Cases2d 1477 (N.D. Ill. 1996) (bus company was not driver's employer where company contracted out operation of service and did not involve itself in day-to-day management of business or exercise significant control over employment relationship); Metzler v. Express 60-Minutes Delivery Servs. Inc., 3 WH Cases2d 1737 (N.D. Tex. 1997) (lack of control of drivers indicates they are not employees.)

However, putative employers do not necessarily have to exercise direct, on-site supervision in order to have sufficient control of their employees to be considered their "employer" under the Act.[51]

In *Cahill v. City of New Brunswick*,[52] a federal district court in New Jersey held that police officers were employees, not independent contractors, when they performed "extra duty jobs" for outside vendors because, even though they worked for private companies in performing these extra duty assignments, they were still under the control of the city. The city oversaw and administered the extra duty jobs program and, for its administrative costs, received a "cut" of the officers' pay for the extra duty jobs.[53] More importantly, though, the city considered the officers to be on "on duty" status during the time they worked these extra duty jobs and admitted that the officers would be eligible for workers' compensation benefits if they were injured while performing an extra duty assignment.[54]

In *Heath v. Perdue Farms, Inc.*,[55] the court found that chicken catchers and their crew leaders were employees and not independent contractors of a poultry operation because, among other reasons, the poultry operation controlled every aspect of the chicken catchers' work.[56] More specifically, the court found that "[the poultry operation] controls the farms they are to go to, the order in which individual [chicken] houses are to be utilized, the times the catchers are to catch, how many chickens are to be caught, and how many chickens are to be placed in each cage."[57]

In *Santelices v. Cable Wiring*,[58] plaintiff, a cable installer, sued Cable Wiring, Inc. (CWI), a "licensed cable installation vendor for TCI of South Florida" and South Florida Cable Contractors, (SFCC), an unaffiliated (with CWI) business, for overtime viola-

---

[51] *Preston*, 90 F. Supp. 2d 1267.

[52] 99 F. Supp. 2d 464 (D.N.J. 2000).

[53] *Id.*

[54] *Id.*

[55] 87 F. Supp. 2d 452, 5 WH Cases2d 1633 (D. Md. 2000).

[56] *Id.* at 457–58, 5 WH Cases2d 1633.

[57] *Id.* at 457, 5 WH Cases2d at 1637.

[58] 147 F. Supp. 2d 1313, 6 WH Cases2d 1855 (S.D. Fla. 2001).

tions, alleging that they were joint employers of plaintiff. CWI and SFCC had entered into a contract under which residential installations for TCI were to be done by persons furnished by SFCC. SFCC had made an agreement with plaintiff for performance of the work. Both defendants argued that plaintiff was an independent contractor and not an employee. The court applied the six-factor economic reality test and found that the nature and degree of control exercised by the installation company, SFCC, created a material fact issue which precluded summary judgment, but that there was insufficient evidence to establish that CWI exercised the degree of control necessary under the economic reality test to substantiate an employment relationship between itself and the cable installers. The court noted that some attributes of plaintiff's work would ordinarily support a conclusion that plaintiff was an independent contractor, e.g., the level of skill required to properly install digital cable, the significant amount of money invested in work tools and equipment, and the maintenance of general liability insurance and federal employer's identification number, but it concluded that the amount of control which the cable company exerted over installers was sufficient to warrant a trial on the employee issue.

In *Chao v. Mid-Atlantic Installation Services, Inc.*,[59] the Fourth Circuit, in an unpublished decision, affirmed a summary judgment in favor of the employer, holding that, under the FLSA's economic reality test, cable installers were independent contractors rather than employees. In applying the six-factor economic reality test, the court concluded that the bulk of the relevant consideration weighed heavily in favor of independent contractor status, while only one factor, the "integral to putative employer's business" factor, favored the conclusion that the installers were employees. The court reasoned that, since no single factor is dispositive, that factor standing alone did not support an employment relationship between the installers and the company.

---

[59]Chao v. Mid-Atlantic Installation Servs., Inc., 2001 WL 739243 (4th Cir. 2001 (unpublished).

Catani v. Chiodi[60] involved a relatively uncommon agreement between an employer and a temporary staffing agency. Under their agreement, the employer, NSPC, would identify the former employees it wanted to hire and would refer the former employees to the staffing agency so that the initial employment applications could be processed. The staffing agency would then process all tax and employment eligibility paperwork prior to sending the employees to their work assignments. Once the employees were given their work assignment, the staffing agency had no control over hiring or firing decisions, work schedules, or rate of pay for any of the employees referred to NSPC. The agency was responsible only for processing payroll for the employees with the time sheets that were sent to the agency by NSPC. Plaintiff, one of the workers, sued the staffing agency for overtime. A federal district court in Minnesota determined that a temporary staffing agency was not an employer of workers placed at NSPC. The court noted that, during the first week of the arrangement, the staffing agency attempted to pay overtime to the temporary employees, but NSPC issued a directive to the agency not to do so. The court granted summary judgment in favor of the agency on the ground that the agency did not exercise any control over the manner in which the temporary workers performed their work. Instead, the evidence unequivocally established that NSPC retained complete control over the employees' work. The court disregarded three of the factors in the economic reality test, relating to profit and loss, special skill and the worker's individual investment because the court concluded that no FLSA case has found any of these factors significant as to whether a temporary employment agency is an "employer." Further, the court held that the factors involving the degree or permanence of the working relationship were "unavailing" because of the unique working relationship between the temporary agency and NSPC.

On a question posed in a factual setting involving several different facets of the question, the Department of Labor issued

[60]2001 U.S. Dist. LEXIS 17023 (D. Minn. 2001).

an opinion[61] that under the accepted tests, the parcel delivery drivers of a private carrier furnishing nationwide package pickup and delivery service were employees rather than independent contractors. Under the agreements between the company and the workers, which provided that the worker was an independent contractor, each worker is assigned a geographic territory for which she is responsible; the worker is permitted to sell off portions of the territory, or hire others to service it. However, the company can reconfigure the driver's assigned service area on relatively short notice. The driver must purchase or lease a truck ordered by the company and showing the company's logo at a cost of $20,000 to $40,000. She must make it available every weekday. When not in service for the company, the trucks may be used for other purposes. The driver may acquire additional vehicles if she chooses. The company determined the rate of the worker's compensation as well as the amount charged for each pickup and delivery. Despite the relatively large investment of the workers in the trucks, and their authority to control their work in a number of other respects, the Department found that the workers were employees and not independent contractors because the company retained significant control over the conditions of the work, including assigning service areas, determining the amount of work which is appropriate for each worker, and significantly controlling the time of performance (by its conditions that no pickup or delivery in the service area be refused, and that all picked up packages be returned to the dock before a particular time in order to meet scheduled departures for other destinations), as well as determining compensation.[62]

2. *Investment*

The investment in equipment used by a worker is a factor considered by courts in determining whether a worker is an

---

[61]WH Op. Letter of December 7, 2000, WHM: 99:8333.

[62]The Department distinguished the Fifth Circuit's decision in *Herman v. Express Sixty-Minutes Delivery Service,* 161 F.3d 299, 5 WH Cases2d 7 (5th Cir. 1998), while at the same time expressing the Department's continuing disagreement with the result there.

employee or independent contractor. In *Heath v. Perdue Farms, Inc.*,[63] the court considered the poultry operation's ownership of the equipment used by the crew leaders and the chicken catchers in performing their duties to be an important factor that weighed in favor of their being employees rather than independent contractors.[64] The court found that the poultry processor owned virtually all of the heavy equipment and machinery required for the catching operation, including the crew cabs, trucks, fork lifts, cages, fans, pens, and nets.[65] In addition, the poultry operation was responsible for the storage, maintenance, repair, fueling, and replacement of all the major equipment. In contrast, the crew leaders' investment in equipment was limited to computers used for bookkeeping and gloves and masks used by the catchers.[66] According to the court, "[t]he crew leaders' relative lack of capital investment in equipment is perhaps one of the strongest indicators that they are employees and not independent contractors."[67]

In *Chao v. Mid-Atlantic Installation Services*,[68] the court held that cable installers were independent contractors, not employees of a cable installation company, because, among other reasons, the installers were required to supply their own trucks, specialized tools, uniforms and pagers. In addition, the installers were responsible for withholding their own employees' federal, state and local taxes as well as payments due for social security, self-employment taxes and unemployment and workers' compensation insurance.

In its opinion[69] addressing the status of package pickup and delivery drivers, the Labor Department pointed out that knowing the amount invested by the worker, $20,000 to $40,000, was not sufficient to determine the "relative investment" of the

---

[63] 87 F. Supp. 2d 452, 5 WH Cases2d 1633 (D. Md. 2001).

[64] *Id.*

[65] *Id.*

[66] *Id.*

[67] *Id.*

[68] 164 F. Supp. 2d 667 (D. Md. 2000), *aff'd mem. sub nom.* Chao v. Mid-Atlantic Installation Servs., Inc., 2001 WL 739243 (4th Cir. 2001).

[69] WH Opinion dated May 8, 2001, WHM 99:8368.

parties since no information had been provided about the capital investment of the company.

3. Opportunity for Profit and Loss

In determining employment status, courts continue to consider, among other factors, the individual's opportunity for profit and loss. In *Heath v. Perdue Farms, Inc.*,[70] the court found that chicken catchers and their crew leaders were employees and not independent contractors of a poultry operation because, among other reasons, the crew leaders of the chicken catchers "[h]ad little opportunity to substantially increase their profit, nor [d]id they expose themselves to much risk of loss."[71] The court noted that the poultry operation paid the crew leaders a carefully calculated piece rate based on the number of chickens caught by the chicken catchers in their crew, assuring a consistent profit margin among crew leaders.[72] Furthermore, because the poultry operation limited the number of chickens to be caught, there was no occasion for extra pay or profit.[73]

In *Chao v. Mid-Atlantic Installation Service*,[74] the court held that cable installers were independent contractors, not employees of a cable installation company, because the installers were no less in control of their net profits than the typical independent contractor whose income derives from how much work someone else wants to give him. Further, the installers' net profit or loss ultimately depended on skill in meeting technical specifications, the installers' decisions on capital investment in tools, equipment and a truck, and the installers' decision to hire employees or work alone.

---

[70] 87 F. Supp. 2d 452, 5 WH Cases2d 1633.

[71] *Id.* at 458, 5 WH Cases2d at 1637.

[72] *Id.* at 452, 5 WH Cases2d at 1633.

[73] *Id.*

[74] 2001 WL 739243 (4th Cir. 2001), *aff'g* Herman v. Mid-Atlantic Installation Servs., Inc., 164 F. Supp. 2d 667 (D. Md. 2000).

4. *Permanency*

In determining employment status, courts continue to consider, among other factors, the permanency of the relationship between the individual and the putative employer. In *Heath v. Perdue Farms, Inc.*,[75] the court found that chicken catchers and their crew leaders were employees and not independent contractors of a poultry operation because, among other reasons, "the crew leaders (and most of the catchers themselves) [had] long-standing, permanent, and exclusive relationships with [the poultry operation]."[76] Most of the crew leaders worked for the poultry operation for at least 10 years, while some longer than 20 years.[77] Moreover, the crew leaders worked exclusively for the poultry operation and the arduous demands of their job made it impractical for them to organize additional crews to work for competitors of the poultry operation.[78]

5. *Skill*

In determining employment status, courts continue to consider, among other factors, the degree of skill required for the job performed by the worker. In *Heath v. Perdue Farms, Inc.*,[79] the court found that chicken catchers and their crew leaders were employees and not independent contractors of a poultry operation because, among other reasons, the crew leaders and the chicken catchers performed unskilled labor.[80] The court noted that (1) there is little doubt that catching chickens is unskilled labor and (2) the fact that the catchers became faster with experience is true of most repetitive tasks, skilled or unskilled.[81] In addition, though the crew leaders possessed certain

---

[75] 87 F. Supp. 2d 452, 5 WH Cases2d 1633.
[76] *Id.* at 458, 5 WH Cases2d at 1637.
[77] *Id.*
[78] *Id.*
[79] *Id.*
[80] *Id.*
[81] *Id.*

supervision and management skills, the court considered this to be "the kind of generalized management skills commonly required of a foreman or supervisor" and not enough skills to render the crew leader position that of an independent contractor.[82]

In *Chao v. Mid-Atlantic Installation Services*,[83] the Fourth Circuit, in an unpublished decision, held cable installers were independent contractors due to the degree of skill required to install and repair cable equipment. The court reasoned that the skills of cable installers are akin to those of carpenters, construction workers and electricians, who are usually considered independent contractors.

In denying summary judgment the federal district court in *Santelices v. Cable Wiring*[84] concluded that, in spite of the company's requirement that cable installers pass a written exam and demonstrate proficiency at digital cable installation, cable installers were employees, not independent contractors, due to the nature and amount of control exerted by the alleged employer over the installer.

6. *"Integral Part of Operation"*

In determining the employment status, some courts consider whether the worker constitutes an integral part of the putative employer's operation.[85] In *Heath v. Perdue Farms, Inc.*,[86] the court found that chicken catchers and their crew leaders were employees and not independent contractors of a poultry operation because, among other reasons, the work of the catchers is highly coordinated with the schedule of the poultry operation's processing plants.[87] The court found that the poultry operation depends on its catching crews for a steady supply

---

[82] *Id.* at 458, 5 WH Cases at 1637.

[83] 2001 WL 739243 (4th Cir. 2001), *aff'g* Herman v. Mid-Atlantic Installation Servs., Inc., 164 F. Supp. 2d 667 (D. Md. 2000).

[84] 147 F. Supp. 2d 1313, 6 WH Cases2d 1855 (S.D. Fla. 2001).

[85] *See* Treatise, Chapter 3, "Coverage" §II.C.6. [Employee or Independent Contractor; "Integral Part of Operations"] at pp. 87–88.

[86] 87 F. Supp. 2d 452, 5 WH Cases2d 1633 (D. Md. 2000).

[87] *Id.* at 459, 5 WH Cases2d at 1637.

of chickens: "Although geographically their work takes place outside [of] the processing plants, the catchers' function, in a real sense, is simply part of the production line."[88]

7. *Other Factors*

Marin v. Travelers Insurance Co.,[89] was a case involving a claim by the wife of an individual who received workers' compensation from an insurance company. She sued for additional wages and overtime for services she provided her disabled husband. In addition to applying a five-factor economic reality test, the state court in Florida considered other factors in holding that there was no employment relationship between plaintiff and the insurance company. The court considered that no interviews were conducted in choosing Mrs. Marin to deliver caregiver services to her husband; there was no supervision of Mrs. Marin's performance and Mrs. Marin did not receive company benefits an employee would otherwise be entitled to receive. The court concluded that the parties had entered into a contractual agreement wherein the claimant's wife would provide the claimant with needed services, but the contract was not one for employment.

8. *Employee Status Found*

A decision that temporary workers hired by an employee-leasing company and provided as unskilled labor to other employers were employees of the leasing company, rather than independent contractors, was upheld by the Labor Department's Administrative Review Board, by a district court, and then by the First Circuit in *Baystate Alternative Staffing v. Herman*.[90] The court noted that in reviewing a Departmental decision under the Administrative Procedure Act, it should set aside the decision only if it is arbitrary, capricious, or an abuse of discretion, and

---

[88] *Id.*

[89] 771 So. 2d 625 (Fla. Dist. Ct. App. 2000).

[90] 163 F.3d 668, 5 WH Cases2d 65 (1st Cir. 1998).

that the appellate and district courts apply the same standard in this regard.[91]

In *Preston v. Settle Down Enterprises, Inc.*,[92] a federal district court in Georgia found that temporary workers were employees of the temporary employment service that placed them in temporary jobs. The temporary workers performed various temporary jobs, including construction work, work in hotels, and stuffing inserts for a local newspaper.[93] The court found that the temporary workers were employees of the temporary employment service because the temporary employment service "recruited, transported, paid, and maintained records" for the temporary workers.[94] More specifically, the temporary employment service "selected workers to send to the job sites"; "told workers when its vans would arrive to take them to the job sites"; and "set the rate of pay [for the workers] and chose to pay its employees by voucher."[95] The court was not persuaded by the temporary employment service's argument that it had no control of the workers once they reached the job site.[96]

In *Herman v. Davis Acoustical Corp.*,[97] a federal district court in New York upheld a special master's determination that under the economic reality test individuals classified as subcontractors were in fact employees entitled to overtime compensation. Factors considered were that supervisors had a high degree of control over the individuals, the individuals had long-standing work relations with the employer, the individuals had no personal investment or opportunity for profit or loss in the construction contracts, and showed no business-like or entrepreneurial skills. Additionally, the alleged subcontractors performed work identical to that performed by employees, and in many cases worked side by side with them. This led the court to view the employer's classification of individuals as subcontractor or employee as arbitrary.

---

[91] *Id.*, 5 WH Cases2d at 69.
[92] 90 F. Supp. 2d 1267 (N.D. Ga. 2000).
[93] *Id.*
[94] *Id.* at 1274.
[95] *Id.*
[96] *Id.*
[97] 21 F. Supp. 2d 130, 4 WH Cases2d 1615 (N.D.N.Y. 1998).

The *Elizondo v. Podgorniak*[98] court granted partial summary judgment for migrant farm worker plaintiffs, holding that they were employees of defendants, owners of a pickling cucumber farm. The migrant farm workers were required to sign agreements that characterized their harvesting work as sharecropping arrangements under which they bought the crops from defendants, then hired defendants to haul them to a manufacturer and arrange sales. The net effect of the transactions was that plaintiffs and defendants would split the proceeds from the sale of crops 50-50. The court rejected the contracts as shams that deliberately misrepresented the actual employment relationship.

Making a careful comparison of the facts in the case before it with those emphasized by the Sixth Circuit in *Donovan v. Brandel*,[99] which found pickle workers to be independent contractors, as well as with those of *Brock v. Lauritzen*[100] and other cases finding pickle and other migrant workers to be employees, the *Elizondo* court applied the standard six-part test to determine whether the migrant workers were employees or independent contractors, considering: (1) the permanency of relationship; (2) the degree of skill required for the work; (3) the workers' capital investment; (4) the workers' opportunity for profit or loss, depending on their skill; (5) the defendant's right to control the work; and (6) whether the work performed was an integral part of the business. After analyzing the factors, the court held that they weighed overwhelmingly in favor of finding an employment relationship.

In *Soto v. McLean*,[101] a federal district court in North Carolina held that a farmer and his farm were employers of migrant farm workers hired to harvest tobacco. The court reasoned that the farmer controlled the workers' work and provided all equip-

---

[98] 70 F. Supp. 2d 758 (E.D. Mich. 1999).

[99] 736 F.2d 1114, 26 WH Cases2d 1309 (6th Cir. 1984).

[100] U.S. Dep't of Labor v. Lauritzen, 835 F.2d 1529, 1538, 28 WH Cases2d 654 (7th Cir. 1987) (pickle farmworkers are employees under FLSA), *cert. denied*, 488 U.S. 898, 109 S. Ct. 243, 102 L. Ed. 2d 232, *reh'g denied*, 488 U.S. 987, 109 S. Ct. 544, 102 L. Ed. 2d 574 (1988).

[101] 20 F. Supp. 2d 901, 4 WH Cases2d 1650 (E.D.N.C. 1998).

ment, the workers invested only their labor, the workers' gains or losses were only dependent upon labor, harvesting tobacco was unskilled labor, and the workers' services were an integral part of the farmer's business.

In *Heath v. Perdue Farms, Inc.*,[102] the court found that chicken catchers and their crew leaders were employees and not independent contractors of a poultry operation because the poultry operation controlled every aspect of the chicken catchers' work; the poultry operation owned virtually all of the equipment used by the catchers; the crew leaders of the chicken catchers had little opportunity to control their profits and losses; the crew leaders and most of the catchers had long-standing, permanent, and exclusive relationships with the poultry operation; the crew leaders and catchers performed unskilled labor; and the chicken catching operation was an integral part of the operation of the poultry processing plants.[103]

In *Richardson v. Genesee County Community Mental Health Services*,[104] a federal district court in Michigan held that plaintiffs, registered nurses under a collective bargaining agreement with defendant, remained employees while working beyond their normal work hours on a paid volunteer basis during the nonbusiness hours of defendant's 24-hour mental health crisis clinic. Applying the six-factor test under *Donovan v. Brandel* adopted by the Sixth Circuit,[105] the court held that plaintiffs did not become independent contractors while performing the paid, nonmandatory work because they continued to be treated as employees, remained under the control of defendant as employer, had no opportunity for profit or loss or any other independent investment in defendant's business, and the services of plaintiffs during that time were integral to defendant's operation of its facilities.

---

[102]87 F. Supp. 2d 452, 5 WH Cases2d 1633 (D. Md. 2000).
[103]*Id.*, 5 WH Cases2d 1633.
[104]45 F. Supp. 2d 610 (E.D. Mich. 1999).
[105]Donovan v. Brandel, 736 F.2d 1114, 26 WH Cases 1309 (6th Cir. 1984).

In *Hefferman v. Illinois Community College District No. 508*,[106] a coach at a community college alleged that Illinois Community College District No. 508 (the "District") violated the Act by not paying him for work he performed.[107] The District moved to dismiss the coach's complaint on the grounds that the coach was not an "employee" of the District, relying on a contract that the coach attached to his complaint between the coach and the District entitled "Independent Contractor."[108] The district court denied the motion to dismiss, noting that "an independent contractor 'label does not necessarily take the worker from the protection of the Act.'"[109]

In *Cahill v. City of New Brunswick*[110] a federal district court in New Jersey held that police officers were employees, not independent contractors, when they performed "extra duty jobs" for outside vendors because, even though they worked for private companies in performing these extra duty assignments, they were still under the control of the city. The city oversaw and administered the extra duty jobs program and, for its administrative costs, received a "cut" of the officers' pay for the extra duty jobs.[111] More importantly, though, the city considered the officers to be on "on duty" status during the time they worked these extra duty jobs and admitted that the officers would be eligible for workers' compensation benefits if they were injured while performing an extra duty assignment.[112]

In *Santelices v. Cable Wiring*,[113] the court denied summary judgment for defendant company, finding a dispute remained on the question of whether a cable installer was an employee or an independent contractor of the cable installation company. There was evidence tending to show that the company con-

---

[106] 2000 WL 631309, 6 WH Cases2d 132 (N.D. Ill. 2000).

[107] *Id.*

[108] *Id.*

[109] *Id.* (quoting Dole v. Amerlink Corp., 729 F. Supp. 73, 76, 29 WH Cases 1019 (E.D. Mo. 1990)).

[110] 99 F. Supp. 2d 464 (D.N.J. 2000).

[111] *Id.*

[112] *Id.*

[113] 147 F. Supp. 2d 1313, 6 WH Cases2d 1853 (S.D. Fla. 2001).

trolled the manner in which the installer performed his work; that the installer had little opportunity to control his profit and losses, and that work performed by plaintiff was an integral part of the operation of the cable installation company's business.

Delivery drivers of a private carrier furnishing nationwide package pickup and delivery service were employees rather than independent contractors, according to a Labor Department opinion letter.[114] The private carrier retained significant control over the conditions of the work, including assigning service areas, determining the amount of work appropriate for each worker, and significantly controlling the time of performance (by its conditions that no pickup or delivery in the service area be refused, and that all picked up packages be returned to the dock before a particular time in order to meet scheduled departures for other destinations), as well as determining compensation.[115]

9. No Employer-Employee Relationship Found

No employment relationship has been found under the FLSA with respect to the "workfare" benefits made available to recipients under a state public assistance plan.[116] Given the economic reality of the particular circumstances presented in the case, the overall nature of the relationship was determined to be that of assistance, not employment.[117]

In *Chao v. Mid-Atlantic Installation Services*,[118] the court found that cable installers were independent contractors, not employees, of a cable installation company because the installers maintained control over their work assignments and managed

---

[114]WH Op. Letter of December 7, 2000, WH Manual 99:8333.

[115]The Department distinguished the Fifth Circuit's decision in *Herman v. Express Sixty-Minutes Delivery Service*, 161 F.3d 299, 5 WH Cases2d 7 (5th Cir. 1998), while at the same time expressing the Department's continuing disagreement with the result there.

[116]Johns v. Stewart, 57 F.3d 1544 (10th Cir. 1995).

[117]*Id.* at 1558–59.

[118]2001 WL 739243 (4th Cir. 2001), *aff'g* Herman v. Mid-Atlantic Installation Servs., Inc., 164 F. Supp. 2d 667 (D. Md. 2000).

their own employees; the installers were required to supply their own trucks, tools, uniforms and pagers; the installers were responsible for their own liability and car insurance, withholding their employees' taxes and social security, self-employment taxes, unemployment and workers' compensation; the installers had control over their profits and losses; and because of the level of skill involved in performing cable installation and repair work.

E. Trainees

A federal district court has found that former homeless individuals who participated in not-for-profit corporations' job training programs were employees under the FLSA and thus entitled to minimum wage.[119] The court found that the not-for-profit entities "treat[ed] the plaintiffs as classic employees for a classic purpose, *i.e.*, to make money."[120] Applying the six-part test for distinguishing trainees from employees used by the Division since *Walling v. Portland Terminal Co.*,[121] the district court found that (1) program participants were in the program for an indefinite period of time, (2) participants performed tasks similar to those of staff employees and often filled in for the full-time staff, (3) the not-for-profit corporations had underbid other commercial businesses because of their cheap labor supply, (4) participants often worked unsupervised, and (5) participants did not receive training similar to that which would be provided at a vocational school.[122] The court also found that the participants reasonably expected compensation for their work and that the corporation received more benefit from the participants than they provided to the participants in training.[123]

---

[119]Archie v. Grand Cent. P'ship, Inc., 997 F. Supp. 504, 4 WH Cases2d 783 (S.D.N.Y. 1998).

[120]*Id.* at 524.

[121]330 U.S. 148 (1947).

[122]997 F. Supp. at 531–32.

[123]*Id.* at 532–33.

In *Herman v. Hogar Praderas de Amor, Inc.*,[124] a federal district court in Puerto Rico held that nurse's aides, maintenance/laundry workers, and kitchen workers that were required to participate in a mandatory two-day "training," which included little, if any, instruction, but considerable productive work, were entitled to compensation for work done during the training sessions. The court relied on the four-factor test set forth in the regulations which outline the conditions for training time of employees to be non-compensable.[125] The court noted that the "similar" six-factor test[126] for whether an individual is an employee or a trainee, which is often used by the courts in these situations, had not been mentioned by the parties in this case before it.

F. Volunteers

The Department of Labor continues to hold the position that there is no permissible volunteering for services to a for-profit employer in the private sector. In an opinion letter from the Wage and Hour Division, the Department of Labor opined once again that, in the private sector, an individual cannot be both a paid employee and an unpaid volunteer while performing the same types of services (i.e., similar or identical services) that the individual is employed to perform for his or her employer.[127]

Since the notion of a volunteer worker is for practical purposes of significance only in the public sector,[128] the application of the "economic reality" test to distinguish a purported "volunteer" from an "employee" in the private sector may be troublesome."[129] For example, whether any profit or loss be-

[124] 130 F. Supp. 2d 257 (D.P.R. 2001).

[125] 29 C.F.R. §785.27 (2000).

[126] U.S. Dep't of Labor, Wage and Hour Division Field Operations Handbook 10(b)11. See Treatise pp. 93–95.

[127] 2000 WL 1537253 (Dep't of Labor May 22, 2000).

[128] *See* Treatise, Chapter 3, "Coverage," §II.F. [Volunteers] at pp. 95–97.

[129] Krause v. Cherry Hill Fire Dist. 13, 969 F. Supp. 270 (D.N.J. 1997) (volunteer firefighters were employees where firefighters worked continuously for township for over three years and were economically dependent on township).

longs to the putative employer or to the individual is meaningless in the case of a volunteer, who theoretically expects no profit at all.[130]

On August 7, 1998, Congress amended the FLSA definition of "employee" by enacting the Amy Somers Volunteers at Food Banks Act.[131] The amendment excludes from the definition of "employee" individuals who volunteer at food banks for humanitarian purposes, even if such individuals receive groceries from the food bank, which might otherwise be considered a form of compensation.

In *Roman v. Maietta Construction*,[132] the U.S. Court of Appeals for the First Circuit considered whether overtime for the employer or volunteer activity was involved in the racing car activities of a construction welder. The employee had obtained his employment though his acquaintance with the company's owner's son, with whom he was associated in stock car racing activities. Despite the company owner's contrary instructions, the plaintiff spent significant on-the-clock time working on the son's stock cars. He also acted as crew chief in connection with the son's racing. At issue was the character of the time spent volunteering as stock car crew chief ; the defendant characterized this time as volunteered time, while the plaintiff characterized it as an extension of his work. The court rejected the plaintiff's contention that, because the weekend crew chief activities included work on the stock cars at the company's car site with the permission of company supervisors, those activities were an extension of work activities and not voluntary. First, the court pointed out, the welder was not obligated to serve as crew chief. Second, any benefits the company received from the son's racing performance were too attenuated to trigger the FLSA

---

[130] *See id.* and discussion therein contrasting application of test to independent contractor determinations vis-à-vis volunteers.

[131] Pub. L. No. 105-221, 112 Stat. 1248 (1998) (codified at 29 U.S.C. §203(e)(5)) provides: "Section 3(e) of the Fair Labor Standards Act of 1938 (29 U.S.C. 203(e)) is amended by adding at the end the following: '(5) The term "employee" does not include individuals who volunteer their services solely for humanitarian purposes to private non-profit food banks and who receive from the food banks' groceries.'"

[132] 147 F.3d 71, 4 WH Cases2d 1293 (1st Cir. 1998).

where the company advertised at the races but did not own the stock cars involved. Finally, the court reasoned, the employee's racing activities were motivated by personal enjoyment rather than by a desire to benefit the company—as was evidenced by his previous volunteer racing activities.

H. Patient-Workers

The Ninth Circuit has held that work that is part of rehabilitative therapy, even if it confers an economic benefit on the putative employer, does not thereby create an employment relationship when there is no express or implied agreement for compensation.[133]

I. Prison Labor

The Eleventh Circuit has joined other circuits[134] in denying prisoners coverage under the FLSA while they do work under the auspices of the prison. Here the case involved prisoners working in industrial work programs operated by a private nonprofit corporation determined to be a "state instrumentality," and the court held that they were "not covered by the [FLSA] and [were] not entitled to receive federal minimum wage for their labor."[135] Distinguishing earlier circuit case law,[136] the court first determined that the private, nonprofit corporation operating the state's prison work program is a state instrumentality,[137] reasoning that the state held ultimate power and control over the prison work program, as well as custody of the inmates. The state's statutory designation of the program "as an instrumentality of the state" was also significant.[138]

---

[133]Williams v. Strickland, 87 F.3d 1064, 1066 (9th Cir. 1996).

[134]*See* Treatise, at p. 100 note 137.

[135]Gambetta v. Prison Rehab. Indus. & Diversified Enters., Inc., 112 F.3d 1119, 1123–25, 3 WH Cases2d 1633 (11th Cir. 1997).

[136]Williams v. Eastside Mental Health Ctr., 669 F.2d 671, 25 WH Cases2d 358 (11th Cir.), *cert. denied*, 459 U.S. 976, 25 WH Cases2d 989 (1982).

[137]112 F.3d at 1123–24.

[138]*Id.*

The Eleventh Circuit relied on decisions from the Fourth,[139] Eighth,[140] and Ninth[141] Circuits holding prisoners not to be "employees" under the FLSA to conclude that the prisoners were not covered, and thus not entitled to the minimum wage, under the FLSA. Noting that the statute's "dual purposes" are "a decent standard of living for all workers and the avoidance of unfair competition," the court observed that neither purpose was served by subjecting state prison work programs to FLSA coverage; states must maintain prisoners at constitutionally mandated living standards and there are criminal statutes to protect private industries from unfair competition by prison-made goods, the court pointed out.[142] It also noted that paying minimum wage to prisoners "could escalate costs enormously and could well compel correctional systems to curtail or terminate their highly-desirable programs."[143]

An Oklahoma state appellate court agreed with the Tenth Circuit and most other circuits when it affirmed the state trial court in holding that prisoners who provide labor to prisons in which they are incarcerated are not "employees" of the prison, even if the prison is privately owned. The court reasoned that a custodial and penological relationship exists between the prisoner and the correctional facility, rather than an employment relationship.[144]

Other courts in five circuits hold that prisoners who provide labor to the prisons in which they are incarcerated are not "employees" of the prison, reasoning that a custodial and peno-

---

[139]Harker v. State Use Indus., 990 F.2d 131, 1 WH Cases2d 508 (4th Cir.), *cert. denied*, 510 U.S. 886 (1993).

[140]McMaster v. Minnesota, 30 F.3d 976, 2 WH Cases2d 294 (8th Cir. 1994), *cert. denied*, 513 U.S. 1157, 3 WH Cases2d 768 (1995).

[141]Hale v. Arizona, 993 F.2d 1387, 1 WH Cases2d 601 (9th Cir.), *cert. denied*, 510 U.S. 946 (1993).

[142]112 F.3d at 1124.

[143]Extending FLSA coverage to prisoners "is a decision for Congress and not the courts." *Id.*

[144]Washington v. Cornell Corrections, Inc., 30 P.3d 1162 (Okla. Civ. App. 2001), *cert. denied.*

logical relationship exists between the prisoner and the correctional facility, rather than an employment relationship.[145]

III. INDIVIDUAL EMPLOYEE COVERAGE

A. General Principles

The reader should be cautioned not only that an employee who fails to meet the individual coverage tests could be covered under the enterprise standard but also that an individual employed by an alleged enterprise that fails to meet the enterprise standard could still be covered under the individual coverage tests. As noted in Chapter 3, §I [Overview] of the main volume of the Treatise, employees are covered by the FLSA if the requirements for *either* individual coverage *or* enterprise coverage are met.[146]

B. "Engaged in Commerce"

An employee of a not-for-profit Pennsylvania corporation that provided residential treatment and foster care placement services to children and teenagers with mental health problems

---

[145] *See* Danneskjold v. Hausrath, 82 F.3d 37 (2d Cir. 1996) (inmate tutor was not "employee"); Reimonenq v. Foti, 72 F.3d 472, 3 WH Cases2d 33 (5th Cir. 1996); Burleson v. California, 83 F.3d 311, 3 WH Cases2d 498 (9th Cir. 1996); Nicastro v. Reno, 84 F.3d 1446, 3 WH Cases2d 526 (D.C. Cir. 1996); Silo v. U.S. Dep't of Labor, 4 WH Cases2d 415 (D.D.C. 1997); *cf.* Villarreal v. Woodham, 113 F.3d 202 (11th Cir. 1997) (pretrial detainee forced to perform translation services was not "employee"); *Gambetta,* 112 F.3d at 1123–25.

[146] Zorich v. Long Beach Fire Dep't & Ambulance Serv., Inc., 118 F.3d 682, 3 WH Cases2d 1799 (9th Cir. 1997) (after determining that the enterprise did not meet the business dollar volume test for enterprise coverage, the district court erroneously granted summary judgment for the employer without first determining whether plaintiffs met the individual coverage tests); Reich v. Stewart, 121 F.3d 400, 405 (8th Cir. 1997) (secretary's complaint based on individual coverage; annual dollar volume test irrelevant); Boekemeier v. Fourth Universalist Soc'y, 86 F. Supp. 2d 280, 285, 6 WH Cases2d 924 (S.D.N.Y. 2000).

could be subject to coverage if, as part of her duties, she transported children across state lines to visit their families.[147]

The Wage-Hour Division issued an Opinion relating to the coverage of persons who, as part of their attendance at non-profit, community-based mental health facilities, participate voluntarily and without compensation in various projects and activities designed to promote mental health. These activities include participation in a kitchen unit, where meals are planned, food is purchased and prepared, and meals are cooked and served; a clerical unit, where a newsletter is planned, written, printed and distributed, and other similar activities are performed; and a maintenance unit where cleaning and maintenance duties are performed on the premises. The question presented was whether the non-staff participants in these activities are covered by the FLSA. After opining that the institution would generally not be subject to enterprise coverage because it did not have a business purpose, the Acting Administrator determined that individual coverage would extend to participants in the clerical unit who regularly and recurrently prepare, work on or handle newsletters, reports, bulletins or magazines that will be sent out of state, or who make bookkeeping entries related to interstate transactions; that participants in the maintenance unit would not be individually covered unless they regularly and recurrently cleaned or maintained the area where the printed materials destined for interstate distribution are prepared or stored; and that participants in the kitchen unit would not be subject to individual coverage.[148]

2. *Regular Use of the Channels of Commerce*

Courts continue to hold that employees who regularly use the channels of interstate or foreign commerce in the course of their operations are covered by the Act. In *Preston v. Settle Down*

---

[147]Johnson-Medland v. Bethanna, 4 WH Cases2d 91 (E.D. Pa. 1996) (Equal Pay Act case).

[148]WH Opinion dated May 8, 2001, WHM: 99:8368.

Enterprises, Inc.,[149] a federal district court in Georgia held that employees who performed billing duties "engaged in commerce" for the purposes of the Act.[150] In *Preston*, the employer was based in Georgia, but it had employees in Houston, Texas, who handled the company's billing.[151]

In *Boekemeier v. Fourth Universalist Society*,[152] a federal district court in New York held that an employee who ordered cleaning supplies and equipment from out-of-state vendors by telephone and facsimile "engaged in commerce" for the purposes of the Act. The court opined that purchases from out-of-state vendors involving "only sporadic and occasional shipments of insubstantial amounts of goods" are not sufficient engagement in commerce to invoke the protection of the Act.[153] However, in *Boekemeier*, the court found that the employee engaged in commerce where he made "recurrent and frequent purchases from out-of-state vendors," including between 14 and 30 purchases made from five different vendors of items such as custodial supplies, a computer, electronic equipment, and a refrigerator.[154]

However, on similar facts, at federal district court in Illinois found that employees of a medical research company were not covered by the Act because they did not "engage in commerce." In *Reed v. Mycopharma, Inc.*,[155] the court considered whether medical researchers who were in the process of developing new biotechnology "engaged in commerce" when they ordered supplies for the laboratory from out of state, and used the phone, mail, and facsimile facilities to communicate out of state while performing their duties. The court held that these employees did not engage in commerce because "the language of the statute clearly conveys that 'engaged in commerce' relates to the goods or services offered by a business, not the services or

[149] 90 F. Supp. 2d 1267 (D. Ga. 2000).
[150] *Id.*
[151] *Id.*
[152] 86 F. Supp. 2d 280, 6 WH Cases2d 924 (S.D.N.Y. 2000).
[153] *Id.* at 287, 6 WH Cases2d at 931.
[154] *Id.*
[155] 2000 WL 1131953 (N.D. Ill. 2000).

products used by a business."[156] The court noted that its position is buttressed by the fact that "enterprise" coverage in Section 3(s)(1) includes coverage for an employer that has employees "engaged in commerce . . . or that has employees handling . . . or otherwise working on goods or materials that have been moved in or produced for commerce by any person . . . ."[157] According to the court, "Congress' omission of similar language for 'individual' coverage further confirms that under these facts none of the plaintiffs was engaged in commerce."[158]

In a case which appeared to turn largely on the district court's determination that the individual plaintiff was "wholly lacking in credibility,"[159] a federal district court in Florida decided, in *Garay v. B&G Volker Corp.*,[160] that an employee of an apartment complex who performed various job duties for the complex, including maintenance and repair, leasing, and collecting rent, did not "engage in commerce." The court reasoned that, although the employee responded to telephone inquiries prompted by local advertisements for the apartment complex, the telephone line provided to the employee was blocked so as to prohibit long-distance dialing and there was no evidence presented at trial that any of the incoming calls originated outside of Florida.[161]

C. "Engaged in the Production of Goods"

3. Whether Goods Are Produced "for Commerce"

Consistent with well-established law, the court in *Figueroa v. America's Custom Brokers, Inc.*,[162] where plaintiff was employed at a wage of $8.50 per hour as a warehouse worker by companies

---

[156] *Id.* at *3.
[157] *Id.*
[158] *Id.*
[159] 2000 WL 1717632, at *4 (S.D. Fla. 2000).
[160] 2000 WL 1717632 (S.D. Fla. 2000).
[161] *Id.* at *4.
[162] 48 F. Supp. 2d 1372 (S.D. Fla. 1999).

whose business was loading and unloading fish, and where the employees' duties included clearing certain goods through customs, sought overtime compensation for hours worked over 40 in a week. Denying defendants' motion to dismiss, the district court referred to "early federal cases" and regulatory guidance in holding that employees who load and unload goods that are part of the stream of commerce are engaged in commerce for purposes of the FLSA.[163]

In *Ristau v. Tours, Inc.*,[164] the Iowa Supreme Court affirmed a trial court decision that an employee who provided management and maintenance services for an apartment building was not covered by the FLSA. The employer's gross annual dollar volume of business was less than $500,000, the Act's threshold figure for enterprise coverage, and the employer solicited business only within the state. With some lack of clarity in distinguishing between being "engaged in commerce" and being "employed by an enterprise engaged in commerce," the court expressed the view that the employee was not engaged in commerce because, among other things, the employer failed to meet the $500,000 threshold. It also stated that in order to be "engaged in commerce" an employer must " 'reasonably expect' its product to 'move or cause movement in interstate commerce.' "[165] Although the employee handled, as part of her job, goods that had traveled in interstate commerce, the court stated that FLSA coverage in these circumstances requires that an employee must perform work on "goods" which are being prepared for introduction into the stream of interstate commerce.

Also consistent with settled authority, one court has held that the local construction of pallets ultimately used to transport goods in interstate commerce would subject an employer to coverage, even when the employer sold the pallets only locally, as the owner was aware of the likely interstate destinations.[166]

---

[163] *Id.* at 1375.
[164] 593 N.W.2d 115, 5 WH Cases2d 318 (Iowa 1998).
[165] *Id.*, 5 WH Cases2d at 319.
[166] Reich v. Stewart, 121 F.3d 400, 4 WH Cases2d 50 (8th Cir. 1997).

In *Lamont v. Frank Soup Bowl, Inc.*,[167] a federal district court in New York granted summary judgment in favor of the employer on the grounds that the food sold to patrons of his restaurant was not goods produced "for commerce" as required by the FLSA. The court considered that the employer did not deliver food or operate outside of New York and that most of the supplies used in the restaurant were purchased and stored on the premises in New York. The court acknowledged the plaintiff's contentions that people who lived outside of New York purchased food prepared at the restaurant and concluded that "that fact alone cannot serve as evidence that Frank's prepares the food for interstate commerce. If that were true, every hot dog vendor in New York would be engaged in producing goods for interstate commerce."[168] The court held that the preparation of food that may have subsequently been sold to a few customers who live outside of New York does not amount to the production of goods for interstate commerce under the FLSA.[169]

IV. ENTERPRISE COVERAGE

A. General Principles

In an unusual decision on the question of whether there were the "two or more" employees required for enterprise coverage, a district court in Pennsylvania apparently counted the plaintiff and her predecessor, and for a later period of time

---

[167] 2001 WL 521815 (S.D.N.Y. 2001).

[168] *Id.* at *2.

[169] While recognizing that federal courts have found that they have jurisdiction over retaliation claims even when there is no FLSA coverage, acknowledging the broad language of §215 and characterizing the question as "closer" on that claim, the court ultimately determined that it had no jurisdiction over the retaliation claim either, finding that there would have been no reason for Congress to have exercised the full extent of its Commerce Clause power to reach a situation where "[n]either Plaintiff nor his employer engaged in the type of commercial activity Congress chose to regulate." *Id.* at *4.

the plaintiff and her successor, as the necessary two to find enterprise coverage.[170]

B. The Interstate Commerce Standard

A not-for-profit corporation may be an "enterprise engaged in commerce" if it engages in commercial activities in competition with the private sector.[171] Alternatively, even if it is not an enterprise, it may be covered through other provisions of the statute. For example, a not-for-profit organization might be covered if it is "an institution primarily engaged in the care of the sick, the aged or the mentally ill or defective who reside on the premises of such institution,"[172] an "activity of a public agency,"[173] etc.

In *Johnson-Medland v. Bethanna*,[174] a district court held that even though a not-for-profit corporation providing residential treatment and foster care placement services to children with mental health problems was not "primarily engaged in the care of . . . the mentally ill" (when only 18 of out 1,000 children served in a given year were in residential treatment and no more than 58 children were in residence at one time), the plaintiff had sufficiently raised factual issues as to whether the employer competed with private sector profit making organizations to defeat summary judgment for the employer.[175]

Similarly, a federal district court in New York has found that three affiliated not-for-profit organizations dedicated to providing services to the homeless constituted an enterprise "engaged in commerce."[176]

---

[170]Walker v. Washbasket Wash & Dry, 2001 WL 770804, at *8, 7 WH Cases2d 482 (E.D. Pa. 2001).

[171]Johnson-Medland v. Bethanna, 4 WH Cases2d 91 (E.D. Pa. 1996).

[172]*Id.* at 95 (quoting 29 U.S.C. §203(s)(1)(B)).

[173]29 U.S.C. §203(s)(1)(C).

[174]4 WH Cases2d 91 (E.D. Pa. 1996).

[175]*Id.* at 95.

[176]Archie v. Grand Cent. P'ship, Inc., 997 F. Supp. 504, 524–25, 4 WH Cases2d 783, 799–802 (S.D.N.Y. 1998).

A district court in North Carolina held that the Act does not extend to "enterprises which are not truly engaged in public competition," thus finding that counselors at a domestic abuse shelter were not covered.[177] Similarly, another court has held that a house parent at a nonprofit group home was not individually covered, nor was the nonprofit employer an enterprise engaged in commerce.[178]

Briggs v. Chesapeake Volunteers in Youth Services, Inc.,[179] involved a claim for overtime pay by an employee of CVYS who had worked over 1,000 hours of overtime for the employer without any premium compensation. The Virginia federal district court granted summary judgment for the employer, holding that the employer was neither an "enterprise engaged in commerce" nor a "public agency" subject to the Fair Labor Standards Act. Citing *Alamo*,[180] it held that a nonprofit corporation that provides community service opportunities for juveniles involved in juvenile court proceedings is not covered as an "enterprise" under the Act because it is not operated for a "business purpose." In reaching this conclusion, the court reasoned that (1) there was no evidence that the nonprofit corporation competed with other commercial ventures or charged its clients for services, and (2) the nonprofit corporation received funding through grants and local fundraising.[181]

But in *Boekemeier v. Fourth Universalist Society*,[182] the court recognized that a nonprofit church could be an "enterprise" because it earned income from renting property "in direct competition with other short and long-term commercial landlords and special event locations."[183]

---

177 Murray v. R.E.A.C.H. of Jackson County, Inc., 908 F. Supp. 337, 339 (W.D.N.C. 1995).

178 Joles v. Johnson County Youth Serv. Bureau, 885 F. Supp. 1169, 3 WH Cases2d 1360 (S.D. Ind. 1995). *Compare* Gaby v. Omaha Home for Boys, 3 WH Cases2d 1674 (D. Neb. 1997) (court assumes coverage and rejects employer's reliance on the educational institution exemption, §13(b)(24)).

179 68 F. Supp. 2d 711, 5 WH Cases2d 1199 (E.D. Va. 1999).

180 Tony & Susan Alamo Found. v. Department of Labor, 471 U.S. 290, 27 WH Cases 209 (1985).

181 68 F. Supp. 2d. at 715.

182 86 F. Supp. 2d 280 (S.D.N.Y. 2000).

183 *Id.* at 286.

In *Reich v. RPT PRN L.L.C.*,[184] a federal district court in California granted partial summary judgment to the Secretary of Labor on the grounds that the employer, which provided physical therapists to various hospitals, was covered by the FLSA because it qualified as "an enterprise engaged in commerce." The court noted that bills for services rendered were transmitted out of state, and the therapists used materials originating outside of California. The court reasoned that the "materials" as defined in the test for enterprise coverage had no "ultimate consumer" exclusion, unlike the definition of "goods" under Section 3(i).

Another court has held that the business of a sole practitioner doctor licensed to practice in only one state may be covered by the Act on the basis of the purchase of out-of-state medical and office supplies.[185]

Courts continue to apply the "handling" standard in Section 3(s) of the FLSA liberally in determining the existence of enterprise coverage. In *Preston v. Settle Down Enterprises, Inc.*,[186] a federal district court in Georgia applied Section 3(s) of the FLSA in holding that a temporary employment service engaged in commerce, for the purposes of enterprise coverage, where the Georgia-based company had employees handling the company's bills, which were sent out from Houston, Texas.[187] Likewise, in *Herman v. Hector I. Nieves Transport, Inc.*,[188] a federal district court in Puerto Rico recognized that truck drivers who transport goods that have moved in or have been produced for commerce purposes are covered under Section 3(s) of the Act.[189] Similarly, in *Tran v. Tran*,[190] a federal district court in New York found that the hotel rooms and the amenities that hotels provided for their guests were "goods produced for commerce," and the hotels had "employees handling, selling, or otherwise working on" these rooms and amenities for the guests.

---

[184]No. SACV96-485-AHS (EEX), 1996 WL 728159, 5 WH Cases2d 903 (C.D. Cal. 1996).

[185]Monaia v. Grinell, 4 WH Cases2d 31 (S.D.N.Y. 1997).

[186]90 F. Supp. 2d 1267 (N.D. Ga. 2000).

[187]*Id.*

[188]91 F. Supp. 2d 435 (D.P.R. 2000).

[189]*Id.* at 444–45.

[190]6 WH Cases2d 507, 2000 WL 1099906, at *6 (S.D.N.Y. 2000).

Courts continue to take an expansive view of "commerce" in applying Section 3(s) of the FLSA to determine the existence of enterprise coverage. A district court in Pennsylvania held in *Walker v. Washbasket Wash & Dry*[191] that Section 3(s) of the FLSA applied to a coin-operated laundromat because it provided washing machines and clothes dryers that had been purchased in interstate commerce, making the laundromat "engaged in commerce" for purposes of coverage.

C. The Business Dollar Volume Test

1. General Principles

Although the purpose of the annual dollar volume test for enterprise coverage was to avoid extending FLSA coverage to small businesses, the exclusion is solely from enterprise coverage. It is not an exclusion from individual coverage. Thus, an employer whose gross annual business volume is less than the statutory minimum may still employ one or more individuals who are subject to the requirements of the FLSA on an individual coverage basis.[192]

The Wage-Hour Division issued an Opinion relating to the coverage of persons who, as part of their attendance at non-profit, community-based mental health facilities, participate voluntarily and without compensation in various projects and activities designed to promote mental health. These activities include participation in a kitchen unit, where meals are planned, food is purchased and prepared, and meals are cooked and served; a clerical unit, where a newsletter is planned, written, printed and distributed, and other similar activities are performed; and a maintenance unit where cleaning and maintenance duties are performed on the premises. The question presented was whether the non-staff participants in these activities are covered by the FLSA. The Acting Administrator opined

---

[191] 2001 WL 770804, 7 WH Cases 2d 482 (E.D. Pa. 2001).

[192] *See, e.g.*, Jensen v. Longwood Towers LLC, 2000 WL 690180, 6 WH Cases2d 671 (N.D. Ill. 2000).

that "private nonprofit institutions providing psychiatric rehabilitation programs would not be covered by the enterprise provisions of the FLSA since their activities are not performed for a 'business purpose' within the meaning of the FLSA, provided that they are not operated in conjunction with a hospital, covered institutions, or school [whose coverage is otherwise provided for.]"[193]

2. *Gross Receipts*

The Seventh Circuit in *Sapperstein v.Hager*[194] reversed the district court's dismissal on jurisdictional grounds of Sapperstein's complaint, which the district court had ordered from the bench. The employer had filed the affidavit of a manager to the effect that gross annual sales for the year preceding the filing of the complaint were $497,253.00. Noting that in the usual case a determination to credit the employer's evidence would be within the trial court's discretion, and that the review of a district court's determination of its jurisdiction is "very deferential," the Court of Appeals went on to state that it was "not reasonable, in the context of a motion to dismiss, to credit an affidavit from the defendants' manager as to the amount of gross sales when the plaintiff had no real opportunity to contest the allegation."[195]

In *Jensen v. Longwood Towers LLC,*[196] a federal district court in Illinois denied "enterprise" coverage because the alleged joint employers did not meet the $500,000 business volume required by Section 3(s)(1)(A). The plaintiff argued that the two defendants constituted a single enterprise and, therefore, the court should add their annual revenues from 1998 together to exceed the $500,000 statutory minimum.[197] The court, however, found that plaintiff's argument was based on "a bit of a ledger legerdemain" because all of the revenues from one of the defendants came from transactions with the other and the

---

[193]WH Opinion dated May 8, 2001, WHM: 99:8368.
[194]5 WH Cases2d 933 (7th Cir. 1999)
[195]*Id.* at 935.
[196]2000 WL 690180, 6 WH Cases2d 671 (N.D. Ill. 2000).
[197]*Id.*

"single revenue pool" for the two defendants in 1998 amounted to less than $500,000.[198] Relying in part on a Department of Labor regulation, the court held that the revenues from these transactions could not be added together for the purposes of meeting the $500,000 threshold under Section 3(s)(1)(A) for enterprise coverage.[199]

In *Boekemeier v. Fourth Universalist Society*,[200] a federal district court in New York considered whether a church met the $500,000 threshold for enterprise coverage. The court noted that the church's rental income and special events income, which amounted to less than $500,000, should be included in the church's gross business volume calculation.[201] However, the court was uncertain as to whether the church's other sources of income, including charitable income, investment income, and miscellaneous income, was "sufficiently related to the Church's business income to warrant inclusion in the gross volume amount."[202] The court denied summary judgment because the parties did not present any evidence regarding the purposes of these other sources of income and their relationship to the church's rental activities.[203] The *Boekemeier* decision suggests that, in analyzing whether a nonprofit company has met the $500,000 gross business volume, courts should closely examine each component of nonbusiness income (*i.e.*, charitable donations, returns on investments, etc.) to determine if the income is used to further a "business" purpose of the nonprofit company. Similarly, in *Garay v. B & G Volker Corp.*,[204] a federal district court in Florida held that an employer cannot be subject to enterprise coverage where the plaintiff failed to put on any evidence at trial that the employer's annual gross volume satisfied the $500,000 threshold business volume during the relevant time period.

---

[198] *Id.*

[199] *Id.*; *see* 29 C.F.R. §779.259(a) ("the dollar amount of an establishment derived from transactions with other establishments in the same enterprise does not ordinarily constitute part of the annual gross volume of the enterprise as a whole").

[200] 86 F. Supp. 2d 280, 6 WH Cases2d 924 (S.D.N.Y. 2000).

[201] *Id.* at 286.

[202] *Id.*

[203] *Id.* at 286–87.

[204] 2000 WL 1717632, at *4 (S.D. Fla. 2000).

In *Lamont v. Frank Soup Bowl*,[205] a federal district court in New York granted summary judgment to the employer holding that the enterprise theory was inapplicable in a restaurant employee's claim for overtime compensation. The court held the restaurant was not an enterprise as defined by the FLSA because it did not have an annual gross volume of sales of at least $500,000.00.

5. Grandfather Coverage

In one case, the Department of Labor asserted "grandfather" coverage of a construction firm. The court, observing that there was no case law regarding Section 3(s) of the Act, concluded that even a firm that was no longer covered on either an enterprise or an individual basis was possibly subject to grandfather coverage, and it directed the parties to address whether the firm indeed was covered as of the effective date of Section 3(s).[206]

E. "Unified Operation" or "Common Control"

"Common control" issues continue to involve a fact-specific inquiry. The Ninth Circuit in one case reversed a district court's decision that one corporation was not a part of the enterprise stipulated to by the other defendants after reviewing the factual findings that supported determinations of related activities, common control or unified operations (common link of ownership, related corporate office holders, hiring of managers, direction of FLSA compliance), and common business purpose.[207]

In *Archie v. Grand Central Partnership, Inc.*,[208] the court found that the defendants, two not-for-profit corporations and a business improvement district, were engaged in related activities under common control in connection with their offering of

[205] 2001 WL 521815 (S.D.N.Y. 2001).
[206] Reich v. Troyer, 3 WH Cases2d 574, 575–76 (E.D. La. 1996).
[207] Reich v. Japan Enters., 91 F.3d 154 (9th Cir. 1996).
[208] 4 WH Cases2d 783 (S.D.N.Y. 1998).

training and other activities for homeless residents of New York. The court found that the entities "sought to benefit the business within their area and provide social services,"[209] that they employed "homeless and formerly homeless people to reach out to their homeless peers in bank vestibules, private properties, and public spaces throughout New York City, to bring them indoors and connect them with social services"[210] and that in doing so they shared "employees, including key executives, office space and operations"[211] under the leadership of a "core group of individuals that controlled the three entities,"[212] that they prepared consolidated financial statements, and that they engaged in their activities for a common business purpose—namely "to further the . . . goals of improving and enhancing the conditions of their districts"[213] and "for the common business purpose of protecting the investments of Grand Central area property owners and enhancing business opportunities for local merchants."[214] The court thus determined that they constituted an enterprise within the meaning of the FLSA.

In *Herman v. Harmelech,*[215] a federal district court in Illinois held that two companies that organized to engage in the retail sale of jewelry at various concessions located in over 50 different Sears stores in numerous states in the Midwest, and two executives of these two companies, together were a single "enterprise" covered by the Act. Specifically, the court found that the companies and the executives engaged in related activities and a common business purpose because all of the concessions sold jewelry, and there was "unified operation and common control" of the various concessions because the managers of the various jewelry concessions reported through a chain of command to the two companies' home offices.[216]

---

[209] *Id.* at 799.
[210] *Id.* at 800.
[211] *Id.* at 787.
[212] *Id.* at 799.
[213] *Id.* at 800.
[214] *Id.* at 797.
[215] 2000 WL 420839 (N.D. Ill. 2000).
[216] *Id.* at *5–6.

In *Preston v. Settle Down Enterprises, Inc.*,[217] the court analyzed the issue of whether a consultant of a temporary employment agency who had control of the day-to-day operations of the company was part of the same "enterprise" as the company for purposes of coverage under the Act.[218] The consultant contended that he could not be part of the "enterprise" because he was an independent contractor.[219] Focusing on the consultant's control of the day-to-day operations of the company, the court found coverage with respect to the consultant because he and the temporary employment agency he controlled were together an "enterprise" under the Act.[220] The court reasoned that "Congress crafted the enterprise liability section of the FLSA to allow businesses to be grouped together so FLSA's coverage could keep up with changes in the national marketplace."[221] It further explained that "[t]he enterprise concept allows the revenues of businesses [sic] entities to be combined to meet the minimum gross sales amount required by the FLSA."[222]

Similarly, in *Herman v. Hector I. Nieves Transport, Inc.*,[223] a federal district court in Puerto Rico held that a company that engaged in the transportation of goods by truck, its president, and its secretary/treasurer, were an "enterprise" covered by the Act because they "engaged in related activities with unified operations or common control for a common business purpose."[224] In *Tran v. Tran*,[225] a federal district court in New York found that a group of hotels in New York constituted an "enterprise" under the Act because the various hotels had common corporate management and shared employees.

---

[217] 90 F. Supp. 2d 1267 (N.D. Ga. 2000).

[218] *Id.*

[219] *Id.* at 1275.

[220] *Id.* at 1275–76.

[221] *Id.* at 1275 (citing Reich v. Gateway Press, Inc., 13 F.3d 685, 694 (3d Cir. 1994)).

[222] *Preston*, 90 F. Supp. 2d at 1275 (citing Patel v. Wargo, 803 F.2d 632, 635 (11th Cir. 1986)).

[223] 91 F. Supp. 2d 435 (D.P.R. 2000).

[224] *Id.* at 444 (citing Falk v. Brennan, 414 U.S. 190, 196 n.8 (1973)).

[225] 2000 WL 1099906 (S.D.N.Y. 2000).

In *Dybevik v. Quality Pork Processors, Inc.*,[226] plaintiffs sought to add as an additional defendant Hormel Foods Inc., either on a joint employer theory[227] or on a "single enterprise" theory. Despite the contested facts as to the extent of "unified operation or common control," and in spite of recognizing the exclusion of "related activities performed . . . by an independent contractor"[228] from consideration, the federal district court allowed the plaintiffs to amend their complaint to include Hormel Foods Inc. as a corporate defendant under the enterprise theory. Allegations of common control included that Hormel was present at the Quality Pork Processors ("QPP") facility daily, oversaw day-to-day operations, instructed QPP employees how to perform their jobs, conducted cost testing in the QPP production area and overrode some supervisory decisions involving QPP employees; that QPP returned any profit it made to Hormel, and was not required to pay rent to Hormel in advance; and that QPP's executive salaries were negotiated with Hormel.

V. Geographic Aspects of Coverage

In *Koren v. Martin Marietta Services*,[229] a federal district court in Puerto Rico considered the Act's applicability to a claim arising while the plaintiff worked on three military installations in Puerto Rico. The court first concluded that the Roosevelt Roads Naval Base, naval facilities located on the island of Vieques, and naval facilities located on the Pico Del Este mountain were subject to federal enclave jurisdiction, although it was unclear when exclusive federal legislative jurisdiction over these areas attached.

When federal enclave jurisdiction is found, state law as it existed at the time that a geographic region became subject to

[226]2001 WL 811124 (D. Minn. 2001).

[227]For discussion of the joint employer analysis, see Chapter 18 (Litigation Issues) IV (Parties) E (Joint Employment) 3 (Other Joint Employers).

[228]29 U.S.C. §206(r).

[229]997 F. Supp. 196, 4 WH Cases2d 712 (D.P.R. 1998).

the exclusive jurisdiction of the federal government continues to apply until a federal law is found to abrogate that state law. Thus, the issue was whether the Act abrogated Puerto Rico wage and hour legislation.[230] Although there was no direct conflict between the FLSA and the Puerto Rico wage and hour laws, the court concluded that because the Puerto Rican laws governing the case had been either repealed or amended since federal legislative jurisdiction attached to the parcels of land at issue, application of the Puerto Rico laws would counter the goal of achieving uniformity between the portions of Puerto Rico that were subject to federal enclave jurisdiction and those that were not. The court also doubted that the Puerto Rican laws would be as favorable to employees as the FLSA, which would interfere with the policy behind the FLSA. Further, the court found that application of repealed or amended laws would place an unreasonable burden on employers who operated in the parcels subject to federal enclave jurisdiction because of the cost of becoming educated about the application of those laws as they existed at the time that federal enclave jurisdiction attached. Finally, the court doubted the Minimum Wage Board's authority to regulate labor under laws that had been repealed or amended, which would leave the parcels of land subject to federal enclave jurisdiction with gaps in the legal framework governing wages and hours. Therefore, the FLSA was found to abrogate the Puerto Rican wage and hour laws in those federal enclaves.

---

[230]The term "abrogation" is not a synonym for preemption but has a similar effect. Preemption will be found only when Congress expressly states an intent to preempt state law or when an actual conflict between state and federal law exists, whether through direct disagreement or an interference with the pervasiveness of federal regulation of a particular area. Abrogation, on the other hand, does not require direct conflict. In conducting its analysis, the court noted that the policies that govern the abrogation inquiry are first, a concern over state law interference with the carrying out of federal law; second, a desire to ensure uniformity between the laws governing the state and the laws governing the parcel subject to federal legislative jurisdiction; and third, a goal of avoiding gaps in the legal framework that operates within the parcel subject to federal legislative jurisdiction.

CHAPTER 4

WHITE-COLLAR EXEMPTIONS

II. LEGAL PRINCIPLES THAT GOVERN ANALYSIS OF EXEMPTIONS

A. Burden of Proving Entitlement to Exemption

Despite the well-settled law that the burden falls on the employer to establish each element of a claimed exemption, two recent district court cases approach the burden issue somewhat differently. In *Morales v. Zondo, Inc.,*[1] a federal district court in New York refused to allow plaintiff to amend her complaint to add an FLSA claim for overtime to a suit originally stating claims under the Pregnancy Disability Act, New York State Human Rights Law, and New York City Human Rights Law. It reached this conclusion on the basis of a finding that such an amendment would be futile because plaintiff was administratively exempt. In reaching that conclusion the court relied on the unusual proposition that to prevail plaintiff would have to prove that "she was an employee who was eligible for overtime, i.e., that she was not exempt from the overtime pay requirements"[2] as well as that she actually worked overtime. The court found that she was an exempt administrative employee, despite plaintiff's evidence tendered to show that she was not paid on a salary basis and that she did significant manual work and exercised little discretion, because she worked directly for the company's proprietor and her primary duties were participating in meetings with customers and the sales staff; coordinating communications with vendors; negotiating prices; arranging deliveries; and maintaining product information files, and because she had conceded (before new information came to her attention) that she was paid on a salary basis. And in an unpublished decision in *Mock v. Tharaldson Property Management, Inc.,*[3] the district court granted

[1]2001 U.S. Dist. LEXIS 508, 6 WH Cases2d 1390 (S.D.N.Y. 2001).
[2]6 WH Cases2d at 1392.
[3]2001 U.S. Dist. LEXIS 3377 (N.D. Iowa 2001).

summary judgment for the employer on plaintiff's claims for unpaid minimum wages and overtime, responding to plaintiff's contention that she did not meet the requirements of the exemption relied on by defendants by noting that she "failed to generate a genuine issue of material fact that she was not a salaried managerial or executive employee exempted from the minimum wage requirements under *29 U.S.C. § 213*(a)(1) . . . ." Although she had apparently put forward at least some evidence that she spent more time on non-exempt work than was permitted by the tests, the plaintiff was found not to have pointed out specific facts in the record which would have led the court to conclude that a genuine factual difference remained for trial.

B. Weight of DOL Regulations

In *Auer v. Robbins*,[4] the Supreme Court deferred to the Secretary's interpretation of the DOL's salary basis regulations, reasoning that "because the salary-basis test is a creature of the Secretary's own regulations, his interpretation of it is, under our jurisprudence, controlling unless 'plainly erroneous or inconsistent with the regulation.'"[5] Under that deferential standard, the Supreme Court gave force of law to the Secretary's view of when an employee's compensation is "subject to reduction" so as to bar a finding of salaried status.[6] The Court also deferred to the Secretary's interpretation of the so-called window of correction (allowing in appropriate circumstances for the restoration of salaried status despite an impermissible salary deduction) as being applicable even where the employer does not repay improper salary deductions immediately.[7]

---

[4] 117 S. Ct. 905, 3 WH Cases2d 1249 (1997).

[5] *Id.* at 911 (quoting Robertson v. Methow Valley Citizens Council, 490 U.S. 332, 359 (1989)).

[6] *Id.*

[7] *Id.* at 912.

Auer has been considered and applied by a variety of circuit and district courts.[8] Most of the cases involve a straightforward application of *Auer's* salary basis holding. A few involve wrinkles.

For example, one district court deferred to the Secretary's interpretation of the window of correction as being unavailable to employers that engaged in a "pattern" of improper deductions.[9] The district court therefore rejected an assertion that the regulatory language[10] effectively grants an absolute right to cure improper deductions retroactively, and thereby avoid overtime liability, whenever a deduction is made for reasons other than lack of work.[11] The Court explained that the Secretary's interpretation of the DOL's own regulations was entitled to deference because

> the Secretary's interpretation, providing that the window of correction is unavailable to employers that have engaged in a "pattern" of improper deductions, rationally expresses the view that such employers lacked a "*bona fide* intent" to treat their employees as exempt.[12]

---

[8]*Second Circuit:* Ahern v. County of Nassau, 118 F.3d 118, 3 WH Cases2d 1822 (2d Cir. 1997); Lilenfeld v. Kiepper, 4 WH Cases2d 307 (S.D.N.Y. 1997); Hoffman v. Sbarro, Inc., 982 F. Supp. 249, 4 WH Cases2d 335 (S.D.N.Y. 1997). *Third Circuit:* Balgowan v. New Jersey Dep't of Transp., 115 F.3d 214, 3 WH Cases2d 1703 (3d Cir. 1997). *Fourth Circuit:* Yuen v. U.S. Asia Commercial Dev. Corp., 4 WH Cases2d 69 (E.D. Va. 1997). *Sixth Circuit:* Aiken v. City of Memphis, 4 WH Cases2d 408 (W.D. Tenn. 1997). *Seventh Circuit:* Haywood v. North Am. Van Lines, Inc., 121 F.3d 1066, 4 WH Cases2d 59 (7th Cir. 1997); Cerbu v. Chicago Bldg. Servs., Inc., 4 WH Cases2d 695 (N.D. Ill. 1998). *Ninth Circuit:* Childers v. City of Eugene, 120 F.3d 944, 3 WH Cases2d 1831 (9th Cir. 1997); Stanley v. City of Tracy, 120 F.3d 179, 3 WH Cases2d 1833 (9th Cir. 1997). *Tenth Circuit:* Carpenter v. City & County of Denver, 3 WH Cases2d 1869 (10th Cir. 1997); Gillette v. Unirex, Inc., 4 WH Cases2d 169 (D. Kan. 1997). *Eleventh Circuit:* Evans v. McClain of Ga., Inc., 131 F.3d 957, 965, 4 WH Cases2d 419 (11th Cir. 1997); Davis v. Hollywood, 4 WH Cases2d 97 (11th Cir. 1997); Arrington v. City of Macon, 4 WH Cases2d 122 (M.D. Ga. 1997).

[9]Hoffmann v. Sbarro, Inc., 982 F. Supp. 249, 4 WH Cases2d 335 (S.D.N.Y. 1997).

[10]29 C.F.R. §541.118(a)(6).

[11]982 F. Supp. at 255, 4 WH Cases2d at 341.

[12]*Id.* at 257, 4 WH Cases2d at 342 (citation omitted).

C. Other Sources of Interpretation

In a decision that illuminates the deference to be given to conflicting Department of Labor opinions offered by different officers of the Department, the Sixth Circuit in *Fazekas v. Cleveland Clinic Foundation Health Care*[13] affirmed the decision of the district court granting summary judgment to the defendants in a case brought by home health care nurses.[14] The question whether the plaintiffs were exempt employees, as claimed by defendants, turned on whether they were or were not compensated on a "fee basis."[15] Deferring to an earlier opinion by the Acting Wage and Hour Administrator, rather than later opinions by counsel and other staff of the Wage and Hour Division, the appellate court ruled that an Acting Administrator's opinion represented the Department's position. The court found that the Acting Administrator's opinion (to the effect that the work involved "unique" (rather than repetitive) tasks and thus the nurses' fixed payments did qualify as fee basis payments) was controlling, as it was not inconsistent with the regulation or plainly erroneous.

IV. THE SALARY BASIS TEST

B. Requirements of the Salary Basis Test

1. General Rule

The Eleventh Circuit rejected the plaintiff's contention that he was not truly salaried because after years as an hourly employee and in the context of a labor organizing campaign, he was given a salary in an attempt to "obviate the requirements of

---

[13]204 F.3d 673 (6th Cir. 2000).

[14]See text at note 157, below.

[15]*See* Supplement, Chapter 4, "White-Collar Exemptions," §IV.E. [Fee Basis Alternative for Professional and Administrative Exemptions] at notes 156–58 and accompanying text, below.

the National Labor Relations Act."[16] The district court had granted summary judgment for the employer, and the court of appeals affirmed, stating:

> We do not believe that an employer's subjective motivations are relevant to the inquiry of whether or not an employee was compensated on a salary basis. The regulations speak in purely objective terms.[17]

In *Haywood v. North American Van Lines, Inc.*,[18] the Seventh Circuit rejected an employee's contention that although she always received a biweekly paycheck in the same amount regardless of the number of hours worked, she was nevertheless not paid on a salary basis for purposes of the Act. She cited four job requirements that she claimed destroyed her salaried status: (1) if she could not work a mandatory Saturday shift and was unable to find a replacement, she was subject to nonmonetary discipline; (2) if she missed work during the regular workweek, she was required to make up the time; (3) if she needed to find a replacement worker for her Saturday shifts, she might have had to pay him or her; and (4) if she failed to make up absence, her salary was deducted.[19] The court rejected the claim for overtime compensation, finding that none of the circumstances alleged indicated she was an hourly, rather than a salaried, employee.

With respect to the first contention—that nonmonetary discipline for failing to work a scheduled shift supports a finding of nonsalaried status—the court concluded that "nothing in the regulations suggests that an employee loses his exempt status simply because his employer disciplines him in a non-monetary fashion for failing to work during his scheduled time. The regulations prohibit monetary discipline of exempt employees; the amount of compensation may not be subject to a reduction because of variations in the quality or quantity of work."[20]

---

[16]Evans v. McClain of Ga., Inc., 131 F.3d 957, 965, 4 WH Cases2d 419 (11th Cir. 1997).

[17]*Id.* at 965 (citation omitted).

[18]121 F.3d 1066, 4 WH Cases2d 59 (7th Cir. 1997).

[19]*Id.* at 1070.

[20]*Id.*

The court rejected the second contention—that the plaintiff was required to make up time before she was able to take additional time off—because had the plaintiff chosen not to make up time before taking additional time off, her salary would not have been reduced. Instead, her sick leave or personal leave would have been reduced, which is not impermissible. The court also noted, "The regulations, moreover, allow employers to deduct from an exempt employee's paycheck for a full day's absence [for personal reasons or if the employer maintains a bona fide sick leave plan]."[21]

Also found unpersuasive was the plaintiff's third contention—that she was not salaried because she had to pay another employee to work in her stead on her mandatory Saturday shifts (three to four per year). The court explained:

> The money that Ms. Haywood agrees to pay her replacement, if any, is simply not a deduction for purposes of the Secretary's regulations; it is a voluntary transaction between Ms. Haywood and another employee by which Ms. Haywood escapes the nonmonetary discipline to which she would be subjected if she neither found a replacement nor showed up for her shift.[22]

Finally, the court found the plaintiff's fourth allegation—that she was threatened with a pay reduction if she did not make up missed time—to be unpersuasive. No deductions were ever made because the plaintiff always worked extra hours before taking time off. The court concluded that the evidence was therefore insufficient to demonstrate the existence of an "employment policy that, 'as a practical matter,' permitted deductions from pay for disciplinary reasons."[23]

In a case involving employees who were never paid at all and who contended that as a result they were not paid on a salary basis within the meaning of the regulations, the court held that the "salary" referred to in the long and short tests is what the employee is owed, not what he actually received.[24]

---

[21] *Id.*
[22] *Id.* at 1071.
[23] *Id.*
[24] Nicholson v. World Bus. Network, Inc., 3 WH Cases2d 1313, 1315 (11th Cir.), *cert. denied*, 118 S. Ct. 368 (1997).

In re Wal-Mart Stores, Inc.[25] arose on review by the district court of recommendations of a magistrate judge. Finding those recommendations thoughtful and in accordance with the law, the court upheld the magistrate's findings and conclusions to the effect that pharmacists employed by the defendant did not qualify for the professional exemption from the FLSA because they were not paid "on a salary basis." In this case, the pharmacists' schedules and compensation were changed prospectively before each pay period.[26] Deposition testimony indicated that the base hours and base pay were reduced in response to business demand, and the court concluded that pay was effectively tied to the actual number of hours worked. The court stated: "[B]usinesses cannot cut hours for their own convenience and still maintain that the employees are salaried. A choice must be made between the convenience of flexible hours or the stability of salaried employees."[27]

The facts in *Caperci v. Rite Aid Corp.*[28] were largely similar but involved only occasional, rather than recurrent, adjustments of the compensation amount agreed to between employer and pharmacists; the case also involved deductions from accrued leave for partial day absences. Plaintiffs sought overtime, asserting that their pay was so tied to their hours of work that the salary basis test was not met. The court adopted and approved the magistrate's findings and recommendations, including the finding that no actual deductions from pay were made for partial day absences and the recommendation that the defendant's motion for summary judgment be granted.

A federal district court in Tennessee held in *Belcher v. Shoney's, Inc.*[29] that the general and assistant managers of Shoney's chain restaurants were not paid on a salary basis where the

---

[25]58 F. Supp. 2d 1219, 5 WH Cases2d 889 (D. Colo. 1999).

[26]The "predetermined salary" claim here is reminiscent of that put forward to, and rejected by, the court in *Thomas v. Fairfax County*, 758 F. Supp. 353, 30 WH Cases 313 (E.D. Va. 1991), *aff'd sub nom.* Allen v. Fairfax County, 16 F.3d 408 (4th Cir. 1994), discussed in the Treatise at p.188.

[27]5 WH Cases2d at 890.

[28]43 F. Supp. 2d 83, 5 WH Cases2d 268 (D. Mass. 1999).

[29]30 F. Supp. 2d 1010, 5 WH Cases2d 134 (M.D. Tenn. 1998).

evidence showed that the chain had a policy of reducing their salaries to cover cash shortages or casualty losses which occurred when the company's cash and deposit management rules had been violated. The company made the novel argument that its deductions did not interfere with payment "on a salary basis" because its rules relating to safekeeping of cash and deposits management were "safety rules of major significance" within the meaning of 29 C.F.R. §541.118(a)(5), inasmuch as violence is the primary cause of injury and death in the workplace, and these rules were adopted for the purpose and had the effect of minimizing the occasions for such violence. The court rejected this claim on the ground that the rules were "not sufficiently related to employee safety"[30] to fall within the provisions of that regulation. Analyzing the deductions evidence, the court reasoned that the restaurant chain had an employment policy that created a substantial likelihood that salaries would be reduced. Management employees were informed in writing about the possibility of such deductions, an internal company form was specifically drafted for the purpose of implementing such salary reductions, and managers were given the form to sign when a loss occurred so that the deduction would be implemented by the accounting department.

In *East v. Bullock's, Inc.*,[31] a federal district court in Arizona, applying *Auer v. Robbins*,[32] found that a manager in a retail store was paid on a salary basis and was thus exempt from the FLSA overtime requirements even though the store's employee manual provided for pay deductions for part-day absences because of sickness, jury duty, participation in a trial as a witness, and temporary military leave. Because no actual deductions were ever taken from the employee's pay and no evidence was presented of improper deductions from the pay of other salaried employees, the court concluded that the manager was salaried.

---

[30] 5 WH Cases2d at 143.
[31] 34 F. Supp. 2d 1176, 5 WH Cases2d 198 (D. Ariz. 1998).
[32] 519 U.S. 452, 3 WH Cases2d 1249 (1997).

Similarly, the Ninth Circuit in *McGuire v. City of Portland*[33] applied *Auer* and reached the conclusion that fire chiefs were exempt because there was no demonstration of a substantial likelihood that inappropriate deductions would be made.

In *Kelly v. City of Mount Vernon*,[34] the Second Circuit, following *Ahern v. County of Nassau*,[35] upheld the district court's decision that detective sergeants and lieutenants in a police department are paid on a salary basis, and are therefore exempt from the FLSA overtime requirements, where the department has neither an "actual practice" nor a "clear and particularized policy" that evidences a "significant likelihood" that it will dock salaried employees' pay for minor violations of department regulations, temporary military leave, or appearing in non-department-related court proceedings.

In *Palazzolo-Robinson v. Sharis Management Corp.*,[36] a manager for a restaurant chain apparently claimed not to be exempt on the ground that she was "paid a salary based upon an hourly rate."[37] The District Court for Western Washington held that a payroll accounting system that calculates an exempt employee's pay on an hourly basis does not indicate that the employee is not salaried.

In *Harris v. Mercy Health Corp.*,[38] a district court in Pennsylvania denied summary judgment for the employer on the salary basis test where the payroll records showed that the employee, a manager of a medical clinic, was an hourly employee and was paid different hourly rates for day, evening, and night work. The employer argued that the payroll management software required assignment of an hourly rate for salaried and nonsalaried employees alike. The employer also argued that the payroll records showed the employee did not have to clock in or clock

[33]159 F.3d 460, 4 WH Cases2d 1736 (9th Cir. 1998) on rehearing. Earlier decisions are reported at 3 WH Cases2d 707 (9th Cir. 1996), and 3 WH Cases2d 1502 (9th Cir. 1997).

[34]162 F.3d 765, 5 WH Cases2d 106 (2d Cir. 1998).

[35]118 F.3d 118, 3 WH Cases2d 1822 (2d Cir. 1997).

[36]68 F. Supp. 2d 1186, 5 WH Cases2d 1561 (W.D. Wash. 1999).

[37]5 WH Cases2d at 1566 (citing Plaintiff's Memo. at 2).

[38]2000 U.S. Dist. LEXIS 11228, 141 Lab. Cas. (CCH) ¶34,146 (E.D. Pa. 2000).

out, as an hourly worker presumably would have to do. However, on summary judgment, the payroll evidence sufficed to create a triable issue.

A pharmacist who is paid on an hourly basis is not an exempt professional, because he is not paid on a salary or fee basis.[39]

The Wage and Hour Division issued additional opinions interpreting and applying the salary basis test. It considered whether a sick leave plan was a bona fide plan for purposes of 29 C.F.R. §541.118(a)(3). The plan under consideration required employment for three months before eligibility to participate. Under the plan, three days would be deposited annually into a sick leave plan. When the leave was exhausted, the employee would be subject to a proportional salary reduction if unable to report because of illness. The plan also had an extended illness bank for absences of more than five consecutive days due to illness, as well as some year-end cash conversion options. The Division held that the plan was bona fide so long as there were no reductions in pay for absences of less than a day.[40]

Along similar lines, the Wage and Hour Division in 1998 reemphasized its long-standing position that reductions in leave banks for less than a day will not defeat the salary basis of compensation so long as "by substituting or reducing such leave 'bank' the employee receives an amount equal to his or her guaranteed salary."[41] The Division also opined that providing additional compensation in a workweek is not inconsistent with payment on a salary basis, nor is the provision of "compensatory time" to exempt employees.[42]

Finally, the Division expressed the view that a work plan by which, under specified circumstances, some exempt employees would have reduced work schedules and thus reduced pay in certain workweeks as a result of economic conditions would not defeat salary basis payment. The Acting Administrator stated

---

[39]Iheanacho v. Safeway, Inc., 2000 U.S. Dist. LEXIS 150156, 142 Lab. Cas. (CCH) ¶34,163 (D. Or. 2000).

[40]WH Admin. Op. (Feb. 19 1998), 1998 WL 852708.

[41]WH Admin. Op. (Feb. 19, 1998), 1998 WL 852706.

[42]WH Admin. Op. (Feb. 27, 1998), 1998 WL 852735.

that "a fixed reduction in salary effective during a period when a company operates a short workweek due to economic conditions would be a *bona fide* reduction not designed to circumvent the salary basis payment."[43]

In *Whitesides v. U-Haul Co. of Alaska*,[44] the Alaska Supreme Court in a case brought under Alaska law vacated a jury verdict for the defendant, U-Haul, and held that U-Haul did not treat the plaintiff manager in a manner consistent with his being an exempt salaried employee as defendant claimed. The state supreme court held that the trial court erred when it denied the manager summary judgment on his claim for overtime compensation. The employee's work for some time had been to service various dealerships dispersed through southern Alaska, which involved a significant amount of travel and work away from the office. After he had had a serious highway accident, he was notified in writing that he had been reassigned to another office, and that his hours would be 8:00 a.m. to 6:00 p.m., Monday through Friday and 8:00 a.m. to 4:00 p.m. on Saturday. The day after receiving this notification, the manager arrived at work fifteen minutes late and was suspended without pay for three days. Although the claim was brought under the Alaska Wage and Hour Act, the court considered the federal regulations and federal caselaw in determining that the "window of correction" did not apply, and that by subjecting the plaintiff to a rigid hourly schedule and strictly enforcing that schedule with disciplinary sanctions, U-Haul treated him like an hourly worker rather than a salaried worker.

Another state law claim came before the Washington Supreme Court in *Drinkwitz v. Alliant Techsystems, Inc.*,[45] where the trial court had certified questions for resolution. There the court held that for purposes of the state statute, the appropriate test of whether an employee was paid on a salary basis was the test incorporated in the federal regulations and (over four dissent-

---

[43]WH Admin. Op. (Feb. 23, 1998), 1998 WL 852696, WHM: 99:8133 (1998).
[44]16 P.3d 729 (Alaska 2001).
[45]140 Wash. 2d 291, 996 P.2d 582, 6 WH Cases2d 1650 (2000).

ing votes) that the "window of correction" was not available under the Washington Minimum Wage Act. The court's majority concluded that the plaintiffs were not exempt.

In *Moss v. Crawford & Co.*,[46] a federal district court in Pennsylvania granted one of plaintiffs' motions for summary judgment, and denied other pending motions for summary judgment. The court determined that plaintiffs, insurance adjusters, monitors and invoice reviewers, were not exempt employees under the salary basis test because their compensation depended upon the number of hours they worked and was calculated at different hourly rates based upon the specific tasks they were performing. In earlier proceedings the court had found that when originally hired, the employees were paid by the project, not on a fixed weekly salary. Subsequently, the employer guaranteed some of them a payment of at least $250 a week. The court stated that before the defendant guaranteed them $250 per week, the plaintiffs were all paid on a commission basis. Thus, the court held that the plaintiffs were entitled to overtime pay.[47]

2. *Permissible Deductions From an Employee's Salary*

In *Baudin v. Courtesy Litho Arts*,[48] the plaintiff failed to receive the full weekly salary for the first week after his promotion to a management position, which happened to be the week in which Thanksgiving fell. The defendant claimed that the plaintiff had taken the Friday after Thanksgiving off for personal reasons and was docked; the plaintiff claimed that the plant was closed on the Friday after Thanksgiving. The district court in Illinois found it unnecessary to resolve this difference even on summary judgment, because in its view the single deduction "under unusual circumstances" would not interfere with salaried status. It said that the "one-time pay deduction does not of

---

[46]2000 WL 33374982 (W.D. Pa. 2000).

[47]The court in this respect disagreed with *Sonnier v. Crawford & Co.*, Civ. A. No. 94-1755 (W.D. Pa. 1997), *aff'd*, No. 97-3096 (3d Cir. 1997), *cert. denied*, 523 U.S. 1107 (1998).

[48]24 F. Supp. 2d 887, 4 WH Cases2d 1830 (N.D. Ill. 1998).

itself mandate a finding that Baudin was not 'on salary.' In interpreting whether an employee's salary was 'subject to reduction' for purposes of the exemption [*Auer*[49]] . . . held that a 'one-time deduction . . . under unusual circumstances' is permissible even for salaried employees."[50]

In *Cowart v. Ingalls Shipbuilding, Inc.*,[51] the Fifth Circuit affirmed the summary judgment granted to the defendant below, holding that the plaintiffs were exempt employees. The plaintiffs contended that the employer's policies, permitting deductions from compensation for personal absences of less than a day where the work time lost was not made up, defeated the exemption. Neither plaintiff had ever experienced a deduction from his fixed compensation, but both had "made up" time they had been absent from work in order to meet the employer's expectations. The appellate court stated that "[a]lthough the salary basis regulation prohibits deductions from an employee's salary for personal absences of less than a day, the regulation does not prohibit an employer from requiring an employee to make up the time he misses."[52] The court also held that the employer's policy that permits salary reductions for absences of eight or more hours over two days does not defeat the salary test. In any event, the court found that the plaintiffs did not show that there was an "actual practice" of taking the deductions or a "significant likelihood" that their salary could be reduced under the policy.

a. During the Initial and Terminal Weeks of Employment

In *Mehrkar v. Daniel Schulmann, Yonkers Karate,*[53] a federal district court in New York held that the failure to pay an employee for his last four days of work is not an impermissible deduction which destroys an employee's exempt status.[54] It

---

[49]519 U.S. 452, 3 WH Cases2d 1249 (1997).

[50]4 WH Cases2d at 1833.

[51]213 F.3d 261, 6 WH Cases2d 161 (5th Cir. 2000).

[52]6 WH Cases2d at 163.

[53]2001 U.S. Dist. LEXIS 717 (S.D.N.Y. 2001).

[54]The discussion of this issue is cursory, but the result is consistent with 29 C.F.R. §541.118(c).

merely exposes the employer to breach of employment contract liability. The plaintiff filed suit under RICO and FLSA for the recovery of overtime payments. Plaintiff conceded that his duties exempted him from the FLSA, but asserted that the defendant's failure to pay him for his last four days of work made him a non-exempt employee entitled to overtime payments. Because he was paid a base weekly salary, the court dismissed his FLSA claim.

c. Deductions From Salary for Absences of a Day or More Due to Sickness or Disability

In *Baudin v. Courtesy Litho Arts,*[55] a federal district court in Illinois held that an employer's deduction from an employee's vacation time for full days he was out sick did not destroy his salaried status. The court found that the deductions were not from pay but rather from the allotment of vacation days, which was permissible under established case law.

e. Deductions From Salary for Absences Due to Violations of Safety Rules of Major Significance

In an Opinion Letter from the Wage and Hour Division,[56] the Department of Labor on June 3, 1999, stated that an employer may not, even prospectively, temporarily reduce the future wages of a salaried employee because he committed "serious misconduct" or for violation of "a significant disciplinary policy." It stated that the only disciplinary-type deduction permissible is one imposed as a penalty in good faith for infractions of *safety* rules of major significance. It distinguished the decision in *Ackley v. Department of Corrections of the State of Kansas*[57] on the ground that the reason for the reduction in salary in that case was not just a single violation of a standard, and noted that even the *Ackley* court had pointed out that "an employee's pay is

[55] 24 F. Supp. 2d 887, 4 WH Cases2d 1830 (N.D. Ill. 1998).

[56] 1999 WL 1002416.

[57] 844 F. Supp. 680, 1 WH Cases2d 1530 (D. Kan. 1994); *see* Treatise Chapter 11, note 225.

not a fixed salary, but contingent, when the employer retains the ability to adjust it 'depending on the quality and the quantity of the work.'"[58]

In *Kelly v. City of New York*,[59] the court analyzed many different disciplinary deductions taken from the compensation of employees over a period of some 10 years. It found that a number of these deductions did not affect the salary basis of compensation of the employees, because they were made for violations of safety rules of major significance, while other deductions did not so qualify. Among others, the court found that the following major safety rules were involved in these cases:

- discipline for sleeping on duty and for being away from their post because it poses a threat to fellow officers;
- discipline for threatening and harassing a fellow officer because it poses a threat to fellow officers;
- discipline for compromising a corruption investigation because it put the officer who reported the corruption at risk;
- discipline for a scheme of breaking into drug dealers' apartments, stealing money from drug dealers, and giving false testimony in proceedings against drug dealers;
- discipline for requesting that fellow officers provide false testimony; and
- discipline for losing a gun, misusing a gun, and interfering with police activities.

No major safety violations, however, were involved in these instances:

- solicitation of bribes where no evidence existed of fellow officers being put at risk;
- being charged with murder of a suspect where the murder charge was dismissed;

---

[58]1999 WL 1002416 (citing 844 F. Supp. at 686).
[59]2000 WL 1150462, 6 WH Cases2d 753 (S.D.N.Y. 2000).

- failure to make reports when a subordinate discharges his firearm;
- solicitation of prostitution, unauthorized off-duty employment, illegal gambling, patronizing unlicensed premises, intoxication while off-duty, cheating on the sergeants' exam, failing to report in sick, insurance fraud, improper fraternization with recruits, and arrests for driving while intoxicated off-duty.

f. Deductions From Leave [New Topic]

In *Cruz v. McAllister Brothers, Inc.*,[60] a federal district court reviewed the state of case law on the subject of deductions from leave balances and concluded, with the majority of courts and the Department of Labor, that deductions from leave balances for partial-day absences do not threaten exempt status.

In an opinion letter from the Wage and Hour Division,[61] the Department of Labor on April 23, 1999, expressed itself on a question apparently on the border between deductions from salary and deductions from leave. The employer in question deducted from leave balances when employees were absent for a partial day, and if the employee had insufficient leave, the employer recorded a negative leave balance. The employer sought the view of the Department on whether it might, consistent with the salary basis test, withhold the appropriate amount (computed on an hour-by-hour basis) from the employee's terminal pay check if the employee left employment with a negative leave balance. The Department found that such a deduction was not permissible.

3. Impermissible Deductions From an Employee's Salary

c. Deductions for Absences of Less Than One Day

i. Deductions From Salary. Under the Secretary's interpretation of the salary basis test, as upheld and applied by the

[60] 52 F. Supp. 2d 269, 290 (D.P.R. 1999).
[61] 1999 WL 10002393.

Supreme Court in *Auer v. Robbins*,[62] employees may not be considered salaried if they are covered by a policy that permits deductions in pay for partial-day absences "as a practical matter."[63] This standard is met in either of two circumstances: (1) when the employer has an actual practice of making such deductions, or (2) when the employer maintains a policy that "creates a 'significant likelihood' of such deductions."[64] A policy creates a "significant likelihood" of impermissible deductions if it "effectively communicates that deductions will be made in specified circumstances."[65]

Emergency medical technician captains and lieutenants subject to a general policy applicable to all employees permitting reductions in pay for partial-day absences and minor disciplinary infractions did not create a significant likelihood of impermissible deductions where there was no evidence that any impermissible deductions had ever been taken from the exempt captains and lieutenants.[66]

A district court held that the plaintiffs had met the *Auer* standard requiring proof of an actual practice of making impermissible deductions, or at the very least a substantial likelihood that such deductions would be made.[67] The plaintiffs introduced evidence of three instances when employees received less than a full week's pay and several occasions when employees were docked pay for fractions of days because of tardiness. This, the court held, was sufficient to show "that as a practical matter deductions in pay are significantly likely on occasion to be invoked against salaried employees."[68]

In *Bowman v. City of Indianapolis*,[69] the Seventh Circuit relied on the defendant's answer to an interrogatory, to the effect that

---

[62] 117 S. Ct. 905, 3 WH Cases2d 1249 (1997).

[63] *Id.* at 911.

[64] *Id.*

[65] *Id.*

[66] West v. Anne Arundel County, 137 F.3d 752, 4 WH Cases2d 641, 646–47 (4th Cir.), *cert. denied*, 119 S. Ct. 607 (1998).

[67] Arrington v. City of Macon, 973 F. Supp. 1467, 4 WH Cases2d 122 (M.D. Ga. 1997).

[68] *Id.* at 1473.

[69] 133 F.3d 513, 4 WH Cases2d 553 (7th Cir. 1998).

a deduction would be made from salary for a partial day's absence if there was no leave available to cover it and the employee did not make up the time, to conclude that the plaintiff was not paid on a salary basis. The disciplinary deduction policy applicable to the plaintiff also failed the salary basis test, as discussed in Section IV.B.3.d [Disciplinary Deductions].

In *Danesh v. Rite Aid Corp.*,[70] a pharmacist had shown that he was subject to pay reductions on an hourly basis for absences from work of less than a day, specifically for tardiness. Consequently, although his employment contract stated he was a salaried employee, the court found that the deduction for his being late to work meant that he was paid in relation to the hours worked and thus was not exempt from the FLSA's minimum wage and overtime provisions.

In *Morales v. Zondo, Inc.*,[71] a federal district court in New York held that the plaintiff, a production manager, was an exempt employee, even though her employer threatened a reduction in pay if she did not work forty hours per week. Throughout her employment the plaintiff's weekly salary was never reduced. "The mere fact that an employee is salaried does not mean that an employer may not expect the employee to work at least 40 hours per week." A threat to dock plaintiff's salary did not, without more, indicate that the plaintiff's salary was subject to reduction, and therefore the plaintiff always remained an exempt employee not entitled to overtime.

ii. Deductions From Leave Accounts. As noted in the Main Volume, most courts that have considered the issue have found that employers do not violate the salary basis test by making deductions from some source other than an employee's salary, such as leave time or vacation time. Recent decisions have generally continued this trend. For instance, in *Graziano v. Society of New York Hospital*,[72] the district court held that an employer's policy of requiring employees to draw on banked "comp" time or accrued vacation time to account for partial-day absences did

[70] 39 F. Supp. 2d 7, 5 WH Cases2d 912 (D.D.C. 1999).
[71] 2001 U.S. Dist. LEXIS 508 (S.D.N.Y. 2001).
[72] 4 WH Cases2d 286 (S.D.N.Y. 1997).

not run afoul of the salary basis test. Similarly, in *Aiken v. County of Hampton*,[73] the district court ruled that it was permissible for an employer to require exempt employees to use holiday or vacation pay to cover partial-day absences because these are fringe benefits, and "not a part of the predetermined pay [p]laintiffs receive each work week." These cases involved fairly straightforward applications of settled precedent.

In an opinion letter from the Wage and Hour Division,[74] the Department of Labor on April 23, 1999, expressed itself on a question apparently on the border between deductions from salary and deductions from leave. The employer in question deducted from leave balances when employees were absent for a partial day, and if the employee had insufficient leave, the employer recorded a negative leave balance. The employer sought the view of the Department on whether it might, consistent with the salary basis test, withhold the appropriate amount (computed on an hour-by-hour basis) from the employee's terminal pay check if the employee left employment with a negative leave balance. The Department found that such a deduction was not permissible.

In *Webster v. Public School Employees of Washington, Inc.*,[75] the plaintiff, a union field representative, appealed the district court's grant of summary judgment for the defendant, a union of school employees. The field representative was paid a weekly salary, but if he worked less than forty hours per week, the union deducted time, in fifteen-minute increments, from his accrued sick or vacation leave. The court held that "compensation" in the FLSA regulations refers to salary, not accrued leave time, and therefore a reduction in paid leave time does not affect an employee's salaried status. The fact that the accrued sick leave time could be converted to cash had no bearing on the union representative's salaried status because deductions from fringe benefits have no effect on the salary basis test.

---

[73] 977 F. Supp. 390, 397 (D.S.C. 1997).
[74] 1999 WL 10002393.
[75] 247 F.3d 910 (9th Cir. 2001).

iii Public Sector Employees and Salary Reductions

In *Demos v. City of Indianapolis,*[76] former city employees brought suit against the city of Indianapolis to recover overtime payments. The city moved for summary judgment claiming that the employees were exempt, salaried employees under the FLSA, even though the plaintiffs' pay was subject to reductions for absences of less than a day. The city contended that such deductions made through its docking system were permissible under the public accountability exemption. The district court followed *Spradling v. City of Tulsa, Oklahoma,*[77] and held that the defendants failed to provide facts to support their claim that the system they employ for docking pay is "established according to . . . a policy or practice established pursuant to principles of public accountability."[78] Therefore, the court would not grant summary judgment on this basis.

In *Johnson v. Ohio Department of Youth Services,*[79] the plaintiff, a regional administrator for the Ohio Department of Youth Services, appealed a trial court finding that she was a salaried employee exempt from the overtime requirements of the FLSA. She was expected to be on the job between 8:30 a.m. and 4:30 p.m. and was docked for arriving late. However, she was able to use accumulated leave time or compensatory time to avoid any reduction in salary. The court found that the employer treated the plaintiff in a manner inconsistent with exempt salaried status. Since the relevant regulation[80] is silent as to the use of comp time, the court reasoned that the use of comp time does not correlate with the DOL's concept of an exempt employee. Therefore, the Ohio Court of Appeals reversed the lower court and held that the plaintiff was not an exempt employee under the FLSA.

---

[76]126 F. Supp. 2d 548 (S.D. Ind. 2000).
[77]95 F.3d 1492 (10th Cir. 1996).
[78]29 C.F.R. §541.5(d).
[79]140 Ohio App. 3d 774 (2000).
[80]29 C.F.R. §541.5(d).

d. Disciplinary Deductions

The Ninth Circuit has issued two decisions applying this aspect of the *Auer* decision. In *Childers v. City of Eugene,*[81] the Ninth Circuit held that executive, administrative, and professional municipal employees were not rendered nonexempt by the city's one-time imposition of a disciplinary suspension on an exempt employee and its lack of a policy prohibiting disciplinary deductions in pay for exempt employees. The court agreed that the city's exempt employees were "nominally" subject to disciplinary suspensions, but found this did not defeat exempt status because "[n]either the City's policy nor the imposition of disciplinary deductions against a single exempt employee in a ten year period created a substantial likelihood that, or an issue of fact whether, exempt employees were 'subject to' such sanctions and therefore rendered nonexempt under the FLSA."[82]

A different panel of the Ninth Circuit applied the Supreme Court's *Auer* decision a few months later in *Stanley v. City of Tracy.*[83] The dispute in *Stanley* centered on a police department policy providing for the possibility of disciplinary suspensions of less than a week's duration. The Ninth Circuit rejected the plaintiffs' overtime claim, noting that, under *Auer,*

> [a] written policy which is nominally applicable to all employees, both salaried and non-salaried, and authorizes deductions which would be proper only for non-salaried employees, does not, without more, communicate as a practical matter that such deductions will be made for employees that otherwise satisfy the salary test.[84]

The court of appeals explained:

> As in *Auer,* the disciplinary policy at issue nominally covers all city personnel, both salaried and non-salaried. No actual suspensions were imposed on any employee in the Mid-Management Unit, and the policy authorizing suspensions does not "effectively communicate" that any employees in that Unit will be suspended in any

[81]120 F.3d 944, 3 WH Cases2d 1831 (9th Cir. 1997).
[82]*Id.* at 947.
[83]120 F.3d 179, 3 WH Cases2d 1833 (9th Cir. 1997).
[84]*Id.* at 184.

> specified circumstance. Rather, the availability . . . of disciplinary suspensions is at the discretion of the City's personnel officers.[85]

The court found the plaintiffs' reliance on their subjective beliefs that they could be suspended for less than a week to be misplaced:

> [T]he controlling factor is not whether the department head or the employees subjectively believed the employees could be subject to improper deductions. Under *Auer*, the dispositive factors are whether there were either actual deductions, or a significant likelihood of deductions.[86]

In *Bowman v. City of Indianapolis*,[87] the Seventh Circuit held that a field captain employed by the Indianapolis police department was not paid on a salary basis, and therefore nonexempt, because he was covered by a "police merit" ordinance explicitly providing for reductions in pay for periods of less than a week. Under the ordinance, the Chief of Police had the authority to discipline "any member of the department" by, among other things, suspending him or her without pay for up to six months. Assistant chiefs, deputy chiefs, and majors were authorized to impose suspensions without pay of up to 10 working days. The court of appeals held:

> Since nothing in the ordinance exempts sergeants, lieutenants or captains from these sanctions, it follows that they are subject to being disciplined by suspension without pay for periods of less than a week. That means, in turn, that their compensation may vary depending on the quality of the work they perform, and thus that they fail the salary basis test for exemption from the FLSA.[88]

---

[85] *Id.* (citation omitted).

[86] *Id.* at 185.

[87] 133 F.3d 513, 4 WH Cases2d 553 (7th Cir. 1998).

[88] *Id.* at 517. Arguably, the Seventh Circuit has taken a broader view of the Supreme Court's holding in *Auer v. Robbins* that the term "subject to reduction" contemplates an actual practice of making impermissible deductions or a policy creating a significant likelihood of such deductions than have the Second, Third, and Ninth Circuits, which seem to hold that a generally applicable deduction policy will not be assumed to cover otherwise exempt white-collar employees.

In *Ahern v. County of Nassau*,[89] the Second Circuit rejected an overtime claim brought by police officers alleging they were not paid on a salary basis because a policy permitted the police commissioner to dock officers' pay or suspend them as a disciplinary measure. The court read *Auer* as requiring proof "of a 'clear and particularized policy—one which effectively communicates that deductions will be made in specified circumstances'" and concluded this standard had not been met.[90] The plaintiffs failed to demonstrate that the disciplinary policy communicated that deductions would be made in specified circumstances. "In other words, the plaintiffs could not point to any rule that stated if they committed a specific infraction, their pay would be docked."[91]

A district court in Tennessee ruled that the salary basis test was satisfied and that police captains were properly classified as exempt employees despite a city policy allowing disciplinary suspension of officers, including captains, without pay for periods less than one day.[92] Noting that no captain had ever been suspended under the policy, the court followed *Auer* and reasoned that because there was no "significant likelihood" that captains would be subjected to such suspensions, the salary basis test was satisfied and the officers retained their exempt status.[93]

Another federal district court held that five suspensions of salaried police officers without pay for less than a week imposed

---

[89]118 F.3d 118, 3 WH Cases2d 1822 (2d Cir. 1997).

[90]*Id.* at 121.

[91]*Id.* at 121–22. *See also* Balgowan v. New Jersey, 115 F.3d 214, 219, 3 WH Cases2d 1703 (3d Cir. 1997) (disciplinary deduction policy that was never actually enforced against exempt managers, and was applicable to nonexempt employees as well, does not show a significant likelihood of deductions to defeat exempt status under *Auer*); Lilenfeld v. Kiepper, 4 WH Cases2d 307, 310–11 (S.D.N.Y. 1997) (managerial employees of city transit authority were paid on a salary basis, despite policy providing for the possibility of pay deductions in connection with disciplinary suspensions, where record reflected only one improper deduction, and employer's unrebutted contention that management's philosophy and practice were to avoid suspensions without pay in disciplinary actions against managers precluded finding of "substantial likelihood" of disqualifying deductions).

[92]Aiken v. City of Memphis, 985 F. Supp. 740, 4 WH Cases2d 408 (W.D. Tenn. 1997).

[93]*Id.* at 743, 4 WH Cases2d at 409.

before the institution of policies to prohibit such suspensions did not establish an actual practice of deductions sufficient to destroy the FLSA exemption for all salaried officers.[94] The court noted that no such suspensions had occurred within the past five years, the suspensions that were imposed occurred under "unusual circumstances," and the suspensions occurred before case law clarified the requirements for the FLSA exemption.[95]

The federal District Court for the Southern District of New York found that the managerial employees of a city transit authority were exempt from the FLSA overtime requirement because they failed to show that they were "subject to" any disqualifying deductions either in "actual practice" or as a "significant likelihood."[96] Under a previous disciplinary policy, the managerial employees were theoretically subject to pay deductions for infractions of rules not directed at major safety violations. Because suspension without pay was one of several possible disciplinary actions for misconduct and the only evidence of an actual deduction taken under the prior disciplinary policy was one non-safety-related disciplinary action, the court found that the record regarding the prior disciplinary policy did not show a "significant likelihood" of a deduction that would disqualify the managerial employees from exempt status.

In *Belcher v. Shoney's, Inc.*,[97] a federal district court in Tennessee held that the general and assistant managers of chain restaurants were not paid on a salary basis where the evidence showed that the chain had a policy of reducing their salaries to cover cash shortages or casualty losses. The court further held that the chain's safety-based explanation of this policy, that it existed to encourage managers to make timely bank deposits to reduce the cash on hand in restaurants and thus reduce the likelihood of robbery attempts, was not sufficiently related to employee safety to fall within the safety-rule provision of the FLSA.

---

[94]DiGiore v. Ryan, 987 F. Supp. 1045, 4 WH Cases2d 481 (N.D. Ill. 1997).
[95]*Id.*, 4 WH Cases2d at 488.
[96]Lilenfeld v. Kiepper, 4 WH Cases2d 307 (S.D.N.Y. 1997).
[97]30 F. Supp. 2d 1010, 5 WH Cases2d 134 (M.D. Tenn. 1998).

In an opinion letter, the Wage and Hour Division expressed the view that deductions from the salary of restaurant managers for unexplained losses in the bank deposit to which the manager had the only access were inconsistent with payment on a salary basis.[98]

A number of courts have continued to hold that public employees met the salary basis test notwithstanding general policies permitting deductions from salary. In *Kelly v. City of Mount Vernon*,[99] the Second Circuit, following *Ahern v. County of Nassau*,[100] held that detective sergeants and lieutenants in a police department are paid on a salary basis, and thus are exempt from the FLSA overtime requirements, where the department has neither an "actual practice," nor a "clear and particularized policy" that evidences a "significant likelihood" that it will start docking salaried employees' pay for minor violations of department regulations, temporary military leave, or appearing in non-department-related court proceedings.

In *DiGiore v. Ryan*,[101] the Seventh Circuit held that police lieutenants and sergeants employed by the state fell within the "white-collar" exemption of the FLSA. The key question was whether the department's general policies of pay deductions for violations of the state's accident, fitness, and discipline policies created a significant likelihood of improper deductions or actually resulted in a practice of improper deductions. The court held that there was no significant likelihood of deductions because the policies in question were general, applying to both salaried and nonsalaried employees, and the state had a policy of reviewing proposed deductions for compliance with the FLSA before making deductions. Additionally, the court held that the state had no actual practice of making deductions, though noting five instances where salary deductions were impermissibly made, because each impermissible deduction was corrected within the statutory "window of correction."

---

[98] Letter of April 1, 1999, signed by John Fraser, WHM: 99:8231.
[99] 162 F.3d 765, 5 WH Cases2d 106 (2d Cir. 1998).
[100] 118 F.3d 118, 3 WH Cases2d 1822 (2d Cir. 1997).
[101] 172 F.3d 454, 5 WH Cases2d 321 (7th Cir. 1999).

In *McGuire v. City of Portland*,[102] the Ninth Circuit found that Portland fire chiefs were paid on a salary basis, even though the city could deduct pay for violations of the city personnel manual or fire bureau policy. There was no actual practice of pay deductions, and the district court had found that there was no significant likelihood that such deductions would be made. The Ninth Circuit affirmed.

In *Spradling v. City of Tulsa*,[103] the Tenth Circuit affirmed summary judgment for defendant holding that District Chiefs of Tulsa's fire department were salaried employees despite a written policy that subjected the plaintiffs' pay to disciplinary deductions, creating a possibility of salary reductions for absences of less than one day. Applying *Auer v. Robbins*,[104] the court found that the plaintiffs were still considered salaried since the city did not maintain an actual practice of making deductions. The court noted that the policy applied to plaintiffs and nonsalaried employees, so it did not "effectively communicate" to plaintiffs that pay deductions are an anticipated form of punishment for employees in "plaintiffs' category." Instead, the court found that no clear inference could be drawn as to the likelihood of sanctions being applied to employees such as the plaintiffs. Moreover, none of the plaintiffs had been subject to a disciplinary reduction in pay, and no employee in the plaintiffs' job position, "district chief," had ever had his or her pay reduced for being absent from work due to any reason other than for violations of a major safety rule.

After the Supreme Court's remand in 1997,[105] litigation in *Yourman v. Giuliani*[106] addressed further aspects of the question whether plaintiffs, managerial employees of various agencies of New York City, were exempt employees. The plaintiffs argued

---

[102]159 F.3d 460, 4 WH Cases2d 1736 (9th Cir. 1998).

[103]198 F.3d 1219 (10th Cir. 2000).

[104]519 U.S. 452 (1997).

[105]In the earlier rounds of the litigation the district court had granted summary judgment for plaintiffs, which was affirmed by the Second Circuit. That decision was vacated and remanded for reconsideration in light of *Auer v. Robbins*, 519 U.S. 114, 53 WH Cases2d 1376.

[106]1999 U.S. Dist. LEXIS 15700, 5 WH Cases 2d 1470 (S.D.N.Y. 1999), *rev'd and remanded*, 229 F.2d 124 (2d Cir. 2000).

that they were not paid on a salary basis because they were subject to disciplinary deductions from salary. The Second Circuit agreed with the district court that because none of the written policies of the relevant city agencies contained rules, applicable only to managers, mandating that if a manager commits a specific infraction, his or her pay will be docked, there was not a significant likelihood of improper disciplinary deductions. However, on appeal (and after seeking the *amicus* views of the Secretary of Labor) the Second Circuit found there was a triable issue as to whether there was an actual practice of imposing disciplinary deductions. The Second Circuit ruled that in determining whether an actual practice existed, a court must determine if the employer has an objective intention of paying its employees on a salary basis. That question cannot be answered by simply dividing the number of impermissible pay deductions by the number of managerial employees, as the district court had done. Rather, the trial court must consider additional factors such as the number of times that other forms of discipline are imposed, the number of employee infractions warranting discipline, the existence of policies favoring or disfavoring pay deductions, the process by which sanctions are determined, and the degree of discretion held by the disciplinary authority. The trial court was also instructed, on remand, to consider evidence of disciplinary deductions made prior to the statute-of-limitations period that it had previously excluded as untimely.

In *Kelly v. City of New York*,[107] the district court applied the Supreme Court's decision in *Auer v. Robbins*,[108] and DOL's regulations regarding permissible deductions for major safety violations,[109] to a variety of fact patterns. The case involved overtime pay claims by captains, corrections captains, deputy inspectors, lieutenants, and sergeants within the New York City police department.

In ruling against all of the plaintiffs, the court first explained that to establish a policy of impermissible deductions

---

[107]2000 WL 1150462, 6 WH Cases2d 753 (S.D.N.Y. 2000).

[108]519 U.S. 452 (1997).

[109]5 C.F.R. §541.118(a)(5).

from employees' salaries, under *Auer,* the employees must demonstrate the existence of a clear and particularized policy that effectively communicates that deductions from employees' salaries will be made in specified circumstances. This requires a finding of "a significant likelihood of [impermissible] deductions." The court then addressed whether certain written policies within the various departments of the police department and corrections department of New York City met this test. The court found that the broad language used in the department policies did not communicate to employees in the positions at issue–captains and other officers–that they were subject to having their pay docked for disciplinary reasons for periods of less than a week. In so ruling, the court ruled that the plaintiffs' subjective beliefs that they were subject to these policies were immaterial.

Next, the court turned to the issue of whether there was sufficient evidence of an actual practice of docking the employees' pay to establish that it had been effectively communicated to the employees that their pay would be subject to being docked. To answer this question, the court first considered the relevant grouping to determine the existence of impermissible disciplinary docking. The court rejected the plaintiffs' argument that the court should view the aggregate number of deductions of all of the positions at issue in the case—captains, lieutenants, sergeants, deputy inspectors, and other high-level officials. Instead, the court viewed the aggregate number of times employees' pay had been docked within each position. The court reasoned that each position is a separate and distinct category within the Civil Service and that promotion to the next rank is through competitive examination.

In *Takacs v. Hahn Automotive Corp.,*[110] the Sixth Circuit affirmed a district court's decision granting summary judgment to twenty-seven managers who sought to recover overtime compensation from an automotive retail chain, holding that they were not exempt employees under the FLSA. Applying the test

---

[110]246 F.3d 776 (6th Cir. 2001).

set forth in *Auer v. Robbins*,[111] the Sixth Circuit held that the managers were not exempt because the employer's disciplinary policy created a significant likelihood of pay deductions from the managers' pay due to disciplinary infractions, and the employer had an actual practice of making such deductions. Managers were subject to suspension without pay for misconduct. Ruling that the specificity of the disciplinary policy made the idea of pay deductions more than a mere theoretical possibility, the court stated that the policy permitted deductions in pay as a practical matter. The evidence showed that the employer had suspended seven members of management without pay over the course of a year and a half, and, thus, that employer had an actual practice of suspending its managers without pay for disciplinary reasons. Therefore, the court held that the managers were non-exempt employees and as such were entitled to overtime wages.

In *Block v. City of Los Angeles*,[112] the Ninth Circuit held that partial week suspensions, even if part of a suspension lasting longer than a week, are inconsistent with treatment of city employees as salaried employees. The defendant argued that only suspensions of less than a week are problematic, and therefore any suspensions of more than a week (e.g., suspensions of 10 working days) were proper. The Ninth Circuit agreed with the district court that although a salaried employee may be suspended without pay for a full week, a salaried employee must receive full salary for any week in which the employee performs any work, and thus that the withholding of pay was impermissible.

In an Opinion Letter dated February 14, 2001,[113] the United States Department of Labor's Wage and Hour Division stated that a public school district was allowed to take deductions from teachers' pay in the form of unpaid disciplinary suspensions for one to four days for reasons not based on infractions of significant safety rules if the teachers qualified for the professional

[111]519 U.S. 452 (1997).
[112]253 F.3d 410 (9th Cir. 2001).
[113]WHM: 99:5417.

exemption because professional teachers were not subject to the $170/week salary requirement under 29 C.F.R. §§ 541.3(e) and 541.314.

e. Other Deductions [New Topic]

Novel and interesting questions were considered by the district courts in *Yuen v. U.S. Asia Commercial Development Corp.*[114] and *Hoffmann v. Sbarro, Inc.*[115] and by the Seventh Circuit in *Haywood v. North American Van Lines.*[116]

In *Haywood,* the Seventh Circuit held that neither nonmonetary discipline for failing to work a scheduled shift nor voluntary payment by one employee to another employee to cover a Saturday shift was an impermissible reduction in salary that would render an individual who received an annual salary a nonexempt employee.[117]

The *Yuen* case concerned a policy prohibiting employees from charging personal long-distance telephone calls to the employer's calling card and charging employees $10 plus the actual cost of any personal long-distance call appearing on the employer's telephone bill. It was undisputed that no salary deductions were made to cover the telephone charges. However, the employer withheld reimbursement for business expenses until the plaintiff paid for her personal long-distance calls and the related $10 charge. The court framed the questions presented as "(i) whether, on the facts of this case, reimbursement for business expenses is 'compensation,' as that term is used in [the] FLSA and its implementing regulations, and, if so, (ii) whether the $10 charge is an impermissible reduction in that 'compensation.'"[118] Addressing the first issue, the district court established as a threshold matter that the "compensation relevant to the 'salary basis' inquiry is an employee's salary; the periodic fixed payments to an employee in return for services

[114]974 F. Supp. 515, 4 WH Cases2d 69 (E.D. Va. 1997).
[115]982 F. Supp. 249, 4 WH Cases2d 335 (S.D.N.Y. 1997).
[116]121 F.3d 1066, 4 WH Cases2d 59 (7th Cir. 1997).
[117]*Id.*
[118]974 F. Supp. at 521.

rendered."[119] From this, the district court concluded that reimbursement of business expenses was not part of the plaintiff's periodic compensation since the amount of reimbursement was not fixed and did not compensate her for services rendered, but rather was an administrative convenience.[120] Turning to the second issue, the district court concluded that the $10 charge was not an impermissible deduction under the salary basis regulations since it was wholly unrelated to the "quality or quantity" of the plaintiff's work. The court explained that "[t]he language and structure of the FLSA implementing regulations point persuasively to the conclusion that the prohibition of disciplinary deductions is limited to reductions based on the 'quality or quantity' of work."[121]

Hoffmann presented the question of whether a policy requiring restaurant managers to make restitution for cash shortages constituted a reduction in their compensation in violation of the salary basis test so as to defeat exempt status.[122] The employer contended that the salary basis test did not prohibit employers from charging employees for shortages of cash or goods of which they were custodians so long as the reimbursement was not made by way of deductions from an employee's base pay. The plaintiffs argued, on the other hand, that the out-of-pocket reimbursements were kickbacks of base pay and therefore should be deemed an improper deduction. Noting that the question posed was somewhat different from that raised in the line of cases involving leave-time deductions, the district court reserved judgment on this complicated and potentially significant issue "until there is a clearer factual record as to what

---

[119] *Id.*

[120] *Id.* at 521–22.

[121] *Id.* at 523.

[122] 982 F. Supp. 249, 4 WH Cases2d 335. *Note:* Deductions for cash register shortages resulting from unaccountable circumstances, mathematical errors, and customers leaving without paying checks have been found to be unlawful where those deductions reduce below the minimum wage the amount of money the employee receives in compensation. *See* Chapter 9, §VI.C. [Potentially Unlawful Deductions].

defendant's policies and practices were, and under what conditions defendant required employees to make out-of-pocket reimbursements or deducted losses directly from salary."[123]

In *Heder v. City of Two Rivers,* [124] a federal district court in Wisconsin held that it was a violation of the FLSA for an employer to require any part of a firefighter's regular wages or overtime compensation, including the costs of training, to be repaid merely because the employee resigned within a specified time. In this case, the employee received mandatory paramedic training. He signed a repayment agreement requiring him to repay the employer for costs associated with his training if he voluntarily resigned within three years of beginning the training. The employee resigned just shy of the three-year period and went to work as a firefighter for another city. The employer withheld money from the employee's pay to recover part of the training costs. The court granted the employee's partial summary judgment motion on his FLSA overtime claim. Additionally, the court held that the training repayment agreement was unenforceable insofar as it did not reduce the amount due over the years that it was in force. The employer's deductions from the final paychecks violated state law and the FLSA's minimum wage requirements.

C. Effect of Making Deductions That Violate the Salary Basis Test—The "Window of Correction"

The Supreme Court held in *Auer v. Robbins*[125] that the window of correction defense is available where impermissible deductions are made inadvertently or for reasons other than lack of work. In *Childers v. City of Eugene,*[126] the Ninth Circuit recognized that *Auer* implicitly overruled that court's restrictive reading of the window of correction in *Abshire v. County of Kern*[127]

[123]982 F. Supp. at 259–60, 4 WH Cases2d at 344.
[124]49 F. Supp. 2d 677 (E.D. Wis. 2001).
[125]117 S. Ct. 905, 3 WH Cases2d 1249 (1997).
[126]120 F.3d 944, 3 WH Cases2d 1831 (9th Cir. 1997).
[127]908 F.2d 483, 29 WH Cases2d 1417 (9th Cir. 1990).

as being inapplicable where an employment policy nominally subjects exempt employees to disciplinary suspensions.[128]

Similarly, in *Davis v. City of Hollywood*,[129] the Eleventh Circuit held that the window of correction was available to an employer where it had made deductions from the compensation of allegedly exempt employees in connection with disciplinary suspensions because the deductions were not for lack of work, the affected employees were subsequently reimbursed, and a written policy was adopted proscribing unpaid suspensions.[130]

However, in *Hoffmann v. Sbarro, Inc.*,[131] the district court held that *Auer* did not overrule the line of cases interpreting the window of correction narrowly and finding the defense applicable only when there is a one-time or inadvertent deduction. The *Hoffmann* court construed *Auer* as limited to its facts, explaining that under any analysis the defendant in *Auer* was entitled to avail itself of the window of correction since the case involved a singular deduction in unusual circumstances. Thus, the district court in *Hoffmann* rejected the defendant's argument that the window of correction gives employers an absolute right to cure improper deductions made for reasons other than lack of work. Rather, the district court deferred "to that portion of the Secretary's interpretation providing that the window of correction is unavailable to employers that have engaged in a 'pattern' of improper deductions."[132]

In *DiGiore v. Ryan*,[133] the court ruled in the alternative that even if prior suspensions of five salaried police officers without pay for less than a week constituted an actual "practice of improper deductions" in violation of the salary basis test, the exempt status of salaried officers was still preserved by the department's compliance with the window of correction.[134] The employer satisfied the requirements for the window of correc-

[128] 120 F.3d at 947.
[129] 120 F.3d 1178, 4 WH Cases2d 97 (11th Cir. 1997).
[130] *Id.* at 1180–81.
[131] 982 F. Supp. 249, 4 WH Cases2d 335 (S.D.N.Y. 1997).
[132] *Id.* at 257.
[133] 987 F. Supp. 1045, 4 WH Cases2d 481 (N.D. Ill. 1997).
[134] *Id.* at 1054–56, 4 WH Cases2d at 488–89.

tion because all five suspensions were for reasons other than lack of work; the five suspended officers were "now being compensated for any days lost not in accordance with the [FLSA]"; and the employer's promise to comply with the FLSA in the future was memorialized in policies it had later adopted to prevent the suspension of exempt employees for periods of less than one week.[135]

In *Gillette v. Unirex Inc.*,[136] a federal district court in Kansas permitted an employer that on two occasions had made improper deductions from the plaintiff's pay for absences from work for less than a day to avail itself of the window of correction even though the employer had not yet reimbursed the plaintiff for the pay that was improperly deducted from the plaintiff's salary. The court noted that there was no evidence that the employer had a policy permitting such deductions or had communicated such a policy to its employees.

In *Freeman v. City of Mobile*,[137] the district court examined the exempt status of city police sergeants and lieutenants suspended under "general orders" of the Mobile police department. The suspensions resulted in disciplinary pay docking for a variety of misbehaviors (including violations of nonsafety rules). The city argued that it had reimbursed sergeants and lieutenants suspended for violations of nonsafety rules under the general orders, thus falling within the window of correction and maintaining the exempt status of the affected sergeants and lieutenants. The sergeants and lieutenants, on the other hand, contended that the city had failed to properly reimburse affected employees, causing a loss of exempt status. The Eleventh Circuit remanded the case for further consideration of *Auer* and development of the record with regard to proper reimbursement, apparently assuming that the window of correction was available to remedy deductions made pursuant to the general orders.

In *Cruz v. McAllister Brothers, Inc.*,[138] a federal district court granted summary judgment for the defendant on the plaintiff's

---

[135] *Id.*
[136] 4 WH Cases2d 169 (D. Kan. 1997).
[137] 146 F.3d 1292, 4 WH Cases2d 1345 (11th Cir. 1998).
[138] 52 F. Supp. 2d 269 (D.P.R. 1999).

claim for overtime pay, holding that the "window of correction" allowed the employer to repay the single salary deduction made from the plaintiff's paycheck that could otherwise have threatened his exempt status. The plaintiff, an engineer for the defendant's tugboat business, had taken partial-day absences as a result of an injury unrelated to his work. The defendant, who consistently maintained that the plaintiff was an exempt employee and not entitled to overtime pay, had deducted pay for the first half-day missed. After the plaintiff complained of the deduction, the defendant paid the amount on the next paycheck and deducted a corresponding amount from the plaintiff's leave account. No further deductions were made from the plaintiff's pay. The court noted that the defendant apparently failed to comply with the "window of correction" requirement that employers must promise to comply in the future with the rule against pay deductions. However, inasmuch as the plaintiff had not alleged the defendant's failure to make such a promise, there was still opportunity for the defendant to make the promise if the plaintiff ever returned to work. The court granted summary judgment for the employer on this issue.

In *Belcher v. Shoney's, Inc.*,[139] a federal district court in Tennessee rejected the employer's contention that the window of correction could be applied to its improper deductions from managers' salaries of restaurant losses. Because of the employer's policy of making deductions for cash shortages and casualty losses, and the many implementations of that policy, the window-of-correction defense was unavailable.

In *Paresi v. City of Portland*,[140] the Ninth Circuit held that the defendant was entitled to invoke the "window of correction" to avoid liability. The defendant had imposed suspension without pay for less than a week as a disciplinary measure on certain police officers. Later, the defendant city conceded that the deductions from salary might have been improper, reimbursed the employees, and adopted a new employment policy that

---

[139] 30 F. Supp. 2d 1010, 5 WH Cases2d 134 (M.D. Tenn. 1998).

[140] 182 F.3d 665, 5 WH Cases2d 694 (9th Cir. 1999).

prohibited supervisors of exempt employees from imposing suspensions of less than a full week. The court found that the facts of the case did not sustain a finding of a pattern or policy of impermissible disciplinary deductions.

In the case of *In re Wal-Mart Stores, Inc.*,[141] a federal district court in Colorado held that the "corrective action" defense was not available for an employer that prospectively changed work schedules and payment before each pay period because work hours and salaries were changed in advance. The court reasoned that the deductions from employee pay were not inadvertent but in response to slow business in certain stores.

In *Danesh v. Rite Aid Corp.*,[142] a federal district court in the District of Columbia found that the employer did not qualify to use the window of correction. A pharmacist had shown that he was subject to pay reductions on an hourly basis for tardiness (i.e., for absences from work of less than a day) and thus he was not paid on a salary basis and was subject to the FLSA's minimum wage and overtime provisions. The defendant had conceded that the deductions were not inadvertent, and in its discussion of the defendant's contention that they were made for "reasons other than lack of work" the court apparently construed that phrase as meaning a lack or absence of work done by the defendant. It found that the deductions were indeed made for the defendant's lack of work on the occasions when he was late. The court concluded accordingly that the window of correction was not available to the employer.

In *Klem v. County of Santa Clara,*[143] the Ninth Circuit adopted the view of the plaintiffs and the Secretary of Labor that the "window of correction" is available only to employers that have demonstrated the objective intention to pay their employees on a salaried basis. When an employer has demonstrated the objective intention, the window of correction is available to cure inadvertent or isolated violations of the salary basis regulations. If an employer cannot demonstrate that objective intention,

---

[141]58 F. Supp. 2d 1219, 5 WH Cases2d 889 (D. Colo. 1999).
[142]39 F. Supp. 2d 7, 5 WH Cases2d 912 (D.D.C. 1999).
[143]208 F.3d 1085 (9th Cir. 2000).

then it cannot, after the fact, use the window of correction to bring itself into compliance with the salary basis regulations and thereby turn nonsalaried employees into salaried employees. Here the court found that the employer had a pattern and practice of improper suspensions resulting in impermissible salary deductions (53 among approximately 5,300 employees), so that it could not establish an objective intention to pay the employees on a salaried basis. Accordingly, the window of correction was not available to the county employer.

After determining that no actual practice of making disciplinary deductions from the compensation of members of the classes of plaintiffs had existed sufficient to defeat the salary basis, the court in *Kelly v. City of New York*[144] considered whether the city could take advantage of the window of correction to avoid backpay liability for those employees whose pay had been improperly docked. The court held that the deductions were made for reasons other than lack of work and, therefore, the window of correction could be utilized. The court interpreted the *Auer* decision to mean that any time a deduction is made for reasons other than lack of work, the window of correction can be utilized. The court noted, however, that this is true only where the employees have failed to establish that an actual practice of making the deductions exists. If the number of impermissible deductions were not found to be sufficiently numerous to constitute an actual practice of making such deductions, the court held that the window of correction could not have been utilized.

In *Takacs v. Hahn Automotive Corp.*,[145] the Sixth Circuit affirmed a district court's ruling that 27 managers who sought to recover overtime compensation from an automotive retail chain were not salaried employees under the FLSA. The employer's policy permitted disciplinary wage deductions and the employer had an actual practice of suspending its managers without pay for disciplinary reasons. The employer claimed that it effectively

---

[144] 2000 WL 1150462, 6 WH Cases2d 753 (S.D.N.Y. 2000).

[145] 246 F.3d 776 (6th Cir. 2001).

utilized the FLSA's window of correction defense by renouncing the practice and reimbursing affected employees. The court affirmed the district court's conclusion that the window of correction defense was unavailable to the employer to preserve the employee's exempt status. Deferring to the Secretary of Labor's statutory interpretation of the window of correction defense, the court held that the defense is not available to this employer, which had both a policy and a practice of making deductions from supposed salaried employees for disciplinary infractions. These facts demonstrate that the employer never had an intention of paying its employees on a salary basis. The window of correction is not available to such an employer.

In *Whetsel v. Network Property Services, LLC*,[146] the trial court granted summary judgment for the employer on the ground that the employer's use of the window of correction restored the exempt status of the employees. On appeal the Seventh Circuit reversed that judgment, holding that where an employer has a policy or practice of making improper deductions, that employer has no objective intention to pay its employees on a salary basis and is not entitled to the executive exemption. The court held that when an employer has a practice or policy of improper deductions the employer cannot utilize the window of correction. Because the court found that the statute was ambiguous as to whether the window of correction was available to correct a policy or practice of docking, the court deferred to the Secretary of Labor's interpretation of the statute.

In *Whitesides v. U-Haul Co. of Alaska*,[147] the Alaska Supreme Court, in a case brought under Alaska law, limited employers' rights to utilize the window of correction by holding that the window usually closes at the start of litigation. The court vacated a jury verdict for the defendant, U-Haul, and held that the company did not treat the plaintiff in a manner consistent with an exempt salaried employee. The manager had been suspended without pay for three days because he arrived late to

---

[146] 246 F.3d 897 (7th Cir. 2001).

[147] 16 P.3d 729 (Alaska 2001).

work. After the manager brought suit to recover overtime wages, U-Haul stated that his pay was "inadvertently reduced" and reimbursed him for the lost wages, plus interest. The refund came two years after the suspension, sixteen months after termination, and four months after the plaintiff filed suit. Finding this type of delay unacceptable, the court held that "the window of correction must be deemed closed when litigation commences." Therefore, the Supreme Court of Alaska found that Whiteside was entitled to summary judgment on his claim for overtime compensation due to the improper deductions from salary.

D. Additional Compensation Permitted

In *Boykin v. Boeing Co.*,[148] the Ninth Circuit adopted the majority view that the payment of additional compensation to exempt employees for overtime work does not defeat exempt status.[149] The court characterized as dictum its earlier statement in *Abshire v. County of Kern*[150] that "additional compensation for extra hours worked is not generally consistent with salaried status."[151]

In *Lee v. Town of Good Hope*,[152] the court granted summary judgment to the employer on the issue of whether a police chief was a salaried employee. The employee argued that he was not paid "on a salary basis" pursuant to the FLSA because his pay was increased by the amount of overtime hours he worked. The court held that where the employee received a consistent amount of base pay each week that could not decrease, the fact that it could increase was not significant to the question of whether he was a salaried employee.

In two opinion letters from the Wage and Hour Division, the Department of Labor on April 1, 1999, reiterated that providing extra compensation for hours worked in excess of 40

---

[148]128 F.3d 1279, 4 WH Cases2d 292 (9th Cir. 1997).
[149]*Id.* at 1281–82.
[150]908 F.2d 483, 29 WH Cases2d 1417 (9th Cir. 1990).
[151]128 F.3d at 1282.
[152]4 WH Cases2d 1392 (N.D. Ala. 1998).

in a workweek—where that payment was in addition to an employee's guaranteed salary—would not defeat an employee's exempt status.[153]

In *Fife v. Harmon*,[154] the Eighth Circuit reversed a district court's grant of summary judgment in favor of plaintiff airport employees and remanded for trial on duties issues. It rejected the claim by the plaintiffs that they were ineligible for the exemption for failure to meet the salary basis test, holding that the fact that employees were paid either hourly overtime (at straight time rate) or comp time, in addition to a fixed salary, for work over 40 hours in a week did not defeat the exemption.

In *Richardson v. Genesee County Community Mental Health Services*,[155] plaintiff registered nurses worked on a salaried basis during regularly scheduled weekly hours and also "volunteered" to work nights and weekends (so that the facility remained professionally staffed, although not fully open for business) at a lower, hourly rate of pay. In the litigation, they sought overtime compensation. Defendants contended that the after-hours work was done on an independent contractor basis, or that if the plaintiffs were employees, they were exempt professionals. After rejecting the independent contractor claim, the federal district court held that the nurses qualified for the "professional" exemption from the FLSA based on their recognized status and professional knowledge through prolonged study. The court stated that the Sixth Circuit had generally indicated that additional compensation paid for work in excess of 80 hours during a biweekly pay period, although seemingly inconsistent with a salaried status, does not jeopardize an employee's exemption.[156] The court accordingly held that the night and weekend hourly work performed by the plaintiffs during the nonbusiness hours of defendant's 24-hour mental health crisis clinic did not affect their exempt status.

---

[153]Letters appear at WHM: 99:8232; WHM: 99:8233.

[154]171 F.3d 1173, 5 WH Cases2d 350 (8th Cir. 1999).

[155]45 F. Supp. 2d 610 (E.D. Mich. 1999).

[156]*Id.* at 616 (citing Michigan Ass'n of Gov't Employees v. Michigan Dep't of Corr., 992 F.2d 82, 84 n.3 (6th Cir. 1993)).

E. Fee Basis Alternative for Professional and Administrative Exemptions

An employee's compensation may meet the regulatory requirements for exemption if it is paid on a "salary or fee basis."[157] In *Fazekas v. Cleveland Clinic Health Care Ventures, Inc.*,[158] a federal district court examined whether registered nurse plaintiffs who were paid flat fees on a per-visit basis for home care services could qualify for the "professional" exemption of the FLSA. Addressing a related question in the context of an earlier administrative opinion, the Department of Labor had stated that fee payments "in a sense resemble piecework payments with the important distinction that generally speaking a fee payment is made for the kind of job which is unique rather than for a series of jobs which are repeated an indefinite number of times and for which payment on an identical basis is made over and over again."[159] Relying on that opinion, the nurses claimed that their payments were for essentially identical repetitive tasks such as those (the administration of stress tests) that the Department had found in its letter did not involve fee basis payments within the meaning of the regulations. The court distinguished the individualized patient care performed by the plaintiffs, which involved the exercise of independent professional assessment and judgment, from rote performance of tasks such as stress tests, and found that the payments to the nurses were "fee" payments within the meaning of the regulation.

The Sixth Circuit affirmed[160] the trial court's summary judgment for the defendant, holding that the registered nurses making home health care visits were paid on a fee basis where they were paid an agreed-upon sum for each visit regardless of the time spent on each visit. The court found that each visit was "unique" given the number of different circumstances unique to

---

[157] 29 C.F.R. §§541.2(e)(1), 541.3(e).

[158] 29 F. Supp. 2d 839 (N.D. Ohio 1998).

[159] WH Administrator's Opinion April 15, 1982; appears at WHM: 99:1317 (Captioned Letter No. 514; cited by court as No. 1567).

[160] 204 F.3d 673 (6th Cir. 2000).

each patient's treatment plan as the patient progresses. This set the plaintiff nurses apart from nurses who perform "a series of jobs which are repeated an indefinite number of times," rendering nurses in such situations exempt.

A different result was reached on superficially similar facts in *Elwell v. University Hospital Home Health Care Service.*[161] There, the district court granted the plaintiff's motion for summary judgment as to liability, finding that a registered nurse making home health care visits was not paid on a fee basis where she was paid on a per-visit basis for patient care, plus an hourly rate for attendance at required or mandatory meetings and on-call duty. The regulation dealing with fee basis does not allow for additional compensation.[162] The district court expressly distinguished the nurse here (*Elwell*) from those in *Fazekas,* on the basis that in *Fazekas,* no additional hourly payments were at issue and that Elwell's services "were not unique."[163]

V. DEFINING THE EXECUTIVE EXEMPTION

C. Factors Under the Tests

1. *Management*

In *Gautier Rodriquez v. Mason Technologies,*[164] the court granted summary judgment to the employer on FLSA claims for over-

[161] 76 F. Supp. 2d 805 (N.D. Ohio 1999).

[162] 29 C.F.R. §541.313, which provides that the requirements for the professional or the administrative exemption may be met by a person compensated on a "fee basis" rather than a "salary basis," and goes on to provide that payments on a "fee basis" "are characterized by the payment of an agreed sum for a single job regardless of the time required for its completion. These payments in a sense resemble piecework payments with the important distinction that generally speaking a fee payment is made for the kind of job which is unique rather than for a series of jobs which are repeated an indefinite number of times and for which payment on an identical basis is made over and over again." No reference is made to additional payments.

[163] 76 F. Supp. 2d at 808.

[164] 931 F. Supp. 114, 116–17, 3 WH Cases2d 733, 735 (D.P.R. 1996).

time where the plaintiffs each supervised nine or more employees and assigned their work, and the plaintiffs had adduced no evidence to show that they were not executive employees within the meaning of the regulations.

In *Anderson v. City of Cleveland,*[165] a district court granted summary judgment for the employer, finding that police lieutenants were exempt managerial employees. The court found that the plaintiffs' primary duty was management because they managed the police department resources (i.e., equipment and staffing) by determining how those resources should be deployed in order to carry out the law enforcement function. The plaintiffs also regularly directed the work of at least two sergeants and several patrol officers, and evaluated or oversaw evaluations of their subordinates for purposes of promotion, demotion, and continued employment with the police department. They also exercised discretion in disciplining their subordinates, determining when work should be delegated, deploying department resources, and determining when to respond to a scene in order to provide backup or take charge, or evaluating the performance of a subordinate. The court also found that, even though the lieutenants performed work that was, for the most part, identical to the work of their subordinates, the "working foreman" regulation (29 C.F.R. §541.115(b)) did not apply. The court considered the "totality of the circumstances" and found that the lieutenants were exempt executive employees because they evaluated their subordinates, had a higher salary range than their subordinates, made personnel and budget decisions, monitored the police radio, backed up their subordinates, and were charged with the responsibility of executing an entire law enforcement function with only general supervision from the captain.

2. *Primary Duty*

In *Jarzeboski v. Brut Plastics,*[166] defendant sought summary judgment against overtime claims on the ground that the plain-

[165]90 F. Supp. 2d 906 (D. Tenn. 2000).
[166]3 WH Cases2d 89 (E.D. Mich. 1995).

tiff was an exempt executive employee, having been promoted to a supervisory position. The plaintiff argued that despite the change in her job title and increase in compensation, her duties as a whole had not changed significantly and that she did not have management as her primary duty. The court ruled that this issue could not be properly determined on summary judgment.

In *Wright v. Rayonier, Inc.*,[167] the court considered whether a lead scaler for a pulp manufacturer was an exempt executive employee. The record reflected that the plaintiff performed several managerial activities, such as scheduling the scalers, completing employee evaluations, and ordering supplies for the scale house. The plaintiff alleged, however, that she spent nearly 75 percent of her time inspecting the wood, calculating the wood inventory, and processing retail shipments of wood, which were the same duties as those assigned to the nonexempt scalers. Given these allegations and the fact that the nonexempt scalers earned more money than the plaintiff, the district court found a material factual dispute existed as to whether the plaintiff's primary duty was management.[168]

A state court applying the FLSA has ruled that a court clerk was properly classified as an exempt executive employee.[169] The court found that the plaintiff's primary duty was management because she spent more than 50 percent of her time handling criminal complaints, setting up the court calendar, acting as custodian of records of the municipal court, assisting the judge while court was in session, preparing the budget applicable to her department, directing the work of three to six employees, planning the work of other employees in the office, attending annual budget meetings, recommending the hiring of additional employees, interviewing new hires, apportioning and assigning work in the office, scheduling vacations and time off work, recommending the firing of employees she had disciplined, and participating in the selection of the computer system

---

[167]972 F. Supp. 1474, 4 WH Cases2d 6 (S.D. Ga. 1997).

[168]*Id.* at 1478–79.

[169]Dimiro v. Township of Montclair, 676 A.2d 627, 3 WH Cases2d 565 (N.J. Super. Ct. Law Div. 1996).

and the automation of the municipal court.[170] Moreover, the plaintiff's argument, that other employees handled duties she performed, was unsuccessful. As the court explained, "[t]he fact that other employees often perform the same duties as a supervisor neither diminishes the delegatory authority of that supervisor, nor minimizes the importance of additional supervisory duties." [171]

In *Trovato v. Metra Electronics Corp.*,[172] a federal district court in Florida held that a wiring department supervisor's primary duty was managerial, and he was an executive employee within the meaning of the FLSA, where the employee regularly managed and supervised thirty to fifty other employees and their work, exercised independent judgment in scheduling work, conducted evaluations of other employees that influenced whether the employees would receive raises or promotions, and unilaterally granted or denied time off to employees.

In *Lee v. Town of Good Hope*,[173] a federal district court granted summary judgment to a town on the issue of whether its police chief was within the executive exemption to the Act's overtime requirements. Although the chief spent less than half his time on management duties, the court found that his primary responsibility and value to the town were the proper training and accreditation of officers, advising the mayor and town council, holding meetings where he set the agenda, and issuing memoranda to department employees regarding complaint procedures, discipline, etc. Thus, judged according to their importance to his employer—the town—the chief's primary responsibilities were executive in nature, and he was paid relatively more than other officers for this reason.

In *East v. Bullock's, Inc.*,[174] a federal district court in Arizona held that where an employee spent more than 50 percent of her working time supervising and training other employees, assist-

---

[170] *Id.* at 630, 3 WH Cases2d 565.
[171] *Id.* at 629, 3 WH Cases2d at 567.
[172] 4 WH Cases2d 1073 (M.D. Fla. 1998).
[173] 4 WH Cases2d 1392 (N.D. Ala. 1998).
[174] 34 F. Supp. 2d 1176, 5 WH Cases2d 198 (D. Ariz. 1998).

ing customers, and interacting with buyers, she had management as her primary duty. The court found that the majority of her duties met the Department of Labor definition of "management" under 29 C.F.R. §541.102 and that the employee satisfied the executive exemption.

In *Baudin v. Courtesy Litho Arts*,[175] a federal district court in Illinois found that an employee's primary duty was in management of the printer-employer's pre-press department. The employee spent a significant amount of his time on management duties, and even though these duties might not have taken up a full 50 percent of his time, they were "undisputably more important to the company's success than Baudin's pure production [work]."[176]

In *Thomas v. Jones Restaurants, Inc.*,[177] a district court granted summary judgment for the employer, finding the plaintiff, a restaurant manager, to be a bona fide executive. The parties disputed whether the plaintiff's "primary duty" was to manage. The court examined the interpretive regulation at 29 C.F.R. §541.103 and found that an employee has management as his or her primary duty under either of two circumstances. First, the employee spends over 50 percent of his or her time on management duties and so is exempt. Here, the court found that the plaintiff provided no evidence that she performed nonexempt work on a regular basis, so no reasonable jury could find that she worked at least 50 percent of her time in nonexempt duties. Second, even where an employee spends more than 50 percent of her time on nonexempt tasks, the court found that it should evaluate "other pertinent factors" such as the relative importance of managerial duties as compared with other types of duties, the frequency with which the employee exercises discretionary powers, the relative freedom of the employee from supervision, and the relationship between the employee's salary and wages paid other employees for the kind of nonexempt

---

[175]24 F. Supp. 2d 887, 4 WH Cases2d 1830 (N.D. Ill. 1998).
[176]*Id.*, 4 WH Cases2d at 1834.
[177]64 F. Supp. 2d 1205 (M.D. Ala. 1999).

work performed; such evaluation might dictate the conclusion that the employee has management as her primary duty. The court viewed the importance of plaintiff's managerial tasks in relation to her nonmanagerial tasks as "monumental."[178] She exercised discretionary powers, like hiring and firing, setting and adjusting work schedules, and apportioning work to employees, and she was relatively free from supervision. Therefore, according to the court, there was no triable dispute as to whether management was her primary duty under either test.

The Supreme Court of Montana, in a 4–3 decision in *Kemp v. State of Montana Board of Personnel Appeals,*[179] reversed the trial court, which had held the employee involved, the "head chef" of the Yellowstone Mine Restaurant, not to be exempt. The Supreme Court decided that she was an exempt executive, despite the fact that she worked only 20 percent of her time managing, and spent the other 80 percent of her work time cooking. The court looked at the "other pertinent factors" to determine that the plaintiff's primary duty was management. The court found that because the plaintiff took care of the duties that needed to be done so that her subordinates could work and the kitchen could operate successfully—like determining how much food to be prepared, scheduling employees, keeping track of inventory, training new cooks, overseeing product quality, helping order major kitchen equipment, setting the prices of daily specials, dealing with customers regarding special requests, dealing with regulatory officers, such as health inspectors, and meeting with customers planning weddings and other special events—her managerial duties were more important than her other duties. The court also found that she exercised discretionary powers on a daily basis because she was in charge of the other cooks and dishwashers, and she determined the quantity of food and supplies to order, the quality of food, and from which company. Although her supervisor hired and fired and purchased major kitchen equipment, the court found that the plaintiff was relatively free from supervision. Finally, the court found the plaintiff to be better compensated because she received health insurance

---

[178] *Id.* at 1213.

[179] 989 P.2d 317, 1999 Mont. LEXIS 259 (1999).

while her subordinates did not. The decision called forth a vociferous dissent that characterized the plaintiff as a nonexempt "straw boss" (working foreman) and distinguished the plaintiff (employed in a single-site restaurant over which the owner exercised managerial authority) from the managers of franchised multisite restaurants such as those involved in *Donovan v. Burger King*[180] and other cases cited by the court where site managers presumably enforce "standardization and uniformity."[181]

In *Kastor v. Sam's Wholesale Club,*[182] a federal district court in Texas granted a defense motion for summary judgment as to a bakery department manager, whom the court found to be an executive employee. According to plaintiff, he spent ninety percent of his time doing "stocking" work, the same as hourly employees. He had no authority to hire or fire, and even some of plaintiff's "managerial" duties were sometimes performed by hourly employees. The court rested its decision in favor of the plaintiff's exempt status on the doctrine that an individual's primary duty is not measured by applying a simple "clock" standard that compares the amount of time each day an employee spends on exempt and non-exempt work. Instead, an employee's primary duty is that which is of principal value to the employer. Here the court weighed the relative importance of the managerial duties compared with the other duties; and found that his primary duty was managerial because his principal value to the company was as manager of the bakery department. He was responsible for supervising bakery employees, tracking and increasing sales, developing production schedules, maintaining inventory and expense controls, maintaining quality assurance, interviewing and training employees, participating in hiring and firing decisions, directing employees' work, and disciplining and evaluating employees.

In *Wemmit-Pauk v. The Beech Mountain Club,*[183] a federal magistrate in the Western District of North Carolina granted

---

[180]675 F.2d 516 (2d Cir. 1982).
[181]989 P.2d at 334.
[182]131 F. Supp. 2d 862 (N.D. Tex. 2001).
[183]140 F. Supp. 2d 571 (W.D. N.C. 2001).

summary judgment for the employer, a company that operated a country club. It was undisputed that plaintiff, a camp director, had spent the majority of her time supervising the entire staff and the participants in the camp's youth recreation program. Accordingly, the district court concluded that the camp director fell within the executive exemption because her primary duty, supervising staff and participants, was managerial.

In *Demos v. City of Indianapolis,*[184] a federal district court in Indiana granted partial summary judgment for the employer as to the city's facilities maintenance supervisor. The plaintiff testified that he spent forty percent of his time supervising workers in the field, and did not dispute that this was managerial activity; a significant amount of the rest of his time was spent on "paperwork," including preparing progress reports. The court found that a significant amount of the paperwork was "directly and closely related" to his exempt work and therefore exempt. He provided input in hiring decisions, and had authority to initiate disciplinary actions and to purchase tools and equipment. Plaintiff urged that he was in fact a "working foreman," and therefore not exempt, but the court found that the applicable collective bargaining agreement largely restricted the work plaintiff was allowed to do, and that the fact that he occasionally did some manual labor alongside the crews did not change the conclusion that he was exempt.

In *Furr v. Well Tech Mid-Continent, Inc.*,[185] a federal district court in Kansas granted summary judgment for the employer, finding that an oil rig supervisor came within the executive exemption. The supervisor had primary responsibility for supervising three rig crews with three members each, insuring that they followed proper production and safety procedures and practices, evaluating crew member performance and recommending promotions or discipline. He also had authority to shut down the work. For these reasons, the court found that plaintiff was an exempt executive employee.

---

[184]126 F. Supp. 2d 548 (S.D. Ind. 2000).
[185]2001 U.S. Dist. LEXIS 6013 (D. Kan. 2001).

3. *Department or Subdivision*

In *Cooper v. Drexel Chemical Co.*,[186] the district court found that a production supervisor was exempt as an executive employee because he was responsible for overseeing the milling process and was the only supervisor for the day shift of the milling operation.[187]

Although there was no consistently used name for the exact collection of employees and work supervised by plaintiff, the "pre-press" department constituted a recognized subdivision of the employer for purposes of the exemption in *Baudin v. Courtesy Litho Arts.*[188] The court noted that "[b]oth the department itself and the employees who worked within it had established goals and functions necessary to keep the business operating. Job duties in pre-press did not change, and the department had a separate physical location within the plant." It found that "[d]espite its various labels, the pre-press department supervised by Baudin existed as a recognized subdivision."[189]

A group of supervised employees whose composition would typically vary from day to day, where the group did not stay with the same supervisor, and that had no official name, was found to "have no permanence" and accordingly not to meet the requirement of being a recognized organizational unit for purposes of the executive exemption in *Adams v. United States.* [190] For that reason, the employees who supervised those units were not exempt.

4. *Customary and Regular Direction of Two or More Employees*

In *Jackson v. Go-Tane Services, Inc.,*[191] the court denied summary judgment to an employer since the evidence raised ques-

---

[186]949 F. Supp. 1275 (N.D. Miss. 1996).
[187]*Id.* at 1281.
[188]24 F. Supp. 2d 887, 4 WH Cases2d 1830 (N.D. Ill. 1998).
[189]*Id.,* 4 WH Cases2d at 1834.
[190]U.S. Court of Federal Claims, No. 96-93C (Sept. 30, 1999), p. 9.
[191]2000 U.S. Dist. LEXIS 12627, 141 Lab. Cas. (CCH) ¶34,138, 6 WH Cases 2d 679 (N.D. Ill. 2000).

tions of whether the plaintiff customarily and regularly directed the work of two or more other employees. Time records showed that in some weeks, the combined total of other employees' hours did not reach 80, which under the Department's interpretive regulations would have been sufficient[192] to show that the equivalent of two or more employees were supervised. After further pre-trial proceedings, the court granted summary judgment for the defendants as to some of the plaintiffs,[193] holding that certain gas station managers qualified for the executive exemption. The managers were paid salaries, were responsible for money received from customers, and handled customer complaints and overall operation of the stations. They regularly supervised at least four or five other full-time employees at the stations, and that supervision included hiring, firing and disciplining, preparing time sheets, and actively supervising at least two on-duty subordinates at all times.

In *Gagnon v. Resource Technology, Inc.*,[194] the Tenth Circuit, in an unpublished decision, affirmed summary judgment for the defendant, a consulting and engineering firm, on grounds other than those relied on by the district court. The plaintiff, an office manager and bookkeeper, was found by the district court to be an exempt executive employee, but the Court of Appeals held that she did not meet the executive exemption because she failed to supervise two or more employees. The appellate court found that she was, however, an exempt administrative employee.

7. *Working Foremen*

The Tenth Circuit in *Hays v. Pauls Valley*[195] reaffirmed the principle that the working foreman provision applies only to employees qualifying under the long test. In that case, the employee at issue qualified under the short test, and therefore he was not entitled to a working foreman jury instruction.[196]

---

[192] 29 C.F.R. §541.105.
[193] 2001 U.S. Dist. LEXIS 10240 (N.D. Ill. 2001).
[194] 2001 WL 909028, 2001 U.S. App. LEXIS 18290 (10th Cir. 2001).
[195] 3 WH Cases2d 97 (10th Cir. 1996).
[196] *Id.* at 100.

Applying the working foreman definition without specific reference to whether the short test or the long test was in question, a court found that senior houseparents were properly viewed as working foremen as opposed to bona fide executives because they spent the bulk of their time doing the same tasks as houseparents, which involved supervising delinquent children. Although the senior houseparents spent some time supervising the other houseparents, the production work of senior houseparents dominated their responsibilities and thus the senior houseparents were not bona fide executives.[197]

8. *Examples of Positions That Are Exempt or Nonexempt*

In *Sack v. Miami Helicopter Service*,[198] the court considered in detail the defendant's claim that the plaintiff, the company's maintenance director, was exempt, either as an executive employee or as an administrative employee. The plaintiff's duties included maintaining an FAA-required technical library, performance of some hands-on mechanical work (which the court estimated as requiring 15 percent of his time), planning repair work, ordering parts, instructing two subordinates, and carrying out inspections of the work done. Considering the plaintiff's primary duty, the court determined first that the plaintiff did not spend 50 percent or more of his time in management activity, and then went on to determine, without reference to the time factor, that management was also not the plaintiff's primary duty. Accordingly, it found that the defendant had not borne its burden of establishing that the plaintiff was an exempt executive.[199]

A store manager was an exempt executive where she prepared the weekly schedule for employees at the store, disciplined and evaluated employees, staffed the store, responded to

---

[197]Adams v. Department of Juvenile Justice of New York, 3 WH Cases2d 295, 298–99 (S.D.N.Y. 1996), *vacated and remanded for further proceedings*, 143 F.3d 61, 4 WH Cases2d 932 (2d Cir. 1998).

[198]986 F. Supp. 1456, 4 WH Cases2d 490 (S.D. Fla. 1997).

[199]*See also* the discussion of the court's analysis of the application of the administrative exemption to this case in text at footnote 267 below.

customer complaints, ordered supplies, had access to the keys to the store's safe and cash register, had authority to recommend that employees be fined or suspended, prepared and delivered the store's bank deposits, and was actively involved in hiring.[200]

A warehouse manager who spent 75 to 90 percent of his work time in manual labor, including cleaning, taking inventory, and loading trucks, was not an exempt executive.[201]

In *Palazzolo-Robinson v. Sharis Management Corp.*,[202] a federal district court in Washington held that a plaintiff employee who had worked as an assistant manager and later as a manager of a restaurant was a member of the business's management and thus exempt under the FLSA. The court held that the employee was exempt even though she spent a significant amount of time, sometimes exceeding 50 percent, performing tasks outside her management duties.

In *Fife v. Harmon*,[203] the Eighth Circuit reversed summary judgment for the plaintiffs and held that there was a sufficient dispute of material fact as to the employees' status to warrant trial. The employees were members of a group called "Airfield Operations Specialists," a unit "created to be the eyes and ears of senior management at all times," and prior statements by the employees themselves had described their role as "acting airport managers" and described their extensive decision-making requirements, contradicting their later assertions that they did not qualify for the administrative or executive exemptions.

In *Copas v. East Bay Municipal Utility District*,[204] a federal district court granted summary judgment for the defendant water utility company on the claims of a "facilities supervisor" who supervised two "facilities technicians." Other employees for whom both the executive and the administrative exemption were claimed were found entitled to the administrative exemption.

---

[200]Haines v. Southern Retailers, Inc., 939 F. Supp. 441, 3 WH Cases2d 872, 876 (E.D. Va. 1996).

[201]L&F Distribs. v. Cruz, 3 WH Cases2d 1158, 1163 (Tex. Ct. App. 1996).

[202]68 F. Supp. 2d 1186 (W.D. Wash. 1999).

[203]171 F.3d 1173, 5 WH Cases2d 350 (8th Cir. 1999).

[204]61 F. Supp. 2d 1017, 6 WH Cases2d 307 (N.D. Cal. 1999).

In an unpublished decision in *Mock v. Tharaldson Property Management, Inc.*,[205] the district court granted summary judgment for the employer on plaintiff's claims for unpaid minimum wages and overtime, responding to plaintiff's contention that she did not meet the requirements of the exemption relied on by defendants by noting that she "failed to generate a genuine issue of material fact that she was not a salaried managerial or executive employee exempted from the minimum wage requirements under *29 U.S.C. § 213*(a)(1) . . . ." Although she had apparently put forward at least some evidence that she spent more time on non-exempt work than was permitted by the tests, the plaintiff was found not to have pointed out specific facts in the record which would have led the court to conclude that a genuine factual difference remained for trial.

VI. DEFINING THE ADMINISTRATIVE EXEMPTION

A. The Short Test

In *Barth v. Wolf Creek Nuclear Operating Corp.*,[206] a federal district court in Kansas rejected the plaintiffs' contention that the long-test factors should be considered in determining whether they, lower-level engineers or engineering specialists, were entitled to overtime. Although they agreed they were paid over $250 per week, plaintiffs argued that the "$250 a week standard is 'outdated,' 'perilously close to minimum wage,' and is no longer a good proxy for the determination of white collar status."[207] The court noted that the use of the short test was mandatory, not permissive, when the payment threshold is met.

---

[205] 2001 U.S. Dist. LEXIS 3377 (N.D. Iowa 2001).
[206] 125 F. Supp. 2d 437 (D. Kan. 2000).
[207] *Id.* at 439.

C. Factors Under the Tests

1. *Office or Nonmanual Work*

In *Morales v. Zondo, Inc.*,[208] a federal district court in New York refused to allow plaintiff to amend her complaint to add an FLSA claim for overtime to a suit originally stating claims under the Pregnancy Disability Act, New York State Human Rights Law, and New York City Human Rights Law. It reached this conclusion on the basis of a finding that such an amendment would be futile because plaintiff was administratively exempt. In reaching that conclusion the court relied on the unusual proposition that to prevail plaintiff would have to prove that "she was an employee who was eligible for overtime, i.e., that she was not exempt from the overtime pay requirements"[209] as well as that she actually worked overtime. The court found that she was an exempt administrative employee, despite plaintiff's evidence tendered to show that she was not paid on a salary basis and that she did significant manual work and exercised little discretion, because she worked directly for the company's proprietor and her primary duties were participating in meetings with customers and the sales staff; coordinating communications with vendors; negotiating prices; arranging deliveries; and maintaining product information files, and because she had conceded (before new information came to her attention) that she was paid on a salary basis.

In *Berg v. United States*,[210] after trial, the Court of Federal Claims held that civilian electronic technicians at Edwards Air Force Base, who maintained and repaired air traffic control equipment, did not meet the test for administrative exemption because a large percentage of their work was manual rather than non-manual. The electronic technicians spent the majority of their work time using testing equipment, tools and cleaning supplies, working off floors and workbenches and following instruction manuals.

---

[208] 2001 U.S. Dist. LEXIS 508, 6 WH Cases2d 1390 (S.D.N.Y. 2001).
[209] 6 WH Cases2d at 1392.
[210] 49 Fed. Cl. 459 (Fed. Cl. 2001).

2. *"Directly Related to Management Policies or General Business Operations"*

The First Circuit affirmed the district court's holding in *Reich v. John Alden Life Insurance Co.*[211] that marketing representatives were exempt administrative employees. This case involved a claim for overtime pay for marketing representatives of a company that designs, creates, and sells various types of commercial insurance policies. The marketing representatives were generally responsible for cultivating an independent agent sales force to act as intermediary between the insurance company and the end-purchaser. The court noted that 29 C.F.R. §541.205(a) "subdivides the first prong of the [administrative exemption's] short test into two subparts: (1) the employee must be engaged in 'administrative' rather than 'production' activity; and (2) this administrative activity must be of 'substantial importance' to management or operations."[212] Finding that the district court had examined the facts and determined that both tests were met, the court of appeals affirmed. Rejecting the Department of Labor's contention that the marketing representatives were "production" rather than "administrative" employees, the First Circuit observed that "the day-to-day activities of marketing representatives are more in the nature of 'representing the company' and 'promoting sales' of John Alden products, two examples of exempt administrative work provided by §541.205(b) of the interpretations."[213] In this regard, the court noted that the marketing representatives were the company's primary contact with the insurance market via the independent agents, and they represented the company by keeping the market informed of changes in product offerings and price structure. Moreover, the court observed that the marketing representatives were engaged in more than routine selling since they advised agents as to which products to market against competitors' offerings and helped the agents put together proposals for bidding on new business.[214]

---

[211] 126 F.3d 1, 4 WH Cases2d 129 (1st Cir. 1997).
[212] *Id.* at 8–9, 4 WH Cases2d at 133.
[213] *Id.* at 10.
[214] *Id.*

The administrative work performed by the marketing representatives was found to be of substantial importance to the management or operation of the business, because the marketing representatives were the "principle [sic] source for information" about the carrier.[215]

Finally, the court held that the marketing representatives exercised sufficient discretion and independent judgment in carrying out their duties to qualify as exempt administrative employees. Choosing which agents to contact on a given day and which products to discuss with each agent, relying on their own knowledge of an agent's business to help tailor proposals for the end-purchasers, and anticipating competing products that the end-purchasers might be considering so as to distinguish the company's offerings from those of competitors were highlighted as duties involving the exercise of such discretion.[216]

The application of the "directly related to management policies" standard was also at issue in *Shaw v. Prentice Hall, Inc.*[217] There, the district court denied an overtime claim made by a production editor/senior production editor of a publishing company who alleged that she was improperly classified as an exempt administrative employee. The court found the requirement of the regulations that an administrative employee's functions be "directly related" to management policies or general business operations was satisfied because the plaintiff was ultimately responsible for managing entire book projects through the editing and production process and was ultimately responsible for the timeliness and quality of the book.[218] In addition, the court agreed with the employer that the plaintiff's primary duty of managing book projects involved the exercise of a substantial amount of discretion and independent judgment. As examples, the court noted that the plaintiff made editorial choices to improve the quality and user-friendliness of the text and the index, approved or disapproved proofreaders' and copy editors' suggested edits, made decisions regarding how to best manage

---

[215] *Id.* at 12.
[216] *Id.* at 13.
[217] 977 F. Supp. 909 (S.D. Ind. 1997).
[218] *Id.* at 916.

the process in order to meet deadlines, made suggestions to her managing editor regarding changing or reprioritizing deadlines, and provided input into the selection of freelance copy editors and technical editors.[219]

In *Scott Wetzel Services, Inc. v. New York State Board of Industrial Appeals,*[220] a state appellate court affirmed a state labor appeals board holding that claims examiners for a company that administered, settled, and paid workers' compensation and general liability claims were production workers, and therefore not exempt from FLSA overtime requirements, because they produced the product offered by the employer to the public. The court distinguished its ruling from a holding that found insurance adjusters for an insurance company to be exempt,[221] noting that those adjusters were not involved in the production of the insurance policies, which were the primary product offered to the public in that case. In a succinct formulation the court stated:

> In applying this production/administrative dichotomy, it is necessary to identify the nature of the employer's business to ascertain whether the employee's job is to produce the product or services the employer's business offers to the public or whether the employee is engaged in servicing the business by performing such tasks as advising management, planning, negotiating, representing the company, purchasing, promoting sales and business research and control.[222]

In *Webster v. Public School Employees of Washington, Inc.*,[223] the Ninth Circuit affirmed the district court's grant of summary judgment in favor of the employer, a union, finding that its field representative was an administrative employee. The plaintiff field representative contended that his work in advising the local units, negotiating bargaining agreements, and handling grievances was the union's principal service to its locals, and thus he was engaged in "production" rather than "administrative," work.

---

[219] *Id.*

[220] 252 A.D.2d 212, 682 N.Y.S.2d 304 (1998).

[221] Blinston v. Hartford Accident & Indem. Co., 441 F.2d 1365 (8th Cir. 1971).

[222] 682 N.Y.S.2d at 305 (citations omitted).

[223] 247 F.3d 910, 914–17 (9th Cir. 2001).

The court noted that a strict application of the administration-production dichotomy of 29 C.F.R. §541.205(a) tended to support plaintiff's argument, but concluded that the regulation, when taken as a whole, showed that the representative's work fell within the types of duties considered to be administrative. Concluding that the purpose of the administration/production dichotomy was to "clarify the meaning of 'work directly related to the management policies or general business operations,' not to frustrate the purpose and spirit of the entire exemption,"[224] the court viewed the representative not as a production employee for his employer union, but as an administrative employee advising and servicing employer's customers, the local bargaining units.

In *Berg v. United States,*[225] the Court of Federal Claims distinguished between the plaintiffs, electronic technicians whose work supported the base's business or "production" mission, flight testing, and other employees whose work supported management services of the base. Electronic technicians supported the production endeavor by repairing and maintaining air traffic control equipment, and that repair and maintenance work was not related to management policies or general business operations.

In *O'Neill-Marino v. Omni Hotels Management Corp.,*[226] a federal district court in New York found that a hotel's Director of Conference Services qualified for the administrative exemption. Her work was "directly related to general business operations" and "of substantial importance to the employer or the employer's customers" because the conference business accounted for approximately ten percent of the hotel's annual revenues, and her responsibilities included extensive client contact and customer service before and during conferences, occasional sales duties, preparation of conference manual, and participation in management meetings and budget planning.

---

[224] *Id.* at 916.
[225] 49 Fed. Cl. 459 (2001).
[226] 6 WH Cases2d 1635 (S.D.N.Y. 2001).

Bell v. Farmers Insurance Exchange[227] was brought by insurance company claims representatives for overtime pay allegedly due under California law. The defendant asserted that the claims representatives were exempt administrative employees. The trial court granted plaintiffs' motion for summary judgment as to this defense, and also awarded interim attorneys fees (under California law); this order was appealed by defendants. The Court of Appeal for the First District held that, under the applicable provisions of California quasi-legislative regulation, and in view of the principle that exemptions from the statutory mandatory overtime provisions are narrowly construed, the trial court correctly determined that the exemption did not apply to plaintiffs. In its decision the court of appeal referred to related provisions of federal law and regulations, and approved the use of federal authorities, including opinion letters, as an aid to interpretations of the administrative exemption under California law.

In *Claes v. Guard Publishing Co.*,[228] a federal district court in Oregon held, after bench trial, that district managers for a newspaper operation were exempt administrative employees. The district managers' primary duty, to create and maintain a reliable system for newspaper delivery within an assigned geographical area, was directly related to management policies because it affected a major and important business operation of Guard Publishing – the delivery system. Each district manager supervised between 30 and 50 route carriers, and was primarily responsible for recruiting, training, and supervising them. The district managers also had responsibility for promoting circulation in their districts. The district managers generally set their own schedules and operated with a degree of freedom in their supervisory and promotional responsibilities. They were paid on a salary basis without set hours. The court found that the occasional need for district managers to perform manual work in delivering on a route in the event of a termination or default by a route carrier did not defeat the exemption.

---

[227]105 Cal. Rptr. 2d 59, 87 Cal. App. 4th 805, 7 WH Cases2d 838, *cert. denied.* 7 WH Cases2d 864 (2001).

[228]2001 U.S. Dist. LEXIS 12840 (D. Or. 2001).

The Wage-Hour Division issued a response to a request for reconsideration of a regional official's opinion to the effect that certain "home office sales consultants" are not exempt administrative employees, concurring with the regional office's reasoning and conclusion. After reviewing extensive factual representations about the work involved, it concluded that the employees were "primarily in the business of selling products and services" and thus performed a production function rather than one relating to the management policies or general business operations of the employer or its customers.[229]

3. *Primary Duty*

In *Adams v. United States*[230] the Court of Appeals for the Federal Circuit addressed whether federal criminal investigators are administratively exempt. The parties had stipulated that the plaintiffs spent 51 percent or more of their time conducting investigations, and the government had argued on its motion for summary judgment that the work of criminal investigation was their primary duty and that they were accordingly administratively exempt. The trial court rejected this theory and based its decision on what it described as the "alternative primary duty" test. Referring to administrative pronouncements of the Civil Service Commission and its predecessor, the Office of Personnel Management, the court described the "alternative primary duty" test as follows: an employee may have as his or her primary duty the one that is "most important, even though it occupies less [than] half of the employee's work time," if it "(1) constitutes a substantial, regular part of a position, and (2) governs the classification and qualification requirements of the position, and (3) is clearly exempt work in terms of the basic nature of the work, the frequency with which the employee must exercise discretion and independent judgment, and the significance of the decisions made." Noting that the plaintiffs had planning and supervision responsibilities as well as responsibilities for con-

---

[229]WH Opinion dated April 18, 2001, WHM: 99:8360.

[230]178 F.3d 1306 (Fed. Cir. 1998).

ducting investigations, the trial court found these duties primary and granted summary judgment for the government. The appellate court upheld the "alternative primary duty" test but reversed the decision below on the ground that the record was devoid of evidence sufficient to support the conclusion that the test was satisfied with respect to the planning and supervision duties of the plaintiffs.

The following are additional examples applying the primary duty test to administrative employees:

- An employee whose primary task was negotiating with customers and their attorneys to settle billing, delay, and cargo damage claims performed work "directly related to management policies or general business relations."[231] The court analogized the employee's tasks to those performed by insurance claims agents and adjusters, who are specifically mentioned by regulation as satisfying the "directly related" test.
- The primary duty of an emergency medical service director was to perform office or nonmanual work directly related to management or general business operations.[232] The court found that the director handled the day-to-day operations of the service, including giving policy advice and recommendations, proposing a budget, sending out and paying bills, determining a schedule for herself and volunteers, making decisions regarding collection, and handling personnel problems. Furthermore, the court emphasized that the director was paid more than the other employees, and worked with little supervision. The court thus found that the issue of whether or not 50 percent or more of the director's time was spent on managerial or administrative tasks was not material.

---

[231]Haywood v. North Am. Van Lines, 121 F.3d 1066, 4 WH Cases2d 59 (7th Cir. 1997) (quoting 29 C.F.R. §541.214).

[232]Mayer v. Board of County Comm'rs, 5 F. Supp. 2d 914, 4 WH Cases2d 1027 (D. Kan. 1998).

In *Lott v. Howard Wilson Chrysler-Plymouth, Inc.*,[233] the Fifth Circuit affirmed the summary judgment granted by the district court to the defendant, on the basis that the plaintiff office manager for an automobile dealership was exempt as an administrative employee. Despite the large amount of time spent by the plaintiff in bookkeeping and clerical work, her primary duties directly related and were important to both management policies and general business operations of the employer and required the exercise of discretion and independent judgment, inasmuch as she was responsible for (1) preparation of all payrolls and various monthly and quarterly returns, reports, and financial statements; and (2) the supervision of four office employees. The plaintiff had a college degree in business administration and held a certified public accountancy certificate and was paid an annual salary of $44,000.

In *Wolf v. Healthcare Compare Corp.*,[234] a district court denied summary judgment for both parties on the issue of whether a proposal specialist was an exempt administrative employee. The evidence showed that the plaintiff, working in the marketing department of a health care product company, was responsible for answering questions in clients' request for proposals. She would first consult the employer's "standard language database" for approved language for sending out a response. If no acceptable standard language was available, she would then contact someone in the appropriate operational department to obtain the applicable information. She would sometimes change the grammar or organization of the information obtained to make it clearer. If she believed the information was inaccurate, she would flag the answer and go elsewhere in the company for the correct information. Based on these duties, the employer argued that the plaintiff's job was to promote the products and services of the company, while the plaintiff argued she was merely an "intelligent clerk" who inserted answers to questions using standard language or information obtained from operational managers. The court found that there was more than one

---

[233] 203 F.3d 326 (5th Cir. 2000).

[234] 1999 U.S. Dist. LEXIS 16191 (N.D. Ill. 1999).

reasonable inference that could be drawn on whether the plaintiff's primary duty was directly related to the management policies or general business operations of the company.

In *Stockman v. Koch Industries, Inc.*,[235] the court denied the employer's motion seeking summary judgment on the plaintiff's overtime claim on the ground that he was an exempt administrative employee. The plaintiff, a pipeline inspector, performed various white-collar tasks such as supervising staff, maintaining documentation of the staff's work, and monitoring safety practices, but also alleged that he performed manual tasks such as blowing down the pipelines, opening and closing valves, and tracing "smart pigs" through the pipelines. The court found that "[w]ithout any type of time reference with respect to the manual versus nonmanual work, the court is unable to make a determination whether the manual work passed over the threshold point [for primary duty] for purposes of the exemption. . . . A material issue of fact remains and summary judgment is thus precluded."[236] The court further found that the plaintiff was not an exempt administrative employee because he was not required to exercise discretion and independent judgment. The plaintiff supervised a contractor's staff, making sure the contractor employees followed procedures and worked in a safe manner. In order to perform that job, the plaintiff was given written and unwritten specifications. If the plaintiff did not think that the work being done met specifications, he would stop the work and have his supervisor look at it. The lead inspectors supervised the plaintiff's work and coordinated his and other inspectors' duties. The court found that the plaintiff's work involved the exercise of skills in applying procedures or specific standards rather than discretion and independent judgment, particularly because the regulation explaining the difference cited an inspector as an example of a nonadministrative, nonexempt employee. Therefore, the court denied the employer's summary judgment motion on this issue.

---

[235]2000 U.S. Dist. LEXIS 4382, 5 WH Cases 2d 1658 (D. Kan. 2000).
[236]5 WH Cases2d at 1677.

In an unpublished decision the Ninth Circuit, in *Cole v. Daniels, Inc.*,[237] affirmed summary judgment for the defendant, holding that an employee's primary duty is "not determined solely by time, but . . . by a number of 'pertinent factors.'"[238] The plaintiff trucking manager's administrative responsibilities were "extremely important," he was almost solely responsible for the company's long-haul trucking operation, and he exercised independent judgment in connection with that responsibility.

In *Berg v. United States,*[239] the Court of Federal Claims found that electronic technicians at Edwards Air Force Base were not administrative employees. Their primary duties were maintaining, repairing and certifying as operational electronic air traffic control equipment. Certain of the employees' duties arguably met the administrative exemption requirements, such as providing technical advice and selecting equipment and parts for acquisition. However, those duties did not involve a significant portion of their work time. They spent the majority of their working time using testing equipment, tools and cleaning supplies, working off floors and workbenches and following instruction manuals. Stand-by time, in which the employees were on-duty but waiting for the need for repair services to arise, constituted a large portion of the time of these employees, and was not counted as time "worked" for the purpose of determining their primary duties.

In *Barth v. Wolf Creek Nuclear Operating Corp.*,[240] a federal district court in Kansas denied a summary judgment by the employer regarding the administrative exemption. The court found itself unable to conclude from the record "that the plaintiffs' primary duties affect management policy, or that they have the responsibility to influence or execute policy decisions."[241] The engineers' primary tasks, such as prioritizing work orders, managing system performance, and preparing reports,

---

[237] 7 Fed.Appx. 634, 2001 WL 294064, 2001 U.S. App. LEXIS 5345 (9th Cir. 2001).

[238] *Id.* at 635.

[239] 49 Fed. Cl. 459 (Fed.Ct.Clms. 2001).

[240] 125 F. Supp. 2d 437, 441-42 (D. Kan. 2000).

[241] *Id.* at 440.

appeared to fall into the production category since they directly affected the plant's energy generation capacity.

In an unpublished decision in *Gagnon v. Resource Technology, Inc.*,[242] the Tenth Circuit affirmed the trial court's judgment for the defendant, a consulting and engineering firm.[243] The plaintiff office manager and bookkeeper was an administrative employee because, inter alia, her primary duty was office or non-manual work related to management policies or general business operations. The office manager/bookkeeper estimated that her bookkeeping duties, which according to regulation[244] are not administrative, absorbed the majority of her time. Nonetheless, the court found that her primary duty was to administer and carry out the office work necessary to run defendant's business. The fact that she alone was charged with those important duties showed that they were of primary importance to defendant. Furthermore, she participated in policy decisions and often executed office policy. She regularly selected and supervised bank accounts, insured completion of personnel and payroll documentation, supervised insurance policies, participated in senior staff meetings, attended applicant interviews, made hiring and firing recommendations, kept and revised the employee manual, and dealt with vendors on behalf of the company. These duties met the substantive element of the duties test, and were a significant part of her employment responsibilities.

In *Demos v. City of Indianapolis*,[245] the district court denied summary judgment for the city with respect to each one of three plaintiffs, because in each case a material issue of fact existed as to at least one of the factors necessary for exemption. Two of the employees were found to meet the duties test of one or another exemption, but a factual question remained in their cases as to

---

[242] 2001 WL 909028, 2001 U.S. App. LEXIS 18290 (10th Cir. 2001).

[243] The court of appeals did not agree with the lower court's findings and conclusion that plaintiff was an exempt executive employee, and the record did not show that she supervised two full-time employees; but did find that she met the conditions of the administrative exemption.

[244] 29 C.F.R. §541.205 (c)(1).

[245] 126 F. Supp. 2d 548, 562–63 (S.D. Ind. 2000).

the salary basis test. After an extensive review of the evidence, the court found that the third employee, who held a number of different jobs, performed some project manager duties that required independent judgment and some secretarial duties which did not. A slight majority of her duties did not require discretion and her supervisor placed priority on her secretarial duties at the expense of her project manager duties. Therefore, there was a question of fact as to whether her "primary duty" was administrative.

In *Claes v. Guard Publishing Co.*,[246] a federal district court in Oregon found that the plaintiff district managers were exempt. They were responsible for selecting, monitoring and terminating the independent contractor delivery staff, and even though they occasionally delivered newspapers when the regular independent contractor route carriers were absent, the district managers' primary duty was to create and maintain a reliable delivery system, and not to engage in the production aspect of delivery itself.

4. *Discretion and Independent Judgment*

An employee who was the only regular paid employee of the county's emergency medical service staffed otherwise by volunteers, and who spent most of her time arranging for and scheduling the volunteers to cover the service's work, exercised sufficient discretion and judgment to qualify as an exempt administrative employee.[247]

a. *Discretion and Independent Judgment As Distinguished From Skills and Procedures*

In *Stockman v. Koch Industries, Inc.*,[248] the court held that even if it could have been determined that the plaintiff's primary duty consisted of nonmanual work, the administrative exemption would be inapplicable because defendant employer Koch had not sufficiently demonstrated that plaintiff employee Stockman's

---

[246] 2001 U.S. Dist. LEXIS 12840 (D. Or. 2001).

[247] Mayer v. Board of County Comm'rs of Chase County, 5 F. Supp. 2d 914, 4 WH Cases2d 1027 (D. Kan. 1998).

[248] 2000 U.S. Dist. LEXIS 4382, 5 WH Cases 2d 1658 (D. Kan. 2000).

work required the use of discretion and independent judgment. Accordingly, the court denied the employer's motion for summary judgment on Stockman's overtime claim.

In a Wage and Hour Opinion Letter,[249] the Department of Labor on May 17, 1999, reiterated that the administrative exemption of Section 13(a)(1) is limited to persons who perform work of substantial importance to the business. The Department noted that "administrative employee" generally means a person who is engaged in the staff function as opposed to the line functions of an employer. The opinion letter concluded that the loan officer employees of a mortgage brokerage company do not qualify for the administrative exemption because they are engaged in carrying out the employer's day-to-day activities as opposed to participating in the formulation or execution of the overall policies of the business. In an Opinion Letter dated February 16, 2001, on request for reconsideration of the May 1999 letter, the Department reached the same conclusion, but with some modification of its reasoning. Relying on additional representations made by the employer, to the effect that the principal responsibility of a loan officer is to advise a borrower in the selection of a loan package, the Department now agreed that the primary duty of the loan officer consists of the performance of office or nonmanual work directly related to the management policies or general business operations of the employer or the employer's customers. However, the Department found that the officers primarily used their skills and knowledge in applying techniques to choose an established loan package for the customer, rather than exercising the necessary discretion or independent judgment to qualify for the exemption.

In *Berg v. United States,*[250] the Federal Court of Claims held that electronic technicians who maintained and repaired air traffic control equipment did not exercise independent judgment and discretion, within the meaning of applicable Office of Personnel Management (OPM) Regulations, in their duties.[251]

---

[249] 1999 WL 1002401, WHM: 99:8249.

[250] 49 Fed.Cl. 459 (2001).

[251] OPM Regulations at 5 C.F.R. §551 differ in detail from DOL regulations at 29 C.F.R. §541.

Rejecting the Department of Defense's contention that they exercised independent judgment by evaluating technical problems, the court found that, although plaintiffs were highly skilled, most of their work consisted of following standard checklists and step-by-step procedures published in manuals to troubleshoot, test and repair the equipment.

In *Gagnon v. Resource Technology, Inc.*,[252] the Tenth Circuit affirmed judgment for the defendant, a consulting and engineering company, concluding that plaintiff, the office manager and bookkeeper, exercised independent judgment and discretion. She evaluated courses of action and made recommendations to senior staff regarding insurance policies; hiring, firing and employment policies; and banking decisions. She also "'actively participated in the Senior Staff meetings and had a say in how the company was run.'"[253]

In *Demos v. City of Indianapolis*, the district court denied summary judgment to the employer with respect to one employee because there was insufficient evidence to demonstrate that she exercised independent judgment and discretion during the period in which she served as a financial advisor.[254] The employee testified that her primary duties involved maintaining records and processing paperwork, which was primarily clerical in nature. While the city contended that she was responsible for compiling a budget for the agency, her testimony showed that she had little discretion in receiving and processing the proposed budgets of the sections she worked with.

b. Decisions in Significant Matters

The applicability of the administrative exemption to a funeral director/embalmer was at issue in *Szarnych v. Theis-Gorski Funeral Home, Inc.*[255] The employer argued that the plaintiff was properly classified as an exempt administrative employee because he was the sole funeral director in charge for over

[252] 19 Fed.Appx. 745, 2001 WL 909028, 2001 U.S. App. LEXIS 18290 (10th Cir. 2001), (unpublished).

[253] *Id.* at 748–49.

[254] 126 F. Supp. 2d 548, 558–60 (S.D. Ind. 2000).

[255] 957 F. Supp. 132, 3 WH Cases2d 1330 (N.D. Ill. 1997).

20 percent of the time and had the "unfettered responsibility" to arrange and direct all aspects of the funerals, including hiring persons needed for the services, supervising other personnel, overseeing paperwork, and reviewing and signing off on death certificates, cremation permits, authorizations for releases, and embalming and funeral purchase contracts. The plaintiff countered that he did not possess independent judgment because he was without authority to commit the funeral home financially.[256] The district court noted that the Department of Labor's regulations "do not require the exercise of discretion and independent judgment at so high a level,"[257] but it found that the extent to which the plaintiff exercised sufficient discretion and independent judgment in performing his duties was contested by the parties. It therefore denied summary judgment.[258]

d. Final Decisions Are Not Necessary

In *Copas v. East Bay Municipal Utility District,*[259] a federal district court granted summary judgment for the defendant water utility company, finding five plaintiffs (three employees in public affairs, one personnel analyst, and one occupational safety and health administrator) to be exempt administrative employees. With regard to all the plaintiffs, the court held that an employee may still exercise the discretion and independent judgment contemplated by the regulation even though the employee's decisions are subject to review or rejection. Although most of these employees were required to clear material with supervisors, they exercised judgment in answering questions and deciding on which substantive policy questions to decline comment in the absence of proper guidance or authorization.

In *Cole v. Daniels, Inc.*,[260] the Ninth Circuit found that the plaintiff exercised independent discretion in managing the

---

[256] *Id.* at 136.
[257] *Id.* (quoting 29 C.F.R. §541.207(d)(2)).
[258] *Id.*
[259] 61 F. Supp. 2d 1017, 6 WH Cases2d 307 (N.D. Cal. 1999).
[260] 2001 WL 294064, 2001 U.S. App. LEXIS 5345 (9th Cir. 2001).

company's trucking operation. Although he was required to consult the company's president on certain matters, he exercised sufficient independent discretion to qualify as an administrative employee because he made recommendations for action. He also made decisions without review regarding drivers, routes and prices.

In *O'Neill-Marino v. Omni Hotels Management Corp.*,[261] a hotel's Director of Conference Services exercised independent judgment where she negotiated contracts within preset limits and her contracts were subject to final approval by the sales manager. She was given substantial discretion within those limits, and she exercised her responsibilities largely without supervision.

In *Claes v. Guard Publishing Co.*,[262] the district court held that district managers for the newspaper circulation department exercised independent judgment and discretion because they had recommending authority regarding contracting, training, supervising, and terminating route carriers. Although zone managers, who supervised the district managers, gave less autonomy to poor performers, all district managers at least made recommendations regarding hiring and retention of route carriers.

6. Examples of Positions That Are Exempt or Nonexempt

The following additional examples illustrate the application of the test for administrative exemption to various job categories; as always, however, each case is analyzed independently on the basis of the particular duties involved:

- A moving company's consumer service coordinator, whom the court analogized to a claims adjuster, has been recognized as an exempt employee.[263] The consumer service coordinator was responsible for negotiating with custom-

---

[261] 6 WH Cases2d 1635 (S.D.N.Y. 2001).

[262] 2001 U.S. Dist. LEXIS 12840 (D. Or. 2001).

[263] Haywood v. North Am. Van Lines, Inc., 121 F.3d 1066, 4 WH Cases2d 59 (7th Cir. 1997).

ers and their attorneys to settle billing, delay, and cargo damage claims. Although supervisors reviewed the employee's work, the court held that neither this review nor the guidelines governing the work prevented the employee from exercising independent professional judgment.

- A store manager who at all relevant times was the highest-ranking employee at a retail store and was responsible for the financial health of the store, maintaining the proper level of inventory, setting prices, placing orders, drafting work schedules, and attending monthly manager meetings satisfied the administrative exemption.[264]
- A technical support engineer who provided "trouble-shooting" advice to her employer's customers met the administrative exemption. She provided assistance relating to the installation, application, and sale of the employer's telecommunications products, which linked her to the employer's "servicing" operations. The engineer's advice did not involve rote applications of previously established procedures; rather, she was given wide latitude to fashion solutions.[265]
- A union vice president who was paid by the employer but who performed no production work, handled employee grievances, and engaged in daily functions to assure the employer followed the terms of the collective bargaining agreement was an exempt administrative employee under FLSA.[266]
- An office accounting manager and clerk is not an exempt administrative employee if her primary duty is the performance of routine clerical and bookkeeping tasks and routine telephone collections. The employer's contention that the employee had discretion to extend credit to customers and set up payment plans did not make the

---

[264]Stricker v. Eastern Off Rd. Equip., 935 F. Supp. 650, 3 WH Cases2d 748, 752 (D. Md. 1996).

[265]Orphanos v. Charles Indus., 3 WH Cases2d 924, 926 (N.D. Ill. 1996).

[266]Douglas v. Argo-Tech Corp., 113 F.3d 67, 3 WH Cases2d 1569 (6th Cir. 1997).

clerk an exempt employee as such duties were rare and the majority of the work was routine in nature.[267]

- The maintenance director of a helicopter company did not fall within the administrative exemption.[268] His duties consisted of maintaining an FAA-required technical library, performance of some hands-on mechanical work (which the court estimated as requiring 15 percent of his time), planning repair work, ordering parts, instructing two subordinates, and carrying out inspections of the work done. Considering the factors that might bring the employee within the administrative exemption notwithstanding his significant expenditure of time on nonadministrative duties, the court referred to its earlier conclusion that the employee failed the primary duty test of the executive exemption, explaining that the analyses under the two exemptions were virtually identical. Although the maintenance director performed certain administrative activities, was relatively free from supervision, and was paid significantly more for hands-on work than his subordinates who performed the same kind of work, he did not exercise discretion on a regular basis and had limited discretion to hire and fire employees beneath him. Therefore, the court concluded that he was not an exempt administrative employee.
- Public relations and community affairs officers, an employee personnel analyst, and an occupational health and safety administrator who monitored companywide OSHA compliance all fell under the administrative exemption because their work did not involve the "production" or "line" work of a water utility, but rather involved the company's general business.[269]

---

[267]Friou v. L.E. Coppersmith Inc., 4 WH Cases2d 1422 (S.D. Tex. 1998).

[268]Sack v. Miami Helicopter Serv., 986 F. Supp. 1456, 4 WH Cases2d 490 (S.D. Fla. 1997). *See also* the discussion of the executive exemption aspects of this case in text at notes 198 and 199 of this chapter.

[269]Copas v. East Bay Mun. Util. Dist., 61 F. Supp. 2d 1017, 6 WH Cases2d 307 (N.D. Cal. 1999).

- A "facilities supervisor" was not exempt because he performed manual labor tasks in the operation of defendant's primary administration building, and he had no role in any financial operations or business management. The fact that the supervisor was responsible for the safety of 750 employees in the building did not transform his manual labor job into an administrative "office" position. This employee was, however, found to be an exempt executive.[270]
- Employees of a visitor center, whose jobs entailed attempting to attract certain categories of visitors or events to the city, were not exempt administrative employees because they did not customarily and regularly exercise discretion and independent judgment. Most of the employees' duties—such as compiling names of prospects for a database, calling prospects, and sending out brochures—were deemed mechanical rather than discretionary. The court likened the visitor center jobs to sales positions, which the court noted are not exempt from the FLSA.[271]
- A member of a company's employee benefits staff had sued for failure to pay overtime under the FLSA. Although his affidavit indicated the contrary, his own deposition established that he (1) was a salaried employee, as he had no expectation that his employer would dock his pay for partial-day absences; (2) was in a position that required the exercise of discretion and independent judgment, in that the plaintiff made judgments by developing methodologies to improve his services, supervised employees, decided among possible courses of action to recommend to clients, and performed other analytical duties; (3) performed duties that influenced the business operations and policies of his employer's clients and also those of the employer (for example, he testified that he

[270] *Id.*, 6 WH Cases2d 307.

[271] Heidtman v. County of El Paso, 171 F.3d 1038, 5 WH Cases2d 385 (5th Cir. 1999).

had played a significant role in helping the firm adopt a voice response system).[272]

- Senior production planners for ship construction projects were found to be exempt administrative employees.[273] The court found that the work performed was predominantly intellectual in nature and involved little manual labor, and that the plaintiffs were responsible for planning in detail all production work in the shipyard, including scheduling craft workers in the construction of battleships.
- The court determined that a senior benefits analyst in the human resources department was an exempt administrative employee.[274] The job duties included, among other things, analyzing plan designs and benefits changes and making appropriate recommendations; conducting plan audits to ensure compliance; developing cost/benefit analysis of various plan design changes; developing and maintaining a standard administrative manual for all benefit programs; administering local network of doctors, hospital, and support services; coordinating customer satisfaction surveys for benefits and related products; reviewing and revising benefit materials; and assisting in developing and providing training on benefits programs and procedures.
- A head athletic trainer who developed and managed a sports medicine program, managed the administration of health care to student athletes, and trained and supervised a staff of student trainees was an exempt administrative employee.[275]
- A resident site manager for an employer that owned and managed a subsidized housing project did not qualify for the administrative exemption where her primary duties

---

[272]Piscione v. Ernst & Young, L.L.P., 35 F. Supp. 2d 106, 5 WH Cases2d 172 (D. Me. 1998).

[273]Cowart v. Ingalls Shipbuilding, Inc., 213 F.3d 261 (5th Cir. 2000).

[274]Furlong v. Johnson Controls World Servs., Inc., 97 F. Supp. 2d 1312 (S.D. Fla. 2000).

[275]Winkle v. Hutchison Cmty. Coll., 2000 WL 1948653 (Kan. Ct. App. 2000).

involved routine clerical duties that resembled work of nonexempt bookkeepers, secretaries, and clerks of various kinds who hold run-of-the-mill positions in any business.[276] The employer had advanced the somewhat creative argument that the employee, who was required to live at the housing complex, should have all her time outside of normal office hours counted as "waiting time" and thus as administrative time in determining whether her primary duty was administrative. The court rejected this argument inasmuch as the employer failed to present any evidence to overcome the presumption created by Department of Labor regulations that an employee who resides on her employer's premises on a permanent basis is not considered to be working all the time she is on the premises. Further, the employer did not object when the jury instructions failed to include the issue of "waiting time" in the primary-duty instruction.

In an April 20, 1999, Opinion Letter,[277] on the question whether college admissions counselors could be exempt administrative employees, the Department of Labor stated: "The work of the college admissions counselors does not satisfy the academic administration prong of 'the primary duty' test because employees who qualify under that part of the test must have as their primary duty work that is directly related to academic administration or general academic operations of the school, i.e., they must perform work directly in the field of education."[278] The letter went on to state that the counselors' principal activity of student recruitment was work directly related to the general business operations of the college, and consequently the counselors met the "business administration" prong of the primary duty standard. Not enough information was supplied to the Department to determine whether they exercised the discretion and independent judgment contemplated by the regulations.

---

[276]Jarrett v. ERC Props., 211 F.3d 1078, 6 WH Cases2d 4 (8th Cir. 2000).
[277]1999 WL 1002391, WHM: 99:8242.
[278]*Id.* (citing 29 C.F.R. §§541.202(e), 541.206(a)).

In a Wage and Hour Opinion Letter,[279] the Department of Labor on May 17, 1999, reiterated that the administrative exemption of Section 13(a)(1) is limited to persons who perform work of substantial importance to the business. The Department noted that "administrative employee" generally means a person who is engaged in the staff function as opposed to the line functions of an employer. The opinion letter concluded that the loan officer employees of a mortgage brokerage company do not qualify for the administrative exemption because they are engaged in carrying out the employer's day-to-day activities as opposed to participating in the formulation or execution of the overall policies of the business. In an Opinion Letter dated February 16, 2001, on request for reconsideration of the May 1999 letter, the Department reached the same conclusion, but with some modification of its reasoning. Relying on additional representations made by the employer, to the effect that the principal responsibility of a loan officer is to advise a borrower in the selection of a loan package, the Department now agreed that the primary duty of the loan officer consists of the performance of office or nonmanual work directly related to the management policies or general business operations of the employer or the employer's customers. However, the Department found that the officers primarily used their skills and knowledge in applying techniques to choose an established loan package for the customer, rather than exercising the necessary discretion or independent judgment to qualify for the exemption.

[279] 1999 WL 1002401, WHM: 98:8249.

VII. DEFINING THE PROFESSIONAL EXEMPTION

C. Types of Professional Employees

1. *The Learned Professional*

As noted in the Treatise (and in the regulations), the "salary basis test" for a professional exemption does not apply to "any plaintiff who holds a law or physician's license and works as a lawyer or doctor."[280]

In *Bolduc v. National Semiconductor Corp.*,[281] the defendant had claimed, but not sufficiently to obtain summary judgment on the claim, that the plaintiff was an independent contractor. The defendant further claimed that the plaintiff, if an employee, was an exempt professional. A federal district court in Maine held that it was a question of material fact whether the plaintiff, a "facilities engineer," qualified for the "learned" branch of the professional exemption. Despite the individual's education and training as an engineer, the court concluded that the question of whether his duties would qualify him as a "learned professional" was one of material fact.

The Seventh Circuit in *Piscione v. Ernst & Young, L.L.P.*[282] upheld a district court's grant of summary judgment in favor of the former employer of a member of the employee benefits staff who had sued for failure to pay overtime under the FLSA. The court found that the employee qualified not only for the administrative exemption but also as an exempt professional, because he performed duties that required advanced knowledge, as evidenced by his college degree in mathematics, his continuing education on changes in tax law, and his membership in the

---

[280]Close v. New York, 3 WH Cases2d 225, 234 (N.D.N.Y. 1996). The decision in this case was subsequently reversed and the case dismissed on the basis of Eleventh Amendment immunity. 125 F.3d 31 (2d Cir. 1997).

[281]35 F. Supp. 2d 106, 5 WH Cases2d 172 (D. Me. 1998).

[282]171 F.3d 527, 5 WH Cases2d 361 (7th Cir. 1999).

Society of Actuaries. Despite plaintiff's assertion that two employees who held that same position possessed no advanced degree, the court found that plaintiff's factual knowledge concerning this claim was quite limited and really amounted only to speculation, insufficient to create an issue requiring trial.

a. "Knowledge of an Advanced Type"

In *Debejian v. Atlantic Testing Laboratories, Ltd.*,[283] a federal district court in New York refused to sustain the defendant company's claim that the plaintiff was an exempt employee. It held that in making the determination as to whether an employee qualifies for the professional exemption, the proper focus is on whether the particular position at issue required advanced knowledge in a field of science or learning, not whether an individual employee actually possessed advanced knowledge.

In an opinion consisting entirely of conclusions and providing no analysis, the Court of Appeals of Kansas affirmed the trial court's decision that a community college head athletic trainer is an exempt administrative employee, exempt "learned professional" and exempt "teacher professional."[284]

c. "Customarily Acquired by a Prolonged Course of Specialized Intellectual Instruction and Study"

In *Rutlin v. Prime Succession, Inc.*,[285] a federal district court in Michigan held that, under the FLSA "short test," a funeral director who was over different periods paid on both a salary and an hourly basis was an exempt professional employee during those periods when he was paid on a salary basis. The court concluded that his duties were of a type that required advanced knowledge gained through prolonged specialized instruction and study—as evidenced by state licensing requirements—that

[283]64 F. Supp. 2d 85 (N.D.N.Y. 1999).

[284]Winkle v. Hutchison Cmty. Coll., 18 P.3d 239, 2000 WL 1948653 (Kan. Ct. App. 2000).

[285]29 F. Supp. 2d 794, 5 WH Cases2d 43 (W.D. Mich. 1998).

his duties as a funeral director/embalmer required the exercise of "discretion and judgment," and that his "primary duty" was the one that was of principal importance to his employer, even if such a duty occupied less than 50 percent of his work time.

In *Owsley v. San Antonio Independent School District,*[286] the Fifth Circuit reversed the trial court's grant of summary judgment to the plaintiffs on the question of their exempt status. The appellate court determined that the plaintiffs, athletic trainers, were exempt learned professionals under the short test, because, in order to qualify, they were required to obtain a state license to be a trainer, and in meeting the license requirements they had to, at a minimum, obtain a bachelor's degree with a minimum of 15 specialized college credits in disciplines such as human anatomy and physiology. Those requirements were, according to the court, sufficient to satisfy the test for a "learned" professional. The appellate court also found that the record showed the trainers exercised sufficient discretion to qualify for the professional exemption.

In *Ragnone v. Belo Corp.,*[287] a federal district court in Oregon held that a helicopter pilot was a non-exempt employee even though he was highly skilled, paid considerably more than most non-exempt employees and had tremendous responsibility. The court likened the pilot's training to a traditional apprenticeship with on-the-job training, rather than the extensive academic training commonly required under the learned professional exemption.

In an Opinion letter, the United States Department of Labor's Wage and Hour Division concluded, in response to an inquiry, that ultrasound technologists earning $750 per week were not professional employees within the meaning of the exemption because their advanced skills were not of the type "customarily acquired by a prolonged course of specialized intellectual instruction and study" as provided by the regulations.[288]

---

[286]187 F.3d 521 (5th Cir. 1999).

[287]131 F. Supp. 2d 1189 (D. Or. 2001).

[288]WH Opinion letter dated November 21, 2000, WHM: 99:8331.

Similarly, it opined that avionics technicians, who "troubleshoot and repair Information technology failures in sophisticated avionics and electrical equipment at a military avionics test facility; service equipment, test [equipment], participate in design and production of the equipment, and recommend improvements; assist in integrating Information technology software and hardware systems and possess significant background and knowledge of many types of software and hardware domains," are not professionals within the meaning of the exemption for the same reason—because their primary duty does not consist of the performance of work requiring knowledge of an advanced type in a field of science or learning customarily acquired by a prolonged course of specialized intellectual instruction and study as required by Section 541.3(a)(1) of the regulations.[289] Their training consisted of seven to twelve months of five-days-a-week classroom instruction with a minimum of 1225 classroom hours, hands-on electronics training, and a follow-on course of 240 to 480 hours in classroom and laboratory.

On January 24, 2001,[290] the United States Department of Labor's Wage and Hour Division stated that social work caseworkers had sufficient advanced learning to satisfy that prong of the exemption for professionals where they had (1)(a) a master's degree in social work or human behavioral science, or (b) a bachelor's degree with a major in human behavioral science with certain courses, and (2) at least one year of experience as a professional caseworker.

2. *The Artistic Professional*

In *Shaw v. Prentice Hall, Inc.*,[291] the district court ruled that a production editor/senior production editor for a publishing company was not covered by the exemption for artistic professionals. The court explained that although the plaintiff "did perform some arguably creative editing tasks, her principal duty

[289]WH Opinion letter dated May 2, 2001, WHM: 99:8366.
[290]WHM: 99:5416.
[291]977 F. Supp. 909 (S.D. Ind. 1997).

was to manage a book project through the editing and publishing process, work which required diligence, good time management, organization and assertiveness, but not invention, imagination or talent in a[n] artistic field of endeavor."[292]

c. *Newspaper Journalists*

In *Truex v. Hearst Communications, Inc.*,[293] after reviewing in some detail the significant recent cases dealing with whether newspaper and television journalists are exempt as artistic professionals,[294] the court denied summary judgment to the employer newspaper in a case involving a reporter on the *Houston Chronicle's* professional baseball beat. The plaintiff wrote three different kinds of articles: stories about Houston Astros' baseball games, an "off-day feature," and a weekly "baseball notebook." After reviewing a representative week of articles submitted by the plaintiff, the court found that there were disputed facts regarding whether the plaintiff's primary duty consisted of "work requiring invention, imagination, or talent." The plaintiff was often given story ideas to pursue, but also originated some himself and to some extent developed the story ideas given to him. The articles showed some analysis, distinctive prose, and even attempts at humor. However, given the factual disputes, the court could not hold that the plaintiff's primary duties were artistic rather than duties requiring only intelligence, diligence, and accuracy.

3. The Teaching Professional

The Department of Labor addressed several questions regarding whether specific employment opportunities qualified under the exemption for teaching professionals. In a letter of September 25, 2000,[295] the Department opined that, where a

[292] *Id.* at 914. As discussed in §VI.C.2. ["Directly Related to Management Policies or General Business Operations"], above, however, the district court in *Shaw* held that the plaintiff was properly classified as an exempt administrative employee.

[293] 96 F. Supp. 2d 652 (S.D. Tex. 2000).

[294] *See* Treatise at pp. 261–66.

[295] WH Opinion letter dated September 25, 2000, WHM: 99:8327.

flight school employer was approved by the Federal Aviation Administration and the instructor was certified under the Federal Aviation Regulations, the instructor would qualify as a teaching professional. A similar result was reached for a certified scuba diving instructor employed by a school certified by a national certification agency such as the National Association of Underwater Instructors or the Professional Association of Dive Instructors.[296]

Preschool "teachers," on the other hand, were found generally not to be exempt.[297] The Department found that "while 'childhood education settings' (for ages 0–5) commonly referred to as preschools may engage in some basic educational activities for the children attending, preschool employees whose primary duty is to protect and care for the needs of the children would not ordinarily meet the requirements for exemption as teachers."

4. The Computer Occupation Professional

The Department of Labor issued an opinion to the effect that a person whose title is Systems Engineer and whose duties "include support services to local businesses; designing computer solutions to fit the client's need . . . (this involves analyzing current equipment and software, identifying equipment and software needs, determining a scope of work for implementation and integration of old with the new, and continuing with support of hardware and software after the implementation is complete)" is not exempt as the employee's primary duty is to identify computer solutions to fit the need of a variety of local businesses, but the employee does not design, create or modify systems or programs (and did not meet alternate conditions of the exemption).[298]

---

[296]WH Opinion letter dated March 5, 2001, WHM: 99:8359

[297]WH Opinion letter dated September 20, 2000, WHM: 99:8327.

[298]WH Opinion letter dated May 11, 2001, WHM: 99:8373.

D. Factors Under the Tests

2. *"Consistent Exercise of Discretion and Judgment"*

Reversing the district court, the Fifth Circuit in *Owsley v. San Antonio Independent School District*[299] found that the plaintiffs, athletic trainers, consistently exercised discretion and judgment. The court noted that the trainers were expected to: (1) establish specific procedures to be carried out by a coach and/or student trainer in the event of an emergency; (2) be responsible for communication with parents, physicians, coordinating trainer, and coaches concerning injured athletes; and (3) determine the athlete's return to practice or playing status following an athletic injury. In addition, they applied discretionary skills within a standards framework to: (1) assess the extent of an injury based on standard treatment guidelines; (2) perform neurological evaluations by assessing consciousness, intellectual performance, sensation, and movement according to standard guidelines; and (3) determine whether the athlete should continue to practice/play after an injury based on well-established tests and criteria when a physician is not present.

In *Barth v. Wolf Creek Nuclear Operating Corp.*,[300] the court found that material issues of fact existed as to, among other things, whether the employees consistently exercised independent judgment and discretion. The employees testified that most of their engineering support work followed standardized written procedures from which they rarely, if ever, deviated, and that if a situation called for a novel approach, they were expected to contact their engineering supervisors to discuss a remedy. The court recognized that in a highly regulated field such as nuclear power, detailed procedures for day-to-day functions might be essential, and held that the reliance on such procedures would not necessarily defeat the exemption. The court concluded, however, that the employer failed to establish con-

[299]187 F.3d 521 (5th Cir. 1999).
[300]125 F. Supp. 2d 437, 441–42 (D. Kan. 2000).

clusively that the employees used or were permitted sufficient independent judgment and discretion in the application or deviation from the procedures to meet the requirements of the exemption.

In an Opinion Letter dated January 24, 2001,[301] the United States Department of Labor's Wage and Hour Division stated that social caseworkers, whose education included a master's degree in social work or behavioral science, exercised sufficient discretion and judgment to satisfy that prong of the exemption for professionals where they received supervisory reviews either monthly or bimonthly and where their job duties included insuring that each child had a permanent safe home, fostering the child's well-being, questioning and investigating allegations of child abuse, assessing the child's needs, developing and recommending appropriate treatment plans, evaluating the child's progress, decision-making regarding outside placement of the child, and determining and recommending whether the child's parental rights should be terminated and the child put up for adoption.

4. Nonexempt Work

In *Flood v. Premier Internal Medicine Assocs.,*[302] a district court denied the employer's motion to dismiss, holding that even though the plaintiff held the title of "registered nurse" and was employed in a medical practice, she had alleged that she performed a variety of duties, some of which may not have been those of a professional, and so she was not necessarily an exempt professional. The plaintiff's duties allegedly included such tasks as greeting patients, escorting patients to and from examination rooms, ordering laboratory tests, copying prescriptions onto patients' charts, phoning druggists, phoning patients to schedule appointments, making daily bank deposits, placing orders for office and medical supplies, collecting payroll records, and phoning information to a payroll service.

---

[301] WH Opinion letter dated January 24, 2001, WHM: 99:5416.
[302] 2000 U.S. Dist. LEXIS 8493 (M.D. Fla. 2000).

VIII. DEFINING THE OUTSIDE SALES EXEMPTION

In a letter dated May 22, 2001, the Wage-Hour Division issued an opinion dealing with the status of route salesmen under the outside sales exemption.[303] It found that the employees in question here, who spent ninety percent of their time visiting customers or en route, customarily and regularly called on customers, obtained orders, delivered products to customers, were the employer's exclusive contact with customers, and whose earnings were, in part, directly attributable to the volume of sales made to customers, would meet the requirements for exemption as outside salesmen within the meaning of section 13(a)(1) of the FLSA.

C. "Incidental to and in Conjunction with" Sales Work

In *Ackerman v. Coca-Cola Enterprises, Inc.*,[304] the Tenth Circuit reversed the district court and held that advance sales representatives and account managers of a soft-drink company fell within the "outside sales" exemption of the FLSA and were therefore exempt from the Act's overtime provisions, despite the fact that a significant percentage (20 percent to 65 percent) of their on-the-job time was spent performing "merchandising" tasks, such as setting up advertising materials, that were also performed by nonexempt employees. The decision turned on whether the plaintiffs' merchandising duties were or were not incidental to their own sales activities, pursuant to the proviso at the end of 29 C.F.R. §541.500(b). The court rejected the plaintiffs' claim that their exempt or nonexempt status should be determined solely by the percentage of time they spent doing merchandising work. As the court pithily said, "what matters is whether the plaintiffs—or someone else—sold Coca-Cola products at the locations where the plaintiffs performed merchandising activities and

---

[303]WH Opinion letter dated May 22, 2001, WHM: 99:8377. *See also* letters of November 16, 1976, WHM: 99:1260, and June 23, 1998, WHM: 99:8173).

[304]179 F.3d 1260, 5 WH Cases2d 651 (10th Cir.), *cert. denied*, 120 S. Ct. 1002 (2000).

whether, if the plaintiffs sold Coca-Cola products at those locations, their merchandising work promoted those sales."[305] The court held that if the sales representatives and account managers performed other nonsales tasks intended to promote their employer's products at locations where they also made sales, then those merchandising tasks were incidental to and in conjunction with their sales tasks and were not subject to the 20 percent test even if they consumed a great deal of the employees' time.

D. Promotion Work

In *Roberts v. Willow Distributors, Inc.*,[306] the plaintiff, a merchandiser, was required to visit stores to stimulate sales of beverages marketed by Willow. The district court held that the plaintiff was exempt under the "outside sales" exemption, granting the employer's motion for summary judgment, to which the plaintiff, who appeared pro se, had not responded. The district court referenced the promotional work regulation ("promotional work which is actually performed incidental to and in conjunction with an employee's own outside sales or solicitations" is included as exempt work under 29 C.F.R. §541.504) in reaching its decision, yet nothing in the decision suggests that plaintiff himself engaged in any sales activity.[307]

Ackerman v. Coca-Cola Enterprises, Inc.,[308] discussed in Section C above, involved promotional activities for Coca-Cola products, as well as merchandising work, carried out by the advance sales representative and account manager plaintiffs. After an extensive review of the Department's regulations interpreting the provisions of the outside sales exemption, and relying particularly on 29 C.F.R. §504, the Tenth Circuit concluded that because plaintiffs' promotional work, like their other merchandising work, was mainly at establishments where

---

[305] *Id.* at 1267.
[306] 967 F. Supp. 904 (N.D. Tex. 1997).
[307] *Id.* at 906–07.
[308] 179 F.3d 1260, 5 WH Cases2d 651.

they themselves made sales, it was "incidental to" their sales work within the meaning of the regulation.

F. Work Performed by Outside Salespersons That Is Considered to Be Nonexempt

2. *The 20-Percent Limitation*

In *Ackerman v. Coca-Cola Enterprises, Inc.*,[309] the Tenth Circuit reversed the district court and held that advance sales representatives and account managers of a soft-drink company fell within the "outside sales" exemption of the FLSA and were therefore exempt from the Act's overtime provisions, despite the fact that a significant percentage (20 percent to 65 percent) of their on-the-job time was spent performing "merchandising" tasks, such as setting up advertising materials, that were also performed by nonexempt employees. The decision turned on whether the plaintiffs' merchandising duties were or were not incidental to their own sales activities, pursuant to the proviso at the end of 29 C.F.R. §541.500(b). The court rejected the plaintiffs' claim that their exempt or nonexempt status should be determined solely by the percentage of time they spent doing merchandising work. As the court pithily said, "what matters is whether the plaintiffs—or someone else—sold Coca-Cola products at the locations where the plaintiffs performed merchandising activities and whether, if the plaintiffs sold Coca-Cola products at those locations, their merchandising work promoted those sales."[310] The court held that if the sales representatives and account managers performed other nonsales tasks intended to promote their employer's products at locations where they also made sales, then those merchandising tasks were incidental to and in conjunction with their sales tasks and were not subject to the 20-percent test even if they consumed a great deal of the employees' time.

---

[309] *Id.*

[310] *Id.* at 1267, 5 WH Cases2d 651.

CHAPTER 5

OTHER STATUTORY EXEMPTIONS

II. SECTION 13(A) EXEMPTIONS FROM THE MINIMUM WAGE AND OVERTIME REQUIREMENTS OF THE ACT

A. Retail and Service Employees

2. *Commission Salespersons*

In *Herman v. Suwannee Swifty Stores, Inc.*,[1] a federal district court sitting in Georgia found that managers of food and household supplies stores were not exempt from overtime requirements as commission salespersons. The court relied on the DOL's interpretation of Section 7(i)'s "*bona fide* commission rate," holding that the DOL's interpretation in 29 C.F.R. §779.416(c) was a permissible construction of Congress' intent. Under the DOL's interpretation, an employer could not rely on the exemption if the employee's commissions "seldom" exceeded the guarantee. The district court found that the store managers' compensation was based mostly upon the number of hours worked rather than the number of sales made, and that the commission rate had an insignificant impact on salary.

In *Salon Enterprises, Inc. v. Langford*,[2] a beauty salon which formerly employed defendant stylist sued both defendant and defendant's new employer for violation of a covenant not to compete, and defendant asserted counterclaims, alleging failure to pay overtime in violation of the Fair Labor Standards Act. Plaintiff argued that defendant was exempt from overtime as a commissioned employee.

Salon paid its former employee a rate of pay connected to the revenue generated by the number of haircuts rather than a flat rate per service. In addition, the employee received 10–15 percent sales commissions on retail product sales. Defendant argued that her pay was partly based on commisions but also partly based on piece work, and that she was entitled to overtime for work over 40 hours in a week. The trial court found wage violations as alleged by defendant. The Kansas Court of Appeals

---

[1] 19 F. Supp. 2d 1365 (M.D. Ga. 1998).

[2] 31 P.3d 290 (Kan. Ct. App. 2000).

relied on the DOL's interpretation of Section 7(i)'s "*bona fide* commission rate" and guidance on the meaning of "goods or services" found in 29 C.F.R. §779.413(b), and reversed the trial court, finding that the defendant employee fell within the commissioned employee exemption under 29 U.S.C. §207(i).

In *Klinedinst v. Swift Investments, Inc.*,[3] the Eleventh Circuit vacated the district court's grant of summary judgment to plaintiff employee in a suit for overtime. Plaintiff, an automobile painter, sued the auto repair and body shop, which defended on the ground that plaintiff was paid on a commission basis and was exempt. The shop compensated Klinedinst on the basis of "flag hours" for each job; "flag hours" are specified for each job in a database used by insurance adjusters and auto repair shops. Klinedinst received payment for the maximum number of flag hours, at his hourly rate, regardless of the number of actual hours worked to complete each project. Relying on 29 C.F.R. §779.413(b) and the DOL Hour Division's Field Operations Manual as persuasive authority on interpretation of "commission," the Eleventh Circuit found the number of hours worked was not relevant to amounts paid to employees under the "flag hour" payment system, and that under this system plaintiff was exempt under the provisions of Section 7(i). The court remanded for a determination on the issue of whether the employee's compensation fell below one and one half times minimum wage.

Erichs v. Venator Group, Inc.,[4] involved a claim for overtime compensation by a group of shoe store managers. The United States District Court for the Northern District of California granted in part and denied in part the employer's motion for summary judgment, finding a genuine issue of material fact as to whether the commission rate paid to the managers was *bona fide* and set in good faith. Defendant claimed its manager employees were exempt under 29 U.S.C. §207(i). Plaintiffs claimed the plan did not meet either of the exemption's requirements as it failed to incorporate a "bona fide commission rate" and provide commissions constituting 50 percent of paid compensation.

---

[3]260 F.3d 1251, 7 WH Cases2d 279 (11th Cir. 2001).

[4]128 F. Supp. 2d 1255 (N.D. Cal. 2001).

Defendant had created its (new and contested) commission plan to stimulate an increase in sales and insulate itself from further litigation relating to the exempt status of retail store managers. The commission pay plan guaranteed managers a minimum hourly rate equal to one and one half times the minimum wage for each hour worked. Managers' earnings were derived from a commission on store sales that decreased as the store's sales increased. Plaintiffs always earned more than one and one half times the applicable minimum wage.

The court's inquiry focused on whether the defendant set its commission rate in good faith.[5] The fact that the plan's commission percentage *decreased* with an increase in sales raised a genuine issue of material fact about defendant's good faith. The court determined that an inevitable consequence of this initial finding resulted in a material dispute as to the second issue of whether more than half of compensation under the plan consisted of commissions on goods and services. Accordingly, summary judgment as to the Section 7(i) exemption was denied.

B. Amusement, Recreational, and Similar Employees

In another piece of litigation involving professional baseball,[6] the Detroit Tigers professional baseball team, although considered a year-round operation, qualified for the recreational or amusement establishment exemption because it was able to demonstrate that its off-season receipts were less than one third of its in-season receipts in the same calendar year.[7]

Bridewell v. Cincinnati Reds[8] was before the Sixth Circuit for a second time after the district court, on remand after an earlier appeal,[9] decided that the team defendant did not qualify for the

---

[5]Id (citing *Herman*, 19 F. Supp. 2d at 1370).

[6]*See* Treatise, Chapter 5, §II.B. [Amusement, Recreational, and Similar Employees], particularly footnotes 49 and 50 and related text at pp. 311–12.

[7]Adams v. Detroit Tigers, Inc., 961 F. Supp. 176, 180 (E.D. Mich. 1997) (batboys lost claim on summary judgment).

[8]155 F.3d 828, 4 WH Cases2d 1601 (6th Cir. 1998).

[9]68 F.3d 136, 2 WH Cases2d 1573 (6th Cir.), *cert. denied*, 516 U.S. 1172 (1996). *See* Treatise at Chapter 5, notes 50–52.

exemption for seasonal recreational establishments. In the earlier appellate decision, the circuit had reversed the district court's determination that the seasonal exemption did apply, reasoning that the proper focus was not on the seven-month baseball season but on the fact that the Reds organization operated year-round with more than 120 employees. On remand the team attempted to rely on the alternative grounds of determining seasonality—namely, that its average receipts for any six months of such year were not more than 33 ⅓ percent of its average receipts for the entire year, as specified in 29 U.S.C. §213(a)(3)(B). The team stipulated that the exemption would be available under this provision only if it was allowed to calculate its "receipts" not according to when the cash was received but according to when the Reds organization recorded the money as income. Although the team regularly used the accrual method of accounting, the district court held that the term "receipts" as used in the statute refers to money as it is actually received by the amusement establishment, and the court of appeals affirmed, relying on the plain language of the statute.

In *Gibbs v. Montgomery County Agricultural Society*,[10] a former maintenance employee of the county fairgrounds sued for overtime and retaliation, and defendant claimed exemption as an amusement or recreational enterprise. Plaintiff conceded that the defendant met the financial test of the second prong of the exemption, but denied that defendant's establishment was "amusement or recreational" in nature. In a straightforward analysis, the district court found that defendant's lease of areas to nonexempt organizations did not result in destroying defendant's exempt status, even though defendant spent time working in these leased areas. It further found that in determining whether the exemption applied, the character of defendant employer's principal, revenue-producing activities was the true inquiry, and that the exact nature of plaintiff's work did not control. The court thus found that the exemption applied, and declined to exercise supplemental jurisdiction over the state law retaliation claim. No federal retaliation claim had been asserted.

---

[10]140 F. Supp. 2d 835 (S.D. Ohio 2001).

In an Opinion Letter dated May 19, 2001,[11] the Department of Labor examined whether the Organizing Committee for the Olympic Games qualified for the exemption under Section 13(b)(3) for certain amusement and recreational establishments. The Department found that, because its average receipts for six months of the year 2000 were less than one third of its receipts for the other six months, the conditions of the exemption were met, and most of the employees would be exempt from the minimum wage and overtime provisions of the FLSA. The letter referred to the FOH at Section 25j13 in noting that "the answer may be different for employees who engage in construction or reconstruction work."[12]

G. Casual-Basis Babysitters and Domestic Companionship Service Providers

2. *Casual Babysitters and Domestic Companions*

b. Companionship Services

As noted in the Treatise,[13] the Department proposed revisions to Part 552 (Domestic Service Regulations) in 1993, and reissued the proposal for further comment in 1995. That proposal was not finalized. A new proposal was issued for comment on January 19, 2001,[14] and the comment period was extended until July 23, 2001, by notice issued in April 2001.[15]

Under the regulations currently in effect, as pointed out in the Treatise,[16] the applicability of this exemption depends on a number of conditions. The principal questions litigated in connection with this potential exemption have been (1) whether companionship services are being rendered in a "private home," (2) whether the services are in fact "companionship" services or

---

[11]WH Opinion Letter dated May 19, 2001, WHM: 99:8376.
[12]*Id.*
[13]*See* Treatise at Chapter 5, text at notes 153 and 154.
[14]66 Fed. Reg. 5481.
[15]66 Fed. Reg. 20,411.
[16]*See* the Treatise at pp. 326–27, especially text at note 134 and following.

instead "general household services," and (3) whether the exception to the exemption for services provided by "trained personnel" applies.

The DOL's proposed clarifications to the regulations relating to companionship services were cited as persuasive authority in *Harris v. Sims Registry.*[17] Plaintiffs sued their former employer, an agency providing "homemaker services" for elderly individuals in their homes, claiming defendant failed to pay minimum wage and overtime compensation in accordance with the FLSA. Plaintiffs and defendant filed cross motions for summary judgment on the issue of whether plaintiffs fell under the FLSA companionship exemption.[18]

i. Private Home [New Topic]. On the question of whether living facilities constitute a "private home," a federal district court in Ohio[19] reached the same conclusion with respect to employer-owned facilities as has been generally reached in similar cases.[20] It refused to extend the definition of private residence to "shared-living facilities" in a case where the defendant operated a shared-living facility consisting of eight buildings that could house up to 12 residents each. The court found that the defendant's facility was not a private residence, and therefore not within the companion services exemption, because the defendant was a for-profit corporation, each of the eight buildings accommodated 12 residents, the buildings had communal dining and other areas, the residents do not maintain the property, and the residents did not have primary control over the residence. Accordingly, the plaintiff was not exempt and therefore was protected by the overtime provisions of the FLSA.

The U.S. Court of Appeals for the Tenth Circuit came to a similar conclusion in *Johnston v. Volunteers of America, Inc.,*[21] when it affirmed a district court's denial of defendant's motion for summary judgment because the employer could not demon-

---

[17]2001 WL 78448 (N.D. Ill. 2001).

[18]29 U.S.C. §215(a)(13).

[19]Gay v. Extended Family Concepts, 102 F. Supp. 2d 449 (N.D. Ohio 2000).

[20]*See* cases cited in the Treatise at note 135.

[21]213 F.3d 559 (10th Cir. 2000), *cert. denied,* 121 S. Ct. 763 (2001).

strate that the employees fit plainly and unmistakably within the overtime exemption for domestic service in private homes. The defendant operated a supported living program in which it selected a location for a shared-living arrangement for a group of developmentally disabled persons and the plaintiffs managed the residence. The court first rejected the plaintiffs' argument that they were entitled to overtime pay because they were not actually employed by the individuals for whom they cared. Nonetheless, the court reasoned that the district court did not err in rejecting the defendant's motion for summary judgment because the defendant had failed to establish as a matter of law that the plaintiffs were working in a "private residence," and therefore were subject to the companionship exemption. The court found that the defendant had not conclusively established that its facilities were "private residences" where the clients of defendant were placed in a residence with other developmentally disabled individuals outside their homes, the residents' diets were controlled by the plaintiffs and not by a family member, and the defendant had a right to use a room in the residence for an office.

On the other hand, in a case[22] raising the question whether a facility that housed 14 marginally mentally and physically handicapped adults was a "private home" for purposes of the Section 13(a)15 exemption to the FLSA, the Supreme Court of Utah observed that the term encompasses a continuum of living arrangements. It determined that in view of the facts that the facility was privately funded, was not open to the public, was organized as a nonprofit corporation, and housed only 14 disabled residents, it did qualify as a private home for purposes of the exemption.[23]

In *Terwilliger v. Home of Hope, Inc.*,[24] employees who provided services to developmentally disabled clients brought suit against their employer for overtime compensation. The court first

---

[22]Bowler v. Deseret Village Ass'n, 922 P.2d 8, 14, 3 WH Cases2d 754 (Utah 1996).

[23]*Id.*

[24]21 F. Supp. 2d 1294, 4 WH Cases2d 1661 (N.D. Okla. 1998).

determined that the residences of the employer's clients were "private homes" because (1) 22 percent of the clients' homes were owned by the client or the client's guardian while the remaining residences were rented in the client's name from third parties, (2) the employer did not co-sign the lease and had no property interest in the client's residence, (3) each client selected and purchased his or her own furniture, (4) the employer maintained a set of keys to the residences to be used only for emergencies, (5) the client chose whether he or she would have a housemate and who that housemate would be, and (6) the employer paid the rent to the landlord from the client's trust account. The court then determined that the employees provided services because they assisted clients with dressing, grooming, and administering medication; performed household chores; and assisted clients in developing skills. The court concluded that the employees fell within the companionship services exemption but that a genuine issue of material fact remained as to whether they fell within the 20 percent household work exception to the exemption.

Madison v. Resources for Human Development, Inc.,[25] reflects that federal courts continue to hold that whether services qualify as exempt under Section 13(a)(15) depends upon whether the domestic or companionship services are provided within a "private" home. In *Madison,* employees of a non–profit corporation providing residential human services programs for mentally ill and mentally retarded adults filed a class action suit alleging their employer improperly calculated their rates of pay under the FLSA. Defendant employer appealed a summary judgment in favor of employees, and the Third Circuit affirmed. The court noted some divergent case law and analysis, but concluded that the Section 13(a)(15) companionship exemption did not exclude the employees from FLSA coverage. In this case, the clients lived in homes rented by the corporation and subleased to the clients. The court looked at factors such as the possessory interest of the client in defendant's homes, whether

[25]233 F.3d 175, 6 WH Cases2d 961 (3d Cir. 2000).

the client had full control of access to the premises, and whether the client maintained "unfettered freedom" in his daily activities. In this case, since clients were not permitted to remain in defendant's homes if the business relationship was terminated, clients did not have full control over others' access to defendant's homes, and clients were required to comply with various rules addressing their daily activities, the court held as a matter of law that the Defendant's residences were not "private homes" under 29 U.S.C. §213(a)(15), and therefore, the exemption did not apply.

ii. Nature of "Companionship" Services [New Topic]. The Sixth Circuit held that a wife who served as a caregiver for her physically disabled husband provided "companionship services" within the meaning of the FLSA and was exempt from the minimum wage and overtime requirements of the Act.[26] The wife helped her husband dress, gave him medication, helped him bathe, assisted him in moving around their home, and cleaned his bedclothes.

General maintenance services—including cleaning laundry areas, general household cleaning, washing vehicles, cleaning garages, and maintaining grounds—constitute general household services, rather than services directly related to disabled individuals, and must not exceed the 20 percent exemption threshold.[27]

iii. "Trained Personnel" Exception [New Topic]. In *Armani v. Maxim Healthcare Services, Inc.*,[28] a federal district court granted summary judgment for defendant, holding that a certified nursing assistant is not within the "trained personnel" exception to the exemption from overtime requirements for workers who provide companionship services. Plaintiff, a certified nursing assistant, claimed he was within the trained personnel exception to the exemption and entitled to overtime pay. Although the Tenth Circuit had not yet decided this question, the court noted

---

[26]Salyer v. Ohio Bureau of Workers' Comp., 83 F.3d 784, 3 WH Cases2d 484 (6th Cir.), *cert. denied,* 117 S. Ct. 386 (1996).

[27]*Bowler,* 922 P.2d at 14–15, 3 WH Cases2d 754.

[28]53 F. Supp. 2d 1120, 5 WH Cases2d 1374 (D. Colo. 1999).

that courts in the Sixth, Seventh, and Ninth Circuits[29] had concluded that nursing aides such as certified nursing assistants are not included within the "trained personnel" exception. To be a trained professional, a companionship service provider must have obtained training comparable in scope and duration to that of a registered or practical nurse. The court noted that the Colorado requirements for certified nursing assistants required either on-the-job training or 75 hours of formal training and 12 hours per year of continuing education. In contrast, registered nurses must have two full years of formal education, and licensed practical nurses needed one year. The court found that plaintiff's training did not place him in the same category as a registered or practical nurse.

III. CURRENT SECTION 13(B) EXEMPTIONS FROM THE OVERTIME REQUIREMENTS OF THE ACT

A. Employees Covered Under the Motor Carrier Act

1. "Subject to the Power of the Secretary of Transportation"

The decision of the Secretary of Transportation to refrain from exercising regulatory authority over a category of carriers (laundry service route salesmen) does not exempt them from his authority.[30] As noted in the Treatise,[31] the Secretary's power to regulate such a category of carriers exists even if unexercised.

In *McGuiggan v. CPC International, Inc.*,[32] a federal district court held that a defendant was a private motor carrier under the provisions of the Motor Carrier Act, and thus certain of its

---

[29] *Salyer*, 83 F.3d 784, 3 WH Cases2d 484; Cox v. Acme Health Servs., Inc., 55 F.3d 1304, 2 WH Cases2d 1249 (7th Cir.1995); McCune v. Oregon Senior Servs. Div., 894 F.2d 1107, 29 WH Cases 1187 (9th Cir. 1990).

[30] Klitzke v. Steiner Corp., 110 F.3d 1465, 1469, 3 WH Cases2d 1537 (9th Cir. 1997).

[31] *See* Treatise at Chapter 5, "Other Statutory Exemptions," §III.A.1. [Employees Covered Under the Motor Carrier Act; "Subject to the Power of the Secretary of Transportation"], text at note 177, p. 334.

[32] 102 F. Supp. 2d 988 (N.D. Ill. 2000).

employees would be exempt from the overtime provisions of the FLSA, even though its primary business was baking and selling bakery goods. The plaintiffs had argued that the defendant was not a "motor carrier" under the Act because transportation was not its primary business. The court relied on cases from the Third and Ninth Circuits that hold that while coverage by the Department of Transportation is limited regarding nontransportation business, coverage continues with relation to working hours and safety of certain drivers. The court reasoned that the transportation within the state, where the goods came from outside the state, was part of the "practical continuity of movement" from suppliers outside the state and thus within the jurisdiction of the Transportation Department. Accordingly, the court held that the defendant's drivers were exempt from the FLSA's overtime provisions.

The Department of Labor issued an opinion letter determining that local armored car drivers were not exempt under Section 13(b)(1). This section of the FLSA provides an exemption from the overtime pay requirement for any employee with respect to whom the Secretary of Transportation has power to establish qualifications and maximum hours of service pursuant to the provision of Section 204 of the Motor Carrier Act. This overtime pay exemption applies to transportation within a single state where the transportation forms a part of a practical continuity of movement across state lines from point of origin to point of destination. The armored drivers in question drove unmarked, customized vans for the purpose of transporting cash, which they picked up from or transported to ATM machines by driving a predetermined route to or from a "central location." The "central location" was a secured vault in an office owned by the company. The drivers normally did not cross state lines.

Under these facts, the Department found that the 13(b)(1) exemption would not apply because the cash was being transported only within the state to a "central location." There was no planned out-of-state movement for the cash once it reached the "central location" and thus there was no interstate commerce necessary for the Secretary of Transportation to establish qualifications and maximum hours of service pursuant to the Motor Carrier Act.

In *Herman v. Hector I Nieves Transport, Inc.*,[33] the Secretary of Labor brought suit against defendant trucking corporation for violation of minimum wage, overtime and reporting requirements of the FLSA. The defendant relied on the Section 13(b)(1) exemption. The First Circuit affirmed the district court's grant of partial summary judgment in favor of the Secretary. In this case of first impression, the question was whether the motor carrier exemption[34] applied to a trucking company whose routes were entirely within the boundaries of Puerto Rico, and the court held that the Secretary of Transportation had no power to "establish qualifications and maximum hours of service pursuant to the provisions of [49 U.S.C. §31502]" for intraisland transportation.

2. *Safety Requirement*

a. Drivers

In *Williams v. Alex's Transportation*,[35] a federal district court held that the employer, which contracts with railroad companies to provide crew hauling services, was entitled to rely on the motor carrier exemption to defeat a driver's claim for overtime compensation. The court found that because there was a "reasonable probability" that the plaintiff would be assigned to an interstate run in the regular course of employment, the plaintiff fell within the Secretary of Transportation's jurisdiction and was thus subject to the motor carrier exemption.[36] En route to determining that there was a "reasonable probability" that the driver would be assigned to an interstate run, the court looked to whether the employer held interstate authority, advertised for interstate work, and assigned drivers indiscriminately to that work. The court rejected the driver's contention that the motor carrier exemption should be applied on an employee-by-employee and week-by-week basis.

---

[33]244 F. 3d 32 (1st Cir. 2001).
[34]29 U.S.C. §213(b)(1).
[35]969 F. Supp. 1142, 4 WH Cases2d 209 (N.D. Ill. 1997).
[36]29 U.S.C. §213(b)(1).

In *Bowe v. SMC Electrical Products, Inc.*,[37] the court denied summary judgment for an employer on its claim that it was exempt from FLSA requirements pursuant to the motor carrier exemption; the court explained that there were genuine issues of material fact regarding how often the employee transported the employer's property in interstate commerce and whether that transportation of property constituted only a minimal aspect of the employee's duties.

Instructors in a for-profit truck driving training school were held covered by the motor carrier exemption because all of the instructors either had engaged in interstate driving or had performed duties related to interstate transportation activities.[38] (These instructors also met the test for the professional exemption.)

Following the reasoning of other courts, the court in *Turk v. Buffets, Inc.*,[39] held that workers who were employed by a company as service technicians for company-owned restaurants fell within the motor carrier exemption because the workers were transported, across state lines to the restaurants, to repair equipment owned by the company. The court held that the workers were exempt even though interstate driving consumed less of their time than did their other duties.[40]

Additional cases have similarly applied these principles to drivers.[41]

In *Mielke v. Laidlaw Transit, Inc.*,[42] a federal district court in Illinois denied the employer's summary judgment motion, holding that the plaintiffs, school bus drivers, were not exempt from the Act's overtime provision under Section 13(b). The defen-

---

[37]935 F. Supp. 1126, 1132–33, 3 WH Cases2d 710, *opin. adhered to on reconsideration,* 945 F. Supp. 1482, 3 WH Cases2d 1310 (D. Colo. 1996).

[38]Gonzales v. New England Tractor Trailer Training Sch., 932 F. Supp. 697, 3 WH Cases2d 758 (D. Md. 1996).

[39]F. Supp. 1255, 3 WH Cases2d 867 (N.D. Ill. 1996).

[40]*Id.* at 1261.

[41]*See, e.g.*, Walton v. Louisiana Compressor Maint., 3 WH Cases2d 1630 (E.D. La. 1997) (repair technician required to transport equipment interstate found to be exempt); Garcia v. Pace Suburban Bus Serv., 955 F. Supp. 75, 3 WH Cases2d 1477 (N.D. Ill. 1996) (although affidavits did not clearly demonstrate whether driver could reasonably be expected to be called upon to make an interstate trip, driver was exempt from FLSA because his employer was a carrier and was subject to regulation by the Department of Transportation).

[42]102 F. Supp. 2d 988 (N.D. Ill. 2000).

dant had contended that it was exempt from the time-and-a-half provision of the FLSA under the Motor Carrier Act because the Department of Transportation had the authority to regulate it. Although it was undisputed that the defendant was a motor carrier, the court rejected the defendant's argument that its bus drivers were exempt because Congress had expressly removed school bus drivers from the Transportation Department's jurisdiction. The defendant had contended that this exemption from the Department of Transportation jurisdiction only applied to tariff, licensing, and rate regulation, and that the school bus drivers were still subject to the Transportation Department's regulations concerning qualifications and hours of service. The court rejected this argument, explaining that while a prior version of the exemption had contained an express statement specifically reserving to the Department of Transportation jurisdiction over qualifications and maximum hours of school bus drivers, Congress had deleted this reservation of Transportation Department jurisdiction in the current version of the statute, indicating its intention that school bus drivers be subject to the provisions of the FLSA.

In *Wilson v. Notheis, Inc.*,[43] a federal district court in Georgia held that hostler-tractor drivers[44] were covered by the Motor Carrier Act and were therefore exempt from the overtime provisions of the FLSA. The plaintiffs' job activities consisted of moving trailers, which were either empty or contained goods in the channels of interstate commerce, between the distribution center loading docks and the trailer staging areas of a client. The plaintiffs took various safety measures and performed multiple safety checks on the trailers. Although the defendant classified the plaintiffs as drivers, the court did not find that they were drivers within the meaning of the statutory and regulatory provisions involved, but it did find that a substantial part of the

---

[43]1999 U.S. Dist. LEXIS 20493, 5 WH Cases2d 1287 (N.D. Ga. 1999).

[44]According to the court, "[h]ostler-tractors are one-seat vehicles, travel at only ten to fifteen miles per hour, do not have speedometers, and are not licensed for use on public highways. Plaintiffs operated the hostler-tractors on public highways only for refueling three blocks away from the Marshalls distribution center, at which time the hostler-tractors were not connected to trailers." *Id.*, 5 WH Cases2d at 1287. The plaintiffs did not drive interstate. *Id.*, 5 WH Cases at 1288.

plaintiffs' duties affected the safety of the transportation of goods in interstate commerce. Accordingly, it granted the employer's motion for summary judgment on the plaintiffs' claims for overtime compensation because the employees' effect on the "safety of transportation of common carriers" subjected them to the coverage of the Motor Carrier Act.

c. *Loaders*

As noted, in *Wilson v. Notheis, Inc.*,[45] a federal district court in Georgia held that hostler-tractor drivers[46] were covered by the Motor Carrier Act and were therefore exempt from the overtime provisions of the FLSA. The plaintiffs' job activities consisted of using hostler-tractors to move trailers, which were either empty or contained goods in the channels of interstate commerce, between the distribution center loading docks and the trailer staging areas of a client. They did not drive interstate. The plaintiffs took various safety measures and performed multiple safety checks on the trailers. Although the defendant classified the plaintiffs as drivers, the court did not find that they were drivers within the meaning of the statutory and regulatory provisions involved, but it did find that a substantial part of plaintiffs' duties affected the safety of the transportation of goods in interstate commerce. Accordingly, it granted the employer's motion for summary judgment on the plaintiffs' claims for overtime compensation because the employees' effect on the "safety of transportation of common carriers" subjected them to the coverage of the Motor Carrier Act.

The district court's decision in *Troutt v. Stavola Bros., Inc.*[47]—holding that an employee of a race car team responsible for moving equipment to the end of transporter, where it was secured by someone else, could not be said to affect safety of operations—was affirmed on appeal.[48]

---

[45] 1999 U.S. Dist. LEXIS 20493, 5 WH Cases2d 1287 (N.D. Ga. 1999).
[46] *See* footnote 44 above.
[47] 2 WH Cases2d 1359 (M.D.N.C. 1995).
[48] 107 F.3d 1104 (4th Cir. 1997).

The Department of Labor issued an opinion letter[49] concerning the applicability of Section 13(b)(1) to "team loaders," who participated in the loading of a racing automobile and parts onto a trailer for transportation. During the 10-month yearly racing season each vehicle is moved, together with the staff responsible for it, approximately every two weeks from one city to another. In evaluating whether the employees in question were safety-affecting employees, which was a necessary factor for exemption, the Department pointed out that an employee "is not a loader 'merely because he furnishes physical assistance when necessary in loading heavy pieces of freight, or because he deposits pieces of freight in the vehicle for someone else to distribute and secure in place . . .'" and stated that "only those 'team loaders' who exercise the judgment and discretion necessary to determine that the automobile and parts have been loaded safely on the trailer would qualify for the section 13(b)(1) overtime exemption."

3. Interstate Commerce Requirement

With respect to ambulance services, courts have followed the Department of Labor in taking the view that ambulances are not subject to regulation by the Department of Transportation, and that, accordingly, ambulance drivers are not exempt from the requirements of the FLSA under the motor carrier exemption.[50]

In *Herman v. Suwannee Swifty Stores, Inc.*,[51] a federal district court sitting in Georgia found that managers of food and household supplies stores were not operating a motor vehicle in interstate commerce when they delivered the employer's checks

---

[49]Opinion Letter of May 5, 2001, by Acting Wage Hour Administrator Markey, WHM 99:8357.

[50]*See* Smith v. F-M Ambulance Serv., Inc., 914 F. Supp. 359, 2 WH Cases2d 1682 (D.N.D. 1995) (ambulance service not exempt from FLSA and employees entitled to proceed on claims for overtime compensation); Bayles v. American Med. Response of Colo., Inc., 937 F. Supp. 1477, 3 WH Cases2d 845 (ambulance service did not fall within motor carrier exemption and was subject to FLSA requirements), *reconsideration granted in part*, 950 F. Supp. 1053, 3 WH Cases2d 1317 (D. Colo. 1996), *on reconsideration*, 962 F. Supp. 1346, 3 WH Cases2d 1567 (D. Colo. 1997).

[51]19 F. Supp. 2d 1365 (M.D. Ga. 1998).

to the local bank. Unlike an armored car service, the managers were delivering checks that belonged to the employer, rather than checks given into their hands by another for delivery. The managers' intent that the checks be placed into interstate commerce after delivery to the bank did not mean that they had already entered interstate commerce during delivery. The district court thus held that the store managers were not exempt from overtime requirements as motor private carriers under Section 13(b)(1).

In *Johnsen v. Allsup's Convenience Stores, Inc.*,[52] a New Mexico court of appeals reversed the trial court's ruling and held that the employer's maintenance man did not engage in significant interstate commerce and thus did not fall within the motor carrier exemption. The plaintiff's duties, which the trial court had found to be in interstate commerce, involved transporting compressor cores manufactured out of state from an in-state wholesaler to the employer, and returning salvageable cores to the wholesaler. The salvageable cores were later reshipped to the out-of-state manufacturer. The appellate court determined that the trial court's decision that the interstate component of the plaintiff's work was not de minimis was not supported by evidence, after noting that it (the court of appeals) had previously determined that the transportation of items already held in stock at local wholesalers' premises constituted intrastate, not interstate, activity, the goods having "come to rest" at the wholesales' warehouses.

The court granted the employer's motion for summary judgment against bus drivers seeking compensation for overtime in *United Transportation Union, Local 759 v. Orange Newark Elizabeth Bus, Inc.*,[53] holding that the defendant bus company was covered by Department of Transportation regulations and thus exempt from the overtime provisions of the FLSA. The court concluded that the ultimate inquiry was whether the defendant operated motor carriers in interstate commerce such that it

---

[52]963 P.2d 533, 4 WH Cases2d 1552 (N.M. Ct. App.), *cert. denied*, 961 P.2d 167 (1998).

[53]111 F. Supp. 2d 514 (D.N.J. 2000).

would be subject to Department of Transportation jurisdiction. Although the defendant acknowledged that its drivers only operated buses in the state of New Jersey, it argued that its participation in "through-ticketing" arrangements, which grant passengers tickets that can also be used in New York, qualified as operating in interstate transportation. This argument persuaded the court, which noted that transportation is interstate even when the vehicle does not cross state lines, so long as the passengers or cargo are in the process of interstate travel. The court further reasoned that the Department of Transportation regulations, the Department of Labor regulations, and the common law all indicate that when an employer participates in a through-ticketing program that results in interstate travel, the employer is engaged in interstate transportation and subject to regulation of the Department of Transportation.

In *McGuiggan v. CPC International, Inc.*,[54] a federal district court, relying on the Ninth Circuit's decision in *Klitzke v. Steiner Corp.*,[55] held that distributors who picked up baked goods in the same state where they delivered the goods were nonetheless subject to regulation by the Department of Transportation where the goods being delivered were baked in another state.

In *The American Federation of State, County and Municipal Employees v. Louisiana*,[56] plaintiff Rhodes, a sergeant in the Louisiana Department of Wildlife and Fisheries Covert Section of the Enforcement Division, filed suit seeking recovery for overtime hours worked. The State argued it was exempt from paying any overtime compensation under Section 13(b)(1) of the FLSA and companion provisions of the Motor Carrier Act of 1935.[57] During his court activities, plaintiff occasionally drove to Mississippi to pretend he was a legitimate seller or purchaser of fish and game illegally caught in the State of Louisiana, and the State raised this travel in support of its argument for a Section 13(b)(1) exemption. The court did not find this argument

[54] 84 F. Supp. 2d 470 (S.D.N.Y. 2000).
[55] 110 F.3d 1465, 1469 (9th Cir. 1997).
[56] 2001 WL 29999 (E.D. La. 2001).
[57] 29 C.F.R. §782.2(b).

to be consistent with the regulations because the travel was primarily related to plaintiff's duties as a law enforcement officer and was not related to interstate commerce.[58]

In *Bilyou v. Dutchess Beer Distributors*,[59] plaintiff who was employed as a route distributor filed a claim for unpaid overtime. Plaintiff's truck route was entirely within New York. Dutchess argued for the application of the motor carrier exemption. The court granted summary judgment for Dutchess and reiterated the application of the motor carrier exemption where the employer is in the business of transporting goods in interstate commerce. It does not matter that the goods are picked up and delivered within the state as long as there exists a "fixed and persisting" intent to transport goods in interstate commerce.

In *Herman v. Hector I Nieves Transport, Inc.*,[60] the Secretary of Labor brought suit against defendant trucking corporation for violation of minimum wage, overtime and reporting requirements of the FLSA. The First Circuit affirmed the district court's granting of partial summary judgment in favor of the Secretary. In this case of first impression, the issue addressed whether the motor carrier exemption[61] includes a trucking company whose routes are entirely within the boundaries of Puerto Rico. The court held that the Secretary of Transportation had no power to "establish qualifications and maximum hours of service pursuant to the provisions of [49 U.S.C. §31502]" for intraisland transportation. Therefore, without the application of the motor carrier exemption, defendant was subject to the overtime provision of the FLSA.

In a May 17, 1999, Wage and Hour Opinion Letter,[62] the Department of Labor stated that an employer in the business of "recovering [i.e., repossessing] and remarketing" leased and financed property from the possession of defaulting parties is entitled to claim the overtime pay exemption afforded under Section 13(b)(1) for its employees performing the actual repos-

---

[58]29 C.F.R. §782.2(b)(2).
[59]2001 WL 286779 (S.D.N.Y. 2001).
[60]244 F.3d 32 (1st Cir. 2001).
[61]29 U.S.C. §213(b)(1).
[62]1999 WL 1002402.

session and return work in 11 western states. The agents fly to a location where property is to be repossessed, pick up a truck and collect the property, and return the property to the home office, doing approximately 90 percent of their work in the field and crossing state lines routinely.

The Department of Labor issued an opinion letter[63] concerning the applicability of Section 13(b)(1) to "team loaders," who participated in the loading of a racing automobile and parts onto a trailer for transportation. During the 10-month yearly racing season each vehicle, together with the staff responsible for it, is moved approximately every two weeks from one city to another. In evaluating whether the employees in question were safety-affecting employees, which was a necessary factor for exemption, the Department pointed out that an employee "is not a loader 'merely because he furnishes physical assistance when necessary in loading heavy pieces of freight, or because he deposits pieces of freight in the vehicle for someone else to distribute and secure in place . . .'" and stated that "only those 'team loaders' who exercise the judgment and discretion necessary to determine that the automobile and parts have been loaded safely on the trailer would qualify for the section 13(b)(1) overtime exemption."

B. Railroad Employees

After holding that the plaintiff was exempt from the FLSA overtime requirements by virtue of being a driver under the Motor Carrier Act,[64] in *Williams v. Alex's Transportation*[65] the federal district court determined that the defendant employer, which provided crew hauling services to railroads, was entitled to rely on the railroad carrier exemptions to defeat the plaintiff's claim for overtime compensation. The court found that the employer's business was incidental to a rail carrier such that the

---

[63]Opinion Letter of May 5, 2001, by Acting Wage Hour Administrator Markey, WHM: 99:8357.

[64]*See* text at note 35, *supra*.

[65]969 F. Supp. 1142, 4 WH Cases2d 209 (N.D. Ill. 1997).

employer was within the rail carrier exemption. A New York State appellate court reversed the trial court's grant of partial summary judgment in favor of former employees of defendants Command Security Corporation (CSC) and British Airways (BA) in *Horkan v. Command Security Corp.*[66] Plaintiffs worked as security officers for both CSC and BA at John F. Kennedy International Airport and claimed entitlement to overtime pay under the FLSA. Finding it "critical" that plaintiffs performed work as subordinate officials under supervision of an air carrier, BA, the appellate court read 45 U.S.C. §181 to extend the Railway Labor Act's provisions to include all officials performing work under the direction or supervision of BA or its agents.

C. Air Transportation Employees

In *Horkan v. Command Security Co.*,[67] the plaintiffs were ground-based employees hired and paid by Command Security and leased to British Airways, which supervised them in their work as undercover security personnel. Against their claim for overtime pay, the defendant relied on the airline exemption. The state court held that, on the pleadings alone, for purposes of a motion to dismiss, it could not be determined as a matter of law that the airline exemption applied, the question of the exempt nature of the work performed being a mixed question of fact and law. Implicit in the holding was the unstated proposition that if the work was exempt work (i.e., traditional airline work which is directly related to the transportation of goods or mail by air in interstate commerce) and occupied more than 80 percent of plaintiffs' work time, both joint employers would be entitled to claim the exemption. A New York State appellate court later reversed the trial court's grant of partial summary judgment in favor of former employees of defendants Command Security Corporation (CSC) and British Airways (BA) in

[66]728 N.Y.S.2d 495, 7 WH 2d 575 (2001). *See* 2001 Cumulative Supplement for review of the trial court decision, 179 Misc.2d 108, 682 N.Y.S.2d 563, 6 WH Cases2d 346 (Sup. Ct. 1998).

[67]179 Misc. 2d 108, 682 N.Y.S.2d 563, 6 WH Cases2d 346 (Sup. Ct. 1998).

Horkan v. Command Security Corp.[68] Plaintiffs worked as security officers for both CSC and BA at John F. Kennedy International Airport and claimed entitlement to overtime pay under the FLSA. Finding it "critical" that Plaintiffs performed work as subordinate officials under supervision of an air carrier, BA, the appellate court read 45 U.S.C. §181 to extend the Railway Labor Act's provisions to include all officials performing work under the direction or supervision of BA or its agents.

In *Verrett v. Sabre Group, Inc.*,[69] a federal district court in Oklahoma held that the defendant airline management information systems company, a corporation previously spun off by the American Airlines group and performing air scheduling and related activities for American and other commercial airlines, was exempt from the overtime provisions of the FLSA as a "carrier" under the Railway Labor Act, and that the company satisfied the two-part test for such coverage. First, the company was under common control with American Airlines. Second, the company's services were transportation-related in that the employees performed and monitored the computer operations critical to airline functions such as flight operations and scheduling.

The Court of Appeals for the Tenth Circuit, in an unpublished decision in *Slavens v. Scenic Aviation, Inc.*,[70] affirmed a district court's decision holding that the defendant, which operated primarily as an air ambulance and charter service, was governed by the Railway Labor Act (RLA) and that the plaintiff was, accordingly, not entitled to overtime under the FLSA. The individual plaintiff was employed in a managerial capacity and his duties involved the medical—rather than the transportation—aspects of the defendant's business. He argued that his duties were "tenuous, negligible, and remote" with respect to the defendant's transportation activities, and that he was an "employer" rather than an "employee" with respect to the

---

[68] 728 N.Y.S.2d 495, 7 WH2d 575. See 2001 Cumulative Supplement for review of the trial court decision, 179 Misc.2d 108, 682 N.Y.S.2d 563, 6 WH Cases2d 346.

[69] 70 F. Supp. 2d 1277, 6 WH Cases2d 143 (N.D. Okla. 1999).

[70] 2000 WL 985933 (10th Cir. 2000).

defendant's air-ambulance business. The court rejected the plaintiff's argument that his status as an "employer" precluded his being an "employee" as well, and noted that the plaintiff's activities—evaluating the medical background of potential medical staff, establishing medical protocols, establishing company policies and procedures, informing hospitals of the services available, and resolving personnel disputes—were "integral" to the defendant's air ambulance services. Because the FLSA exempts from its overtime provisions any employee of a carrier by air subject to the Railway Labor Act, and because the defendant was such a carrier subject to the RLA, the plaintiff was not entitled to overtime under the provisions of the FLSA.

In *Thibodeaux v. Executive Jet International, Inc.*[71] plaintiff alleged overtime violations pursuant to the FLSA and defendant moved for summary judgment, claiming an exemption from the FLSA's overtime provisions under 29 U.S.C. §213(b)(3) and its status as a "common carrier by air" under the Railway Labor Act.[72] Declining to determine whether defendant was a common carrier based upon an analogy to a sister company, the court focused on the ultimate finding necessary even if it were to find defendant a "common carrier by air." The court explained the exemption at issue would be defeated if plaintiff spent more than 20 percent of his time during the workweek performing nonexempt work. Accordingly, the court denied defendant's motion for summary judgment, finding a genuine issue of material fact existed as to whether plaintiff spent more than 20 percent of his time per workweek performing nonexempt work.

F. Certain Employees of Automobile, Truck, or Farm Implement Dealers; Salespersons of Trailers, Boats, and Aircraft

In *Viart v. Bull Motors, Inc.*,[73] a former employee brought an action against his former employer, an automobile dealership,

---

[71]2001 WL 699653 7 WH Cases2d 254 (E.D. La 2001).

[72]45 U.S.C. §181.

[73]149 F. Supp. 2d 1346 (S.D. Fla. 2001).

alleging violations of FLSA overtime provisions. Defendant employed plaintiff as a predelivery inspection technician. Plaintiff's duties included checking interior lights, gauges and other interior items, checking the air conditioning, battery and steering, and working through a 46-point checklist to ensure new vehicles were ready for delivery to customers. Defendant paid plaintiff a flat, "flag" rate for each car regardless of the actual time worked to complete each inspection. Defendant contended that the provisions of Section 13(b)(10)(A), exempting certain "salesmen, partsmen and mechanics," exempted plaintiff from overtime.

After a jury verdict in favor of plaintiff, the trial court considered defendant's timely motion for judgment as a matter of law and found that the issue of plaintiff's exempt status was a legal question for the court. Employing *Chevron*[74] deference to the DOL regulations, the court held that plaintiff fit within the definition of mechanic.[75] The court also cited as persuasive authority the DOL's Dictionary of Occupational Titles' definition of "get-ready mechanic"[76] and legislative history indicating plaintiff's duties were covered by the Section 13(b)(10)(A) exemption. The trial court accordingly granted defendant's motion for judgment as a matter of law.

In *Gieg v. Howarth,*[77] the Ninth Circuit reversed the judgment of the district court which had held plaintiff to be exempt under Section 13(b)(10)(A). Plaintiff was an auto dealership employee described as a finance writer, and his primary job responsibilities included determination of the type of financing appropriate to customers, and sales of credit-life insurance and service contracts. He sued for overtime under the FLSA and Oregon wage and hour laws. Defendant claimed a Section 13(b)(10) exemption from the Act's overtime provisions. The district court granted summary judgment in favor of defendant.

---

[74]Chevron, U.S.A., Inc. v. Natural Resources Defense Council, Inc., 467 U.S. 837, 842–43, 104 S. Ct. 2778, 81 L. Ed. 2d 694 (1984).

[75]29 C.F.R. §779.372(c)(3) (2000).

[76]U.S. DEP'T OF LABOR, DICTIONARY OF OCCUPATIONAL TITLES 806.361.026 (4th ed. 1991).

[77]244 F.3d 775, 6 WH Cases2d 1618 (9th Cir. 2001).

Defendant paid plaintiff commissions on finance and insurance products sold, but plaintiff did not receive any payment associated with sales of the cars themselves. Plaintiff also received a "draw" as an advance on expected commissions. In its analysis of the 13(b)(10) exemption, the court focused on the legislative history of the provision, noting particularly the 1966 amendments to the FLSA. These amendments repealed language of the provision indicating that "any employee" of an automobile sales establishment was exempt, and replaced this with language specifying "salesmen, partsmen and mechanics"[78] as the positions covered by this exemption. Acknowledging that the auto industry might have changed significantly since 1966, the Ninth Circuit concluded nevertheless that Congress intended to narrow the exemption through the 1966 amendments and, accordingly, held that the plaintiff was not exempt under 29 U.S.C. §213(b)(10)(A).

H. Taxicab Drivers

In *Herman v. Brewah Cab*,[79] a federal district court in Wisconsin held that a company providing transportation for the elderly and handicapped did not fall within the taxicab exemption to overtime provisions of the FLSA. The court distinguished the transportation that the defendant provided from taxicabs on the grounds that: (1) the drivers of defendant's vehicles were required to adhere to a daily work schedule prearranged by the company rather than the driver; (2) the drivers were not free to pick up passengers who had not prearranged services; (3) the defendant's vehicles were unmetered, did not have vacancy signs, and were specially equipped for wheelchairs; (4) the defendant's vehicles were not advertised as taxicabs; (5) unlike taxicab companies, the defendant qualified for various elderly and handicapped subsidy and co-payment programs; (6) the defendant's drivers could not receive tips; (7) the defendant was

[78]Pub. L. No. 89-601, §§209(b), 212(a) (1966).

[79]992 F. Supp. 1054, 4 WH Cases2d 653 (E.D. Wis.), *motion to amend denied,* 179 F.R.D. 577 (1998).

not registered with the city as a cab company; and (8) the defendant's drivers were specially trained to assist elderly and handicapped customers.[80]

L. Employees of Amusement or Recreational Establishments Located in a National Park, National Forest, or on Land in the National Wildlife Refuge System

In *Chessin v. Keystone Resort Management*,[81] the Tenth Circuit affirmed the district court's holding that a company's two ski resorts on national forest land were separate "establishments" under the FLSA, even though the resorts were less than six miles apart, operated under a joint marketing strategy, sometimes exchanged employees, and provided shuttle bus service between the two areas. Citing Supreme Court and Tenth Circuit precedent, the court noted that under the FLSA, "establishment" means a distinct physical place of business rather than a business enterprise, which might take place at two or more distinct locations. The plaintiffs also argued that one of the two establishments was not an amusement or recreational establishment, as it derived substantial income from sales of food, lodging, and retail items as well as a convention center. The court declined to follow a percentage-of-revenue test and distinguished the analysis under Section 13(b)(29) from that made under Section 13(a)(3) (relating to employees of amusement, recreational, and similar establishments generally). It stated that for purposes of Section 13(b)(29) the test was "whether lodging and other services like restaurants and retail shops, viewed in the context of Keystone's operations on or near national forest land, have a recreational nature."[82] Finally, the court adopted a strict construction of the 56-hour proviso of the exemption, holding specifically that for any workweek in which any plaintiff had worked more than 56 hours without time-and-one-half compensation, that plaintiff was entitled to time-and-

---

[80] *Id.* at 1059–60, 4 WH Cases2d 653.
[81] 184 F.3d 1188, 5 WH Cases2d 739 (10th Cir. 1999).
[82] *Id.*, 5 WH Cases2d at 742.

one-half compensation for each hour over 40 in that week, and not, as defendants contended, merely for each hour over 56.

A county agency responsible for managing county fairgrounds and mounting the county fair fell within the "amusement or recreational establishment" exemption of the FLSA and Ohio fair wage statutes in *Gibbs v. Montgomery County Agricultural Society.*[83] A former maintenance employee conceded defendant met the second prong of the 13(a)(3) exemption, averaging less than 33 ⅓ percent of its receipts during its six slowest months of the year. Plaintiff claimed defendant failed to meet the first requirement of the exemption, that it be an amusement or recreational establishment.

In a straightforward analysis, the district court found that defendant's lease of areas to nonexempt organizations did not result in destroying defendant's exempt status, even though defendant spent time working in these leased areas. It further found that in determining whether the exemption applied, the character of defendant employer's principal, revenue–producing activities was the true inquiry, and that the exact nature of plaintiff's work did not control. The court thus found that the exemption applied, and declined to exercise supplemental jurisdiction over the state law retaliation claim. No federal retaliation claim had been asserted.

IV. SECTION 7 EXEMPTIONS FROM THE OVERTIME REQUIREMENTS OF THE ACT

D. Employees of a Hospital or Establishment Engaged in Care of the Sick [New Section]

The Department of Labor issued an opinion letter[84] concerning the applicability of Section 7(j) of the Act to the employees of a multisite medical testing laboratory which did

[83] 140 F. Supp. 2d 835 (S.D. Ohio 2001).

[84] Opinion Letter of Sept. 14, 2000, by member of Office of Enforcement Policy, WHM: 99:8325.

much of its work for hospital patients. The facts involved five hospitals and a central laboratory location not within any of the hospitals. The five hospitals were owned by a single entity, and the central laboratory was owned by that entity and another organization. Eighty percent of the employer's laboratory employees worked in the hospitals on a full-time basis and performed their work in connection with tests administered to hospital patients; the other 20 percent of the employees worked at the central laboratory facility. The Department concluded that the operation constituted a single enterprise under the Act, and that employees of the enterprise who spent virtually all their time on the premises of the hospitals were entitled to be treated as exempt under Section 7(j). With respect to the employees who worked at the central laboratory facility, the Department determined that not enough information had been provided to draw a conclusion as to the applicability of Section 7(j), and that the identity of the co-owner and the source of the laboratory work done by those employees could be relevant to that decision.

Chapter 6

AGRICULTURAL EXEMPTIONS

II. General Scope of Agriculture

B. "Primary" Agriculture

5. Raising Livestock, Bees, Fur-Bearing Animals, or Poultry

Baldwin v. Iowa Select Farms, L.P.[1] is an interesting decision exploring the scope of "agriculture" under pertinent statutory, case law, and regulatory authority. In *Baldwin,* a district court granted summary judgment, holding that a sow farm technician in a "confinement feeding" pork production operation was an agricultural worker exempt from the Act's overtime requirements. The employer engaged in the complete process of raising hogs and maintained ownership and control over the hogs for their entire lives. In this case of modern, segmented, and quasi-industrial agriculture, the court observed:

> Although there may be some appeal to Baldwin's assertion that industrialized hog production operations that bear a greater resemblance to Ford Motor Company than to a "farm" should not be able to invoke the "employed in agriculture" exemption from overtime pay requirements of the FLSA, that argument is better addressed to Congress than to this court in light of the language of the statute and the governing interpretations.[2]

---

[1] 6 F. Supp. 2d 831, 4 WH Cases2d 1119 (N.D. Iowa 1998).
[2] *Id.* at 842, 4 WH Cases2d at 1127.

C. "Secondary" Agriculture

3. *"Such Farming Operations" of the Farmer*

The necessity that the "practices . . . performed by a farmer or on a farm" be performed as an incident to or in conjunction with "such farming operations" to come within the secondary meaning of "agriculture" was underscored by a district court in *Adkins v. Mid-American Growers, Inc.*[3] In that case, exemption from overtime requirements under Section 13(b)(12) was claimed for employees of a large greenhouse operation. The court, however, held that work performed by the employees on nursery plants obtained by the greenhouse from other growers and then resold was not primary or secondary agriculture and was therefore not exempt.[4] The defendant failed to carry its burden of establishing that the work performed was "agriculture" because the greenhouse operation did not systematically and consistently perform work relating to plants obtained from other growers that were calculated to produce growth to maturity or substantial maturity, or to acclimate the plants to the local climate.[5] Because the employees performed some of this nonexempt work and the employer failed to record employees' time spent on such work, the exemption was found unavailable to shield the employer from the requirement to pay overtime to these employees.[6]

---

[3] 965 F. Supp. 1076 (N.D. Ill. 1997), *aff'd in part, vacated in part,* 167 F.3d 355, 5 WH Cases2d 129 (7th Cir. 1999). For a discussion of the regulations relating to nursery operations as agriculture, see §II.D.2. [General Scope of Agriculture; Specific Situations; Nursery and Landscaping Operations] in the Main Volume of the Treatise.

[4] 965 F. Supp. 1076.

[5] *Id.* at 1088.

[6] As the court noted, the regulations recognize that a variety of tasks performed by nursery employees relating to the handling of plants may be within the secondary meaning of agriculture, but only if such work is performed "only [on] products grown by their employer[.]" *Id.* at 1085 n.12 (quoting 29 C.F.R. §780.149). The court further recognized that to determine whether the work performed by the greenhouse employees related to "growing," as opposed to merely handling, caring for, or preserving the plants while they are on the employer's premises, it is necessary to consider several factors, including the stage of development of the plant at the time it is obtained; the nature and purpose of the operations performed on the plant; and the length of time the plant is retained from the time it is obtained to the time of sale or other disposition and the stage of development at that time. *Id.* at 1087.

5. *Performance of the Practice "As an Incident to or in Conjunction With" Farming Operations*

An example of an incidental practice that is within the secondary meaning of agriculture is work by employees of a large greenhouse operation relating to "hard goods" such as soil, fertilizer, and planting pots. Where the sale of such goods constitutes a negligible portion of the employer's business and investment of its resources relative to its farming operations, the work is performed by the same employees who perform agricultural tasks relating to propagating and tending plants, and the goods sold are horticultural or related to horticulture, such work qualifies as secondary agriculture and does not defeat an exemption under Section 13(b)(12).[7]

On the other hand, work by greenhouse employees on the owner's residence, including lawn mowing and landscaping, car washing, furniture moving, cleaning, unloading and storing hay for the owner's horses (who were not used in the greenhouse operation), car maintenance and repair, and babysitting were not secondary agriculture.[8] Even though it might be argued that the "traditional view" of farming operations would include "mowing the lawn at the farmhouse," such tasks as those listed were not performed incidental to or in conjunction with farming operations.[9]

In an Opinion Letter dated January 17, 2001,[10] the Department of Labor's Wage and Hour Division addressed questions involving processing operations performed on a farm. In this factual scenario, the farmer raised and slaughtered poultry, processed the poultry skins, dyed and trimmed the processed pelts, and packed and shipped the final product for use in fly fishing.[11] Interpreting the exemption provided in Section 13(b)12 of the statute and the regulation at 29 C.F.R. §780.106, and applying those to the facts presented, the Department

---

[7]*Id.* at 1089–90 (citing Maneja v. Waialua Agric. Co., 349 U.S. 254 (1955)).
[8]*Id.* at 1090–91.
[9]*Id.*
[10]WH Opinion Letter dated Jan. 17, 2001, 2001 WL 58865.
[11]*Id.*

opined that, while raising poultry is clearly "primary agriculture," and slaughtering "secondary agriculture" if performed by the farmer on the farm, once the poultry were slaughtered and the pelts were being processed, the activity was "more akin to manufacturing than agriculture"[12] (as provided in the regulatory provision) and thus not performed as an incident to or in conjunction with the farmer's farming operations, and not exempt from the overtime provisions of the FLSA.

E. Examples of Functions As "Agricultural" or "Nonagricultural" Work

As noted in the Main Volume of the Treatise, drivers working for a vertically integrated poultry enterprise who carried feed from the enterprise's mill to independently operated farms that were under contract to raise the enterprise's chickens were not engaged in agriculture because their work was performed neither "on a farm," nor "by a farmer."[13]

In 1996, the Supreme Court revisited the question of the dividing line between the agricultural and the nonagricultural for the purposes of the FLSA in *Holly Farms Corp. v. NLRB.*[14] *Holly Farms* was not an FLSA case. Rather, it involved a dispute over the classification of certain workers under the National Labor Relations Act (NLRA). Nevertheless, as the court explained:

> Annually since 1946, Congress has instructed, in riders to Appropriations Acts for the Board "[A]gricultural laborer," for NLRA §2(3) purposes, shall derive its meaning from the definition of "agriculture" supplied by §3(f) of the Fair Labor Standards Act of 1938 (FLSA).[15]

The *Holly Farms* Court relied heavily on its decision in *Bayside Enterprises.* It found that the "live-haul" employees of Holly Farm, who caught chickens at the contract farm and delivered them to Holly Farm's processing plants, were not

[12] *Id.*

[13] Bayside Enters. Inc. v. NLRB, 429 U.S. 298, 303 (1977).

[14] 517 U.S. 392 (1996)

[15] *Id.* at 397.

themselves engaged in raising poultry. The Court then found that live-haul crews were not engaged in secondary activity "on the farm" that was "incidental to or in conjunction with" farming operations, because those activities, while on the farm, were incidental to and in conjunction with Holly Farms' slaughtering and processing operations, and hence did not constitute "farming" under the statute.[16]

In January and February 2000, three federal district courts issued decisions recognizing the applicability of the *Holly Farms* decision to cases involving chicken catchers' claims for overtime compensation under the FLSA. In two of those cases, the Secretary brought suit against poultry companies, alleging that the companies' failure to pay its live-haul crews overtime pay violated the FLSA.[17] In February 2000, a class action was brought against an employer by more than 100 chicken-catcher employees for FLSA overtime violations. The employer argued that its chicken catchers and crew leaders working on crews to catch and deliver live chicken to poultry processors fell within the agricultural laborer exception to the overtime provisions of the FLSA.[18] In each of these cases, the federal district courts relied upon the Supreme Court decision in *Holly Farms* in reaching its decision.

In *Herman v. Continental Grain Co.*, Chief Judge Albritton thoroughly reviewed the *Holly Farms* decision and ruled that in order to decide the question of whether the live-haul crews came within the exemption, the court would need to examine "the specific nature of the work in question, and this would require resorting to facts not contained in the Complaint."[19] In denying the defendant's motion to dismiss, the court wrote: "[I]t is inappropriate for the court to determine at this stage in the litigation whether Continental's employees fall within the agricultural exemptions."[20]

---

[16] *Id.* at 401.

[17] Herman v. Continental Grain Co., 80 F. Supp. 2d 1290 (M.D. Ala. 2000); Herman v. Tyson Foods, Inc., 82 F. Supp. 2d 631 (E.D. Tex. 2000).

[18] Heath v. Perdue Farms, 87 F. Supp. 2d 452 (D. Md. 2000).

[19] 80 F. Supp. 2d at 1295.

[20] *Id.* at 1296.

In *Herman v. Tyson Foods,* the defendant also moved to dismiss on the ground that chicken catchers are agricultural laborers exempt from the FLSA provisions, citing the Fifth Circuit's decision in *Coleman v. Sanderson Farms.*[21] The Secretary argued that the Supreme Court's *Holly Farms* decision implicitly overruled *Coleman.* In denying the defendant's motion to dismiss, the court wrote: "Given the choice of following conflicting authority of the Fifth Circuit and of the Supreme Court of the United States, this court chooses to follow Supreme Court authority."[22]

In *Heath v. Perdue Farms,* Perdue Farms sought to distinguish *Holly Farms* primarily on the ground that Holly Farms was decided under the NLRA, and not the FLSA. However, the Maryland district court adopted the rationale of *Holly Farms* regarding the definition of agricultural laborer and noted that "federal courts have consistently held that the *Holly Farms* decision is applicable to cases arising under the FLSA."[23]

IV. SECTION 13(B) EXEMPTIONS FROM THE OVERTIME REQUIREMENTS OF THE ACT

B. Agricultural Workers and Those Employed in Operating or Maintaining Irrigation Systems for Agricultural Purposes

Employees connected with the operation or maintenance of ditches, canals, reservoirs, or waterways used for supplying and storing water for agricultural purposes may be exempt from the FLSA overtime requirements, even if the provider supplies water for other than agricultural purposes. In the Department of Labor Appropriations Act of 1998,[24] Congress amended Section 13(b)(12) of the FLSA by allowing the exemption to cover any

---

[21] 629 F.2d 1077 (5th Cir. 1980).
[22] *Tyson Foods,* 82 F. Supp. 2d at 632.
[23] 87 F. Supp. 2d at 460.
[24] Pub. L. No. 105-78, 111 Stat. 1467 (1997).

provider who supplies up to 10 percent of its water for other than agricultural purposes during the preceding calendar year.[25] The exemption still applies only where the irrigation system is operated on a nonprofit or sharecrop basis.

The Tenth Circuit has joined the Ninth Circuit in applying the regulations to deny the exemption for specified irrigation activities where the water delivered by the irrigation system was not used exclusively for supplying and storing water for agricultural purposes.[26]

---

[25]Pub. L. No. 105-78,111 Stat. 1467, 1477 (1997). The amendment provides:

> Section 13(b)(12) of the Fair Labor Standards Act of 1938 (29 U.S.C. 213(b)(12)) is amended by striking "water for agricultural purposes" and inserting in lieu thereof "water, at least 90 percent of which was ultimately delivered for agricultural purposes during the preceding calendar year."

Id.

[26]Sanders v. Elephant Butte Irrigation Dist., 112 F.3d 468, 3 WH Cases2d 1573 (10th Cir. 1997) (citing Dole v. West Extension Irrigation Dist., 909 F.2d 349, 29 WH Cases 1449 (9th Cir. 1990); applying 29 C.F.R. §780.408).

CHAPTER 7

SPECIAL CERTIFICATES

I. OVERVIEW

As indicated in the Main Volume of the Treatise, on December 9, 1997, the Department of Labor issued a final rule on Section 14 certification programs, effective February 9, 1998.[1] The final rule eliminates 29 C.F.R. Part 527 and consolidates former 29 C.F.R. Parts 520, 521, 522, and 523 into a single Part 520. The changes effected by this regulatory activity are discussed in Chapter 7 of the Main Volume at pages 441–63.

[1] 62 Fed. Reg. 64,956 (1997).

CHAPTER 8

DETERMINING COMPENSABLE HOURS WORKED

II. Principles for Determining Hours Worked

D. Statutory Exceptions That Narrow the Concept of Hours Worked

1. Section 3(o) of the FLSA

A number of cases have turned on issues involving the effect, in terms of the practical realities of various industries, of Section 3(o) on claims of unionized workers for overtime arising from matters which may or may not be covered by the section's language. Questions relating both to the scope of "changing clothes or washing"[1] and of the meaning of "by the express terms of or by custom or practice under"[2] a collective bargaining agreement continue to be litigated, and the effect of statements of interpretation by the Department of Labor[3] have also entered the picture.

In *Pressley v. Sanderson Farms, Inc.*,[4] the plaintiffs, poultry processing employees, claimed they should be compensated for time spent changing clothes, sanitizing tools and garments, and

---

[1]Metzler v. IBP, Inc., 127 F.3d 959, 4 WH Cases2d 229 (10th Cir. 1997), *earlier litigation involving these matters decided sub nom.* Reich v. IBP, Inc., 38 F. 3d 1123, 2 WH Cases2d 641 (10th Cir. 1994); Reich v. Montfort, 144 F.3d 1329, 4 WH Cases2d 1106 (10th Cir. 1998).

[2]Turner v. City of Phila., 262 F.3d 222, 225–27 (3d Cir. 2001), *aff'g* 96 F. Supp. 2d 460 (E.D. Pa. 2000); Bernard v. IBP, Inc. of Neb., 154 F.3d 259 (5th Cir.1998); Arcadi v. Nestle Food Corp., 38 F.3d 672, 2 WH Cases2d 644 (2d Cir. 1994).

[3]WH Opinion Letter dated Dec. 3, 1997, WHM 99:8107; WH Opinion Letter dated Jan. 15, 2001, 2001 WL 58864.

[4]143 Lab. Cas. ¶34,262 (S.D. Tex. 2001), 2001 WL 850017, *aff'd,* No. 01-20527 (5th Cir. Mar. 7, 2002).

walking to and from workstations before and after shifts and during unpaid meal periods. The court granted summary judgment in favor of the employer. The court held that "as a matter of law the time spent by Plaintiffs walking, . . . donning, doffing, and cleaning their equipment, is not compensable work under the FLSA," and is excluded from compensable time by the Portal-to-Portal Act. In addition, the court disregarded the plaintiffs' contentions that they spent seven to 20 minutes per day donning, doffing, and sanitizing, finding instead that the activities took "minimal time" and, therefore, were de minimis as a matter of law but it rejected defendant's argument under Section 3(o) that its collective bargaining agreement with plaintiff-employees completely barred plaintiffs' claims that the defendant failed to pay them for all hours worked. After noting that the defendants had failed to bring to the court's attention all the pertinent and arguably controlling circuit court case law, it rested its partial denial of defendant's summary judgment motion on the finding that a factual issue existed as to whether all plaintiffs were covered by the collective bargaining agreement.

In *Anderson v. Pilgrim's Pride Corp.*,[5] a Texas federal district court entered judgment in a chicken processing company's favor following a bench trial on the production employees' claims that the company failed to pay them for donning and doffing time. The court held that such clothes changing time was excluded from compensable work time under Section 3(o) because the collective bargaining agreements under which the employees worked did not provide for payment for clothes changing time, the employees at the company had not been compensated for clothes changing time during the period covered by the collective bargaining agreements, and the employees' collective bargaining agent had proposed paying employees for such time during collective bargaining negotiations, but the company had rejected the proposal.

The Third Circuit joined the Second and the Fifth Circuits[6] in taking a broad view of the phrase "custom or practice under

---

[5]147. F. Supp. 2d 556 (E.D.Tex 2001).

[6]*Arcadi*, 38 F. 3d 672, 2 WH Cases2d 644 (2d Cir. 1994); *Bernard*, 154 F.3d 259 (5th Cir. 1998).

a collective bargaining agreement" when it affirmed the district court's determination that a "custom or practice" of non-payment for clothes changing time existed in *Turner v. City of Philadelphia.*[7] There summary judgment had been granted against the claim of plaintiffs, corrections officers, for overtime for time spent changing into and out of their uniforms. The court held that the city's 30-year policy of not compensating the corrections officers for clothes changing time may be excluded from measured working time as a "custom or practice under a bona fide collective-bargaining agreement" under Section 3(o) even though this policy was neither specified in a collective-bargaining agreement nor ever raised in contract negotiations. The court reasoned that a particular custom or practice can become an implied term of a labor agreement through a mere prolonged period of acquiescence.

2. The Portal-to-Portal Act

In *Steelman v. Telco Telephone Co., Inc.,*[8] a federal district court in Oregon denied summary judgment motions filed by both parties where a telephone network systems installer brought suit for overtime compensation against his employer telephone company for the time he traveled directly to the first customer site from home, and directly home from the last customer work site. The employer argued that this travel time was not compensable under Section 4(a)(1) of the Portal-to-Portal Act.[9] The employee contended that while he was traveling he carried indispensable equipment and tools for his job.[10] The court noted that under Section 4(a)(1), travel time from the employee's home to a customer's site may be compensable if it is "integral and indispensable" to the employee's principal activity.[11] To determine whether an activity is integral and indispensable, the

[7] 262 F.3d 222, 225–27 (3d Cir. 2001), *aff'g* 96 F. Supp. 2d 460 (E.D. Pa. 2000).
[8] 2001 WL 21361 (D. Or. 2001).
[9] *Id.* at *2.
[10] *Id.*
[11] *Id.*

court considered whether the employer requires the employee to do the work, to what degree the employer benefits from the work, and to what extent the activity is indispensable to the primary goal of the employee's work.[12] The court ultimately concluded that disputed issues of fact remained as to whether the particular travel time at issue was integral and indispensable to the employee's principal activity.[13]

III. APPLICATION OF PRINCIPLES

A. "Suffer or Permit to Work"

1. *Knowledge*

In *Darrikhuma v. Southland Corp.*,[14] a federal district court in Maryland held that an employee had failed to prove that his employer had actual or constructive knowledge of his off-the-clock work hours. Although a field consultant for the employer saw the plaintiff working on weekends, this was insufficient to demonstrate that the consultant knew about the plaintiff's off-the-clock work. Furthermore, the plaintiff did not offer more than his own unsupported allegations that he had advised his employer of his working unpaid hours on the job.

In *Robertson v. Board of County Commissioners*,[15] the plaintiffs, deputy sheriffs and a dispatcher working in the sheriff's office, sued for uncompensated overtime for hours spent on call, but only one of the plaintiffs produced any evidence that the employer knew that they were on call. The court granted partial summary judgment for the employer as to all other plaintiffs, noting that an employer is not required to pay for time worked when the employer truly did not know, and had no reason to know, the work was being performed.

---

[12] *Id.* at *3.

[13] *Id.*

[14] 975 F. Supp. 778, 4 WH Cases2d 277 (D. Md.), *aff'd*, 129 F.3d 1258 (4th Cir. 1997).

[15] 78 F. Supp. 2d 1142, 1160, 5 WH Cases2d 1449 (D. Colo. 1999).

B. Waiting Time

2. *Off Duty*

One court has concluded that police trainees confined to barracks during their training were free to use their time as they wished and thus were not entitled to compensation for periods during which they were confined to their barracks.[16]

In *United Transportation Union Local 1745 v. Albuquerque*,[17] plaintiffs were local bus drivers working for the defendant City of Albuquerque, New Mexico, who sued for compensation for the non-working time between the "split" (morning *and* evening rush hour) shifts they were required to work, and for the time spent riding city buses from and to the end-points of their driving routes. The Tenth Circuit affirmed the district court's holding that, with the exception of the shuttle times after the morning shift and before the afternoon shift, the time bus drivers spent outside the two shifts in a day was not compensable. The court reasoned that the drivers had a three- to five-hour period between shifts in which they were free to do anything they wanted (except drink alcohol). The drivers were "completely relieved from duty" during this period, which the court reasoned was "long enough to enable [them] to use the time effectively for [their] own purposes."

The Sixth Circuit affirmed the district court's decision that a city's "location when ill" policy, under which police officers on paid sick leave for periods of illness or on-the-job injury were required to stay at home unless they received permission to leave, did not violate the FLSA by failing to compensate officers for every waking hour they were confined at home.[18] The court found this situation analogous to on-call situations and, applying the predominant benefit test, determined that the city's policy was not so onerous as to prevent employees from effectively

---

[16] Banks v. City of Springfield, 959 F. Supp. 972, 3 WH Cases2d 1507 (C.D. Ill. 1997).

[17] 178 F.3d 1109, 5 WH Cases2d 555 (10th Cir. 1999).

[18] Aiken v. City of Memphis, 190 F.3d 753, 5 WH Cases2d 961 (6th Cir. 1999), *cert. denied,* 528 U.S. 1157, 5 WH Cases2d 1632 (2000).

using their time for personal pursuits. Likewise, in *DeBraska v. City of Milwaukee*,[19] the Seventh Circuit held that time police officers spent at home pursuant to the city's sick leave policy, requiring police officers on sick or injury leave to remain at home unless they obtained permission, was not equivalent to compensable "on call" time. Because the sick and injured officers were not fit to work, the court ruled that they were not "engaged to wait" for work and, therefore, their time at home was not compensable.

In *Monserrate v. City of New York*,[20] a federal district court in New York granted the employer's motion to dismiss where police officers sued the City of New York (the "City") for overtime compensation allegedly accrued on sick days. The employees claimed they should be compensated for the shifts they spent at home pursuant to the City's policy mandating that employees who report sick and/or unable to work because of illness or disability are required to remain at home for the entire 24-hour work day associated with their shift.[21] In granting the City's motion to dismiss, the court was persuaded by reasoning found in decisions of the Sixth[22] and Seventh[23] Circuits that being required to stay at home was not "work" entitling the employees to compensation because the restriction was not so onerous as to prevent the employees from effectively using the time for their own pursuits,[24] noting that the policy only applied to officers who claimed to be unable to perform limited duty assignments.

3. *On-Call Time*

In an opinion letter, the Wage and Hour Division considered an on-call arrangement in which employees would wear a

---

[19]189 F.3d 650, 652, 5 WH Cases2d 982 (7th Cir. 1999).

[20]2000 WL 1741673 (S.D.N.Y. 2000).

[21]*Id.* at *1.

[22]Aiken v. City of Memphis, 190 F.3d 753 (6th Cir. 1999), *cert. denied,* 528 U.S. 1157, 5 WH Cases2d 1632 (2000).

[23]Debraska v. City of Milwaukee, 189 F.3d 650 (7th Cir. 1999).

[24]*Monserrate,* 2000 WL 1741673, at *2–3.

beeper and check the employer's merchandise levels remotely via laptop computer. The Division expressed the view that if the time was compensable on-call time, then associated "on-call" pay could not be excluded from the regular rate of pay.[25]

In another opinion letter,[26] the Department of Labor addressed the question whether the on-call time of electricians and maintenance engineers was compensable under two scenarios. Under the first scenario, service calls occurring outside of normal work hours were handled by a voluntary on-call system under which employees were given beepers and the ability to accept or refuse calls at their discretion. Calls averaged two per 24 hours on the weekends and one per 16-hour period during the workweek. The Division expressed the view that the time spent awaiting calls on the beeper was not compensable time worked because the employees could accept or refuse calls and were free to engage in a full range of personal activities during the periods when they were on call.[27] Under the second scenario, an employee was designated for stand-by status by the employer and during the period of this assignment was required to handle service calls during weekends and evening hours. The stand-by employee was required to remain within reach by telephone and respond to calls within 10 minutes or report to the job site within one hour. Beepers were not issued. Only one employee was on call at a time, and employees were not permitted to trade on-call duties with other employees. The volume of call-outs was the same as described in the first scenario. The Division stated that time under this mandatory on-call system was compensable because it unduly restricted employees' freedom to use the on-call time for their own benefit.[28] On the other hand, the Division also stated that it would not consider the time to be compensable hours worked if employees were provided beepers, pagers, or cell phones and were free to engage in personal activities both

---

[25]Wage-Hour Admin. Op., 1998 WL 852812 (June 23, 1998). *See also* Chapter 10, §III.F.5. ["Call-Back" Pay].

[26]1999 WL 1788156 (Dep't of Labor Sept. 3, 1999).

[27]*Id.*

[28]*Id.*

at home and away from home during a period of idleness, unless the calls were so frequent or the on-call restrictions were so restrictive that employees could not effectively use the on-call time for their own purposes.[29] The Division's opinion was the same when the hypothetical was altered so that three to six employees were on designated on-call status at a time, the call-outs were spread evenly among the employees, and employees were permitted to trade on-call duty and to answer calls within 15 minutes by phone or report to the job site within two hours.[30] In addition, the Division stated that premium pay for on-call time was not a factor in determining whether the on-call time was compensable hours worked.[31]

a. *Cases Finding That On-Call Time Is Compensable*

- Genuine issues of material fact were raised by evidence that emergency medical technicians had short response time, had to wear a uniform to calls, and could not leave the island on which the services were performed while on call.[32]
- Genuine issues of material fact were raised when an employee had to make an "inordinate" number of daily commutes to projects, and was severely hampered in his personal activities.[33]
- With respect to one deputy sheriff out of several plaintiffs, evidence that he was required to be on call for two hours prior to his regular shift, averaged two calls per week while on call, was required to remain within the county, and had to be available by phone or pager was sufficient to raise an issue of fact as to whether his on-call time was compensable.[34]

---

[29] *Id.*

[30] *Id.*

[31] *Id.*

[32] Spencer v. Hyde County, 959 F. Supp. 721, 3 WH Cases2d 1515 (E.D.N.C. 1997) (compensability "boils down" to whether an employee is waiting to be engaged, or engaged to wait).

[33] Brown v. Luk Inc., 3 WH Cases2d 560 (N.D.N.Y. 1996).

[34] Robertson v. Board of County Comm'rs, 78 F. Supp. 2d 1142, 1160, 5 WH Cases2d 1449, 1463 (D. Colo. 1999).

- In *Rutlin v. Prime Succession, Inc.*,[35] the Sixth Circuit reversed and remanded to the district court its ruling that a funeral director was not eligible for compensation for some of his time spent on call for a funeral parlor. During the periods of his employment in which he was not exempt, the employee was on call two nights a week, and sometimes all weekend, and answered between 15 and 20 calls per night, taking up about an hour of his time. The employee argued that his on-call time "severely restricted" him, preventing him from "drinking alcohol, visiting his children, or boating, and that his meals, evening activities, and sleep were disrupted by his on-call duties." The employer argued that the employee "was free to engage in personal activities while on call" because it gave the employee a pager so he could leave his home if he wanted and the employee could switch on-call shifts with other employees if needed. The Sixth Circuit held that the employee was entitled to compensation for that part of his on-call time spent answering the 15 to 20 phone calls per night. "Answering these phone calls was not typical on-call time; rather, [the employee] was actually working, albeit from home. There is no question that the time [the employee] spent on those phone calls was primarily for the benefit of [the employer]." [36] The remainder of his on-call time was ruled to be noncompensable as the restrictions on his time were not "onerous."[37]
- In *Pabst v. Oklahoma Gas & Electric Co.*,[38] the Tenth Circuit affirmed the district court's ruling that the on-call time for electronic technicians of a gas company was compensable where the employees received three to five calls per on-call period, responded to pages within 10 to 15 minutes, and spent an average of 45 minutes responding to each call. According to the court, the short response

[35]220 F.3d 737, 6 WH Cases2d 359 (6th Cir.), *reh'g and suggestion for reh'g en banc denied* (Sept. 11, 2000).

[36]*Id.* at 744.

[37]*Id.*

[38]228 F.3d 1128, 6 WH Cases2d 609 (10th Cir. 2000).

time, coupled with unreliable pagers, required the on-call employees to remain at or near their homes while on call.[39] In addition, the frequency of the calls and the time employees spent responding to calls severely disrupted the employees' sleep habits and, even during waking hours, the employees were unable to pursue many activities because of the need to come home and check their computers every 15 minutes.[40]

b. Cases Finding That On-Call Time Is Not Compensable

- A federal district court sitting in Georgia concluded that city police officers were not entitled to be compensated for their time spent on-call.[41] Although during their on-call time the officers were required to be readily accessible, to notify dispatchers of their whereabouts any time they left their homes, to remain in a geographical area that would allow for radio or pager or telephone contact, and to respond to a call within 30 minutes, the court held that these restrictions were not so onerous and did not restrict their free time so severely that their on-call time should be construed as work time under the FLSA. There was no indication that the employees were subject to frequent calls or were unable to use their on-call time predominantly for their own benefit.
- In both *Shepard v. City of Burlington*[42] and *Bartholomew v. City of Burlington,*[43] the U.S. District Court for the District of Kansas held that a city need not compensate patrol officers for 8-hour on-call periods spent after their regular shifts although (1) it was difficult to trade such on-call duties with other officers, and (2) the patrol officer claimed to have been precluded from travel away from home by the combination of the city's prohibition against

[39]*Id.* at 1131.

[40]*Id.*

[41]Arrington v. City of Macon, 986 F. Supp. 1474, 4 WH Cases2d 348 (M.D. Ga. 1997).

[42]4 WH Cases2d 1149 (D. Kan. 1998).

[43]5 F. Supp. 2d 1161, 4 WH Cases2d 1156 (D. Kan. 1998).

personal use of the patrol car with the requirement that the patrol officer respond immediately. A significant factor making the on-call time noncompensable was that the patrol officer was merely required to stay within the limits of the city and was thus free to travel or to remain at home. Therefore, the on-call time was spent primarily for the officer's benefit. Other factors making the on-call time noncompensable were the following: (1) the officer was required to return to work only two to three times per week; (2) the requirement of returning "as soon as possible" allowed more flexibility than a fixed 5- to 10-minute response time; and (3) the officer carried out personal activities during the on-call period.

- In *Ingram v. County of Bucks*,[44] the Third Circuit held that sheriffs' deputies were not entitled to compensation while on call. The employees' ability to use the time for personal pursuits was not effectively restricted, the court reasoned, because they (1) could wear beepers, (2) were summoned infrequently and had no fixed time within which they were required to respond, (3) could easily trade on-call shifts with other deputies to freely enjoy personal time, and (4) could engage in personal activities while on call. The court noted that its determination was proper on summary judgment—provided the issue of how an employee spent on-call time was not in dispute.
- A state highway employee's on-call time was not compensable where the employee was not required to do any affirmative act while on call, was called upon only once per week during the winter season, could predict when he would be called on the basis of weather conditions, was not required to live on the employer's premises, was not required to wear a pager, and was permitted nearly an hour to respond.[45]

---

[44]144 F.3d 265, 4 WH Cases2d 1011 (3d Cir. 1998).

[45]Darrah v. Missouri Highway & Transp. Comm'n, 885 F. Supp. 1307, 1313, 2 WH Cases2d 1264 (W.D. Mo. 1995).

- The on-call time of an emergency medical technician (EMT) was not compensable where the EMT was required to work four 12-hour on-call shifts immediately following his regular four 12-hour duty shifts per week, could trade on-call shifts with other EMTs, was required to carry a pager, could reasonably predict when he would be called, was required to remain clean and appropriately attired (although not required to report in uniform) and sober, was required to respond only within a reasonable time and was called to service only on 16.18 percent of his on-call shifts in 1993 and 22.96 percent of his on-call shifts in 1994.[46]
- Nonholiday time for sheriffs who did not need to stay near their station and could eat, shop, and visit friends while on call was not compensable.[47]
- On-call time of ambulance workers who were not required to be on premises and responded on average .6 times per day, despite a 10-mile limit on their beeper range and some loss in personal freedom, was not compensable.[48]
- A city line supervisor's on-call time was not compensable where the evidence showed that he owned his own business and fished and hunted while on call, indicating that the time spent was predominantly for his benefit.[49]
- A funeral director, during the time he was paid on an hourly basis and not exempt, was not entitled to compensation for his on-call time.[50] During on-call periods, the employer's telephone number was "switched" to plaintiff's home, and he received between 15 and 20 calls per night, consuming an average of an hour's time, for which he

---

[46]Andrews v. Town of Skiatook, 123 F.3d 1327, 1328–29, 4 WH Cases2d 65 (10th Cir. 1997).

[47]Ingram v. Bucks County, 3 WH Cases2d 1611 (E.D. Pa. 1997). This was so even though the collective bargaining agreement characterized such time during the holidays as compensable.

[48]Kartchner v. Town of Kearny, 3 WH Cases2d 1153 (D. Ariz. 1996).

[49]Priddy v. City of Kiowa, 3 WH Cases2d 1463 (D. Kan. 1997).

[50]Rutlin v. Prime Succession, Inc., 29 F. Supp. 2d 794, 5 WH Cases2d 43 (W.D. Mich. 1998).

received no compensation; the telephone calls, however, rarely resulted in his being called to duty, and when he was, he did receive additional compensation. On the other hand, the plaintiff was usually able to swap on-call schedules with a co-worker and could use phone-forwarding and a beeper while on call so that he could go out. He was also able to watch television, use the computer, and engage in significant amounts of personal activity at his home while on call. On these facts, the court held that the on-call time was not compensable.

- Emergency medical technicians (EMTs) who were part of a "first-out crew" and were required to arrive at their hospital within 7 minutes of being paged could not count their on-call time as hours worked under the FLSA.[51] Noting the rural location of the hospital and distinguishing the impact of such a time limit when used in a major metropolitan area, the court held that their on-call time in this location could be used for many, though not all, personal activities. The court also noted that the EMTs had sought the "first-out" status because of its relatively high earnings potential and had agreed with the hospital in advance to both their compensation scheme and the restrictions on their on-call time. The court stated that, "[a]lthough the FLSA overrides contracts, in close cases [such as this one] it makes sense to let private arrangements endure."[52]
- The on-call time of EMTs was not compensable where the EMTs were required to carry hand-held radios, stay within 5 minutes' traveling time of the ambulance garage, arrive for any call sober, remain call-ready in their work uniforms, and respond to an average of 1.2 ambulance calls per shift.[53] The court found that the minimal number of

---

[51]Dinges v. Sacred Heart St. Mary's Hosps., Inc., 164 F.3d 1056, 5 WH Cases2d 78 (7th Cir. 1999).

[52]*Id.* at 1059.

[53]Sletten v. First Care Med. Servs., 2000 WL 1196199 (D. Minn. 2000).

calls per shift, on the average, did not discourage a wealth of activities that could be performed within five minutes of the ambulance garage. As such, the court found that the on-call time was not predominantly for the employer's benefit but, rather, that the employees were waiting to be engaged.

- A federal district court in North Dakota concluded that nurses were not entitled to be compensated for their time spent on call.[54] Employees were not required to remain on the premises while on call; there were no excessive geographic limitations placed on employees; the response time was 20 minutes; employees were allowed to trade calls; employees used pagers, cell phones, or left numbers where they could be reached; employees were not frequently called in more than once per on-call shift; employees were not required to perform any affirmative acts while on call; the longest period of on-call time was a weekend; and employees were able to engage in personal pursuits. The employees' main restriction was that they could not use alcohol or take mind-altering drugs.
- In *Pabst v. Oklahoma Gas & Electric Co.*,[55] the Tenth Circuit affirmed the district court's ruling that the on-call time for electronic technicians of a gas company was compensable where the employees received three to five calls per on-call period, were required to respond to pages within 10 to 15 minutes, and spent an average of 45 minutes responding to each call. According to the court, the short response time, coupled with unreliable pagers, required the on-call employees to remain at or near their homes while on call.[56] In addition, the frequency of the calls and

[54]Wisnewski v. Champion Healthcare Corp., 2000 WL 1474414 (D.N.D. 2000). In this case, the hours in question were being compensated, but at a rate less than the minimum wage, and the plaintiffs contended that, having a contract of employment with the defendant, and being paid for their "work," they were required to be paid at least the minimum wage. The court rejected that argument and in effect approved the arrangement.

[55]228 F.3d 1128, 6 WH Cases2d 609 (10th Cir. 2000).

[56]*Id.* at 1131.

the time employees spent responding to calls severely disrupted the employees' sleep habits and, even during waking hours, the employees were unable to pursue many activities because of the need to come home and check their computers every 15 minutes.[57]

C. Rest and Meal Periods

2. *Meal Periods*

In assessing the compensability of meal periods, the previously noted trend away from strict application of the Labor Department's "completely relieved from duty" test continues. For the most part, the courts continue to *refer to* the Department of Labor's rule but *actually apply* the looser "predominant benefit" test.

Perhaps the most striking example of this trend is found in the Tenth Circuit, where, following its earlier decision in *Lamon v. City of Shawnee*,[58] the court reiterated its view that a law enforcement employee "is completely relieved from duty during a meal period . . . when the employee's time is not spent predominantly for the benefit of the employer."[59] The court in *Bates* also went beyond *Lamon* by refusing to apply other requirements—namely, that to be noncompensable, a meal period must be scheduled, occur at a regular time, and be at least 30 minutes in length—which had been applied in *Lamon* in light of 29 C.F.R. §553.223(b).[60]

The Second Circuit has also clearly rejected the "completely relieved from duty" test—in the context of a private employer[61]—explaining that "[Section] 785.19, as literally construed, fails to persuade us primarily because the completely-

---

[57] *Id.*

[58] 972 F.2d 1145, 30 WH Cases 1665 (10th Cir. 1992).

[59] Bates v. Department of Corr. of Kan., 81 F.3d 1008, 1011, 3 WH Cases2d 460 (10th Cir. 1996) (quoting *Lamon*, 972 F.2d at 1157).

[60] 81 F.3d 1008, 3 WH Cases2d at 462.

[61] Reich v. Southern New England Telecomms. Corp., 121 F.3d 58, 4 WH Cases2d 33 (2d Cir. 1997).

removed[sic]-from-duty standard is inconsistent with controlling Supreme Court precedent defining 'work.'"[62]

Some other courts continue to apply the "completely relieved from duty" standard as it is written,[63] and another district court, taking an approach similar to that of the Tenth Circuit, set forth the "completely relieved from duty" test but discussed the facts in a way that signaled its intention to apply, after supplemental submissions of fact were filed, a "predominant benefit" test.[64]

One court has applied the "predominant benefit" test to breaks—as opposed to meals—of 30 minutes or longer.[65]

In *Hoffman v. St. Joseph's Hospital of Atlanta, Inc.*,[66] a federal district court sitting in Georgia held that the "predominant benefit" test only applies in the law enforcement context. However, this decision was vacated by the court pursuant to an agreement by the parties.[67]

In *Nelson v. Waste Management of Alameda County, Inc.*,[68] a federal district court ruled that when a collective bargaining agreement provided garbage truck drivers with a half-hour meal period away from work and the break was interrupted by duties in contravention of the agreement, the time did not have to be added to the total hours of the workday because every hour during which they were punched in—including the half-hour meal period—was already counted toward the 40-hour-per-week trigger of overtime. The court determined that requiring work during the lunch period may have violated the collective bargaining agreement, but it did not violate the FLSA.

---

[62]*Id.*, 4 WH Cases2d at 33, 37.

[63]*See, e.g.*, Abendschein v. Montgomery County, 984 F. Supp. 356, 4 WH Cases2d 327 (D. Md. 1997).

[64]Arnold v. Arkansas, 910 F. Supp. 1385, 1397, 3 WH Cases2d 146 (E.D. Ark. 1995).

[65]Marti v. Grey Eagle Distribs., Inc., 937 F. Supp. 845, 851, 3 WH Cases2d 834 (E.D. Mo. 1996) (holding that breaks of at least 30 minutes are not compensable if the activities during the break are not predominantly for the employer).

[66]4 WH Cases2d 972 (N.D. Ga. 1998).

[67]Order of July 19, 1999.

[68]2000 WL 868523 (N.D. Cal. 2000).

In *Brown v. Howard Industries, Inc.*,[69] the federal district court found that the mere fact that employees were restricted to their employer's premises during their lunch break did not make the time compensable. In granting the employer's motion to dismiss, the court, relying in part on 29 C.F.R. §785.19(b), stated that the plaintiffs did not state a cause of action because there were no allegations that any duties were imposed on the plaintiffs during their lunch break.

In a matter involving fairly unusual facts, the Department of Labor recognized an exception to the general rule contained in FLSA regulations that a meal period should last at least 30 minutes in order to be bona fide. In an opinion letter[70] from the Enforcement Policy Office, the Department opined that employees of a production operation do not have to be compensated for a meal period of only 15 minutes where (1) the employees are completely relieved of duty, (2) the building has numerous readily accessible lunch rooms so that no employee is more than a minute's walk from a place to eat, (3) there are no eating establishments within a 30-minute drive, and (4) the employees requested the shortened meal period because it serves as an adequate meal period and allows them to end the day earlier.

In *Summers v. Howard University*,[71] a district court for the District of Columbia denied a summary judgment motion filed by university police officers who brought suit for unpaid overtime compensation for meal breaks. After a comprehensive review of the current law in this regard, the court decided to apply the "predominant benefit" test, which it found to be "a flexible standard that is consistent with the language of the FLSA and governing case law."[72] The plaintiffs had produced evidence to show that while on their meal breaks, they had to remain in uniform, respond to emergency situations and public inquiries,

---

[69]116 F. Supp. 2d 764 (S.D. Miss. 2000).

[70]Opinion Letter dated Sept. 25, 2000, by member of the Office of Enforcement Policy, WHM 99:8329, 2000 WL 33126561.

[71]127 F. Supp. 2d 27, 6 WH Cases2d 1278 (D.D.C. 2000).

[72]*Id.* at 33.

and, if they wished to leave the campus, were required to spend 10–15 minutes checking out equipment. On that record the court found that whether the restrictions imposed on plaintiffs during their meal periods caused them to "engage in activities predominantly for the benefit of defendant" was unclear, and that the issue was accordingly not suitable for summary judgment.[73]

In *Schwertfeger v. Village of Sauk Village*,[74] police officers claimed that their employer violated the FLSA by refusing to compensate them for mandatory 15-minute roll-call periods before the beginning of each shift. The police department employer argued that it was legal to set off the 15-minute daily roll call against the officers' break periods and lunch. The officers contended that their break periods, totaling one hour a day, were entirely compensable time. The department's primary summary judgment argument was the exemption in 29 U.S.C. §207(k) for employees on a regularly recurring work period of 28 days. The court held that the roll calls were clearly compensable time, but it was unclear whether the department compensated the officers for that time. The court held that roll calls could be set off against meal periods, if the meal periods were non-compensable time. While eating lunch, police officers were required to remain in uniform, respond to emergency calls, and be within a certain range of distance. Therefore, the court found a genuine issue of material fact with regard to the compensability of the officers' lunch period. Additionally, the record did not establish a regularly recurring work period of 28 days, or any duration, as required by the FSLA. Consequently, the court held that the department's 29 U.S.C. §207(k) defense must also be determined by a jury.

a. Cases Finding That a Meal Period Is Compensable

In *AFSCME Local 889 v. Louisiana*,[75] the Fifth Circuit affirmed a ruling that the state of Louisiana was required under

---

[73] *Id.*

[74] 2001 WL 293115 (N.D. Ill. 2001).

[75] 145 F.3d 280, 4 WH Cases2d 1355 (5th Cir. 1998).

the FLSA to compensate correction officers for lunch periods, because the officers were required to eat lunch in the cafeteria with inmates and were required to be prepared to react to disturbances or other needs.

In *Hoffman v. St. Joseph's Hospital of Atlanta Inc.*,[76] a federal district court sitting in Georgia held that respiratory therapists should be compensated for their 30-minute meal breaks. The court held that the fact that the employees were required to wear pagers during their meal breaks and that failure to respond to pages subjected the employees to discipline established that the employees were not "fully relieved of their responsibilities during their meal period." However, this decision has been vacated and may no longer be cited.

In *Bernard v. IBP Inc.*,[77] the Fifth Circuit affirmed the decision of the district court based on a jury finding that maintenance employees at a meat processing plant were entitled to compensation for meal breaks. The district court had determine that although a bona fide meal break of (in this case) 30 minutes is not to be considered time worked, the burden of proof is on the employer to show that such a meal period is primarily for the benefit of the employee. The court had denied the defendant's proffered instruction, and refused to permit argument to the jury, that plaintiffs were entitled to pay only for those lunch periods which were actually interrupted by problems requiring their immediate attention.[78] The jury determined that the meal breaks were predominantly for the employer's benefit because employees were required to wear their radios and tools during lunch, could not leave the site, and had their lunch breaks interrupted frequently by work demands. The court also upheld a jury instruction stating the critical issue for determining whether the meal breaks are compensated "is whether the employee can use the time effectively for his or her own purposes."

---

[76] 4 WH Cases2d 972 (N.D. Ga. 1998), *order vacated* (July 26, 1999).
[77] 154 F.3d 259, 4 WH Cases2d 1604 (5th Cir. 1998).
[78] *Id.* at 265–66.

In *Hartsell v. Dr. Pepper Bottling Co.*,[79] the Fifth Circuit affirmed the trial court's ruling that employees who worked as merchandisers building and stocking displays in stores were entitled to compensation for meal periods. The district court's finding that the time was spent predominantly for the benefit of the employer was supported by employees' testimony that they rarely took their meal period and that they were verbally disciplined when they took their meal period.

In *Herman v. Hogar Praderas de Amor, Inc.*,[80] a federal district court in Puerto Rico held that nurses' aides and maintenance employees were entitled to compensation for portions of meal breaks in which they worked. The employees would sign out for an hour at lunch time but would continue to work for approximately 30 minutes.[81]

b. *Cases Finding That a Meal Period Is Not Compensable*

In *Roy v. County of Lexington,*[82] the Fourth Circuit, applying the predominant benefit test, affirmed the trial court's ruling that emergency medical service paramedics and technicians were not entitled to compensation for meal periods. The trial court had found that the paramedics had no official responsibilities during the meal periods other than to respond to emergency calls and that they were permitted to go anywhere within their 82-square-mile response zone during meal time.[83]

In *McKnight v. Kimberly Clark Corp.*,[84] the Tenth Circuit ruled that a lunch break was primarily for the benefit of the employee and therefore not compensable, despite the contention that the employee was not allowed to leave work during lunch and was on call during his lunch break.

---

[79]207 F.3d 269, 5 WH Cases2d 1700 (5th Cir. 2000).

[80]130 F. Supp. 2d 257 (D.P.R. 2001).

[81]*Id.* at 267.

[82]141 F.3d 533, 4 WH Cases2d 869 (4th Cir. 1998).

[83]*Id.* at 545 (in the event of an emergency, the paramedics were paid for the entire meal period).

[84]149 F.3d 1125, 4 WH Cases2d 1297 (10th Cir. 1998).

In *Arrington v. City of Macon*,[85] a federal district court considered whether police officers were entitled under the FLSA to compensation for meals times and held that they were not, despite the fact that they were (1) subject to immediate call into service during meal breaks, (2) required to remain in uniform, (3) subject to interruptions by inquiries from citizens, and (4) required to maintain constant radio contact. The court found insufficient evidence that the predominant benefit of the meal period was for the city or that the officers were unable to utilize their meal periods for the intended purpose of eating a meal. The court, however, did find that the officers were entitled to compensation on those occasions when they were actually called from their lunch breaks to work, or when they received no lunch break at all.

In *Powell v. Simon Management Group*,[86] the Kansas Supreme Court also applied the predominant benefit test in holding that shopping mall security guards and a maintenance worker who monitored their radios during their lunch breaks and were to respond to calls if no one else was available or if an emergency situation occurred were not entitled to compensation for their meal periods under the FLSA. The court determined that the services provided by the security guards and maintenance workers during their lunch breaks did not "eclipse[ ] the central purpose of the break as a time for the employees to relax and eat."[87] On those occasions when the employees are deprived of time to eat and relax, they are eligible for compensation.

In *Leahy v. City of Chicago*,[88] police officers' 30-minute meal periods were held not compensable. Restrictions on the officers

---

[85]986 F. Supp. 1474, 4 WH Cases2d 348 (M.D. Ga. 1997).

[86]960 P.2d 212, 4 WH Cases2d 1200 (Kan. 1998).

[87]*Id.* at 221.

[88]785 F. Supp 1724, 30 WH Cases 1656 (N.D. Ill. 1992), *aff'd on other reasoning,* 96 F.3d 228, 231, 3 WH Cases2d 801 (7th Cir. 1996), *cert. denied,* 117 S. Ct. 1818 (1997). The court of appeals decision in this case, involving the effect of the collective bargaining agreement on FLSA overtime entitlement, where the agreement guaranteed overtime compensation for hours worked in excess of 8 in a day but did not include meal periods as compensable, is discussed in the Treatise in Chapter 11, "Government Employment," §V.C.2. [Special Provisions That Apply to Fire Protection and Law Enforcement Employees of Public Agencies; Compensable Hours of Work Rules; Meal Time].

during meal breaks included the following: (1) permission was necessary to take a meal break; (2) permission was necessary for an officer to leave an assigned district during a meal break; (3) officers were required to remain in uniform during a meal period; (4) no more than two officers were permitted to congregate during a meal break without permission; (5) two-person units were required to break at the same time; (6) officers were required to end their meals upon request; (7) officers were required to respond to emergencies and requests for assistance; and (8) officers were required to be available to the dispatcher by radio.

In *Bayles v. American Medical Response of Colorado, Inc.*,[89] ambulance drivers' hour-long meal breaks were found not compensable. The court noted that ambulance drivers were permitted to leave the premises during meal times to eat at restaurants or run personal errands; the only restrictions placed on the employees were that they had to maintain radio contact with their dispatch center and remain with or near the ambulance and within the district. The court applied the predominant benefit test and concluded that because the employees could comfortably and adequately pass the meal time, the time was not compensable.

In *Hahn v. Pima County,*[90] an Arizona appellate court affirmed the trial court's decision granting summary judgment in favor of Pima County (the "County") after it was sued by corrections officers seeking overtime compensation for unpaid meal breaks. The court found that the employees did not establish that they spent their meal time for the predominant benefit of the County, even though the corrections officers were implicitly required to carry their portable radios and service revolvers, were expected to respond to emergency situations or citizen inquiries, and were subject to calls and interruptions from fellow

---

[89]937 F. Supp. 1477, 1485–87, 3 WH Cases2d 845 (D. Colo.), *reconsideration granted in part,* 950 F. Supp. 1053, 3 WH Cases2d 1317 (D. Colo. 1996), *on reconsideration,* 962 F. Supp. 1346, 3 WH Cases2d 1567 (D. Colo. 1997).

[90]24 P.3d 614, 7 WH Cases2d 434 (Ariz. Ct. App. 2001).

employees, inmates and visitors.[91] The court explained that, at most, the record reflected employees "enjoyed something less than unfettered freedom during meal periods," but the employees did not provide evidence as to how often and to what extent the theoretical restrictions interfered with employees' primary lunch-break activity of eating.[92] In addition, a longtime corrections officer had acknowledged that employees' primary activity during their meal periods was consuming meals.

In *Salon Enterprises, Inc. v. Langford*,[93] a Kansas appellate court reversed the trial court and determined that a salon stylist's meal breaks were not compensable. The salon stylist sued her former beauty salon employer in a Kansas state court alleging a claim under the FLSA to recover unpaid wages as a result of her not being compensated for meal breaks. The employee successfully argued at a bench trial that she should have been compensated for her meal breaks because she had to be "available" to work over lunch.[94] The court noted that the evidence did not establish that the employee was required to be available during her meal break; rather, the employee had the choice as to whether to work during her break, and was compensated for the occasions when she did work during her meal break.[95]

In *Brown v. Howard Industries*,[96] a federal district court in Mississippi granted the employer's motion to dismiss where production workers sued their employer under the FLSA seeking compensation for their 30-minute lunch breaks. The employees alleged that, by remaining on their employer's premises, their lunch breaks were primarily for their employer's benefit, and the failure to pay them for the time on their lunch breaks violated the FLSA.[97] In rejecting this argument, the court held that the mere fact that the employees were restricted to the

---

[91] *Id.* at 616–20.
[92] *Id.* at 619.
[93] 31 P.3d 290 (Kan. Ct. App. 2000).
[94] *Id.* at 293.
[95] *Id.*
[96] 116 F. Supp. 2d 764 (S.D. Miss. 2000).
[97] *Id.* at 765.

employer's premises during their lunch period did not make the lunch period compensable, and noted that, to sustain a cause of action, "Plaintiffs must allege that some duty imposed upon Plaintiffs during the lunch break benefited Defendant, not merely that the fact that Plaintiffs were required to remain on the premises during the lunch break benefited Defendant."[98]

D. Sleeping Time and Certain Other Activities

2. *Duty Period of 24 Hours or More*

The Fourth Circuit has ruled that emergency medical service paramedics and technicians were not entitled to compensation for an 8-hour sleep period where only 35 percent of sleep periods were interrupted such that the paramedics received less than 5 hours' sleep.[99] (The paramedics were paid for hours actually worked during the scheduled sleep time.)

In *Braziel v. Tobosa Development Services*,[100] the Tenth Circuit upheld the district court's holding that residential assistants for developmentally disabled people were not entitled to compensation under the FLSA for sleep time in their patients' homes, whether their shifts consisted of more or fewer than 24 hours. The court had found that there was an "implied agreement" as to the noncompensability of sleep time because at the time of hiring, each of the plaintiffs was aware of defendants' policy of not paying for sleep time, and, although some of them complained to their supervisors, none grieved the policy, although they were aware of the grievance procedure. The court held that the Department of Labor regulation concerning the deduction of sleep time from hours worked, 29 C.F.R. §785.23, applied to residential assistants with work shifts of less than 24 hours. It pointed out that the regulation does not require permanent residence, only that the employee reside on the premises "for extended periods of time."

---

[98] *Id.* at 767.

[99] Roy v. County of Lexington, 141 F.3d 533, 546, 4 WH Cases2d 869, 878 (4th Cir. 1998).

[100] 166 F.3d 1061, 5 WH Cases2d 97 (10th Cir. 1999).

In *Salazar v. Life Ambulance Service, Inc.*,[101] a Texas district court denied cross motions for summary judgment and held that it is a jury question whether designating 23 hours of a 24-hour shift as a "sleeping period" provides a bona fide sleeping period as required under the FLSA. Former and current Emergency Medical Technicians (EMTs) alleged that their employer had illegally docked hours for "sleep time" under the FLSA. Although no more than 8 hours of any 24-hour shift was allocated to uncompensated sleep time, the employer provided that the first hour of a 24-hour shift would be compensable and thereafter deducted hours if an EMT had a period of 5 hours or more uninterrupted by an emergency call. The time was deducted regardless of whether an employee had a meaningful opportunity to sleep. On cross motions for summary judgment the employer argued that the court need determine only whether more than 8 hours was ultimately deducted from any employee's compensation. However, the court found that the FLSA required the employer to provide a bona fide regularly scheduled sleeping period for the employees. A reasonable jury could find that designating 23 hours of a 24-hour shift as a "sleeping period" does not provide a bona fide, regularly scheduled sleep period under the statute.

3. *Employee Residing on Employer's Premises or Working at Home*

In *Gaby v. Omaha Home for Boys*,[102] the Eighth Circuit held that an agreement between houseparents and a group home was "reasonable" when it provided that the houseparents were compensated for 60 hours with overtime payments for hours over 40. The court rejected the houseparents' contention that they worked considerably more than 10 hours per day during the 6-day workweek. For support, the court cited testimony that, with two houseparents, one parent could often respond to the occa-

---

[101] 2001 WL 685755 (W.D. Tex. 2001).

[102] 140 F.3d 1184, 1189–90, 4 WH Cases2d 865, 867 (8th Cir. 1998). As noted in the Treatise, p. 491, "any reasonable agreement between the parties that takes into consideration all the pertinent facts" is acceptable. 29 C.F.R. §785.23.

sional demand or problem and that in this way it was possible to "cover" even more than 10 hours of activity in any given day.[103]

In *Shannon v. Pleasant Valley Community Living Arrangements*,[104] a federal district court held that employees whose shifts required them to reside at group homes for mentally retarded persons from 3:00 p.m. on Wednesday until 10:00 a.m. the following Wednesday resided at the homes for "extended periods of time" for purposes of the regulation (29 C.F.R. §785.23), allowing employers to enter into a reasonable agreement regarding sleep time with employees who reside for extended periods on employer's premises, even if employees had periods of complete freedom from all duties. Statements in the employer's personnel manual that no contract was created and that terms of employment were "unilaterally adopted" by the employer did not preclude a finding that exclusion of sleep time in calculation of overtime was a result of employee-employer agreement for purposes of allowing the employer to enter into a reasonable agreement regarding sleep time with employees. However, the court found that summary judgment was precluded because there were genuine issues of material fact as to whether the employer paid overtime only if an employee received less than 8 hours' sleep and whether the employer told employees not to turn in any other overtime for sleep interruptions.

Responding to a question raised on behalf of a homeless shelter, which contemplated hiring a "night emergency response worker" to be on the premises from 10:00 p.m. until 8:00 a.m. five nights a week, as to whether the hours during which the employee was not actually attending clients could, pursuant to 29 C.F.R. §785.23, be treated as sleep time and thus not compensated, the Wage and Hour Division opined that it could not.[105] The Division noted that although the shift—10 p.m. to 8 a.m.—involved hours the employee might be sleeping, the time did not qualify for the work-time exclusion because the employee did not have complete freedom from all duties and was required to

---

[103] 140 F.3d at 1189–90.
[104] 82 F. Supp. 2d 426 (W.D. Pa. 2000).
[105] 2000 WL 1537274 (Jan. 6, 2000).

be physically on the premises. Therefore, all of his time would be compensable.

E. Preparatory and Concluding Activities

In *AFSCME Local 889 v. Louisiana,*[106] the Fifth Circuit held that a 15-minute roll-call period for field officers at state correctional facilities was compensable. The state had argued that the roll-call period was offset by a compensated lunch period. The court, however, concluded that the state was required to compensate the officers for the lunch period because of the circumstances of the case, and it therefore held that the field officers were entitled to additional compensation for the roll-call period.

Continuing the development of the law concerning the compensability of clothes changing and associated activities in the meat-packing industry, *Metzler v. IBP, Inc.,*[107] involved a meat slaughter and packing employer that failed to record and compensate its meat-processing employees for time spent performing various pre- and post-shift activities. In determining the amount of damages, the district court had made the following findings on the average reasonable time to perform each compensable activity: (1) 3 minutes to wait for and exchange knives; (2) 3 minutes to put on and take off personal protective equipment; (3) 3 minutes of wait time at wash stations to clean protective equipment; (4) 2 minutes for post-shift cleaning of protective equipment; and (5) 3 minutes of preshift and post-shift compensable walk time.

On appeal, the employer challenged the district court's factual finding that 3 minutes was a reasonable amount of time for employees to don and doff the required safety equipment because employees who were being compensated for the time taken to wash this specialized equipment and time spent to wait

---

[106]145 F.3d 280, 4 WH Cases2d 1355 (5th Cir. 1998).

[107]127 F.3d 959, 4 WH Cases2d 229 (10th Cir. 1997), *earlier litigation involving these matters decided sub nom.* Reich v. IBP, Inc., 38 F. 3d 1123, 2 WH Cases2d 641 (10th Cir. 1994).

for the washing facilities to open actually removed the equipment while waiting to wash or during the washing itself, and thus the court had double-counted the time needed to remove the safety equipment. Therefore, half the time allotted for putting on and taking off the protective gear (1.5 minutes) should be subtracted from the amount of time used to calculate the backpay award, the employer asserted. The U.S. Court of Appeals for the Tenth Circuit held that the district court's estimate of 3 minutes for putting on and taking off the required safety equipment was not clearly erroneous. The Tenth Circuit first noted that the employer had failed to present evidence that the employees were required to remove the equipment while waiting to wash or that the equipment could not have been removed at another site before washing up. Second, the employer's own time-study estimates accounted for a separate amount of time to remove the equipment. Third, all the estimates and demonstrations showed that the time to put on the equipment far exceeded the time to remove it.

In another meat-packing industry case,[108] the defendant conceded on appeal that the similar activities involved would be compensable if they were not of a de minimis nature. The district court had concluded that 10 minutes per day should be compensated, and the defendant appealed. Although both the trial and the appellate courts found that the time would be administratively difficult to record, the court of appeals determined that the total amount of time involved, both on a per-employee basis (10 minutes per day over 3 years) and on an aggregate basis for all of the employees as a group (which the employer had contended was not appropriately taken into account) would properly be considered substantial, and that the regularity of the activities involved also weighed against a de minimis finding. It therefore affirmed the district court's decision.

In contrast to the meat-packing industry cases,[109] a district court in Texas found "line time" to be an acceptable measure of

[108]Reich v. Monfort, 144 F.3d 1329, 4 WH Cases2d 1106 (10th Cir. 1998).

[109]See The Fair Labor Standards Act 2001 Cumulative Supplement Chapter 8, III.E., pages 174–75.

compensable time in the poultry industry. In *Anderson v. Pilgrim's Pride Corp.*,[110] two issues were before the court: (1) whether the manner in which the employer utilized line time to measure hours worked complied with the recordkeeping provisions of the FLSA, and (2) whether the donning, doffing, and cleaning of the various items of clothing worn by the line employees prior to the shift, during breaks, and after the shift required compensation. After a bench trial, the court ruled in favor of the employer on all issues. Neither the FLSA, nor any regulation interpreting it, prohibited the employer's use of line time to capture compensable hours. Also, because the donning and doffing of work clothes did not involve physical or mental exertion and took only seconds, the time was not compensable. In addition, the issue had been rejected in collective bargaining agreement negotiations. The non-compensability of these activities was both practice and custom in the industry.

In another poultry workers case, *Pressley v. Sanderson Farms, Inc.*,[111] the plaintiffs, poultry processing employees, claimed they should be compensated for time spent changing clothes, sanitizing tools and garments, and walking to and from workstations before and after shifts and during unpaid meal periods. The court granted summary judgment in favor of the employer. The court held that "as a matter of law the time spent by Plaintiffs walking, . . . donning, doffing, and cleaning their equipment, is not compensable work under the FLSA," and is excluded from compensable time by the Portal-to-Portal Act. In addition, the court disregarded the plaintiffs' contentions that they spent 7 to 20 minutes per day donning, doffing, and sanitizing, finding instead that the activities take "minimal time" and, therefore, are de minimis as a matter of law, but it rejected defendant's argument under Section 3(o) that its collective bargaining agreement with plaintiff-employees completely barred plaintiffs' claims that the defendant failed to pay them for all hours worked. After noting that the defendants had failed to bring to

---

[110] 147 F. Supp. 2d 677 (E.D. Tex. 2001).

[111] 143 Lab. Cas. ¶34,262 (S.D. Tex. 2001), 2001 WL 850017, *aff'd,* No. 01-20527 (5th Cir. Mar. 7, 2002).

the court's attention all the pertinent and arguably controlling circuit court case law, it rested its partial denial of defendant's summary judgment motion on the finding that a factual issue existed as to whether all plaintiffs were covered by the collective bargaining agreement.

Courts continue to hold that training and care of police dogs after hours is compensable. In *Holzapfel v. Town of Newburgh,*[112] for instance, the Second Circuit stated that such activity could be "work" because "walking, feeding, training, grooming and cleaning up are integral and indispensable parts of the handler's principal activities." The court further noted that the determination of the amount of time actually spent in such activities was a question for the jury. The court concluded that if the work was required by—or was primarily for the benefit of—the employer, then the activity would be compensable, but that any time spent by the employee for personal pleasure or to inflate earnings would not be compensable.

That court also held that the employer must have actual and constructive knowledge that its officers were providing care and training outside normal work hours. Thus, a jury could have determined an amount of time worked after hours for which the employees should have been compensated.

In *DeBraska v. Milwaukee,*[113] a federal district court sitting in Wisconsin considered whether the time that canine unit police officers spent transporting their dogs to and from work was preparatory or concluding compensable time, or merely involved "preliminary" and "postliminary" time under the Portal-to-Portal Act. In declining to grant either party's motion for summary judgment, the court stated that at least part of the time spent transporting the dogs might be considered compensable time if the city (1) required the officers to respond to emergency calls or to maintain contact with the police dispatcher during their commutes, and (2) prohibited the officers from making personal stops during their commute.

---

[112]145 F.3d 516, 4 WH Cases2d 1097 (2d Cir.), *cert. denied,* 119 S. Ct. 619 (1998).
[113]11 F. Supp. 2d 1020, 4 WH Cases2d 1377 (E.D. Wis. 1998).

The court in *Debraska* also addressed the question whether the time canine officers spend caring for their dogs outside work is compensable, or whether such time constitutes "preliminary" and "postliminary" activities. Under the facts of that case, the city compensated the officers for 30 minutes of canine care per day. Referring to the Second Circuit's decision in *Holzapfel v. Town of Newburgh*,[114] the court asked three main questions: first, whether the city required the officers to spend more than 30 minutes per day performing canine care; second, whether the time spent was for the officer's own benefit or for the city's benefit; and third, whether the city knew that the officers spent more than 30 minutes per day. Based on the police officers' presentation of evidence that the city required them to care for their dogs in a certain way, combined with evidence that the officers spent more than 30 minutes per day caring for their dogs, the court granted partial summary judgment to the officers on this issue.

The Federal Circuit in *Bobo v. United States*[115] held that Immigration and Naturalization Service border patrol agent dog handlers were not entitled to compensation for commuting to and from work with their assigned dogs because restrictions placed on handlers while commuting—such as a prohibition on making personal stops, a need to make stops to allow their dogs to exercise and relieve themselves, and a requirement to monitor their radios—were de minimis.

In *Jerzak v. City of South Bend*,[116] a federal district court in Indiana held that a canine officer was not entitled to overtime for time involving the transport of his police dog to and from work. The court stated, however, that travel to and from the veterinarian might be compensable, but whether it was compensable and whether that time was de minimis were issues properly left for the jury.

Other cases involving the care of canines include *Karr v. City of Beaumont*[117] (holding that officers' care and transportation of

[114]145 F.3d 516, 4 WH Cases2d 1097.

[115]136 F.3d 1465 (Fed. Cir. 1998), *aff'g* 37 Fed. Cl. 690, 3 WH Cases2d 1587 (1997).

[116]996 F. Supp. 840, 4 WH Cases2d 736 (N.D. Ind. 1998).

[117]950 F. Supp. 1317, 1322–33 (E.D. Tex. 1997).

dogs and related maintenance of the police vehicles was an integral and indispensable part of officers' duties, but denying summary judgment because a material issue of fact remained in dispute over amount of damages); *Mayhew v. Wells*[118] (holding that dog-care time was overtime and should be compensated at a "half time" rate); *Rudolph v. Metropolitan Airport Commission*[119] (agreement as to the amount of time to be spent caring for dogs was reasonable; officers were not entitled to additional compensation); and *Helmers v. Vestal, New York*[120] (off-duty care of dogs is compensable; commuting time in a marked car is not; and there were genuine issues about time spent on "making and receiving dog-related phone calls").

In *Baker v. Barnard Construction Co.*,[121] the Tenth Circuit noted the difficulty of determining a precise standard for the compensability of activities performed outside employees' normal working hours. Defendants argued that the return travel of employee welders, during which they refueled and restocked their welding rigs, was ordinary home-to-work travel, which is not compensable under the Portal-to-Portal Act absent a contract or custom of compensability. Plaintiffs contended that because the travel was indispensable to the performance of their jobs, it was a principal activity and therefore compensable under the FLSA. The court held that on remand the jury must determine whether such travel time was an "integral and indispensable" part of the welders' principal duties.[122] In making this determination, the jury must resolve factual disputes, including the issues whether the plaintiffs (1) were truly free to go where they wanted at the end of the workday and to use any means of transportation that they chose, and (2) could have left the rig at the work site to be refueled and restocked at the site.

In *Robertson v. Board of County Commissioners*,[123] a federal district court held that genuine issues of material fact existed as to whether sheriff's deputies were denied compensatory time

---

[118]125 F.3d 216, 217 (4th Cir. 1997).

[119]103 F.3d 677, 3 WH Cases2d 1089 (8th Cir. 1996).

[120]3 WH Cases2d 1837 (N.D.N.Y. 1997).

[121]146 F.3d 1214, 4 WH Cases2d 1249 (10th Cir. 1998).

[122]*Id.* at 1219–20.

[123]78 F. Supp. 2d 1142, 5 WH Cases2d 1449 (D. Colo. 1999).

for preshift briefings where there was evidence that the sheriff 's deputies were told to record preshift briefings on their time records but no individual time records were submitted.

In *Aiken v. City of Memphis,*[124] the Sixth Circuit ruled that commuting time of canine officers was not compensable absent evidence that the officers spent more than a de minimis amount of time during their commutes engaged in true dog-care activities such as feeding, training, or walking the dog. The court noted the officers "occasionally" had to stop to feed their dogs, let the dogs out of the cars, clean up after them while driving to work, and discipline them. However, the court did not consider this to be sufficient time to be compensable under the FLSA.

In *Schwertfeger v. Village of Sauk Village,*[125] police officers claimed that their employer violated the FLSA by refusing to compensate them for mandatory 15-minute roll-call periods before the beginning of each shift. The police department argued that it was legal to set off the 15-minute daily roll call against the officers' break periods and lunch. The officers contended that their break periods, totaling one hour a day, were entirely compensable time. The department's primary summary judgment argument was the exemption in 29 U.S.C. §207(k) for employees on a regularly recurring work period of 28 days. The court held that the roll calls were clearly compensable time, but it was unclear whether the department compensated the officers for that time. The court held that roll calls could be set off against meal periods, if the meal periods were non-compensable time. While eating lunch, police officers were required to remain in uniform, respond to emergency calls, and be within a certain range of distance. Therefore, the court found a genuine issue of material fact with regard to the compensability of the officers' lunch period. Additionally, the record did not establish a regularly recurring work period of 28 days, or any duration, as required by the FSLA. Consequently, the court held that the department's 29 U.S.C. §207(k) defense must also be determined by a jury.

---

[124]190 F.3d 753, 5 WH Cases2d 961 (6th Cir. 1999), *cert. denied,* 528 U.S. 1157, 5 WH Cases2d 1632 (2000).

[125]2001 WL 293115 (N.D. Ill. 2001).

F. Lectures, Meetings, and Training Programs

In *Dade County v. Alvarez,*[126] the Eleventh Circuit held that physical training conducted off duty in order to maintain required physical fitness standards is not compensable work within the meaning of the FLSA. The plaintiffs were police officers assigned to a "special response team" (SRT). SRT officers' physical conditioning was evaluated monthly. Notwithstanding the employer's restrictions on on-duty training, SRT officers were instructed to do whatever was necessary to maintain adequate cardiovascular and strength levels. SRT supervisors, however, never directed SRT officers to engage in any specific off-duty routine or training. The court, applying the four-prong test described in the Treatise, and relying on two opinions of the Wage and Hour Administrator, determined that time spent training was not compensable.

Of particular note is the *Alvarez* court's discussion of the voluntariness and "directly related to" factors. On the issue of voluntariness, the court found that the physical training was voluntary because (1) there was no evidence the officers were required to spend a certain amount of time on training or to perform certain exercises; (2) there were no adverse employment consequences from not training while not on duty, provided they passed the fitness test; and (3) the officers enjoyed complete discretion in the type, location, and duration of off-duty training. With regard to "directly related to," the court held that the county did not require the officers to develop a specific skill unique to their employment as SRT officers. Rather, the off-duty training "also provides the individual officers with benefits that extend beyond their employment position."[127]

In an opinion letter[128] signed by a member of the staff of the Office of Enforcement Policy, the Department of Labor discussed the application of 29 C.F.R. §785.27 to the case of an

---

[126]124 F.3d 1380, 4 WH Cases2d 225 (11th Cir. 1997), *cert. denied,* 118 S. Ct. 1904 (1998).

[127]*Id.* at 1385, 4 WH Cases2d 225.

[128]Opinion Letter dated Feb. 16, 2001, WHM: 20010216.

employee assigned to the Corrections Division of the Sheriff's Department, and who hoped at a later time to be transferred to the Road Patrol Division, spending off-duty time "riding with" a Road Patrol Deputy and participating in assignments. The letter found that the first two conditions (voluntariness and outside regular duty hours) were met, that the third condition (directly related to current employment) might or might not be met (insufficient information having been provided), but that the fourth condition, that no productive work be done, was not met because the "ride along" deputy would undoubtedly be giving hands-on assistance to the road deputy if the occasion presented itself.

In another opinion letter[129] on this issue the Department addressed the compensability of state-mandated training attended by local school district bus drivers. Reviewing the conditions of 29 C.F.R. §785.27, the letter found that the first and fourth conditions were met, that the third condition might be met if it was the type of training that corresponded to courses offered by independent educational institutions (as appeared might be the case), and that the second condition, voluntariness, would be met where the requirement was imposed by the state directly on the individuals involved in the employment, rather than on or by the employer. Thus it appeared that the time was probably not compensable.

In *Herman v. Hogar Praderas de Amor, Inc.*,[130] the Secretary of Labor's case included a claim that employees should have been paid for the first two days of their employment, during which the employer considered them to be trainees and did not pay them. During this period the court found that the employer offered little or no instruction, and that the employees would perform the regular duties of the position without any special supervision or instruction. Accordingly the court found that each worker was entitled to additional compensation for the "training" time.

---

[129]Opinion Letter dated May 3, 2001, signed by member of Office of Enforcement Policy staff, WHM: 20010503. *See also* staff Opinion Letter dated Sept. 14, 2000, WHM: 99:5414.

[130]130 F. Supp. 2d 257 (D.P.R. 2001).

1. *Involuntary Attendance*

In *DeBraska v. Milwaukee*,[131] a federal district court in Wisconsin held that police officers' voluntary appearances at predisciplinary hearings and meetings were not compensable. The city had a practice of conducting a "Loudermill hearing"[132] prior to imposing discipline, and the plaintiffs contended that their attendance was as a practical matter involuntary. The court found that there was no formal requirement that the officers attend the hearings or meetings,[133] and the officers failed to demonstrate any infringement of their personal freedom as a result of attendance at the hearings or meetings.

2. *"Directly Related to" Employee's Job*

The Wage and Hour Division opined that although training for licensed vocational nurses (LVNs) was clearly related to their job, it would not be compensable outside of working hours because it corresponded to courses offered by independent bona fide institutions of learning.[134]

G. Travel Time

1. *Preliminary and Postliminary Travel*

In *DeBraska v. Milwaukee*,[135] a federal district court in Wisconsin considered whether the time police officers in a canine unit spent transporting their dogs to and from work was preparatory or concluding compensable time, or merely involved

---

[131]F. Supp. 2d 1020, 4 WH Cases2d 1377 (E.D. Wis. 1998).

[132]In *Cleveland Board of Education v. Loudermill*, 470 U.S. 532, 544–45 (1985), the U.S. Supreme Court decided that public employees are constitutionally entitled to some form of hearing before the involuntary termination of their employment.

[133]The court made no reference to the Labor Department regulations, 29 C.F.R. §785.28, which provide that attendance is required if the employee is "led to believe that . . . continuance in employment would be adversely affected by nonattendance." *See* Treatise, §III.F.1. [Application of Principles; Lectures, Meetings, and Training Programs; Involuntary Attendance] at p. 495.

[134]1999 WL 1788164 (Dep't of Labor Sept. 30, 1999).

[135]11 F. Supp. 2d 1020, 4 WH Cases2d 1377.

"preliminary" and "postliminary" travel. Declining to grant either party's motion for summary judgment on this issue, the court stated that at least part of the time spent transporting the dogs might be considered compensable if the city required the officers to respond to emergency calls or to maintain contact with the police dispatcher, and if the city prohibited the officers from making personal stops during their commute.

In *Baker v. Barnard Construction Co.*,[136] the Tenth Circuit noted the difficulty of applying a definite standard for determining the compensability of activities performed outside employees' normal working hours. The defendants argued that the return travel of employee welders, during which they refueled and restocked their welding rigs, was ordinary home-to-work travel, which is not compensable under the Portal-to-Portal Act absent a contract or custom of compensability. The plaintiffs contended that because the travel was indispensable to the performance of their jobs, it was a "principal" activity and therefore compensable under the FLSA. The court held that on remand, the jury must determine whether such travel time was an "integral and indispensable" part of the welders' principal duties.[137] In making this determination, a jury must resolve factual disputes, including whether the plaintiffs were truly free to go where they wanted at the end of the workday, to use any means of transportation that they chose, and whether they could have left the rig at the work site to be refueled and restocked at the site.

In *Abeyta v. Phelps Dodge Corp.*,[138] the court was required to decide whether certain travel by mine employees to the place of the morning lineup was compensable under an exception to the Portal-to-Portal Act's noncompensability provisions for activities made compensable pursuant to "a custom or practice in effect, at the time of such activity, at the establishment or other place where such employee is employed."[139] Finding that the custom

---

[136] 146 F.3d 1214, 4 WH Cases2d 1249 (10th Cir. 1998).
[137] *Id.* at 1219–20.
[138] 3 WH Cases2d 1422 (D. Ariz. 1997).
[139] 29 U.S.C. §254(a).

in question provided compensation for a related but different activity (namely, travel from the lineup site to the work site, rather than from the beginning of transportation to the lineup site, where previously the lineup site was reached by the employees before company transportation began), the court held the time noncompensable.

In *United Transportation Union Local 1745 v. Albuquerque,*[140] the Tenth Circuit held that time bus drivers spent on a shuttle bus traveling from the terminal point of the first shift, and to the commencement point of the later shift during the course of a split-shift work day, was compensable. The court reasoned that "there is a meaningful distinction between time spent shuttling to or from a relief point, where a working shift just ended or is about to begin, and the remainder of the drivers' split shift periods, during which they have an extended block of time in which to pursue, as most testified they do, purely personal pursuits."[141] During this period, "the drivers are not free to do whatever they wish—they must spend that time traveling to or from a location dictated by the City, and situated to serve the City's need to provide an efficient and useful bus transportation system."[142] Thus, this time was part of the drivers' "principal activity."

In *Aiken v. City of Memphis,*[143] the Sixth Circuit affirmed a ruling that police officers' commute time to work was not compensable. The police officers contended that they should be compensated because they had to respond to emergencies that they observed or that were communicated by radio dispatch while driving to work. They also contended that they should be compensated because the presence of marked police vehicles on the streets deterred crime. The court held the commute time not to be compensable because the officers were compensated for emergencies if the response time was 30 minutes or longer, the amount of work involved in monitoring the police radio was

---

[140] 178 F.3d 1109, 5 WH Cases2d 555 (10th Cir. 1999).

[141] *Id.*, 5 WH Cases2d at 562.

[142] *Id.*

[143] 190 F.3d 753, 5 WH Cases2d 961 (6th Cir. 1999), *cert. denied,* 528 U.S. 1157, 5 WH Cases2d 1632 (2000).

de minimis, and the deterrent effect of marked police cars on the streets was irrelevant for FLSA purposes.

In *Kavanagh v. Grand Union Co.*,[144] the Second Circuit affirmed the district court's summary judgment for the employer in the case of a supermarket refrigerator repairer who worked at various sites across a three-state region, and who claimed but had been denied overtime compensation for the 7 to 8 hours a day he spent traveling to the first work site and home from the last site of the day. Acknowledging the employee's situation was "inequitable,"[145] the court nevertheless concluded that the FLSA did not permit a construction that would require the employer to compensate the employee regardless of the length of that distance or the benefit to the employer of having only one employee cover such a large geographic area. The court stated that the Department of Labor regulation providing "normal travel" from home to work is not compensable is not an objective standard, but a subjective standard defined by what is usual within the confines of a particular employment relationship.

In *Steelman v. Telco Telephone Co., Inc.*,[146] a federal district court in Oregon denied summary judgment motions filed by both parties where a telephone network systems installer brought suit for overtime compensation against his employer telephone company for the time he traveled directly to the first customer site from home, and directly home from the last customer work site. The employer argued that this travel time was not compensable under Section 4(a)(1) of the Portal-to-Portal Act.[147] The employee contended that while he was traveling he carried indispensable equipment and tools for his job.[148] The court noted that under Section 4(a)(1), travel time from the employee's home to a customer's site may be compensable if it is "integral

[144]192 F.3d 269, 5 WH Cases2d 1089 (2d Cir. 1999).

[145]"Although Kavanagh's situation strikes us as inequitable, nothing in the pertinent statutes and regulations requires Grand Union to compensate Kavanagh for his travel time." *Id.*, 5 WH Cases2d at 1090.

[146]2001 WL 21361 (D.Or. 2001).

[147]*Id.* at *2.

[148]*Id.*

and indispensable" to the employee's principal activity.[149] To determine whether an activity is integral and indispensable, the court considered whether the employer requires the employee to do the work, to what degree the employer benefits from the work, and to what extent the activity is indispensable to the primary goal of the employee's work.[150] The court ultimately concluded that disputed issues of fact remained as to whether the particular travel time at issue was integral and indispensable to the employee's principal activity.[151]

3. *Overnight Travel*

In *Imada v. City of Hercules*,[152] the plaintiff police officers were required to attend training away from Hercules a few times a year. Depending on the location involved, they sometimes made trips daily and sometimes stayed overnight. The court considered whether the FLSA required the city to compensate police officers for the time that the officers spent traveling to the training locations. Where the travel was to a destination that required an overnight trip, the court held, "[t]he regulations plainly exempt from compensation an employee's travel to a location where he or she must stay overnight unless it cuts across the normal workday or the corresponding hours on nonworking days,"[153] and thus it affirmed summary judgment for the employer on this point.

4. *Special One-Day Trips*

In *Imada v. City of Hercules*,[154] the court also considered whether the FLSA requires a city to compensate police officers for the time that the officers spent commuting from their homes to mandatory off-site training locations when that time ex-

---

[149] *Id.*
[150] *Id.* at *3.
[151] *Id.*
[152] 138 F.3d 1294, 4 WH Cases2d 705 (9th Cir. 1998).
[153] *See* 29 C.F.R. §785.39 (1997).
[154] 138 F.3d 1294, 4 WH Cases2d 705 (9th Cir. 1998).

ceeded their regular commuting time. The court recognized the regulation providing for compensation of travel time when an employee goes on certain kinds of trips: "Section 785.37 provides such an exception for an unusual 1-day assignment in another city to meet a special need."[155] However, the court found that the conditions of this exception did not apply and rejected the plaintiffs' contention, finding first that the travel was not unusual, but rather normal, contemplated, and in fact required by the officers' collective bargaining agreement. On this point, the court also noted that travel need not occur frequently to be considered normal or usual. Second, the court found that the travel was not undertaken to meet a special need of the employer. Although the travel to the off-site training facility conferred benefits on the city, the court concluded that the officers realized an equivalent, if not greater, benefit from the training because they were required to attend the training sessions in order to maintain their state law enforcement certifications. Because it was neither unusual nor specialized, the travel time fell outside the regulatory exception and was considered uncompensable ordinary home-to-work travel time.

5. Travel "All in a Day's Work"

In *DeBraska v. Milwaukee*,[156] a federal district court in Wisconsin addressed whether the time that officers spent commuting from one work location to another was compensable time. The officers claimed that they drove their own cars to the district stations to pick up department vehicles, which were necessary for the completion of their duties, and then drove those department squad cars to the substations to which they were assigned. These facts fairly match those given as an illustration in the regulations, where the travel is characterized as "part of the day's work."[157] The city agreed that officers working in certain departments—namely, the background investigation unit and the

[155] *Id.*, 4 WH Cases2d at 706 (citing 29 C.F.R. §785.37).
[156] 11 F. Supp. 2d 1020, 4 WH Cases2d 1377 (E.D. Wis. 1998).
[157] 29 C.F.R. §785.38.

senior citizens unit—were not in fact compensated for this travel time, and conceded that they should be. As to these officers, the district court granted summary judgment. As to officers assigned to other departments, the city argued that since the officers appeared for roll call at the district stations, their compensation began at that time and not when they arrived at their substations. Therefore, according to the city, these officers were compensated for their travel time between the district stations and their assigned substations. The district court accepted this claim, granting the city summary judgment as to the officers who reported to the district station for roll call.

In *Breen v. Concrete by Wagner, Inc.*,[158] a federal district court in Illinois held that the defendant's conduct was willful when the defendant was aware of the FLSA but never investigated whether the FLSA was violated by its policies of paying travel time to a jobsite at a flat rate that was lower than the regular hourly rate and not including the time spent in travel as hours worked, and of not paying any compensation at all for return travel from a jobsite at the end of the day.

6. *Private Automobile and Employer Vehicle Use*

Relying on the 1996 amendment to the Portal-to-Portal Act,[159] a federal district court has held that a city did not violate the FLSA by failing to compensate police officers for time they spent commuting to and from work in city-owned vehicles.[160] Additionally, the court determined that the officers were not entitled to compensation for time spent on vehicle maintenance.[161]

In both *Shepard v. Burlington*[162] and *Bartholomew v. City of Burlington*,[163] the U.S. District Court for the District of Kansas held that patrol officers were not entitled to overtime compen-

[158]1999 WL 1016267 (N.D. Ill. 1999).

[159]29 U.S.C. §254(a).

[160]Aiken v. Memphis, 985 F. Supp. 740, 743–44, 4 WH Cases2d 408, 410 (W.D. Tenn. 1997).

[161]*Id.* at 740, 4 WH Cases2d at 410.

[162]4 WH Cases2d 1149 (D. Kan. 1998).

[163]5 F. Supp. 2d 1161, 4 WH Cases2d 1156 (D. Kan. 1998).

sation for time spent driving to and from work in a city patrol car—even though the officers conducted briefings on the way to work with an officer going off duty. The court first found that under Section 4 of the Portal-to-Portal Act, an officer is not entitled to compensation for travel to and from work when an agreement exists regarding the officer's use of city vehicles. Second, the court held that time spent commuting in city vehicles was noncompensable when the use of such vehicles for travel was within the "normal commuting area" and the city had an agreement with employees regarding use of city vehicles as required by the Employee Commuting Flexibility Act.

The Sixth Circuit affirmed the lower court's ruling[164] that a municipal employer did not violate the FLSA by failing to compensate police officers for time they spent on cleaning and scheduling the maintenance of city-owned vehicles used by officers for commuting to and from work. The court cited the 1996 amendments to the statute, which provide among other things that "the use of an employer's vehicle for travel by an employee and activities performed by an employee which are incidental to the use of such vehicle for commuting shall not be considered part of the employee's principal activities . . . [provided certain conditions are met]."[165]

In *Manners v. State of New York*,[166] a New York state court addressed the issue of whether time spent by a state employee traveling to and from his home to the actual place of performance of his principal activities in his employer's vehicle was compensable when the employee's use of the employer's vehicle was nonconsensual. The court held that if there is not an employer-employee agreement, then the 1996 amendment to the FLSA[167]—requiring an employer-employee agreement for the time to be noncompensable—is inapplicable and the issue

---

[164] Aiken v. City of Memphis, 985 F. Supp. 740, 743–44, 4 WH Cases2d 408, 410 (W.D. Tenn. 1997), *aff'd on other grounds,* 190 F.3d 753, 5 WH Cases2d 961 (6th Cir.), *cert. denied,* 528 U.S. 1157, 5 WH Cases2d 1632 (2000).

[165] 5 WH Cases2d 961, 965 (6th Cir. 1999).

[166] 703 N.Y.S.2d 375 (Ct. Cl. 2000).

[167] 29 U.S.C. §254.

of the compensability of the commuting time is decided by analyzing the activities involved. Imposing that analysis on the facts presented, the court found that the employee was merely traveling to and from his home to the actual place of the performance of his principal activities and was not involved in any conduct that was integral and indispensable to his principal employment activities. Simply commuting to and from work in an employer's vehicle, without more, is not compensable and is not made compensable by an employer's restricting or prohibiting the personal uses to which the vehicle may be put during the course of the commute.

A New York appellate court[168] has held that, although the FLSA required employers to pay employees for all work performed, under the Portal-to-Portal Act, time spent by the employee commuting to and from work, even in an employer-provided vehicle, was not compensable. In this case, the employee was reimbursed $200 per week for daily commuting expenses prior to June 1996. As a cost savings method, the State assigned the employee a State vehicle and directed him to use it for all reimbursable mileage. The employee, who was a construction superintendent for the New York Office of General Services, contended that the State, by requiring him to use a State vehicle to commute to and from his assigned work station, was obligated to pay him overtime for his commute time. The court found that any activity which preceded or followed the employee's principal work activity was not compensable. As there was no dispute that the employee was not engaged in any work-related activity while commuting to and from his assigned work station, his travel time was not compensable.

[168]Manners v. State of N.Y., 727 N.Y.S.2d 547 (2001).

H. Other Situations

1. Adjusting Grievances

In *DeBraska v. Milwaukee,*[169] the Seventh Circuit upheld the trial court's ruling that police officers' time spent making voluntary appearances at preliminary disciplinary hearings, or in voluntarily drafting written submissions for consideration during such hearings, was not compensable. The city conducts two hearings before disciplining an officer—a formal hearing, which the city conceded involved compensable time, and a preliminary informal hearing for which officers' participation is not compensated. The district court held that time spent in the preliminary phase was not compensable because the city did not require attendance and could not control what officers did during their own time. The court of appeals noted that the outcome of a preliminary hearing "does not adversely affect either working conditions or the continuation of employment,"[170] and thus affirmed the decision of the district court.

In an opinion letter from the Wage and Hour Division,[171] the Department of Labor expressed its opinion that licensed vocational nurses (LVNs) who are required by state law to undergo 30 hours of nursing skills continuing education every two years need not be compensated for time spent in training if all criteria in 29 C.F.R. §785.27 are met: (1) attendance must be outside the employee's regular working hours; (2) attendance must be voluntary; (3) the training must not be directly related to the employee's job; and (4) the employee must not perform any productive work during attendance. Where a state requires individuals to take training as a condition of employment with any employer, attendance would be voluntary provided the employer does not impose additional requirements. However, where a state requires employers to provide training as a condition of the employers' license to remain open for business, the training time is considered involuntary.

---

[169]189 F.3d 650, 5 WH Cases2d 982 (7th Cir. 1999).
[170]*Id.*, 5 WH Cases2d at 984.
[171]1999 WL 1788164 (Dep't of Labor Sept. 30, 1999).

IV. RECORDING WORKING TIME

B. The De Minimis Rule

Time spent by border patrol canine handlers caring for their dogs during the commute to and from work was found to be de minimis because of the administrative difficulties in tracking such time and because the time spent on such activities, although generally not long, was widely varied.[172]

In *Reich v. Monfort Inc.*,[173] the Tenth Circuit held that preliminary and postliminary activities amounting to 10 minutes per day for each meat processing company employee, including putting on and taking off safety gear, were not de minimis. Although both the trial and the appellate courts found that the time would be administratively difficult to record, the court of appeals determined that the total amount of time involved, both on a per-employee basis (10 minutes per day over 3 years) and on an aggregate basis for all the employees as a group (which total the employer contended was not appropriately taken into account) would properly be considered substantial. The court also decided that the regularity of the activities involved weighed against a de minimis finding. It thus affirmed the district court's decision that the time was compensable. The Tenth Circuit explicitly stated that it was proper to apply the de minimis rule in relation to the aggregate amount of time worked by all employees involved in the litigation, but also noted that it was a "close case."[174] The backpay award involved was over $1.5 million plus interest.

In *Shepard v. Burlington*[175] and in *Bartholomew v. City of Burlington*,[176] the U.S. District Court for the District of Kansas held that, under the de minimis doctrine, patrol officers were

---

[172]Aguilar v. United States, 38 Fed. Cl. 431, 4 WH Cases2d 83 (1997), *appeal dismissed*, 155 F.3d 565 (Fed. Cir. 1998).

[173]144 F.3d 1329, 4 WH Cases2d 1106 (10th Cir. 1998).

[174]*Id.*, 4 WH Cases2d at 1109.

[175]4 WH Cases2d 1149 (D. Kan. 1998).

[176]5 F. Supp. 2d 1161, 4 WH Cases2d 1156 (D. Kan. 1998).

not entitled to overtime compensation for time spent on briefings conducted on the way to work between an officer going off duty and a replacement officer. The court first found that under Section 4 of the Portal-to-Portal Act an officer is not entitled to compensation for travel to and from work when an agreement exists regarding the officer's use of city vehicles. The court then noted several factors that made the time spent in these briefings de minimis. First, the court found that the amount of time spent above and beyond necessary travel time was small. Second, the officer benefited from using the city's vehicles for commuting. Third, it is administratively difficult to record travel time. Fourth, the officer was only occasionally required to spend up to an additional 15 minutes in preparing for work by participating in the briefings.

Time spent by police officers monitoring a police radio in order to respond to possible emergencies arising during their commutes to work was found to be de minimis and not compensable.[177]

---

[177]Aiken v. City of Memphis, 190 F.3d 753, 759, 5 WH Cases2d 961 (6th Cir. 1999), *cert. denied,* 528 U.S. 1157, 5 WH Cases2d 1632 (2000).

CHAPTER 9

DETERMINING THE MINIMUM WAGE PAYMENT

III. PAYMENT OF THE MINIMUM WAGE

C. "Free and Clear" Payments

In *Cardenas v. Benter Farms,*[1] the plaintiff agricultural workers sued the couple who owned the farm on which they worked. Among other violations they asserted that workers in each family group were collectively paid by a single check, rather than each worker being paid individually. The farmers asserted that they followed this practice based on farm workers' specific requests; this was denied by the workers. Without resolving the factual

[1]2000 WL 1372848, 6WH Cases 2d 817 (S.D. Ind. 2000).

difference but giving respect to the Department of Labor's letter (which the employer contended should be stricken) stating that "one payment to the head of the family or other family member, rather than to each individual worker" would "not comply with the provisions of [AWPA]," and holding that this letter is "consistent with the language in the FLSA which requires every employer to 'pay to each of his employees . . . wages'"[2] the court granted summary judgment for plaintiffs on this issue.

In *Heder v. City of Two Rivers,*[3] a federal district court in Wisconsin held that it was a violation of the FLSA for an employer to require any part of a firefighter's regular wages or overtime compensation, including the costs of training, to be repaid merely because the employee resigned within a specified time. In this case, the employee received mandatory paramedic training. He signed a repayment agreement requiring him to repay the employer for costs associated with his training if he voluntarily resigned within three years of beginning the training. The employee resigned just shy of the three-year period and went to work as a firefighter for another city. The employer withheld money from the employee's pay to recover part of the training costs. The court granted the employee's partial summary judgment motion on his FLSA overtime claim. Additionally, the court held that the training repayment agreement was unenforceable insofar as it did not reduce the amount due over the years that it was in force. The employer's deductions from the final paychecks violated state law and the FLSA's minimum wage requirements.

D. Time of Payment

In *United States Department of Labor v. Micro-Chart, Inc.,*[4] the administrative law judge held that the fact that employees accepted their jobs knowing "that payroll could be irregular" was no defense to liability. The court also ruled that financial

[2] *Id.* (citing 29 USC §206).
[3] 49 F. Supp. 2d 677 (E.D. Wis. 2001).
[4] 4 WH Cases2d 511, 514 (U.S. Dep't of Labor 1997).

hardship is "not sufficient to avoid liability under the Act." On appeal, the Department's Administrative Review Board held that the Act requires payment of wages on the regular payday.[5] The ARB expressly accepted the Ninth Circuit's reasoning in *Biggs v. Wilson.*[6]

In *Rogers v. City of Troy,*[7] the Second Circuit held that a series of 1-day delays in payment caused by an employer's attempt to change the pay schedule did not automatically violate the FLSA. The appellate court set forth conditions necessary to make such a change lawful: (1) the change was made for a legitimate business reason; (2) there is no unreasonable delay in payment; (3) the employer intends the change to be permanent; and (4) the change does not have the ultimate effect of avoiding the minimum wage and overtime requirements. Although withholding judgment on the first three factors, the court concluded that the delay did not evade the minimum wage and overtime requirements because no payments were permanently skipped and the wages paid for a workweek exceeded the minimum wage even when discounted for the delay. However, the court vacated the district court's dismissal of the case and remanded so that evidence could be adduced on the question whether the other conditions had been met. One member of the three-judge panel dissented, arguing that the Act demands prompt payment on the regular payday, and that any delay, reasonable or not, violates this requirement.

IV. Calculating the Minimum Wage

C. Commission Payments

The courts continue to hold that no violation of Section 206 occurs so long as the weekly total of commissions and hourly wages, if any, results in an average hourly pay that meets or exceeds the minimum hourly requirement.

---

[5]Case No. 95-FLS-12 (DOL ARB 1998).
[6]1 F.3d 1537, 1540 (9th Cir. 1993).
[7]148 F.3d 52, 4 WH Cases2d 1089 (2d Cir. 1998).

When a commissioned employee is also paid a "base" or hourly wage that is below the minimum, an employer should keep complete and detailed records of the total wages paid and hours worked. In one case, a court considered an employer's argument that the employee's hourly wage plus commissions far exceeded the minimum wage. The employee, however, claimed she had worked more hours than were reflected on the employer's wage statements. Finding that the employee's claims raised issues of credibility, the court denied summary judgment to the employer.[8]

2. *Monthly Commission Period*

One district court disallowed an employer's attempt to reduce its minimum wage liability by retroactively changing the settlement period for paying commissions to its sales employees.[9] Following an investigation by the Department of Labor and a demand for payment of back wages to its sales employees, the employer entered into an agreement with the employees whereby the commission settlement period was retroactively changed from 7 to 28 days. The result of the change was to increase the likelihood that an employee would have sales during the settlement period that would generate commissions in excess of the minimum wage. (The employee was entitled to receive a commission for a period only if the employee sold one or more automobiles during the period.) The court held that the employer's attempt to amend its commission settlement period retroactively was an impermissible attempt to decrease retroactively the wages already owed to its employees. Because the employer had set the settlement period at 7 days, the minimum wage became vested and was owed to the employees at the completion of the settlement period.

---

[8]Birch v. Kim, 977 F. Supp. 926 (S.D. Ind. 1997).

[9]Reich v. Scherer Buick Co., 887 F. Supp. 1142 (C.D. Ill. 1997).

D. Piece Rates

When an employer/contractor of piece rate workers failed to pay minimum wages, the concept of joint employment has been applied to render the companies that contracted with the employer potentially liable to the contractor's employees.[10] Piece rate workers in the garment industry claimed that clothing manufacturers (including retailers, designers, and distributors) had contracted for the production of garments at prices too low to permit payment of minimum wages to the contractors' employees. The court found that the "economic reality" of the garment business resulted in the workers' being dependent upon the manufacturers for the payment of the minimum wage, notwithstanding the fact that the contractor would be entirely responsible for hiring and supervising the workers.

VI. ALLOWABLE AND DISALLOWABLE DEDUCTIONS FROM WAGES

A. Deductions Allowable Under Section 3(m) of the Act

1. Meals

In *Herman v. Collis Foods Inc.*,[11] the Sixth Circuit joined the Fifth[12] and Eleventh[13] Circuits when it affirmed the decision of the district court rejecting the voluntariness provision of the Section 3(m) credit regulation as applied to meals, holding that that section permits an employer to deduct the average cost of meals offered to employees regardless of whether the employees accept the meals. In addition, and going beyond those decisions, *Collis* held that the employer could properly take a meal credit for each employee for each shift based on the average cost of all

[10]Bureerong v. Uvawas, 922 F. Supp. 1450, 3 WH Cases2d 383 (C.D. Cal. 1996).
[11]176 F.3d 912, 5 WH Cases2d 545 (6th Cir. 1999).
[12]Donovan v. Miller Props., Inc., 711 F.2d 49, 26 WH Cases 514 (5th Cir. 1983).
[13]Davis Bros., Inc. v. Donovan,700 F.2d 1368, 26 WH Cases 29 (11th Cir. 1983).

meals provided (as opposed to the average cost of all meals provided to employees only) where the employer kept detailed records of the cost of food on hand and food acquired on a weekly basis. The court repeatedly emphasized that the statutory provisions relating to in-kind payments focus entirely on the conduct of the employer, rather than on the conduct or preferences of the employees.

The Sixth Circuit in *Herman v. Palo Group Foster Home Inc.*[14] affirmed the decision of the District Court for the Western District of Michigan, which had found that the defendants had violated the minimum wage and overtime requirements by claiming excessive and unjustified meal credits. The court held that these violations warranted the award of statutory liquidated damages when the defendants had previously been investigated twice by the Department of Labor for the same kinds of activities, had previously paid back wages and been informed of the requirements of the law by the Department, and had engaged in the same or similar conduct a third time. On each of the two prior occasions, the Labor Department had disallowed some portion of the meal credits taken by defendants. In the most recent investigation prior to the one out of which the current suit arose, an investigation which related to 1983–85, the Department had reconstructed from defendants' records an approximation of the costs of the meals provided during that period, for which defendants had not maintained adequate records, and allowed $0.62 per meal, advising defendants that for the future, complete and accurate records were required, and that the $0.62 could not be used prospectively. In its 1995 investigation, the Department discovered that the defendants were still using the $0.62 meal credit and had not maintained adequate records. The court upheld the disallowance of the meal credit.

[14]183 F.3d 468, 5 WH Cases2d 837 (6th Cir. 1999).

C. Potentially Unlawful Deductions

3. Uniforms and Uniform Cleaning

In *Ayres v. 127 Restaurant Corp.*,[15] the court denied the defendant employer's motion for summary judgment on the plaintiffs' claims that they were entitled to reimbursement for the costs of purchasing and maintaining their uniforms. Under the FLSA, employees are entitled to compensation for the purchase and maintenance of a required uniform if such costs would reduce their wages to below minimum wage. Here, the court found that a reasonable jury could conclude that the employer's required attire of white shirt, khaki pants, black shoes, and black socks constituted a "uniform" under the FLSA. Although such items could be part of an employee's ordinary wardrobe, the facts showed that at least some of the employees had to purchase these items with their own funds and that dry cleaning costs for such items were clearly the employees' responsibility.

VII. PAYMENT OF WAGES TO TIPPED EMPLOYEES

B. Statutory Provisions With Regard to Tipped Employees

The Sixth Circuit upheld the district court's approval of an employer-imposed tip pool distributed to hosts, bus persons, and bartenders in *Kilgore v. Outback Steakhouse*,[16] holding that the steakhouse had satisfied the FLSA requirement that it first "inform" employees (although not necessarily "explain" to employees) that it would treat tips toward satisfying the minimum wage requirements because it had provided employees with a tip policy page that explained that tips would be credited toward the

---

[15] 12 F. Supp. 2d 305, 4 WH Cases2d 1255 (S.D.N.Y. 1998).
[16] 160 F.3d 294, 4 WH Cases2d 1729 (8th Cir. 1998).

minimum wage. However, the court reversed and remanded for trial the summary judgment granted the employer in the case of three individual employees as to whom there was evidence that they had not received, or had been discouraged from reading, the information otherwise provided. The court held that, in this case, a genuine issue of material fact precluded summary judgment.

In an opinion letter the Department of Labor addressed the question whether tips which are included in a customer's credit card payment are "still considered tips if the employee chooses to have contributions to a 401(k) plan and payments for insurance, and for federal and state taxes" withheld from the amounts in question.[17] The letter states that since 1974 the tips are the property of the employee, and are not considered wages paid by the employer. Without the employer's losing the right to claim the tip credit, assuming the appropriate conditions are met, the employee may, because the tips are his or her own property, voluntarily direct the tips to any of the matters mentioned by the inquirer.[18]

G. Tip Pooling

In *Ayres v. 127 Restaurant Corp.*,[19] the plaintiffs challenged the employer's tip pooling practices, asserting that the conditions for taking the tip credit were not met because employees had not been allowed to keep all of their tips. The court granted summary judgment to the plaintiff employees on this issue, finding as a matter of law that the employer did not meet the FLSA's requirement for tip credits that "all tips received by [an] employee have been retained by the employee."[20] Here, it was undisputed that the employees for whom the tip credit was taken did not retain all of their tips because a portion went to the

[17]Opinion Letter dated April 19, 2001, signed by staff member of Office of Enforcement Policy, WHM: 8363.

[18]*Id.*

[19]*Id.*

[20]*Id.* at 308, 4 WH Cases2d at 1257.

restaurant's general manager through the restaurant's tip pooling arrangement. Under New York state law, the general manager was an employer, barred from participating in tip pooling.

In *Austin v. Colonial Williamsburg Hotel Properties,*[21] the court considered the FLSA claim of employee "wine runners" at the Regency Dining Room, Colonial Williamsburg, who contended that the employer was not authorized to take the tip credit against their hourly wage because the only amount they actually received by way of tips was an allocation to them of 10 percent of the wine charge on the bill, out of whatever tip was left on the whole check, collected by the server and "tipped out" to the wine runners pursuant to provisions of a collective bargaining agreement. The evidence showed that even under this method of allocation, the wine runners actually received an average of more than $7.00 per hour in tips. The court noted that the unfairness perceived by the wine runners was in actuality a matter to be taken up with their union, which had agreed on their behalf to the arrangement, and did not involve a violation of the FLSA.

In *Kilgore v. Outback Steakhouse,*[22] the court upheld a 3-percent-of-gross-sales tip-out requirement applied to servers as against the plaintiffs' argument that the amount was excessive and therefore failed to be "customary and reasonable," a requirement that appears in Department of Labor opinion letters construing the tip credit provision from shortly after its enactment.[23] The court found that the letters referred to no statutory basis for that requirement and were not persuasive; it affirmatively refused *Chevron*[24] deference to the two opinion letters, and referred with apparent approval to a district court decision from another circuit[25] holding that a tip-out requirement that resulted in servers' tipping out 40 percent of their tips did not

---

[21] 3 WH Cases2d 579 (E.D. Va. 1996).

[22] 160 F.3d 294, 4 WH Cases2d 1729.

[23] Opinion Letter WH-380, Mar. 26, 1976; Opinion Letter WH-468, Sept. 5, 1978.

[24] Chevron U.S.A. Inc. v. Natural Res. Def. Council, Inc., 467 U.S. 837 (1984).

[25] Dole v. Continental Cuisine, 751 F. Supp. 799, 803, 30 WH Cases 163 (E.D. Ark. 1990).

violate the FLSA. The *Kilgore* court refused to follow the opinion letters because "[t]he [c]ourt can find no statutory or regulatory authority for the Secretary's opinion that contributions in excess of 15% of tips or 2% of daily gross sales are excessive."[26]

In *Kilgore* the Sixth Circuit also upheld the use of a tip pool even though the restaurant hosts receiving payments from tip receipts were not themselves permitted to accept tips. The court in *Kilgore* found that these hosts were engaged "in an occupation in which [they] customarily and regularly receiv[e] tips" because they worked in an industry where undesignated tips were common.[27]

---

[26]160 F.3d 294, 4 WH Cases2d at 1735.
[27]*Id.* at 301, 4 WH Cases2d 1729.

CHAPTER 10

DETERMINING OVERTIME COMPENSATION

II. OVERTIME PAY REQUIREMENTS

A. Introduction

1. General Principles

In *Figueroa v. America's Custom Brokers, Inc.*,[1] plaintiff was employed at a wage of $8.50 per hour as a warehouse worker by companies whose business was loading and unloading fish, and sought overtime compensation for hours worked over 40 in a week. Denying the defendants' motion to dismiss, the district court held that the employer's argument that paying wages greater than one and one-half times the minimum wage satisfied the statutory requirements was "wholly without merit."[2]

2. Determining the Workweek

While an employer's failure to pay employees on the regular payday gives rise to an FLSA claim, the Act does not generally prohibit an employer from changing its payday.[3] Following the

---

[1]48 F. Supp. 2d 1372 (S.D. Fla. 1999).

[2]*Id.* at 1377.

[3]Rogers v. City of Troy, 949 F. Supp. 118, 3 WH Cases2d 1105 (N.D.N.Y. 1996), *aff'd as to this conclusion, with additional requirements articulated,* 4 WH Cases2d 1089 (2d Cir. 1998).

DOL's interpretation,[4] the court held that a change in the pay period is permissible under the FLSA if various requirements are met, notably that the change must be intended to be permanent and must not be for purposes of evading the requirements of the FLSA.[5]

B. Principles for Computing Overtime Pay Based on the "Regular Rate"

1. *The "Regular Rate"—Payment of Wages Based on an Hourly Rate*

The Ninth Circuit held that supplemental payments, designed to bring the wage of a partially disabled worker up to his or her predisability wage level, should be included in the base figure upon which the regular rate, and thus overtime pay, is calculated.[6] Relying on 29 C.F.R. §778.109, the court ruled that the supplemental payments—which were tied not to hours but to the worker's predisability regular weekly compensation—must be counted in calculating the regular hourly rate. The court found it made no difference whether the supplemental payments were tied to a weekly rate or an hourly wage.

b. Employees Paid at Two or More Hourly Rates

In *Wisnewski v. Champion Healthcare Corp.*,[7] the district court gives an extensive analysis of the correct calculation of overtime in rejecting an argument by plaintiffs that the example given by the Labor Department in 29 C.F.R. §778.110 is incorrect.

The Supreme Court of Nebraska also relied on Section 778.109 in finding the employee's regular rate was higher than what the employer contended.[8] In a suit brought for overtime

---

[4] 29 C.F.R. §778.105.

[5] *Rogers*, 949 F. Supp. 118, 3 WH Cases2d 1105.

[6] Local 246 Utility Workers Union of Am. v. Southern Cal. Edison Co., 83 F.3d 292, 3 WH Cases2d 449 (9th Cir. 1996).

[7] 2000 WL 1474414, 141 Lab. Cas. ¶ 34,095 (D.N.D. 2000).

[8] Kreus v. Stiles Serv. Ctr., 550 N.W.2d 320, 3 WH Cases2d 687 (Neb. 1996).

pay, the court found, contrary to the lower court's conclusions and the employer's contention that the employee was paid $5.00 per hour plus overtime, that the employee had received pay at the rate of either $6.00 per hour or later $6.25 per hour in every paycheck. These facts were found to meet the standard definition of "regular rate" (i.e., total remuneration per workweek divided by the number of hours worked in that week, as set forth in Section 778.109).

2. *The "Regular Rate"—Payment of Wages Based on a Nonhourly Rate*

a. Piece Rates Generally

The Department of Labor responded to a puzzling inquiry about whether what the inquirer describes as "coefficient overtime" can be used for calculating the correct total pay of a piece rate worker. The Department's response explained that the inquirer's explication of the method bears no resemblance to the practice correctly used for calculating overtime for workers paid a fixed amount for straight time for all hours worked, which is sometimes called the "coefficient method" and involves paying additional half time for the hours over 40. The letter describes a correct calculation of overtime for a piece rate worker using some of the facts supplied by the inquirer, and pointing out why the method described by the inquirer is not lawful.[9]

c. Day Rates and Job Rates

In contrast to certain other provisions of the regulations governing payment on a basis other than hourly,[10] the Department of Labor regulation concerning overtime when payment is made on a "day rate" basis does not specifically require employee understanding or agreement to this method of pay. In

---

[9]WH Opinion Letter of May 1, 2001, 2001 WL 1592792, WHM: 99:8356.

[10]*See, e.g.*, 29 C.F.R. §778.114(c), relating to payment on a fluctuating workweek basis.

DuFrene v. Browning-Ferris, Inc.,[11] the Fifth Circuit affirmed a district court's decision upholding this regulation[12] as a permissible construction of Section 7(a)(1) of the Act[13] and refused to read Section 778.114(c)'s mutual agreement requirement into Section 778.112, finding that the "triggering requirement [under Section 778.112] is solely that employees are paid a day or job rate."[14] Although the policy considerations that prompted the inclusion of the understanding requirement[15] in the fluctuating workweek regulation appear to be equally applicable to day rates, the court was guided by the "plain language"[16] used in the regulation.

The plaintiffs in *DuFrene* also contended that their employer impermissibly calculated the regular rate using the day rate method because, in addition to their salaries, they received sick days, paid vacation, and other fringe benefits. Section 778.114 permits the use of the day rate method only where an employee "receives no other form of compensation for services" above and beyond his or her salary. Noting that the regulations expressly exclude sick days and other such fringe benefits from the regular rate of pay,[17] the court rejected the plaintiffs' argument that their employer's provision of such benefits precluded resort to the day rate method.

In a companion case issued the same day as *DuFrene*, the Fifth Circuit vacated and remanded in part a decision based on a jury verdict after a district court had given a jury instruction to the effect that employee agreement is a prerequisite to application of the day rate method.[18] The district court erred in giving

---

[11]207 F.3d 264, 5 WH Cases2d 1697 (5th Cir.), *cert. denied*, 121 S. Ct. 72 (2000).

[12]29 C.F.R. §778.112.

[13]29 U.S.C. §207(a)(1).

[14]207 F.3d at 268.

[15]Employee "clearly understands that the salary covers whatever hours the job may demand in a particular workweek," 29 C.F.R. §778.112, which by analogy would be "whatever hours the job may demand in a day," rather than, as here, where the collective bargaining agreement defines a day as 8 hours.

[16]5 WH Cases2d at 1699. The regulation provides that employee "is paid a flat sum for a day's work . . . without regard to the number of hours worked in the day."

[17]*See* 29 C.F.R. §778.218.

[18]Hartsell v. Dr. Pepper Bottling Co., 207 F.3d 269, 5 WH Cases2d 1700 (5th Cir. 2000).

such an instruction because, as the Fifth Circuit held in *DuFrene*, Section 778.112 "does not require that employee and employer have a mutual understanding concerning the 'regular rate' of pay."[19]

d. Salaried Employees Generally

Premium payments included in annual salary will receive close scrutiny by courts, who must satisfy themselves that wage agreements between employers and employees are not a sham. In *Adams v. Department of Juvenile Justice*,[20] the Second Circuit held that the parties must intend for the agreed salary to include the regular rate and the overtime rate or the arrangement will not fall under the overtime exemption. The minimum wage requirement must also be met when the salary is calculated on an hourly basis for the total number of hours worked. Thus, where the employer docked pay for hours missed on a pro rata basis but paid time and a half for hours worked beyond the regular shift, the court held that there might be a sham, reasoning that when an employee's regular schedule included hours intended to be compensated by the overtime premium in the set salary, it was inconsistent to treat any time missed as regular time and dock on a pro rata basis and at the same time pay time and a half for hours worked in excess of the regularly scheduled hours.

In *Albanese v. Bergen County*,[21] plaintiff police officers had established by collective bargaining a monthly stipend to compensate canine officers for their at-home, off-the-clock dog care activities. In this suit for overtime, on the question whether that stipend should be included in the officers' regular rate, the court held that it should not, recognizing that the decision conflicted with the Labor Department's regulation on the matter. Emphasizing that the stipend was collectively agreed to and that its inclusion would produce a "windfall" for the officers, the court stated, "Although the Court normally grants the Depart-

[19]*Id.* at 273.
[20]143 F.3d 61, 67–68, 4 WH Cases2d 932, 936 (2d Cir. 1998).
[21]991 F. Supp. 410 (D.N.J. 1997).

ment of Labor's regulations great deference, . . .[t]he Court finds that the Department of Labor's regulation as applied in this case would lead to an unjust result, and is therefore an impermissible construction of the statute."[22]

In *Theisen v. City of Maple Grove*,[23] a federal district court in Minnesota discussed a number of issues relating to the determination of the regular rate for certain law enforcement officers. The officers contended generally that all the types of pay involved should be included in the determination, while the defendant advanced various arguments for the exclusion of longevity pay, special pay for canine handlers, payments in lieu of increased contributions to insurance, and acting supervisor or field training officer rates. The court held that

- "Longevity payments" should be included in the regular rate because such payments were made on a nondiscretionary basis, as required by the applicable collective bargaining agreement, and therefore were not discretionary bonuses.
- Monthly payments made to plaintiffs as canine handlers should be included in the regular rate. Defendant cited *Albanese v. Bergen County*[24] in support of its argument that the payments should be excluded from the regular rate. The court noted that *Albanese* had specifically declined to follow Department of Labor regulations, and it declined to disregard those clear guidelines.[25] The defendant had argued that, as in *Albanese*, the payments were established to constitute payment for the time spent caring for the dogs at the plaintiffs' homes. The court held that the jury finding that no agreement had been reached between the parties as to compensation for home care of the dogs led to the conclusion that the payments were compensation for the increased training and responsibilities of the

---

[22] *Id.* at 423.
[23] 41 F. Supp. 2d 932 (D. Minn. 1999).
[24] 991 F. Supp. 410.
[25] 29 C.F.R. §778.207.

officers as canine handlers, and not for home care given to the dogs.

- Monthly payments to the plaintiffs made in lieu of increased insurance contributions should be excluded from the regular rate because the amounts were fixed on a monthly basis and did not depend on hourly amounts worked.
- Rates for field training and supervisory work on a temporary basis should be excluded from the regular rate because, although the collective bargaining agreement did set a specific amount to be paid for supervisory work, the plaintiffs had failed to produce any evidence that they had actually worked such time.

In *Cowan v. Treetop Enterprises, Inc.*,[26] after earlier decisions establishing, among other things, that plaintiff unit managers were not exempt employees as contended by defendant,[27] the court addressed the overtime compensation owed where plaintiffs and defendant had agreed as to the regular number of hours to be worked per week, for which plaintiffs would be compensated by a fixed salary, and where the actual number of hours worked averaged from some 87 to some 91 per week. Finding that the agreed workweek was 53 hours, the court determined that the regular rate was to be ascertained by dividing the salary received by 53, and that the overtime due was one and one half times the regular rate for the hours over 53 worked each week, which amounted to approximately 36 hours, and half the regular rate for the 13 hours between 40 and 53. In responding to defendant's contention that the fluctuating workweek method should be applied to the calculation of overtime, the court noted that there could not have been a "clear understanding" between plaintiffs and defendant as to the use of this method since the defendant understood the plaintiffs to be exempt.

---

[26]163 F. Supp. 2d 930 (M.D.Tenn. 2001).

[27]Unreported. Docket Entry numbers appear in decision.

e. Salaried Employees—Fluctuating Hours

In *DuFrene v. Browning-Ferris,*[28] the court upheld the federal regulations that provide the method for calculating overtime compensation for workers who receive a fixed salary for fluctuating hours.[29] The court concluded that the regulations were a reasonable interpretation of the FLSA.

Courts continue to require that the regular rate be determined from hours actually worked.[30]

Courts continue to address the "clear mutual understanding" requirement of Section 778.114 of the regulations in a variety of ways. The Fourth Circuit has interpreted Section 778.114 as not requiring that an employee understand the precise manner in which his or her overtime pay is calculated. It also has found no requirement that the employer secure some written acknowledgment by employees indicating that the fluctuating pay plan had been explained before the plan was adopted.[31] The court decided that to meet the requirements of Section 778.114, it was sufficient that the employees were generally aware that their salary was intended as compensation for whatever hours they worked.

One district court in the Fourth Circuit vacated an earlier order after the Fourth Circuit clarified issues regarding the fluctuating workweek method of pay.[32] The court found the salary arrangement was clear to the employees and the fact that the employees were not informed and did not understand how their overtime was calculated was irrelevant under Section 778.114. Thus, the court found the employer did not err by paying the employees on a fluctuating workweek basis.

---

[28]994 F. Supp. 748, 4 WH Cases2d 729 (E.D. La. 1998), *cert. denied,* 531 U.S. 825 (2000).

[29]29 C.F.R. §778.114.

[30]Adams v. Department of Juvenile Justice, 143 F.3d 61, 67–68, 4 WH Cases2d 932, 936 (2d Cir. 1998).

[31]Bailey v. County of Georgetown, 94 F.3d 152, 3 WH Cases2d 776 (4th Cir. 1996).

[32]Roy v. County of Lexington, 948 F. Supp. 529, 3 WH Cases2d 1214 (D.S.C. 1996).

One court denied summary judgment for the employer, finding a material fact question regarding whether the employee and the employer had a clear mutual understanding that her fixed salary agreement limited her right to overtime to an additional 50 percent of her regular rate.[33] The employee testified that the individuals who hired her explained that she would be paid "time-and-a-half" if she worked more than 40 hours in a week. The employee's testimony also suggested that she periodically asked to be compensated for overtime but was refused.

Another district court granted the employer's motion for summary judgment, finding the employer had met the requirements of Section 778.114.[34] The court found the employer's practice of making reductions in deputies' and jailers' leave time and holiday pay for partial-day absences did not affect their status as salaried employees. The court also found that the fact that the employer kept hourly accounts of employees' time did not indicate they were hourly employees. The court further found that the employees' receiving 8 hours' pay for legal holidays did not indicate they were hourly employees. The court held that the fact that the employees never worked less than 40 or 43 hours each workweek did not preclude the use of the fluctuating workweek method. Finally, the employer's limited use of a minimum wage adjustment was found not to indicate noncompliance with the minimum wage requirements for use of the fluctuating workweek method.

The Fourth Circuit found a "clear mutual understanding" required by Section 778.114 between the employer and the employee that the fixed salary is to be compensation for all straight time hours worked, whether few or many.[35] The court, in so finding, held that the existence of such an understanding may be "based on the implied terms of one's employment agreement if it is clear from the employee's actions that he or she

[33]Szymula v. Ash Grove Cement Co., 941 F. Supp. 1032, 3 WH Cases2d 918 (D. Kan. 1996).

[34]Aiken v. County of Hampton, 977 F. Supp. 390 (D.S.C. 1997).

[35]Mayhew v. Wells, 4 WH Cases2d 103 (4th Cir. 1997).

understood the payment plan in spite of after-the-fact verbal contentions otherwise." The former employee's testimony demonstrated that he knew he would never be paid any different amount than his fixed salary no matter how many hours he worked because the employer's policy was only to allow compensatory time off.

The required fluctuation for purposes of Section 778.114 does not require proof that the employee has worked different hours every week and that the employer has not set a fixed, predictable schedule.[36] It is thus possible for an employee's hours to fluctuate from week to week even though the employee worked pursuant to a fixed schedule. The Fourth Circuit, in rejecting the plaintiff's contention that the term "fluctuate" in Section 778.114 included a requirement of "utter unpredictability," relied in part on a 1996 Wage and Hour Division's letter ruling.[37]

In *Aiken v. County of Hampton*,[38] the Fourth Circuit affirmed the district court's grant of summary judgment in favor of the employer.[39] The appellate court held that to invoke the fluctuating workweek method, fluctuating base hours were not necessary. Thus, Section 778.114 applies to situations where fixed base hours are coupled with fluctuating overtime. The court also held that an employee's schedule need not fluctuate in an unpredictable manner. Thus, an employer may use the fluctuating workweek method where employees are paid based on fixed-schedule alternating workweeks. The court further held that the employer's practice of making reductions in deputies' and jailers' leave time and holiday pay for partial-day absences did not preclude use of the fluctuating workweek method. In addition, the employer's practice of calculating vacation pay and leave time by dividing the weekly pay rate by the number of regularly scheduled hours or requiring employees to keep track of their hours worked did not indicate that the employees were

---

[36]Flood v. New Hanover County, 125 F.3d 249, 252, 4 WH Cases2d 139 (4th Cir. 1997).

[37]*Id.*

[38]172 F.3d 43, 6 WH Cases2d 896 (4th Cir. 1998) (unpublished opinion).

[39]*See* Aiken v. County of Hampton, 977 F. Supp. 390 (D.S.C. 1997).

hourly employees. Finally, the employer's limited use of a minimum wage adjustment was found not to indicate noncompliance with the minimum wage requirements for use of the fluctuating workweek method.

The requirements for a fluctuating hours plan were clarified in *Griffin v. Wake County*,[40] a case involving emergency medical technicians (EMTs) whose rotating schedule required them to work 24 hours, have 24 hours off, work 24 hours, have 24 hours off, work 24 hours, and have 96 hours off. The EMTs' hours thus fluctuated between 48 and 72 hours per week, for which they were paid a flat salary and half-time overtime. The Fourth Circuit rejected the EMTs' claims that the plan did not meet the requirements of Section 778.114. First, the court held that Section 778.114 does not require a schedule to be unpredictable for it to meet the "fluctuation" requirement. The court then stated that the "clear mutual understanding" requires only that the employee understand the basic features of the plan. An explanatory memorandum issued at a mandatory employee meeting when the plan was instituted, a policy of explaining the plan to potential employees, the plan's implementation 8 years before the lawsuit, and the county's requirement that employees sign a statement that the plan had been explained combined to prove that the EMTs had a clear understanding of the plan. The court further explained that Section 778.114 does not require an employer to explain the precise details of the administration of a fluctuating hours plan, and thus a challenge related to an occasional misstatement or alleged confusion about the technical details of administering the plan would fail. Finally, the court concluded that Section 778.114 does not prohibit deductions from leave accounts.

Contrary to the prevailing approach, a federal district court in Texas held in *Cash v. Conn Appliances*[41] that the definition of "salaried basis" used for the fluctuating workweek method is not governed by the definition of "salaried basis" used in determin-

---

[40] 142 F.3d 172, 4 WH Cases2d 929 (4th Cir. 1998).

[41] 2 F. Supp. 2d 884, 4 WH Cases2d 941 (E.D. Tex. 1998).

ing whether an employee falls under the white-collar overtime exemption. The court concluded that when an employer intends to pay employees a fixed amount at regular intervals regardless of the amount of time that they are scheduled to work, they are paid on a "salaried basis" under the fluctuating workweek method. The court held that occasional deductions from fixed salary for an employee's absences due to illness, personal business, or other reasons during scheduled work times are allowed under the fluctuating workweek method. The court noted that such deductions could occur only occasionally and apply only to willful absences from work.

The court further stated that evidence of isolated instances when the regular rate fell below minimum wage for individual employees was insufficient to preclude the use of the fluctuating workweek method, provided that the shortfall was cured. The court followed prior cases in holding that the employee is required only to have a clear understanding of the fluctuating workweek payment method and need not have obtained that understanding by any particular means. The court explained that a written example combined with an oral explanation of the policy was sufficient, and the employer was under no obligation to explain its docking policy or the possibility that the hourly rate might occasionally fall below the minimum wage.

In *Local 359 Firefighters v. Gary*,[42] the plaintiffs were scheduled to work 24 hours on and then be off for 48 hours; they were paid a fixed salary for a fluctuating workweek, and they worked both scheduled and unscheduled overtime. For each hour of scheduled overtime, they were paid additional half time (since their pay already included straight time for those hours), which the court approved; for unscheduled overtime, they were first paid pursuant to an idiosyncratic method (the details of which are described in the decision) and later, for budget reasons, were paid on the same basis for the unscheduled as for the scheduled overtime hours. The court found that this ran afoul of the Act because there was no clear understanding of the

[42] 3 WH Cases2d 1846 (N.D. Ind. 1995).

method of compensation.[43] Although the city attempted to justify its use of this system as an example of fixed pay for a fluctuating workweek, the court found that even the city had admitted that it was not using this method, that accordingly no mutual understanding was possible, and that additional compensation was due.

Hergenreter v. City of Fort Dodge[44] involved a dispute over the regular rate of pay of city firefighters who were paid a base salary based on a 56-hour workweek, which translated into 216 hours per 27-day pay period. The city allowed the firefighters 12 hours of paid time off during each pay period to reduce their hours worked to the 204—the threshold number of hours for paying overtime with a 27-day period—under the FLSA's Section 7(k) exemption. The firefighters and the city disputed whether the base salaries were intended to compensate for 204 hours or the full 216 hours of their 27-day work period. The court concluded that there was a genuine issue of material fact on this issue and therefore denied the parties' cross-motions for partial summary judgment.

"A 'clear mutual understanding' as to the use of the fluctuating hours method for unscheduled overtime work was impossible because the City itself admits that it did not use this method."[45]

Where there is a valid fluctuating hours arrangement, the regular rate is determined by dividing total base pay by the hours actually worked.[46]

In *Valerio v. Putnam Associates, Inc.*,[47] the First Circuit affirmed the district court's decision on plaintiff's claim for overtime. The court had found that there was a clear mutual understanding at the time of hiring that plaintiff's weekly hours would fluctuate and that the fixed salary provided straight time compensation for all hours worked. The court found that the

[43]*Id.* at 1851.

[44]987 F. Supp. 1141, 4 WH Cases2d 1759 (N.D. Iowa 1997).

[45]*Local 359,* 3 WH Cases2d at 1851.

[46]Parisi v. Town of Salem, 3 WH Cases2d 1460 (D.N.H. 1997).

[47]173 F.3d 35, 5 WH Cases2d 389, *amended and reh'g denied,* 5 WH Cases2d 1024 (1st Cir. 1999).

employee was told that work days could last longer than 8 hours and that the employer did not intend to pay her overtime if she worked more than 40 hours a week. Although the employee was initially denied overtime payment, the final overtime payment in her severance package was more than the amount required (to add half-time to the salary previously paid). The court thus found that the employer had properly calculated the overtime owed by using the fluctuating workweek method set out in 29 C.F.R. §778.114.

In *Samson v. Apollo Resources, Inc.*,[48] the Fifth Circuit affirmed the district court's judgment for the defendant, holding, in a case of first impression, that it is the employee who bears the burden of proving that the employer failed to properly administer the requirements of the fluctuating workweek method. The court further concluded that the "clear mutual understanding" requirement was satisfied where there was a clear mutual understanding between the parties that the fixed salary included compensation for all the hours worked during the week, regardless of the actual number of hours worked during the week by the employee.[49] The fact that the plaintiffs alleged that they were misled as to the actual number of hours they would have to work during the week and that they were allegedly not told that they would not get paid for weeks during which they did no work, did not alter the existence of a clear mutual understanding between the parties. To the court, all the employees had to understand was that their fixed weekly salary was meant to compensate them for all hours worked regardless of the actual number of hours they worked during the week.

In *Samson*, the court also held that the fluctuating workweek method could be used by an employer even if the employees worked more than 60 hours in a given week and the overtime premium paid was not more than 50 percent of the regular hourly rate. The plaintiffs argued that when an employee worked in excess of 60 hours in a workweek, the employer was required to pay an overtime rate of more than one-half the regular rate of

---

[48] 242 F.3d 629 (5th Cir. 2001).
[49] *Id.* at 637.

pay; otherwise, the rate of pay for each overtime hour would be less than the rate of pay for non-overtime hours. The plaintiffs argued that the hourly rate for non-overtime pay should be determined by dividing the fixed weekly salary by 40 hours. The court held this to be an incorrect interpretation of the regulation and found that under the fluctuating workweek method, the fixed salary was to be divided by the actual number of hours worked, whatever they may be. The court found that even defendant's "deductions for tardiness" for willful absences did not defeat the use of the fluctuating workweek method.

In *Cowan v. Treetop Enterprises, Inc.*,[50] the court held that the fluctuating workweek method could not be applied because there was evidence of an express agreement that the employees' weekly compensation was intended to cover an average workweek of 53 hours, rather than "whatever hours [the employee] is called upon to work in the workweek, whether many or few."[51] Moreover, as the employer had considered the employees to be exempt, it could not have had a "clear mutual understanding" with the employees as to the application of the fluctuating workweek method of compensation.[52]

In *Heder v. City of Two Rivers*,[53] the district court granted summary judgment to plaintiffs for overtime of one and one half times the regular rate for hours worked over 216 in the applicable Section 7(k) pay period. The applicable collective bargaining agreement provided for fluctuating hours but did not expressly state that the employees' salaries covered all of the hours worked; instead it provided that overtime would be paid at one and one half times the regular rate as opposed to half-time for all hours worked in excess of 40 per week. For these reasons, the court concluded that the collective bargaining agreement did not express a "clear mutual agreement" that the fluctuating workweek method was to be used to calculate overtime payments.

---

[50] 163 F. Supp. 2d 930 (M.D. Tenn. 2001).
[51] 29 C.F.R. §778.114.
[52] *Cowan,* 163 F. Supp. 2d at 940.
[53] 149 F. Supp. 2d 677 (E.D. Wis. 2001).

III. SUPPLEMENTAL PAYMENTS NOT INCLUDED IN THE REGULAR RATE

A. Exclusions From the Regular Rate—Statutory Provisions

There have been no changes in the seven types of payments that are statutorily excluded from the "regular rate." The Sixth Circuit has held that "the list of exclusions in Section 7(e) is exclusive."[54]

1. Extra Compensation Paid for Overtime

a. Premium Pay for Hours Worked in Excess of the Daily or Weekly Standard

A district court has held that "minimum manning payments" to firefighters in excess of the contractual rate were not excluded from the regular rate under Section 7(e)(5) because such payments were not for hours in excess of the standard.[55]

The Department of Labor has indicated in an opinion letter that where a premium payment for hours worked in excess of the regular workweek creates an incentive for employees to work additional hours, and they begin to do so on a regular basis, the premium payment may have to be included in the regular rate of pay, and may no longer be credited against accrued overtime. In this interesting letter, which provides little analysis, the Division was presented with a situation where an employer had a regular workweek of 36 hours, during which employees were paid $20 per hour, but the employer offered $25 per hour for hours over 36 in the week.[56] The premium pay had the effect of inducing employees to work 44 hours a week on a "regular" basis—rather than the 36 hours the employer usually had identified as the normal workweek. Despite apparently contrary

---

[54]Featsent v. City of Youngstown, 70 F.3d 900, 905, 2 WH Cases2d 1697 (6th Cir. 1995).

[55]Abbey v. City of Jackson, 883 F. Supp. 181, 185, 2 WH Cases2d 1235 (E.D. Mich. 1995).

[56]1999 WL 33210914 (Dep't of Labor Oct. 21, 1999).

language in the statute,[57] which the letter quotes, the Division opined that "[a]s a result of this change to the employees' regular working hours, the additional . . . [amount] paid per hour worked over 36 in a week must be included in determining the regular rate . . . ." The opinion letter does not indicate such factors as how regularly the employees worked the expanded hours, whether or not working the additional hours was entirely voluntary, or other possible factors that might affect the result.

In *Herman v. City of St. Petersburg, Florida, Police Department*[58] a district court granted the Secretary of Labor's motion for summary judgment, holding that the defendant had paid insufficient overtime as a result of its failure to include shift differential payments in the regular rate.

In *Lee v. Vance Executive Protection, Inc.*,[59] security agency employees regularly worked 12-hour shifts and occasionally worked more than 12 hours in a given day. The employer paid a fixed amount per shift, regardless of the number of hours worked. At issue was the calculation of overtime. While the plaintiffs contended that they were paid a day rate, the employer claimed that the shift payment consisted of two parts, a straight time rate for the first 8 hours and "double time" for the following 4 hours. The district court determined that the employer's approach was not prohibited by the FLSA, and awarded no relief. On the plaintiffs' appeal, the Fourth Circuit noted the regulatory prohibition on "compensation schemes in which 'the normal workday is artificially divided into a "straight time" period to which one rate is assigned, followed by a so-called "overtime" period for which a higher rate is specified'"[60] and concluded that the agents were in fact paid a day rate. Accordingly the judgment was reversed in part so that some of the overtime claimed would be awarded. The appellate court affirmed that portion of the district court's decision that held there was insufficient evidence relating to unrecorded hours allegedly worked by plaintiffs to award overtime for those hours.

---

[57] 29 U.S.C. §207(e)(5).
[58] 131 F. Supp. 2d 1329 (M.D. Fla. 2001).
[59] 2001 WL 108760 (4th Cir. 2001) (unpublished opinion).
[60] 7 Fed. Appx. at 164 (quoting 29 C.F.R. §778.202(c)).

In *Nolan v. City of Chicago*[61] the district court held, after trial "on the papers" by a magistrate judge, that premium pay for hours worked in excess of the normal workday (8 hours) and the normal workweek (40 hours) may be excluded from the regular rate of pay and credited against statutorily required overtime pay.

b. Premium Pay for Hours Worked on Saturdays, Sundays, and Other Special Days

In *Nolan v. City of Chicago*[62] the district court held, after trial "on the papers" by a magistrate judge, that premium pay for hours worked on holidays may be excluded from the regular rate of pay and credited against statutorily required overtime pay.

B. Bonuses

1. Inclusion and Exclusion of Bonuses in Computing the "Regular Rate"

A state supreme court has held that an employer's assurance that "'he would see to it that he [Kreus] averaged $6 per hour'" was "a prior agreement or promise to pay Kreus a 'bonus' at a set amount, making any 'bonus' amount paid nondiscretionary [and not excludable] under the meaning of the FLSA."[63]

The court in *Herman v. Anderson Floor Co.*[64] held that an employer's "premium payments" made to employees were not discretionary bonuses excludable from computation of the employees' regular rate of pay. The court found that the employer's practices and specific provisions in the labor agreement between the employer and his employees created on the part of the employees an expectation of premium pay on a regular basis.

---

[61] 125 F. Supp. 2d 324 (N.D. Ill 2000).

[62] *Id.*

[63] Kreus v. Stiles Serv. Ctr., 550 N.W. 2d 320, 326–27, 3 WH Cases2d 687 (Neb. 1996).

[64] 11 F. Supp. 2d 1038, 136 Lab. Cas. (CCH) ¶33,751 (E.D. Wis. 1998).

According to a Division opinion letter, regularly paid incentive bonuses for attaining educational and other job-related credentials must be included in an employee's regular rate of pay.[65]

In *Heder v. City of Two Rivers*,[66] the city offered premium payments for required paramedic training, and also required the execution of a repayment agreement. The agreement between the firefighter and the city provided that the premium payments were not to be included as part of the employee's base salary for purposes of calculating his regular rate of pay. Citing a Wage Hour Division opinion letter providing that regularly paid incentive bonuses for attaining education and other job related credentials must be included in an employee's regular rate of pay,[67] the district court in Wisconsin held that the training premiums had to be included in the employee's base salary in order to calculate his regular rate of pay.

The Department of Labor stated in a letter[68] that biannual nondiscretionary variable bonuses given to employees if the company met a "savings" goal of reduced costs compared to a benchmark of costs incurred in a previous year, need not be incorporated into the employees' regular hourly rate and thus would not require a recalculation of overtime under the FLSA.

2. *Discretionary Bonuses*

In *Theisen v. City of Maple Grove*,[69] a federal district court in Minnesota held "longevity payments" made to plaintiff police officers were not discretionary bonuses because such payments were made on a nondiscretionary basis, pursuant to provisions in the applicable collective bargaining agreement. Therefore, such payments should be counted toward the "regular rate" used to calculate overtime pay.

---

[65] 1999 WL 1788163 (Dep't of Labor Sept. 30, 1999).

[66] 149 F. Supp. 2d 677, 7 WH Cases2d 242 (E.D. Wis. 2001).

[67] 1999 WL 1788163.

[68] Letter of Feb. 5, 2001, signed by staff member of Office of Enforcement Policy, 2001 WL 1558953, WHM: 99:8324.

[69] 41 F. Supp. 2d 932 (D. Minn. 1999).

An employer's practice of paying a bonus year after year at the same time may suggest the existence of an understanding between employee and employer that will render a bonus nondiscretionary and thus not excludable from the regular rate. Finding in one recent opinion letter that an employer's practice of paying bonuses every year at the same time (*and* paying the bonuses from a specific pool of assets into which the employer made regular contributions) indicated that "an arrangement to pay the bonuses . . . exists . . . [such that] the bonuses must be included in the regular rate." The Division concluded: "Although regularity or repetitive payment is not in itself sufficient to destroy the discretionary nature of a bonus, where there is a custom or practice of paying a bonus with regularity sufficient to imply an understanding on the part of employees that they will regularly receive a bonus, the employer will be considered to have arranged to pay such bonus."[70]

3. Gifts and Special Occasion Bonuses

The Nebraska Supreme Court held that the extra payments to an employee did "not qualify as excludable 'gifts' under the FLSA because they were paid pursuant to an agreement between the parties, and the amount 'given' was directly dependent on the amount of hours worked."[71]

In an opinion letter dated February 14, 2001,[72] the Department of Labor's Wage and Hour Division stated that a company employing cashiers whom it provided to retail and service establishments was required to include a so-called "finder's fee" in the cashiers' regular rate of pay under Section 7(e) of the

[70]1999 WL 33210906 (Dep't of Labor Nov. 5, 1999). The bonus at issue in this opinion also appeared to be performance-based. This, perhaps more than the nondiscretionary character of the bonus, led the Division to conclude that the employer had to include the bonus in the regular rate. For a recent opinion letter in which the Division did find that a bonus was discretionary within the meaning of the applicable interpretative guideline (29 C.F.R. §778.211(c)), see 2000 WL 1537273 (Dep't of Labor May 19, 2000).

[71]Kreus v. Stiles Serv. Ctr., 550 N.W.2d 320, 327, 3 WH Cases2d 687, 692 (Neb. 1996).

[72]WH Opinion Letter dated Feb. 14, 2001, 2001 WL 1558771, WHM: 99:8346.

FLSA and 29 C.F.R. §778.331. The company paid a cashier $50.00 for each credit card recovered after confirming that the credit card was unauthorized, ostensibly as an advance because the credit card company would later pay the employer company a fee for recovering and turning over the unauthorized credit card. The Department concluded that the "finder's fee" was effectively a prize awarded for job performance or efficiency and was therefore includible remuneration. The Department also stated that the amount would still be includible as remuneration even if it was paid directly from the credit card company instead of from the employer company.

D. Profit-Sharing, Thrift, and Savings Plans

In an opinion letter from the Wage and Hour Division,[73] the Department of Labor on February 12, 1999, stated that a one-time stock option plan (where the employees had the right to purchase company stock at a grant price) did not qualify for any of the exclusions from the regular rate as defined in Section 7(e)(1) of the FLSA. Nor did the one-time stock option plan qualify as a bona fide profit-sharing plan or trust or a bona fide thrift savings plan. It also did not meet the criteria for a discretionary bonus. The value of employee stock options should be included in regular pay rates for the purpose of overtime calculation. The employee's profit from selling stock options would be allocated over the time period between when the option was exercised and when the employee became eligible to purchase the shares. The profit was not to be allocated over more than the previous two years, however.[74]

The Division also addressed a situation where an employer's profit-sharing plan distributed benefits at uneven levels to employees at different plants. The distribution was based upon each plant's productivity (although employees within a given

[73] 1999 WL 1002365.

[74] The controversy sparked by this opinion letter resulted in the amendment of the statute not long thereafter through the Worker Economic Opportunity Act, S. 2323/H.R. 4182, 106th Cong. (2000).

plant apparently received equal bonuses). In its opinion letter, the Division concluded that this feature of the plan, along with the employer's failure to satisfy the Division that all plan funds were derived from profits, as required by Section 549.1(c) of the regulations, indicated that the payments "may be designed to reward employees for increased production . . . and may not be tied exclusively to profits."[75] This apparent production criterion, concluded the Division, disqualified the plan as a bona fide profit-sharing plan under Section 549.2(e) of the regulations. The Division also questioned whether the contributions to the plan were derived from profits of the entire company or instead particular branches/divisions, and, if the latter, whether each such branch/division "is recognized as such for general business purposes and for which profits are separately and regularly calculated in accordance with accepted accounting practice"[76] as required under Section 549.1(c)(1) of the regulations.

In an opinion letter dated February 14, 2001,[77] the Department of Labor's Wage and Hour Division stated that an employer's profit sharing plan, which "meets the requirements in 29 CFR §547.1(b)-(f), except that under certain conditions the employer's contributions can exceed the total amount deferred by the participants," and which has none of the disqualifying characteristics of Section 547.2, was a plan that qualified as bona fide and thus the employer's contributions to it did not have to be included in the calculation of the regular rate under Section 7(e)(3)(b) of the statute.

E. Benefit Plans

In 1996, the Ninth Circuit considered "whether certain supplemental payments, designed to bring the wage of a partially disabled worker up to his or her predisability wage level, should be included in the [regular rate]."[78] Pursuant to its

---

[75] 1999 WL 33210911 (Dep't of Labor Oct. 29, 1999).

[76] *Id.*

[77] WH Opinion Letter dated Feb. 14, 2001, 2001 WL 1558785, WHM: 99:8347.

[78] Local 246, Utility Workers Union of Am. v. Southern Cal. Edison Co., 83 F.3d 292, 294, 3 WH Cases2d 449 (9th Cir. 1996).

collective bargaining agreements, the employer paid the difference between the predisability and postdisability wage rate to employees who, because of disability, were unable to continue working at a job in a higher-paying classification. Because the supplemental payments were not made irrevocably to a trust, the court held that the supplemental wage payments did not meet a fundamental requirement of the Section 7(e)(4) benefit plan exception and "must be included in calculating the employees' regular rate of pay."[79]

Madison v. Resources for Human Development Inc.[80] involved current and former employees' suit against a nonprofit corporation that provides its clients—mentally ill and mentally retarded adults—with human services programs such as community health centers, transportation services, and community living facilities and assistance. The Third Circuit affirmed the district court's decision that the FLSA applied to the defendant and that the domestic companionship exemption, relied on by the defendant, was not available. However, according to the appellate court, the district court's decision that the defendant was required to include in the plaintiffs' regular rate the contributions made by the defendant to its cafeteria-type benefit plan,[81] which had a cash option, was reached through reliance on 29 C.F.R. §778.215(a)(5), which the district court had treated as a formal agency regulation, when in fact it is "merely an interpretative guideline of the agency."[82] Accordingly, it remanded for further consideration in light of the Supreme Court's recent deference decision.[83] In its opinion, the Third Circuit reiterated that "there is a statutory presumption . . . that remuneration in any form is included in the regular rate calculation. The burden is on the employer to establish that the remuneration in question falls under an exemption."

---

[79] *Id.* at 296, 3 WH Cases2d at 452.

[80] 233 F.3d 175, 187, 6 WH Cases2d 961 (3d Cir. 2000).

[81] A cafeteria-type plan is one in which employees are permitted to allocate the sums credited to their accounts among several designated plans such as health care, child care, and vacation pay. A cash option is frequently available in such plans.

[82] 6 WH Cases2d at 967.

[83] Christensen v. Harris County, 529 U.S. 576, 5 WH Cases2d 1825 (2000).

F. Payments Made When No Work Is Performed

1. Reimbursement for Expenses

In *Montana Public Employees' Ass'n v. Montana DOT*,[84] the Montana Supreme Court ruled that the amount fixed by a collective bargaining agreement as reimbursement for travel from home to job reporting stations for certain state construction bureau employees must be included in the regular rate for purposes of calculating overtime.[85] However, the time employees spent traveling to and from work did not have to be counted as time worked.[86]

An employer that provides an employee with an on-site apartment and requires the employee to occupy it should not include the cost of the apartment in the employee's regular rate of pay. The Division will deem a residential facility to be for the employer's benefit, and hence excludable from the regular rate, where (1) the employer requires the employee to occupy the facility for the employer's benefit, (2) the employer provides the facility at no cost, and (3) "it is understood that the furnishing of the apartment is not considered a part of the employee's wages."[87] A different result obtains, the Division made clear, "where payments are made to employees in the form of facilities which are regarded as part of wages." In such cases, Section 778.116 of the regulations requires that the cost of such facilities be included in the regular rate.

5. "Call-Back" Pay

In an opinion letter, the Division considered an on-call arrangement in which employees would wear a beeper and check the employer's merchandise levels remotely via laptop computer. The Division expressed the view that if the time were

---

[84]954 P.2d 21, 4 WH Cases2d 691 (Mont. 1998).
[85]*Id.* at 695, 4 WH Cases2d 691.
[86]*Id.*
[87]1999 WL 1788149 (Dep't of Labor Sept. 1, 1999).

compensable on-call time, then associated on-call pay could not be excluded from the regular rate of pay.[88]

7. *Other Similar Payments*

The Seventh Circuit has considered the meaning of "other similar payments" as used in the last clause of Section 7(e)(2).[89] That provision excludes from the regular rate "other similar payments to an employee which are not made as compensation for his hours of employment."[90] The court held that the word "similar" "refers to other payments that do not depend at all on when or how much work is performed."[91] Specifically, the court held that "earned work credits" paid by the bakery to employees who did not receive two consecutive days off in a week were not excluded under Section 7(e)(2) because the credits were "tied to work schedules that employees dislike."[92]

Similarly, the Ninth Circuit has rejected an employer's argument that "certain supplemental payments, designed to bring the wage of a partially disabled employee up to his or her predisability wage level" should be excluded from the regular rate as "other similar payments" within the meaning of "the final clause of 29 U.S.C. §207(e)(2)."[93] Pursuant to its collective bargaining agreements, the employer paid the difference between the predisability and postdisability wage rate to employees who, because of disability, were unable to continue working at a

---

[88]Wage-Hour Admin. Op. (June 23, 1998), 1998 WL 852812. *See also* Main Volume of Treatise, Chapter 8, "Determining Compensable Hours Worked," §III.B.3. [Application of Principles; Waiting Time; On-Call Time] at p. 479.

[89]Reich v. Interstate Brands Corp., 57 F.3d 574, 2 WH Cases2d 1281 (7th Cir. 1995), *cert. denied*, 116 S. Ct. 699, 3 WH Cases2d 64 (1996). *See also* Featsent v. City of Youngstown, 70 F.3d 900, 904, 2 WH Cases2d 1697 (6th Cir. 1995) ("the 'similar payments' clause of Section 7(e)(2) was not intended to exclude bonuses from inclusion in the regular rate when those bonuses are understood to be compensation for services even when they are 'not directly attributable to any particular hours of work'").

[90]29 U.S.C. §207(e)(2).

[91]57 F.3d at 578, 2 WH Cases2d 1284.

[92]*Id.*

[93]Local 246, Utility Workers Union of Am. v. Southern Cal. Edison Co., 83 F.3d 292, 3 WH Cases2d 449 (9th Cir. 1996).

job in a higher-paying classification. "Because the [supplemental] payments are compensation for that lower classification work, they are not exempt under Section 7(e)(2)."[94]

The Division has addressed the issue of whether payments tendered in consideration of an employee's agreement to a noncompetition agreement must be included in the regular rate. The agreement at issue prohibited employees from competing both during their employment and for a 30-month period after their terminations, in exchange for which the employees received additional quarterly payments during the period of their employment. The Division viewed the payments as "promised bonuses that are part of the remuneration for employment"[95] and thus could not be excluded from the regular rate.

The Division also addressed the status of payments made "in lieu of holiday pay"—a sum provided during each pay period to employees who did not receive time off for official holidays. The Division concluded that such pay must be included in an employee's regular rate of pay.[96]

H. Stock Options [New Topic]

In response to a much-criticized Division opinion letter holding that the value of employer-granted stock options must be included in the regular rate,[97] Congress amended the Fair Labor Standards Act by passing the Worker Economic Opportunity Act with overwhelming bipartisan support.[98] President Clinton signed the bill into law on May 18, 2000. As a result of the amendment, the Act now excludes from the regular rate an eighth category of benefits, namely:

---

[94]*Id.* at 296, 3 WH Cases2d 451.
[95]1999 WL 33210905 (Dep't of Labor Nov. 23, 1999).
[96]1999 WL 1788163 (Dep't of Labor Sept. 30, 1999).
[97]1999 WL 1002365 (Dep't of Labor Feb. 12, 1999).
[98]Pub. L. No. 106-202 (codified at 29 U.S.C. §207(e)(8)).

> any value or income derived from employer-provided grants or rights provided pursuant to a stock option, stock appreciation right, or bona fide employee stock purchase program which is not otherwise excludable under any of paragraphs (1) through (7) [of 29 U.S.C. §207(e)] if—
>
> (A) grants are made pursuant to a program, the terms and conditions of which are communicated to participating employees either at the beginning of the employee's participation in the program or at the time of the grant;
>
> (B) in the case of stock options and stock appreciation rights, the grant or right cannot be exercisable for a period of at least 6 months after the time of grant (except that grants or rights may become exercisable because *of an employee's death, disability, retirement, or a change in corporate ownership, or other circumstances permitted by regulation),* and the exercise price is at least 85 percent of the fair market value of the stock at the time of grant;
>
> (C) exercise of any grant or right is voluntary; and
>
> (D) any determinations regarding the award of, and the amount of, employer-provided grants or rights that are based on performance are—(i) made based upon meeting previously established performance criteria (which may include hours of work, efficiency, or productivity) of any business unit consisting of at least 10 employees or of a facility, except that, any determinations may be based on length of service or minimum schedule of hours or days of work; *or* (ii) *made based upon the past performance* (which may include any criteria) of one or more employees in a given period so long as the determination is in the sole discretion of the employer and not pursuant to any prior contract.[99]

While the amendment took effect 90 days after its May 18, 2000 enactment date,[100] Congress did give the amendment some retroactive effect: An employer will not be liable for failure to include any income or value derived from a stock option, stock appreciation right, or employee stock purchase program if "(1) the grants or rights were obtained before the effective

---

[99] 29 U.S.C. §207(e)(8) (emphasis added).
[100] *See* 29 U.S.C. §207 (note).

date;" "(2) the grants or rights were obtained within the 12-month period beginning on the effective date . . . so long as such program was in existence on the date of enactment . . . and will require shareholder approval to modify such program to comply with [the stock option amendment to the Act];" or "(3) [the grants or rights were] . . . provided under a collective bargaining agreement that is in effect on the effective date."[101]

No published federal decisions or Division opinion letters have addressed the Worker Economic Opportunity Act, and the Secretary of Labor has not to date promulgated any regulations or any interpretive guidelines. Employers must ensure that the grant of stock options to nonexempt employees is done in strict conformity with the above rules.[102]

IV. SPECIAL PROBLEMS CONCERNING THE REGULAR RATE

F. Gap Time [New Topic]

An issue involving gap time arises whenever an employee is paid a fixed salary for a number of hours in the week which is less than the statutory overtime threshold, and actually works more hours than the number for which the salary is paid. The employee may work more than 40 hours in the week or merely some number of hours less than the 40 but more than the number for which the salary is agreed payment. The issue more commonly arises in cases where public employees are paid under a Section 7(k) plan,[103] but it can also arise in the private sector when, for example, employees are hired on the basis of a 35-hour workweek.

---

[101] *Id.*

[102] The Employee Benefits Committee of the American Bar Association's Section of Taxation has recently raised questions about the relationship between the Worker Economic Opportunity Act and the Internal Revenue Code and, in particular, whether restricted stock may be excluded from the regular rate under the Act. *See FLSA: ABA Benefits Committee Members Seek Clarification of Employee Stock Treatment*, DAILY LAB. REP. Jan. 2, 2001, at A-5.

[103] *See* Treatise, Chapter 11, "Government Employment," §V.B. [Special Provisions That Apply to Fire Protection and Law Enforcement Employees of Public Agencies; The Section 7(k) Exemption] at pp. 687–89.

The Department of Labor regulations provide that overtime compensation "cannot be said to have been paid to an employee unless all the straight time compensation due him for the non-overtime hours under his contract (express or implied) . . . has been paid."[104] The Department takes the view, on the basis of this provision, that in overtime weeks, the employee's gap time must have been compensated at the regular rate (rather than only at something equal to or in excess of the statutory minimum wage) before any computation can be made of whether the overtime due has been paid. The Department's view on whether or not there is a duty to pay gap time at the regular rate in nonovertime weeks has not been clarified, but in the absence of any direct expression on this question, one might assume that the Department does not consider that to be a requirement under the FLSA.

In *Monahan v. County of Chesterfield, Virginia,*[105] plaintiff police officers were paid under a Section 7(k) plan, were regularly scheduled for fewer hours per period than the applicable Section 7(k) threshold number for the period, and regularly worked more hours than scheduled. When they worked more hours than the threshold number, they received overtime. The plaintiffs brought this suit for back wages at the regular rate for hours worked between the number scheduled and the number actually worked—the so-called gap time—whether they worked more than the overtime threshold of hours in the period or not. They relied in part for their claim on Sections 778.315 and .317 of the regulations, which provide in effect that overtime has not been properly paid until all straight time hours have been compensated at the regular rate. The Fourth Circuit rejected these claims, and with them implicitly the regulatory provisions, holding that there is no minimum wage violation so long as, for all hours below the overtime threshold, the total straight time compensation divided by the total number of hours worked

[104]29 C.F.R. §778.315.
[105]95 F.3d 1263, 3 WH Cases2d 806 (4th Cir. 1996).

exceeds the statutory minimum wage, and that if there is a "clear understanding" between the employer and employee as to the terms of compensation, there is no requirement that gap time be compensated at the regular rate even in overtime weeks. The court ruled that the existence of a clear understanding under Section 778.114 can be based on the implied terms of one's employment agreement if it is clear from the employee's actions that he or she understood the payment plan.

In *Braddock v. Madison County*,[106] a federal district court in Indiana held that where employees worked in excess of their agreed-upon hourly requirements but were still below the overtime threshold of 40 hours, the FLSA did not require the payment of gap time to employees as long as the employees' salaries exceeded the FLSA's minimum wage requirements when applied to the actual hours worked. The court stated that the FLSA does not provide a federal remedy for any and all breaches of payment obligations under employment contracts. It held that as long as minimum wage levels and entitlement to overtime pay for work above specified maximum hours are met, additional payment for gap time is not required.

In *Robertson v. Board of County Commissioners of County of Morgan*,[107] where the plaintiffs challenged various aspects of the defendants' use of the provisions of 29 U.S.C. §207(k),[108] the district court found that the plaintiffs, who were paid a salary to cover all hours worked up to 171 in a 28-day period, as permitted under the Section 7(k) rules, were not entitled to be paid overtime for the "gap time" between 160 and 171 hours, as the salary exceeded the product of the minimum wage times the total number of hours worked.

---

[106]34 F. Supp. 2d 1098 (S.D. Ind. 1998).

[107]78 F. Supp. 2d 1142 (D. Colo. 1999).

[108]Section 207(k) provides a special rule for the numbers of hours that may be worked by law enforcement and fire employees before overtime premium is payable.

V. EXCEPTIONS FROM THE REGULAR RATE PRINCIPLES

A. Using Basic Rates for Regular Rates

1. Requirements for a Basic Rate

The Sixth Circuit implicitly rejected a district court's finding that employer/employee agreements on the basic rate of pay are permissible only when overtime calculations are difficult because of the way nonovertime compensation is computed.[109] In beginning its discussion of basic rates, the court of appeals stated, "Section 7(g) of the FLSA, however, allows employers and employees to negotiate and agree upon a mutually acceptable 'basic rate.'"[110] The court went on to allow and disallow certain exclusions from the regular rate, on the assumption that the "basic rate" agreement was valid.[111]

In that case, the district court had held that shift differential pay and incentive bonuses must be included in overtime calculations, even if not covered by a basic rate agreement. These holdings were affirmed by the Sixth Circuit. However, the circuit court reversed the lower court's holding regarding awards for nonuse of sick leave and bonuses for the absence of medical claims, instead holding that such awards and bonuses can be excluded from overtime calculations.

2. Methods for Calculating Basic Rates

b. Averaging Earnings for a Period Other Than a Workweek

In *Firestone v. Southern California Gas Co.*,[112] the Ninth Circuit affirmed the district court's dismissal of the plaintiffs' FLSA claims to the effect that the employer's practice of calculating the basic rate on a daily basis, pursuant to a complicated for-

---

[109]Featsent v. City of Youngstown, 70 F.3d 900, 2 WH Cases2d 1697 (6th Cir. 1995).

[110]*Id.* at 903, 2 WH Cases2d at 1699.

[111]*Id.* at 903–04, 2 WH Cases2d at 1699–1700.

[112]219 F.3d 1063, 6 WH Cases2d 371 (9th Cir. 2000).

mula[113] set forth in a collective bargaining agreement, violated the Act. They alleged that the basic rate would often "fluctuate wildly" as a result of the employer's method of calculation and relied upon Section 548.2(e) of the regulations, which provides that an employee's basic rate must be "substantially equivalent" to an employee's average earnings "over a representative period of time." The court rejected the plaintiffs' argument, emphasizing that Section 548.3(b) expressly allows an employer to calculate "an employee's 'regular rate' . . . on the basis of the employee's average earnings over one of any number of periods, including a day."[114] The Ninth Circuit also explained that Section 548.2(e) provides that the basic rate must be substantially equivalent to the average earnings over a "representative period of time" *or* authorized by Section 548.3. Because the employer's practice was in accord with Section 548.3(b), the employer was not required to establish that the basic rate was derived from average earnings over a representative period of time.

VII. SPECIAL OVERTIME PROVISIONS

B. Hospital and Residential Care Establishments

The Department of Labor issued an opinion letter[115] concerning the applicability of Section 7(j) of the Act to the employees of a multi-site medical testing laboratory which did much of its work for hospital patients. The facts involved five hospitals and a central laboratory location not within any of the hospitals. The five hospitals were owned by a single entity, and the central laboratory was owned by that entity and another organization. Eighty percent of the employer's laboratory em-

---

[113]Discussion of the formula is found in 6 WH Cases2d at 373.

[114]219 F.3d at 1068.

[115]Opinion Letter dated Sept. 14, 2000 by member of Office of Enforcement Policy, WHM: 99:8325.

ployees worked in the hospitals on a full time basis, and performed their work in connection with tests administered to hospital patients; the other 20 percent of the employees worked at the central laboratory facility. The department concluded that the operation constituted a single enterprise under the Act, and that employees of the enterprise who spent virtually all their time on the premises of the hospitals were entitled to be treated as exempt under Section 7(j). With respect to the employees who worked at the central laboratory facility, the Department determined that not enough information had been provided to draw a conclusion as to the applicability of Section 7(j), and that the identity of the co-owner and the source of the laboratory work done there by those employees could be relevant to that decision.

In an opinion letter[116] the Department of Labor responded to an inquiry concerning payment arrangements for tribal nurse employees working at tribal health facilities under contract with the Indian Health Service. The requestor sought a waiver of the overtime requirements so that these employees could be paid the same as federal employees. After pointing out that the administration of the FLSA with respect to both federal and tribal nurses is carried out by the Office of Personnel Management, and that the Department of Labor has no authority to grant waivers of overtime, the letter discussed Sections 13(a)(1) and 7(j) of the Act, pointing out how Section 7(j) if applicable permits nine-five-four scheduling without any overtime liability if the workweek is set to begin and end in the middle of the 8-hour day which separates the two sets of four 9-hour days of the 2-week work period.

[116]WH Opinion Letter dated June 1, 2001, WHM: 99:8378.

CHAPTER 11

GOVERNMENT EMPLOYMENT

II. COVERAGE ISSUES

A. Definitions

In *Benshoff v. City of Virginia Beach*,[1] a federal district court in Virginia determined that volunteer firefighter rescue squads were not public agencies under the FLSA even though the squads were coordinated by the city's department of medical services. The plaintiffs sought to have counted as hours worked for their public employer the time spent in fire squads. The squads had various relationships with, and were coordinated by but were not a direct part of, the city system. The court focused on the following facts. First, the squads were independently organized, private nonprofit organizations and thus not created by the state. Second, the city had no appointment or removal authority over the squad's board of directors and the board retained control over the squads' finances and fundraising activities. Third, the squads' board, and not the city, controlled who became a squad member. Fourth, the city defined the squads as private entities. Thus, the court concluded that the squads were not public employers and that, because the squads were private, the firefighters who were seeking overtime compensation for hours worked on the squads had not impermissibly volunteered their time to the "same public agency which employed them."[2]

---

[1]9 F. Supp. 2d 610, 4 WH Cases2d 1310 (E.D. Va. 1998).

[2]As discussed in the Treatise at Chapter 11, §II.C.3. [Volunteers; Employment by the Same Public Agency], pp.654–58, public employees may not "volunteer" to perform the "same services" for the "same public agency" by which they are employed. These tests require detailed factual analysis.

Courts still apply the *Hawkins County* factors to determine whether an organization providing a public service is a "public agency" under the FLSA.[3]

In *Briggs v. Chesapeake Volunteers in Youth Services, Inc.*,[4] the court declined to find that a nonprofit corporation that provided community service opportunities to juveniles in the juvenile court system was covered as an enterprise under the FLSA as a "public agency." The former employee claimed the nonprofit corporation was an "arm" of the city of Chesapeake because, among other things, (1) the corporation received some funding from the city, (2) the board members of the nonprofit corporation were appointed by members of an advisory council who were appointed by a juvenile court judge, (3) the former employee's paychecks were drawn from the city, and (4) the former employee received benefits from the Virginia Retirement System.[5] Despite these facts, the court found that the nonprofit corporation was not a "public agency" because a majority of its funding came from private sources, it was created by a group of private individuals (not by the city of Chesapeake of the Commonwealth of Virginia), and it appointed its own board members and hired and fired its own employees.[6]

In *Robertson v. Board of County Commissioners of County of Morgan*,[7] a federal district court in Colorado considered whether certain deputy sheriffs were employees of the Board of County Commissioners for Morgan County. The court applied the four-factor "economic reality" test and found that the first factor, the authority to hire and fire, weighed in favor of the deputies not being employees of the board because the Morgan County sheriff (not the board) had sole authority to hire and fire deputy sheriffs.[8] However, the court found that the remainder of the

---

[3] *In re* Lower Marion Township Fire Dep't Labor Standards Litig., 972 F. Supp. 315, 4 WH Cases2d 142 (E.D. Pa. 1997) (publicly funded volunteer fire departments are not "public agencies" because they are not responsible to general public or to public officials).

[4] 68 F. Supp. 2d 711, 5 WH Cases2d 1199.

[5] *Id.* at 716–17, 5 WH Cases2d at 1202–03.

[6] *Id.* at 716–18, 5 WH Cases2d at 1203.

[7] 78 F. Supp. 2d 1142, 5 WH Cases2d 1449 (D. Colo. 1999).

[8] *Id.* at 1151, 5 WH Cases2d at 1456.

factors indicated that the deputies were employees of the board because: (1) though the sheriff controlled the day-to-day activities of the deputies and other employees, the board set some conditions of employment (such as the overtime pay and compensatory time policies); (2) the board approved the rates and frequency of pay fixed by the sheriff; and (3) though the sheriff maintained separate pay records of the employees, the board maintained the "permanent" and "official" records used to calculate pay and compensatory time.[9] Weighing all the factors, and in light of the "expansive" view of the terms "employee" and "employer" under the Act, the court concluded that the board was an employer of the deputy sheriffs.[10]

In *Taylor v. County of Fluvanna,*[11] a federal district court in Virginia came to the opposite conclusion and held that the county of Fluvanna was not the employer of a deputy sheriff who sued the county and the sheriff for unpaid overtime wages. Applying the four-factor "economic reality" test, the court granted summary judgment for the county on the grounds that the county was not the deputy's employer due to its insufficient control over the deputy sheriff, his working conditions, his workplace, and his pay.[12] Specifically, the court found that "the county does not (1) hire, fire, supervise, or discipline the deputy sheriffs; (2) supervise or control the deputies' work schedules or conditions of employment; (3) set rates of pay or method of employment; or (4) maintain employment records other than payroll-related records."[13] The court noted that the strongest factor in favor of the county was the fact that it maintained some of the employment records.[14] However, the court opined that "mere maintenance, by itself, of employment records is not sufficient to bestow employer status under the four-part test . . . ."[15] Instead, the court found that the sheriff had exclusive control of

---

[9] *Id.* at 1151–52, 5 WH Cases2d at 1456.
[10] *Id.* at 1152, 5 WH Cases2d at 1456.
[11] 70 F. Supp. 2d 655, 5 WH Cases2d 1255 (W.D. Va. 1999).
[12] *Id.* at 658–59, 5 WH Cases2d at 1258.
[13] *Id.* at 658, 5 WH Cases2d at 1258.
[14] *Id.*
[15] *Id.*

the deputy's "day-to-day shift scheduling, job duties, and method of job performance."[16]

A federal district court in New Jersey held in *Cahill v. City of New Brunswick*[17] that police officers were employees, not independent contractors, when they performed "extra duty jobs" for outside vendors because, even though they worked for private companies in performing these extra duty assignments, they were still under the control of the city. The city oversaw and administered the extra duty jobs program and, for its administrative costs, received a "cut" of the officers' pay for the extra duty jobs.[18] More importantly, though, the city considered the officers to be on "on-duty" status during the time they worked these extra duty jobs and admitted that the officers would be eligible for workers' compensation benefits if they were injured while performing an extra duty assignment.[19]

Of course the label that the parties give to their relationship is not controlling. In *Hefferman v. Illinois Community College District No. 508,*[20] a coach at a community college alleged that Illinois Community College District No. 508 violated the FLSA by not paying him for work he performed. The district moved to dismiss the coach's complaint on the grounds that the coach was not an "employee" of the district, relying on a written contract between the parties that the coach attached to his complaint entitled "Independent Contractor." The district court denied the motion to dismiss, noting that an independent contractor label does not necessarily remove the worker from the protection of the Act.[21]

---

[16]*Id.* Under Virginia law, sheriffs are independent constitutional officers whose power does not derive from the state or the county. *Id.* at 656, 5 WH Cases2d at 1256.

[17]99 F. Supp. 2d 464 (D.N.J. 2000).

[18]*Id.*

[19]*Id.*

[20]2000 WL 631309, 6 WH Cases2d 132 (N.D. Ill. 2000).

[21]6 WH Cases2d at 133.

B. Exclusions

2. *Personal Staff of Elected Officials*

A district court has ruled that a deputy sheriff did not fall within the personal staff exemption to the Act.[22] The only evidence the sheriff produced to support his claim for this exemption was the testimony of a major in the department that the plaintiff ranked 13th out of 260 deputies. In reaching its conclusion, the court applied the Fifth Circuit's six-factor test[23] to determine whether an employee falls under the personal staff exemption, and decided that the sheriff had failed to adduce evidence sufficient to support the claimed exemption.

The question whether deputy sheriffs are members of the "personal staff" of the sheriff was again presented in *Baker v. Stone County, Missouri.*[24] There the court analyzed the different approaches taken by the Fourth[25] and Tenth[26] Circuits, and the opinions issued by the Labor Department,[27] and decided that

---

[22]29 U.S.C. §203(e)(c)(ii). *See* Oliver v. Layrisson, 2 WH Cases2d 1246 (E.D. La. 1995), and 3 WH Cases2d 316 (E.D. La. 1996).

[23]The test is set forth in *Montgomery v. Brookshire,* 34 F.3d 291, 295, 65 FEP Cases 1866 (5th Cir. 1994), an ADEA case, where a similar but not identical personal staff exemption is applicable. The factors are: (1) whether the elected official has plenary powers of appointment and removal; (2) whether the person in the position at issue is personally accountable to only that elected official; (3) whether the person in the position at issue represents the elected official in the eyes of the public; (4) whether the elected official exercises a considerable amount of control over the position; (5) the level of the position within the organization's chain of command; and (6) the actual intimacy of the working relationship between the elected official and the person filling the position. These are the same factors as appeared in *Rodriguez v. Township of Holiday Lakes,* 866 F. Supp. 1012, 2 WH Cases2d 667 (S.D. Tex. 1994), a Title VII case, discussed in the Main Volume at §11.II.B.2 [Coverage Issues; Personal Staff of Elected Officials] p. 647. As noted by the court in *Oliver,* the exemptions under the ADEA and Title VII are identical.

[24]41 F. Supp. 2d 965, 5 WH Cases2d 414 (W.D. Mo. 1999).

[25]Curl v. Reavis, 740 F.2d 1323, 35 FEP Cases 930 (4th Cir. 1984); Brewster v. Barnes, 788 F.2d 985, 28 WH Cases 1110 (4th Cir. 1986); United States v. Gregory, 818 F.2d 1114, 46 FEP Cases 1743 (4th Cir.), *cert. denied,* 484 U.S. 847, 108 S. Ct. 143, 49 FEP Cases 1640 (1987).

[26]Nichols v. Hurley, 921 F.2d 1101, 30 WH Cases 125 (10th Cir. 1990).

[27]Brief filed by the Secretary of Labor as amicus curiae in *Nichols* and W-H Administrative Opinions of July 12, 1985, and Mar. 10, 1986. *See* 6 Wage and Hour Manual 91:404.

the mere fact that the sheriff had exclusive power to hire and fire the deputies was insufficient to establish the kind of "intimate and personal relationship" on which the personal staff exemption relies. The sheriff did not personally supervise the deputies, and it was the sheriff's chief deputy who exercised day-to-day supervision over the employees, including scheduling work shifts and responding to requests for overtime, time off, or comp time. The sheriff never scheduled meetings with employees to discuss official office policy or practice, and many of the employees would not have contact with the sheriff for weeks at a time or at all.

In *Renna v. County of Fresno,*[28] a board member assistant to a county supervisor was found to be exempt from the FLSA as a member of the personal staff of an elected official. Although under the Labor Department regulations[29] that address this personal-staff exemption, the employee might have been found nonexempt, the court analyzed the issue under a provision of Title VII of the Civil Rights Act[30] as construed by the Fifth Circuit in *Teneyuca v. Bexar County*[31] and concluded that the exemption applied.[32] The six factors applied in *Teneyuca,* which the court stated "take[] into account" the Labor Department rule, are:

> (1) [W]hether the elected official has plenary powers of appointment and removal,
>
> (2) [W]hether the person in the position at issue is personally accountable to only that elected official,

---

[28] 78 Cal. App. 4th 1, 92 Cal. Rptr. 2d 586 (2000).

[29] "The statutory term 'member of personal staff' generally includes only persons who are under the direct supervision of the selecting elected official and have regular contact with such official. The term typically does not include individuals who are directly supervised by someone other than the elected official even though they may have been selected by the official. For example, the term might include the elected official's personal secretary, but would not include the secretary to an assistant." 29 C.F.R. §553.11(b).

[30] 42 U.S.C. §2000e(f).

[31] 767 F.2d 148, 151 (5th Cir. 1985).

[32] In the apparently unrelated case of *Rodriguez v. Township of Holiday Lakes,* 866 F. Supp. 1012, 2 WH Cases2d 667 (S.D. Tex. 1994), discussed in the Treatise at p. 647, the district court similarly relied on a Title VII analysis to conclude that a police chief was a personal staff member of the city council that employed him.

(3) [W]hether the person in the position at issue represents the elected official in the eyes of the public,

(4) [W]hether the elected official exercises a considerable amount of control over the position,

(5) [T]he level of the position within the organization's chain of command, and

(6) [T]he actual intimacy of the working relationship between the elected official and the person in the position.[33]

The court noted that these factors are not intended to be exclusive, but instead are guidelines. Applying these factors, the court concluded that the plaintiff had a close working relationship with the board member for whom she worked, which the court found to be the most important factor among those listed in *Teneyuca*; represented the board member in the public's eyes; and was dependent for her work on that board member. The court rejected the employee's argument that, because she also performed work for other board members, she could not be considered the personal assistant to any one member.

C. Volunteers

1. *Definition of "Volunteer"*

In *Benshoff v. City of Virginia Beach*,[34] the court held that because firefighters employed by the city joined privately organized volunteer rescue squads primarily out of civic and charitable motivations and did not expect compensation for services rendered, they were "volunteers" under the FLSA. Additionally, the court found that the city's understanding that the rescue squad work was voluntary contributed to the firefighter's volunteer status. In this case, the city did not require firefighters to give up outside employment that interfered with their rescue squad

[33]767 F.2d at 151.
[34]9 F. Supp. 2d 610, 4 WH Cases2d 1310 (E.D. Va. 1998).

activities, nor did the city have the power to approve or dismiss rescue squad members. Thus, it was "obvious that the City does not hold the rescue squad members out as 'employees.'"

In *Benshoff v. City of Virginia Beach,*[35] the Fourth Circuit held that firefighters employed by the city who were also members of all-volunteer medical rescue squads were not entitled to overtime compensation under the FLSA for time spent working on the rescue squads. The plaintiffs argued that their work for the rescue squads was controlled by the city through a municipal department, the Department of Emergency Medical Services (DEMS), that had been established by the city to certify emergency medical technicians who practice within the jurisdiction and to coordinate and schedule the rescue squads' services to city residents. The plaintiffs also argued that their work for the rescue squads was compensable regardless of whether it was controlled by the city because these services primarily benefited the city and were substantially similar to those services they provided the city as paid firefighters. They contended that these facts precluded the city from claiming that the plaintiffs served on the rescue squads as "volunteers" within the meaning of 29 U.S.C. §203(e)(4)(A), which excludes from the definition of "employee" any individual "who volunteers to perform services for a public agency if . . . (ii) such services are not the same type of services which the individual is employed to perform for such public agency."

The court rejected each of these arguments. First, it held that the plaintiffs were not employed by the city by virtue of the city's control over the rescue squads through the DEMS, on grounds that the rescue squads, and not DEMS, accepted, disciplined, and discharged the rescue squad workers. The court also held that the city's control over the squads' scheduling and services, and its power to certify rescue squad members, was too limited to create an employment relationship between the city and the rescue squad workers. In reaching this conclusion, the court was careful to emphasize that the DEMS possessed no

---

[35]180 F.3d 136, 5 WH Cases2d 657 (4th Cir. 1999).

control over the minimum training and service requirements imposed by the individual rescue squads or the hours worked by the squad members.

The court also rejected the plaintiffs' argument that they were not volunteers under Section 203(e)(4)(A), finding that the plaintiffs' services primarily benefited the rescue squads, and not the city, and that the rescue squads are not "public agency" employers within the meaning of the FLSA. The court rejected the plaintiffs' argument that the only relevant inquiry to the application of Section 203(e)(4)(A) was whether their services benefited the city, and concluded that this interpretation of the volunteer exception would prohibit public agencies from ever allowing their employees to volunteer similar services for the benefit of a public agency.

Finally, the court rejected the Secretary of Labor's amicus curiae contention that the rescue squad members should be compensated by the city "as a practical matter" because the city derived a substantial benefit from their services. Rather, the court held that Congress did not intend Section 203(e)(4)(A) to relieve a plaintiff of the burden of demonstrating the existence of an employment relationship as a prerequisite to claiming compensation. The court concluded that judges should be able to "ferret out" cases where there is a "sham" private volunteer corporation placed between an employer and its employees to avoid the requirements of the Act.[36]

Todaro v. Township of Union[37] was a case in which the plaintiffs had "volunteered" their services to the township for 4 hours a week, without pay, as "special law enforcement officers," as a consequence of which they were eligible for referral to "jobs-in-blue," a program in which both regular employed police officers and the plaintiffs were eligible to be hired by private employers as security guards, etc. As of October 1995, the township notified the group to which the plaintiffs belonged that they would no longer be eligible for the jobs-in-blue program; however, the plaintiffs continued to work the customary

---

[36] *Id.*, 5 WH Cases2d at 666–67.

[37] 40 F. Supp. 2d 226, 6 WH Cases2d 281 (D.N.J. 1999).

4 hours per week. Their motive, as revealed by deposition testimony, was largely the hope that their eligibility for referral to jobs-in-blue would be restored. When it was not, after 2 years, the plaintiffs brought suit to be paid for the time they had worked as employees.

The federal district court in New Jersey court held that in determining whether an individual working for a public agency is an employee or a volunteer, the statutory definitional requirement that a volunteer be motivated by "civic, charitable, or humanitarian purposes" should be construed as requiring only that the individual be motivated "at least in part" by such purposes. The court stated that "it offends rationality" to suggest that an individual motivated by reasons of "personal purpose or pleasure" rather than the specified charitable purposes should be found an employee by virtue of that motivational discrepancy, noting that nothing in the language of the definition requires that the individual be exclusively, or even predominantly, motivated by civic, charitable, or humanitarian reasons. Further, commenting on the plaintiffs' argument concerning their expectations regarding compensation, the court noted that

> a person who performs services in the face of a regulation or stated policy that specifies that such services will be unpaid, yet who nevertheless persists in "expecting" to receive compensation, should not be permitted to satisfy the definition of "employee" simply by unreasonably insisting that he has a subjective expectation of receiving wages.... [T]here must be a point at which a person's subjective expectations and motivations are so unfounded and conjectural as to be insufficient to support a finding of reasonableness, and at this point the Court must rely on common-sense standards and objective indicia.[38]

Thus the court held that the plaintiffs were volunteers as a matter of law.

---

[38] *Id.* at 230, 6 WH Cases2d 281.

In an opinion letter dated September 14, 2000,[39] after summarizing the general rules applicable to the volunteering of services by public employees, the Department of Labor reiterated its policy that it will take no enforcement action in the case of a full- or part-time employee of a public school district who performs "volunteer" work in the classroom of, or in an activity where, the employee's own child is a participant, even if the employee regularly performs the same services for the employer, so long as the performance of services is entirely voluntary on the part of the employee and not the result of employer pressure or coercion to perform such volunteer activities.

2. *Receipt of Expenses, Reasonable Benefits, or a Nominal Fee*

In a May 17, 1999, opinion letter,[40] the Department of Labor, after noting that volunteers may be paid expenses, reasonable benefits, a nominal fee, or any combination thereof without losing their status as volunteers, found that a payment of $40 for a 24-hour standby period on-call, plus additional specified amounts for services actually performed, with a maximum payment of $50 per 12-hour shift, would qualify as a "nominal" fee. The Department also stated that where total compensation for volunteers from any combination of payments yields compensation that meets or exceeds the minimum wage, the issue of volunteer status becomes moot.

3. *Employment by the Same Public Agency*

In *Benshoff*,[41] the district court found that the firefighters, who were employed by the city and who volunteered time to

---

[39]WH Opinion Letter of Sept. 14, 2000, WHM: 99:5412, 2000 WL 33128584; following WH Opinion Letter of Aug. 3, 1995, WHM: 99:5301, which states "the Wage and Hour Division will not assert FLSA violations for time spent by a public school employee, who is also the parent of the child in that school system, volunteering in their own child's classroom or in activities directly involving their own child's education without expectation of compensation so long as there is no coercion or pressure on the employee by the employer to do so."

[40]1999 WL 1002403 (DOL Wage-Hour May 17, 1999).

[41]9 F. Supp. 2d 610 (E.D. Va. 1998).

privately organized volunteer rescue squads in the same geographic area, were not entitled to overtime compensation for volunteering their time to the "same public agency." The court emphasized that (1) the rescue squads for which the firefighters volunteered were independently organized, nonprofit organizations; (2) they were not controlled by the city; and (3) the city had no control over who was a member of the squad.

Affirming, the Fourth Circuit[42] held that city-employed firefighters who also were members of all-volunteer rescue squads were not entitled to overtime compensation under the FLSA for the time they gave to the rescue squads. The rescue squads were private entities, separate from the city, and so the volunteer arrangement did not run afoul of the FLSA's stipulation that an individual cannot be considered a volunteer for performing the same types of services for the same public agency for which the individual normally works.

5. Private Individuals As Volunteers for Public Agencies

Todaro v. Township of Union,[43] a case in which the plaintiffs had "volunteered" their services to the township for 4 hours a week, without pay, as "special law enforcement officers," and so became eligible for referral to "jobs-in-blue," a program in which both regular employed police officers and the plaintiffs were eligible to be hired by private employers as security guards, etc., the court held that the plaintiffs were volunteers as a matter of law, since they were motivated at least in part by civic, charitable, or humanitarian purposes and never had any realistic expectation of receiving compensation, whatever their hopes might have been in that regard.

---

[42] 180 F.3d 136, 5 WH Cases2d 657 (4th Cir. 1999).
[43] 40 F. Supp. 2d 226, 6 WH Cases2d 281 (D.N.J. 1999).

III. EXEMPTIONS FROM OVERTIME REQUIREMENTS IN THE PUBLIC SECTOR

A. Section 7(o)—Compensatory Time

1. Statutory Provisions

The Supreme Court held in *Christensen v. Harris County*[44] that neither the plain language of Section 7(o) nor the Department of Labor's regulations prohibit an employer from compelling employees to use compensatory time that the employees accrued under the Act.

The Court held that the FLSA addresses only the conditions under which employers must grant employees' requests to use comp time and is silent on the issue of whether or not employers can compel employees to use their accrued comp time. The Court noted that the FLSA permits employers to "cash out" accrued comp time whenever the employer wishes and nothing in the FLSA prohibits employers from requiring employees to take time off from work. The Court reasoned that compelled use of comp time "merely involves doing both of these steps at once."[45] It thus rejected the employees' argument that Section 7(o)(5), which requires employers to reasonably accommodate employee requests to use compensatory time, provides the exclusive means of using compensatory time, unless the employees and employer agreed otherwise, as well as the Department of Labor's argument that the Court should defer to the Department's position on this issue as it had been expressed in prior Wage and Hour Division opinion letters. The Court determined that deference to the agency's position is warranted only when the language of the statute or the implementing agency's

[44]529 U.S. 576, 5 WH Cases2d 1825 (2000).
[45]*Id.* at 586.

regulations is ambiguous. Because neither the statute nor the DOL regulations address this issue at all, the Court held that the deference to the DOL that the Court granted in *Auer v. Robbins*[46] was unwarranted.

In *Robertson v. Board of County Commissioners of County of Morgan,*[47] a federal district court held that genuine issues of material fact existed as to whether sheriff's deputies were denied compensatory time for preshift briefings where there was evidence that the deputies were told to record preshift briefings on their time records but no individual time records were submitted.

In *Alexander v. City of Evansville,*[48] the Seventh Circuit held that language in a collective bargaining agreement granting the city the right to handle overtime "as allowed by the FLSA" did not unambiguously compel the conclusion that the city must meet its overtime obligations by giving compensatory time off.

2. *Prior Agreement or Understanding*

In *Baker v. Stone County, Missouri,*[49] a federal district court concluded that the FLSA was not violated where the sheriff's department compensated employees with compensatory time off rather than cash for overtime worked, despite the fact that the policy pursuant to which this was done was adopted unilaterally by the county. When the county was made aware that its prior overtime policies violated the FLSA, it adopted a Section 7(k) plan and at the same time advised all employees that the "Sheriff and the Stone County Commission retain the right to determine how hours worked beyond the limit of 171 hours will be compensated (by either being paid compensation or compensatory time off)."[50] In its review of the "agreement," the court noted, "Each Plaintiff testified that he or she understood at or near the time of hiring that compensatory time is received as

---

[46]519 U.S. 452 (1997).
[47]78 F. Supp. 2d 1142, WH Cases2d 1449 (D. Colo. 1999).
[48]120 F.3d 723, 4 WH Cases2d 1 (7th Cir. 1997).
[49]41 F. Supp. 2d 965, 5 WH Cases2d 414 (W.D. Mo. 1999).
[50]*Id.,* 5 WH Cases2d at 434.

compensation for overtime. Every Plaintiff except for one testified that he or she never complained regarding the compensatory time system. Only Plaintiff Nina Stults testified that she complained about receiving compensatory time instead of pay, but she never refused a paycheck or refused to work overtime."[51] Finding that "Section 553.23(3) indicates that an agreement or understanding with individual employees need not be in writing but a record of its existence must be kept pursuant to §553.50,"[52] and finding considerable written evidence of the operation of the policy, the court found an implied agreement to accept the comp time in lieu of overtime pay.

In *Robertson v. Board of County Commissioners of County of Morgan*,[53] the court denied summary judgment to plaintiff deputy sheriffs and dispatchers who claimed that they had been improperly paid comp time for overtime work. The employees claimed that comp time was improper because there was no explicit agreement to award comp time, they had never signed such an agreement, and their employer never told them they had the option to preserve, use, or cash out comp time pursuant to Section 7(o). The employer claimed, however, that it had submitted a memo to the employees explaining its comp time policy. In denying the plaintiffs' motion for summary judgment, the court noted that the agreement or understanding may properly be evidenced by a memorandum, and that nothing in the FLSA requires a written comp time agreement, let alone one signed by the employee.

4. Rate of Accrual

In a somewhat unclear opinion letter dated January 8, 2001,[54] the Department of Labor stated that a compensation program to which paramedic employees had agreed in advance, and under which they earned one-half hour of "comp time" for each hour worked over 40 in a week when their salary already

---

[51] *Id.* at 435.
[52] *Id.* at 434.
[53] 78 F. Supp. 2d 1142 (D. Colo. 1999).
[54] Letter of Jan. 8, 2000 by staff member of Office of Enforcement Policy, WHM: 99:5415, 2001 WL 1558758.

compensated them for the straight time pay of all hours worked, would satisfy Section 7(o) of the FLSA.

6. *Conditions for Using or Cashing Out Comp Time*

Although a requirement to use accrued comp time by signing up for days off in a logbook sometimes resulted in police officers' being denied comp time, a federal district court in Tennessee held that the policy did not violate the FLSA's requirement that public employees be permitted to take comp time within a "reasonable period."[55] This was because the police and the city had agreed to the logbook method, and the logbook defined what constituted a "reasonable period" under Section 553.25 of the Code of Federal Regulations.[56]

In *AFSCME Local 889 v. Louisiana*,[57] the Fifth Circuit held that a state practice of requiring employees to exhaust compensatory time before taking annual leave did not violate Section 7(o) of the FLSA. Relying on the Eighth Circuit's decision in *Heaton v. Moore*,[58] the union argued that Section 7(o) created a property right in compensatory time that fell under the dominion of the employee, prohibiting the employer from mandating that time off be deducted first from compensatory time. The Fifth Circuit distinguished *Heaton*, rejecting the argument that Congress intended Section 7(o) to create new property rights in employees. The purpose of Section 7(o)'s authorization of the use of compensatory time, according to the court, was to balance the interests of employees against the unique burden imposed on public employers which would result from the payment of cash overtime. The Fifth Circuit agreed with the district court that allowing public employees to bank compensatory time until it reached the statutory limit, thus requiring the payment of cash, would upset this balance and impose an undue burden on public employers.

---

[55]Aiken v. Memphis, 985 F. Supp. 740, 745–46, 4 WH Cases2d 408, 412 (W.D. Tenn. 1997).

[56]*Id.* at 746, 4 WH Cases at 412.

[57]145 F.3d 280, 4 WH Cases2d 1355 (5th Cir. 1998).

[58]43 F.3d 1176, 2 WH Cases2d 801 (8th Cir. 1994).

The Fifth Circuit also declined to follow the Eighth Circuit's rule in *Moreau v. Harris County*.[59] The court reasoned that Congress had not intended in Section 7(o) to create a property right in accrued comp time and that Section 7(o) did not prohibit employers from setting uniform employment policies with respect to comp time in the absence of a negotiated agreement to the contrary. In particular, the court found that, on the facts before it, the Harris County police department was permitted to require its employees to reduce their accrued comp time when it rose above a predetermined level. According to the Fifth Circuit in *Moreau v. Harris County*, the 1985 amendments to the FLSA do not give public employees a right to choose when they will use accrued comp time. It upheld a county policy that required employees to use accrued comp time rather than receive overtime pay. The court reasoned that the statute was silent and that absent such a statutory restriction or a negotiated agreement to the contrary, the employer could set workplace rules.[60] In doing so, the court rejected the Eighth Circuit holding in *Heaton v. Moore*.[61]

The Ninth Circuit affirmed a district court's decision to the same effect in a Washington case involving firefighters, *Collins v. Lobdell*.[62]

In *Aiken v. City of Memphis*,[63] the Sixth Circuit affirmed the district court in upholding the city of Memphis' policy of preventing police officers from taking accrued FLSA comp time when too many officers had signed up to take a particular day off. The court analyzed the case in the context of whether the employer granted the employees' request to use comp time within "a reasonable period" after making the request rather than on the basis of whether the request "unduly disrupted" the employer's operations. The court found that the city's policy

---

[59]158 F.3d 241 (5th Cir. 1998), *aff'd*, 120 S. Ct. 1655, 5 WH Cases2d 1825 (2000).

[60]*Id.* On certiorari, this decision was affirmed by a divided Supreme Court in *Christensen v. Harris Co.*, 120 S. Ct. 1655, 5 WH Cases2d 1825 (2000).

[61]43 F.3d 1176.

[62]188 F.3d 1124, 5 WH Cases2d 929 (9th Cir. 1999).

[63]190 F.3d 753, 5 WH Cases2d 961 (6th Cir. 1999), *cert. denied*, 528 U.S. 1157, 5 WH Cases2d 1632 (2000).

merely reflected the city's collective bargaining agreement with the police union that defines when the use of comp time will be permitted. The court held that it should defer to the agreement as to whether a request had been granted within a reasonable period of time pursuant to the meaning of Section 7(o)(5) and the Department of Labor regulations.[64] The court found that the union and the city reached this agreement to ensure that each shift was adequately staffed. Under the agreement, the commanding officer of each precinct monitored the station log book with regard to staffing. Requests to use comp time could be made beginning 30 days before the date requested to use the time. Once the requests became sufficiently numerous that staffing levels at a precinct adversely affected the functioning of the unit, the commanding officer could deny comp time requests for that day. The police officers argued that it was not unduly disruptive to an employer within the meaning of the Act to pay overtime to one officer so that another could use comp time. They argued that the city could have called in other officers to work overtime if granting an officer's request affected staffing needs. The court rejected this argument. The court first noted that Section 7(o)(5) permits an employee to use compensatory time only within a reasonable period of time after the request is made. The court then found that the agreement between the union and the city that set forth the procedures for using comp time merely defined whether a request was granted within a reasonable period of time after the request was made.

In *DeBraska v. City of Milwaukee*,[65] the court considered whether a city could prohibit police officers from using their comp time when doing so would require the city to call in another officer to work overtime. The city had argued that DOL regulations did not require a public employer to honor an employee's request for compensatory time off if to do so would be "unduly disruptive" to the employer's operations.[66] Before

---

[64] 29 C.F.R. §553.25(d).

[65] 131 F. Supp. 2d 1032, 142 Lab. Cas. (CCH) ¶34,212 (E.D. Wis. Sept. 26, 2000).

[66] *See* 29 C.F.R. §553.25(d).

making its decision, the court requested an *amicus* brief on the issue from the DOL.[67] Giving deference to the DOL's interpretation of its own regulations, the *Debraska* court found that the city had not in fact considered each request to see if the individual request "would impose an unreasonable burden 'during the time requested.'"[68] Rather, the city had simply automatically denied any request for comp time when it would require another officer to work overtime.[69] Thus the court could not agree with the city that granting such requests would be "unduly disruptive."

Further, the *Debraska* court found that the DOL's 1987 preamble to its own regulations supported and clarified the DOL's current interpretation of "unduly disrupt." The 1987 preamble acknowledged "that situations may arise in which overtime may be required of an employee to prevent another employee to use compensatory time off. However, such a situation, in and of itself, would not be sufficient for an employer to claim that it is unduly disruptive."[70]

8. Records to Be Kept of Compensatory Time

American Federation of State, County and Municipal Employees v. Louisiana,[71] involved the claim of a sergeant in the Wildlife and Fisheries Enforcement Division of the state service. Neither the employee nor the employer kept contemporaneous records of overtime worked by the sergeant. The employer had a policy of non-payment for overtime and relied on an "honor system" in which the employee was to take compensatory time off for the hours worked as overtime.[72] The employee-plaintiff claimed that he had too much work and therefore was unable to use his accumulated compensatory time. Though sympathetic to the

[67]131 F. Supp. 2d at 1033.
[68]*Id.* at 1035.
[69]*Id.* at 1035.
[70]*Id.* at 1036 (quoting 52 Fed. Reg. 2012, 2017 (1987))
[71]2001 WL 29999 (E.D. La. Jan. 9, 2001).
[72]*Id.* at *11.

plaintiff's supervisor, who was "caught between the non-overtime policy and accomplishing results,"[73] the court nevertheless found the employer guilty of violating FLSA's overtime requirements because the plaintiff had not taken the appropriate amount of compensatory time off and the employer had not otherwise paid him for the overtime. Further, although the plaintiff did not actually request to use compensatory time until thousands of hours had accumulated, the court found that this did not excuse the employer's asserted ignorance of the overtime worked.[74]

B. Section 7(p)(2)—Occasional or Sporadic Employment

2. *Provisions in the Regulations*

a. "Occasional or Sporadic"

In *Johnson v. Unified Government of Wyandote County/Kansas City*,[75] police officers challenged the city's use of the "special detail" exemption provided by 29 U.S.C. §207(p)(1). Section 207(p)(1) provides that when government employees engaged in fire protection or law enforcement agree to and do work, on a part-time basis, for "a separate and independent" employer under arrangements made or facilitated by their regular employing agency, the hours worked in the other job are not added to the hours worked at the regular jobs for purposes of overtime compensation. Plaintiffs had volunteered for and were regularly assigned to special duty on the premises controlled by the Housing Authority. Plaintiffs were also paid directly by the Housing Authority for the work. Plaintiffs challenged the city's use of the exemption by claiming first that their "special details" were not covered by the exemption because they were not sporadic occurrences, but were instead regular and recurring;

---

[73] *Id.* at *12.
[74] *Id.* at *6.
[75] 127 F. Supp. 2d 1181 (D. Kan. 2000).

second, they challenged the "separate and independent" nature of the Housing Authority as related to their regular employer; and, finally, they asserted that they were required to and did perform their regular duties as officers for the Unified Government while on "detail" to the Housing Authority, and therefore did not qualify for the exemption. After extensive review of the pertinent facts before it, the district court found that each of plaintiffs' claims required the resolution of disputed factual issues, and thus denied defendants' motions for summary judgment. The court did conclude as a matter of law that to qualify for the Section 7(p)(1) exemption a "special detail" assignment need not be sporadic or occasional as required by a related exemption set forth in Section 7(p)(2) of the Act.

Another case involving Section 7(p)(1) is *Nolan v. City of Chicago*,[76] where the district court addressed whether the time spent by police officers working for the Chicago Transit Authority (CTA) and the Chicago Housing Authority (CHA) pursuant to a City of Chicago program entitled the "Voluntary Special Employment Program" (VSEP), constituted the type of special detail employment arranged or facilitated by the employer which need not be consolidated with regular hours worked under 29 U.S.C. §207(p)(1). The court concluded that the CHA and CTA were in fact separate entities from the City, as they were each established separately under state law; they each had the authority to issue tax notes; they could each pass ordinances and promulgate regulations; and they could each be sued or sue on their own behalf. Accordingly, the court ruled that the police officers' time spent working for the CHA and CTA constituted outside employment under Section 207(p)(1), and therefore the police officers' hours did not need to be combined with their time spent working for the City of Chicago when computing their entitlement to FLSA overtime pay.

---

[76] 125 F. Supp. 2d 324 (N.D. Ill. 2000).

IV. OTHER FLSA EXEMPTIONS IN THE PUBLIC SECTOR[77]

A. The "White-Collar" Exemption

1. Executive Employees

Police patrol and special lieutenants were held to be exempt under the executive exemption in *Anderson v. City of Cleveland.*[78] In so ruling, the court cited the plaintiffs' testimony that all of them were "in charge" of their assigned units, directed the work of officers under their supervision, assigned work at roll call, and spent the rest of the day monitoring the employees' work.

In *Adams v. United States,*[79] the Court of Federal Claims addressed the issue of whether certain supervisory border patrol agents were exempt under the executive exemption. The court ruled that field operations supervisors who supervised lower-level employees; assigned them to work with supervisory border patrol agents; and were responsible for time and attendance, pay raises recommendations, performance evaluations as well as recommendations for bonuses met the test for executive employees under the Act. The court ruled that the first-line supervisory border patrol agents, however, did not qualify for the executive exemption because they did not supervise a recognized organizational unit with a continuing function. Instead, each day they were assigned a group of six to eight agents to supervise in the field. The agents whom they supervised changed from day to day because the first-line supervisory agents supervised geographic areas rather than a particular group of employ-

[77]The reader is reminded that many of the exemptions applicable to public sector employees are also applicable to private sector employees, and the principal discussion of the issues raised by these exemptions is in Chapters 4 and 5 of both the Treatise and the Supplement.

[78]90 F. Supp. 2d 906 (E.D. Tenn. 2000).

[79]44 Fed. Cl. 772, 6 WH Cases2d 1097 (1999). *See* 29 C.F.R. §541.102 ("In the vast majority of cases the bona fide executive employee performs managerial and supervisory functions which are easily recognized as within the scope of the exemption.").

ees. The court concluded that supervision of a recognized organizational unit with a continuing function is a requirement of the test for the executive exemption, which the supervisory agents did not meet.

In *Kavanagh v. City of Phoenix*,[80] the court ruled that the head of the Phoenix police department's legal unit was exempt under the Act as an executive employee, "because he supervises the Legal Unit with virtually no supervision."[81]

2. *Administrative Employees*

In *Kavanagh v. City of Phoenix*,[82] the court ruled that the head of the Phoenix police department's legal unit and a legal specialist within the legal unit were exempt under the Act as administrative employees. One of them spent over 90 percent of his time either dispensing legal advice, which constitutes "analyzing data and drawing conclusions" as well as "making recommendations," or coordinating the department's defense by other attorneys, which involves "representing" the department and "negotiating" on its behalf; acting as liaison between the police department, the city's law department, and private law firms; and serving as a witness in cases against the department; he also advised the department's executive heads on legal issues, which constitutes "advising management," and oversaw the legal unit's publications, which constituted a "major assignment." The other employee, a legal specialist, was also exempt as an administrative employee, as he spent approximately 60 percent of his time lobbying on behalf of the police department and 30 percent of his time providing legal advice to the department.

---

[80] 87 F. Supp. 2d 958, 6 WH Cases2d 661 (S.D. Tex. 2000).

[81] *Id.*, 6 WH Cases2d at 666. There is no discussion of the number of employees in the Legal Unit. The court refers to 29 C.F.R. §541.102, concluding that "in the vast majority of cases the bona fide executive employee performs managerial and supervisory functions which are easily recognized as within the scope of the exemption."

[82] *Id.*

3. *Professional Employees*

In *Kavanagh v. City of Phoenix,*[83] the court ruled that the head of the Phoenix police department's legal unit qualified for exemption as a professional (as well as qualifying as an executive and administrative employee) because the evidence reflected that he spent 70 percent of his time providing legal advice and 25 percent of his time acting as a liaison between the police department, the city's law department, and outside law firms. A legal specialist in the same department was an exempt professional since he spent 30 to 34 percent of his time providing legal advice and 60 percent lobbying.

In *Owsley v. San Antonio Independent School District,*[84] the Fifth Circuit reversed the trial court's grant of summary judgment awarding overtime benefits to a school district's athletic trainers, determining that the trainers were exempt professionals. The trainers fit the first prong of the short test because they had to obtain a state license to be a trainer, and in meeting the license requirements they had to, at a minimum, obtain a bachelor's degree with specialized training in human anatomy and physiology. Those requirements were enough to satisfy the "learned" prong.

5. *Issues Under the Salary Basis Test*

In *Kavanagh v. City of Phoenix,*[85] the court rejected the plaintiff's argument that he was not paid on a salary basis. The plaintiff was head of the Phoenix police department's legal unit. He admitted he received a salary of $77,000 per year without regard to the number of hours worked, but claimed that since his paid leave was accrued and deducted in hourly increments, he should be considered to be paid hourly. In rejecting this argument, the court cited Ninth Circuit case law to the effect that charging the use of paid leave on an hourly basis does not defeat an employee's status as a salaried employee.

---

[83]87 F. Supp. 2d 958 (D. Ariz. 2000).
[84]187 F.3d 521 (5th Cir. 1999).
[85]87 F. Supp. 2d 958.

An Ohio court of appeal ruled in *Worley v. City of Cincinnati*[86] that assistant fire chiefs for the city of Cincinnati were paid on a salary basis despite deductions for less than a day's absence for personal reasons. The court based its decision on 29 C.F.R. §541.5d, which carves out an exception to the salary requirement set forth in 29 C.F.R. §541.118(a) for public employees. It provides that a public employee otherwise meeting the salary test will not be disqualified from a white-collar exemption when an employee's pay is reduced for personal absences of less than one day as long as the pay system is founded upon public-accountability laws or principles. The concept of public accountability derives from the desires of taxpayers that their government be accountable to them for expenditures from the public treasuries. The court found that even though the city did not have a written policy relating to public accountability, it was able to show that it had an existing policy of refusing to pay its employees for work not performed.

The Tenth Circuit affirmed summary judgment for the defendant in *Spradling v. City of Tulsa*,[87] holding that district chiefs of Tulsa's fire department were salaried employees despite a written policy that subjected the plaintiffs' pay to disciplinary deductions, creating a possibility of salary reductions for absences of less than one day. Applying *Auer v. Robbins*,[88] the court found that the plaintiffs were still considered salaried since the city did not maintain an actual practice of making deductions. The court noted that the policy applied to the plaintiffs and nonsalary employees, so it did not "effectively communicate" to the plaintiffs that pay deductions are an anticipated form of punishment for employees in "plaintiffs' category." Instead, the court found that no clear inference could be drawn as to the likelihood of sanctions being applied to employees such as the plaintiffs. Moreover, none of the plaintiffs had been subject to a disciplinary reduction in pay, and no employee in the plaintiffs' job position, district chief, had ever had his pay

---

[86]2000 Ohio App. LEXIS 3856 (Ohio Ct. App. 2000).
[87]198 F.3d 1219 (10th Cir. 2000).
[88]519 U.S. 452 (1997).

reduced for being absent from work due to any reason other than violations of a major safety rule.

In *Kelly v. City of New York*,[89] the district court applied the Supreme Court's decision in *Auer v. Robbins*,[90] and the Department of Labor's regulations regarding permissible deductions for major safety violations,[91] to a variety of fact patterns. The case involved overtime pay claims by captains, corrections captains, deputy inspectors, lieutenants, and sergeants within the New York City police department.

In ruling against all of the plaintiffs, the court first explained that to establish a policy of impermissible deductions from employees' salaries, under *Auer*, the employees must demonstrate the existence of a clear and particularized policy that effectively communicates that deductions from employees' salaries will be made in specified circumstances. The court found that the broad language used in the department policies did not communicate to employees in the positions at issue—captains and other officers—that they were subject to having their pay docked for disciplinary reasons for periods of less than a week. In so ruling, the court ruled that the plaintiffs' subjective beliefs that they were subject to these policies were immaterial.

Next, the court turned to the issue of whether there was sufficient evidence of an actual practice of docking the employees' pay to establish that it had been effectively communicated to the employees that their pay would be subject to being docked. To answer this question, the court first considered the relevant grouping to determine the existence of impermissible disciplinary docking. Rejecting the plaintiffs' argument that the court should aggregate the number of deductions of all of the positions at issue in the case (captains, lieutenants, sergeants, deputy inspectors, and other high-level officials), the court instead examined the dockings in each position-category separately over a 10-year period. The court did not consider any of the dockings that it determined had been made for violations of

---

[89]2000 WL 1150462, 6 WH Cases2d 753 (S.D.N.Y. 2000).
[90]519 U.S. 452.
[91]5 C.F.R. §541.118(a)(5).

major safety violations, discussed below, and with those exclusions determined that the number was insufficient to establish an actual practice of docking in any of the categories.

The court determined the following deductions among others to have been made for major safety violations:

- discipline for sleeping on duty and for being away from the post, because it poses a threat to fellow officers;
- discipline for threatening and harassing a fellow officer, because it poses a threat to fellow officers;
- discipline for compromising a corruption investigation because it put the officer who reported the corruption at risk;
- discipline for a scheme of breaking into drug dealers' apartments, stealing money from drug dealers, and giving false testimony in proceedings against drug dealers;
- discipline for requesting that fellow officers provide false testimony; and
- discipline for losing a gun, misusing a gun, and interfering with police activities.

The court found that the following disciplinary deductions did not fall within the exception for major safety violations:

- solicitation of bribes where no evidence existed of fellow officers being put at risk;
- being charged with murder of a suspect where the murder charge was dismissed;
- failure to make reports when a subordinate discharges his firearm; and
- solicitation of prostitution, unauthorized off-duty employment, illegal gambling, patronizing unlicensed premises, intoxicated while off-duty, cheating on sergeants' exam, failing to report in sick, insurance fraud, improper fraternization with recruits, and arrests for driving while intoxicated off-duty.

The court then considered whether the city could take advantage of the window of correction to avoid backpay liability for those employees whose pay had been improperly docked. The court held that the deductions were made for reasons other than lack of work and, therefore, the window of correction could be utilized. The court interpreted the *Auer* decision to mean that any time any deduction is made for reasons other than lack of work, the window of correction can be utilized. The court noted, however, that this is true only where the employees have failed to establish that an actual practice of making the deductions exists. If the court had found the number of impermissible deductions to be sufficiently numerous to constitute an actual practice of making such deductions, according to the court, the window of correction could not have been utilized.

On remand from the Supreme Court, the district court in *Yourman v. Giuliani*[92] granted summary judgment to the city in an action brought by managerial employees employed by several municipal agencies. The plaintiffs argued that they were not paid on a salary basis because they were subject to improper disciplinary deductions. The Second Circuit agreed with the district court that because none of the written policies of the relevant city agencies contained rules applicable only to managers, mandating that if a manager commits a specific infraction, his or her pay will be docked, there was not a significant likelihood of improper disciplinary deductions being made. However, the Second Circuit found there was a triable issue as to whether there was an actual practice of imposing disciplinary deductions. The appellate court ruled that in determining whether an actual practice existed, a court must determine if the employer has an objective intention of paying its employees on a salary basis. That question cannot be answered by simply dividing the number of impermissible pay deductions by the number of managerial employees, as the district court had done. Rather, the trial court must consider additional factors such as the number of times that other forms of discipline are imposed, the number of employee infractions warranting discipline, the existence of policies favoring or disfavoring pay deductions, the process by which sanctions are determined, and the degree of

---

[92]1999 U.S. Dist. LEXIS 15700, 5 WH Cases2d 1470 (S.D.N.Y. 1999), *rev'd and remanded,* 229 F.3d 124 (2d Cir. 2000).

discretion held by the disciplinary authority. The trial court was also instructed, on remand, to consider evidence of disciplinary deductions made prior to the statute-of-limitations period that it had previously excluded as untimely.

In *Klem v. County of Santa Clara,*[93] the Ninth Circuit adopted the view of the plaintiffs and the Secretary of Labor that the "window of correction" is available only to employers that have demonstrated the objective intention to pay their employees on a salaried basis. When an employer has demonstrated the objective intention, the window of correction is available to cure inadvertent or isolated violations of the salary basis regulations. If an employer cannot demonstrate that objective intention, then it cannot, after the fact, use the window of correction to bring itself into compliance with the salary basis regulations and thereby turn nonsalaried employees into salaried employees. Here the court found that the employer had a pattern and practice of improper suspensions resulting in impermissible salary deductions (53 among approximately 5,300 employees), so that it could not establish an objective intention to pay the employees on a salaried basis. Accordingly, the window of correction was not available to the county employer.

In *Block v. City of Los Angeles,*[94] the Ninth Circuit examined disciplinary suspensions in light of the DOL's interpretation of the salary basis test as stated in its amicus brief filed with the Supreme Court in *Auer v. Robbins.*[95] According to the DOL's interpretation, employees may lose the exempt status under FLSA if the employer has either a practice or a policy of making disciplinary or other deductions in salary.[96] In *Block,* the Ninth Circuit affirmed the district court's findings that the city did not have a policy that led to a significant likelihood of disciplinary deductions, but held that the city did have an "actual practice" of making such improper disciplinary deductions.[97] The Ninth Circuit also affirmed the district court's determination that, because the improper deductions involved an "actual prac-

---

[93]208 F.3d 1085 (9th Cir. 2000).

[94]253 F.3d 410, 7 WH Cases2d 4 (9th Cir. 2001).

[95]519 U.S. 452, 117 S. Ct. 905 (1997), discussed *supra.*

[96]*Id.*

[97]253 F.3d at 414, 7 WH Cases2d 4.

tice,"[98] the city could not avail itself of the "window of correction" otherwise provided for in the regulations.[99]

The *Block* decision also discussed whether disciplinary suspensions in any amounts of time other than "full-week increments" violated the salary basis test, and held that partial week suspensions, even if part of a suspension lasting longer than a week, are inconsistent with treatment of city employees as salaried employees. The defendant argued that only suspensions of less than a week are problematic, and therefore any suspensions of more than a week (e.g., suspensions of 10 working days) were proper. The district court had found the city's argument entirely without merit on the basis of the regulation which states that a salaried employee "must receive his full salary for any week in which he performs any work, without regard to the number of days or hours worked."[100] The appellate court was uncertain that the regulatory language relied on by the district court entirely disposed of the matter, but found that it did not need to reach this question to decide the case, and thus did not do so, although it stated that it did "agree with the district court that suspensions of more than a week run afoul of the salary basis test."[101]

In *Anthony v. State of Iowa*,[102] the Iowa Supreme Court determined that the "window of correction" was not available to the public employer that had a general policy of making disciplinary deductions from the pay of the employees in question. The various decisions[103] preceding this one were reversed or withdrawn.

---

[98] *Id.* at 420, 7 WH Cases2d 4.

[99] *See* 29 C.F.R. §541.118(a)(6).

[100] 253 F.3d 410, 7 WH Cases2d at 9 (quoting the decision below).

[101] *Id.* at 10.

[102] 7 WH Cases2d 389.

[103] In addition to federal litigation ultimately dismissed after the decision in *Seminole Tribe*, 517 U.S. 44, and before the state litigation was filed, there was state litigation challenging the state courts' jurisdiction on sovereign immunity grounds. The Iowa Supreme Court here decided that the state had waived its immunity. On the salary issue, this decision deals with the matters decided in 6 WH Cases2d 1334, *aff'g trial court decision; withdrawn on grant of reh'g*, Apr. 13, 2001 *and superseded*, 7 WH Cases2d 389, *cert. denied*, 7 WH Cases2d 1152 (2002).

In *Demos v. City of Indianapolis*,[104] former city employees brought suit against the City of Indianapolis to recover overtime payments. The City moved for summary judgment claiming that the employees were exempt, salaried employees under the FLSA, even though the plaintiffs' pay was subject to reductions for absences of less than a day. The City contended that such deductions were permissible under the public accountability exception. The district court found that requiring employees to work at least 8 hours each day "strongly suggests" that the employee should be classified as non-exempt rather than exempt.[105] It further determined that the city had not offered any evidence to support its argument that principles of "public accountability"[106] were the basis for the docking system. Accordingly, the court denied the City's motion for summary judgment.[107]

In *Johnson v. Ohio Department of Youth Services*,[108] the plaintiff, a regional administrator for the Ohio Department of Youth Services, appealed a trial court finding that she was a salaried employee exempt from the overtime requirements of FLSA. She was expected to be on the job between 8:30 a.m. and 4:30 p.m. and was docked for arriving late. However, she was able to use accumulated leave time or compensatory time to avoid any reduction in salary. The court found that the employer treated the plaintiff in a manner inconsistent with exempt salaried status. Since the relevant regulation[109] is silent as to the use of comp time, the court reasoned that the use of comp time does not correlate with the DOL's concept of an exempt employee. Therefore, the Ohio Court of Appeals reversed the lower court and held that the plaintiff was not an exempt employee under the FLSA.

[104] 126 F. Supp. 2d 548 (S.D. Ind. 2000).
[105] *Id.* at 553.
[106] *See* 29 C.F.R. §541.5d(a).
[107] 126 F. Supp. 2d at 554.
[108] 140 Ohio App. 3d 774 (Ohio Ct. App. 2000).
[109] 29 C.F.R. §541.5(d).

V. SPECIAL PROVISIONS THAT APPLY TO FIRE PROTECTION AND LAW ENFORCEMENT EMPLOYEES OF PUBLIC AGENCIES

B. The Section 7(k) Exemption

The Section 207(k) exemption is limited to public agencies and does not apply to any private organization engaged in providing fire protection or law enforcement services. A federal district court in Pennsylvania addressed the question of how to determine whether particular volunteer fire departments are public agencies entitled to exemption from the FLSA overtime pay exemption.[110] The court held that paid firefighters of five volunteer fire departments were not employees of public agencies for purposes of Section 207(k)'s partial overtime exemption. In examining the relationship of the fire departments and the Pennsylvania township in which they were located, the court looked at the factors identified in *Wilcox v. Terrytown Fifth District V.F.D., Inc.*,[111] and *Conway v. Takoma Park V.F.D., Inc.*[112] The court noted that the fire departments received much of their funding from, and were regulated by, the township. The court, however, stated that this "merely show[ed] a conditional grant of money, and not a parent-subsidiary relationship." Next, the court found that the members of the governing boards of the departments were not elected by the public or appointed by a public official. Therefore, the departments were not directly responsible to the general public or to a public official. Furthermore, the court found significant a Pennsylvania court decision[113] under the National Labor Relations Act in which the state court held that the township was not a "joint employer" with the fire departments of the firefighters.

---

[110] *In re* Lower Marion Fire Dep't Litig., 972 F. Supp. 315, 4 WH Cases2d 142 (E.D. Pa. 1997).

[111] 897 F.2d 765, 29 WH Cases 1218 (5th Cir. 1990).

[112] 666 F. Supp. 786, 28 WH Cases 314 (D. Md. 1987).

[113] International Ass'n of Firefighters v. Commonwealth, 504 A.2d 422 (Pa. Commw. Ct. 1986).

Several decisions construe the Section 7(k) partial overtime exemption. In *Spradling v. City of Tulsa*,[114] the Tenth Circuit upheld the district court's ruling that the city had failed to establish its entitlement to a Section 7(k) partial exemption for Tulsa fire chiefs who worked shifts of 24 hours on duty followed by 48 hours off duty.[115] The Tenth Circuit stated that the public employer had the burden to prove that it had established a Section 7(k) work period, either by "an appropriate public declaration of intent to adopt a work period of between 7 and 28 days"[116] or "as long as its employees actually work a regularly recurring cycle of between 7 and 28 days."[117] Because the evidence failed to support the city's claim that it had adopted a 9-day work period, the city failed to sustain its burden.[118]

A state appellate court considered a complicated formula under which Louisiana police officers were paid during a 14-day work period straight time pay for the first 80 hours worked, credited for 1 hour compensatory time off at the straight-time rate for each of the next 6 hours worked, and paid overtime cash compensation for all hours worked in excess of the 86th hour.[119] The court rejected the employees' contention that the department had established an 80-hour, 14-day work period rather than an 86-hour, 14-day work period. The employees' contention was based on the fact that they were regularly scheduled to work 80 hours and thus were entitled to be paid overtime if called upon to work longer than 80 hours.[120] The court held that an 86-hour, 14-day work period had been established because the employees worked regularly recurring 14-day work cycles in which they were not paid overtime until the 87th hour worked.[121]

---

[114]95 F.3d 1492, 3 WH Cases2d 823 (10th Cir. 1996), *cert. denied*, 117 S. Ct. 1081 (1997).

[115]*Id.* at 1505.

[116]*Id.* (quoting McGrath v. City of Philadelphia, 864 F. Supp. 466, 476 (E.D. Pa. 1994)).

[117]*Id.* (quoting *McGrath*, 864 F. Supp. at 476).

[118]*Id.*

[119]Futral v. Louisiana, 699 So. 2d 1089, 1092 (La. Ct. App.), *writ denied*, 703 So. 2d 1317 (La. 1997).

[120]*Id.* at 1095.

[121]*Id.*

The department's policy of granting the compensatory straight-time rate for work performed after the 80th but before the 87th hour did not defeat the exemption.

In *Barefield v. Village of Winnetka*,[122] the Seventh Circuit held that the Section 7(k) exemption applied to police officers even though the employer had adopted the work schedule before the enactment of Section 7(k).[123] The court stated that "it is enough that Winnetka's police department met all of the factual criteria for §7(k)" and that "Winnetka need not have had the 7(k) exemption in mind when it adopted a 28-day work period."[124]

In *Freeman v. City of Mobile*,[125] the Eleventh Circuit found that the Mobile police department was entitled to an exemption under Section 7(k) of the FLSA. The employer demonstrated the city commission's adoption of a resolution "establish[ing] a Fourteen (14) Day work period for all members of the Mobile Police Department." Also, the city paid its police officers, sergeants, and lieutenants every other Friday, reflecting a 14-day pay period. Finally, the Mobile police chief had issued a memorandum in 1993 in response to police officers who sought overtime pay which stated that "[s]ince the Police Department has an established pay period of at least 7 days (ours is actually 14 days), the Department is not required to pay overtime compensation unless you work more than 86 hours during those 14 days." The police officers, sergeants, and lieutenants who argued against a 7(k) exemption presented no evidence demonstrating that the city did not have a 14-day work period. The court rejected the argument that the city was required to affirmatively adopt a resolution containing language explicitly referring to a 7(k) compensation plan, and found that the above evidence adequately demonstrated that the city had in fact adopted a 14-day work period.

In *AFSCME Local 889 v. Louisiana*,[126] the Fifth Circuit held that the state's adoption of a 14-day work period was reflected by

[122] 81 F.3d 704, 3 WH Cases2d 353 (7th Cir. 1996).
[123] *Id.* at 710.
[124] *Id.*
[125] 146 F.3d 1292, 4 WH Cases2d 1345 (11th Cir. 1998).
[126] 145 F.3d 280, 4 WH Cases2d 1355 (5th Cir. 1998).

its practice of averaging the number of hours worked by corrections employees acting as "compound officers" over a 2-week span. These employees worked 60 hours during the first week of the pay period and 24 hours during the second week. The state chose to pay the compound officers overtime for hours exceeding 80 during a 2-week pay period, even though Section 7(k)[127] did not require overtime payment until the number of hours worked during a 2-week period exceeded 86 hours. The employees argued that the state's choice to pay overtime for hours exceeding 80 during a pay period resulted in a forfeiture of the benefits of Section 7(k), but the Fifth Circuit rejected this claim, holding that the pay scheme complied with the requirements for a 7(k) exemption.

In *Jerzak v. City of South Bend*,[128] a federal district court in Indiana held that a city police department had met its burden of proving that it had adopted a Section 7(k) workweek exemption because the department's evidence included a notice provided to its employees informing them that the department had elected a 27-consecutive-day work period under Section 7(k). Furthermore, the evidence also included an interoffice memorandum that stated that the department had adopted a 9-day work cycle, and the plaintiff in his deposition stated that he was on a 27-day work cycle with 6 days on and 3 days off.

The Eighth Circuit in *Christian v. City of Gladstone*[129] considered the relationship of Section 553.212(a)[130] of the regulations and the Section 7(k) partial exemption in the context of para-

---

[127]29 U.S.C. §207(k) (1998).

[128]996 F. Supp. 840, 4 WH Cases2d 736 (N.D. Ind. 1998).

[129]108 F.3d 929, 133 Lab. Cas. (CCH) ¶33,508, 3 WH Cases2d 1441 (8th Cir.), *cert. denied*, 118 S. Ct. 557, 4 WH Cases2d 416 (1997).

[130]Section 553.212(a) states:

> Employees engaged in fire protection or law enforcement activities as described in §553.210 and 553.211, may also engage in some nonexempt work which is not performed as an incident to or in conjunction with their fire protection or law enforcement activities. . . . A person who spends more than 20 percent of his/her working time in nonexempt activities is not considered to be an employee engaged in fire protection or law enforcement activities for purposes of this part.

29 C.F.R. §553.212(a).

medics who were certified firefighters. The initial issue the court resolved was whether the paramedics were employees in fire protection activities as defined in Section 7(k). The court stated that Section 553.210(a)[131] of the regulations provides the definition of "employee in fire protection activities" and concluded that the paramedics met the four-part test set forth in that regulation.[132] In applying the four-part test to the paramedics, the court stated that the test "has no requirement that firefighting be the employees' only or primary duty, and the fact that the paramedics are also able to provide medical services while at fires and elsewhere does not eliminate their responsibility for firefighting."[133]

Next, the court considered the paramedics' argument that Section 553.212(a) (also known as the "80/20 rule") of the regulations applied and defeated the partial overtime exemption because over 20 percent of their work time involved "nonexempt activities." In considering the meaning of "nonexempt activities," the court examined the two competing tests respectively applied by the Fourth[134] and Eleventh[135] Circuits. The court rejected the Eleventh Circuit's approach, which broadly defines nonexempt work as "any work that 'generally inures to the benefit of the employer . . . which the employer requires its

---

[131]Section 553.210(a) states that the term "employee in fire protection activities" includes:

> any employee (1) who is employed by an organized fire department or fire protection district; (2) who has been trained to the extent required by State statute or local ordinance; (3) who has the legal authority and responsibility to engage in the prevention, control or extinguishment of a fire of any type; and (4) who performs activities which are required for, and directly concerned with, the prevention, control or extinguishment of fires, including such incidental non-firefighting functions as housekeeping, equipment maintenance, lecturing, attending community fire drills and inspecting homes and schools for fire hazards.

29 C.F.R. §553.210(a). The provision further states that the term "employee in fire protection activities" also includes "rescue and ambulance service personnel if such personnel form an integral part of the public agency's fire protection activities. *See* §553.215." *Id.*

[132]*Christian*, 108 F.3d at 932.

[133]*Id.*

[134]Schmidt v. County of Prince William, 929 F.2d 986, 30 WH Cases2d 377 (4th Cir. 1991).

[135]O'Neal v. Barrow County Bd. of Comm'rs, 980 F.2d 674 (11th Cir. 1993).

employees to do while they are not engaged in activities related to their fire protection or law enforcement duties.'"[136] The court, agreeing with the Fourth Circuit, found that the better approach in determining what constitutes nonexempt work is to consider whether the work is "'distinct from and unrelated to fire protection activities' and whether 'the essential nature of the firefighter's job changes and he is required to perform tasks unrelated to his job.'"[137] Because the facts showed that "the paramedics respond to fires, fight them, and provide paramedic services at those fires, as well as on calls not involving fires [and] [n]early all of their time is spent on such activities, related training, support services, and waiting for calls," the court held that Section 553.212 did not apply to defeat the Section 7(k) partial exemption in this case.[138]

A district court within the Fourth Circuit, however, held that the Section 7(k) partial overtime exemption did not apply to the county's emergency medical service (EMS) workers, who worked in an agency that was independent of fire protection or law enforcement.[139] For its EMS workers to qualify for the 7(k) exemption, the county had to show that the workers met the "substantially related" test of Section 553.215 and the "80/20" test of Section 553.212 of the regulations.[140] The court held that the county had failed to meet either of these tests.[141] First, the EMS workers were not "substantially related" to fire protection or law enforcement services. The evidence showed that 69.5 percent of EMS calls were on matters without a law enforcement or fire response and that 10 percent of working hours were spent on law enforcement and fire calls;[142] it did not show the total number of police and fire calls or the percentage of these which involved EMS workers. The court concluded that it had not been shown that EMS workers were "regularly dispatched to fires,

[136]108 F.3d at 933 (quoting *O'Neal*, 980 F.2d at 681).
[137]*Id.* (quoting *Schmidt*, 929 F.2d at 990).
[138]*Id.* at 934.
[139]Roy v. County of Lexington, 928 F. Supp. 1406, 3 WH Cases2d 613 (D.S.C.), *vacated in part*, 948 F. Supp. 529, 3 WH Cases2d 1214 (D.S.C. 1996).
[140]*Id.* at 1413. *See also* 29 C.F.R. §§553.215, 553.212.
[141]928 F. Supp. at 1416.
[142]*Id.* at 1414.

crime scenes, riots, natural disasters and accidents;"[143] and therefore, they did not qualify for the Section 7(k) exemption. Second, the county had failed to establish that the employees spent at least 80 percent of their time performing law enforcement or fire protection activities because the court calculated that the EMS workers spent 22.62 percent of work time on nonexempt activities (i.e., activities other than fire protection or law enforcement).[144]

Hergenreter v. City of Fort Dodge[145] involved a dispute over the regular rate of pay of city firefighters who were paid a base salary based on a 56-hour workweek, which translated into 216 hours per 27-day pay period. The city allowed the firefighters 12 hours of paid time off during each pay period to reduce their hours worked to 204—the threshold number of hours for paying overtime with a 27-day period—under the FLSA's Section 7(k) exemption. The firefighters and the city disputed whether the base salaries were intended to compensate for 204 hours or the full 216 hours of their 27-day work period. The court concluded that there was a genuine issue of material fact on this issue and therefore denied the parties' cross-motions for partial summary judgment.

The Eleventh Circuit has held that a district court erred in granting summary judgment to a municipal employer where the district court had concluded only that a "majority" of time was spent on fire protection activities.[146]

The Fourth Circuit has held, in the context of a Section 7(k) case, that "gap time" claims—that is, claims for compensation at the regular (straight time) rate for hours other than overtime hours—fail if the minimum wage was paid for the relevant hours.[147]

---

[143] *Id.* at 1413 (quoting 29 C.F.R. §553.215, and citing Spires v. Ben Hill County, 980 F.2d 683, 689 n.36 (11th Cir. 1993), and Justice v. Metropolitan Gov't of Nashville, 4 F.3d 1387, 1392 (6th Cir. 1993)).

[144] *Id.* at 1415–16.

[145] 987 F. Supp. 1141, 4 WH Cases2d 1759 (N.D. Iowa 1997).

[146] Jones v. Columbus, 120 F.3d 248, 4 WH Cases2d 99 (11th Cir. 1997). *See also* Craig v. Chattanooga, 910 F. Supp. 384, 3 WH Cases2d 220 (E.D. Tenn. 1996).

[147] Monahan v. County of Chesterfield, 95 F.3d 1263, 3 WH Cases2d 806 (4th Cir. 1996).

A federal district court considered a state law setting for Texas police officers a maximum workweek, which was less than the number of hours allowed under Section 7(k) of the FLSA.[148] The district court held that under Section 218(a) of the FLSA,[149] the city could not rely on the 7(k) exemption to excuse its noncompliance with the Texas statute.[150]

Ruling that federal firefighters' entire 24-hour shift, consisting of 8 hours of actual work and 16 hours of standby time, must be counted toward overtime, the Claims Court in *Adams v. United States*[151] also ruled that standby time (even if spent sleeping or performing mundane chores) was so closely related to overtime-exempt work that it was also exempt. Agreeing with other courts, the court noted, "[I]t is the nature of a firefighter's work to be ready and alert for emergencies."[152]

In *Milner v. City of Hazelwood*,[153] the Eighth Circuit held per curiam that the FLSA's Section 7(k) exemption for publicly employed police officers applied, despite the fact the city manager's memorandum establishing the 28-day work period was not made public and that the city paid "daily overtime," a practice whose details are not made clear but which would arguably be inconsistent with reliance on a Section 7(k) work period. The court affirmed the district court's holding that "a city does not forfeit its §207(k) exemption by paying overtime more generously than the Secretary's regulations would require" and that "the exemption need not be established by public declaration."[154]

---

[148]Karr v. City of Beaumont, 950 F. Supp. 1317, 133 Lab. Cas. (CCH) ¶33,511 (E.D. Tex. 1997).

[149]29 U.S.C. §218(a) provides: "No provision of [the FLSA] or of any order thereunder shall excuse noncompliance with any Federal or State law or municipal ordinance establishing . . . a maximum workweek lower than the maximum workweek established under this [Act]."

[150]950 F. Supp. at 1324.

[151]36 Fed. Cl. 91, 3 WH Cases2d 647 (1996).

[152]*Id.* at 99 (internal quotation marks omitted; quoting Birdwell v. City of Gadsden, 970 F.2d 802, 809, 30 WH Cases 1745 (11th Cir. 1992)). *See also* Armour & Co. v. Wantock, 323 U.S. 126, 132–33, 4 WH Cases 862 (1944) ("Readiness to serve may be hired . . . and time spent lying in wait for threats to the safety of the employer's property may be treated by the parties as a benefit to the employer.").

[153]165 F.3d 1222, 5 WH Cases2d 133 (8th Cir. 1999).

[154]*Id.* at 1223.

Adair v. City of Kirkland[155] involved a claim for overtime for required 10-minute briefings prior to police officers' shifts on duty. The city and the officers had, by collective bargaining agreement, established that each officer would work four 12-hour shifts in each 8-day period and receive a fixed salary for that work. The officers claimed that the 10-minute period was not included in the compensation provided under the agreement. The city contended, and the district and appellate courts agreed, that the agreement established a valid Section 7(k) 8-day work period. Under Section 7(k), the overtime threshold for law enforcement officers for an 8-day period is 49 hours. Accordingly, the court of appeals held, there was no overtime owing even if the four 10-minute periods were not intended to be included in the fixed salary, since the officers worked only four 12 hour-and-40-minute shifts per pay period, and the total amount[155A] they received for that time was more than 48 2/3 times the minimum wage.

In *American Federation of State, County and Municipal Employees v. State of Louisiana,*[156] which involved the claim of a sergeant working in an undercover operation in the Wildlife and Fisheries Enfocement Division of the State service, the court, at the parties' request, applied a method which provided straight time pay for hours worked between 80 and 86 hours in a two-week pay period, and time and one half pay for hours worked beyond 86 hours. This was based on an agreement by the parties as to the correct application of Section 7(k) to plaintiff's employment.

In *Franklin v. City of Kettering,*[157] the Sixth Circuit Court of Appeals affirmed the trial court's grant of summary judgment for the defendant in a case addressing the issue whether an employer's work period, adopted under Section 7(k), was required to correspond with the employees' duty cycle or the length of the work period as provided by a collective bargaining agreement. The officers actually worked a 42-day work cycle.

---

[155] 185 F.3d 1055, 5 WH Cases2d 883 (9th Cir. 1999).

[155A] The 48 2/3 hours worked is less than the 49-hour threshold.

[156] 2001 WL 29999 (E.D. La. Jan. 9, 2001)

[157] 246 F.3d 531 (6th Cir. 2001)

The City used a 28-day work period for purposes of computing FLSA overtime for the plaintiff police officers. Pursuant to the collective bargaining agreement with the police officers' union, however, the City paid the police officers at time and one half their hourly rates of pay when they worked more than 40 hours per week, or beyond the regular workday. The Union contract also provided for various shift differentials that the City did not include in computing the police officers' regular rate of pay. When computing the police officers' FLSA overtime pay based on the 28-day work period, the City credited itself with the time and one half payments made based on the 40-hour workweeks under the contract. As a result, despite its failure to include shift differentials in the police officers' regular rates of pay, the City claimed that it did not owe the police officers any overtime payments. The trial court had found that the 7(k) work period need not coincide with the actual work period of the employees, and the court of appeals affirmed this conclusion, relying on a provision of 29 C.F.R. §553.224(a) as follows: "[T]he [Section 7(k)] work period can be of any length [between 7 and 28 days], and it need not coincide with the duty cycle or pay period or with a particular day of the week or hour of the day."

In *Nolan v. City of Chicago*,[158] the court held that the City of Chicago was entitled to offset its FLSA overtime liability with premium payments for work on holidays made under a collective bargaining agreement. The court held that premium payments made beyond the requirements of the FLSA that are made in accordance with the terms of a collective bargaining agreement can be used to offset FLSA overtime liability incurred within the same work period.

In *Adair v. City of Kirkland*,[159] police officers appealed the district court's decision that the city did not violate the FLSA by refusing to compensate the police officers for time spent in pre-shift briefings. The case turns on the whether the employer had established a Section 7(k) work period, because, if it had, there

---

[158] 125 F. Supp. 2d 324 (N.D. Ill. 2000). This case is dicussed further in V.C.4.
[159] 2001 WL 821021 (9th Cir. 2001) (unpublished decision).

would be no overtime pay due (since the number of hours worked by the officers, including the additional time worked in attending briefings, was less than the number of hours which must be worked before any overtime is due under Section 7(k)). The Ninth Circuit agreed with the district court that the provisions of the collective bargaining agreement, together with the actual work assignments followed, showed that the Section 7(k) work period had indeed been established. The plaintiffs' various arguments to the contrary, such as that the payroll administrator was unfamiliar with Section 7(k), that the employer's recordkeeping practices were deficient and did not show a Section 7(k) work period, etc., were rejected. The court had no difficulty with the district court's conclusion that the definition of salary in the collective bargaining agreement was intended to compensate the officers for their time spent in pre-shift briefings as well as their other work periods. The appellate court also found that the plaintiffs' attempt to raise a gap time claim for the first time on appeal was unavailing.

C. Compensable Hours of Work Rules

1. *Sleep Time*

A district court in the Fourth Circuit held that an employer who failed to prove that shifts were in excess of 24 hours was not able to avail itself of the "sleep time" exemption. In that case, the employer contended that by policy, shifts were actually 24 hours and 15 minutes, but the court found no evidence that the policy was in fact implemented.[160]

In *Allen v. City of Greenville*,[161] city firefighters challenged the exclusion of 8 hours' sleep time per shift under 29 U.S.C. §207(k) and 29 C.F.R. §553.222, applicable to municipal firefighters. The firefighters here were assigned 24½-hour shifts and argued that their tour of duty was not more than the

[160]Carter v. Charleston, 4 WH Cases2d 448 (D.S.C. 1997).

[161]1999 U.S. Dist. LEXIS 20207 (N.D. Miss. 1999).

required 24 hours because of their employer's policy of permitting them to leave prior to the conclusion of their shifts based on the express condition that their replacement had already reported for duty. The federal district court found the city had properly adopted and employed a shift of 24 ½ hours, thereby meeting the 24-hour requirement to claim the sleep exclusion. The court also ruled that the firefighters' continued employment constituted an implied agreement to the sleep time rules when the sleep time deductions were reflected in their paychecks, they did not contest that the paychecks were ample notice of the pay plan, they did not complain either internally or to the Department of Labor, and they continued to accept their checks and report for duty for years. However, the court held that since there were genuine issues of material fact with regard to the adequacy of sleeping quarters, the firefighters' ability to enjoy uninterrupted sleep, and the calculation of work time sleep interruptions, trial would be appropriate on these issues, and summary judgment should be denied.

2. *Meal Time*

In *Leahy v. City of Chicago*,[162] the Seventh Circuit, by holding that the provisions of a police officers' collective bargaining agreement[163] governed whether meal time would be compensated, in effect avoided having to decide whether the officers' meals were compensable work time. The court stated that the FLSA permits employers and employees to make "reasonable provisions of contract [to guide] the computation of work hours where precisely accurate computation is difficult or impossible."[164] Because the court found that that the contract assumed

---

[162]96 F.3d 228, 3 WH Cases2d 801 (7th Cir. 1996), *cert. denied*, 117 S. Ct. 1818 (1997).

[163]The agreement provided that "'[a]ll time in excess of the hours worked in a normal workday (8 hours) and the normal workweek (40 hours) shall be compensated' at the rate of time-and-one-half." *Id.* at 232 (quoting from the collective bargaining agreement).

[164]*Id.* (quoting Tennessee Coal, Iron & R. Co. v. Muscoda Local No. 123, 321 U.S. 590, 603 (1944); alteration in original).

that officers were not working during meal time but provided for compensation when an officer actually worked during the meal time, the court held that the collective bargaining agreement fully protected the police officers' FLSA rights; therefore, the agreement served as a complete defense for the city to the officers' FLSA lawsuit.[165]

A dissenter argued that the ruling "would leave the determination of whether the officers' meal periods constitute 'work' to case-by-case grievance arbitration."[166] "[T]he assertion that merely by providing for overtime pay in its collective bargaining agreement an employer may insulate itself from FLSA scrutiny borders on the preposterous."[167]

In *Baker v. Stone County, Missouri,*[168] a U.S. district court concluded that, on the basis of the small number of actual interruptions which occurred, meal time for the sheriff's deputies need not be counted as compensable. However, the department had previously counted those hours in determining the compensatory time off to which the sheriff's deputies would be entitled. Holding that nothing in the statute authorized the retroactive deduction of compensation previously authorized, whether required or not, the court rejected the defendant's effort to deduct the hours previously credited for meal breaks from the sheriff's deputies' accrued comp time.

In *Hahn v. Pima County,*[169] an Arizona appellate court affirmed the trial court's decision granting summary judgment in favor of Pima County (the "County") after it was sued by corrections officers seeking overtime compensation for unpaid meal breaks. The court found that the employees did not establish that they spent their meal time for the predominant benefit of the County, even though the corrections officers were implicitly required to carry their portable radios and service revolvers, were expected to respond to emergency situations or citizen inquiries, and were subject to calls and interruptions

---

[165] *Id.*
[166] *Id.* at 234 (Cudahy, J., dissenting).
[167] *Id.* at 235 (Cudahy, J., dissenting).
[168] 41 F. Supp. 2d 965, 5 WH Cases2d 414 (W.D. Mo. 1999).
[169] 24 P.3d 614, 7 WH Cases2d 434 (Ariz. Ct. App. 2001).

from fellow employees, inmates and visitors.[170] The court explained that, at most, the record reflected employees "enjoyed something less than unfettered freedom during meal periods," but the employees did not provide evidence as to how often and to what extent the theoretical restrictions interfered with employees' primary lunch break activity of eating.[171] In addition, a longtime corrections officer had acknowledged that employees' primary activity during their meal periods was consuming meals.

4. Outside Employment

In *Nolan v. City of Chicago,*[172] the district court addressed whether the time spent by police officers working for the Chicago Transit Authority (CTA) and the Chicago Housing Authority (CHA) pursuant to a City of Chicago program entitled the "Voluntary Special Employment Program" (VSEP), constituted the type of special detail employment arranged or facilitated by the employer which need not be consolidated with regular hours worked under 29 U.S.C. §207(p)(1). Under the VSEP, the officers performed law enforcement and patrol functions and wore their City of Chicago police uniforms. The police officers were paid for this work by the City by separate check. The wages, however, were paid out of monies paid to the City by the CTA and CHA. For purposes of computing the police officers' FLSA overtime pay, the VSEP work time was not combined with the police officers' work time as City police officers.

The court's analysis centered on whether the CTA and CHA were separate entities from the City. In finding that they were separate entities the court reviewed the six-factor test set forth in *Barajas v. Unified Government.*[173] The factors are (1) whether the entities maintain separate payrolls, (2) whether they have separate budgets, (3) whether they maintain arm's-length dealings

---

[170] *Id.* at 616–20.
[171] *Id.* at 619.
[172] 125 F. Supp. 2d 324 (N.D. Ill. 2000).
[173] 87 F. Supp. 2d 1201, 1204 (D. Kan. 2000).

regarding employment, (4) whether the entities participate in separate retirement systems, (5) whether they are independent entities under state law, and (6) whether they can be sued or sue. The court determined that these factors were to be considered separately and that not all of the factors needed to be met for the entities to be considered separate entities for purposes of Section 7(p)(1).

Applying the six-factor *Barajas* test, the court concluded that the CHA and CTA were in fact separate entities from the City. They were each established separately under state law; they each had the authority to issue tax notes; they could each pass ordinances and promulgate regulations; and they could each be sued or sue on their own behalf. Accordingly, the court ruled that the police officers' time spent working for the CHA and CTA constituted outside employment under Section 207(p)(1), and therefore the police officers' hours did not need to be combined with their time spent working for the City of Chicago when computing their entitlement to FLSA overtime pay.

In another case involving a similar issue, *Johnson v. Unified Government of Wyandote County/Kansas City*,[174] police officers challenged the city's use of the "special detail" exemption provided by 29 U.S.C. §207(p)(1). Section 207(p)(1) provides that when government employees engaged in fire protection or law enforcement agree to and do work, on a part-time basis, for "a separate and independent" employer under arrangements made or facilitated by their regular employing agency, the hours worked in the other job are not added to the hours worked at the regular jobs for purposes of overtime compensation. Plaintiffs had volunteered for and were regularly assigned to special duty on the premises controlled by the Housing Authority. Plaintiffs were paid directly by the Housing Authority for the work. Plaintiffs challenged the city's use of the exemption by claiming first that their "special details" were not covered by the exemption because they were not sporadic occurrences, but were instead regular and recurring; second, they challeged the "separate and independent" nature of the Housing Authority as

[174] 127 F. Supp. 2d 1181 (D. Kan. 2000).

related to their regular employer; and, finally, they asserted that they were required to and did perform their regular duties as officers for the Unified Government while on "detail" to the Housing Authority, and therefore did not qualify for the exemption. After extensive review of the pertinent facts before it, the district court found that each of plaintiffs' claims required the resolution of disputed factual issues, and thus denied defendants' motions for summary judgment. The court did conclude as a matter of law that to qualify for the Section 7(p)(1) exemption a "special detail" assignment need not be sporadic or occasional as required by a related exemption set forth in Section 7(p)(2) of the Act.

5. Animal Care [New Topic]

Although there is no provision of the FLSA dealing specifically with the issues arising in connection with the use of animals in employment, typically in law enforcement, litigation persists over what constitutes compensable work for law enforcement officers and firefighters who care for these working animals.[175] Recently, this issue has been heavily litigated in the context of canine officers, who claim they are entitled to compensation for commuting time to and from work with a police dog and/or for time spent caring for the animal. Courts have reached varying conclusions on this issue depending upon the particular facts.[176]

---

[175]See the Treatise for a discussion of cases involving these issues, in Chapter 8, "Determining Compensable Hours," at footnote 147 and accompanying text.

[176]In addition to the cases discussed here, and those from the Treatise at Chapter 8, note 147, see also *Rudolph v. Metropolitan Airports Commission,* 103 F.3d 677, 133 Lab. Cas. (CCH) ¶33,478, 3 WH Cases2d 1089 (8th Cir. 1996) (holding that § 785.23 of the regulations permits parties to enter into agreement on amount of time to be compensated for caring and feeding of police dog as long as agreement is reasonable; additional work in caring and feeding of animal over and above that specified in the agreement is not work that is "suffered or permitted" by employer); *Karr v. City of Beaumont,* 950 F. Supp. 1317, 133 Lab. Cas. (CCH) ¶33,511 (E.D. Tex. 1997) (holding that off-shift time spent on care and transportation of dogs and dog-related maintenance of vehicles is a "principal activity" rather than a preliminary or postliminary activity and thus is compensable); *Bolick v. Brevard County Sheriff's Department,* 937 F. Supp. 1560 (M.D. Fla. 1996) (holding that time spent in transporting police dogs to and from work as part of ordinary commute was not compensable where there was no evidence the officers expended significant time or effort to care for the dogs during the commute; dogs were merely "four-legged

In *Holzapfel v. Town of Newburgh,*[177] the Second Circuit Court of Appeals stated that animal care activity could be "work" because "walking, feeding, training, grooming and cleaning up are integral and indispensable parts of the handler's principal activities." The court further noted that how much of the time claimed by the employee was actually work was a question for the jury.

In *DeBraska v. Milwaukee,*[178] a federal district court in Wisconsin considered whether the time that police officers in a canine unit spent transporting their dogs to and from work was compensable or was merely "preliminary" and "postliminary" time under the Portal-to-Portal Act. In declining to grant either party's motion for summary judgment, the court stated that at least part of the time spent transporting the dogs might be considered compensable time if the city required the officers to respond to emergency calls or to maintain contact with the police dispatcher, and if the city prohibited the officers from making personal stops during their commute.

The *DeBraska* court also addressed whether the time canine officers spent caring for their dogs away from the workplace was compensable. The city compensated the officers for 30 minutes of canine care per day. Referring to the Second Circuit's decision in *Holzapfel,*[179] the court asked three major questions: first, whether the city required the officers to spend more than 30 minutes per day performing canine care; second, whether the time spent was for the officer's own benefit or for the city's benefit; and third, whether the city knew that the officers spent

---

passengers"); *Aguilar v. United States,* 38 Fed. Cl. 431, 4 WH Cases2d 83 (1997) (holding that commuting time to work during which the border patrol officer cared for the dog is not compensable under the de minimis doctrine because evidence showed that amount of time expended caring for the animal during the commute was uncertain in length and frequency and involved a minimal amount of time, and tracking such time would be administratively difficult); *Truslow v. Spotsylvania County Sheriff,* 783 F. Supp. 274, 30 WH Cases 1259 (E.D. Va. 1992); *Nichols v. City of Chicago,* 789 F. Supp. 1438, 30 WH Cases 1444 (N.D. Ill. 1992) (relying on and finding the *Truslow* court's analysis "highly persuasive"); *Levering v. District of Columbia,* 869 F. Supp. 24, 2 WH Cases2d 838 (D.D.C. 1994).

[177] 145 F.3d 516, 4 WH Cases2d 1097 (2d Cir.), *cert. denied,* 119 S. Ct. 619 (1998).

[178] 11 F. Supp. 2d 1020, 4 WH Cases2d 1377 (E.D. Wis. 1998).

[179] 145 F.3d 516, 4 WH Cases2d 1097.

more than 30 minutes per day. On the basis of the police officers' presentation of evidence that the city required them to care for their dogs in a certain way, combined with evidence that the officers spent more than 30 minutes per day caring for their dogs, the court granted partial summary judgment to the officers on this issue.

In *Jerzak v. City of South Bend*,[180] the city police department did not argue that the canine officer's care of his police dog was not compensable work time but contended that the officer was already compensated an additional paid hour each day allotted for the care of the dog and that any additional work beyond the allotted hour was de minimis. The court concluded that the extent to which the officer's dog-care activities were reasonably necessary, were de minimis, or were compensable overtime was a question of fact properly left to a jury to decide.

In *Albanese v. Bergen County*,[181] plaintiff police officers had established by collective bargaining a monthly stipend to compensate canine officers for their at-home, off-the-clock dog care activities. In this suit for overtime, on the question of whether that stipend should be included in the officer's regular rate, the court held that it should not, recognizing that the decision conflicted with the Labor Department's regulation on the matter. Emphasizing that the stipend was collectively agreed to and that its inclusion would produce a "windfall" for the officers, the court stated, "Although the Court normally grants the Department of Labor's regulations great deference, ... [t]he Court finds that the Department of Labor's regulation as applied in this case would lead to an unjust result, and is therefore an impermissible construction of the statute."[182]

In *Theisen v. City of Maple Grove*,[183] a federal district court in Minnesota held that agreed-to payments to canine officers which were over and above their base pay should be counted toward the "regular rate" used to calculate overtime pay. The

---

[180] 996 F. Supp. 840, 4 WH Cases2d 736 (N.D. Ind. 1998).
[181] 991 F. Supp. 410 (D.N.J. 1997).
[182] *Id.* at 423.
[183] 41 F. Supp. 2d 932 (D. Minn. 1999).

defendant cited *Albanese* in support of its argument that the payments should be excluded from the regular rate. The court distinguished *Albanese,* pointing out that that case had declined to follow clear governmental guidance. The defendant argued that the payments should be viewed as meant specifically to compensate the plaintiffs for the time spent caring for the dogs at the plaintiffs' homes. The court held that, given the jury's finding that no agreement had been reached between the parties as to compensation for home care of the dogs, the payments were to be treated as compensation for the increased responsibilities of the officers as canine handlers and not for home care given to the dogs.

In *Aiken v. City of Memphis,*[184] the Sixth Circuit affirmed a district court's ruling that canine police officers were not entitled to compensation for time spent commuting with their assigned dogs. The court found that the officers' affidavits demonstrated that they only occasionally stopped to feed, walk, or clean up after the dogs during their commutes and that the officers were generally responsible for disciplining them. The court rejected this as proving more than a de minimis amount of work time.

6. *On-Call Time [New Topic]*

In *Robertson v. Board of County Commissioners of County of Morgan,*[185] the plaintiffs claimed backpay for on-call time and waiting time. The district court held that, with the exception of one plaintiff who had submitted an affidavit dealing with his assigned on-call time, the plaintiffs had adduced no evidence showing that the employer-board (as opposed to the sheriff) had any knowledge that the plaintiffs were required to be on call, or, even assuming such knowledge, that the requirements for being on call were so restrictive as to convert the time to work time. Summary judgment was granted for defendants against all but one of the plaintiffs on this claim.

---

[184]190 F.3d 753, 5 WH Cases2d 961 (6th Cir. 1999), *cert. denied,* 528 U.S. 1157, 5 WH Cases2d 1632 (2000).

[185]78 F. Supp. 2d 1142, 5 WH Cases2d 1449 (D. Colo. 1999).

VI. DETERMINING WHETHER EMPLOYEES ARE EMPLOYED IN FIRE PROTECTION OR LAW ENFORCEMENT ACTIVITIES

A. Fire Protection Activities

In *Mathias v. Addison Fire Protection District No. 1,*[186] a federal district court granted summary judgment for the defendant, holding that wages paid to the plaintiffs who were employed as both firefighters and fire inspectors did not violate FLSA overtime rules; the plaintiffs were paid overtime rates for fire inspector work based on lower hourly wages for that work than for their non-overtime firefighter work. The court held that Section 7(g) of the FLSA allowed the fire district to pay plaintiffs differing rates of pay for firefighter and fire inspector work, and that the plaintiffs' overtime work could be compensated accordingly. This was because (1) the two kinds of work had sufficient qualitative differences, despite certain minimal overlaps (the plaintiffs were required to devote an average of 5 out of 1,040 annual hours worked as inspectors as backup firefighters on ride-alongs); (2) the rate for fire inspectors was a bona fide rate, having been established through a survey of rates paid to fire inspectors in nearby municipalities; (3) the fire district and the plaintiffs had agreed to the rate structure prior to performance of work; and (4) the wages paid for the fire inspector work were one and one-half times the rate established for non-overtime work.

In *Lockwood v. Prince George's County, Maryland,*[187] a federal district court in Maryland held that fire investigators whose duties did not actually include prevention, extinguishment, or control of fires, and who did not perform activities that were required for prevention, control, or extinguishment of fires, were not employees engaged in fire protection services for purposes of the Section 7(k) partial overtime exemption, even though the fire investigators were required to have experience

---

[186]43 F. Supp. 2d. 916 (N.D. Ill. 1999).
[187]58 F. Supp. 2d 651 (D. Md. 1999).

as firefighters and were theoretically required to assist firefighters when called upon to do so.

B. Law Enforcement Activities

In *Baker v. Stone County, Missouri,*[188] a federal district court concluded, consistent with prevailing law, that dispatchers employed by the county sheriff's department and jailer/dispatchers who spent more than 20 percent of their time as dispatchers were not employees in law enforcement activities for purposes of the Section 7(k) partial overtime exemption. The court distinguished these employees from deputies and jailers/dispatchers who spent less than 20 percent of their time working as dispatchers.

C. Twenty-Percent Limit on Nonexempt Work

Ruling that federal firefighters' entire 24-hour shift, consisting of 8 hours of actual work and 16 hours of standby time, must be counted toward overtime, the Claims Court in *Adams v. United States*[189] also ruled that standby time (even if spent sleeping or performing mundane chores) is so closely related to overtime-exempt work that it is also exempt. Agreeing with other courts, the court noted, "[I]t is the nature of a firefighter's work to be ready and alert for emergencies."[190]

In *Baker v. Stone County, Missouri,*[191] a U.S. district court concluded that dispatchers employed by the county sheriff's department and jailer/dispatchers who spent more than 20 percent of their time as dispatchers were not employees in law enforcement activities for purposes of the Section 7(k) partial overtime exemption.

---

[188] 41 F. Supp. 2d 965, 5 WH Cases2d 414 (W.D. Mo. 1999).

[189] 36 Fed. Cl. 91, 3 WH Cases2d 647 (1996).

[190] *Id.* at 99 (internal quotation marks omitted; quoting Birdwell v. City of Gadsden, 970 F.2d 802, 809, 30 WH Cases 1745 (11th Cir. 1992)). *See also* Armour & Co. v. Wantock, 323 U.S. 126, 132–33, 4 WH Cases 862 (1944) ("Readiness to serve may be hired . . . and time spent lying in wait for threats to the safety of the employer's property may be treated by the parties as a benefit to the employer.").

[191] 41 F. Supp. 2d 965, 5 WH Cases2d 414.

E. Trainees

In *Heder v. City of Two Rivers,*[192] a federal district court in Wisconsin held that it was a violation of the FLSA for an employer to require any part of a firefighter's regular wages or overtime compensation, including the costs of training, to be repaid merely because the employee resigned within a specified time. In this case, the employee received mandatory paramedic training. He signed a repayment agreement requiring him to repay the employer for costs associated with his training if he voluntarily resigned within three years of beginning the training. The employee resigned just shy of the three-year period and went to work as a firefighter for another city. The employer withheld money from the employee's pay to recover part of the training costs. The court granted the employee's partial summary judgment motion on his FLSA overtime claim. Additionally, the court held that the training repayment agreement was unenforceable insofar as it did not reduce the amount due over the years that it was in force. The employer's deductions from the final paychecks violated state law and the FLSA's minimum wage requirements.

F. Paramedics, Emergency Medical Technicians, and Ambulance Employees

The Eighth Circuit in *Christian v. City of Gladstone*[193] considered the relationship of Section 553.212(a)[194] of the regulations

---

[192]49 F. Supp. 2d 677 (E.D. Wis. 2001).

[193]108 F.3d 929, 3 WH Cases2d 1441 (8th Cir.), *cert. denied,* 118 S. Ct. 557, 4 WH Cases2d 416 (1997).

[194]Section 553.212(a) states:

> Employees engaged in fire protection or law enforcement activities as described in §553.210 and 553.211, may also engage in some nonexempt work which is not performed as an incident to or in conjunction with their fire protection or law enforcement activities. . . . A person who spends more than 20 percent of his/her working time in nonexempt activities is not considered to be an employee engaged in fire protection or law enforcement activities for purposes of this part.

29 C.F.R. §553.212(a).

and the Section 7(k) partial exemption in the context of paramedics who were certified firefighters. The initial issue the court resolved was whether the paramedics were employees in fire protection activities as defined in Section 7(k). The court stated that Section 553.210(a) of the regulations[195] provides the definition of "employee in fire protection activities" and concluded that the paramedics met the four-part test set forth in that regulation.[196] In applying the four-part test to the paramedics, the court stated that the test "has no requirement that firefighting be the employees' only or primary duty, and the fact that the paramedics are also able to provide medical services while at fires and elsewhere does not eliminate their responsibility for firefighting."[197]

Next, the court considered the paramedics' argument that Section 553.212(a) (also known as the "80/20 rule") of the regulations applied and defeated the partial overtime exemption because over 20 percent of their work time involved "nonexempt activities." In considering the meaning of "nonexempt activities," the court examined the two competing tests, respectively, applied by the Fourth[198] and Eleventh[199] Circuits. The court rejected the Eleventh Circuit's approach, which broadly defines nonexempt work as "any work that 'generally inures to

---

[195]Section 553.210(a) states that the term "employee in fire protection activities" includes:

> any employee (1) who is employed by an organized fire department or fire protection district; (2) who has been trained to the extent required by State statute or local ordinance; (3) who has the legal authority and responsibility to engage in the prevention, control or extinguishment of a fire of any type; and (4) who performs activities which are required for, and directly concerned with, the prevention, control or extinguishment of fires, including such incidental nonfirefighting functions as housekeeping, equipment maintenance, lecturing, attending community fire drills and inspecting homes and schools for fire hazards.

29 C.F.R. §553.210(a). The provision further states that the term "employee in fire protection activities" also includes "rescue and ambulance service personnel if such personnel form an integral part of the public agency's fire protection activities. *See* §553.215." *Id.*

[196]*Christian*, 108 F.3d at 932.

[197]*Id.*

[198]Schmidt v. County of Prince William, 929 F.2d 986, 30 WH Cases2d 377 (4th Cir. 1991).

[199]O'Neal v. Barrow County Bd. of Comm'rs, 980 F.2d 674 (11th Cir. 1993).

the benefit of the employer . . . which the employer requires its employees to do while they are not engaged in activities related to their fire protection or law enforcement duties.'"[200] The court, agreeing with the Fourth Circuit, found that the better approach in determining what constitutes nonexempt work is to consider whether the work is "'distinct from and unrelated to fire protection activities' and whether 'the essential nature of the firefighter's job changes and he is required to perform tasks unrelated to his job.'"[201] Because the facts showed that "the paramedics respond to fires, fight them, and provide paramedic services at those fires, as well as on calls not involving fires [and] [n]early all of their time is spent on such activities, related training, support services, and waiting for calls," the court held that Section 553.212 did not apply to defeat the Section 7(k) partial exemption in this case.[202]

A district court within the Fourth Circuit, however, held that the Section 7(k) partial overtime exemption did not apply to the county's emergency medical service (EMS) workers, who worked in an agency that was independent of fire protection or law enforcement.[203] For its EMS workers to qualify for the 7(k) exemption, the county had to show that the workers met the "substantially related" test of Section 553.215 and the "80/20" test of Section 553.212 of the regulations.[204] The court held that the county had failed to meet either of these tests.[205] First, the EMS workers were not "substantially related" to fire protection or law enforcement services. The evidence showed that 69.5 percent of EMS calls were on matters without a law enforcement or fire response and that 10 percent of working hours were spent on law enforcement and fire calls;[206] it did not show the total number of police and fire calls or the percentage of these which involved EMS workers. The court concluded that it had not been

---

[200] *Christian*, 108 F.2d at 933 (quoting *O'Neal*, 980 F.2d at 681).

[201] *Id.* (quoting *Schmidt*, 929 F.2d at 990).

[202] *Id.* at 934.

[203] Roy v. County of Lexington, 928 F. Supp. 1406, 3 WH Cases2d 613 (D.S.C.), *vacated in part*, 948 F. Supp. 529, 3 WH Cases2d 1214 (D.S.C. 1996).

[204] *Id.* at 1413. *See also* 29 C.F.R. §§553.215, 553.212.

[205] 928 F. Supp. at 1416.

[206] *Id.* at 1414.

shown that EMS workers were "regularly dispatched to fires, crime scenes, riots, natural disasters and accidents,"[207] and therefore they did not qualify for the Section 7(k) exemption. Second, the county had failed to establish that the employees spent at least 80 percent of their time performing law enforcement or fire protection activities because the court calculated that the EMS workers spent 22.62 percent of work time on nonexempt activities (i.e., activities other than fire protection or law enforcement).[208]

In *Lang v. City of Omaha,*[209] the Eighth Circuit affirmed a district court's decision that found that city paramedics employed by the fire department were "engaged in fire protection activities," even though the plaintiffs claimed they performed only medical services at fires. It was undisputed that the plaintiffs had been trained and were qualified to fight fires, and could be pressed into firefighting duty if a situation required, although most of the calls they responded to were not fire calls and they had been ordered even at fires not to engage in direct fire suppression but just to perform medical duties. The court indicated that standby duties performed by trained firefighting personnel are activities which are required for and directly concerned with the control or extinguishment of fires. The district court had found that the paramedics were included under either the four-part test or the "including" test of 29 C.F.R §553.210(a), despite the suggestion of the "including" test that it applies only to paramedics employed by agencies other than the fire department; but the appellate court found it unnecessary to decide the applicability of the "including" test, relying on the four-part test alone.[210]

---

[207] *Id.* at 1413 (quoting 29 C.F.R. §553.215, and citing Spires v. Ben Hill County, 980 F.2d 683, 689 n.36 (11th Cir. 1993), and Justice v. Metropolitan Gov't of Nashville, 4 F.3d 1387, 1392 (6th Cir. 1993)).

[208] *Id.* at 1415–16.

[209] 186 F.3d 1035, 5 WH Cases2d 865 (8th Cir. 1999).

[210] *Id.*, 5 WH Cases2d at 866 n.3.

The U.S. Court of Appeals for the Eleventh Circuit examined the application of DOL's "80/20" test to dual-role, cross-trained firefighters/emergency medical technicians in *Falken v. Glynn County*.[211] The issue in *Falken* was whether the county could apply Section 7(k) to the firefighters/emergency medical technicians where fewer than 80 percent of the calls to which the firefighter/emergency medical technicians responded were fire-related. To answer this question, the court first examined DOL's regulations defining "fire protection activities." The court explained that for employees whose sole function is to respond to emergency medical calls, it is clear that the partial overtime exemption set forth under Section 7(k) does not apply. The court noted, however, that there are two provisions in DOL's regulations in which emergency medical technician workers can be included in the definition of fire protection workers. One exception is under 29 C.F.R. §553.210(a), where the employees form an integral part of the public agency's fire protection activities. The other exception is where their services are "substantially related to fire fighting."[212] The court then explained that each of these exceptions must be read in light of DOL's "80/20" regulation, 29 C.F.R. §553.212(a), in which an employee must spend 80 percent or more of his or her work time engaged in fire protection activities for the Section 7(k) exemption to apply. Examining these regulations and the case law interpreting them, the court held that the work time of employees who are cross-trained, dual-role firefighter/emergency medical technicians is evaluated differently for purposes of the 80/20 test than it is for employees who function exclusively as emergency medical technicians. In the case of cross-trained, dual-role firefighters/emergency medical technicians, the work time spent responding to emergency medical and rescue calls is considered to be a fire protection activity. In so ruling, the court emphasized that this test applies only to employees who are trained and engaged in firefighting as part of their job, and who are regularly dispatched to firefighting-related emergencies.

---

[211] 197 F.3d 1341, 5 WH Cases2d 1417 (11th Cir. 1999).

[212] 197 F.3d at 1346, 5 WH Cases2d 1417 (citing 29 C.F.R. §553.215).

In December 1999, Public Law No. 106-151 was passed to clarify the overtime exemption for employees engaged in fire protection activities. Section 3 of the FLSA was amended to provide the following:

> (y) "Employee in fire protection activities" means an employee, including a firefighter, paramedic, emergency medical technician, rescue worker, ambulance personnel, or hazardous materials worker, who
>
> (1) is trained in fire suppression, has the legal authority and responsibility to engage in fire suppression, and is employed by a fire department of a municipality, county, fire district, or State; and
>
> (2) is engaged in the prevention, control, and extinguishment of fires or response to emergency situations where life, property, or the environment is at risk.

According to congressional floor debate, this amendment responds to several court decisions that held that firefighters working as emergency medical services personnel did not come within the exemption because they spent the majority of their time in non-fire protection activities. This legislation clarifies that firefighters who are cross-trained as emergency medical technicians still fall within the exemption.

2. *The "Substantially Related" Test*

b. *Requirement of Being Regularly Dispatched to Fires, Crime Scenes, Riots, Natural Disasters, and Accidents*

In *West v. Anne Arundel County*,[213] the Fourth Circuit also held that county EMTs, who spent at least 80 percent of their time responding to emergency calls that did not involve any fire suppression and were "prohibited by standard operating procedure from engaging in fire suppression activities," did not fall within the "fire protection activities" exception. The court also

[213] 137 F.3d 752, 4 WH Cases2d 641 (4th Cir.), *cert. denied*, 119 S. Ct. 607 (1998).

ruled that medical services "which are not rendered at the scene of any fire do not qualify as exempt activities."[214]

VII. THE FEDERAL SECTOR

In a case involving questions of the proper scope of the jurisdiction of the U. S. Court of Federal Claims, that court held in *El-Sheikh v. United States*[215] that the plaintiff's action for backpay under the FLSA against an Air Force officers' club did not fall within the court's Tucker Act jurisdiction for two reasons. First, the Tucker Act grants the U.S. Court of Federal Claims jurisdiction over claims for money against only certain enumerated nonappropriated fund instrumentalities (NAFIs)[216] such as the Army and Air Force Exchange Service, Navy Exchanges, Marine Corps Exchanges, Coast Guard Exchanges, or Exchange Councils of the National Aeronautics and Space Administration. The court found that the NAFI in this case, however, was not among the enumerated NAFIs. Therefore, the court lacked jurisdiction over the action because the plaintiff's complaint did not state a claim against the "United States." Second, the court stated that even if the officers' club was a NAFI specifically listed in the Tucker Act, the court's jurisdiction over those NAFIs was limited to claims alleging the existence of an express or implied contract. Because the plaintiff did not prove that he was employed under either an express or implied contract, the court did not have jurisdiction over the plaintiff's claim.

In *Yamin v. United States*,[217] a federal district court in New York addressed whether Foreign Service employees must exhaust the grievance procedures set forth in the Foreign Service Act[218] (FSA) before they may obtain district court review. The

---

[214] *Id.* at 761, 4 WH Cases2d 641.

[215] 39 Fed. Cl. 1, 4 WH Cases2d 180 (1997).

[216] Nonappropriated funds are monies that have not been deposited into the U.S. Treasury and that are maintained independently of the public fisc. A case involving a successful FLSA suit against a NAFI is discussed in the Treatise at p. 881.

[217] 982 F. Supp. 958, 4 WH Cases2d 441 (S.D.N.Y. 1997).

[218] 22 U.S.C. §§4131–4140 (1998).

government argued that the FSA requires plaintiffs to initially bring their complaints before the Foreign Service Grievance Board. Although no section of the FSA states that the Act's grievance procedures are a Foreign Service employee's exclusive remedy to recover unpaid overtime compensation, the government argued that the FSA should be construed and applied in accordance with the Civil Service Reform Act,[219] under which the procedures set forth in a collective bargaining agreement provide the exclusive administrative procedures for resolving grievances. The court rejected this argument because there was no showing that the plaintiffs were parties to a collective bargaining agreement.

The court in *Yamin* also relied on *Ososky v. Wick*[220] to conclude that the FLSA does not include an exhaustion requirement for federal employees attempting to recover unpaid minimum wage and overtime compensation. The D.C. Circuit in *Ososky* noted that in contrast to Title VII, when Congress extended the scope of FLSA to cover federal employees, it did not add language to the statute expressly requiring federal employees to exhaust administrative remedies before filing an action in federal district court.

Abbott v. United States[221] involved a claim of unfair representation against a union that entered into a memorandum of understanding (MOU) with the U.S. government settling the overtime claims of employees who had opted to join the union's grievance procedure. The employees who had not joined the grievance procedure were foreclosed by the MOU from seeking overtime back pay under the FLSA and Back Pay Act. The foreclosed employees argued that they had been misled by the union into believing that these claims would not be foreclosed if they opted out of the grievance procedures and that an unfair representation claim under the FLSA should therefore be allowed against the union. The First Circuit, however, held that

---

[219]Pub. L. No. 95-454, 92 Stat. 1111 (codified as amended in scattered sections of 5 U.S.C.).

[220]704 F.2d 1264 (D.C. Cir. 1983).

[221]144 F.3d 1, 4 WH Cases2d 1163 (1st Cir. 1998).

federal claims under the FLSA against a union involving overtime pay and the alleged failure of the union to meet its duty of fair representation were precluded by the Civil Service Reform Act's comprehensive regulatory scheme. Any duty-of-fair-representation claim against the union lies within the jurisdiction of the Federal Labor Relations Authority. Moreover, that matter ended when the FLRA's general counsel decided not to issue a complaint.

The court also held that the federal employee's FLSA overtime claims against the government were barred by the Act's 2-year statute-of-limitation period despite the employees' contention that the statute of limitations was tolled while they exhausted administrative grievance proceedings. The court based its decision on *Unexcelled Chemical Corp. v. United States,*[222] in which the Supreme Court held that the FLSA's statute of limitations "is not subject to tolling on the basis of administrative proceedings." The *Abbott* court rejected the employees' argument that *Unexcelled* should not apply to their dispute because it predates the Civil Service Reform Act and therefore could not have contemplated that Act's required negotiated grievance procedure.

The Civil Service Reform Act provides that a collective bargaining agreement may provide the exclusive procedures to resolve employee grievances which are covered by the agreement. The Federal Court of Claims held in *Martin v. United States*[223] that it did not have jurisdiction over a former federal employee's FLSA action for compensation for sick leave, regular time, and overtime pay, because the governing collective bargaining contract provided the exclusive grievance procedures. The court noted that a three-part inquiry determined the exclusivity of the bargaining contract: (1) the employee was "covered" by the agreement, (2) the dispute was "grievable" within the terms of the agreement, and (3) the agreement did not specifically exclude the claims being made by the employee.

---

[222]345 U.S. 59, 11 WH Cases 271 (1953).
[223]40 Fed. Cl. 726, 4 WH Cases2d 1077 (1998).

A. White-Collar Exemptions

In *Adams v. United States,*[224] the U.S. Court of Federal Claims considered a challenge to the Office of Personnel Management's exemption regulations, which do not include a salary basis test or the disciplinary-deduction exception to the salary basis test. Border agents and supervisory aircraft pilots brought suit for overtime compensation arguing that because they could be suspended without pay for non-safety-rule violations, they should not be exempt from the FLSA's overtime provisions. Because they did not meet the Department of Labor's salary basis test, they urged that their entitlement to overtime pay should be assessed under DOL, rather than OPM, regulations. The U.S. Court of Federal Claims rejected the plaintiffs' argument that DOL's regulations control when they conflict with OPM regulations. Accordingly, the court upheld OPM's rules.

In *Adams v. United States*[225] the Court of Appeals for the Federal Circuit addressed whether federal criminal investigators are administratively exempt. The parties had stipulated that the plaintiffs spent 51 percent or more of their time conducting investigations, and the government had argued on its motion for summary judgment that the work of criminal investigation was their primary duty and that they were accordingly administratively exempt. The trial court rejected this theory and based its decision on what it described as the "alternative primary duty" test. Referring to administrative pronouncements of the Civil Service Commission and its predecessor, the Office of Personnel Management, the court described the "alternative primary duty" test as follows: an employee may have as his or her primary duty the one that is "most important, even though it occupies less [than] half of the employee's work time," if it "(1) constitutes a substantial, regular part of a position, and (2) governs the classification and qualification requirements of the position, and (3) is clearly exempt work in terms of the basic nature of the

---

[224] 40 Fed. Cl. 303 (1998).
[225] 178 F.3d 1306 (Fed. Cir. 1998).

work, the frequency with which the employee must exercise discretion and independent judgment, and the significance of the decisions made." Noting that the plaintiffs had planning and supervision responsibilities as well as responsibilities for conducting investigations, the trial court found these duties primary and granted summary judgment for the government. The appellate court upheld the "alternative primary duty" test but reversed the decision below on the ground that the record was devoid of evidence sufficient to support the conclusion that the test was satisfied with respect to the planning and supervision duties of the plaintiffs.

The Federal Court of Claims ruled that federal supervisory firefighters were exempt from FLSA's overtime provisions as executive employees, even though 16 hours of every 24-hour shift was standby time and the supervisors passed the time sleeping or engaged in the same activities as their subordinates.[226] The court reasoned:

> It is who they [the supervisors] are that gives plaintiffs their utility during standby time. . . . [T]heir "work" is simply to be present, so that, in the event of an emergency, they can be activated, in their supervisory capacity, to respond to the emergency. Their "doing" consists in "being." That work cannot be performed by non-supervisory firefighters. Their presence accomplishes a different function.[227]

B. Hours of Work

Under the Portal-to-Portal Act,[228] commuting to and from work and preliminary and postliminary activities are not compensable work under the FLSA. Thus, the Court of Claims ruled that INS border patrol agents' travel time with their dogs is not compensable, even though they actually perform "work" during the commute time.[229] The "work" alluded to was the act of

---

[226]Adams v. United States, 36 Fed. Cl. 91, 3 WH Cases2d 647 (1996).
[227]*Id.* at 100.
[228]29 U.S.C. §§251–262.
[229]Aguilar v. United States, 36 Fed. Cl. 560, 3 WH Cases2d 897 (1996).

transporting the dogs. Noting that "[t]he mere presence of a dog does not make the commute compensable," the court stated that to rule otherwise would mean "that all time [the agents] spent with their dogs was compensable."[230] The court concluded, "[C]ommon sense tells us that employees should not be compensated for doing what they would have to do anyway—getting themselves to work."[231] To be compensable, according to the court, commute time must be an integral and indispensable part of their principal job activities and be compelled by vital considerations such as health, hygiene, and personal safety.[232]

Standby time for federal firefighters and their supervisors is "worktime" and compensable.[233]

F. Liquidated Damages

In *Adams v. United States,*[234] the Court of Federal Claims held that the normal presumption that the government acted in good faith does not apply in determining whether liquidated damages should be awarded, because it runs directly contrary to a statutory presumption that employees deprived of proper wages are entitled to liquidated damages unless the employer demonstrates that it acted in good faith and with reasonable basis to believe its conduct complied with the law. Next, the court found that the government willfully violated the law with respect to agents who did not supervise the requisite number of employees mandated by the Office of Personnel Management's regulations. The court noted that the government classifier was aware of this criterion but the agency made no effort to determine

---

[230] *Id.* at 566, 3 WH Cases2d 897 (internal quotation marks omitted; quoting Reich v. New York City Transit Auth., 45 F.3d 646, 652, 2 WH Cases2d 833 (2d Cir. 1995)).

[231] *Id.* at 566–67 (internal quotation marks omitted; quoting Andrews v. DuBois, 888 F. Supp. 213, 218, 2 WH Cases2d 1297 (D. Mass. 1995)).

[232] *Id.* at 569. *See also* Adams v. Bowsher, 946 F. Supp. 37, 133 Lab. Cas. (CCH) ¶33,531 (D.D.C. 1996) (congressional intent to equate federal workers' rights to those of private sector employees regarding commuting time, based on considerations of cost and fairness, had legitimate purpose accomplished by rational means).

[233] Adams v. United States, 36 Fed. Cl. 91, 3 WH Cases2d 647 (1996).

[234] 46 Fed. Cl. 616, 6 WH Cases2d 1110 (2000).

whether the employees met this requirement. With regard to the other employees, however, the court found that the classifier had analyzed the relevant criteria, albeit wrongly, and that the agents' job duties often changed. As a result, it found that the classifier acted in good faith in classifying the plaintiffs as exempt.

IX. UNIQUE CONSTITUTIONAL DEFENSES

As in the cases challenging the constitutionality of the retroactive imposition of a new national statute of limitations by the Portal-to-Portal Act,[235] the constitutionality of a congressional change in the time allowed for federal employees to make claims with the General Accounting Office (from 6 years to either 2 or 3 years) was challenged in *Adams v. Hinchman.*[236] There the D.C. Circuit held that this retroactive change did not violate the due process or equal protection rights of the federal employees whose claims were pending but had not been acted on by the GAO at the time of the legislation, and it remanded to permit the district court to consider the propriety of its exercise of jurisdiction (in light of the allocation of jurisdiction between the district court and the Court of Federal Claims under the Tucker Act[237] and Little Tucker Act[238]) over the plaintiffs' Fifth Amendment claim that they had been deprived of property without just compensation.

A. The Tenth Amendment

Lower courts continue to follow *Garcia v. San Antonio Metropolitan Transit Authority.*[239] In *Adams v. Department of Juvenile*

---

[235] *See* Treatise Chapter 1 at pp. 18–19.
[236] 154 F.3d 420, 5 WH Cases2d 568 (D.C. Cir. 1999).
[237] 28 U.S.C. §1491.
[238] 28 U.S.C. §1346(a)(2).
[239] 469 U.S. 528 (1985).

Justice,[240] the Second Circuit, following *Garcia*, rejected a claim that New York's complicated collective bargaining and impasse procedures prevented application of the FLSA under the Tenth Amendment, or that such application would upset the federal-state balance of power.

The Fourth Circuit rejected the argument that the Supreme Court's 1997 decision in *Printz v. United States* (cited below) justified a Tenth Amendment defense to suits against states and local governments under the FLSA.[241] Following *Garcia,* it held that the Tenth Amendment provided state and local governments with no defense to FLSA actions.[242]

In *Bunch v. Robinson*,[243] Maryland probation agents sought overtime pay for work exceeding 40 hours per week. The trial court dismissed the claim, holding that it lacked subject matter jurisdiction and that the Tenth Amendment precluded the FLSA from being applied to the states under the Supreme Court's decision in *Seminole Tribe of Florida v. Florida.*[244] The trial court interpreted *Seminole Tribe* as a disapproval of federal intrusion on the states' sovereign immunity. The Maryland Court of Special Appeals reversed, holding that *Garcia* remained good law until the Supreme Court (again) reversed itself, and criticized the trial court for effectively abrogating Supreme Court precedent.

Despite the decision of the Fourth Circuit in *West,* the defendants in *Lockwood v. Prince George's County, Maryland,*[245] contended that *Printz v. United States*[246] and related cases implied that the application of the FLSA to local governments in connection with payment issues was unconstitutional. Noting that it was bound by *West,* the federal district court in Maryland denied this

[240]143 F.3d 61, 65, 4 WH Cases2d 932, 935 (2d Cir. 1998).

[241]West v. Anne Arundel County, 137 F.3d 752, 4 WH Cases2d 641 (4th Cir.), *cert. denied,* 119 S. Ct. 607 (1998).

[242]*Id.* at 760, 4 WH Cases2d at 645.

[243]712 A.2d 585, 4 WH Cases2d 1300 (Md. Ct. Spec. App.), *cert. granted,* 718 A.2d 234 (Md. 1998).

[244]517 U.S. 44, *cert. denied,* 116 S. Ct. 1415 (1996).

[245]58 F. Supp. 2d 651 (D. Md. 1999).

[246]521 U.S. 898 (1997).

constitutional challenge, reemphasizing that neither *Printz* nor any other case had overruled *Garcia v. San Antonio Metropolitan Transit Authority,*[247] which was directly on point.

B. The Eleventh Amendment

Since *Seminole Tribe v. Florida,*[248] every court that has addressed the issue has ruled that state employees may not sue their states under the FLSA because Congress did not have power, under either the Article I Commerce Clause or the enforcement clause of the Fourteenth Amendment, to abrogate states' Eleventh Amendment sovereign immunity.[249] All courts that have considered the issue of waiver have refused to find a waiver

[247] 469 U.S. 528 (1985).

[248] 517 U.S. 44.

[249] Mills v. Maine, 118 F.3d 37, 3 WH Cases2d 1802 (1st Cir. 1997); Close v. New York, 125 F.3d 31, 4 WH Cases2d 108 (2d Cir. 1997); Balgowan v. New Jersey, 115 F.3d 214, 3 WH Cases2d 1703 (3d Cir. 1997); Wilson-Jones v. Caviness, 99 F.3d 203, 3 WH Cases2d 929 (1996), *opinion amended,* 107 F.3d 358, 3 WH Cases2d 1501 (6th Cir. 1997); Moad v. Arkansas State Police Dep't, 111 F.3d 585, 3 WH Cases2d 1540 (8th Cir. 1997); Roper v. Iowa, 115 F.3d 623, 3 WH Cases2d 1727 (8th Cir. 1997); Bergemann v. Rhode Island, 958 F. Supp. 61, 3 WH Cases2d 1495 (D.R.I. 1997); Palotai v. University of Md. Coll. Park, 959 F. Supp. 714 (D. Md. 1997); Taylor v. Virginia, 951 F. Supp. 591, 3 WH Cases2d 1199 (E.D. Va. 1996); AFSCME v. Virginia, 949 F. Supp. 438, 3 WH Cases2d 1191 (W.D. Va. 1996); Frazier v. Courter, 958 F. Supp. 252, 3 WH Cases2d 1662 (W.D. Va. 1997); Chauvin v. Louisiana, 937 F. Supp. 567, 3 WH Cases2d 927 (E.D. La. 1996); Arndt v. Wisconsin Dep't of Corrs., 972 F. Supp. 475 (W.D. Wis. 1996); Digiore v. Illinois, 962 F. Supp. 1064, 3 WH Cases2d 1542 (N.D. Ill. 1997); Rehberg v. Department of Pub. Safety, 946 F. Supp. 741, 3 WH Cases2d 1149 (S.D. Iowa 1996), *aff'd,* 117 F.3d 1423 (8th Cir. 1997); Arnold v. Arkansas, 957 F. Supp. 185 (E.D. Ark. 1996); Adams v. Kansas, 934 F. Supp. 371, 3 WH Cases2d 626 (D. Kan. 1996), *aff'd,* 116 F.3d 489, 3, WH Cases2d 1792 (10th Cir. 1997); Blow v. Kansas, 929 F. Supp. 1400, 3 WH Cases2d 627 (D. Kan. 1996), *aff'd,* 116 F.3d 489, 3 WH Cases2d 1792 (10th Cir. 1997); Whalen v. Arizona, 962 F. Supp. 1218 (D. Ariz. 1997); Walden v. Florida Dep't of Corrs., 975 F. Supp. 1330 (N.D. Fla. 1996). *Cf.* Timmer v. Michigan Dep't of Commerce, 104 F.3d 833, 72 FEP Cases 1471 (6th Cir. 1997) (Congress had power under Fourteenth Amendment to make Equal Pay Act enforceable against states in federal court); Ussery v. Louisiana, 962 F. Supp. 922 (W.D. La. 1997) (same); Varner v. Illinois State Univ., 972 F. Supp. 458 (C.D. Ill. 1997) (same); Gehrt v. University of Ill., 974 F. Supp. 1178, 74 FEP Cases 961 (C.D. Ill. 1997) (ADEA and EPA claims not barred). *But see* Larry v. Board of Tr. of Univ. of Ala., 975 F. Supp. 1447 (N.D. Ala. 1997) (Congress did not have power to make EPA enforceable against states in federal court because Fourteenth Amendment requires discriminatory intent and EPA is strict liability statute).

either by implication, by application of states' general waiver statutes, or by application of Tenth Amendment jurisprudence (congressional exercise of power over states does not affect sovereign immunity).[250] The *Ex parte Young*[251] doctrine is unavailing because only prospective declaratory and injunctive relief is available through that avenue of redress, and Congress has expressly prohibited private actions for injunctive relief, limiting such remedy to actions by the Department of Labor.[252] Some state courts have held, furthermore, that states cannot be sued under the FLSA even in that forum.[253]

However, in *Luder v. Endicott*,[254] the court ruled that certain correctional officers in the state correctional system who were sued as individuals were not immune from liability in actions under the FLSA. The court first examined the law subjecting individuals to liability under the FLSA. Then, the court determined that the exception to immunity found under *Ex parte Young*,[255] which applies to constitutional violations, should be extended to violations of federal statutory law such as the FLSA. The court rejected an analysis of whether the individual officials were acting in an official capacity or an individual capacity as not being useful in the context of an FLSA suit. The court stated that it was unquestioned that the individuals being sued had the power to order overtime work without compensation. Thus, these defendants qualified as employers under the FLSA regard-

---

[250]*Close*, 125 F.2d 31, 4 WH Cases2d 108; *Wilson-Jones*, 99 F.3d 203, 3 WH Cases2d 929; *Arndt*, 972 F. Supp. 475; *AFSCME*, 949 F. Supp. 438, 3 WH Cases2d 1191; *Taylor*, 951 F. Supp. 591, 3 WH Cases2d 1199; *Palotai*, 959 F. Supp. 714; *Digiore*, 962 F. Supp. 1064, 3 WH Cases2d.

[251]209 U.S. 123 (1908).

[252]29 U.S.C. §211(a); *Mills*, 118 F.3d 37, 3 WH Cases2d 1802; *Frazier*, 958 F. Supp. 252, 3 WH Cases2d 1661; *Bergemann*, 958 F. Supp. 61, 3 WH Cases2d 1495. *Contra Balgowan*, 115 F.3d 214, 3 WH Cases2d 1703; *Digiore*, 962 F. Supp. 1064, 3 WH Cases2d 1542 (neither of which addressed 29 U.S.C. §211(a)).

[253]Bunch v. Robinson, No. 97006017 (Md. Cir. Ct. (Baltimore), Sept. 11, 1997); German v. Wisconsin Dep't of Transp., No. 96-CV-96-751 (Me. Super. Ct., July 18, 1997); Mossman v. Donahey, 46 Ohio St. 2d 1, 346 N.E. 2d 305 (1976); Weppler v. Dade County Sch. Bd., 311 So. 2d 409, 410 (Fla. Ct. App. 1975).

[254]86 F. Supp. 2d 854 (W.D. Wis. 2000).

[255]209 U.S. 123 (1908).

less of whether or not they acted *ultra vires.* Because the plaintiffs did not claim that the individuals sued were following state policy, the court held that if the plaintiffs were successful, they would be awarded damages payable by the defendants.[256]

In *Quillin v. Oregon,*[257] the Ninth Circuit refused to find an express or implied waiver from the state's failure to raise the immunity defense before the district court because *Seminole Tribe* had not been decided at the time. Furthermore, the court rejected the employees' request to avoid the inherent unfairness of dismissal of their FLSA action. Although the statute of limitations for filing a new claim in state court had passed, the *Quillin* court stated that it might be possible that the state courts would invoke principles of equitable tolling to allow them to review the claim.

In *Mueller v. Thompson,*[258] the Seventh Circuit held that Wisconsin wage and hour provisions adopted before *Seminole Tribe* that were identical to the FLSA and authorized suit to be brought in "any court of competent jurisdiction" did not effect a waiver of the state's Eleventh Amendment immunity from suit in federal court under the FLSA.

In *Robertson v. Board of County Commissioners of County of Morgan,*[259] a Colorado federal district court considered whether a political subdivision of a state is entitled to share in the immunity from suit enjoyed by the state. In determining whether the governmental entity was entitled to Eleventh Amendment immunity, the court considered the following factors: (1) the characterization of the entity under state law; (2) the guidance and control exercised by the state; (3) the degree of state funding received by the entity; (4) whether the entity may levy taxes or issue bonds; and (5) of most importance, and whether

---

[256] *See* Knussman v. Maryland, 65 F. Supp. 353 (D. Md. 1999) (case against state and individuals sued in their official capacity dismissed pursuant to principles of sovereign immunity in FMLA case; award against persons sued in their individual capacity, however, upheld).

[257] 4 WH Cases2d 296 (9th Cir. 1997).

[258] 135 F.3d 1063, 4 WH Cases2d 558 (7th Cir. 1998).

[259] 985 F. Supp. 980, 4 WH Cases2d 443 (D. Colo. 1997), *aff'd,* 166 F.3d 1222, 5 WH Cases2d 671 (10th Cir. 1999).

a judgment against the entity would be paid from the state fisc. The court held that the board of county commissioners was not entitled to share Colorado's Eleventh Amendment immunity from FLSA suits because the board had broad powers and the state retained relatively narrow control over the board's actions, the degree of state funding provided to the board was not significant, the board had power to levy taxes and to issue revenue bonds, and judgment against a board would be paid by levy of tax upon county property or by a warrant drawn upon the county fund in the county treasury. Therefore, the court refused to grant the defendant board of county commissioners' motion to dismiss for lack of subject matter jurisdiction.

In *Kimel v. Florida Board of Regents*,[260] the Supreme Court held that Congress exceeded its authority under Section 5 of the Fourteenth Amendment when it subjected states to monetary damage suits by their employees under the Age Discrimination in Employment Act. *Kimel* involved an action by faculty members claiming age discrimination by their state university employer. The Court concluded that the language of the ADEA makes clear Congress's intention to abrogate the states' immunity from suit. The Court cited the ADEA's statement in Section 626(c) that its provisions shall be enforced with the penalty, remedies, and procedures provided under certain provisions of the FLSA, including the right under Section 16(b), 29 U.S.C. §216(b), to pursue an action in a federal or state court of competent jurisdiction. Despite finding Congress's clear interest to abrogate the states' immunity, the Court held that Congress nonetheless lacked the power to effectuate that intent. The same five-person majority that ruled in *Seminole Tribe v. Florida*[261] held that the ADEA is not appropriate legislation under Section 5. The Court found that the substantive provisions not to discriminate contained in the ADEA were disproportionate to any unconstitutional conduct that could be targeted by the ADEA. In other words, the types of discrimination prohibited by the ADEA were

---

[260]528 U.S. 62 (2000).
[261]517 U.S. 44 (1996).

far greater than the types of discrimination that would be found unconstitutional under an equal protection, rational basis standard.

Next, the court found that congressional prohibitions against age discrimination by states could pass Section 5 analysis if such legislation was in response to difficult and intractable problems of discrimination that Congress had identified. The Court reviewed the legislative record to the ADEA to determine whether Congress had identified patterns or practices of discrimination by the states in enacting this legislation. The Court found that Congress had not.

In *Mercado v. Puerto Rico*,[262] the First Circuit held that Puerto Rico as a territory is to be treated no differently than the states with regard to Congress's power to abrogate states' Eleventh Amendment immunity from private individuals' suits in federal court. The plaintiffs, employees of the Commonwealth of Puerto Rico, argued that the Supreme Court's decision in *Seminole Tribe v. Florida*[263] did not apply to territorial possessions of the United States. The employees argued that since Congress has plenary power with respect to territories and possessions under the Territorial Clause, Congress's relationship with entities such as Puerto Rico is different than it is with the states. Thus, the employees concluded, the Eleventh Amendment immunity from suit available to the states did not apply to Puerto Rico.

The First Circuit rejected this argument as raising a "seductive lure of deceptively simple solutions."[264] The court examined the purpose of the FLSA's enforcement provisions and determined that Congress intended Puerto Rico to be treated as a state rather than a mere territory with regard to the application of the FLSA. Accordingly, the court concluded that the language in the FLSA that the Supreme Court deemed insufficient to abrogate states' immunity from suit is insufficient to abrogate Puerto Rico's immunity from suit under the Eleventh Amendment.

---

[262]214 F.3d 34, 6 WH Cases2d 118 (1st Cir. 2000).
[263]517 U.S. 44 (1996)
[264]214 F.3d at 40.

The *Seminole Tribe* result has been extended by the recent decision of the Supreme Court in *Alden v. Maine*.[265] In that litigation, the Maine Supreme Judicial Court had ruled that the Eleventh Amendment protects states from having to defend FLSA suits not only in federal court but also in state court.[266] The ruling effectively barred jurisdiction over any FLSA suit against the state of Maine. The court reasoned, per the U.S. Supreme Court's *Seminole* decision, that if Congress lacked the authority to abrogate state sovereign immunity in federal court, then it similarly lacked authority to abrogate such immunity in a state's own courts. Rejecting recent contrary decisions in other states,[267] which emphasized the federal Supremacy Clause, the Supreme Court in its affirmance of the Maine tribunal stated that "the States' immunity from suit is a fundamental aspect of the sovereignty which the States enjoyed before the ratification of the Constitution, and which they retain today (either literally or by virtue of their admission into the Union upon an equal footing with the other States) except as altered by the plan of the Convention or certain constitutional Amendments."[268]

In a dissenting opinion in *Abril v. Virginia*,[269] Judge Butzner argued that the Eleventh Amendment does not bar state employees from suing in federal court to enforce provisions of the FLSA. Judge Butzner would find that the FLSA meets the *Seminole* requirements that Congress clearly indicate its intent to abrogate state immunity and act through a "valid exercise of power" granted to it by the Fourteenth Amendment. Judge

---

[265] 527 U.S. 706, 5 WH Cases2d 609 (1999).

[266] Alden v. Maine, 715 A.2d 172, 4 WH Cases2d 1417 (Me.), *aff'd*, 527 U.S. 706, 5 WH Cases2d 609 (1999).

[267] Jacoby v. Arkansas Dep't of Educ., 962 S.W.2d 773, 4 WH Cases2d 686, 688–89 (Ark. 1998); Whittington v. State of N.M. Dep't of Pub. Safety, 966 P.2d 188, 4 WH Cases2d 1739 (N.M. Ct. App.), *cert. denied*, 972 P.2d 353 (N.M. 1998) (court of appeals of New Mexico held Eleventh Amendment did not give the state Department of Public Safety sovereign immunity in state court from suit based upon FLSA violations); Bunch v. Robinson, 712 A.2d 585, 4 WH Cases2d 1300 (Md. Ct. Spec. App. 1998) (reversing state trial court's dismissal on Eleventh Amendment grounds, emphasizing federal Supremacy Clause).

[268] 527 U.S. 706, 5 WH Cases2d at 610.

[269] 145 F.3d 182, 4 WH Cases2d 1110 (4th Cir. 1998) (Butzner, J., dissenting).

Butzner cited the Supreme Court's explanation in the *Slaughter-house Cases*[270] that the privileges of state citizenship include government protection to pursue happiness and safety. Concluding that the privileges of national citizenship are no less significant, Judge Butzner found that Congress had validly exercised its power to protect the privileges of national citizenship guaranteed by the Privileges and Immunities Clause of the Fourteenth Amendment in enacting the FLSA.

In *Ahern v. New York*,[271] the plaintiffs timely filed an action for overtime pay in federal court against the state police. The case was later dismissed on Eleventh Amendment grounds, and the plaintiffs subsequently filed suit in New York state court within 90 days of dismissal from federal court.[272] The state court, applying federal tolling principles, held that the 90-day statute of limitations prescribed by state law for the filing of such claims was equitably tolled by the timely filing of the federal suit, and the plaintiffs' suit in state court would not be dismissed for failure to file within the statute of limitations.[273]

In *Commonwealth of Virginia v. Luzik*[274] the Virginia Supreme Court held that the commonwealth did not waive its immunity nor consent to suit for unpaid FLSA overtime by waiving its immunity for contract debt. Similarly, in *King v. States of Nebraska*,[275] the Supreme Court of Nebraska ruled that a Nebraska statute permitting suit against the state "in any matter founded upon or growing out of a contract"[276] did not constitute a waiver of immunity to suit by state employees under the FLSA. In both *King* and *Luzik* the courts relied upon the long-established principles that waivers of sovereign immunity are strictly construed and must be pursuant to express language rather than by implication.

---

[270] 83 U.S. (16 Wall.) 36 (1873).

[271] 662 N.Y.S. 2d 684, 4 WH Cases2d 667 (Ct. Cl. 1997), *aff'd*, 676 N.Y.S.2d 232 (App. Div. 1998).

[272] *Id.* at 685, 4 WH Cases2d at 667–68.

[273] *Id.* at 686–87, 4 WH Cases2d at 668–69.

[274] 524 S.E.2d 871, 5 WH Cases2d 1735 (Va. 2000).

[275] 614 N.W.2d 341 (Neb. 2000).

[276] *Id.* at 347.

In *Whittington v. State of New Mexico*,[277] the Court of Appeals for New Mexico ruled that the state was immune from FLSA suits by state employees. The court noted, however, that its decision should not be interpreted as precluding the employees from asserting that the written employment policy of the employing state agency may constitute a contract within meaning of the state statutes governing contractual liability and that the provisions of the FLSA were incorporated into the contract between employees and the agency.

In *Butterfield v. State of Oregon*,[278] the Court of Appeals of Oregon did not reach the question of whether the state waived its immunity from suits by private parties under the FLSA. Instead, the court ruled that any such waiver would be encompassed by the Oregon Tort Claims Act (OTCA). The OTCA contains certain notice requirements that the plaintiff employees failed to meet. As a result, the court dismissed the suit.

In *Lawson v. University of Tennessee*,[279] the Court of Appeals of Tennessee rejected the argument that the state waived its immunity from FLSA suits for the University of Tennessee. The university employees argued that the legislature's creation of the Tennessee Claims Commission, with jurisdiction over negligent deprivation of rights established under Tennessee law, constituted an express waiver of sovereign immunity. The court rejected this argument, finding that the FLSA was not a statutory right "under Tennessee law."

In *Speers v. New York*,[280] the Court of Claims in New York found a partial waiver of the state's immunity from FLSA suits by state employees. The court ruled that the state was subject to suits by private parties under the FLSA, and that it was subject to the liquidated damages and attorneys' fees provisions of the Act. The court also held, however, that the employees pursuing actions against the state as an employer were bound by the New York Court of Claims Act's requirement that the claim be filed

---

[277] 4 P.3d 668, 6 WH Cases2d 1023 (N.M. Ct. App. 2000).
[278] 987 P.2d 569, 5 WH Cases2d 1173 (Or. Ct. App. 1999).
[279] 2000 WL 116312 (Tenn. Ct. App. 2000).
[280] 705 N.Y.S.2d 858 (2000).

within 180 days of the date it accrued. The court held that New York's waiver of immunity is expressly conditioned upon meeting the jurisdictional limitations contained in the state's Court of Claims Act.

In *Cash v. Granville County Board of Education*,[281] the North Carolina Supreme Court ruled that North Carolina sheriffs and deputies function as state employees. Accordingly, the court found that the state was immune from suit by these employees.

In *Bunt v. Texas General Land Office*,[282] the court ruled that Eleventh Amendment immunity barred an employee's FLSA suit against his state agency employer.

In *Hartman v. Regents of the University of Colorado*,[283] the Colorado Court of Appeals ruled that employees of the state university could be sued individually under the FLSA and that overtime pay claims did not fall within the state's immunity statute for tort claims. The court did find that the state was immune from suit involving retaliation claims under the FLSA because these claims fell within the tort immunity statute, but that individual state employees who qualified as employers under the FLSA were not immune from suit.

In *Dick v. Merillat*,[284] a former member of the county sheriff's department sued the county sheriff and County Board of Commissioners alleging that he was entitled to overtime under the FLSA for the time he spent after work caring for his police dog.[285] The Court of Appeals of Ohio concluded that the Supreme Court's holding in *Alden v. Maine*,[286] barring FLSA suits against the states on the basis of the Eleventh Amendment, did not apply in the instant case because the police officer had brought suit against the county sheriff and the County Commissioners and not the state of Ohio.[287] The court further concluded that Ohio state statutes regarding sovereign immunity did not bar the FLSA lawsuit.

---

[281] 2000 U.S. Dist. LEXIS 4852 (E.D.N.C. 2000).
[282] 72 F. Supp. 2d 735 (S.D. Tex. 1999).
[283] 2000 WL 890411 (Colo. App. 2000).
[284] 139 Ohio App. 3d 716, 745 N.E. 2d 507 (Ohio Ct. App. 2000).
[285] *Id.* at 507–508.
[286] 527 U.S. 706 (1999).
[287] *Dick*, 745 N.E. 2d at 510.

In *Lopez Rosario v. Puerto Rico Police Department*,[288] civilian employees of the Puerto Rico Police Department and Security Commission brought suit against the police department, the police superintendent and the Security Commission, the Office of Labor Advice and various others, including individuals in both their official and their personal capacities, alleging FLSA and Equal Pay Act violations, and a variety of other violations based on the same set of facts.[289] Defendants moved to dismiss all claims on Eleventh Amendment and related grounds. The trial court, relying on the holdings of *Seminole Tribe of Florida v. Florida*,[290] *Alden v. Maine*,[291] and *Mills v. Maine*,[292] first noted that for Eleventh Amendment purposes Puerto Rico is considered a "state." It therefore concluded that plaintiffs' FLSA claims were barred.[293] It found that *Ex parte Young* suits could not be maintained because of the FLSA's detailed remedial scheme providing for injunctive relief to be available only to the Secretary, and declaratory judgment to be unavailable because its sole purpose would be to provide a res judicata "end run" around the Eleventh Amendment jurisprudence. The court then held that, although the Equal Pay Act claim was not barred by the Eleventh Amendment, plaintiffs had failed to establish a prima facie Equal Pay Act violation because they had not alleged that defendants were paying different wages to employees of different sexes.[294] Other claims such as a violation of constitutional Equal Protection and violations of 28 U.S.C. §§1981 and 1985 were disposed of, and the plaintiffs' complaint was dismissed.

In *Kess v. State of Maryland*,[295] current and former law enforcement officers employed at Baltimore-Washington International Airport sued the State of Maryland and various state

---

[288] 126 F. Supp. 2d 167 (D.P.R. 2000).
[289] *Id.* at 169.
[290] 517 U.S. 44 (1996).
[291] 527 U.S. 706 (1999).
[292] 118 F.3d 37 (1st Cir. 1997).
[293] *Lopez Rosario*, 126 F. Supp. 2d at 170–71.
[294] *Id.* at 172–73.
[295] 2001 WL 85179 (D. Md. Jan. 29, 2001).

agencies for alleged FLSA violations.[296] The trial court, relying on *Seminole Tribe*[297] and *Alden v. Maine*,[298] granted defendants' motion to dismiss on Eleventh Amendment grounds.[299] The trial court rejected plaintiffs' argument that the defendant state agencies were not "arms of the state." The trial court rendered such a conclusion because the state's treasury would be affected by any adverse judgment entered against the agencies.[300]

In *Adams v. United States*,[301] current and former Border Patrol employees brought suit for unpaid overtime pursuant to the FLSA.[302] The issue here involved the award of interest on back pay which had been awarded by a previous order. The Court of Federal Claims concluded that Congress had not expressly waived, through the Back Pay Act,[303] the federal government's immunity from interest on FLSA back pay awards to federal employees.[304]

In *Cash v. Granville County Board of Education*,[305] a high school secretary/bookkeeper sued the County Board of Education for unpaid overtime under the FLSA.[306] The trial court concluded that the County Board was an "arm of the state" and dismissed the suit on Eleventh Amendment grounds.[307] The Fourth Circuit Court of Appeals reversed.[308] The appellate court emphasized that the most important factor in determining whether an agency is in fact an "arm of the state" is whether a judgment against the entity would have to be paid from the state's treasury.[309] Because all the parties involved in the suit

---

[296] *Id.* at *1.

[297] 517 U.S. 44 (1996).

[298] 527 U.S. 706 (1999).

[299] *Kess*, 2001 WL 85179, at *2.

[300] *Id.*

[301] 48 Fed.Cl. 602 (2001).

[302] *Id.* at 604.

[303] 5 U.S.C. §5596(b)(1). The Back Pay Act provides a monetary remedy, i.e., back pay, to federal employees who are subjected to unlawful personnel actions which resulted in a reduction in pay.

[304] *Adams*, 48 Fed.Cl. at 610.

[305] 242 F.3d 219 (4th Cir. 2001).

[306] *Id.* at 221.

[307] *Id.*

[308] *Id.*

[309] *Id.* at 223.

agreed that the state would not be legally obligated to satisfy a judgment against the County Board, the court held that the Board was not an "arm of the state" and was therefore not immune from an FLSA suit.[310]

The New Jersey Supreme Court in a 4-to-2 per curiam decision held, in *Allen v. Fauver*,[311] that New Jersey had not waived its sovereign immunity so as to subject itself to suit under the FLSA. This was a case brought by state corrections officers against the state, the state governor and the state corrections commissioner for alleged unpaid overtime.[312] The Supreme Court affirmed the trial court's and intermediate appellate court's holdings. Neither the New Jersey Wage and Hour Law, under which the state is not an "employer," nor the Contractual Liability Act,[313] since the plaintiffs' suit did not sound in contract, could be said to have displaced the state's sovereign immunity which protected it from the assertion of back pay liability.

In *Luder v. Endicott*,[314] state prison employees sued their prison supervisors, in their individual capacities, to recover alleged unpaid wages, pursuant to the FLSA.[315] In the district court the defendants moved to dismiss on the grounds of sovereign immunity but that motion was denied. The Seventh Circuit Court of Appeals reversed and dismissed the suit.[316] Judge Posner first concluded, without much difficulty, that the supervisors were "employers" for FLSA purposes.[317] He then determined that the Eleventh Amendment barred the suit because the state, whether by indemnifying the individual defendants or by modifying its practices to rectify the alleged FLSA violations, would be the actual entity disbursing any monies as a result of the suit.[318] Therefore, the effect of the lawsuit would be

---

[310] *Id.* at 224–25.
[311] 786 A.2d 1055 (N.J. 2001).
[312] *Id.* at 1057.
[313] N.J.S.A. 59:13-1 to 13-10. The Act provides that "if a state official, having the legal authority to do so, makes a written or implied in fact contractual commitment, that contractual undertaking will be enforced."
[314] 253 F.3d 1020 (2001).
[315] *Id.* at 1021–22.
[316] *Id.* at 1025.
[317] *Id.* at 1022.
[318] *Id.* at 1024.

the same as if the plaintiffs had directly sued the state of Wisconsin;[319] and, because a direct suit against the state would be barred by the Eleventh Amendment, so would the present suit against the prison supervisors.[320]

In *Chao v. Virginia Department of Transportation*,[321] the trial court recognized that, pursuant to *Seminole Tribe* and *Alden*, individuals could not sue a state or state agency for FLSA violations.[322] It noted, however, that

> although VDOT, as an employer, is immune from suits by private parties, it does not enjoy "a concomitant right to disregard the Constitution or valid federal law. The States and their officers are bound by obligations imposed by the Constitution and by federal statutes that comport with the constitutional design."[323]

The court accordingly held that sovereign immunity did not prevent the United States, through the secretary [of Labor], from seeking a restitutionary or prospective injunction against a state under Section 217 [of the FLSA].[324]

---

[319] *Id.*

[320] *Id.*

[321] 157 F. Supp. 2d 681, 7 WH Cases2d 347 (E.D. Va. 2001).

[322] *Id.* at 694, 7 WH Cases2d 347.

[323] *Id.* at 681, 7 WH Cases2d 347, 356 (E.D. Va 2001) (quoting Alden v. Maine, 527 U.S. 706, 755 (1999)).

[324] *Id.* at 694, 7 WH Cases2d 347.

CHAPTER 12

CHILD LABOR

IV. Child Labor Amendments

J. 1998 [New Topic]

Section 13(c) of the Act, relating to child labor, was amended in 1996 and in 1998. The 1996 amendments[1] modified the effect of the prohibitions of Child Labor Hazardous Order 12 to permit children 16 and 17 years old to load boxes and other paper products into paper balers and paper box compactors, but not to unload or operate the machines, so long as the machines meet certain design specifications.[2]

The 1998 amendments[3] modified the application of Hazardous Order 2, relating to operation of motor vehicles. Employees under 17 years of age are prohibited from driving automobiles or trucks on public roadways, but employees 17 and 18 years of age are permitted to do so under the restrictions and conditions newly set forth. Employees who are 17 years of age or older may drive automobiles and trucks on public roadways only if (1) such driving is restricted to daylight hours; (2) the employee holds a valid state license for the type of driving involved and has no record of moving violations at the time of hire; (3) the employee has successfully completed a state-approved driver education course; (4) the vehicle is equipped with a seat belt for the driver and any passengers, and the employee's employer has instructed the employee that seat belts must be used when driving the vehicle; (5) the vehicle does not exceed 6,000 pounds of gross vehicle weight; and (6) the driving does not involve (a) the towing of vehicles; (b) route deliveries or route sales; (c) the transportation for hire of property, goods, or passengers; (d) urgent, time-sensitive deliveries; (e) more than two trips away from the primary place of employment in any single day for the purpose of delivering goods of the employer to a customer; (f) more than two trips away from the primary

---

[1]Compactors and Balers Safety Standards Modernization Act, Pub. L. No. 104-174, 110 Stat. 1553 (1996).

[2]These specifications are set forth in the statute. *See* Appendix A.3 in this supplement.

[3]Drive for Teen Employment Act, Pub. L. No. 105-334, 112 Stat. 3137 (1998).

place of employment in any single day for the purpose of transporting passengers; (g) transporting more than three passengers; or (h) driving beyond a 30-mile radius from the place of employment; and (7) such driving is only occasional and incidental to the employee's employment.

The amendment goes on to define the term "occasional and incidental" in connection with (7) above as meaning no more than one-third of an employee's work time in any workday and no more than 20 percent of an employee's work time in any workweek. This definition applies to any case, action, citation, or appeal pending on the date of enactment of the amendment (October 31, 1998), unless the case, action, citation, or appeal involves property damage or personal injury.

VI. WORK RESTRICTIONS BY AGE AND OCCUPATION

A. Nonagricultural Occupations

1. Minors Under Age 18

c. Further Discussion of Selected Hazardous Orders

i. HO 2: Occupation of Motor Vehicle Driver and Outside Helper. Pursuant to the 1998 Drive for Teen Employment Act,[4] children who are 17 years of age may drive automobiles or trucks on public roadways subject to specific restrictions.[5] The restrictions are:

(1) that the driving is restricted to daylight hours;

(2) that the employee holds a valid state license for the type of driving involved and has no record of moving violations at the time of hire;

(3) that the employee has successfully completed a state-approved driver education course;

(4) that the vehicle is equipped with a seat belt for the driver and any passengers, and the employee's employer has

---

[4] *Id.*

[5] *Id.*

instructed the employee that seat belts must be used when driving the vehicle;

(5) that the vehicle does not exceed 6,000 pounds of gross vehicle weight;

(6) that the driving does not involve

(a) the towing of vehicles;

(b) route deliveries or route sales;

(c) the transportation for hire of property, goods, or passengers;

(d) urgent, time-sensitive deliveries;

(e) more than two trips away from the primary place of employment in any single day for the purpose of delivering goods of the employer to a customer;

(f) more than two trips away from the primary place of employment in any single day for the purpose of transporting passengers;

(g) transporting more than three passengers; or

(h) driving beyond a 30-mile radius from the place of employment; and

(7) that the driving is only occasional and incidental to the employee's employment.

The amendment explicitly defines the term "occasional and incidental," which appears in the last condition, as no more than one-third of an employee's work time in any workday and no more than 20 percent of an employee's work time in any workweek. This definition applies to any case, action, citation, or appeal pending on the date of enactment of the amendment (October 31, 1998), unless the case, action, citation, or appeal involves property damage or personal injury.

In *Acura of Bellevue v. Reich*,[6] the Ninth Circuit affirmed the district court's dismissal of an action by car dealers who had sought judicial review of an administrative determination that car dealers violated Hazardous Occupation Order No. 2 by employing minors between the ages of 16 and 18 as lot attendants, because the lot attendants' duties included driving cars

---

[6]90 F.3d 1403, 3 WH Cases2d 673 (9th Cir. 1996), *cert. denied,* 117 S. Ct. 945, 3 WH Cases2d 1312 (1997).

on the dealers' premises, moving cars to different lots, driving to get gas, and transporting customers. Because the plaintiffs had previously filed an administrative appeal which was still pending, the court held that the dealers' action was not ripe for judicial review because the agency action was not final. The court rejected the dealers' claim of financial hardship, stating that a showing of financial hardship is insufficient to justify a finding of ripeness.

vi. HO 12: Operating Paper Product Machines. The 1996 Compactors and Balers Safety Standards Modernization Act[7] modified the effect of the prohibitions of Child Labor Hazardous Order 12 to permit children 16 and 17 years old to load boxes and other paper products into paper balers and paper box compactors, but not to unload or operate the machines, so long as the machines meet certain design specifications.[8]

In *Administrator v. Ahn's Market,*[9] the Department of Labor's Administrative Review Board upheld a fine levied against a defendant who employed 10 minors under the age of 18 to load and/or operate a scrap paper baler. The defendant had argued that its conduct was permissible under an August 1996 amendment to the FLSA that allowed 16- and 17-year-old minors to load scrap paper balers under certain circumstances. An administrative law judge (ALJ) found that the defendants had sought to impermissibly apply the 1996 amendment retroactively because the violations had occurred before the amendment was enacted into law. The Board upheld the ALJ's ruling, finding that there was no evidence in the legislative history or the Act itself that indicated that Congress intended to apply the amendments retroactively. As an alternative holding, the Board found that the defendant had not established that its baler fell within the exemption contained in the 1996 amendment. The defendant had tried to argue that the government had the burden of establishing that the baler did not meet the amendment's

---

[7]Pub. L. No. 104-174, 110 Stat. 1553 (1996).

[8]These specifications are set forth in the statute. *See* Appendix A.3 in this supplement.

[9]ARB No. 99-024, ALJ No. 97-CLA-33, 2000 WL 1074299 (DOL ARB July 28, 2000).

requirements. The Board rejected this contention, finding that a party seeking protection from liability via an exemption has the burden of proving compliance with the conditions of the exemption.

B. Agricultural Occupations

1. Minors Under Age 16

a. The Hazardous Occupations

In *Administrator v. Elderkin,*[10] a farmer was accused of illegally employing eight minors, one of whom had been involved in a serious accident while operating farm machinery specifically prohibited by DOL regulations. Due to the severity of the incident, the Wage and Hour Division levied a fine of $71,100 against the defendant. The defendant sought review before a Department administrative law judge, arguing that the minors were not "employees" of the farm. The ALJ rejected this argument, but reduced the penalty to $29,050 because the financial resources of the defendant's business were not properly taken into account. Both sides appealed to the Administrative Review Board. The Board, as had the ALJ, rejected the defendant's contention that the minor was not an employee at the time of the accident. It found that despite alleged inconsistencies in the minor's testimony, there was sufficient support for the ALJ's finding that the farmer had violated the FLSA. In addition, the Board conducted a de novo review of the ALJ's reduction of the defendant's penalty. It held for the first time that "once a [civil monetary penalty] has been challenged before an ALJ the issue is not whether the penalty assesed by the Administrator comports with the [W-H published grid contained in Form W-H 266]. Rather the question is whether the assessed penalty complies with the statutory provision regarding CMP and the CMP regulations."[11] It found that the ALJ had misjudged the serious-

---

[10]ARB Nos. 99-033, 99-048, ALJ No. 95-CLA-31, 2000 WL 960261 (DOL ARB June 30, 2000).

[11]ARB 99-033, 99-048, June 30, 1999, at p.10.

ness of the defendant's violations, specifically, the young ages of the children, the large number of record-keeping violations, and the dangerous work the children performed. In light of that evidence, the Board found that the original fine levied was appropriate.

XI. ENFORCEMENT

B. Civil Money Penalties

In appellate administrative proceedings, the Secretary in 1996 found that civil money penalties were mandatory for child labor violations. He reinstated penalties that had been reversed by an ALJ, while criticizing both the Administrator and the ALJ for the manner in which penalties were assessed and then reversed.[12]

The Department's Administrative Review Board revised an ALJ's reduction of civil money penalties imposed on an employer, reasoning that the FLSA's legislative history regarding civil money penalties did not restrict maximum civil money penalties to the most egregious cases.[13]

In *Administrator v. Thirsty's Inc.*,[14] the Administrative Review Board deferred to the Administrator's use of a grid and matrix providing for the calculation of civil money penalties.

An ALJ declined to reduce a civil money penalty against an employer because of the employer's history of violation and its failure to cooperate in the administrative proceeding.[15]

In *Thirsty's, Inc. v. United States Department of Labor,*[16] a suit to set aside the civil money penalty imposed by the Department for child labor violations, the defendant claimed that Form WH-

---

[12]Administrator v. Navajo Mfr., 92-CLA-13 (Sec'y Feb. 28, 1996) <http://204.245.136.2/libtrad.htm> (visited Feb. 12, 1998).

[13]Administrator v. Sayler, 93-CLA-18,—22,—23 (ARB Sept. 27, 1996).

[14]94-CLA-65, 1997 WL 453588 (ARB May 14, 1997).

[15]United States Dep't of Labor v. Jerral D. Parris, 95-CLA-8 (ALJ May 24, 1996), *aff'd in part and rev'd in part,* 1997 WL 144082 (ARB Mar. 27, 1997) <http://204.245.136.2/libtrad.htm> (visited Feb. 12, 1998).

[16]57 F. Supp. 2d 431, 6 WH Cases2d 340 (S.D. Tex. 1999).

266, a form used by the Wage and Hour Division in calculating penalties, failed to take into account all the factors required to be considered in assessing a penalty under the statute. The case came to the court after an ALJ had accepted the employer's argument and reduced the penalty by 75 percent, and the Department's Administrative Review Board subsequently reversed the ALJ's decision and reinstated all but 25 percent of the originally imposed penalty. After analyzing the form itself and the regulations governing the imposition of penalties, the court concluded that the form did take into account the necessary factors and that the assessment process permitted the assessing officer to excercise discretion in assessing the penalty. The court found that the Administrative Review Board's decision was entitled to deference and that Form WH-266 was appropriately used to calculate penalties for child labor violations.[17]

D. No Private Remedy

Courts continue to hold that the FLSA does not create a private right of action for violations involving child labor. In *Henderson v. Bear*,[18] a case involving the death by electrocution of a minor working in violation of the child labor prohibitions, a Colorado state court held that the FLSA did not create an implied private right of action that superseded the exclusivity provisions of the state workers' compensation act. The court applied the four-factor test in *Cort v. Ash*[19] for determining if a private right of action had been created and concluded that it had not in this fact situation. It stated, "Questions as to the inadequacy of that [state workers' compensation] remedy do not justify the creation of a new federal remedy in addition to the criminal penalties provided by the FLSA."[20]

---

[17]*Id.* at 436–37, 6 WH Cases2d 340.
[18]968 P.2d 144, 4 WH Cases2d 1756 (Colo. Ct. App. 1998).
[19]422 U.S. 66 (1975).
[20]968 P.2d 144, 4 WH Cases2d at 1758.

CHAPTER 13

HOMEWORK

There are no developments to report.

Chapter 14

HOT GOODS VIOLATIONS

I. OVERVIEW

The Department of Labor in 1996 and 1997 conducted a high-profile compliance campaign in the garment industry. Entitled "No Sweat," this initiative relied in part on the threatened use of the "hot goods" provision against manufacturers using contractors whose employees had not been paid in accordance with the FLSA.[1] In at least one case, the Department successfully enjoined a manufacturer during the pendency of an enforcement action from receiving hot goods.[2] The court in that case imposed numerous specific requirements on the manufacturer, including the obligation to review the feasibility of proposed price terms with contractors.[3]

IV. DEFINITIONS USED IN THE HOT GOODS PROVISIONS

A. Building Blocks of the Hot Goods Ban of Section 12(a)

3. *"Goods"*

Herman v. Hospital Staffing Services, Inc.,[4] was a hot goods injunction action brought by the Department after defendant company, which was in bankruptcy, had missed two payrolls and closed down its operations in several states. The Secretary sought to enjoin the shipment in commerce of records—including patient clinical reports and billing records—of the defendant company, which records the unpaid employees had worked on. The trustee in bankruptcy and others moved to dismiss the complaint. On the jurisdictional question—whether the exclusive jurisdiction of the bankruptcy court deprived the district court of jurisdiction—the district court held that the Secretary's hot goods action was within the "police powers" exception, Section 362(b)(4), to the exclusivity provision of the bankruptcy code because it was brought to enforce the public policy goals inherent in the minimum wage and overtime provisions of the

---

[1] *See, e.g.*, U.S. Department of Labor Garment Enforcement Report (Jan. 1997—Mar. 1997) <http:/www.dol.gov/dol/era/public/nosweat/garment/htm> (visited Feb. 24, 1998).

[2] Herman v. Fashion Headquarters, Inc., 1998 WL 47823, 4 WH Cases2d 649 (S.D.N.Y. 1998).

[3] *Id.* at *4, 4 WH Cases2d 649.

[4] 236 B.R. 377 (Bankr. W.D. Tenn. 1999).

FLSA.[5] On the question whether the documents were "goods" within the meaning of the statute, the court held that clinical patient reports and billing documents constituted goods of a kind that could be subject to a "hot goods" action under the FLSA. It noted that the records and documents were articles of trade, were not internal documents, were produced as an objective of the defendant's business, and were produced for multiple purposes, including use by the treating physician to develop a plan of care. Because of these factors, the court held that the records were sufficiently related to the defendant's business to be classified as goods.

VI. Enforcement of the Hot Goods Ban

D. Reliance on the Hot Goods Provisions in Matters Not Seeking a Hot Goods Remedy [New Topic]

Despite the lack of a private right of action under the FLSA's hot goods provisions, its provisions have been successfully invoked in at least one private case to support a state law claim based on a negligence per se theory. In *Bureerong v. Uvawas*,[6] a group of immigrant workers who alleged that they had been held in involuntary servitude and forced to work in a garment manufacturing complex brought an action against the operators of the complex and the manufacturer who contracted with the operators to produce the garments. Among the claims alleged by the plaintiffs was a claim that the defendants were liable to them under a California negligence per se theory because their conduct violated a statute—namely, the FLSA's hot goods provisions. The plaintiffs further asserted that the conduct in question proximately caused them injury and that they were in the class of persons for whose benefit the statute was

---

[5] *Id.* at 382–83.

[6] 959 F. Supp. 1231 (C.D. Cal. 1997).

adopted.[7] The court determined that the plaintiffs had pleaded the necessary elements of a cause of action for negligence per se.

---

[7]*Id.* at 1236. At an earlier point in this litigation, 922 F. Supp. 1450, 3 WH Cases2d 383 (C.D. Cal. 1996), the defendants had moved to dismiss the negligence per se claim, arguing that the plaintiffs had not stated a claim upon which relief could be granted because (1) a claim for negligence per se under California law cannot be based upon a statute which has no private right of action, (2) plaintiffs' injuries were not of the type that the hot goods provisions were designed to prevent, and (3) the hot goods provisions were intended not to protect individual employees but to protect interstate commerce from the competitive injury occasioned by the sale of goods manufactured under substandard labor conditions. The court held that it *is* possible to state a claim for negligence per se under California law based upon violation of the FLSA's hot goods provisions. The district court reasoned that the FLSA *was* intended to protect individual laborers and the plaintiffs' injuries were arguably within the scope of injuries intended to be remedied by the FLSA. However, because the plaintiffs failed to allege all four essential elements of a state negligence per se claim, the court dismissed the claim without prejudice to allow plaintiffs to further amend the complaint.

CHAPTER 15

RETALIATION

II. PARTIES

A. Plaintiffs

1. *"Any Employee"*

In *Glover v. City of North Charleston*[1] the district court held that "employee" did not include two firefighters who had been employed by fire districts before the city took over the fire protection responsibilities from the districts, and who had been the lead FLSA plaintiffs against the districts, on the ground that with respect to the city they were job "applicants" who had never been employed by the city.

In *Contreras v. Corinthian Vigor Insurance*,[2] a federal district court in California held that an employee whose employer reported her to the Immigration and Naturalization Service because she had filed a wage claim under California law was protected under the retaliation provision of the FLSA. Reiterating in forceful terms the prevailing view, the court stated, "There is no question that the protections provided by the FLSA apply to undocumented aliens. *See e.g., In re Reyes,* 814 F.2d 168, 170 (5th Cir. 1957), *cert. denied,* 487 U.S. 1235 ('[I]t is well established that the protections of the Fair Labor Standards Act are applicable to citizens and aliens alike and whether the alien is documented or undocumented is irrelevant. An employee is "any individual employed by an employer."')."[3]

B. Defendants

The court in *Glover* found that the city of North Charleston qualified as a "person" for the purposes of an FLSA retaliation claim under Section 15(a)(3).[4]

---

[1]848 F. Supp. 911, 1 WH Cases2d 1651 (D. Colo. 1994).

[2]25 F. Supp. 2d 1053, 4 WH Cases2d 1793 (N.D. Cal. 1998).

[3]25 F. Supp. 2d 1053, 4 WH Cases2d at 1794–95.

[4]848 F. Supp. 911, 1 WH Cases2d 1651.

The Seventh Circuit in *Sapperstein v. Hager*[5] reversed the district court's dismissal on jurisdictional grounds of Sapperstein's complaint, which asserted among other things a claim for retaliatory dismissal. The district court had dismissed on jurisdictional grounds, finding that the employer's annual dollar volume of sales failed to meet the jurisdictional amount. The court of appeals pointed out that the prohibitions of Section 15(a)(3) extend to "any person" and that, accordingly, they extend beyond the covered employers to whom the substantive provisions of Sections 6 and 7 apply. The court held that "there is no required amount to be a 'person' under §215."[6]

In *Cheng v. IDEAssociates., Inc,*[7] the plaintiff had, while employed by the defendant, complained to her supervisor and to the EEOC about what she claimed were underpayments under the Equal Pay Act. In this FLSA retaliation case brought after the plaintiff's employment was terminated, the federal district court held that the company's president and vice-president, co-founders of the corporation, each of whom had a significant ownership interest and operational control over the company's daily functions, could be held liable, despite their contentions that neither knew of the plaintiff's complaint and that the president did not participate in the decision to terminate the plaintiff's employment.

In *Oi Kwan Lai v. Eastpoint International, Inc.*,[8] a garment industry suit, the plaintiff sought to hold liable, in addition to the contractor that directly employed her, the manufacturer, Donna Karan, for whom the goods worked on were produced. The court held that in the context of garment industry subcontracting practices, the manufacturer, while not the direct employer, might be liable for retaliation as a joint employer, but granted Karan's motion to dismiss because the plaintiff had failed to establish a prima facie case of retaliation against Karan.

---

[5]5 WH Cases2d 933 (7th Cir. 1999).

[6]*Id.* at 936.

[7]6 WH Cases2d 654 (D. Mass. 2000).

[8]2000 WL 1234595 (S.D.N.Y. 2000).

In an unpublished decision the Tenth Circuit in *Hinsdale v. City of Liberal, Kansas,*[9] affirmed in part and reversed and remanded in part the district court's summary judgment in favor of the defendants, the acting city manager and several city commissioners sued as individuals. The plaintiffs asserted claims of retaliation under the FLSA and a variety of other claims including claims based on freedom of association under the First and Fourteenth Amendments, procedural due process, substantive due process, and equal protection. Plaintiffs, Mr. and Mrs. Hinsdale, had been employed as chief of police and in a staff position at the Housing Authority, respectively. Some time after Mrs. Hinsdale filed suit for overtime under the FLSA, the Commission became aware that Mr. Hinsdale intended to testify in the case. This resulted, eventually, in Mr. Hinsdale's being first demoted from the position of chief of police to court administrator, with a reduction in pay; and, after his testimony, being fired from that position.

The trial court had held that the demotion from chief of police to court administrator was not retaliatory within the meaning of the FLSA on the ground that it occurred at a time when no protected activity had yet occurred. (The testimony came later.) The court of appeals decided that the decision to testify, which came to the Commission's attention, should have been considered protected activity, and that summary judgment for defendants on the first claim should be reversed. On the firing claim, the district court had found that a prima facie case of retaliation had been made out, but that defendants had offered a non-discriminatory reason other than retaliation (lack of funding for the new position) for the act, and that plaintiffs' counter-evidence was insufficient for a jury to find the defendants' reason pretextual. After reviewing the evidence, the appellate court rejected this analysis and held that a jury question as to actual motive for the firing had been made out; thus summary judgment on this claim was also reversed. Finally, the individual defendants argued that they enjoyed absolute legislative immunity for their actions. The court found that the record

[9]2001 WL 980781 (10th Cir. 2001) (unpublished opinion).

was insufficient to support a claim that they had acted within the scope of legislative immunity, and declined to consider that contention, leaving defendants free to make the case that they acted in a strictly legislative manner on the remand.

A district court in New York held in *Lamont v. Frank Soup Bowl, Inc.*[10] that when an employer is not covered by the FLSA, that same employer is not subject to the FLSA anti-retaliation provision. The employer here operated a small take-out restaurant in the Bronx. The single location served local patrons only and had annual gross sales of less than $500,000. Therefore, the employer was not engaged in interstate commerce or subject to the FLSA. The court acknowledged the contrary rule (that the FLSA's anti-retaliation prohibition extends to "any person," whether or not wage and overtime coverage independently exists), but attempted to distinguish *Sapperstein v. Hager,*[11] and *Wirtz v. Ross Packaging Co.,*[12] on their facts. Moreover, it found that "neither of those [appellate] cases considered the clear intent of Congress to limit the reach of the FLSA or the constitutional issues that arise from extending jurisdiction beyond the area in which Congress chose to legislate."[13]

III. CONDUCT FOUND TO BE PROTECTED

C. Informal Workplace Complaints

Section 15(a)(3) extends protection to an employee who "has filed any complaint or instituted or caused to be instituted any proceeding under or related to [the Act], or has testified or is about to testify in any such proceeding, or has served or is about to serve on an industry committee."[14] Courts disagree on the question of whether Section 15(a)(3) protects informal complaints in the workplace.

---

[10]2001 WL 521815, 143 Lab. Cas. (CCH) ¶34,259 (S.D.N.Y. 2001).
[11]188 F.3d 852 (7th Cir. 1999), reported in the Supplement.
[12]367 F.2d 549, 550–51 (5th Cir. 1966).
[13]2001 WL 521815, 143 Lab. Cas. (CCH) ¶34,259.
[14]29 U.S.C. §215(a)(3).

The majority view declines to give a literal reading to Section 15(a)(3) but rather extends protection to the informal assertion of rights under the FLSA. For example, in *Conner v. Schnuck Markets, Inc.*,[15] the Tenth Circuit reaffirmed its holding in *Love v. RE/MAX of America, Inc.*,[16] that Section 15(a)(3) protects the "unofficial assertion of rights through complaints at work."[17]

In *Valerio v. Putnam Associates, Inc.*,[18] the First Circuit reversed the district court's dismissal of plaintiff's claim for retaliation, holding in this case of first impression on the issue in this circuit that internal complaints to the employer are protected under the FLSA. The court reviewed the state of the law in the other circuits[19] and sided with the majority of them, reasoning that remedial statutes should be construed broadly and noting that the definition of "file a complaint" could include an internal complaint made with the expectation that it will be "placed on file" with the employer's official records.

Similarly, the Ninth Circuit en banc affirmed the decision of the district court for the Western District of Washington in *Lambert v. Ackerley*,[20] joining six other circuits in holding that the anti-retaliation provision of the FLSA protects employee complaints to an employer. The question had previously been noted, but not addressed, by a panel of the circuit in *Knickerbocker v. Stockton*.[21] Judge Reinhardt, writing for the en banc court, reasoned that the FLSA was a remedial statute that should be construed broadly and should be interpreted to address em-

[15] 121 F.3d 1390 (10th Cir. 1997).

[16] 738 F.2d 383, 387 (10th Cir. 1984).

[17] 121 F.3d at 1394. *See also* Ruccolo v. BDP Int'l, 3 WH Cases2d 941, 943 (D.N.J. 1996) (proximity of request for overtime pay to termination states claim for retaliation). Further discussion of the role of temporal proximity in respect to causation in retaliation cases is found at §V. [Prima Facie Case and Burden of Proof] of this chapter, Treatise at p. 911.

[18] 173 F.3d 35, 5 WH Cases2d 389 (1st Cir. 1999), *corrected*, 173 F3d 35, 5 WH Cases2d 1024 (1st Cir. 1999).

[19] 173 F.3d 35, 5 WH Cases2d at 393.

[20] 180 F.3d 997, 5 WH Cases2d 677 (9th Cir. 1999).

[21] 81 F.3d 907, 912 n.3, 3 WH Cases2d 453 (9th Cir. 1996), noted in Treatise at Chapter 15, note 296.

ployee fears of economic retaliation for raising complaints. The court noted that only the Second Circuit had adopted a narrower interpretation.

A different result was reached in *Clevinger v. Motel Sleepers, Inc.*,[22] where a Virginia federal district court held that an employee alleging that she was fired for complaining to her employer about its failure to pay minimum wage did not state a claim for retaliation under the FLSA. Since the Fourth Circuit had not addressed this issue, the district court adopted the minority view and held that informal complaints to an employer did not meet the Act's requirements. The statute protects from retaliation any employee who "has filed any complaint,"[23] and the court reasoned that the word "filed" "clearly denotes a procedure other than oral."[24] The court also concluded that the other activities mentioned in the context of the provision involved "formal endeavors" and thus "a more verifiable activity is required than merely an oral complaint to a supervisor."[25]

Written complaints to the employer about possible Equal Pay Act violations in addition to informal oral complaints and a complaint to the EEOC resulting in an investigation of the employer have been held to be protected activities pursuant to 29 U.S.C. §15(a)(3).[26]

In *Truex v. Hearst Communications, Inc.*,[27] the federal district court followed the majority rule in holding that an oral, internal complaint was sufficient to trigger the protection of Section 15(a)(3). The plaintiff sought the guidance of the Department of Labor and spoke with a representative who advised him to try to resolve the matter with his employer before filing a formal complaint. The court also observed that employees must feel free to communicate with federal authorities about their grievances.

---

[22] 36 F. Supp. 2d 322, 5 WH Cases2d 165 (W.D. Va. 1999).
[23] 29 U.S.C. §215(a)(3).
[24] 36 F. Supp. 2d 322, 5 WH Cases2d at 166.
[25] *Id.*, 5 WH Cases2d at 167.
[26] Cheng v. IDEAssocs., Inc., 6 WH Cases2d 654 (D. Mass. 2000).
[27] 96 F. Supp. 2d 652 (S.D. Tex. 2000).

Another federal district court in Illinois[28] denied the employer's summary judgment motion by following the same majority rule where the plaintiff's retaliation claim was predicated on his complaint to the defendant's human resource manager.

In *Ellis v. HarperCollins Publishers, Inc.*,[29] the plaintiff's claim of retaliation was dismissed in accordance with the minority rule that a retaliation claim under the FLSA is limited to retaliation for filing formal complaints, instituting a proceeding, or testifying—not making a complaint to a supervisor. The plaintiff, a human resource manager, had only verbally complained to her supervisor that the employer was failing to pay other employees overtime compensation.

The Eleventh Circuit has also held, affirming a district court, that a one-time statement by a worker's counsel to the effect that the worker was an employee who had claims under the FLSA, which may have been described in words as vague as "Fair Labor" or "Wage Labor Hour or something like that," was "too indefinite" to establish an actual assertion of FLSA rights before an alleged retaliatory termination.[30]

In *Cartwright v. Tacala, Inc.*[31] the district court denied summary judgment for the employer on plaintiff's FLSA retaliation claim, relying on Eleventh Circuit precedent holding that an informal complaint to the employer about pay violations is protected by the FLSA's anti-retaliation provision.[32]

In *Dronet v. Lafarge Corp.*[33] a claim for retaliatory discharge was advanced by plaintiff truck driver who had for several years complained about various aspects of the employer's compensation system, about the lack of truck maintenance and cleaning facilities, and about other aspects of his treatment by the em-

---

[28] DeGrange v. Richard Wolf Med. Instruments Corp., 2000 WL 1368043, 141 Lab. Cas. ¶34,147 (N.D. Ill. 2000).

[29] 2000 WL 802900, 141 Lab. Cas. ¶59,020 (S.D.N.Y. 2000). See *Lambert v. Genessee Hospital*, 10 F.3d 46, 55 (2d Cir. 1993), for the minority rule.

[30] Wolf v. Coca-Cola Co., 200 F.3d 1337, 1339 (11th Cir. 2000).

[31] 2000 WL 33287445 (M.D. Ala. 2000).

[32] EEOC v. White & Son Enters., 881 F.2d 1006, 1011 (11th Cir. 1989).

[33] 2001 WL 699384 (E.D. La. 2001).

ployer, all of which culminated in his discharge after a warning to behave more cooperatively in the workplace and then a final confrontation with his supervisor which resulted in an on-the-spot suspension. The district court granted summary judgment for the defendants on the retaliation complaint, finding that under Fifth Circuit precedent complaints to the employer were not protected activity. Further, even if the complaint activity had been protected, the plaintiff had failed to make out a prima facie case of retaliation since no causality could be inferred from the time sequence of many complaints over years with no action, and then termination with no connected complaint. Finally, the court noted that the employer had advanced a non-discriminatory explanation for the firing which plaintiff had not shown to be pretextual.

D. Conduct Opposed Need Not Be Unlawful

The Seventh Circuit in *Sapperstein v. Hager*[34] reversed the district court's dismissal of the complaint in this case. In its ruling from the bench, the district court, commenting on the retaliation claim, stated that the conduct about which Sapperstein had complained to state authorities "was not a violation." In reversing, the court of appeals noted that "Congress might have put the risk on the employee to do his or her homework and make sure that there was actually a violation before going to the authorities, but it instead protected the employee regardless."[35]

F. Testimony [New Topic]

The prohibition against discrimination of Section 15(a)(3) extends to any person who "has testified or is about to testify" in a proceeding under or related to the FLSA. The Act does not, however, protect potential testimony in lawsuits that have not been instituted but have only been contemplated. In *Ball v.*

---

[34] 5 WH Cases2d 933 (7th Cir. 1999).
[35] *Id.* at 936.

Memphis Bar-B-Q Co.,[36] the plaintiff alleged that a coworker was preparing to bring an FLSA action against the employer for minimum wage and overtime violations and that the plaintiff had been fired because the employer discovered that the plaintiff's testimony would be adverse to the employer. The employer argued that the plaintiff did not have a cognizable claim of retaliation under the FLSA because he failed to allege that such a proceeding ever existed and thus did not sufficiently allege that he was "about to testify" in an FLSA proceeding.

The court held that an individual can receive the benefit of the FLSA's prohibition on retaliating against an employee who "is about to testify in any such proceeding" only when the employee has testified in an FLSA proceeding or is scheduled to testify in a then-pending FLSA proceeding. Because the plaintiff failed to allege that he was subpoenaed to testify or even that he was told he would be called upon to testify, and failed to allege that any FLSA proceeding had ever been initiated, the court held that the plaintiff failed to state a claim on which relief could be granted.

In an unusual case, *Perdomo v. Sears, Roebuck & Co.*,[37] an FLSA trial was in progress between the parties on a claim for overtime when the plaintiff offered the testimony of two employees of the defendant, not themselves plaintiffs, which included testimony, objected to by the defendants, that the witnesses called by plaintiff were not being paid their regular wages by the defendant for their time in court under subpoena (on the theory that they were not during that time working for the defendant), whereas the witnesses called by the defendant were being paid their regular wages (on the theory that while present to testify for the defendant, they were "working" for the defendant). In the course of ruling on the objection, the court examined the defendant's policies regarding the payment of its employees while testifying and concluded that the policy as applied in this case was discriminatory within the meaning of Section 15(a)(3).

---

[36] 34 F. Supp. 2d 342, 5 WH Cases2d 184 (E.D. Va. 1999).
[37] 5 WH Cases2d 1021 (M.D. Fla. 1999).

The court also relied in part on the provisions of 42 U.S.C. §1985(2), a civil rights statute that "prohibits conspiracies to deter, by force, intimidation, or threat, any party or witness in any court of the United States from attending such court, or from testifying to any matter pending therein, freely, fully, and truthfully, or to injure such party or witness in his person or property on account of his having so attended or testified."[38] Continuing, the court ordered the defendant to "continue to pay the witnesses called or subpoenaed by Defendant to appear before this Court."[39] Thus the court's ruling had the effect of requiring the payment of regular wages to all of the defendant's employees who were called to testify in the matter, except for the plaintiffs themselves.

In *Ball v. Memphis Bar-B-Q Co.*,[40] a fellow-employee of the plaintiff had let it be known that he anticipated filing a suit against the defendant. The plaintiff's supervisor had inquired whether, if the suit were brought, the plaintiff would testify in a specified way, and the plaintiff advised that he would not. The plaintiff was fired five days later. The Fourth Circuit interpreted the term "proceeding" in Section 15(a)(3) to require a pending, as opposed to an impending or anticipated, "proceeding." Because the other employee had not yet filed a lawsuit or complaint, the Fourth Circuit upheld the district court's dismissal of the plaintiff's suit, reasoning that to hold otherwise would expand the scope of the FLSA beyond that which Congress intended.[41] In reading the statute literally and narrowly, the Fourth Circuit suggested that the FLSA anti-retaliation coverage is less broad than the anti-retaliation protections in Title VII at 42 U.S.C. §2000e-3(a).

In *E.E.O.C. v. Swift Transportation Co.*[42] the plaintiff brought suit to remedy alleged pay discrimination between male and female dispatchers. It included a claim that defendant had discriminated against one of the female dispatchers by transfer-

---

[38] *Id.* at 1023.
[39] *Id.* at 1024.
[40] 228 F.3d 360 (4th Cir. 2000).
[41] *Id.* at 364.
[42] 120 F. Supp. 2d 982 (D. Kan. 2000).

ring her from the dispatcher position to a customer service position after EEOC notified the employer of the initial charge received. The district court granted a defense summary judgment motion as to this Section 215(a)(3) retaliation claim, finding that the individual's transfer occurred before there was any contact between the EEOC and the individual involved, or any effort to set up such contact. The court adopted the interpretation of the provision's "about to testify" clause in *Ball v. Memphis Bar-B-Q Co.*,[43] and concluded that plaintiff was not actively participating in or assisting the EEOC in its investigation.

In an unpublished decision the Tenth Circuit in *Hinsdale v. City of Liberal, Kansas*,[44] reversed and remanded that part of the district court's summary judgment in favor of the defendants, the acting city manager and several city commissioners sued as individuals, on plaintiffs' claims of retaliation under the FLSA. Plaintiffs, Mr. and Mrs. Hinsdale, had been employed as chief of police and in a staff position at the Housing Authority, respectively. Some time after Mrs. Hinsdale filed suit for overtime under the FLSA, the Commission became aware that Mr. Hinsdale intended to testify in the case. This resulted, eventually, in Mr. Hinsdale's being first demoted from the position of chief of police to court administrator, with a reduction in pay; and, after his testimony, being fired from that position.

The trial court had held that the demotion from chief of police to court administrator was not retaliatory within the meaning of the FLSA on the ground that it occurred at a time when no protected activity had yet occurred. (The testimony came later.) The court of appeals decided that the decision to testify, which came to the Commission's attention, should have been considered protected activity, and that summary judgment for defendants on the first claim should be reversed. On the firing claim, the district court had found that a prima facie case of retaliation had been made out, but that defendants had offered a non-discriminatory reason other than retaliation (lack of funding for the new position) for the act, and that plaintiffs'

---

[43] 228 F. 3d 360.

[44] 2001 WL 980781 (10th Cir. 2001) (unpublished opinion).

counter-evidence was insufficient for a jury to find the defendants' reason pretextual. After reviewing the evidence, the appellate court rejected this analysis and held that a jury question as to actual motive for the firing had been made out; thus summary judgment on this claim was also reversed.

G. Complaints to Persons Other Than the Employer or the Department of Labor [New Topic]

In *Sapperstein v. Hager*[45] the Seventh Circuit held for the first time that a complaint made to a state agency is sufficient to trigger the retaliation protections of Section 15(a)(3). Other courts have reached this conclusion without specifically addressing the issue,[46] and in some cases have found that complaints to other outsiders, such as an international union,[47] could qualify for protection.

A complaint to the EEOC, which then began an investigation, qualified as "instituting or causing to be instituted a proceeding" pursuant to 29 U.S.C. §215(a)(3).[48]

In *Contreras v. Corinthian Vigor Insurance Brokerage, Inc.*,[49] a complaint to the California Labor Commissioner against Contreras' employer for unpaid wages and overtime pay sufficed to meet the requirement of "filing a complaint or instituting a proceeding 'under or related' to the FLSA."[50]

In *Lamont v. Frank Soup Bowl, Inc.*,[51] the district court granted summary judgment for the employer on the basis, in part, that plaintiff had complained only to the New York Department of Labor. It refused to extend Section 215(a)(3) protection to such complaints, and suggested that plaintiff file in state court under state law.

---

[45]5 WH Cases2d 933 (7th Cir. 1999).

[46]*See, e.g.*, Contreras v. Corinthian Vigor Ins., 25 F. Supp. 2d 1053, 4 WH Cases2d 1793 (N.D. Cal. 1998).

[47]See, for example, *Legutko v. Teamsters Local 816*, 606 F. Supp. 352 (E.D.N.Y.), *aff'd on other grounds*, 853 F.2d 1046 (2d Cir. 1985), discussed in Treatise at p. 893.

[48]Ball v. Memphis Bar-B-Q Co., 228 F.3d 360, 364 (4th Cir. 2000).

[49]103 F. Supp. 2d 1180 (N.D. Cal. 2000).

[50]*Id.* at 1184 (citing 29 U.S.C. §215(a)(3)).

[51]2001 WL 521815 (S.D.N.Y. 2001).

IV. CONDUCT FOUND TO BE PROHIBITED

A. Constructive Discharge

In *Campbell v. HSA Managed Care System, Inc.*,[52] a federal district court in Illinois held that the plaintiff failed to establish a prima facie case of retaliation under Section 15(a)(3) of the FLSA where she alleged that after trying to resolve her overtime compensation issue, she felt she was being "set up," "games were being played," and certain employer actions were rude, upsetting, or seemingly intrusive. The court concluded that these actions did not rise to the level of a materially adverse employment action as they had no impact on her wages, benefit levels, job title, or job responsibilities and privileges. Determining whether an action is materially adverse "must be cast in objective terms."

Furthermore, the court rejected the plaintiff's constructive discharge theory of retaliation. It found that her vague allegations of being "set up" and other wrongdoing not only failed to suggest the inference of a retaliatory motive but also failed to show that her working conditions were so intolerable that a reasonable person would have been compelled to resign.

B. Harrassing Acts at Work

In *Cartwright v. Tacala, Inc.*,[53] the magistrate judge denied a defense summary judgment as to the plaintiff's FLSA retaliation claim where the evidence showed that the employer had reduced plaintiff's hours shortly after her complaint to her manager about unpaid overtime. The temporal proximity between the complaint and the adverse employment action was sufficient to establish the prima facie element of causation.

---

[52]4 WH Cases2d 365 (N.D. Ill. 1997).
[53]2000 WL 33287445 (M.D. Ala. 2000).

C. Wage Reductions

In an unpublished decision the Tenth Circuit in *Hinsdale v. City of Liberal, Kansas,*[54] reversed and remanded that part of the district court's summary judgment in favor of the defendants, the acting city manager and several city commissioners sued as individuals, on plaintiffs' claims of retaliation under the FLSA. Plaintiffs, Mr. and Mrs. Hinsdale, had been employed as chief of police and in a staff position at the Housing Authority, respectively. Some time after Mrs. Hinsdale filed suit for overtime under the FLSA, the Commission became aware that Mr. Hinsdale intended to testify in the case. This resulted, eventually, in Mr. Hinsdale's being first demoted from the position of chief of police to court administrator, with a reduction in pay; and, after his testimony, being fired from that position.

As to the demotion with reduced pay, the trial court had held that it was not retaliatory within the meaning of the FLSA on the ground that it occurred at a time when no protected activity had yet occurred. (The testimony came later.) The court of appeals decided that the decision to testify, which came to the Commission's attention, should have been considered protected activity, and that summary judgment for defendants on the first claim should be reversed.

In *Cartwright v. Tacala, Inc.,*[55] the magistrate judge denied a defense summary judgment as to the plaintiff's FLSA retaliation claim where the evidence showed that the employer had reduced plaintiff's hours shortly after her complaint to her manager about unpaid overtime. The temporal proximity between the complaint and the adverse employment action was sufficient to establish the prima facie element of causation.

In *E.E.O.C. v. Swift Transportation Co.,*[56] the plaintiff brought suit to remedy alleged pay discrimination between male and female dispatchers. It included a claim that defendant had discriminated against one of the female dispatchers by transfer-

[54] 2001 WL 980781 (10th Cir. 2001) (unpublished opinion).
[55] 2000 WL 33287445 (M.D. Ala. 2000).
[56] 120 F. Supp. 2d 982 (D. Kan. 2000).

ring her from the dispatcher position to a customer service position after the EEOC notified the employer of the initial charge received. The district court granted a defense summary judgment motion as to this Section 215(a)(3) retaliation claim, finding that the individual's transfer occurred before there was any contact between the EEOC and the individual involved, or any effort to set up such contact. The court adopted the interpretation of the provision's "about to testify" clause in *Ball v. Memphis Bar-B-Q Co.*,[57] and concluded that plaintiff was not actively participating in or assisting the EEOC in its investigation.

D. Postemployment Misconduct

Employees cannot sustain a claim of retaliatory termination where they tendered their letters of resignation before filing an action under the FLSA, even where the employer terminates employment before the employees' intended last day.[58]

In *Contreras v. Corinthian Vigor Insurance Brokerage, Inc.*,[59] a federal district court held that a *former* employee was still protected by the FLSA from her employer's adverse actions. Contreras voluntarily terminated her employment with Corinthian before filing a claim for wages and before Corinthian reported her status ("undocumented worker") to the Immigration and Naturalization Service and the Social Security Administration. Such conduct "clearly affects the former employee's ability to maintain employment" and thereby constituted adverse actions under the FLSA.[60]

V. PRIMA FACIE CASE AND BURDEN OF PROOF

In *Cartwright v. Tacala, Inc.*,[61] the magistrate judge denied a defense summary judgment as to the plaintiff's FLSA retaliation

---

[57] 34 F. Supp. 2d 342 (E.D. Va. 1999), *aff'd* 228 F. 3d 360 (4th Cir. 2000).

[58] Ayres v. 127 Restaurant Corp., 12 F. Supp. 2d 305, 4 WH Cases2d 1255 (S.D.N.Y. 1998).

[59] 103 F. Supp. 2d 1180 (N.D. Cal. 2000).

[60] *Id.* at 1185.

[61] 2000 WL 33287445 (M.D. Ala. 2000).

claim where the evidence showed that the employer had reduced plaintiff's hours shortly after her complaint to her manager about unpaid overtime. The temporal proximity between the complaint and the adverse employment action was sufficient to establish the prima facie element of causation.

In an unpublished decision the Tenth Circuit in *Hinsdale v. City of Liberal, Kansas,*[62] affirmed in part and reversed and remanded in part of the district court's summary judgment in favor of the defendants, the acting city manager and several city commissioners sued as individuals. The plaintiffs asserted claims of retaliation under the FLSA and a variety of other claims including claims based on freedom of association under the First and Fourteenth Amendments, procedural due process, substantive due process, and equal protection. Plaintiffs, Mr. and Mrs. Hinsdale, had been employed as chief of police and in a staff position at the Housing Authority, respectively. Some time after Mrs. Hinsdale filed suit for overtime under the FLSA, the Commission became aware that Mr. Hinsdale intended to testify in the case. This resulted, eventually, in Mr. Hinsdale's being first demoted from the position of chief of police to court administrator, with a reduction in pay; and, after his testimony, being fired from that position.

The trial court had held that the demotion from chief of police to court administrator was not retaliatory within the meaning of the FLSA on the ground that it occurred at a time when no protected activity had yet occurred. (The testimony came later.) The court of appeals decided that the decision to testify, which came to the Commission's attention, should have been considered protected activity, and that summary judgment for defendants on the first claim should be reversed. On the firing claim, the district court had found that a prima facie case of retaliation had been made out, but that defendants had offered a non-discriminatory reason other than retaliation (lack of funding for the new position) for the act, and that plaintiffs' counter-evidence was insufficient for a jury to find the defen-

---

[62]2001 WL 980781 (10th Cir. 2001) (unpublished opinion).

dants' reason pretextual. After reviewing the evidence, the appellate court rejected this analysis and held that a jury question as to actual motive for the firing had been made out; thus summary judgment on this claim was also reversed.

In *Dronet v. Lafarge Corp.*[63] a claim for retaliatory discharge was advanced by plaintiff truck driver who had for several years complained about various aspects of the employer's compensation system, about the lack of truck maintenance and cleaning facilities, and about other aspects of his treatment by the employer, all of which culminated in his discharge after a warning to behave more cooperatively in the workplace and then a final confrontation with his supervisor which resulted in an on-the-spot suspension. The district court granted summary judgment for the defendants on the retaliation complaint, finding that under Fifth Circuit precedent complaints to the employer were not protected activity. Further, even if the complaint activity had been protected, the plaintiff had failed to make out a prima facie case of retaliation since no causality could be inferred from the time sequence of many complaints over years with no action, and then termination with no connected complaint. Finally, the court noted that the employer had advanced a non-discriminatory explanation for the firing which plaintiff had not shown to be pretextual.

A. Pretext Cases

Once the plaintiff has made out a prima facie case of retaliation, the burden of producing evidence shifts to the defendant to articulate a legitimate nondiscriminatory reason for its action.[64]

---

[63] 2001 WL 699384 (E.D. La. 2001).

[64] *See, e.g.,* Bowe v. SMC Elec. Prods., 935 F. Supp. 1126, 1136, 3 WH Cases2d 710 (D. Colo. 1996); Conner v. Schnuck Mkts. Inc., 121 F.3d 1390, 4 WH Cases2d 43 (10th Cir. 1997); Knickerbocker v. Stockton, 3 WH Cases2d 453 (9th Cir. 1996); Cross v. Bally's Health & Tennis Corp., 945 F. Supp. 883, 3 WH Cases2d 1067 (D. Md. 1996); Cannella v. Anodyne Corp., 3 WH Cases2d 1972 (N.D. Ill. 1996); Marti v. Grey Eagle Distribs., 937 F. Supp. 845, 3 WH Cases2d 834 (E.D. Mo. 1996).

To defeat a defendant's showing of a "legitimate, non-discriminatory reason for discharge," the plaintiffs must show that such a reason is a "pretext" for retaliation. Courts have recognized genuine issues of material fact raised by a "temporal proximity" between the protected conduct and the adverse action;[65] and understand that an employer's "singling out" a complaining employee by requiring him to reconstruct time records,[66] or enforcing work rules especially harshly,[67] could be evidence of pretext.

In *Knuf v. ATC/Vancom*,[68] a federal district court in Nevada held that the plaintiff had failed to establish the necessary causal connection between her change in shifts, suspension, and ultimate termination and the filing of a written complaint regarding the manner in which defendant assigned overtime to its drivers. The plaintiff filed suit against her employer alleging retaliation for filing the complaint. The defendant claimed that the plaintiff had notice of some of the allegedly retaliatory activity (e.g., her change in shifts) before filing her complaint. With respect to the acts that occurred after the complaint was filed, the court recognized that temporal proximity should be taken into account, but here the suspension and termination came three months after the complaint. Therefore, a causal connection could not be reasonably inferred from the proximity alone as plaintiff urged. The employer proffered two reasons for plaintiff's termination: her surveillance of a coworker and her failure to cooperate in a company investigation. The plaintiff failed to offer any substantial evidence that the defendant's reasons were merely pretext. The court granted summary judgment for the defendant.

Plaintiff was unable to prove that defendant's proffered reasons for the allegedly retaliatory termination were pretextual

---

[65]O'Brien v. DeKalb-Clinton Counties Dist. Ambulance, 3 WH Cases2d 37 (W.D. Mo. 1995).

[66]Bowe v. SMC Elec. Prod., 935 F. Supp. 1126, 3 WH Cases2d 710 (D. Colo. 1996).

[67]Angleton v. Beech Aircraft Corp., 4 WH Cases2d 150 (D. Kan. 1997).

[68]4 WH Cases2d 1274 (D. Nev. 1998).

in *E.E.O.C. v. Swift Transp., Co., Inc.*[69] Evidence beyond mere conjecture that the defendant's explanation is pretext is necessary to survive summary judgment. A comment by a co-employee, one not involved in the decision making, is insufficient evidence of pretext. Nor does mere temporal proximity prove pretext.

In an unpublished decision the Tenth Circuit in *Hinsdale v. City of Liberal, Kansas,*[70] reversed and remanded that part of the district court's summary judgment in favor of the defendants, the acting city manager and several city commissioners sued as individuals, on plaintiffs' claims of retaliation under the FLSA. On that claim the district court had found that a prima facie case of retaliation had been made out, but that defendants had offered a non-discriminatory reason other than retaliation (lack of funding for the new position) for the act, and that plaintiffs' counter-evidence was insufficient for a jury to find the defendants' reason pretextual. After reviewing the evidence, the appellate court rejected this analysis and held that a jury question as to actual motive for the firing had been made out; thus summary judgment on this claim was reversed.

In *Dronet v. Lafarge Corp.*[71] a claim for retaliatory discharge was advanced by plaintiff truck driver who had for several years complained about various aspects of the employer's compensation system, about the lack of truck maintenance and cleaning facilities, and about other aspects of his treatment by the employer, all of which culminated in his discharge after a warning to behave more cooperatively in the workplace and then a final confrontation with his supervisor which resulted in an on-the-spot suspension. The district court granted summary judgment for the defendants on the retaliation complaint, finding that under Fifth Circuit precedent complaints to the employer were not protected activity. Further, even if the complaint activity had been protected, the plaintiff had failed to make out a prima facie

---

[69] 120 F. Supp. 2d 982 (D. Kan. 2000).
[70] 2001 WL 980781 (10th Cir. 2001) (unpublished opinion).
[71] 2001 WL 699384 (E.D. La. 2001).

case of retaliation since no causality could be inferred from the time sequence of many complaints over years with no action, and then termination with no connected complaint. Finally, the court noted that the employer had advanced a non-discriminatory explanation for the firing which plaintiff had not shown to be pretextual.

C. Immediate Cause/Motivating Factor

In *Ramirez de-Arellano v. American Airlines, Inc.*,[72] the plaintiff submitted a written grievance to his employer concerning his termination, pursuant to the internal grievance procedure set forth in the employee handbook. The employer upheld the termination and denied the plaintiff's appeal on the basis of an untimely application. The plaintiff subsequently filed suit for retaliatory dismissal under the FLSA. The district court, giving res judicata effect to the employer's internal grievance procedure, granted summary judgment to the employer. The First Circuit upheld the district court's dismissal of the claim on different grounds—namely, that the record showed that the plaintiff had failed to meet his burden of proving discrimination or retaliation, and that the plaintiff's misconduct furnished "ample just cause" for his dismissal.[73]

In *Wolf v. Coca-Cola Co.*,[74] the Eleventh Circuit affirmed the district court's summary judgment for the defendant on plaintiff's retaliation claim. The plaintiff failed to show that she would not have been terminated but for her complaint, and the court rejected the plaintiff's argument that the motivating factor for her termination was her counsel's assertion that she was an employee with an FLSA claim, where the only evidence of that assertion was a vague comment during a meeting.

---

[72] 133 F.3d 89 (1st Cir. 1997).

[73] *Id.* at 91.

[74] 200 F.3d 1337, 1343, 5 WH Cases2d 1441 (11th Cir. 2000).

In *Bick v. Harrah's Operating Co.*,[75] the plaintiff claimed that she was discharged in retaliation for her complaints about the defendants' policy of demanding that employees work "off the clock." The defendants did not dispute that the plaintiff engaged in protected conduct or that the plaintiff suffered an adverse action, namely, her termination. However, the plaintiff was terminated over two-and-a-half months after she complained, and the record revealed several other issues over which the plaintiff and her fellow-workers or her supervisors had had difficulties. Assessing the impact of the chronological nexus between the protected activity and the termination, the district court recognized that a one-week period between the protected activity and the adverse action usually proves a causal link, and that a lapse of four or five months is usually too long to establish causation. This case fell in the middle, thus requiring the plaintiff to present additional proof of causation. The plaintiff presented no compelling evidence suggesting an inference of a causal nexus. Moreover, the defendants offered several reasons for the termination including disclosure of confidential information in violation of company policy, improper tape recording of conversations at work, and continual gossiping in violation of company policy. The plaintiff tendered no evidence going to pretext and therefore summary judgment was granted for the defendant.

In *Scott v. Sunrise Healthcare Corp.*,[76] the Seventh Circuit upheld the district court's grant of summary judgment to the employer on the plaintiff's FLSA retaliation claim finding that the plaintiff failed to show a causal connection between her discharge and her complaint. While the court noted that "circumstantial evidence [temporal proximity] may be used to allow a plaintiff to survive a summary judgment motion," the plaintiff's failure here to pin down the time period of her complaint did not allow an inference that her discharge was retaliatory.[77]

---

[75] 2000 WL 204222 (N.D. Ill. 2000).

[76] 195 F.3d 938 (7th Cir. 1999).

[77] *Id.* at 941.

VI. DEFENSES AND OTHER RESPONSES

D. Waiver and Release

An employer accused by a former employee of retaliatory discharge who waived the right to remove the case to federal court by letting the time for filing a timely petition to remove expire is not barred from joining a timely petition to remove filed by a later-joined defendant.[78]

VII. REMEDIES

A. Reinstatement and Other Injunctive Remedies

An employee was not entitled to a preliminary and permanent injunction barring his employer from retaliation against the employee for filing an FLSA claim for overtime wages because only the Secretary of Labor has the statutory authority to seek injunctions under the FLSA.[79]

2. *Reinstatement Pending a Trial on the Merits*

In *Bailey v. Gulf Coast Transp., Inc.*,[80] plaintiff taxi drivers brought suit against Gulf for back wages, and shortly thereafter the relationship between the putative employer and the plaintiffs was terminated.[81] The plaintiffs then added a claim for retaliatory discharge to their complaint, and sought preliminary injunctive relief reinstating them. The district court determined it could not grant a preliminary injunction to a private litigant,

---

[78]Collings v. E-Z Serve Convenience Stores, 936 F. Supp. 892, 894, 3 WH Cases2d 861 (N.D. Fla. 1996).

[79]Bjornson v. Daido Metal U.S.A., Inc., 12 F. Supp. 2d 837, 4 WH Cases2d 1428 (N.D. Ill. 1998).

[80]139 F. Supp. 2d 1358, 7 WH Cases2d 964 (M.D. Fla. 2001).

[81]While plaintiffs claimed to be employees, the defendant claimed that the relationship it had with them was that they were independent contractors, and that they were not covered by the wage provisions of the Act.

citing the relatively recent decision of the Eleventh Circuit in *Powell v. State of Florida,*[82] which holds that "'the right to bring an action for injunctive relief under the [FLSA] rests exclusively with the United States Secretary of Labor.'"[83] Because *Powell* "neither limits its conclusion to enforcement of specific sections of the FLSA nor limits its holding to the particular facts of *Powell*,"[84] the court denied plaintiffs' motion for a preliminary injunction.[85]

B. Monetary Damages

2. *Front Pay*

A Florida federal district court required evidence that an award of front pay would effectuate the purposes of Section 15(a)(3) before awarding such damages.[86] The defendant admitted a willful violation of Section 15(a)(3) by virtue of its default. Although the plaintiff is entitled to an award of liquidated damages on his claim, an award of front pay on a Section 15(a)(3) claim is left to the discretion of the court. The plaintiff must present evidence that he is entitled to front pay. Otherwise, an award of front pay on top of liquidated damages can cause overcompensation. The district courts have been cautioned that they should "guard against being 'overly generous' when awarding front pay in cases where an employee receives liquidated damages."[87]

4. *Compensatory Damages*

In *Lambert v. Ackerley,*[88] a case involving the retaliatory discharge from employment of six ticket sales employees who

---

[82] 132 F.3d 677, 4 WH Cases2d 638 (11th Cir.), *cert. denied,* 524 U.S. 916 (1998).

[83] 7 WH Cases2d at 966 (quoting *Powell,* 132 F.3d at 678).

[84] *Id.* at 968.

[85] On Jan. 29, 2002, the Eleventh Circuit reversed and remanded.

[86] Miller v. Paradise of Port Richey, Inc., 75 F. Supp. 2d 1342 (M.D. Fla. 1999).

[87] *Id.* at 1346–47 (citing Judge Posner in Avitia v. Metropolitan Club of Chicago Inc., 49 F.3d 1219, 1231–32, 2 WH Cases2d 993 (7th Cir. 1995)).

[88] 180 F.3d 997, 5 WH Cases2d 677 (9th Cir. 1999).

had been employed for the Seattle SuperSonics basketball team, the Ninth Circuit concluded that awarding $75,000 for emotional distress to each employee terminated in retaliation for protected complaints was not excessive. The court noted that each plaintiff had given evidence concerning the emotional toll of the terminations, and the court could not, in light of that evidence, conclude that the damages for emotional distress were either "grossly excessive or monstrous."[89]

5. *Liquidated Damages*

The federal district court in *Miller v. Paradise of Port Richey, Inc.*,[90] held that in retaliation claims under Section 15(a)(3), an award of liquidated damages is mandatory unless the court explicitly finds that the defendant acted in good faith in violating the FLSA. The court found that since liquidated damages are allowed in nonpayment of overtime, minimum wages, or equal pay cases, they should also be allowed when an employee is illegally discharged and no longer receives any pay from the employer. The plaintiff alleged that he was terminated in retaliation for voicing opposition to violation of the FLSA and that the defendant willfully violated the Act. As a defaulted party, the defendant admitted the allegations of willfulness, and liquidated damages were therefore appropriate.

6. *Punitive Damages*

b. Actions by Private Plaintiffs

In *Shea v. Galaxie Lumber & Construction Co.*,[91] the Seventh Circuit held, in a case involving a jury verdict where the verdict form itself was unclear, and no compensatory damages had been awarded under Section 15(a)(3), that the punitive damages fixed by the jury could have been properly awarded on the Sec-

---

[89] *Id.*, 5 WH Cases2d at 687.
[90] 75 F. Supp. 2d 1342 (M.D. Fla. 1999).
[91] 152 F.3d 729, 4 WH Cases2d 1473 (7th Cir. 1998).

tion 15(a)(3) retaliation claim even though no compensatory damages had been awarded for that violation.[92] The appellate court reversed and remanded the trial court's decision denying liquidated and punitive damages on the FLSA retaliation claim.

In *Contreras v. Corinthian Vigor Insurance*,[93] a federal district court in California rejected the defendant's motion to strike the plaintiff's claim for punitive damages under the FLSA. The court stated that the Seventh Circuit, the only court to address the issue at the time, had allowed such claims in *Travis v. Gary Community Mental Health Center, Inc.*,[94] and that the Ninth Circuit, which had not yet addressed the issue, had historically taken an expansive view of remedies available under federal labor laws.

In *Lambert v. Ackerley*,[95] the Ninth Circuit noted that the Seventh Circuit opinion[96] permitting punitive damages under the FLSA was persuasive, but stated that it need not reach the question because the defendants had waived the issue of punitive damages by failing to raise it sufficiently with the trial court. The district court had reduced a jury award of $12 million in punitive damages to just over $4 million. The Ninth Circuit found that $4 million was not an excessive amount, given the conduct of the defendant and its substantial financial assets.

In *Snapp v. Unlimited Concepts, Inc.*,[97] the Eleventh Circuit addressed for the first time the question of whether punitive damages may be awarded to a plaintiff who has proven a violation of the FLSA's anti-retaliation provision. The court found that all of the relief provided in Section 16(b) is compensatory in nature, and noted that punitive damages are not compensatory in nature. It pointed out that Congress provided

---

[92]The only possible place on the verdict form at which compensatory damages for retaliation could have been awarded specified "For compensatory damages for the humiliation, inconvenience and emotional suffering sustained for complaining about not receiving overtime wages." Shea v. Galaxie Lumber, 3 WH Cases2d 1431 (N.D. Ill. 1997).

[93]25 F. Supp. 2d 1053, 4 WH Cases2d 1793 (N.D. Cal. 1998).

[94]921 F.2d 108 (7th Cir. 1990).

[95]180 F.3d 997, 5 WH Cases2d 677 (9th Cir. 1999).

[96]*Travis*, 921 F.2d 108.

[97]208 F.3d 928, 5 WH Cases2d 1761 (11th Cir. 2000).

separately for punitive sanctions (fines and/or imprisonment) in Section 16(a). The court also relied on a Fifth Circuit decision holding that punitive damages are not available in an age discrimination (ADEA) case.[98] The court concluded that the FLSA should be interpreted similarly to preclude an award of punitive damages.[99]

A federal district court in *Lanza v. Sugar Land Run Homeowners Ass'n*[100] also found, in the context of a motion to dismiss, that punitive damages were not available as a remedy for violations of the FLSA's anti-retaliation provisions. In its discussion of the matter, the court provided citation to and analysis of the governing legislation and all of the pertinent cases in this area.

C. Attorneys' Fees and Costs [New Topic]

Former employees who prevail in an action alleging retaliatory discharge against an employer are entitled to an award of attorneys' fees under Section 216(b) of the FLSA. A state appeals court held that where the trial court did not comply with federal precedent by first calculating the lodestar amount and then clearly explaining any adjustments, it abused its discretion in its award of attorneys' fees.[101]

VIII. Preemption of Wrongful Discharge Actions

In *Williamson v. General Dynamics Corp.*,[102] the plaintiffs alleged that their employer dissuaded them from participating in a class action settlement of FLSA overtime claims by falsely promising that their manufacturing facility would remain open,

---

[98]Dean v. American Sec. Ins. Co., 559 F.2d 1036 (5th Cir. 1977).

[99]*Snapp* does not address the availability of emotional distress damages.

[100]97 F. Supp. 2d 737, 6 WH Cases2d 175 (E.D. Va. 2000).

[101]Stanley v. McDaniel, 913 P.2d 76, 79, 3 WH Cases2d 422 (Idaho Ct. App. 1996).

[102]208 F.3d 1144, 6 WH Cases2d 8 (9th Cir.), *cert. denied,* 531 U.S. 929, 6 WH Cases2d 736 (2000).

and indicating that joining the class action would harm their otherwise-viable careers. After the plant was closed, they brought suit in state court asserting common law fraud, and the employer removed to federal court. The employer there argued that the plaintiffs' "career fraud" claims could not be entertained, as the FLSA's anti-retaliation provisions preempted the common law of fraud as applied to the employment at issue. The Ninth Circuit, in a decision of first impression in the circuit, reversed the lower court's dismissal of the claims, noting at the same time that "[c]laims that are directly covered by the FLSA (such as overtime and retaliation disputes) must be brought under the FLSA."

CHAPTER 16

RECORD-KEEPING

II. Requirements Generally Applicable to Employers of Workers Subject to the FLSA's Minimum Wage or Minimum Wage and Overtime Pay Requirements

A. Form of Records and Record-Keeping Systems

The Division opined that automated record-keeping systems based on intranet or telephone-prompted entries made by employees would satisfy the FLSA's record-keeping requirements.[1]

---

[1]Wage-Hour Admin. Op. (Feb. 6, 1998), 1998 WL 852676.

C. Preservation of Records

4. Recomputation and Reports at the DOL's Request

Herman v. Harmelech[2] was a case brought by the Secretary of Labor to recover back wages and to seek an injunction against future violations of the statute. During the course of the proceedings, the Secretary first served a demand, and then a subpoena, calling for the production of hours-worked and payroll records. These were never produced. One of the defendants, who had been held to be liable under the FLSA as an employer, asserted that within the defendant corporations, she had no obligation with respect to records or record-keeping and, thus, that she was not liable for the failure of the corporate defendants to produce the records. The court noted that the duty to maintain records is an affirmative duty and that an employer cannot shirk her responsibility by isolating herself from the daily operations of the company.

F. Enforcement of Record-Keeping Requirements [New Topic]

No private right of action exists to allow an employee to enforce the Act's record-keeping requirements, according to the court in *East v. Bullock's, Inc.*[3] The court reasoned that there was no evidence that Congress intended to create a private right of action under Section 15(a)(5), and given the specification of other private rights of action in the FLSA, Congress apparently did not intend to create a private right to enforce the record-keeping provisions.

Chao v. Virginia DOT[4] was a suit brought by the Secretary of Labor to enjoin withholding of back pay and for other injunctive relief including prospective restraint of record-keeping viola-

---

[2] 2000 WL 420839 (N.D. Ill. 2000).
[3] 34 F. Supp. 2d 1176, 5 WH Cases2d 198 (D. Ariz. 1998).
[4] 157 F. Supp. 2d 681 (E.D. Va. 2001).

tions. It was instituted after private plaintiffs had unsuccessfully attempted to pursue their claims against the state first in federal and then in the state courts, these attempts having been unsuccessful as a result of the Eleventh Amendment developments. The district court had found the statute of limitations tolled in connection with the wage claims previously vigorously pursued by private plaintiffs. The defendants claimed that the record-keeping claims were barred by the limitations period as the private plaintiffs had never asserted a record-keeping claim. The court held that the Secretary's claim was not barred, as the 2- and 3-year limitations periods only apply to wage claims and not to record-keeping.

IV. OTHER SPECIAL RECORD-KEEPING REQUIREMENTS

C. Deductions for Board, Lodging, or Other Facilities

In *Herman v. Collis Foods Inc.*,[5] the Sixth Circuit held that a restaurant chain's record-keeping of a meal-credit plan where the average cost of a meal was deducted from an employee's paycheck satisfied the FLSA. This was so even though the deduction was based on estimated cost and applied on a uniform basis, regardless of the actual cost of what the employee ate. The court stated that Section 3(m) allowed employers to use average costs to themselves or average value to employees as a measure of reasonable costs.

Meal-credit deductions were found to be inadequately supported by employer records in *Herman v. Palo Group Foster Home Inc.*[6] There the Sixth Circuit affirmed the decision of the district court that the employer had failed to meet its burden of substantiating the cost of meals provided where it continued to claim, in 1995, a credit of $0.62 per meal provided, in the absence of any pertinent employer records and based exclu-

---

[5]176 F.3d 912, 5 WH Cases2d 545 (6th Cir. 1999).
[6]183 F.3d 468, 5 WH Cases2d 837 (6th Cir. 1999).

sively on the fact that $0.62 was the amount used by the Department of Labor in 1985 to compute an allowable meal credit when the defendant's records were inadequate even then, 10 years earlier. In view of the fact that the Labor Department had merely attempted to accommodate the defendant's previous record-keeping violations, and had explicitly advised the defendant of the requirements of the law, the defendants' arguments concerning the permissibility of these deductions were without merit.

V. VIOLATION OF RECORD-KEEPING REQUIREMENTS

A. Failure to Keep Records

The courts continue to follow the rule that where an employer fails to maintain adequate records, damages may be awarded based on the just and reasonable inferences drawn from the evidence presented. The burden shifts to the employer to show otherwise.[7]

However, even when the employer does not have records, a successful defense against a claim of underpayment is possible. In *Bates v. Old Time Coffee Co.*,[8] the employer did not keep hourly records for the plaintiff while he was a salaried employee. Although the plaintiff claimed to have worked 46 hours per week for most weeks of his employment, and he was only paid for 40, the defendants' evidence included two corporate employees and the plaintiff's wife, who testified that the plaintiff's regular routines would not have been consistent with the work time he claimed. A federal district court in California held that, although

[7]Reich v. Stewart, 121 F.3d 400, 405 (8th Cir. 1997); Herman v. Palo Group Foster Home, Inc., 976 F. Supp. 696 (W.D. Mich. 1997); Herman v. Hector I. Nieves Transp., Inc., 91 F. Supp. 2d 435 (D.P.R. 2000). The court in *Herman v. Harmelech*, 2000 WL 420839 (N.D. Ill. 2000), assessed backpay for 101 truck drivers based on the testimony of 14 employees, determining the backpay owing from available payroll checks and employee statements summarized by a DOL compliance officer.

[8]2000 WL 41223 (N.D. Cal. 2000).

the employee need not "provide as specific evidence of hours worked as he would otherwise be required"[9] to do if the employer fails to keep accurate time records, here the plaintiff's estimates did not meet his burden of proof by a preponderance of the evidence that he performed work for which he was not properly compensated.

[9] *Id.* at *7.

CHAPTER 17

ENFORCEMENT AND REMEDIES

II. ADMINISTRATIVE ENFORCEMENT

A. Assessment of Civil Money Penalties

1. Repeated or Willful Minimum Wage or Overtime and Child Labor Violations

In an appeal of a district court's decision upholding the Department of Labor's Administrative Review Board (ARB) decision that treating certain employees as independent contractors constituted a repeated or willful violation, the First Circuit reversed and remanded for further consideration in *Baystate Alternative Staffing v. Herman.*[1] The company had been investigated before for the same activity, had been given Labor Department publications concerning the employment relationship, and had entered into an agreement by which it undertook to keep required records for "all employees"; however, the agreement contained language to the effect that performance under it was "without prejudice to the Company's position."[2] The company attorney continued to advise that the temporary workers in question were not employees, and the company continued to treat them as independent contractors. The ARB found this reliance by the company to be unjustified, in light of the information it had been given by the Wage and Hour Division and its failure to take further steps to ascertain the lawfulness of its conduct. In upholding the penalty, the ARB relied on the provisions of 29 C.F.R, §578.3(c), a regulation based on the *Richland Shoe*[3] definition of willfulness. However, the court found the examples given in the regulation to be incongruous with the *Richland Shoe* decision and construed them to apply a negligence standard in some cases, despite the fact that negligence was expressly rejected as a basis for willfulness in *Richland Shoe.* It directed a remand to the ARB for reconsideration of the case in light of the willfulness standard of *Richland Shoe.*

---

[1]163 F.3d 668, 5 WH Cases2d 65 (1st Cir. 1998).

[2]163 F.3d 668, 5 WH Cases2d at 67.

[3]McLaughlin v. Richland Shoe Co., 486 U.S. 128 (1988).

B. Administrative Law Judge Proceedings Contesting Civil Money Penalties

1. *Child Labor and Repeated or Willful Minimum Wage and Overtime Violations*

An administrative law judge declined to reduce a civil money penalty against an employer because of the employer's history of violation and its failure to cooperate in the administrative proceeding.[4]

C. Appeals to the Secretary

1. *Repeated or Willful Minimum Wage or Overtime and Child Labor Violations*

In *Administrator v. Thirsty's Inc.*,[5] the Department's Administrative Review Board deferred to the Administrator's use of a grid and matrix providing for the calculation of civil money penalties.

The Administrative Review Board revised an ALJ's reduction of civil money penalties imposed on an employer, reasoning that the FLSA's legislative history regarding civil money penalties did not restrict maximum civil money penalties to the most egregious cases.[6]

In *Administrator v. Ahn's Market*,[7] the Department of Labor's Administrative Review Board upheld a fine levied against a defendant who employed 10 minors under the age of 18 to load and/or operate a scrap paper baler. The defendant argued that its conduct was permissible under an August 1996 amendment to the FLSA that allowed 16- and 17-year-old minors to load scrap

---

[4]U.S. Dep't of Labor v. Jerral D. Parris, 95-CLA-8, (ALJ May 24, 1996), *aff'd in part and rev'd in part*, 1997 WL 144082 (ARB Mar. 27, 1997) <http://204.245.136.2/libtrad.htm> (visited Feb. 12, 1998).

[5]94-CLA-65 1997 WL 453588 (ARB May 14, 1997).

[6]Administrator v. Sayler, 93-CLA-18, — 22, — 23 (ARB Sept. 27, 1996).

[7]ARB No. 99-024, ALJ No. 97-CLA-33, 2000 WL 1074299 (DOL ARB July 28, 2000).

paper balers under certain circumstances. An administrative law judge had found that the defendants had sought to impermissibly apply the 1996 amendment retroactively because the violations had occurred before the amendment was enacted into law. The Board upheld the ALJ's ruling, finding that there was no evidence in the legislative history or the Act itself that indicated that Congress intended to apply the amendments retroactively. As an alternative holding, the Board found that the defendant had not established that its baler fell within the exemption contained in the 1996 amendment. The defendant had tried to argue that the government had the burden of establishing that the baler did not meet the amendment's requirements. The Board rejected this contention, finding that a party seeking protection from liability via an exemption has the burden of proving compliance with the conditions of the exemption.

In *Administrator v. Elderkin,* [8] a farmer was accused of illegally employing eight minors, one of whom had been involved in a serious accident while operating farm machinery specifically prohibited by DOL regulations. Due to the severity of the incident, the Wage and Hour Division levied a fine of $ 71,100 against the defendant. The defendant sought review before a Department administrative law judge, arguing that the minors were not "employees" of the farm. The ALJ rejected this argument, but reduced the penalty to $29,050 because the financial resources of the defendant's business were not properly taken into account. Both sides appealed to the Administrative Review Board. The Board, like the ALJ, rejected the defendant's contention that the minor was not an employee at the time of the accident. It found that despite alleged inconsistencies in the minor's testimony, there was sufficient support for the ALJ's finding that Elderkin had violated the FLSA. In addition, the Board conducted a de novo review of the ALJ's reduction of the defendant's penalty. It held for the first time that "once a CMP has been challenged before an ALJ the issue is not whether the penalty assesed by the Administrator comports with the [W-H

---

[8]ARB Nos. 99-033, 99-048, ALJ No. 95-CLA-31, 2000 WL 960261 (DOL ARB June 30, 2000).

published grid contained in Form W-H 266]. Rather the question is whether the assessed penalty complies with the statutory provision regarding CMP and the CMP regulations."[9] It found that the ALJ had misjudged the seriousness of the defendant's violations, specifically the young ages of the children, the large number of record-keeping violations, and the dangerous work the children performed. In light of that evidence, the Board found that the original fine was appropriate.

D. Judicial Review of Civil Money Penalties

Once an aggrieved party exercises the right to file an exception to the Administrator's decision, the party cannot simultaneously pursue a court challenge.[10]

F. Double Jeopardy and Civil Money Penalties [New Topic]

There is some question whether the Double Jeopardy Clause of the Fifth Amendment[11] bars the government from assessing a civil money penalty after the government has criminally prosecuted the employer for the same conduct under Section 16(a)(1) of the Act. Similarly, the Double Jeopardy Clause may bar the government from criminally prosecuting the employer if the employer has already been assessed a civil money penalty.[12]

---

[9] *Id.*

[10] Acura of Bellevue v. Reich, 90 F. 3d 1403, 1407, 3 WH Cases2d 673 (9th Cir. 1996), *cert. denied,* 117 S. Ct. 945 (1997) (holding that the exercise of filing an exception renders the Administrator's decision nonfinal and unripe for purposes of judicial review under the APA).

[11] U.S. CONST. amend. V (providing that no "person [shall] be subject for the same offence to be twice put in jeopardy of life or limb").

[12] *See* United States v. Morse, No. S1 96 Cr. 732 (RPP), 1997 U.S. Dist. LEXIS 4765 (S.D.N.Y. Apr. 11, 1997) (SEC civil money penalty bars subsequent criminal prosecution for same offense).

A non-FLSA Supreme Court decision, however, provides some insight on this issue. In *Hudson v. United States*,[13] the Supreme Court held that the Double Jeopardy Clause did not bar the government's subsequent criminal prosecution against bank officer defendants even though the Office of Comptroller of Currency (OCC) had already imposed a monetary penalty on these bank officers for violating banking statutes.[14]

In *Hudson*, the Court held that the OCC's monetary penalty was not a criminal punishment and thus that the Double Jeopardy Clause did not bar the subsequent criminal prosecution for the same conduct. The Court, in concluding that the OCC monetary penalty is a civil penalty, relied on the following factors: (1) Congress intended the OCC money penalty to be civil in nature as evidenced by the applicable statute's express designation of the money penalty as "civil";[15] (2) the money penalty is not "so punitive in form and effect as to render [it] criminal despite Congress' intent to the contrary"[16] because the sanction historically has not been viewed as punishment and "payment of fixed or variable sums of money [is a] sanction which ha[s] been recognized as enforceable by civil proceedings since the original revenue law of 1789";[17] (3) the sanctions do not impose "affirmative disability or restraint" as that term is normally understood;[18] (4) scienter is not a requisite for the sanction;[19] and (5) the OCC money penalty sanctions conduct that may also be criminal.[20]

Although the Supreme Court has not directly addressed double jeopardy in the FLSA civil money penalty context, it is unlikely after *Hudson* that the Double Jeopardy Clause will bar a civil money penalty following a criminal prosecution or a criminal prosecution of the employer following imposition of a civil

---

[13] 118 S. Ct. 488 (1997).

[14] *Id.* at 495.

[15] *Id.*

[16] *Id.* at 495–96 (quoting United States v. Usery, 116 S. Ct. 2135, 2148 (1996)).

[17] *Id.* at 496 (quoting Helvering v. Mitchell, 303 U.S. 391, 400 (1938) (alterations in original)).

[18] *Id.*

[19] *Id.*

[20] *Id.*

money penalty for the same FLSA offense because, like the OCC penalty in *Hudson*, it is specifically designated as a "civil" penalty by Congress,[21] and each of the other factors enumerated as significant in that case also applies to FLSA civil money penalties.

III. ACTIONS FOR INJUNCTIONS

A. General

1. Plaintiff in Injunction Actions

Courts continue to hold that only the Secretary of Labor, not private parties, including unions, may bring injunction suits under the FLSA.[22]

In *Luder v. Endicott*,[23] the plaintiffs, corrections department employees of the Wisconsin Department of Corrections, sued both the department and certain individual managerial employees, asserting that they were not paid for performing certain essential duties of their positions. The district court granted summary judgment against plaintiffs' claims for injunctive relief for the asserted FLSA violations. It held that the plaintiffs' argument that the exception to sovereign immunity under *Ex parte Young*, [24] which allows a court to order prospective injunctive relief to restrain state officials sued in their official capacities from violating the U.S. Constitution even when the state itself is immune from suit under the Eleventh Amendment, provides no basis for injunctive relief in state employees' FLSA action against state corrections officials, since the FLSA's statutory language indicates that only the Secretary of Labor may pursue claims for injunctive relief under the Act.[25]

---

[21]29 U.S.C. §216(e) (specifically referring to "civil penalties" for child labor and for repeated or willful minimum wage and overtime violations). *See also* 29 U.S.C. §211(d) (ratifying "all existing [homework] regulations and orders" of the Secretary which did use the term "civil" money penalties at that time and still do).

[22]UFCW Local 1564 v. Albertson's, Inc., 207 F.3d 1193, 5 WH Cases2d 1705 (10th Cir. 2000).

[23]86 F. Supp. 2d 854, 5 WH Cases2d 1581 (W.D. Wis. 2000).

[24]209 U.S. 123 (1908).

[25]*See* 29 U.S.C. §§211(a) and 217.

After a careful analysis of the general unavailability of injunctive relief to private plaintiffs for wage claims under the FLSA, the Tenth Circuit in *UFCW Union, Local 1564 v. Albertson's, Inc.*,[26] reluctantly concluded, reversing the district court, that there was no federal jurisdiction to determine a union's declaratory judgment action seeking to invalidate a collective bargaining provision calling for compulsory unpaid training time.[27] The court reserved the question of whether 29 U.S.C. §207(o), which expressly provides for a potential role for a union in implementing compensatory time arrangements for public employee members, might create a limited exception to the representative action bar in an action alleging a violation of that section.

The Treatise indicates that employees may seek reinstatment and equitable relief in retaliation actions under Sections 215(a)(3) and 216.[28] However, a federal district court in Florida recently rejected this approach.[29] In *Bailey v. Gulf Coast Transportation, Inc.*,[30] plaintiff taxi drivers brought suit against Gulf for back wages, and shortly thereafter the relationship between the putative employer and the plaintiffs was terminated.[31] The plaintiffs then added a claim for retaliatory discharge to their complaint, and sought preliminary injunctive relief reinstating them. The district court determined it could not grant a preliminary injunction to a private litigant, citing the relatively recent decision of the Eleventh Circuit in *Powell v. State of Florida*,[32] which holds that "'the right to bring an action for injunctive relief under the [FLSA] rests exclusively with the United States

---

[26]207 F.3d 1193, 5 WH Cases2d 1705.

[27]While the case was pending, the Supreme Court held that §301 of the Labor Management Relations Act, 29 U.S.C. §1851(a), did not afford federal courts jurisdiction over declaratory judgment suits alleging the invalidity but not the violation of a collective bargaining agreement provision. Textron Lycoming Reciprocating Engine Div. v. UAW Int'l & Local 787, 563 U.S. 653 (1998).

[28]Treatise, pp. 1020, 1054.

[29]Bailey v. Gulf Coast Transp., Inc., 139 F. Supp. 2d 1358, 7 WH Cases2d 964 (M.D. Fla. 2001).

[30]*Id.*

[31]While plaintiffs claimed to be employees, the defendant claimed that the relationship it had with them was that they were independent contractors, and that they were not covered by the wage provisions of the Act.

[32]132 F.3d 677, 4 WH Cases2d 638 (11th Cir.), *cert. denied*, 524 U.S. 916 (1998).

Secretary of Labor.'"[33] Because *Powell* "neither limits its conclusion to enforcement of specific sections of the FLSA nor limits its holding to the particular facts of *Powell*,"[34] the court denied plaintiffs' motion for a preliminary injunction.[35]

2. *Defendants in Injunction Actions*

The definition of "employer" was held in *Bureerong v. Uvawas*[36] to include clothing manufacturer defendants who contracted with other defendants (the "operator" defendants) who actually operated a California garment facility in which immigrant employees from Thailand were employed under conditions allegedly amounting to involuntary servitude. The employees alleged in their pleadings that the manufacturer defendants, who were located elsewhere in the United States, contracted with the operators to produce garments at prices too low to permit payment of minimum wages and overtime.[37] The pleadings also alleged that the manufacturers directly and indirectly employed the plaintiffs and exercised meaningful control over the work the employees performed.[38] The court looked at "economic realities" rather than "technical concepts"[39] and determined that employees had sufficiently pleaded that the manufacturers were "employers" under the Act.

Similarly, the Department of Labor's Administrative Review Board concluded in 1996 that a referral agency was a joint employer for purposes of FLSA liability because of a variety of roles that it played, including the collection of time slips and payment of wages.[40]

---

[33]139 F. Supp. 2d 1358, 7 WH Cases2d at 966 (quoting *Powell*, 132 F.3d at 678).

[34]*Id.*, 7 WH Cases at 968.

[35]On Jan. 29, 2002, the Eleventh Circuit reversed and remanded.

[36]922 F. Supp. 1450, 132 Lab. Cas. (CCH) ¶ 33,411, 3 WH Cases2d 383 (C.D. Cal. 1996).

[37]*Id.* at 1468, 3 WH Cases2d 383.

[38]*Id.* at 1469, 3 WH Cases2d 383.

[39]*Id.* at 1467, 3 WH Cases2d 383 (quoting Hale v. State of Ariz., 993 F.2d 1387, 1393 (9th Cir.), *cert. denied*, 510 U.S. 946 (1993)).

[40]Reich v. Baystate Alternative Staffing, Inc., No. 97-FLS-22, 1996 WL 737281 (DOL. Off. Adm. App. Dec. 19, 1996).

B. Prospective Injunctions

1. Generally: Specificity and Discretion

In *Herman v. Brewah Cab*,[41] the district court permanently enjoined an employer held to have violated the Act from future violations of the FLSA, despite the employer's then-current compliance with the Act, applying the well-established principle that the defendant's then-current compliance was not an adequate assurance that the company would not violate the statute again in the future.[42]

Similarly, in *Metzler v. IBP, Inc.*,[43] which involved a meat slaughter and packing employer that unlawfully failed to record and compensate employees for time spent performing preshift and postshift activities, the U.S. Court of Appeals for the Tenth Circuit held that the district court did not abuse its discretion in granting a permanent prospective injunction forbidding IBP from violating the FLSA's overtime and record-keeping provisions. Noting that "[t]he purpose of an injunction against future violations is remedial rather than punitive," the Tenth Circuit stated that the mere fact that a company is in current compliance does not require a court to deny an injunction.[44] The court pointed out that the district court had cited the following factors as supporting an injunction: (1) IBP's failure to enter into a compliance agreement with the Secretary; (2) its failure to compensate or record any of the compensable preshift and postshift time even after the district court's findings that such time was compensable were affirmed by the Tenth Circuit in an earlier decision;[45] and (3) testimony by IBP's own director of industrial engineering indicating that IBP still did not record or

---

[41] 992 F. Supp. 1054, 1060, 4 WH Cases2d 653, 658 (E.D. Wis.), *motion to amend denied*, 179 F.R.D. 577 (E.D. Wis. 1998) (denying request for additional relief).

[42] *Id.*

[43] 127 F.3d 959, 4 WH Cases2d 229 (10th Cir. 1997).

[44] *Id.* at 963, 4 WH Cases2d 229.

[45] *Id.* at 964, 4 WH Cases2d 229. *See* Reich v. IBP, Inc., 38 F.3d 1123, 2 WH Cases2d 641 (10th Cir. 1994).

compensate employees for the work activities found to be compensable.[46]

However, the court in *Reich v. Newspapers of New England, Inc.*,[47] affirmed the lower court's denial of a prospective injunction after finding that the employer's violations were traceable in part to the indeterminate status of FLSA exemptions for the field of journalism.

In *Herman v. City of St. Petersburg, Florida, Police Department*,[48] the Secretary of Labor sued the defendant police department alleging the department failed to pay proper overtime by excluding shift pay differentials or premiums from the regular rate calculation. The applicable collective bargaining agreement provided that shift differential payments did not apply to overtime hours. The Secretary moved for partial summary judgment seeking, in part, an injunction prohibiting future violations of the FLSA and prohibiting the withholding of back wages. The district court held that the police department had violated the FLSA by failing to include shift differentials in calculating overtime. The court concluded that the Secretary was entitled to a permanent injunction to prevent the department from committing future violations of the FLSA and requiring the payment of back wages.

In *Chao v. Virginia Department of Transportation*,[49] the Secretary of Labor sought a prospective injunction against defendant based on alleged violations of the FLSA for failure to pay overtime to transportation construction inspectors for travel time between work sites. During the litigation the plaintiff conceded that defendant was no longer violating the statute and there was no evidence that defendant would violate the Act in

---

[46]127 F.3d at 965, 4 WH Cases2d 229. *See also* Reich v. Scherer Buick Co., 887 F. Supp. 1142, 1147, 2 WH Cases2d 1755 (C.D. Ill. 1995), in which the court granted a permanent injunction against the employer from committing future violations of record-keeping and minimum wage requirements because defendants failed to "provide the Court with reasons why they should not be enjoined from further violations of the FLSA."

[47]44 F.3d 1060, 131 Lab. Cas. (CCH) ¶33,314, 2 WH Cases2d 897 (1st Cir. 1995).

[48]131 F. Supp. 2d 1329 (M.D. Fla. 2001).

[49]157 F. Supp. 2d 681, 7 WH Cases2d 347 (E.D. Va. 2001).

the future. Defendant moved to dismiss and for summary judgment. The court observed that while the Secretary, as the party asserting jurisdiction, bears the burden of satisfying the court that an injunction is necessary, it is clear that a district court is empowered to issue a prospective injunction against violating the FLSA in the absence of a finding of current violations.[50] Citing the Tenth Circuit's decision in *IBP*[51] and other authorities therein, the court enumerated factors which bear on the question of whether an injunction is appropriate, including "the employer's previous conduct, its current conduct, and the reliability of its promises of future compliance."[52] The court noted that in this case defendant allegedly violated the rights of over 100 employees over the course of several years, and the Secretary and the defendant were engaged in a continuing dispute over the applicability of a related statute.[53] Finding that the question as to whether or not a prospective injunction should issue depended on other facts to be found in the future, the court held there was no current basis for dismissing or disposing of the Secretary's claim for that relief and denied defendant's motions.

In *Herman v. Hogar Praderas de Amor, Inc.*,[54] the Secretary of Labor tried a five-day bench trial against a nursing home and its owner for failure to pay minimum wages or overtime compensation, and for record-keeping violations. The district court held that the defendants had violated the FLSA and granted back pay relief. However, the district court denied the Secretary's request for a prospective injunction to restrain future FLSA violations. The court noted that such injunctions are discretionary under Section 217.[55] Here, evidence showed that defendants had been in contact with the Puerto Rico Department of Labor, which at no time informed Hogar that any of their pay rates were less than the minimum wage rates set by federal law, and in fact advised

[50] *Id.*, 7 WH Cases2d at 352.
[51] 127 F.3d 959, 963–64, 4 WH Cases2d 229 (10th Cir. 1997).
[52] *Chao*, 157 F. Supp. 2d 681, 7 WH Cases2d at 352.
[53] The Employee Commuting Flexibility Act of 1996, 29 U.S.C. §254(a).
[54] 130 F. Supp. 2d 257 (D.P.R. 2001).
[55] *See* Treatise at §17.III.B.1, nn.190–202.

that the federal minimum wage did not apply to Hogar. Moreover, Hogar had made prompt efforts to comply with the FLSA once they were notified they were in violation, and there was no evidence of any risk of future violations.

2. *Record-Keeping Violations*

In *Reich v. Scherer Buick Co.*,[56] the court granted a prospective injunction because the "[d]efendants d[id] not inform the Court if they are currently complying with the FLSA's record keeping requirements."

C. Restitutionary Injunctions

1. *Nature and Purpose*

A motion to amend an injunction enjoining an employer from violating Section 207(a)(1) by including a provision enjoining the employer from "withholding back wages due defendants' employees" was improper under Rule 60(a), Federal Rules of Civil Procedure because the "omission" was not of a clerical nature and was not intended by the court to be included.[57]

In *Chao v. Virginia Department of Transportation*,[58] the Secretary of Labor also sought a restitutionary injunction against the continued withholding of back pay from transportation construction inspectors for past travel time between work sites. Defendant contended that in the absence of a prospective injunction, no restitutionary injunction could issue. Noting several decisions to the contrary, the court pointed out that United States Court of Appeals for the Ninth Circuit had explained, "[t]he contention that an injunctive restraint against further withholding of past due overtime compensation may be awarded only as part and parcel of an injunction against future violations is predicated upon a narrow, technical and untenable

[56] 887 F. Supp. 1142, 130 Lab. Cas. (CCH) ¶33,264 2 WH Cases2d 1755 (C.D. Ill. 1995).

[57] Herman v. Brewah Cab, 179 F.R.D. 577, 4 WH Cases2d 1279 (E.D. Wis. 1998).

[58] 157 F. Supp. 2d 681, 7 WH Cases2d 347 (E.D. Va. 2001).

interpretation of the Act."[59] The court found that even if a prospective injunction were not issued, or even if its own analysis concerning the propriety of issuing a prospective injunction were wrong, the court nevertheless had the ability to issue a restitutionary injunction independent of a prospective injunction, in keeping with the basic tenet that the FLSA, as a remedial statute, "must not be interpreted or applied in a narrow, grudging manner."[60]

5. Interest

c. Computation and Rate

In proceedings to hold the defendant in contempt of an earlier consent decree, the district court in *Herman v. Davis Acoustical Corp.*[61] adopted the recommendation of the special master to deny the defendants' motion to toll the accrual of prejudgment interest during periods of delay in the litigation allegedly attributable to the Department of Labor. Although affirming the power of the court to withhold interest on such grounds, the court approved the master's view that "prejudgment interest serves the goal of making whole the employees who have been deprived of rightful wages, and it also serves to divest the errant employer of the competitive advantage it gained over law-abiding businesses by not properly paying its [employees],"[62] and awarded interest for the whole time involved.

In that same proceeding, the Secretary of Labor objected to the master's decision to compute the interest by simple annual compounding, and it sought a determination that daily compounding of interest should have been used. The district court, citing many authorities, upheld the decision to use simple interest, finding no statutory or common law precedent for using daily compounding for interest on a back wage award.

---

[59] 7 WH Cases2d at 353 (quoting Wirtz v. Milton J. Wershow Co., 416 F.2d 1071, 1072, 19 WH Cases 165 (9th Cir. 1969)).

[60] *Id.* at 354 (quoting Tennessee Coal, Iron & R.R. Co. v. Muscoda Local No. 123, 321 U.S. 590, 59, 4 WH Cases 293 (1944)).

[61] 21 F. Supp. 2d 130, 4 WH Cases2d 1615 (N.D.N.Y. 1998).

[62] 4 WH Cases2d at 1619.

D. Other Issues

4. Contempt

a. Civil Contempt

(iii) Remedies. On the appeal in *Herman v. Davis Acoustical Corp.*,[63] the Second Circuit reversed the district court and held that a federal district court has inherent power to award the Secretary of Labor attorneys' fees incurred in prosecuting a contempt motion against an employer.[64] The district court had thought that there was a lack of statutory basis or clear precedent for such an award, and it observed that Congress had specifically provided for recovery of attorneys' fees in Section 16 enforcement actions by individual plaintiffs but not in Section 17 actions by the Secretary. Without addressing the question of whether attorneys' fees could be recovered in a simple enforcement action by the Secretary, the Second Circuit held that the court could award attorneys' fees in a contempt action as part of its inherent power unless such an award was forbidden by Congress.[65]

IV. ACTIONS FOR BACK WAGES

A. Statutory Plaintiffs

1. Secretary

b. Right to a Jury Trial

In *Reich v. Southern New England Telecommunications Corp.*,[66] the court rejected the employer's contention that the Secretary sought only equitable relief pursuant to Section 17 as "a mischaracterization of the Secretary's complaint," noting that

---

[63] 196 F.3d 354, 5 WH Cases2d 1249 (2d Cir. 1999).

[64] The decision is consistent with others involving similar issues, discussed in the Treatise at Chapter 17, p. 1071, notes 378–81 and accompanying text.

[65] 196 F.3d at 357, 5 WH Cases2d 1249.

[66] 121 F.3d 58, 70, 4 WH Cases2d 33 (2d Cir. 1997).

relief had been sought under both Section 17 and Section 16(c) and that nothing precludes the Secretary from seeking both legal and equitable relief under these two sections. Moreover, the court noted, "in response to [employer's] motion to strike the claim for liquidated damages, the Secretary invited [employer] to request a trial by jury," but it had deliberately chosen not to do so.[67]

2. *Private Plaintiffs*

Courts continue to hold that, generally, unions lack standing to bring representative suits on behalf of their members for violations of the FLSA.[68]

Does I thru XXII v. Advanced Textile Corp.[69] was a suit initiated on behalf of 23 unnamed plaintiffs who were residents of China recruited to work on Saipan. They allegedly had sworn never to complain about their treatment, on pain of immediate return to China. The district court found that the alleged risks to the plaintiffs "did not outweigh `the prejudicial effect on defendants' ability to investigate and defend against claims by unnamed plaintiffs,' and the public's interest in a 'case [of] widespread implications.'"[70] It dismissed the plaintiffs' complaint but stayed final action so that the plaintiffs might amend to include the actual names of the plaintiffs. The Ninth Circuit reversed, holding that the decision constituted an appealable collateral order final in effect, and that in the case before it, the collective action under the FLSA could proceed without the plaintiffs identifying themselves. While noting that the "[p]laintiffs' use of fictitious names runs afoul of the public's common law right of access to judicial proceedings,"[71] the court

---

[67] *Id. See also* Reich v. Scherer Buick Co., 887 F. Supp. 1142, 1143, 1147, 2 WH Cases2d 1755 (C.D. Ill. 1995) (unopposed summary judgment granting liquidated damages under Section 16(c) in Secretary's "action for injunctive relief and liquidated damages").

[68] UFCW Local 1564 v. Albertson's, Inc., 207 F.3d 1193, 5 WH Cases2d 1705 (10th Cir. 2000).

[69] 214 F.3d 1058, 6 WH Cases2d 97 (9th Cir. 2000).

[70] *Id.*, 6 WH Cases2d at 100.

[71] *Id.*, 6 WH Cases2d at 103. *See also* Nixon v. Warner Communications, Inc., 435 U.S. 589, 598–99 (1978).

recognized that parties could "proceed anonymously when special circumstances justify secrecy,"[72] and reversed the lower court for abuse of discretion.[73] It observed that in weighing the interests of the respective parties in concealment versus disclosure, the factors to be weighed included: (1) the severity of the threatened harm; (2) the reasonableness of the anonymous party's fears; and (3) the anonymous party's vulnerability to retaliation.[74] The court further opined that the trial court must "determine the precise prejudice at each stage of the proceedings to the opposing party, and whether proceedings may be structured so as to mitigate that prejudice. Finally, the [trial] court must decide whether the public's interest in the case would be best served by requiring that the litigants reveal their identities."[75]

In *Bureerong v. Uvawas,*[76] the U.S. District Court for the Central District of California held that Secretary Reich's decision to sue only the operators of a garment facility for unpaid minimum wage and overtime compensation did not preclude the employees' action against additional defendants, the manufacturers that contracted with the operators.[77] The court interpreted Sections 216(b) and (c) broadly and adopted the interpretation advanced by the plaintiffs that the sections are "employer-specific."[78] Therefore, because there may be more than one "employer" for FLSA purposes,[79] the Secretary's suit against the operators did not terminate the employees' suit against the manufacturers.[80]

---

[72]214 F.3d at 1068, 6 WH Cases2d 97.

[73]*Id.*

[74]214 F.3d 1058, 6 WH Cases2d at 104.

[75]*Id.*

[76]922 F. Supp. 1450, 3 WH Cases2d 383 (C.D. Cal. 1996).

[77]*Id.* at 1465–66, 3 WH Cases2d 383. The employees' action against the operators, however, was precluded by the Secretary's suit.

[78]*Id.* at 1466–67, 3 WH Cases2d 383.

[79]*Id.* at 1468, 3 WH Cases2d 383.

[80]*Id.* at 1466–67, 3 WH Cases2d 383.

C. Monetary Damages

In *Morales v. Zondo Inc.*[81] plaintiff brought suit for the termination of her employment under the federal Pregnancy Disability Act, the New York State Human Rights Law, and the New York City Human Rights Law. Approximately 3 months after the answer to the complaint was filed, plaintiff changed attorneys. Shortly after entering an appearance and attending a conference with the court, the new attorney filed a motion on behalf of plaintiff to amend the complaint to add a claim under the FLSA. The district court denied this motion, stating that "a motion for leave to amend may be denied where the amendment would be 'futile' or has 'no colorable merit.'"[82] Although the plaintiff offered evidence tending to show (a) that her salary was subject to reduction on account of her failure to work a full 40 hours per week, and (b) that she did manual work to an extent possibly rendering her ineligible for the administrative exemption, the court decided both these issues on the evidence before it, without trial, and went on to decide that there was no set of circumstances under which the plaintiff could recover overtime under the FLSA because she was an exempt administrative employee.

2. *Liquidated Damages*

Restating the general rule that liquidated damages are generally to be awarded to the plaintiffs in cases under Section 216(b) unless the defendant proves both elements of the defense under Section 11 of the Portal-to-Portal Act[83] and persuades the court to exercise its discretion to reduce the amount of, or eliminate, the award, the court in *Bureerong v. Uvawas*[84] denied the defendants' motion to strike a claim for liquidated damages.

---

[81]2001 U.S. Dist. LEXIS 508, 6 WH Cases2d 1390 (S.D.N.Y. 2001).
[82]2001 U.S. Dist. LEXIS 508, 6 WH Cases2d at 1392.
[83]29 U.S.C. §260.
[84]922 F. Supp. 1450, 3 WH Cases2d 383 (C.D. Cal. 1996).

One district court provided a detailed explanation of the employer's substantial burden of proving good faith in order to avoid or diminish an award of liquidated damages.[85] "It is not enough, for instance, to plead and prove ignorance of the wage requirements.... Good faith requires some duty to investigate potential liability under the FLSA.... Lack of good faith is demonstrated when an employer 'knows, or has reason to know, that his conduct is governed by the [FLSA].'"

In *Sack v. Miami Helicopter Service,*[86] the district court determined that it had discretion to award partial liquidated damages in a "close case" in which the employer had demonstrated that it had "acted in good faith and that [its] decision as to applicability of the overtime pay requirements was not unreasonable."[87] The court also noted that a large liquidated damages award was inappropriate because the plaintiff knew that he had stopped receiving overtime pay, "but did not object or complain . . . about the unpaid overtime wages until after he left his employment more than a year later."[88]

a. Availability

In *Uphoff v. Elegant Bath, Ltd.,*[89] the Seventh Circuit reversed a denial of liquidated damages by the district court. The lower court had relied on the facts, "undisputed by the parties, that Defendants gave [plaintiffs] numerous cash payments as well as access to [company] vehicles and materials for personal use."[90] The defendants claimed at trial that these payments and other benefits were compensation for the plaintiffs' overtime and that the defendants had acted in good faith and reasonably. The court of appeals held that even assuming the defendants' good faith, they had failed to meet the burden of demonstrating the reasonableness of their conduct, having adduced no evidence to

---

[85] Karr v. City of Beaumont, 950 F. Supp. 1317, 1325–26 (E.D. Tex. 1997).
[86] 986 F. Supp. 1456, 4 WH Cases2d 490 (S.D. Fla. 1997).
[87] *Id.* at 1473, 4 WH Cases at 502–03.
[88] *Id.*, 4 WH Cases at 503.
[89] 176 F.3d 399, 5 WH Cases2d 467 (7th Cir. 1999).
[90] *Id.*, 5 WH Cases2d at 470.

show that they believed the monetary payments and other benefits satisfied their obligations under the law.

The Sixth Circuit in *Herman v. Palo Group Foster Home Inc.*[91] affirmed the decision of the District Court for the Western District of Michigan finding that the defendants' violations warranted an award of statutory liquidated damages. The defendants had previously been investigated twice for the same kinds of activities by the Department of Labor, had previously paid back wages and been informed of the requirements of the law by the Department, and engaged in the same or similar conduct a third time.

In *American Federation of State, County, and Municipal Employees v. State of Louisiana,*[92] the district court awarded plaintiff liquidated damages after trial. Plaintiff, a state law enforcement agent, sued for uncompensated overtime hours during which he had performed undercover operations as a buyer and seller of illegal fish and wildlife. The district court concluded that plaintiff was due overtime compensation and awarded back overtime pay plus liquidated damages. Supervisors knew plaintiff was working overtime and approved the time, encouraging plaintiff to utilize a "loose" honor system of using compensatory time in lieu of overtime. The court imposed liquidated damages despite the finding that the employer acted in good faith in denying the overtime sought. Rather the court found the supervisors to be "negligent" and "less than reasonable" in handling these claims.

In *Herman v. Hogar Praderas de Amor, Inc.,*[93] the Secretary of Labor succeeded at trial in proving that a nursing home and its owner failed to pay minimum wages or overtime for training and meal times. The court addressed the liquidated damages issue separately for each type of violation. With regard to the minimum wage claim, the court held that defendants had met their burden of showing the requisite good faith and reasonableness based on evidence that defendants had received orientation on

---

[91] 183 F.3d 468, 5 WH Cases2d 837 (6th Cir. 1999).
[92] 2001 U.S. Dist. LEXIS 437 (E.D. La. Jan. 10, 2001).
[93] 130 F. Supp. 2d 257 (D.P.R. 2001).

wage issues from the Puerto Rico Department of Labor, had submitted proposals to Puerto Rican government agencies in which they disclosed the wages they intended to pay, had been given tacit approval for the wage rates, and had promptly changed their pay rates to comply with the law once challenged. The court imposed prejudgment interest as to this claim. With regard to the claims for overtime based on training and mealtimes, the court found that defendants had not offered evidence to show their good faith, but instead asserted that compensation at straight time rates in cases of this kind was consistent with industry practice. The court found that "[a] showing of conformity with an industry-wide practice does not establish good faith"[94] and it awarded liquidated damages.

In *Pabst v. Oklahoma Gas & Electric Co.*,[95] electronic technicians employed by a utilities company were awarded overtime compensation for their on-call time but denied liquidated damages. The district court held that defendant's actions, while a violation of the FLSA, were reasonable and in good faith because defendant paid double time for overtime reported; it permitted plaintiffs to report an hour every time they responded to an alarm, even if they spent only a few minutes; and defendant was not fully aware of the burden of the on-call responsibilities on plaintiffs until some time in 1997, after which it took corrective action. The Tenth Circuit reviewed this decision under the abuse of discretion standard and, while noting that it might have decided the matter differently, affirmed. The district court did not abuse its discretion because the analysis of on-call time under the FLSA is fact-sensitive and the facts relied upon by the district court provided some support for its decision.

In *Bjerke v. Nash Finch Co.*,[96] plaintiff proved violations of the Equal Pay Act (EPA) at a jury trial. The district court granted plaintiff liquidated damages on her EPA claim in accordance with Section 216(b) of the FLSA, holding that defendant had

---

[94] *Id.* at 268 (citing Reich v. Southern New England Telecomms., 121 F.3d 58, 71 (2d Cir. 1997)).

[95] 228 F.3d 1128 (10th Cir. 2000).

[96] 2000 U.S. Dist. LEXIS 19777, 84 FEP Cases 1350 (D.N.D. 2000).

not met its burden of proving good faith and reasonableness. Specifically, defendant had no evidence that it took any action to ascertain whether its practice of paying female packing room workers less than male general warehouse workers violated the law, even though the alleged violation had been brought to its attention on a number of occasions.

In its unpublished decision in *Ackler v. Cowlitz County*,[97] the Ninth Circuit reversed the district court's denial of liquidated damages to 31 deputy sheriffs, concluding that even if it deferred to the district court's view of the defendant's good faith, defendant had not established reasonable grounds for believing that its conduct complied with the FLSA. In explaining its decision, the opinion noted that the employer had failed to adhere to the "clear requirement"[98] to pay employees overtime for hours worked over 40 in a week, and had relied on the collective bargaining agreement and the employees' failure to complain for the belief that its conduct was acceptable. "Because Cowlitz County knew that employees were working overtime without additional pay and knew or at least recklessly disregarded the fact that a collective bargaining agreement's terms cannot waive the requirements of the FLSA, the County acted willfully. The County's argument regarding its motivation—that it acted to satisfy the desires of employees for a certain schedule—has no legal relevance."[99] Thus liquidated damages were required.

b. Computation

In *Braswell v. El Dorado*,[100] the Eighth Circuit held that a federal district court had improperly failed to award the full amount due as liquidated damages. After the district court had granted summary judgment against the defendants on the liability aspect of the plaintiffs' overtime claim, the defendant paid the plaintiffs some $55,000, contending that that sum

---

[97] 2001 U.S. App. LEXIS 2672, 7 Fed. Appx. 543 (9th Cir. 2001) (unpublished).
[98] *Id.*, 7 Fed. Appx. at 544.
[99] *Id.*, 7 Fed. Appx. at 545.
[100] 187 F.3d 954, 5 WH Cases2d 868 (8th Cir. 1999).

constituted the full amount of back wages due plus certain interest. The plaintiffs claimed the overtime due was some $58,000. At trial, the jury determined that the back wages owing were, as the plaintiffs contended, $58,000. In making its judgment, the district court awarded liquidated damages only on the $3,000 difference between what the plaintiffs had been owed and the amount the defendants had paid before trial. The Eighth Circuit noted, in accordance with prevailing law, that the district court, after having found that the defendants failed to demonstrate their good faith and reasonable belief in their compliance with the law, was bound to award full liquidated damages.

In *Jarrett v. ERC Properties*,[101] the Eighth Circuit required an award of liquidated damages. Following the general rule and citing *Braswell v. City of El Dorado*,[102] the court held that an award of liquidated damages for FLSA violations "is mandatory unless the employer can show good faith and reasonable grounds for believing that it was not in violation of the FLSA."[103]

3. *Interest*

a. Prejudgment Interest

The Fourth Circuit's approach to prejudgment interest appears to be that "the decision to award prejudgment interest is a discretionary one for the trial court, which should consider the equities of the particular case."[104] Whether a finding of good faith on the part of the employer precludes an award of prejudgment interest has not been decided by the Fourth Circuit,[105] but

---

[101]211 F.3d 1078, 6 WH Cases2d 4 (8th Cir. 2000).

[102]187 F.3d 954, 5 WH Cases2d 868.

[103]*Id.* at 957, 5 WH Cases2d 868. *See also* Tran v. Tran, 2000 WL 1099906, at *9 (S.D.N.Y. 2000) (double damages are the norm, single damages the exception).

[104]Quirk v. Baltimore County, 895 F. Supp. 773, 790, 2 WH Cases2d 1500 (D. Md. 1995) (quoting Thomas v. County of Fairfax, 758 F. Supp. 353, 368 (E.D. Va. 1991)). *See also* Masters v. Maryland Mgmt. Co., 493 F.2d 1329, 21 WH Cases 604 (4th Cir. 1974).

[105]*Quirk*, 895 F. Supp. at 790, 2 WH Cases2d 1500.

Maryland district courts have held that "an employer's good faith is not a sufficient reason for denial of pre-judgment interest."[106]

In *Uphoff v. Elegant Bath, Ltd.*,[107] the Seventh Circuit held that the federal district court had abused its discretion in failing to award liquidated damages to the plaintiffs. It accordingly declined to rule on the plaintiffs' appeal of the court's denial of their claim for prejudgment interest under the FLSA, expressing adherence to the view of the majority of circuits, that "the FLSA does not permit successful plaintiffs to obtain prejudgment interest in addition to liquidated damages because that would enable them to obtain double recovery."[108]

In *Pabst v. Oklahoma Gas & Electric Co.*,[109] electronic technicians employed by a utilities company were awarded overtime compensation for their on-call time, denied liquidated damages, and awarded prejudgment interest. The Tenth Circuit reviewed this decision under the abuse of discretion standard. The district court held that defendant's actions, while a violation of the FLSA, were reasonable and in good faith. Defendant paid double time for overtime reported; it permitted plaintiffs to report an hour every time they responded to an alarm, even if they spent only a few minutes; and defendant was not fully aware of the burden of the on-call responsibilities on plaintiffs until some time in 1997, after which it took corrective action. The appellate court, while noting that it might have decided the matter differently, affirmed. The district court did not abuse its discretion because the analysis of on-call time under the FLSA is fact-sensitive and the facts relied upon by the district court provided some support for its decision.

---

[106] *Id.*, 2 WH Cases2d 1500 (quoting Marshall v. Board of Educ., 470 F. Supp. 517, 519 (D. Md. 1979), *aff'd*, 618 F.2d 101 (4th Cir. 1980), and citing Marshall v. Gerwill, Inc., 495 F. Supp. 744, 755 (D. Md. 1980)).

[107] 176 F.3d 399, 5 WH Cases2d 467 (7th Cir. 1999).

[108] *Id.*, 5 WH Cases2d at 470 (citing Gibson v. Mohawk Rubber Co., 695 F.2d 1093, 1102, 30 FEP Cases 859 (8th Cir. 1982), and noting that the First, Fourth, Fifth, Sixth, Eighth, and Tenth Circuits agree, while the Second, Third, Ninth, and Eleventh do not).

[109] 228 F.3d 1128 (10th Cir. 2000).

V. ATTORNEYS' FEES AND COSTS

In *Uphoff v. Elegant Bath, Ltd.*,[110] the Seventh Circuit upheld a district court's decision to reduce the requested fee rates to those that the court had previously awarded in a recent FLSA case involving the same attorneys. The court stated that it was highly deferential to the trial court's determination on this issue, that review was only for abuse of discretion, and that "the district court is in the best position to determine the worth of the attorneys practicing before him." The court also upheld the district court's denial of recovery of the cost of fees paid a nontestifying accountant hired to calculate damages, reasoning that the expenses related to the accountant were akin to those of an expert witness, recoverable only if the court appointed or approved the expert.

In *DiGiore v. Ryan*,[111] one plaintiff, who was an exempt employee during his usual assignments, was detailed to the Secret Service and during the period of the detail was not paid overtime. In a suit by a group of plaintiffs for back wages, the defendant successfully claimed the exemption for most of the plaintiffs but agreed that this plaintiff was not exempt during the period of his detail and agreed to pay the back wages due and to comply in the future. After granting summary judgment for the defendant, the trial court dismissed the individual plaintiff's claim as moot, given the unusual circumstances of the violation. The Seventh Circuit affirmed but pointed out that although the defendant-employer had prevailed, costs of the action could not be assessed against the individual employee who had appealed the lower court's determination that his case was moot because the state had compensated him retroactively, as to do so would permit the state to "alleviate both the claim and the costs they incurred as a result of it."[112]

---

[110] 176 F.3d 399, 5 WH Cases2d 467.

[111] 172 F.3d 454, 5 WH Cases2d 321 (7th Cir. 1999).

[112] *Id.*, 5 WH Cases2d at 330.

B. Specific Factors That Affect Attorneys' Fees Awards

1. Prevailing Plaintiff Requirement

An employer that made impermissible deductions from exempt employees' paychecks but preserved employees' status by exercising a window of correction was not liable for attorneys' fees because the plaintiffs were not the prevailing party.[113]

The relationship between success on the merits and the award of attorneys' fees can be followed in the series of decisions in *Shea v. Galaxie Lumber & Construction Co.*[114] In the first decision, [115] the district court reversed an award of punitive damages where the jury had awarded nothing to the plaintiff on the compensatory damages (for retaliation) claim, $1,200 in overtime, and significant punitive damages, holding that punitive damages were not available on the overtime claim and could not be awarded on the claim for which no compensatory damages had been allowed. On appeal, the Seventh Circuit reinstated the award of punitive damages, holding that "punitive damages may be awarded on an FLSA §216(b) retaliation claim even without a separate award of compensatory damages."[116] On the plaintiff's appeal of the district court's original award of attorneys' fees, which was only about 20 percent of the amount sought, the appellate court remanded for further consideration in light of its disposition on the merits. On the subsequent appeal[117] of an increased attorneys' fee award by the district court,[118] the appellate court affirmed an upward revision to the fee award because of the increased success of the plaintiff's FLSA claim, finding defensible the district court's increase in the amount of attorneys' fees from 20 percent to 60 percent of the lodestar amount. The circuit court opined that the plaintiff's

---

[113]Arrington v. City of Macon, 986 F. Supp. 1474, 4 WH Cases2d 113 (M.D. Ga. 1997).

[114]2000 WL 868605 (7th Cir. 2000).

[115]*See* discussion in Treatise at Chapter 15, p. 942, text at notes 429 and 430.

[116]152 F.3d 729, 4 WH Cases2d 1473 (7th Cir. 1998).

[117]2000 WL 868605 (unreported decision).

[118]6 WH Cases2d 1435 (N.D. Ill. 1999).

success on her FLSA claims in the appellate court had increased her success overall, but it was still a limited increase that justified the district court's limited increase of attorneys' fees.

In *Wisnewski v. Champion Healthcare Corp.*,[119] the district court accorded prevailing-party status to a class of plaintiffs whose suit served as the catalyst for the defendants to adjust the calculation of overtime in accordance with the FLSA. Although no relief was awarded by the district court, the defendant had significantly modified its overtime calculations during the pendency of the suit. The court noted that the decision as to which party prevailed would be relied on in the determination of whether attorneys' fees would be awarded under the FLSA, and used the analysis discussed in *Tyler v. Corner Construction Corp.*[120] for determining a prevailing party. [121]

2. **Hensley v. Eckerhart** *and the Fee-Shifting Standard*

In a case in which the defendant church parish conceded liability and judgment in the amount of $1,000 for unpaid overtime, the plaintiff's lawyer received 10 percent of his requested fee.[122] The court arrived at this figure through the lodestar method after reducing the attorney's requested billing rate and finding that most of the time billed was not "reasonable and necessary."

---

[119]2000 WL 1474414, 141 Lab. Cas. ¶34,095 (D.N.D. 2000).

[120]167 F.3d 1202 (8th Cir. 1999).

[121]Under *Tyler,* if a defendant has changed his or her behavior to the benefit of the plaintiff after a suit commences, making the plaintiff's claim moot, a plaintiff is a prevailing party if the suit was "a catalyst for the defendant's voluntary compliance and the defendant's compliance was not gratuitous, meaning that the plaintiff's suit was neither 'frivolous, unreasonable, nor groundless.'" *Id.* at 1205 (citing Little Rock Sch. Dist. v. Pulaski County Special Sch. Dist. No. 1, 17 F.3d 260, 262 (8th Cir. 1995)).

[122]Spegon v. Catholic Bishop, 989 F. Supp. 984, 4 WH Cases2d 568 (N.D. Ill. 1998).

3. *Attorneys' Fees for Non-FLSA Claims Made in FLSA Litigation*

In *DeLeon v. Trevino*,[123] the district court adopted the magistrate's report, granting summary judgment to plaintiffs on their claim that defendant failed to compensate them for time worked as agricultural workers, in violation of the FLSA and the Migrant and Seasonal Agricultural Worker Protection Act (AWPA), 29 U.S.C. §1801 et seq. The court awarded plaintiffs attorneys' fees for work performed on the entire case, even though the AWPA does not provide for attorneys' fees. In doing so, the district court relied on a Fifth Circuit decision that provides that recovery of attorneys' fees under the FLSA "'extends to time spent on non-FLSA issues to the extent that those issues interrelate and overlap with FLSA ones.'"[124]

4. *Attorneys' Fees for Appellate Work*

With respect to attorneys' fees on appeal, *Sanders v. Elephant Butte Irrigation District of New Mexico*[125] held, after affirming in part and remanding in part the district court's decision for the plaintiff, that plaintiff had prevailed on the appeal and was entitled "to a substantial portion of his attorneys' fees incurred for defending the appeal."[126] However, the court refused to award fees for the time spent calculating overtime due the plaintiff, noting that issues surrounding the calculation of overtime should have been addressed by the attorneys in the district court, thereby obviating the need for remand.[127]

---

[123]163 F. Supp. 2d 682 (S.D. Tex. 2001).

[124]*Id.* (quoting Diaz v. Robert Ruiz, Inc., 808 F.2d 427, 429 (5th Cir. 1987) (punctuation added)).

[125]112 F.3d 468, 3 WH Cases2d 1573 (10th Cir. 1997).

[126]*Id.* at 472, 3 WH Cases2d 1573.

[127]*Id.*

5. *Calculating "Reasonable" Attorneys' Fees*

Former employees who prevail in an action alleging retaliatory discharge against an employer are entitled to an award of attorneys' fees under Section 216(b) of the FLSA. A state appeals court held that where the trial court did not comply with federal precedent by first calculating the lodestar amount and then clearly explaining any adjustments, it abused its discretion in its award of attorneys' fees.[128]

In accordance with prevailing law, a state appellate court reversed a denial of fees to the attorney for a prevailing plaintiff and remanded for the trial court to determine, after receiving evidence, an appropriate fee award.[129] The court pointed out that the FLSA mandates the award of fees to a prevailing party but leaves the reasonableness of the amount to the trial court's discretion.

In *Cunningham v. Gibson Electric Co.*,[130] a federal district court in Illinois held that in determining reasonable attorneys' fees the court must (1) determine the prevailing market rates in the relevant community, and (2) not be bound by any lower rate that the lawyers' law firm may charge to its other clients because of other factors such as the firm's social commitments. The court stated that while each court should arrive at its own determination as to a proper fee, rates awarded in similar cases are clearly evidence of an attorney's market rate.[131]

In *Stanley v. McDaniel*,[132] the Idaho Supreme Court held that a plaintiff with a federal FLSA claim in state court is entitled under state procedural law to interest on attorneys' fees from the date the district court makes a final determination on the amount of attorneys' fees. The state supreme court held that state procedural law is controlling for deciding issues of calculat-

---

[128]Stanley v. McDaniel, 913 P.2d 76, 79, 3 WH Cases2d 422 (Idaho Ct. App. 1996).

[129]Dutcher v. Randall Foods, 546 N.W.2d 889, 895 (Iowa 1996).

[130]63 F. Supp. 2d 891 (N.D. Ill. 1999).

[131]*Id.* at 893 (citing People Who Care v. Rockford Bd. of Educ., 90 F.3d 1307, 1312 (7th Cir. 1996)).

[132]7 P.3d 1107 (Idaho 2000).

ing attorneys' fees in a federal FLSA claim brought in state court. Further, the court held that, under state procedural law, postjudgment interest does not accrue after the original decision of the district court if that decision is later revised on appeal or remand.

In *Tran v. Tran,*[133] a federal district court in New York, after a bench trial on claims under the FLSA and RICO,[134] awarded judgment for the plaintiff on the RICO claim in the amount of some $600,000. The court had also found a violation of the FLSA, on which the backpay and liquidated damages would have amounted to under $100,000. Both claims arose out of the same conduct by the defendant, except that a longer period was considered in the RICO claim, and under RICO, the actual damages were tripled. The court did not award the plaintiff any damages on the FLSA claim, in order to prevent the plaintiff from recovering twice for the same injury and because the RICO damages covered the entire period of the FLSA damages. Subsequently, the plaintiff applied for attorneys' fees, provided for under both statutes, and such fees were allowed in substantial part despite a variety of objections by the defendant.

a. Calculating the Lodestar Figure

In two of the several decisions in the litigation between these parties, the Seventh Circuit in *Dormeyer v. Comerica Bank-Illinois*[135] affirmed a fee award cutting by 80 percent the fees applied for in a case involving claims under the FLSA, FMLA, and the Pregnancy Discrimination Act, among others, and then sanctioned the attorney for the plaintiff for pursuing a frivolous appeal. In the underlying FLSA case, the plaintiff accepted a $1,152 offer of judgment before trial; her remaining claims were decided adversely on summary judgment. The plaintiff's attorney then applied for almost $35,000 in fees. The lower court was

---

[133] 2000 WL 1099906, 6 WH Cases2d 507 (S.D.N.Y. 2000).

[134] Racketeer Influenced and Corrupt Organizations Act (RICO).

[135] 223 F.3d 579, 6 WH Cases2d 435; 226 F.3d 915, 6 WH Cases2d 548 (7th Cir. 2000).

"aghast" that counsel allocated half of his entire time on the case to the FLSA claim and determined, as had a previous court in another case, that the plaintiff's attorney had engaged in the "dishonest practice of joining two small valid claims, here the plaintiff's FLSA claim, large invalid and even frivolous claims, and seeking a larger award of attorneys' fees for services ostensibly devoted to the small claim but actually devoted to the large."[136]

In *Turner v. Progressive Corp.*,[137] the state appellate court reversed the trial court's second order awarding attorneys' fees. After a settlement of the underlying claim for the amount of $5,000, the original attorneys' fee award of $3,000, on a claim for $17,940, was reversed on appeal and the trial court was instructed to "provide a concise but clear explanation of its reasons for the fee award . . . listing the factors it took into consideration and stating the basis for the fee determination."[138] On remand, the trial court reiterated that it had taken into account all relevant factors, and raised the award to $4,500, noting that the issues presented were "neither difficult nor novel" and that it had considered the amount recovered. The plaintiff's second appeal asserted that the trial court abused its discretion in failing to articulate the factors on which it relied. The appellate court agreed and reversed, pointing out that "as far as the record reveals herein, the trial court failed to make a lodestar determination," and stating that, the plaintiff having presented evidence of a reasonable hourly rate, the court must under *Hensley v. Eckerhart*[139] provide a clear explanation for a deviation from it[140]

In *Batt v. Micro Warehouse, Inc.*,[141] the prevailing plaintiffs appealed the amount of attorneys' fees ($4,280) awarded by the district court post-settlement. The Seventh Circuit affirmed the trial court, finding no abuse of discretion in the reduction of the

---

[136]223 F.3d at 584, 6 WH Cases2d 435.
[137]1999 WL 980395 (Ohio Ct. App. 1999).
[138]*Id.* at *2.
[139]461 U.S. 424, 437 (1983). *See* discussion in Treatise at p. 1104.
[140]1999 WL 980395, at *4 (Ohio Ct. App. 1999).
[141]241 F.3d 891 (7th Cir. 2001).

number of hours allowed because much of the time was unnecessary, clerical, or inaccurate. Further, the district court did not abuse its discretion in reducing the number of hours billed to the fee petition from 10.5 hours to two hours given the relatively few number of hours spent on the merits of the case. Finally, the court was within its discretion in setting the hourly rate at $350/hour rather than $375/hour where evidence for the higher rate claimed was "thin and not well substantiated."

In *Loughner v. University of Pittsburgh*,[142] the Third Circuit vacated the trial court's award of attorneys fees ($88,655) after the parties had settled on the eve of trial, and had stipulated that plaintiff was the prevailing party. The court remanded the case for further consideration, concluding that the district court's findings were inadequate. "The District Court performed scant analysis, if any, of the hours in Hoover's petition."[143] Although the district court did reduce significantly the fees claimed, the fees awarded were more than triple the actual settlement amount. The appellate court found particularly suspect 120 hours of communication between plaintiff and her attorney. The trial court also erred in assigning a flat hourly rate of $175/hour for the wide range of tasks performed. Finally, the appellate court found the costs petition was insufficiently detailed to support an award.

In *Guity v. C.C.I. Enterprise, Co.*,[144] the Texas state appellate court reversed the trial court's grant of summary judgment on attorneys' fees. Plaintiff's counsel had submitted an affidavit claiming fees of $8,325. Defense counsel's affidavit asserted that $500 was a reasonable fee and the court awarded this amount. On remand, the trial court was directed to determine a reasonable fee award using the established *Johnson v. Georgia Highway Express, Inc.*[145] factors.

---

[142]260 F.3d 173, 7 WH Cases2d 200 (3d Cir. 2001).

[143]7 WH Cases2d at 204.

[144]54 S.W.3d 526, 7 WH Cases2d 446 (Tex. App. 2001). *See* Treatise pp. 1112–15.

[145]488 F.2d 714 (5th Cir. 1974).

In *Small v. Richard Wolf Medical Instruments Corp.*,[146] the Seventh Circuit determined that the district court did not abuse its discretion in reducing the plaintiff's claimed attorneys' fees by more than half through a combination of reducing the hourly rate from the $425 claimed to $300, and reducing the number of hours. The court found the case to have been "neither novel nor complex."[147] Where the evidence showed that plaintiff's attorney had been awarded rates of $280 to $300 in other non-complex FLSA cases, the district court did not abuse its discretion in reducing the hourly rate from $425 to $300; and where the plaintiff's "self proclaimed highly experienced FLSA attorney" billed 111 hours for his own time but only a total of 10.4 hours for the time of three subordinate attorneys, it was "understandable that the judge would assume that much of the more routine work would be delegated to competent attorneys in the firm who charge at a much lower hourly rate."[148] The district court's explanation for reducing the number of hours billed as excessive was limited but sufficient.

In its unpublished decision in *Ackler v. Cowlitz County*,[149] the Ninth Circuit held that the district court did not abuse its discretion in considering a settlement offer made by defendants and rejected by plaintiffs when the court made its award of attorneys' fees. The court pointed out that it is appropriate to consider the benefits obtained by the attorney, which depends at least in part on comparison of the results obtained by going to trial compared to the settlement offer. However, in light of the fact that the appeal resulted in the plaintiffs' becoming entitled to liquidated damages and a potential extra year of actual damages, the district court on remand should reconsider the attorneys' fees award in light of the new amount to be awarded to plaintiffs.

---

[146]264 F.3d 702, 7 WH Cases2d 385 (7th Cir. 2001).

[147]*Id.*, 7 WH Cases2d at 388.

[148]*Id.*

[149]2001 U.S. App. LEXIS 2672, 7 Fed. Appx. 543 (9th Cir. 2001) (unpublished).

b. Adjusting the Lodestar Amount—The 12-Factor Test

In *Spegon v. Catholic Bishop of Chicago,*[150] the Seventh Circuit upheld a district court's decision to disallow certain attorneys' fees because of the attorney's lack of "billing judgment," one of the twelve factors in the test to determine the proper amount of attorneys' fees. Because the FLSA violation was undisputed and the amount involved small, the attorney was deemed to have billed an excessive amount of time on litigating the matter.

In *Heidtman v. County of El Paso,*[151] the Fifth Circuit overruled a district court that had increased the lodestar amount of attorneys' fees by 50 percent. The trial court decision referred to "time limitations, complexity of issues, results obtained, and preclusion of other employment by the attorney" as factors warranting the enhancement. The court of appeals pointed out that the Supreme Court has stated that two of those factors, "complexity of the issues" and "results obtained," are "presumably fully reflected in the lodestar amount, and thus cannot serve as independent bases for increasing the basic fee award."[152] Accordingly, the circuit had previously held that enhancement based on complexity of the issues and results obtained is appropriate only in "rare and exceptional circumstances" and must be supported by both specific evidence in the record and detailed findings by the lower court, and noted that no such specific evidence or detailed findings were present in the case at bar.[153] Turning to the other two factors, the court pointed out that the Fifth Circuit had previously noted that "preclusion of other employment" is generally subsumed within the lodestar amount,[154] and it found nothing to distinguish the case at hand. Finally, it found that although the case had proceeded from filing to trial in only about eight months, there was insufficient basis for enhancement due to time limitations.

---

[150] 175 F.3d 544, 5 WH Cases2d 457 (7th Cir. 1999).

[151] 171 F.3d 1038, 5 WH Cases2d 385 (5th Cir. 1999).

[152] *Id.,* 5 WH Cases2d at 388 (citing Pennsylvania v. Delaware Valley Citizens' Council for Clean Air, 478 U.S. 546, 565, 106 S. Ct. 3088, 3098 (1986)).

[153] *Id.* (citing Shipes v. Trinity Indus., 987 F.2d 311, 319–22 & n.9 (5th Cir. 1993)).

[154] *Id.* (citing *Shipes,* 987 F.2d at 321–22).

In *Perdomo v. Sears, Roebuck & Co.*,[155] the court rejected a defense contention that a fee award should be reduced due to the plaintiffs' failure to prevail on all claims. The court used the lodestar method to calculate attorneys' fees with the reasonable hourly rate multiplied by the number of hours reasonably expended. The court determined that the hourly rate proffered by the plaintiffs was reasonable on a national average. The court further determined that the number of hours expended by the plaintiffs was reasonable. However, the court deducted time spent on notice and opt-in procedures and the unsuccessful plaintiffs' claims, which was time, the court reasoned, normally not charged to a client. In addition, the court awarded all the costs to the plaintiff. The court focused the fee determination on the overall results obtained by the plaintiffs and did not require that the plaintiffs divide up the time spent on certain minutiae, which otherwise would be burdensome to both the court and the plaintiff, and not in the spirit of the court's awarding of fees that focus on the success achieved as a whole.

In *Scott v. Sunrise Healthcare Corp.*,[156] the court calculated the attorneys' fee for the plaintiff based on the success of her small FLSA claim as linked to her larger unsuccessful wrongful termination claim. The court reasoned that, in calculating attorneys' fees based on the lodestar formula, modifying factors may be added, including the degrees of success obtained and the actual difficulty in obtaining that success. The court concluded that, despite losing her larger, wrongful termination claim, the plaintiff should be fairly compensated for the actual costs of succeeding on her FLSA claim. The court denied the plaintiff's request for attorneys' fees as too disproportionate from what the court noted as the amount of time necessary to reasonably execute the steps that could have been taken by the plaintiff's attorney in pursuing both claims. The court used what it surmised was the appropriate amount of time for the plaintiff to have pursued both claims and calculated the attorneys' fees based on her

---

[155] 1999 U.S. Dist. LEXIS 20881 (M.D. Fla. 1999).
[156] 1999 U.S. Dist. LEXIS 15073 (N.D. Ill. 1999).

limited success with one claim as modified by the degree of difficulty of her failed claim.

6. *Contempt [New Topic]*

In *Herman v. Davis Acoustical Corp.*,[157] the Second Circuit held that a federal district court had inherent power to award the Secretary of Labor attorneys' fees incurred in prosecuting a contempt motion against an employer.[158] The district court had thought that there was a lack of statutory basis or clear precedent for such an award, and it observed that Congress had specifically provided for recovery of attorneys' fees in Section 16 enforcement actions by individual plaintiffs but not in Section 17 actions by the Secretary. Without addressing the question of whether attorneys' fees could be recovered in a simple enforcement action by the Secretary, the Second Circuit held that the court could award attorneys' fees in a contempt action as part of its inherent power unless such an award was forbidden by Congress.

C. Costs

The Eleventh Circuit has held that, because costs do not include attorneys' fees under the FLSA, a district court did not retain jurisdiction to award fees once an offer of judgment was accepted under Federal Rules of Civil Procedure 68.[159]

In *Uphoff v. Elegant Bath, Ltd.*,[160] the court upheld the district court's denial of recovery of the cost of fees paid by plaintiff to a nontestifying accountant hired to calculate damages, reasoning that the expenses related to the accountant were akin to those of an expert witness, recoverable only if the court appointed or approved the expert.

---

[157]196 F.3d 354 (2d Cir. 1999).

[158]The decision is consistent with others involving similar issues, discussed in Treatise at Chapter 17, p. 1071, notes, 378–81 and accompanying text.

[159]Arencibia v. Miami Shoes Inc., 113 F.3d 1212, 3 WH Cases2d 1695 (11th Cir. 1997).

[160]176 F.3d 399, 5 WH Cases2d 467 (7th Cir. 1999).

VI. ACTIONS FOR DECLARATORY JUDGMENT AND JUDICIAL REVIEW

In a case of first impression, the federal district court in *Herman v. Excel Corp.*,[161] held that an employer being sued by the Department of Labor under the FLSA for failing to properly compensate its employees at one of its employment sites could file a counterclaim against the Secretary for a declaratory judgment on the issue that would be applied consistently to all of the defendant's employment sites. The Secretary's reliance on sovereign immunity was rejected because, the court found, the combination of an opinion letter by the Labor Secretary, a letter from the Secretary's counsel to the employer's counsel, and the filing of the FLSA lawsuit constituted "final agency action," which therefore subjected the Secretary to judicial review under the Administrative Procedure Act, in which Congress waived sovereign immunity in equitable cases. However, the employer did not have a basis for its counterclaim under (1) supplemental jurisdiction, (2) federal question jurisdiction, or (3) jurisdiction based on the fact that the FLSA regulates commerce, since the FLSA provides for no such cause of action. Furthermore, the Secretary's decision to file an FLSA action against the employer (alone) was not itself final agency action subjecting the Secretary to a counterclaim.

After a careful analysis of the general unavailability of injunctive relief to private plaintiffs (except in retaliation cases) under the FLSA, the Tenth Circuit in *UFCW Union, Local 1564 v. Albertson's, Inc.*,[162] reluctantly concluded, reversing the district court, that there was no federal jurisdiction to determine a union's declaratory judgment action seeking to invalidate a collective bargaining provision calling for compulsory unpaid training time.[163] The court reserved the question of whether 29

[161] 37 F. Supp. 2d 1117, 5 WH Cases2d 161 (C.D. Ill. 1999).

[162] 207 F.3d 1193, 5 WH Cases2d 1705 (10th Cir. 2000).

[163] While the case was pending, the Supreme Court held that §301 of the Labor Management Relations Act, 29 U.S.C. §1851(a), did not afford federal courts jurisdiction over declaratory judgment suits alleging the invalidity but not the violation of a collective bargaining agreement provision. Textron Lycoming Reciprocating Engine Div. v. UAW Int'l & Local 787, 563 U.S. 653 (1998).

U.S.C. §207(o), which expressly provides for a potential role for a union in implementing compensatory time arrangements for public employees it represents, might create a limited exception to the representative action bar in an action alleging a violation of that section.

In *Media General Operations, Inc. v. Herman*[164] the owner of a television station brought suit against the Secretary of Labor for a declaratory judgment that its television reporters were exempt employees. The Secretary moved to dismiss on the ground that the court lacked subject matter jurisdiction. The court noted that neither the FLSA itself nor the Declaratory Judgment Act provided an independent basis of jurisdiction, and so turned its attention to the Administrative Procedure Act, which provides jurisdiction to review "final agency action." At issue was whether a Department of Labor investigator's conclusion that FLSA violations were found, or that the reporters were not exempt, constituted such "final agency action." The court was not troubled by the conflicting positions of the parties as to what was said about the finality of the investigator's action, noting that "finality depends on the actual effect of the agency's determination."[165] Based on affidavit evidence as to the actual procedures in effect with respect to such investigations, the court found that the case file was subject to further administrative review, and that the agency process was not yet completed. Accordingly, it dismissed the action.

---

[164] 152 F. Supp. 2d 1368 (S.D. Ga. 2001).
[165] *Id.* at 1375–76.

CHAPTER 18

LITIGATION ISSUES

II. JURISDICTION

B. Federal Courts

1. Original Jurisdiction

The Fifth Circuit in *Barnes v. Levitt*[1] affirmed dismissal of an Equal Pay Act claim against the chairman of the U.S. Securities and Exchange Commission in his official capacity. The claim demanded in excess of $10,000. Under the Tucker Act,[2] the district court lacked jurisdiction of the case, which should have been filed in the Court of Federal Claims.[3]

Contrastingly, in a case involving questions of the proper scope of the jurisdiction of the U.S. Court of Federal Claims, that court held in *El-Sheikh v. United States*[4] that the plaintiff's action for back pay under the FLSA against an Air Force officers' club did not fall within the court's Tucker Act jurisdiction for two reasons. First, the Tucker Act grants the U.S. Court of Federal Claims jurisdiction over claims for money against only certain enumerated nonappropriated fund instrumentalities (NAFIs)[5] such as the Army and Air Force Exchange Service, Navy Ex-

---

[1] 118 F.3d 404 (5th Cir. 1997).

[2] 28 U.S.C. §1491.

[3] 118 F.3d at 410.

[4] 39 Fed. Cl. 1, 4 WH Cases2d 180 (1997).

[5] Nonappropriated funds are monies that have not been deposited into the U.S. Treasury and that are maintained independently of the public fisc. A case involving a successful FLSA suit against a NAFI is discussed in the main volume of the Treatise at p. 881.

changes, Marine Corps Exchanges, Coast Guard Exchanges, or Exchange Councils of the National Aeronautics and Space Administration. The court found that the NAFI in this case, however, was not among the enumerated NAFIs. Therefore, the court lacked jurisdiction over the action because the plaintiff's complaint did not state a claim against the United States. Second, the court stated that even if the officers' club was a NAFI specifically listed in the Tucker Act, the court's jurisdiction over those NAFIs is limited to claims alleging the existence of an express or implied contract. Because the plaintiff did not prove that he was employed under either an express or implied contract, the court did not have jurisdiction over the plaintiff's claim.

2. *Supplemental Jurisdiction*

Citing the Fifth Circuit's "general rule . . . to dismiss state claims when the federal claims to which they are pendent are dismissed," the court in *Roberts v. Willow Distributors, Inc.*,[6] declined to exercise supplemental jurisdiction over the plaintiff's state claims when the plaintiff's federal claims under the FLSA and Title VII were dismissed before trial.

In *Ansoumana v. Gristede's Operating Corp.*[7] a group of §216(b) FLSA paintiffs, who asserted supplemental claims under state law, sought certification under Rule 23 of a class of workers with state law claims similar to their own. The court found that the Rule 23(b) criteria were met, and certified the class, despite defendant's objections. Defendant argued that the class should not be extended to plaintiffs having no federal claim of their own, citing an Eighth Circuit case;[8] however, the court found that the class members would not be "parties" within the usual meaning of that phrase, and, noting that the Eighth Circuit case was not binding, the court declined to follow it. The attempt by defendants to extend the certification restrictions applicable to

---

[6]967 F. Supp. 904, 908 (N.D. Tex. 1997).

[7]201 F.R.D. 81 (S.D.N.Y. 2001).

[8]Fiedler v. Credit Acceptance Co., 188 F.3d 1031 (8th Cir. 1999).

diversity litigation to this case was rejected by the court as a "tortured" reading of the authority advanced by defendant to support its argument. In response to the argument that the court should exercise its discretion to refuse supplemental jurisdiction because there would be novel questions of state law presented, the court pointed out that the plaintiffs had agreed to waive the potential claims raising that issue. The court noted that any potential class member who did not agree with the proposed waiver could opt out of the class, thereby preserving his individual rights. Finally, the court rejected the defendant's argument that the jury would be confused by the presentation of state and federal claims in one proceeding. The court judged that there was little risk of jury confusion while, in contrast, separate trials in state and federal courts presented great potential for confusion and inconsistency.

III. VENUE

B. Removal From State to Federal Court

Most courts continue to hold that FLSA actions commenced in state court are removable to federal court. In *Bingham v. Newport News Shipbuilding*,[9] for example, a Virginia federal district court noted that the "overwhelming majority" of jurisdictions allow removal of FLSA claims from state court. The court further noted that while the general removal statute allows for such removal unless expressly prohibited by act of Congress, no such express rejection of removal of FLSA claims had occurred.

In *Smith v. K-Mart Corp.*,[10] the defendants removed a complaint alleging FLSA and state law claims to federal court, and plaintiff moved to remand the state claims to state court. The court denied the remand motion and found all of the claims arose out of the "same nucleus of operative facts," giving it

---

[9] 3 F. Supp. 2d 691, 4 WH Cases2d 1182 (E.D. Va. 1998).
[10] 899 F. Supp. 503, 3 WH Cases2d 156 (E.D. Wash. 1995).

supplemental jurisdiction of the state claims.[11] The court refused to decline to exercise jurisdiction over the state claims, finding that none of the four factors in Section 1367(a) of the venue statute,[12] which would justify declining to exercise jurisdiction, were satisfied.[13]

H & R Block, Ltd. v. Housden[14] was a case originally brought in state court by the company, H&R Block, against a group of former employees for violating a covenant not to compete. The defendant employees counter-claimed against both the plaintiff and four other parties, alleging FLSA violations. Two of the newly added parties removed the case to the federal court, and the original plaintiff consented to the removal. The former employees moved to remand on two grounds, and the court denied their motion. With respect to the first ground advanced by the employees for remand—namely, that FLSA cases are not removable from state to federal court on federal question grounds because Congress provided that such cases may be maintained in either state or federal courts—the district court reviewed the widely split opinions on this issue. It noted that its own circuit, the Fifth, had ruled that removal was not precluded in a case under the Age Discrimination in Employment Act (ADEA),[15] and it found that the better reasoned view would allow such removal. The employees argued as a second ground for remand that the new parties had no standing to remove the case, as only the original defendants (the employees) could remove. The cases cited by the employees in support of this view were found by the district court to have distinguished between original plaintiffs and new parties and to have precluded removal only by original parties. The court also cited Fifth Circuit authority for upholding the standing to remove of a counterclaim defendant who was not an original plaintiff,[16] and on this basis, it rejected the motion to remand.

---

[11] *Id.* at 507, 3 WH Cases2d 156.

[12] 28 U.S.C. §1367(a).

[13] 899 F. Supp. at 504, 3 WH Cases 2d 156.

[14] 24 F. Supp. 2d 703, 5 WH Cases2d 190 (E.D. Tex. 1998).

[15] 29 U.S.C. §§621–634.

[16] 24 F. Supp. 2d at 705, 5 WH Cases2d 190 (citing Baldwin v. Sears, Roebuck & Co., 667 F.2d 458, 461, 27 FEP Cases 1624 (5th Cir. 1982)).

In *Pauly v. Eagle Point Software Co., Inc.*,[17] the court held that FLSA actions cannot be removed to federal court, following the Eighth Circuit's decision in *Johnson v. Butler Bros.*[18] *Pauly* declined to follow the contrary result of *Waldermeyer v. ITT Consumer Financial*,[19] because it "contains no reference to the holding in *Johnson*, nor any discussion as to why the *Johnson* case is no longer good authority." The majority rule is to the contrary.[20]

A state wage claim may not be removed to federal court on the basis of preemption of state law by the FLSA.[21]

In *Mincy v. Staff Leasing, L.P.*,[22] a federal district court in Arizona held that once a federal court has obtained jurisdiction over a claim, there is no statutory authority to remand an FLSA overtime pay claim to state court along with causes of action for breach of express and implied contract, quantum meruit, and breach of covenant of good faith and fair dealing despite the fact that each of the state claims has a common nucleus of operative fact with the FLSA claim and each arises from the defendants' alleged failure to pay plaintiffs properly. The court analysed the 1990 amendment to 28 U.S.C. §1441(c), relating to removal, and the commentary on the new provision, relied on by plaintiffs in seeking remand, which it found did not "explain what was the legislative purpose" of the amendment but rather "raise[d] many questions."[23]

Lopez v. Wal-Mart Stores, Inc.,[24] held that because FLSA Section 16(b) provides that an action "may be maintained . . . in any Federal or State court of competent jurisdiction,"[25] removal to federal court is not permitted, because the statute "plainly

---

[17]958 F. Supp. 437, 3 WH Cases2d 1565 (N.D. Iowa. 1997).

[18]162 F.2d 87, 6 WH Cases2d 1015 (8th Cir. 1947).

[19]767 F. Supp. 989, 55 FEP Cases 1598 (E.D. Mo. 1991).

[20]Brown v. Luk Inc., 3 WH Cases2d 560 (N.D.N.Y. 1996); Barrios v. Hilton Title, 3 WH Cases2d 893 (E.D. La. 1996).

[21]Morales v. Showell Farms, 910 F. Supp 244, 3 WH Cases2d 85 (M.D.N.C. 1995).

[22]100 F. Supp. 2d 1050 (D. Ariz. 2000).

[23]*Id.* at 1057.

[24]111 F. Supp. 2d 865 (S.D. Tex. 2000). *See* Treatise at Chapter 18, pp. 1150–52, note 27, collecting cases.

[25]*Id.* at 866.

implies that the plaintiff is given a right to not only institute a suit in state court, but to keep it there until a final judgment is rendered, despite defendant's desire to remove it to a federal court."[26] The court noted the long-standing split of authority on the removal question, and that neither the Supreme Court nor the Fifth Circuit had ruled on the issue, and concluded that the better reasoned authority read the word "maintained" as precluding the removal.

Following the majority rule, in *Whitlock v. BMP America, Inc.*,[27] a federal district court in Oregon held that an FLSA claim and a state law claim for overtime pay are subject to removal to federal court under 28 U.S.C. §1441(a) because the federal courts have original jurisdiction over FLSA claims.

More recently in *Brown v. Sasser*,[28] *Valdivieso v. Atlas Air, Inc.*,[29] and *Roseman v. Best Buy Co. Inc.*,[30] the district courts denied plaintiffs' motions to remand to state court after removal by defendants of suits originally filed there. In addition to the common arguments to the effect that the words "may be maintained" in Section 216(b) carry the implication that plaintiffs are entitled to have the court respect their choice of forum, the plaintiffs in *Sasser* claimed that the defendants had acted sufficiently in the federal forum to be deemed to have waived their demand for remand. The court reviewed the defendant's conduct and found that merely having answered, asserted affirmative defenses, and engaged in discovery was not sufficient to demonstrate clearly an intent to waive the right to remove. The *Roseman* court provided a comprehensive review of decisions on the question of the propriety of remand both before and since the amendment of 28 U.S.C. §1441, and noted its agreement with the decision in *Cosme Nievas v. Deshler*,[31] which resolved the matter by denying remand in light of those amendments.

---

[26] *Id.* at 867.
[27] 1999 WL 1491474 (D. Or. 1999).
[28] 128 F. Supp. 2d 1345, 6 WH Cases2d 1457 (N.D. Ala. 2000).
[29] 128 F. Supp. 2d 1371, 6 WH Cases2d 1249 (S.D. Fla. 2001).
[30] 140 F. Supp. 2d 1332 (S.D. Ga. 2001).
[31] 786 F.2d 445 (1st Cir. 1986).

IV. PARTIES

A. Standing

In *Robertson v. Board of County Commissioners of County of Morgan*,[32] moreover, current and former employees of the sheriff had standing to sue a board of county commissioners for FLSA violations.[33] The court explained that because the board had authority to approve employees' salaries and because the board funded and approved the sheriff's budget, it had control over the elected sheriff.[34] The court also noted that the plaintiffs had been injured in fact by the failure of the board to pay them overtime, compensatory time, on-call time, and "waiting" time.[35] The plaintiffs thus had standing to sue the board for violations related to their compensation.[36]

A prisoner plaintiff did not have standing to challenge a reduction of wages for mental health patients working at a state hospital because prisoners employed by their correctional authorities are not covered as employees under the FLSA and cannot bring an action for compensation under the Act.[37] "To qualify as an employee under the statute, a prisoner must show that he freely contracted with a non-prison employer to sell his labor."[38] Because the prisoner did not allege that he was employed in such capacity, he lacked standing under the FLSA.[39]

---

[32]985 F. Supp. 980, 4 WH Cases2d 443 (D. Colo. 1997), *aff'd*, 166 F.3d 1222 (10th Cir. 1999) (finding that the board of county commissioners' power to approve and fund the sheriff's budget provided the board with practical and effective control over the sheriff's personnel actions and thus provided the sheriff's office's employees with standing to sue the board in suits pertaining to personnel matters).

[33]*Id.* at 984–85, 4 WH Cases2d 443.

[34]*Id.* at 983, 4 WH Cases2d 443.

[35]*Id.*, 4 WH Cases2d 443.

[36]*Id.*

[37]Silo v. U.S. Dep't of Labor, 4 WH Cases2d 415 (D.D.C. 1997). *See* Chapter 3, Coverage, §II.I. [The Employer-Employee Relationship; Prison Labor] for a discussion of the coverage issue.

[38]*Silo*, 4 WH Cases2d 415.

[39]*Id.*

In *Bureerong v. Uvawas*[40] a federal district court held that garment worker employees did not have a private right of action to enforce Section 215(a)(5) of the FLSA,[41] which provides that it is unlawful to violate any regulation or order pursuant to Section 211(d).[42] Section 211(d) empowers the Secretary of Labor to promulgate regulations related to industrial homework, and, in this case, the plaintiffs asserted that the defendants had violated an applicable regulation.[43] The court noted Section 215(a)(5)'s silence as to whether a litigant can sue under the provision, whereas Sections 216 and 217 recognize several rights of action.[44] The court said that because it found no evidence of congressional intent to create a private right of action to enforce Section 215(a)(5), it was unwilling to imply a right and dismissed plaintiffs' suit with respect to that section.[45]

1. Actions by Unions

In *DeBraska v. Milwaukee*,[46] a Wisconsin federal district court granted the defendants' motion to dismiss the Milwaukee Police Association, a union which represented Milwaukee police officers, as a plaintiff. Relying on Section 216(b) of the FLSA, the court concluded that the union lacked standing. The court rejected the union's argument that it was suing not in its representative capacity but rather as a party to the collective bargaining agreement at issue in the case. In addition, the court rejected the union's argument that Section 7(o), which provides that a public agency's ability to provide compensatory time is contingent upon the existence of a provision in a collective bargaining agreement, confers standing upon a union. Although agreeing that Section 7(o) expands the role of unions in ensuring that public employers comply with the FLSA, the court held that this provision did not grant the union standing.

---

[40] 922 F. Supp. 1450, 3 WH Cases2d 383 (C.D. Cal. 1996).
[41] *Id.* at 1473, 3 WH Cases2d 383.
[42] *Id.* at 1471, 3 WH Cases2d 383.
[43] *Id.*, 3 WH Cases2d 383.
[44] *Id.* at 1472, 3 WH Cases2d 383.
[45] *Id.* at 1472–73, 3 WH Cases2d 383.
[46] 11 F. Supp. 2d 1020, 4 WH Cases2d 1377 (E.D. Wis. 1998).

In *UFCW Union, Local 1564 v. Albertson's, Inc.*,[47] the Tenth Circuit reversed the decision of the district court in a declaratory judgment suit and held that a labor union cannot sue for declaratory relief, injunctive relief, or damages on behalf of its members because the FLSA does not permit suits for injunctive relief by private parties or representative actions by labor organizations.

A contrary and unusual decision was reached in *Local 1035, International Brotherhood of Teamsters v. Pepsi-Cola Allied Bottlers, Inc.*[48] Applying general principles of Declaratory Judgment Act jurisprudence and traditional principles of standing, and without consideration of the FLSA's failure to give a right to seek injunctive relief to private wage plainiffs, a federal district court in Connecticut denied the defendant's motion to dismiss and held that a union had associational standing to bring state law overtime pay claims and FLSA claims because the court could order equitable relief designed to enjoin the defendants from continuing illegal practices that might impact members of the union.

D. Opt-In Procedures

Consistent with prevailing law, the district court in *Kelley v. SBC, Inc.*,[49] held that the opt-in provision of the FLSA was not a bar to class certification under Fed. R. Civ. P. 23 of separate pendent state law claims which the employee-plaintiffs had joined with their FLSA overtime claims.

In *Ansoumana v. Gristede's Operating Corp.*[50] a group of Section 216(b) FLSA paintiffs, who asserted supplemental claims under state law, sought certification under Rule 23 of a class of workers with state law claims similar to their own. The court

---

[47]207 F.3d 1193, 5 WH Cases2d 1705 (10th Cir. 2000) (collecting cases and noting that the FLSA does not bar unions from providing organizational and/or financial support to the legal efforts of its members).

[48]83 F. Supp. 2d 301 (D. Conn. 1999).

[49]No 97-CV-2729 CW, 1998 WL 928302, 5 WH Cases2d 16 (N.D. Cal. Nov. 13, 1998).

[50]201 F.R.D. 81 (S.D.N.Y. 2001).

found that the Rule 23(b) criteria were met, and certified the class, despite defendant's objections. Defendant argued that the class should not be extended to plaintiffs having no federal claim of their own, citing an Eighth Circuit case;[51] however, the court found that the class members would not be "parties" within the usual meaning of that phrase and, noting that as the Eighth Circuit case was not binding, the court declined to follow it. The attempt by defendants to extend the certification restrictions applicable to diversity litigation to this case was rejected by the court as a "tortured" reading of the authority advanced by defendant to support its argument. In response to the argument that the court should exercise its discretion to refuse supplemental jurisdiction because there would be novel questions of state law presented, the court pointed out that the plaintiffs had agreed to waive the potential claims raising that issue. The court noted that any potential class member who did not agree with the proposed waiver could opt out of the class, thereby preserving his individual rights. Finally, the court rejected the defendant's argument that the jury would be confused by the presentation of state and federal claims in one proceeding. The court judged that there was little risk of jury confusion while, in contrast, separate trials in state and federal courts presented great potential for confusion and inconsistency.

In a case where the court has already approved of notice being sent to persons who are or were employees "within the last three years," a person does not fail to be "similarly situated" to the named plaintiff for purposes of opting in merely because that person's employment commenced after the named plaintiff's employment terminated.[52]

---

[51]Fiedler v. Credit Acceptance Co., 188 F.3d 1031 (8th Cir. 1999).

[52]Jackson v. Go-Tane Servs., Inc., 2001 U.S. Dist. LEXIS 10240 (N.D. Ill. 2001).

1. Comparison With the Procedural Requirements of Rule 23 of the Federal Rules of Civil Procedure

Courts continue to hold that the provisions of Rule 23 are inapplicable to any action brought pursuant to Section 16(b) of the FLSA.[53]

2. Discovery of Names and Addresses of Similarly Potential Plaintiffs

In *Bayles v. American Medical Response of Colorado, Inc.*,[54] the court highlighted four approaches that have been taken in defining "similarly situated" plaintiffs under Section 16(b) of the Act. The first approach considers plaintiffs to be similarly situated if they meet the commonality and typicality requirements of Rule 23(a), Federal Rule of Civil Procedure. Second, class members are similarly situated if they meet all the requirements of Rule 23 that do not conflict with Section 16(b) requirements. Third, the class members are similarly situated if they meet all the requirements for a "spurious" class under pre-1996 Rule 23. Finally, plaintiffs are similarly situated if they fall within the plain meaning of the term in light of the purposes of a collective action.[55]

The court in *Bayles* rejected the first approach outright, insisting that a more stringent test is appropriate for Section 16(b).[56] As to the second approach, which looks at all the Rule 23 requirements, the court explained that this approach was also wrong because there is no valid explanation for using modern Rule 23 standards. Next, the court analyzed the pre-1966 spurious class action approach, but concluded that Congress, in 1938,

---

[53]Alix v. Shoney's, 3 WH Cases2d 1532 (E.D. La. 1997); Wyatt v. Pride Offshore Inc., 3 WH Cases2d 892 (E.D. La. 1996); Zelaya v. J.M. Macias Inc., 175 F.R.D. 625, 4 WH Cases2d 89 (E.D.N.C. 1997).

[54]950 F. Supp. 1053, 3 WH Cases2d 1317 (1996), *on reconsideration*, 962 F. Supp. 1346, 3 WH Cases2d 1567 (D. Colo. 1997).

[55]*Id.* at 1058, 3 WH Cases2d 1317.

[56]*Id.* at 1059–60, 3 WH Cases2d 1317.

must have intentionally constructed Rule 23(a) differently from the newly enacted Section 16; thus, Rule 23, "regardless of vintage," should not even be considered in defining "similarly situated."[57]

The court then considered the fourth, ad hoc, approach, which it ultimately supported.[58] The ad hoc approach contemplates whether certification serves the purposes, and provides the benefits, of a collective action under Section 16(b). It balances the benefits against prejudice to the defendants and any judicial inefficiencies that may result from allowing the plaintiffs to proceed collectively.[59] The court explained that despite the unpredictability of an ad hoc approach, it found no basis for using the Rule 23 framework in analyzing Section 16(b).[60]

In *McNeil v. District of Columbia*,[61] the plaintiffs, guards employed by the Department of Corrections, sought to require the defendant to produce in discovery the names and addresses of employees who might be similarly situated, relying on *Hoffmann-LaRoche v. Sperling*.[62] The defendants contended that *Hoffmann* applied only to Rule 23 actions, not to opt-in actions under the FLSA. The court, noting that *Hoffmann* had been brought under ADEA, the enforcement of which is closely related to FLSA enforcement, pointed out that "[i]f the Supreme Court held that a court in an ADEA action could assist in the notification of potential claimants, it would have to follow that it can do so in an FLSA action itself,"[63] and that the benefits available through such notice were the same, whether a Rule 23 or an opt-in action was involved. Accordingly, the court granted the motion.

In *Miklos v. Golman-Hayden Companies, Inc.*,[64] plaintiff moved, without having sought class certification, for discovery of the names and addresses of all "logistics coordinators" at defendant's

---

[57] *Id.* at 1066, 3 WH Cases2d 1317.
[58] *Id.* at 1066–67, 3 WH Cases2d 1317.
[59] *Id.*, 3 WH Cases2d 1317.
[60] *Id.* at 1067, 3 WH Cases2d 1317.
[61] No. CIV. A. 98-3142 HHKJM, 1999 WL 571004 (D.D.C. Aug. 5, 1999).
[62] 493 U.S. 165 (1989).
[63] 1999 WL 571004, at *1.
[64] 2000 WL 1617969 (S.D. Ohio 2000).

15 locations throughout the United States. The court determined that the job description of a logistics coordinator generally was consistent from one office to another and that all logistic coordinators seemed to perform the same job facilitating the transportation of shipments. The court allowed the discovery.

3. *Judicial Supervision of Notice, Discovery, and Class Certification*

The ever-growing number of cases raising issues concerning the certification of a "class" of individuals, for purposes of discovery, for discovery and trial, or conditionally, makes it possible to discern some apparent trends in judicial approaches to these matters. First, similar factual circumstances seem to make a case for certification more easily than a similar legal issue surrounded by potentially divergent factual conditions. Secondly, a disproportion between the variety of experience among the named plaintiffs (or purported representatives) and the expected variety in the class sought to be represented may defeat a certification request. Third, very large potential classes may be subjected to greater scrutiny, or require a higher degree of "similarity" due to manageability problems than more modest potential classes. Fourth, large numbers of named or opt-in plaintiffs appearing before the notice is sought lends weight to the request for certification. The recent cases are reviewed in light of these observations.

In addition to the many decisions discussed below, we note two significant appellate opinions in ADEA collective actions brought pursuant to 29 U.S.C. §216(b): *Thiessen v. General Electric Capital Corp.*[65] *("Thiessen III")* and *Hipp v. Liberty National Insurance Co.*[66] These cases will no doubt be cited widely on FLSA collective action issues. *Thiessen III* explicitly adopts the two-step approach described in *Mooney v. Aramco Services, Inc.*[67] Significantly, *Thiessen III* reversed the trial court's decertification order

---

[65] 267 F.3d 1095 (10th Cir. 2001).
[66] 252 F.3d 1208 (11th Cir. 2001).
[67] 54 F.3d 1207, 68 FEP Cases 421 (5th Cir. 1995).

at *Mooney*'s step two (pre-trial). *Hipp* also endorsed *Mooney* but counseled trial courts that they were at liberty to use other approaches so long as they exercised sound discretion. *Hipp* affirmed both the trial court's initial certification of the opt-in ADEA class and its refusal to decertify the class at trial.

a. Similarity of Facts Alleged [New Topic]

At the notice stage of an FLSA suit against a former employer for unpaid overtime, the plaintiffs seeking to discover similarly situated employees need only show a similarity, and not an identity, of wage and pay provisions in order to have notice of their suit sent to current or former employees of that employer.[68] In *Harrison,* former management assistants of the employer were entitled to have notice of their suit sent to current and former management assistants of that company where declarations of original and opt-in plaintiffs showed that they performed the same tasks, under the same conditions and with the same pay.[69] The court rejected the company's argument that management assistants performed too wide and varied a range of tasks to be considered a class of similarly situated employees.[70]

In *Realite v. Ark Restaurants Corp.,*[71] a New York federal district court authorized a class notice in an FLSA action, finding that the plaintiffs met the burden of demonstrating that potential class members were "similarly situated." The plaintiffs were current and former hourly paid, nonmanagerial employees of 15 restaurants owned and/or managed by the defendant in the New York City metropolitan area. The restaurants, which were not theme restaurants, had different names, menus, and atmospheres. The plaintiffs, some of whom had worked at more than one of the restaurants, held a variety of positions, including

---

[68]Harrison v. Enterprise Rent-A-Car Co., 4 WH Cases2d 1339 (M.D. Fla. 1998). *See also* Realite v. Ark Restaurants Corp., 7 F. Supp. 2d 303, 4 WH Cases2d 1207 (S.D.N.Y. 1998) (modest showing of similarity sufficient at discovery stage).

[69]4 WH Cases2d at 1341.

[70]*Id.*

[71]7 F. Supp. 2d 303, 4 WH Cases2d 1207. *See also Harrison,* 4 WH Cases2d 1339 (modest showing of similarity sufficient at discovery stage).

waiter, porter, dishwasher, cook, backwaiter, bartender, runner, pizza maker, busboy, and security guard. The plaintiffs alleged that a scheme to avoid paying minimum wage and overtime was undertaken at all 15 restaurants with the knowledge and approval of the corporate parent and that the parent controlled the employment practices at each of the 15 restaurants. The court noted that at the preliminary notice stage, the burden in demonstrating that potential class members are similarly situated can be met by "making a modest factual showing sufficient to demonstrate that they and potential plaintiffs together were victims of a common policy or plan that violated the law." Therefore, the court approved the class definition proposed by the plaintiffs for notice purposes.

The court ruled that the plaintiffs were entitled to have notice of their FLSA action sent to all hourly paid, nonmanagerial employees who worked at any of the 15 restaurants during the past 6 years and who (1) worked overtime, (2) did not receive minimum cash wages for all hours worked, (3) did not have working time properly recorded, (4) had to purchase or maintain uniforms, (5) did not receive agreed-upon vacation time, (6) were not allowed meal breaks, or (7) were not informed about tip credit rules or were required to pool tips with managerial or nonservice employees. The court found that the plaintiffs had established enough of a factual nexus between their situation and those of other hourly paid workers to demonstrate that they were similarly situated. The court, however, emphasized that it was certifying the proposed class for notice and discovery purposes only.

As in *Realite*, above, in *Edelen v. Shoney's, Inc.*,[72] the court made a "preliminary" decision that the members of the class were situated similarly to the plaintiffs. It considered whether notice should be sent to a group of managers and assistant managers where the original plaintiffs claimed that the defendant had intentionally treated all managerial employees as

---

[72]4 WH Cases2d 980 (M.D. Tenn. 1998). *See also* Hoffman v. Sbarro, Inc., 982 F. Supp. 249, 261–62, 4 WH Cases2d 335 (S.D.N.Y. 1997) (notice permitted though claims not necessarily meritorious).

hourly workers, rather than as salaried, and therefore owed them unpaid overtime. The court stated,

> Although it is clear that a court may supervise notice to potential class members, the lower courts have not agreed as to the factual showing that must be made by a plaintiff to show who is "similarly situated" at the notice stage. Some courts hold that a plaintiff can demonstrate that potential class members are "similarly situated," for purposes of receiving notice, based solely upon allegations in a complaint of class-wide illegal practices.[73] Other courts hold that a plaintiff meets this burden by demonstrating some factual support for the allegations before issuance of notices.[74] This Court finds it unnecessary to adopt either of the competing standards because the Plaintiffs have made a sufficient showing under either standard that the individuals to whom they seek to send notice of this lawsuit are "similarly situated" to them to warrant the issuance of court-supervised notice. The Court is not holding at this time, however, that all members of the potential class who will be sent notices are, in fact, similarly situated to Plaintiffs.[75]

In *Thiebes v. Wal-Mart Stores, Inc.*,[76] a federal district court in Oregon held that in order to have the case certified as a collective action for notice and discovery purposes, the plaintiffs need only show some factual nexus that they and the putative class were victims of a common policy or plan that violated the FLSA. In this case, the employees provided evidence that hourly employees were "working off the clock" in some 23 Wal-Mart stores with the acquiescence of management. Although the court allowed the case to proceed as a collective action for notice and discovery, the court deferred ruling on whether the plaintiffs and potential opt-in plaintiffs were similarly situated under the FLSA and on the plaintiffs' request to certify a Rule 23 class

---

[73] 4 WH Cases2d at 981 (citing Allen v. Marshall Field & Co., 93 F.R.D. 438, 442–45 (N.D. Ill. 1982)). Plaintiffs claimed that the defendant intentionally treated them as hourly workers, rather than salaried management employees, and therefore owed them unpaid wages and overtime compensation and other damages.

[74] *Id.* (citing Jackson v. New York Tel. Co., 163 F.R.D. 429, 431 (S.D.N.Y. 1995)).

[75] *Id.*

[76] 1999 WL 1081357 (D. Or. 1999).

under a pendent state law overtime claim based on the same facts until after the collective action notice procedure was concluded.

In *Kane v. Gage Merchandising Services,*[77] the district court explicitly adopted the two-step approach from *Mooney v. Aramco Services Co.*[78] The named plaintiff was a crew coordinator who supervised employees refurbishing interiors of commercial retail stores. Plaintiff relied on an affidavit which identified 51 potential class members who allegedly were not properly paid. Additionally, plaintiff provided an affidavit asserting that a manager had informed the crew coordinators that they would never be paid overtime. Applying the "lenient" standard, the court determined that this was sufficient evidence of similarly situated employees and ordered the production of names and addresses of crew coordinators as well as notice.

In *Krieg v. Pell's Inc.,*[79] the district court granted plaintiff's notice motion. The named plaintiff, a manager at one of the defendant's 140 shoe repair stores, alleged that defendant had failed to pay him and other similarly situated managers overtime pay. In support of his motion, plaintiff submitted the affidavit of a former payroll administrator reflecting that the majority of store managers were paid on a salary basis, and were not paid overtime. The evidence of this one employee, given his position, was sufficient for the court to order notice to all store managers employed by defendant during the same time period as plaintiff, allowing 120 days to file opt-in notices. The court also rejected the defendant's request to include an admonition in the notice that opt-in plaintiffs were at risk of costs being imposed.

Garza v. Chicago Transit Authority[80] further illustrates the lenient standard for authorizing class notice under Section 216(b). Here the court granted the plaintiffs' motion for notice to similarly situated rail employees who had been denied compensation for required training classes in addition to their 40-hour workweeks. The court rejected the transit authority's

---

[77]138 F. Supp. 2d 212 (D. Mass. 2001).

[78]54 F.3d 1207, 1213–14 (5th Cir. 1995); *see* Treatise p. 1168, note 103.

[79]2001 WL 548394 (S.D. Ind. 2001).

[80]2001 WL 503036 (N.D. Ill. 2001).

argument that a Rule 23 analysis was required and held that the "similarly situated" standard under Section 216(b) was met with "a modest factual showing sufficient to demonstrate the [plaintiffs] and potential plaintiffs together were victims of a common policy or plan that violated the law."[81] Because of the common treatment they received in that respect, potential plaintiffs were "similarly situated" for purposes of notice although there were many differences in their circumstances, including that they had different jobs, earned different amounts and received different training. *Garza* mandated notice to potential claimants for the full three-year limitations period and ordered the employer to post the notice at Chicago Transit Authority terminals (in addition to mailing the notice to former employees). The court did revise the plaintiffs' proposed notice to include the statement: "[I]f the Court rules in favor of CTA, you will be entitled to no relief if you join this action."

An Oregon district court granted a motion to allow notice to potential class members in *Ballaris v. Wacker Silttronic Corp.*[82] The court found the detailed allegations of the complaint, along with two affidavits, to be sufficient to meet the "less stringent" and "modest factual showing" standards. The two-step approach was explicitly adopted, ordering a collective action only for notice to and discovery concerning employees required to change into uniforms and/or "bunny suits" for work in "clean rooms." A further ruling on whether such employees were "in fact, similarly situated" was deferred to the completion of discovery.

Despite the fact that more than 16,000 employees in several states were to be included, the court in *Trotter v. Perdue Farms, Inc.*[83] ordered FLSA collective action notice to all present and former non-exempt employees of defendant's chicken processing plants. The court also certified related ERISA and state wage law class claims, where plaintiffs contended (and defendants did not deny) that no payment was made for donning and doffing protective equipment required for the work by OSHA rules.

---

[81] 7 F. Supp. 2d 303, 306 (S.D.N.Y. 1998) (quoting Realite v. Arkansas Rests. Corp.).

[82] 2001 U.S. Dist LEXIS 13354, 144 Lab. Cas. (CCH) ¶34,351 (D. Or. 2001).

[83] 2001 U.S. Dist. LEXIS 13212, 144 Lab. Cas. (CCH) ¶34,364 (D. Del. 2001).

In *Miklos v. Golman-Hayden Companies, Inc.,*[84] plaintiff moved, without having sought class certification, for discovery of the names and addresses of all "logistics coordinators" at defendant's 15 locations throughout the United States. The court determined that the job description of a logistics coordinator generally was consistent from one office to another and that all logistic coordinators seemed to perform the same job facilitating the transportation of shipments. The court allowed the discovery.

In *Rodolico v. Unisys Corp.,*[85] an action under state law and the ADEA, after finding that the state law claims could be maintained as a Rule 23 class action, the court found that for the liability phase of the ADEA case, an opt-in collective action was authorized, despite the claims of the defendant that separate defenses were to be advanced as to each defendant and that different decision-makers were involved. The court stated that "[w]eighing very strongly in favor of a collective action is the fact that the challenged employment practice, termination, is the same for each of the members,"[86] and noted that all were terminated on the same date, worked at the same plant, and had the same basic job. The court also found that the extent to which common evidence would be relied upon was significant. Of the 173 potentially in the class, 120 had filed opt-in notices without there having been any judicially supervised notice.

b. Similarity of Legal Issues Alleged [New Topic]

In *Morisky v. Public Serivce & Gas Co.,*[87] a federal district court in New Jersey refused to certify a collective action under the FLSA or a Rule 23 class action under the New Jersey Wage and Hour Law by employees at a nuclear generating plant who alleged that they had been misclassified as exempt administra-

---

[84] 2000 WL 1617969 (S.D. Ohio 2000).

[85] 199 F.R.D. 468 (E.D.N.Y. 2001).

[86] *Id.* at 483.

[87] 111 F. Supp. 2d 493 (D.N.J. 2000) (distinguishing age discrimination certification matters from cases where a collective action would only be appropriate where class members perform work at least somewhat similar to that of the original plantiffs).

tive employees. The court used a heightened scrutiny of the collective action evidence because discovery in the case had closed prior to the motion's being filed. The court held that it would have to conduct an individualized determination of each employee's job responsibilities to determine whether a statutory exemption applied. The court noted that the plaintiffs failed to provide any proof that the representative plaintiffs' job duties were similar to those of the putative class which consisted of employees in a wide variety of job titles.

In *Pfaahler v. Consulations for Architects, Inc.*,[88] the plaintiffs moved for conditional certification of a class consisting of persons classified as independent contractors by the employer. The federal district court in Illinois held that certification of a collective action under the FLSA is inappropriate when the court would be required to make a "fact-intensive, individual determination of the nature of each potential claimant's employment relationship" to determine if the claimant is an employee or an independent contractor, where the plaintiff failed to show that the work of the other potential opt-in plaintiff was similar to the work he himself performed.

In *Jackson v. Go-Tane Services, Inc.*,[89] a federal district court in Illinois held that a collective action was appropriately certified for notice purposes to include the representative plaintiff who worked as a "manager" at a car wash and other managers who worked for the same employer at gas stations and convenience stores. The exemption at issue was the executive exemption. The court also denied the defendant's request that notice to potential opt-in plaintiffs include a provision warning those opting in that they might have to pay the defendant's costs. The court noted that Section 16(b) specifically refers to attorneys' fees awards only as to prevailing plaintiffs and is silent on defense costs, and it concluded that a provision in the notice might unreasonably chill participation.

---

[88]2000 WL 198888 (N.D. Ill. 2000).

[89]2000 U.S. Dist. LEXIS 12627, 6 WH Cases2d 679 (N.D. Ill. 2000).

c. Proportionality Between Representative and To-Be-Represented Classes [New Topic]

Following prevailing law, a federal district court in Florida held, in *Baum v. Shoney's, Inc.*,[90] that the plaintiffs who were seeking notification of a potential class were "similarly situated," that FLSA violations had occurred outside the country in which the plaintiffs worked, or that the potential class members were the victims of a single decision, policy, or plan. The plaintiffs' only evidence of commonality consisted of five nearly identical affidavits, all from employees who worked in restaurants in a single country.

In *Harper v. Lovett's Buffet, Inc.*,[91] a federal district court again denied a motion for conditional class certification for past and current employees of defendant's chain of restaurants, who brought minimum wage and overtime claims alleging eight types of violations, including improper timekeeping, pay rate, and tip practices, but it granted a conditional class certification limited to employees at the single restaurant at which all the named plaintiffs worked or had worked for the three-year period in question. Although the plaintiffs alleged that a corporate management incentive plan encouraged violations, they offered no proof of existence or effect of such a plan. The court held that the evidence relating to the one restaurant was insufficient to establish a class of similarly situated individuals among the large number of restaurants, absent proof of any corporate policy connecting them in such a way as would encourage violations.

In *Santelices v. Cable Wiring*,[92] the district court overruled the plaintiff's objection to the magistrate's denial of his notice motion. The plaintiff had submitted only his own affidavit to support his motion. The court determined that the affidavit failed to meet the evidentiary burden required to establish the existence of similarly situated employees who want to opt in.

---

[90]No. 98-423-CV-ORL-19B, 1998 WL 968390, 5 WH Cases2d 127 (M.D. Fla. Dec. 3, 1998).

[91]185 F.R.D. 358 (M.D. Ala. 1999).

[92]6 WH Cases2d 1864 (S.D. Fla. 2001).

In *Camper v. Home Quality Management, Inc.*,[93] the court addressed the threshold issue of whether a sufficient preliminary factual showing had been made for notice. The 11 plaintiffs presented evidence that the company had a corporate policy of automatically deducting 30 minutes for meal breaks, although some employees worked during the meal break time and employees also did unpaid work prior to clocking in. These allegations were supported by deposition and declarant testimony. The court noted that factual disputes would not negate the appropriateness of notice. The court granted plaintiffs' motion, but limited it to one facility rather than the company's 47 nursing home facilities. The evidence of employer knowledge of unpaid work was limited to supervisors at one facility being aware of employees working off the clock.

d. Very Large Potential Classes [New Topic]

In an action by assistant managers in a motel chain, the court adopted the recommendation of the magistrate and declined to authorize the sending of notice to a proposed class of between 1,000 and 1,500 present and former assistant managers at 775 nationwide properties, even though the plaintiffs alleged that all the assistant managers were employed by the same corporate entity pursuant to similar managerial plan. The magistrate had noted that the assistant managers work in five different regions, in at least 20 states, and at a minimum of 39 different properties that vary widely in numerous ways, that the amount of overtime worked varies between assistant managers, and that the alleged illegal overtime plan is not necessarily carried out through central management. The court was of the view that the discrepancies between managers' employment circumstances and the significant manageability problems inherent in trial of 1,000-plus individuals demonstrated the inappropriateness of proceeding as class, and so denied class certification.[94]

---

[93]200 F.R.D. 516 (D. Md. 2000).

[94]Ray v. Motel 6 Operating, Ltd. P'ship, 4 WH Cases2d 573 (D. Minn. 1996).

Despite the fact that more than 16,000 employees in several states were to be included, the court in *Trotter v. Perdue Farms, Inc.*[95] ordered FLSA collective action notice to all present and former non-exempt employees of defendant's chicken processing plants. The court also certified related ERISA and state wage law class claims, where plaintiffs contended (and defendants did not deny) that no payment was made for donning and doffing protective equipment required for the work by OSHA rules.

e. Large Numbers of Named or Opt-In Plaintiffs [New Topic]

In *De Asencio v. Tyson Foods, Inc.*,[96] the district court granted plaintiffs' notice motion. Poultry processors asserted that they had not been paid for time spent when the production line was not working, time spent putting on safety equipment (boots, coveralls and gloves), time spent reporting to group leaders, and time spent cleaning out lockers. Plaintiffs supported the motion with four declarations showing a consistent pattern of unpaid work performed when the production lines were not in operation. Defendant submitted detailed declarations purporting to show that potential plaintiffs were not similarly situated to the representative plaintiffs. However, given the plaintiffs' declarations and the 94 opt-in forms already filed, plaintiffs had advanced sufficient evidence to meet their low burden for facilitated notice.

In *Volek v. Hannan*,[97] the district court granted plaintiff's motion pursuant to 29 USC §216(b). Sixty-three former warehouse workers from the same facility had filed opt-in notices with supporting affidavits alleging that they had worked in excess of 40 hours per week but were not paid overtime wages and sought identical relief. The court considered evidence that plaintiffs may have worked for two separate but related entities. The court determined that this might be germane to a later stage of litigation, but did not have an impact on class certification.

---

[95] 2001 U.S. Dist. LEXIS 13212, 144 Lab. Cas. (CCH) ¶34,364 (D. Del. 2001).
[96] 130 F. Supp. 2d 660, 6 WH Cases2d 1330 (E.D. Pa. 2001).
[97] 2000 WL 33370239 (W.D. Pa. 2000).

In *Rodolico v. Unisys Corp.*,[98] an action under state law and the ADEA, after finding that the state law claims could be maintained as a Rule 23 class action, the court found that for the liability phase of the ADEA case an opt-in collective action was authorized, despite the claims of the defendant that separate defenses were to be advanced as to each defendant and that different decision-makers were involved. The court stated that "[w]eighing very strongly in favor of a collective action is the fact that the challenged employment practice, termination, is the same for each of the members,"[99] and noted that all were terminated on the same date, worked at the same plant, and had the same basic job. The court also found that the extent to which common evidence would be relied upon was significant. Of the 173 potentially in the class, 120 had filed opt-in notices without there having been any judicially supervised notice.

f. Other Issues [New Topic]

In *Yates v. Wal-Mart Stores, Inc.*,[100] a federal district court in Colorado followed the recommendation of the magistrate and allowed the pharmacists claiming unpaid overtime wages to proceed with a class action, even though they had failed to opt in to a previously filed class action then pending in the same district court on the same issue. The court reasoned that allowing the second class action would promote judicial economy, since otherwise the plaintiffs would sue individually on their separate claims. The court stated that "[u]nlike Rule 23, the opt-in provision of section [216] provides for no legal effect on those parties who choose not to participate."[101]

Does I thru XXII v. Advanced Textile Corp.,[102] was a suit initiated on behalf of 23 unnamed plaintiffs who were residents of China recruited to work on Saipan. They allegedly had sworn never to complain about their treatment, on pain of immediate return to

[98] 199 F.R.D. 468 (E.D.N.Y. 2001).
[99] *Id.* at 483.
[100] 58 F. Supp. 2d 1217, 5 WH Cases2d 892 (D. Colo. 1999).
[101] *Id*, 5 WH Cases2d at 893.
[102] 214 F. 3d 1058, 6 WH Cases2d 97 (9th Cir. 2000).

China. The district court found that the alleged risks to the plaintiffs "did not outweigh 'the prejudicial effect on defendants' ability to investigate and defend against claims by unnamed plaintiffs,' and the public's interest in a 'case [of] widespread implications.'"[103] It dismissed the plaintiffs' complaint but stayed final action so that the plaintiffs might amend to include the actual names of the plaintiffs. The Ninth Circuit reversed, holding that the decision constituted an appealable collateral order final in effect, and that in the case before it, the collective action under the FLSA could proceed without the plaintiffs identifying themselves. While noting that the "[p}laintiffs' use of fictitious names runs afoul of the public's common law right of access to judicial proceedings,"[104] the appellate court recognized that parties could "proceed anonymously when special circumstances justify secrecy,"[105] and reversed the lower court for abuse of discretion.[106] It observed that in weighing the interests of the respective parties in concealment versus disclosure, the factors to be weighed included: (1) the severity of the threatened harm; (2) the reasonableness of the anonymous party's fears; and (3) the anonymous party's vulnerability to retaliation.[107] The court further opined that the trial court must "determine the precise prejudice at each stage of the proceedings to the opposing party, and whether proceedings may be structured so as to mitigate that prejudice. Finally, the [trial] court must decide whether the public's interest in the case would be best served by requiring that the litigants reveal their identities."[108]

In *Gordon v. Trace Ambulance, Inc.*,[109] the district court granted the defense motion to dismiss, to the extent of striking the Section 216(b) class allegations, on the basis that in the

[103] *Id.*, 6 WH Cases2d at 100.
[104] *Id.*, 6 WH Cases2d at 103. *See also* Nixon v. Warner Communications, Inc., 435 U.S. 589, 598–99 (1978).
[105] 214 F.3d at 1068, 6 WH Cases2d 97.
[106] *Id.*
[107] 214 F.3d 1058, 6 WH Cases2d at 104.
[108] *Id.*
[109] 2001 U.S. Dist. LEXIS 3140, 143 Lab. Cas. ¶34,230 (N.D. Ill. 2001).

13 months since the filing of the complaint no other written consent to join forms had been filed with the court.

4. Decertification of Certified or Provisionally Certified Class [New Section]

In *Thiessen v. General Electric Capital Corp.*[110] *(Thiessen III),* an ADEA case, the court of appeals reversed the trial court's decertification order for abuse of discretion. It reviewed the three factors identified by the district court as bearing on the question and determined that the district court's failure to "recognize the pattern-or-practice nature of the class claim . . . adversely impacted its 'similarly situated' analysis" and resulted in an abuse of discretion.[111]

In another ADEA case, *Hipp v. Liberty National Insurance Co.,*[112] the court of appeals affirmed both the trial court's initial certification of the opt-in ADEA class and its refusal to decertify the class for trial.

In *Moss v. Crawford & Co.,*[113] the district court addressed the defendant's motion to decertify a Section 216(b) class of monitors, adjusters, and invoice receivers who had worked on the Exxon Valdez oil spill clean-up. Seventy-four individuals had opted in and twenty-four had been deposed. Defendant's motion to decertify the class after discovery was denied. The court noted that when seeking to decertify a class, it could look at disparate factual and employment settings of individual plaintiffs, various defenses available which would appear to be individual to each plaintiff, as well as fairness and procedural considerations. In this case, the court determined that the differences which may have existed in plaintiffs' employment duties, location, and pay did not undermine the purpose of collective actions under Section 216(b). Further, the statute of limitation defenses would apply to all members of the class and

[110] 267 F.3d 1095 (10th Cir. 2001).
[111] *Id.* at 1105.
[112] 252 F.3d 1208 (11th Cir. 2001).
[113] 201 F.R.D. 398 (W.D. Pa. 2001).

it would be a more cost-effective use of the court's resources to try the case both as to the exemption and statute of limitations issues as a collective action.

The decision in *Cowan v. Treetop Enterprises, Inc.*[114] shows that, in earlier proceedings, the court had denied a motion for class decertification after receiving testimony from seventeen members of the provisionally certified class (unit managers), several district managers, one division manager and other personnel.

In *Cardenas v. Benter Farms,*[115] the plaintiff agricultural workers, who had sued the couple who owned the farm on which they worked, sought to hold them liable principally for alleged violations of the Migrant and Seasonal Agricultural Worker Protection Act (AWPA), and also for certain violations of the FLSA. Many of the violations were alleged to have been perpetrated directly by the owners' crew chief,[116] a registered farm labor contractor who was hired to perform recruiting and supervision of the crew, and certain of the contractor's associates who were involved in plaintiffs' recruitment and transportation. The court examined plaintiffs' asserted theories of joint employment, of liability for the acts of their farm labor contractor, and of agency. The district court rejected the first two theories. On the joint employer issue, the court held that the AWPA "was not intended to be applied"[117] in a situation where the agricultural employer admitted that it employed the plaintiff workers. On the vicarious liability issue, the court construed the plaintiff's argument as being one of per se liability for actions of a farm labor contractor, found no cases upholding such a theory, and distinguished the cases cited by plaintiff in which such liability

---

[114]163 F. Supp. 2d 930, 932 (M.D. Tenn. 2001).

[115]2000 WL 1372848, 6 WH Cases2d 817 (S.D. Ind. 2000).

[116]Although joined as a defendant himself, the crew chief had not been served and the court issued an Order to Show Cause why he should not be dismissed. *Id.,* 6 WH Cases2d at 821.

[117]*Id.,* 6 WH Cases2d at 822 (citing numerous cases in which farm owners resisting liability had litigated whether they were joint employers with farm labor contractors who had been determined to be employers, and having found no cases proceeding in the other direction).

was found for actions of the employer's contractor on an agency theory. Finally, examining an agency theory of liability, the court found that the record would support a finding that the crew leader was a "general" rather than a "special" agent of the owners, and thus that defendant farm owners would be liable for his acts within the "ordinary scope of recruiting, acquiring and supervising workers" even if he violated instructions of the farm owner, provided the plaintiffs were unaware that he had exceeded his authority. The court found that there were factual issues in dispute on the scope of the agency involved and thus denied summary judgment on some of the issues.

E. Joint Employment

3. *Other Joint Employers*

The court in *Barfield v. Madison County*[118] found that a county sheriff and the county were joint employers of the sheriff's department's employees. First, the court found the sheriff, in his individual capacity, to be the plaintiffs' employer. The court relied on a Fifth Circuit decision[119] holding that the sheriff in that case clearly fell within the class of managerial personnel considered employers by the FLSA because Mississippi law grants a county sheriff the power to appoint and remove deputies and fix their compensation subject to budgetary constraints.

The court then determined the employer status of the county by applying the following factors:[120] (1) the power to hire and fire the employee, (2) supervision and control of the employee's work schedule or conditions of employment, (3) determining the rate and method of payment for the hours worked, and (4) maintenance of employment records. The

---

[118]984 F. Supp. 491, 4 WH Cases2d 426 (S.D. Miss. 1997).

[119]Lee v. Coahoma County, 937 F.2d 220 (5th Cir. 1991), *amended in part*, 37 F.3d 1068 (5th Cir. 1993).

[120]Because in an earlier part of the opinion the court found the sheriff to be an employer, it did not analyze in depth the four factors as applied to him, although it did note that the sheriff "hired and fired his employees; he supervised their schedules and conditions of employment; and he determined their rate of pay." 984 F. Supp. at 497 n.13, 4 WH Cases2d at 431 n.13.

court found that (1) the county had control over hiring and firing by allocating funds to the sheriff to operate his department, (2) the board of supervisors and/or the chancery clerk instructed the sheriff not to report any overtime for his employees, (3) the county had ultimate authority for approving the funds for paying overtime, and (4) the county had some responsibility for employment records because the chancery clerk received time cards and prepared the employees' paychecks. Therefore, the court concluded that the sheriff, in his individual capacity, and the county were the joint employers of the plaintiffs.[121]

In another case, however, a municipal bus company that contracted with another business for bus services was found not to be a joint employer of a bus driver who was hired, trained, disciplined, and terminated by the latter business.[122] There, although the contract between the companies specified the bus routes, the bus company at issue did not involve itself in the day-to-day management of the other business, it did not set the employees' work schedules, it did not issue the employees' paychecks, and it did not exercise significant control over the employment relationship.[123]

Suit was brought in *Barajas v. Unified Government of Wyandotte County/Kansas City*[124] by police officers of the Kansas City police department for overtime pay for hours voluntarily worked over and above their normal police shifts for the Kansas City Housing Authority. Both the police department and the housing authority are units of the Unified Government defendant. The district court granted in minor part and denied in substance the defendant's motion for summary judgment. In order to decide whether overtime pay was due, it was necessary to determine whether the exemption for "special detail work" provided under

[121] *Id.* at 496, 4 WH Cases2d 426. *Cf.* Robertson v. Board of County Comm'rs, 985 F. Supp. 980, 4 WH Cases2d 443 (D. Colo. 1997), *aff'd*, 166 F.3d 1222 (10th Cir. 1999) (finding that the board of county commissioners' power to approve and fund the sheriff's budget provided the board with practical and effective control over the sheriff's personnel actions and thus provided the sheriff's office's employees with standing to sue the board in suits pertaining to personnel matters).

[122] Garcia v. Pace Suburban Bus Serv., 955 F. Supp. 75, 76, 3 WH Cases2d 1477 (N.D. Ill. 1996).

[123] *Id.*

[124] 87 F. Supp. 2d 1201 (D. Kan. 2000).

Section 207(p)(1) was applicable, and this in turn required a decision whether the agencies involved were "separate and independent." The court, following the seven-factor test set forth in a DOL opinion letter to determine whether two governmental agencies were separate and independent employers for the FLSA, held that, among other things, the extent of control of an agency's budget by another agency and the extent to which an agency's operating functions are financed by another agency are relevant in making the determination of whether the agencies are separate and independent. The court also decided that the defendant had failed to demonstrate the absence of material factal disputes on these topics, so that a trial was required to explore those issues.

In *Robertson v. Board of County Commissioners,*[125] a federal district court in Colorado applied the Supreme Court's "economic realities" test to determine that a board of county commissioners and the sheriff were joint employers of deputy sheriffs even though the sheriff had sole authority to hire and fire the deputies. In this case, the board set the conditions of employment, approved the sheriff's department budget, and maintained the payroll records for that department.

In *Liu v. Donna Karan International, Inc.,*[126] plaintiff garment workers sued both their immigrant-owned sewing shop employers and Donna Karan International, the company to which significant amounts of the produced goods were provided. The plaintiffs asserted each was liable as a joint employer of plaintiffs for FLSA and New York state labor law violations. The district court denied Donna Karan's Rule 12(b)(6) motion to dismiss. Discussing an earlier Second Circuit case[127] and a more recent garment worker case in the southern district of New York,[128] the court concluded that the garment case more closely paralleled the case before it. In *Liu,* Chinese immigrant garment factory

[125] 78 F. Supp. 2d 1142 (D. Colo. 1999).

[126] 2001 WL 8595, 6 WH Cases2d 1142 (S.D.N.Y. 2001).

[127] Carter v. Dutchess Cmty. Coll., 735 F.2d 8, 25 WH Cases 1239 (2d Cir. 1984) (FLSA claim of a prisoner working outside the prison while serving his term of incarceration).

[128] Lopez v. Silverman, 14 F. Supp. 2d 405, 6 WH Cases2d 186 (S.D.N.Y. 1998).

workers alleged that they were not paid overtime or minimum wage by their employers while working 80 hour workweeks. Plaintiffs, asserting factors similar to those relied on in the New York case, alleged that 60 percent to 100 percent of the clothing they produced in factories owned and operated by co-defendants was made for Donna Karan, that Donna Karan had representatives in the factories on a daily basis, and that Donna Karan controlled wages and hours of the workers through setting low prices and making large output demands. The court applied the economic realities test and determined that plaintiffs' allegations sufficiently alleged joint employment under the expansive rules established in 29 C.F.R. §791.2(a).

In another case involving manufacture of clothing for Donna Karan enterprises, *Bravo v. Eastpoint International, Inc.*,[129] the court dismissed claims by garment workers against all the Donna Karan defendants except Karan International. This case was brought by garment workers for unpaid wages and overtime against Eastpoint, their employer, Karan International and related corporate defendants, for which goods were produced, and Donna Karan, individually. After reciting plaintiffs' allegation that the defendants "controlled plaintiffs' wages and hours through 'establishing contract prices and dates of production'" and also that the Karan defendants "supplied all of the 'materials, assembly instructions, patterns, cutting control sheets, tags, zippers, buttons, pre-cut pieces of fabric [and] care labels'" and "had a representative present in the factory at least once a day," the court stated the black letter law that entities are liable as joint employers only if they possess the power to control the workers involved. The court found that plaintiffs had made no allegations of fact supporting the power of control. The court's decision referred the plaintiffs' counsel to the case of *Herman v. RSR Security Services* Ltd.[130] "where the Court applies the 'economic reality' test."[131] It granted the motion to dismiss all the Karan defendants except International.[132]

[129]7 WH Cases2d 28 (S.D.N.Y. 2001).
[130]172 F.3d 132, 5 WH Cases2d 257 (3d Cir. 1999).
[131]7 WH Cases2d at 29.
[132]*Id.* at 30.

In *Santelices v. Cable Wiring,*[133] plaintiff, a cable installer, sued Cable Wiring, Inc.(CWI), a "licensed cable installation vendor for TCI of South Florida," and South Florida Cable Contractors (SFCC), a business unaffiliated with CWI, for overtime violations, alleging that they were joint employers of plaintiff. CWI and SFCC had entered into a contract under which residential installations for TCI were to be done by persons furnished to the jobs by SFCC. Both defendants argued that plaintiffs were independent contractors and not employees. The court found insufficient evidence of "dependence" in the relationship between Santelices and CWI, and thus granted summary judgment for CWI. After reviewing the standard ecomomic reality factors the court determined that there were material issues of fact as to several aspects of the relationship between Santelices and SFCC, especially concerning the amount of control exercised by SFCC over Santelices. It therefore denied the SFCC motion for summary judgment.

Plaintiffs sued both an individual, Mary Chiodi, who operated a temporary staffing agency, and National Steel Pellet Corporation (NSPC), a company to whom Chiodi referred employees, for overtime violations in *Catani v. Chiodi.*[134] The district court granted summary judgment in favor of the individual defendant Chiodi. The evidence before the court showed that Chiodi, pursuant to her arrangement with NPSC, referred only those employees that NSPC requested by name, had nothing to do with the training, supervising, or disciplining of employees, and no control over the manner in which they performed their work. She processed payroll and cut paychecks on the basis of information furnished by NSPC, and had been instructed by NSPC not to pay overtime. The court applied the "economic realities" test, distinguished the payroll processing function performed by Chiodi from the joint employment relationships inherent in more traditional temporary staffing arrangements, and concluded that Chiodi was not an employer of plaintiffs.

---

[133] 147 F. Supp. 2d 1313, 6 WH Cases2d 1853 (S.D. Fla. 2001).
[134] 2001 WL 920025 (D. Minn. 2001).

In *Dybevik v. Quality Pork Processors, Inc.*,[135] plaintiffs sought to add Hormel Foods Inc., as an additional defendant either on a joint employer theory or on a "single enterprise" theory.[136] The court granted plaintiffs' motion under the joint employer theory, after reviewing allegations that a Hormel employee was in charge of overseeing Quality Pork Processors (QPP) operations on a daily basis. A Hormel employee in charge of yields and new products visited the QPP production floor on a daily basis and occasionally instructed employees on how to do their jobs, and Hormel employees had the authority to tell QPP supervisors to add or remove employees from particular jobs. The court determined that the plaintiff had pleaded sufficient facts to establish that Hormel exercised sufficient control over QPP and its employees to support the joint employer allegation.

Responding to a 1999 request for an opinion, the Wage and Hour Division concluded[137] that where private duty nurses are hired by patients or their representatives to provide care to patients while they are in the hospital, and where the hospital is legally required to provide certain oversight of the private duty nurses and the responsibility for the care of the patient remains with the hospital, the hospital is a joint employer of the nurses.

F. Individual Corporate Officers and Indemnification

In *Enright v. CGH Medical Center*,[138] an Illinois federal district court dismissed an employee's claims under the FLSA against two medical center directors, finding that the directors were not employers within the meaning of the Act. The court reasoned that the directors were not liable for failure to provide compensation to the employee during meal periods and time worked at home because there was no indication that the directors knew of the failure to provide adequate compensation, or that either

---

[135] 2001 WL 811124 (D. Minn. 2001).

[136] For a discussion of the single enterprise analysis, see Chapter 3, Coverage, IV, Enterprise Coverage, E ["Unified Operation" or " Common Control"].

[137] WH Opinion letter dated May 11, 2001, signed by staff member of Office of Enforcement Policy, WHM: 99:8370.

[138] 4 WH Cases2d 1080 (N.D. Ill. 1998)

director exercised control over the day-to-day operation of the medical center such that he would have notice that the center's policies were being unlawfully applied.

An individual can be personally liable as an employer under the FLSA if the individual had supervisory authority over the complaining worker and was responsible in whole or in part for the alleged violation, or had control over the employer's compliance with the Act.[139]

In *Reich v. Harmelech,*[140] the district court determined that two individuals were employers for FLSA purposes. One person was considered an employer because he was the controlling shareholder, director, and officer of a company; he signed the company's payroll; he signed a letter written to employees attesting to the company's financial stability; he had knowledge and authority to act on employees' complaints about payroll and salary nonpayments; and he had authority to establish the salary of officers.[141] The other individual was considered an employer under FLSA because she was an officer and director of the company; she had knowledge that the company employees received payroll checks drawn on inadequate funds; and, having that knowledge, she wrote and deposited payroll checks made out to the company from accounts at other banks.[142]

Subsequent proceedings in the same matter, styled *Herman v. Harmelech,*[143] resulted in a decision on the effect of failure to produce subpoenaed hours-worked and payroll records. One of the defendants, who had been held to be liable under the FLSA as an employer, asserted that within the corporations she had no obligation with respect to records or record-keeping, and thus that she was not liable for the failure of the corporate defendants

---

[139]Welch v. Laney, 57 F.3d 1004, 1010–11 (11th Cir. 1995); Bergstrom v. University of N.H., 943 F. Supp. 130, 135 (D.N.H. 1996). *Cf.* Freemon v. Foley, 911 F. Supp. 326, 2 WH Cases2d 1665 (N.D. Ill. 1995) (employee's temporary supervisor lacked sufficient control to be FMLA employer); Johnson v. A.P. Prods., Ltd., 934 F. Supp. 625, 3 WH Cases2d 914 (S.D.N.Y. 1996) (dismissing FMLA complaint against manager of human resources absent allegation of control over ability to take leave).

[140]3 WH Cases2d 597 (N.D. Ill. 1996).

[141]*Id.*

[142]*Id.*

[143]2000 WL 420839 (N.D. Ill. 2000).

to produce the records. The court noted that the duty to maintain records is an affirmative duty and that an employer cannot shirk her responsibility by isolating herself from the daily operations of the company.

In *Lambert v. Ackerley*,[144] the Ninth Circuit upheld a ruling that a chief operating officer and chief executive officer of the defendant company were personally liable for punitive damages in a retaliation case involving termination of employees for protected complaints. The jury had heard evidence that the corporate officers had a long-standing policy of refusing to pay overtime compensation, that the officers had participated in the overtime dispute with the employees, and that one officer stated he didn't "care what the laws are" and he would not pay overtime but would "wait until someone sue[d] [him]." The court thought this evidence reasonably supported the jury determination that the individual officers acted with reckless disregard of the law in respect to the plaintiffs.

After all the defendants were found liable for back pay for FLSA violations, the attorney who had had operational control of the company sought, and was denied, contribution by other defendants for the amount of the judgment against him. On appeal, in *Herman v. RSR Security Services*, [145] the Second Circuit held that there was no right of contribution or indemnification against the company president and vice president where the attorney's status as an FLSA employer placed him outside the statute's intended protection, regardless of the status of the parties from whom he sought contribution. The court noted that the FLSA makes no provision for contribution or indemnification, that the statute was designed to regulate conduct of employers for benefit of employees, and that, accordingly, employers cannot be said to be members of a class for whose benefit FLSA was enacted. It found that the Act's comprehensive remedial scheme strongly counseled against judicially adding such remedies and also preempted New York law, which recognizes a right to contribution or indemnification.

---

[144]180 F.3d 997, 5 WH Cases2d 677 (9th Cir. 1999).

[145]5 WH Cases2d 257 (2d Cir. 1999).

The First Circuit reiterated its more nuanced view of the circumstances under which an individual corporate officer is properly held an employer in *Baystate Alternative Staffing v. Herman.*[146] There review was sought by two individual corporate officers of the decision of Wage-Hour in a civil penalty assessment case, which had been affirmed by the Labor Department administrative law judge and Administrative Review Board and thereafter by the district court. Finding that the ARB had relied for its decision on the statute's broad definition of employer, under which in the circuit's view any corporate manager could be held responsible for FLSA violations regardless of that manager's degree of control, the appeals panel reversed the district court and remanded for return to the ARB for reconsideration in light of the proper legal standard, which the court said it had articulated in *Donovan v. Agnew.*[147] The factors to be considered include the ownership interest of the corporate officers in question; their operational control of significant aspects of the corporation's day-to-day functions, including compensation of employees; and whether they personally made decisions resulting in the violations.[148]

In *Preston v. Settle Down Enterprises, Inc.*,[149] suit was brought against the corporate employer and a "consultant" who had no ownership interest in the employer and who claimed to be an independent contractor, and not an employee, of the business. The federal district court in Georgia held nevertheless that the consultant, an individual "who knew the most about the labor pools and was responsible for day-to-day operations of the business,"[150] was a joint employer for FLSA purposes.

---

[146]163 F.3d 668, 5 WH Cases2d 65 (1st Cir. 1998).
[147]712 F.2d 1509, 26 WH Cases 466 (1st Cir. 1983).
[148]*Id.* at 1511–14, 26 WH Cases 466.
[149]90 F. Supp. 2d 1267 (N.D. Ga. 2000).
[150]*Id.* at 1275.

Courts continue to hold liable as employers individuals with varying amounts of equity in and control over the employers and activities challenged in these cases.[151]

In *Herman v. Hogar Praderas de Amor, Inc.*, [152] the trial court imposed individual liability upon Carmen Diaz, who was both the president of the defendant nursing home and the president of its board of directors. The parties had stipulated that Diaz hired and fired employees, set their work hours, directed their activities and had the power to set their wages. Additionally, on behalf of defendant, Diaz had signed an agreement to waive the statute of limitations. Defendant Diaz essentially did not contest the secretary's allegations against her. Applying the factors of significant ownership interest, personal responsibility for decisions leading to violations of the Act, and control over significant aspects of daily operations, including compensation of the employees, the court determined that Diaz should be held individually liable.

---

[151]Cheng v. IDEAssocs., Inc., 2000 WL 1029219, 6 WH Cases 654 (D. Mass. 2000) (executives may be personally liable under the Act as employers because they had significant control over the day-to-day functions of the company); Stewart v. Intem, Inc., 2000 WL 1140517 (D. Or. 2000) (following Ninth Circuit authority that an individual who exercises control over the nature and structure of the employment relationship, or has economic control over the relationship, is an employer under the Act); Herman v. Harmelech, 2000 WL 420839 (N.D. Ill. 2000) (directors and officers had sufficient control of corporation's operations to be individually liable as employers); Herman v. Hector I. Nieves Transport, Inc., 91 F. Supp. 2d 435 (D.P.R. 2000) (president and secretary-treasurer who actively controlled and managed the company by regulating its personnel were employers); Luder v. Endicott, 86 F. Supp. 2d 854, 5 WH Cases2d 1581 (W.D. Wis. 2000) (holding that individual state government supervisors who controlled and directed the work of employees were FLSA employers); Samborski v. Linear Abatement Corp., 1999 WL 739543 (S.D.N.Y. 1999) (holding that president and sole owner of company had "operational control" of the company and therefore was an employer in his individual capacity); Mosley v. Douglas County Corr. Ctr., 192 F.R.D. 282, 6 WH Cases2d 241 (D. Neb. 2000) (state government supervisor may be liable under FLSA as an employer); Hartman v. Regents of the Univ. of Colo., 2000 WL 890411 (Colo. Ct. App. 2000) (college dean and assistant dean individually liable under FLSA and do not enjoy sovereign immunity). *Cf.* Reed v. Mycopharma, Inc., 2000 WL 1131953 (N.D. Ill. 2000) (part-time president of company not an employer where he did not directly supervise employees and was not responsible, in whole or in part, for the alleged FLSA violation); Derewiecka v. Zlored, Inc., 1999 WL 767203, at *2 (S.D.N.Y. 1999) (president's signature on a waiver-of-lien form not sufficient evidence by itself to show that the president personally liable as employer).

[152]130 F. Supp. 2d 257 (D.P.R. 2001).

In *Bravo v. Eastpoint International, Inc.*,[153] the court dismissed claims by garment workers against all the Donna Karan defendants except Karan International. The case was brought by garment workers for unpaid wages and overtime against Eastpoint, their employer, Karan International and related corporate defendants, for which goods were produced, and Donna Karan individually. After reciting plaintiffs' allegations that the defendants "controlled plaintiffs' wages and hours through 'establishing contract prices and dates of production'" and also that the Karan defendants "supplied all of the 'materials, assembly instructions, patterns, cutting control sheets, tags, zippers, buttons, pre-cut pieces of fabric [and] care labels'" and "had a representative present in the factory at least once a day," the court stated the black letter law that entities are liable as joint employers only if they possess the power to control the workers involved. The court found that plaintiffs had made no allegations of fact supporting the power of control. The court referred the plaintiffs' counsel to the case of *Herman v. RSR Security Services* Ltd.[154] "where the [c]ourt applies the 'economic reality' test."[155] It granted the motion to dismiss all the Karan defendants except International "without prejudice" to allow plaintiffs properly to state their claims if they so wish."[156]

G. Successors

Herrera v. Singh,[157] involves a father-son corporate successorship which threatened to leave the plaintiffs, ten farm workers, without the opportunity to recover the $160,000 judgment they obtained in their AWPA suit. Plaintiffs had commenced the litigation at a time when the farm property was being operated by its owner, individually, under the name Ram Farms. During the course of the litigation a corporation was formed under the name Ram Investments LLC (RI) in which the ownership be-

[153] 7 WH Cases2d 28 (S.D.N.Y. 2001).
[154] 172 F.3d 132, 5 WH Cases2d 257 (3rd Cir. 1999).
[155] 7 WH Cases2d at 29.
[156] *Id.* at 30.
[157] 118 F. Supp. 2d 1120 (E.D. Wash. 2000).

longed 1 percent to the original owner of the farm, and 49.5 percent each to his two sons. The original owner then transferred the farm property to RI by quitclaim deed, and mortgaged other parcels of his land for the benefit of RI. Plaintiffs moved for an Order of Successorship, by virtue of which they would be entitled to enforce their judgment against the original owner. RI defended against this motion on the basis that the court lacked jurisdiction over it, since it had never been properly served, and also cited a 2000 Supreme Court case, *Nelson v. Adams USA,*[158] for the proposition that the order sought by plaintiffs could not be lawfully granted. The district court distinguished *Nelson* on a number of grounds, and then examined the motion under Rule 25(c) of the FRCP, which provides for substitution of parties when property interests are transferred. It reviewed the three requirements for permitting substitution, namely 1) the purported successor is a *bona fide* successor based upon business continuity; 2) there has been notice of the potential liability to the successor; and 3) the predecessor was unable to provide adequate relief. In this case, the defendants contested only the last factor, arguing that substitution was inappropriate because the original defendant had sufficient assets to satisfy the judgment. The court reviewed the status of those assets and determined that outstanding liens on the assets precluded, or rendered unlikely, satisfaction of the judgment from them. It then granted plaintiffs' motion, providing for execution on RI to the extent of the transferred assets, in reliance on Rule 25(c). Although the court had found no prior case in which the substitution principle had been applied in a suit under AWPA, it pointed out that the doctrine had been applied to "'almost every employment law statute,'"[159] noting particularly an FLSA case, *Steinbach v. Hubbard,*[160] and observing that the FLSA and AWPA have similar purposes, to protect workers' standards of living. Both statutes are remedial and are to be broadly construed to effectuate their purposes.[161]

---

[158] 529 U.S. 460, 120 S.Ct. 1579, 146 L.Ed.2d 530 (2000).
[159] 118 F. Supp. 2d at 1124.
[160] 51 F.3d 843 (9th Cir.1995).
[161] *Id.*

I. Government Officers [New Topic]

Prickett v. DeKalb County[162] was an overtime suit by fire and rescue employees; named as defendants were the county itself and several named county officers individually, who were sued "in their official capacity." Granting a motion to dismiss filed on behalf of the individual defendants, the court stated that while the matter was believed to be of first impression under the Fair Labor Standards Act, the numerous authorities standing for the proposition that in federal courts "a lawsuit against a government official in his official capacity is an action against the underlying governmental entity"[163] were indistinguishable from the case before the court.

J. Consolidation [New Topic]

The district court granted defendant Unified Government's motion to consolidate for purposes of discovery and pretrial proceedings the cases of *Johnson v. Unified Government of Wyandotte County/Kansas City*[164] and *Barajas v. Unified Government of Wyandotte County/Kansas City*.[165] The Johnson plaintiffs had joined the Kansas City Housing Authority as a defendant, but the *Barajas* plaintiffs had not. After the consolidation, the defendants in *Barajas* contended that Housing Authority, by virtue of being a party to the consolidated proceedings, was entitled to reply to the allegations in the *Barajas* complaint. The federal district court in Kansas held that the consolidation had not made the Housing Authority a party to the *Barajas* litigation and that it was not entitled to respond to the *Barajas* allegations.

---

[162] 5 WH Cases2d 63 (N.D. Ga. 1998).

[163] *Id.* at 63 (citing Will v. Michigan Dep't of State Police, 491 U.S. 58, 71 (1989) and other cases from the Eleventh Circuit and from Alabama, California, Colorado, Florida, Mississippi, Puerto Rico, and Texas).

[164] 1999 WL 1096038 (D. Kan. 1999).

[165] 87 F. Supp. 2d 1201 (D. Kan. 2000).

V. BURDEN OF PROOF

A. Generally

In *Bernard v. IBP, Inc.*,[166] the court held that although a bona fide meal break of (in this case) 30 minutes is not to be considered time worked, the burden of proof is on the employer to show that such a meal period is primarily for the benefit of the employee and thus not compensable.

B. The Prima Facie Wage Case

Bailey v. County of Georgetown[167] follows established law in maintaining that the burden is on the plaintiffs to prove that their employer actually or constructively knew that they were working unrecorded overtime hours.

The plaintiffs must be permitted sufficient time to conduct discovery before a court grants a defendant employer's summary judgment motion. In *Jones v. City of Columbus*,[168] for example, the Eleventh Circuit reversed the district court's summary judgment for the defendant because the plaintiffs were not given the opportunity, prior to the ruling, to examine requested documents or to depose city officials whose affidavits were offered to support the summary judgment motion.[169] It held that the lower court had abused its discretion by allowing the city to block the plaintiffs' efforts to gain necessary information through normal discovery procedures.[170]

In *Gale v. Levi Strauss & Co.*,[171] a federal district court in Georgia denied the defendant's motion for summary judgment on the plaintiff's overtime claims. Although plaintiff was sched-

---

[166]154 F.3d 259, 265 (5th Cir. 1998) (citing and following Roy v. County of Lexington, 141 F.3d 533, 544 (4th Cir. 1998)).

[167]94 F.3d 152, 157, 3 WH Cases2d 776 (4th Cir. 1996).

[168]120 F.3d 248, 253, 4 WH Cases2d 99 (11th Cir. 1997).

[169]*Id.*, 4 WH Cases2d 99.

[170]*Id.*

[171]No. 1:97 CV 3636 TWT, 1999 WL 438470, 5 WH Cases2d 513 (N.D. Ga. Apr. 26, 1999).

uled and compensated for 40 hours a week, and the defendant had memoranda instructing her to stay within her scheduled hours and not work overtime, and although the plaintiff had no records to substantiate her claim, the plaintiff herself testified that she worked 65 hours per week. She produced affidavits from her co-workers that they had worked unpaid overtime and observed the plaintiff working overtime, an affidavit from an ex-spouse that the plaintiff had frequently worked at home at night and on weekends, and an e-mail message from a supervisor that referred to weekend work. Despite the absence of corroborating documents, the plaintiff's evidence was sufficient to make out a case for trial.

C. Inadequate or Inaccurate Records

Courts continue to hold that an employer cannot complain about the speculative nature of damages where the imprecision arises from the employer's failure to maintain the required records.[172]

Although responsibility for keeping adequate records of employee activities lies with the employer, the employer's failure to keep such records does not require that time be considered compensable where the employees' own accounts of their activities do not support their claims.[173]

Affirming in all but one respect the trial court's rulings leaving intact a jury verdict for the defendant on the plaintiff's overtime claims in *Etienne v. Inter-County Security Corp.*,[174] the Eleventh Circuit reversed the district court's failure to grant judgment n.o.v. as to a claim for $18.62, which the defendant had admitted it owed. The court stated that, in all other respects, the case had involved crediblility issues that the jury had resolved against the plaintiff. The court affirmed the district court's decision not to give an instruction of the type used in *Anderson*

---

[172]Reich v. Stewart, 121 F.3d 400, WH Cases2d 50 (8th Cir. 1997).

[173]Powell v. Simon Mgmt. Group, 960 P.2d 212, 4 WH Cases2d 1200, 1207 (Kan. 1998).

[174]5 WH Cases2d 859 (11th Cir. 1999), *vacating and substituting in part into* 173 F.3d 1372, 5 WH Cases2d 454 (11th Cir. 1999).

v. Mt. Clemmons Pottery,[175] holding that even though the plaintiff employee had shown the employer's records were inaccurate (for one pay period because of a clerical error and for another pay period because they were missing), and even though the plaintiff had shown he had performed work for which he was not properly compensated by $18.62, the burden of proof did not shift to the defendant.

In *Bates v. Old Time Coffee Co.*,[176] the plaintiff sued for overtime for hours over 40 per week allegedly worked during a period in which he was compensated by a salary but not exempt. Neither the plaintiff nor the employer had any records concerning the hours worked by the plaintiff. Conflicting estimates of the plaintiff's work time were offered at a 1-day bench trial of the matter, the plaintiff testifying that he worked approximately 46 hours per week for the weeks in question, the plaintiff's wife testifying somewhat inconsistently with the plaintiff as to his hours, and the plaintiff's supervisor testifying that the work should take approximately 7 hours per day. A federal district court in California held that an employee has the burden of proving by a preponderance of the evidence that he performed work for which he was not compensated and, without focusing on the defendant's failure to comply with its record-keeping duties, found as a fact that the plaintiff did not work for more than 40 hours per week. The court acknowledged that the employee need not "provide as specific evidence of hours worked as he would otherwise be required"[177] to do if the employer failed to keep accurate time records. Here, however, the court dismissed the plaintiff's claim for failure of proof.

In *American Federation of State, County and Municipal Employees v. State of Lousiana*,[178] a federal district court in Louisiana awarded a covert operative in the Louisiana Department of Wildlife and Fisheries $21,438.19 for unpaid overtime, liquidated damages of an equal sum, and reasonable attorneys' fees and costs. Neither

---

[175] 328 U.S. 680, 66 S. Ct. 1187, 6 WH Cases 83 (1946).

[176] 2000 WL 41223 (N.D. Cal. 2000). See also cases reported herein at Chapter 16, §V.A, regarding the shifting burden of proof of damages in cases where the employer failed to keep required records.

[177] *Id.* at *7.

[178] 2001 WL 29999, 142 Lab. Cas. (CCH) ¶34,195 (E.D. La. 2001).

the employer nor the employee kept accurate records. The employer authorized the employee to work overtime by instructing him to work the hours necessary to complete the undercover operations and then, using the "honor system," to take any overtime hours as compensatory time off. The employer's time sheets reflected only 80 hours per two-week pay period because the employee had been instructed to record his time this way and to keep a separate log of his overtime hours. The employee failed to keep such a log, but supported his claim with documentation from his actual work records. These records included his daily log, his vehicle log, his time sheets, his expense accounts and his case reports. None of these records, however, kept consistent track of the employee's work hours. In determining the amount of uncompensated overtime, the court applied the burden shifting analysis adopted in *Anderson v. Mt. Clemens Pottery Co.*[179] The court determined that the employee produced sufficient evidence to warrant an award and that the employer failed to produce sufficient evidence to rebut the plaintiff's claim. However, the court reduced the amount of damages by almost 50 percent because it had some concerns about the reliability of the employee's recollections. The court indicated that it could expect better records from a law enforcement officer, who is, in effect, a trained, professional record-keeper.

In *Barios v. Brooks Range Supply, Inc.*,[180] the Alaska Supreme Court affirmed the trial court's finding that a former office worker had not worked any unpaid overtime, and thus was entitled to no relief under Alaska law. While the employer did not have any written records of the employee's hours because it had mistakenly assumed she was exempt, the employer was able to meet its "considerable" burden under the federal *Mt. Clemens Pottery* burden shifting analysis. The employer presented credible testimony from the plaintiff's supervisor and two co-workers that plaintiff was consistently late for work, had as many as 150 medical appointments, and that there was insufficient work to warrant overtime.

---

[179]328 U.S. 680, 6 WH Cases2d 83 (1946).

[180]26 P.3d 1082 (Alaska 2001).

In the damages phase of a bifucated trial, the court in *Cowan v. Treetop Enterprises*[181] addressed the question of the number of hours for which the plaintiffs were owed back pay. The district court had earlier granted plaintiffs' motion for summary judgment as to liability, finding that the workers defendant claimed were exempt managers were, in fact, cooks and not exempt. Here, after a bench trial, the federal district court in Tennessee found that the plaintiffs had presented sufficient evidence of an average of 89.04 hours of work per week. The employer conceded that it did not have any actual records because it had classified the plaintiffs as exempt. The court based its finding on testimony by numerous plaintiffs as to their hours worked and on the restaurants' staffing practices. The court then applied the computed 89-hour weekly average time worked to the entire class. The court further noted that the employer would not be heard to complain about the exactness and precision of the measurement because it had failed to keep adequate records, citing *Mt. Clemens Pottery*.

VI. AFFIRMATIVE DEFENSES

A. Generally: Exemptions, Deductions, and Credits

In *Barfield v. Madison County*,[182] the defendant sheriff asserted that he was entitled to qualified immunity from individual liability for any alleged violations of the FLSA. A federal district court in Mississippi rejected this contention and stated that "[the defendant] has not cited, and the Court has not found, any cases recognizing qualified immunity as a defense to a claim for violation of the FLSA."[183]

Courts can make a determination concerning an FLSA exemption issue based solely upon joint submission because a party is estopped from arguing that more information is re-

---

[181]163 F. Supp. 2d 930 (M.D. Tenn. 2001), *appeal pending*, 6th Circuit, No. 1-6308.

[182]984 F. Supp. 491, 4 WH Cases2d 426 (S.D. Miss. 1997).

[183]*Id.*, 4 WH Cases2d at 430 n.8.

quired once such submissions are submitted to the court specifically for the purpose of making such a determination.[184]

In *Magana v. Commonwealth of the Northern Mariana Islands,*[185] the court held that a Section 13(a) exemption from overtime was unavailable because it was not pleaded in a response to a pleading as required by the rules.

B. Statute of Limitations

In *Fisher v. Vassar College,*[186] the Second Circuit declined to consider a statute-of-limitations defense raised for the first time on appeal, observing that the defense had been waived.

In a case brought for backpay under the Alaska Wage and Hour Law, the Alaska Supreme Court held that the FLSA's statute of limitations applies only to causes of action brought under that statute, and cases under state statutes governing overtime pay, minimum wages, and damages are governed by their own statutes of limitations.[187] The Alaska limitations period is not preempted by the FLSA.[188] In this case, certain of the plaintiff's claimed damages were barred by the Alaska 2-year statute of limitations, but the supreme court remanded to permit the plaintiff to amend the complaint to state a claim under the FLSA and thereby take advantage of the 3-year statute if the defendant's conduct was willful.[189]

To the extent private FLSA claims against a state are still viable after *Alden v. Maine,*[190] a statute of limitations set by state rather than federal law may apply. For example, in New York, FLSA claims against the state are viable only to the extent such claims comply with the limitations set forth in the Court of

[184]Adams v. United States, 38 Fed. Cl. 572, 575 (1997).

[185]107 F.3d 1436, 3 WH Cases2d 1413 (9th Cir. 1997).

[186]70 F.3d 1420, 1452 (2d Cir. 1995), *cert. denied,* 118 S. Ct. 851 (1998).

[187]Quinn v. Alaska State Employees Ass'n, 944 P.2d 468, 471, 4 WH Cases2d 215 (Alaska 1997). *See also* Ahern v. State, 662 N.Y.S.2d 684, 686 (Ct. Cl. 1997) (noting that the accrual of a cause of action based on a federal statute is governed by federal law).

[188]*Quinn,* 944 P.2d at 471, 4 WH Cases2d at 217.

[189]*Id.*

[190]527 U.S. 706 (1999).

Claims Act.[191] This Act requires a claimant to file a claim within six months after its accrual.[192] Thus, wage claims filed against the state beyond this limitations period will be dismissed.

1. *Period for Nonwillful Violations*

In *Adams v. Hinchman*,[193] the D.C. Circuit upheld congressional action that retroactively changed the statute of limitations for FLSA claims for federal employees that were filed with the General Accounting Office from 6 years to 2 or 3 years. The court found Congress was acting to standardize the statute of limitations for government and private workers. The court rejected constitutional challenges based on due process and equal protection. However, the court was unwilling to affirm that portion of the district court's decision holding "that plaintiffs' 'property' had not been taken without just compensation, in violation of the Fifth Amendment to the Constitution,"[194] holding that it was without jurisdiction to decide the issue. After noting that "[t]he usual remedy for unconstitutional takings is 'a suit for money damage (i.e., the `just compensation' that the Constitution assures) under the Tucker Act in the Court of Federal Claims, 28 U.S.C. §1491 . . .' [citation and note omitted],"[195] the court remanded the matter to the district court for consideration of its jurisdiction in light of these statutory provisions.

2. *Period for Willful Violations*

To trigger the 3-year statute of limitations, an employee generally must show that the employer either knew or demonstrated reckless disregard for whether the conduct was prohibited by the FLSA.[196]

---

[191]N.Y. Ct. Cl. Act §8 (2001).
[192]*Id.* Act §10(4) (2001).
[193]154 F.3d 420, 5 WH Cases2d 568 (D.C. Cir. 1999).
[194]*Id.*, 5 WH Cases2d at 571.
[195]*Id.*, 5 WH Cases2d at 572.
[196]Karr v. City of Beaumont, 950 F. Supp. 1317, 1325 (E.D. Tex. 1997); L&F Distribs. v. Cruz, 941 S.W.2d 274, 283, 3 WH Cases2d 1158 (Tex. App.—Corpus Christi, 1997).

When an employer acts recklessly by not making an honest attempt to ascertain what the FLSA requires and to comply with it, actions on claims for violations of the FLSA will be governed by the 3-year statute of limitations for "willful" acts.[197]

In *Bliss v. Bobich*,[198] the Alaska Supreme Court affirmed a lower court ruling that a willful violation of the FLSA would not be found for purposes of extending the statute of limitations from 2 to 3 years where the plaintiffs failed to offer any specific evidence relating to the third year prior to the filing of the complaint. The plaintiffs had won a directed verdict on their claim for overtime violations for the period between the filing of their complaint in September 1991 and September 1989, and their only evidence of willfulness, according to the court, related to some time in or after December 1990. Moreover, the court had ruled in limine that no evidence could be offered on the defendant's violations of the FLSA in his conduct of other businesses without a specific offer of proof at trial; on appeal, the plaintiffs provided no "meaningful discussion of the court's specific rulings excluding proffered evidence and fail[ed] to demonstrate that any particular ruling amounted to an abuse of discretion."[199] Thus, the rejection of evidence was upheld.

The court also rejected plaintiffs' claims that a state statute that entitles workers to receive all unpaid back wages within 3 days of termination took their action outside the FLSA's statute of limitations. The employer had signed a "payroll recap" statement in 1991 reflecting unpaid overtime dating back to 1988. Without dealing directly with the argument that entitlement arose anew under the Alaska statute at the date of termination, in 1992, the court held that the claim was without merit on the ground that "[b]ecause the Blisses pursued their overtime claim under the FLSA and the [Alaska Wage and Hour Act], the specific statutes of limitation set out in those acts governed their causes of action."[200]

---

[197]Ayres v. 127 Rest. Corp., 12 F. Supp. 2d 305, 4 WH Cases2d 1255 (S.D.N.Y. 1998).

[198]971 P.2d 141 (Alaska 1998).

[199]*Id.* at 145.

[200]*Id.* at 146.

In *Schwertfeger v. Village of Sauk,*[201] the plaintiffs sued for overtime under the FLSA for regular 15-minute preshift briefing sessions they were required to attend. They sought back pay for 3 years. They did not explicitly plead willful conduct by the defendant. In an unusual decision, the federal district court in Illinois held that if 3 years of damages are sought, a complaint must allege willfulness in order for the claims to survive a motion to dismiss. It dismissed without prejudice, allowing the plaintiffs 14 days to amend.

In an unpublished opinion, *Ackler v. Cowlitz County,*[202] the Ninth Circuit reversed a district court's decision that the 2-year statute of limitations applied to deputy sheriffs' claims for overtime, finding that the county knew or should have known that a collective bargaining agreement (under which the payments made were computed) cannot waive the requirements of the FLSA, and thus that the county acted willfully in adhering to those CBA provisions. The court observed, "[t]he County's argument regarding its motivation—that it acted to satisfy the desires of employees for a certain schedule—has no legal relevance."[203]

3. Willful and Nonwillful Conduct Distinguished

In *Edelen v. Shoney's, Inc.,*[204] a Tennessee federal district court held that the rescission of a compensation deduction policy, the effect of which was to defeat a claimed deduction, was insufficient to bar employees' claims made more than 2 but fewer than 3 years after the rescission, where the plaintiffs presented evidence that the original adoption of the policy was willful. Rather than examining only the date that the policy was implemented (1990) and barring claims made almost 8 years later, the court allowed the plaintiffs to proceed for the purposes of issuing notice. The court stated that the employees had presented sufficient evidence that the employer knew that its

---

[201] 2000 WL 224746 (N.D. Ill. 2000).
[202] 7 Fed.Appx. 543, 2001 WL 115019 (9th Cir.(Wash.)).
[203] *Id.* at 545.
[204] 4 WH Cases2d 980 (M.D. Tenn. 1998).

compensation deduction policy was illegal up to 4 years before rescission of the policy in July 1995. [205] Thus, the plaintiffs' lawsuit in December 1997 might be within the 3-year statute of limitations for willful conduct.

In *Reich v. Monfort Inc.*,[206] the Tenth Circuit found that a meat processing company's failure to pay employees for preliminary and postliminary activities was a willful violation of the FLSA, despite the company's contention that it believed that the de minimis doctrine applied. The Tenth Circuit held that the employer's conduct was willful under the standard of *McLaughlin v. Richland Shoe Co.*,[207] that the employer "knew or showed reckless disregard for the matter of whether its conduct was prohibited by the [FLSA]," where an audit of the employer's slaughter division in 1984 disclosed identical violations and an incident at a sister plant in 1989 resulted in the payment of back wages and an agreement to comply with the FLSA. The Tenth Circuit also held that earlier violations could be established through sources other than litigation, such as audits, to establish that later violations were willful.

In *Herman v. RSR Security Services Ltd.*,[208] the Second Circuit held that the reliance by appellant, an attorney who was chairman of the board of the corporate employer, on the statements of his co-board-members that the business was complying with the FLSA constituted, under the circumstances, reckless disregard of the risk that the business was actually not complying and thus involved a willful violation of the statute. The court noted that the attorney knew that one of the business's board members had conducted earlier business activities in an illegal manner, had extensive knowledge of the FLSA, was aware that some employees had been improperly classified as independent contractors, and could have easily looked into the actual wage rates the company was paying.

---

[205] *Id.*
[206] 4 WH Cases2d 1106 (10th Cir. 1998).
[207] 486 U.S. 128 (1988).
[208] 172 F.3d 132, 5 WH Cases2d 257 (2d Cir. 1999).

In *Cunningham v. Gibson Electric Co.*,[209] a federal district court held that a willful FLSA violation occurs when an employer either knew about or showed reckless disregard for conduct prohibited by the statute. In determining whether an employer's actions are willful, the term should be viewed as synonymous with "voluntary," "deliberate," and "intentional." The court found that the president of the defendant company had actual knowledge of a failure to comply with overtime requirements. During certain assignments, he was instructed to report 40 hours of work whether he worked that full amount, less than that amount, or more than that amount. During other assignments, the plaintiff was not allowed to report 40 hours of work if he did not actually complete them, but was also not allowed to report and collect overtime for time over 40 hours per week. The court held that the defendant was knowledgeable or reckless in not knowing that the plaintiff had been changed from an exempt to a nonexempt pay arrangement and, despite this change, was not allowed to collect overtime. The court held that an employer who has notice that an employee is working overtime cannot stand idly by and allow the work without providing overtime compensation, even if a claim is not made. Furthermore, an employee is not estopped from asserting a claim if the court finds that the employer knew or had reason to know that the reported hours were not correct.

In *Debejian v. Atlantic Testing Laboratories, Ltd.*,[210] a federal district court in New York refused to apply the available 3-year statute of limitations for willful FLSA claims, finding insufficient proof that the employer either knew or showed reckless disregard for whether its conduct was prohibited by the statute. The defendant had claimed the professional exemption for the plaintiff, an engineer; ultimately the court determined that, although the plaintiff had an advanced education, his position was not one which necessitated such knowledge, and partly for that reason the exemption was not available. The plaintiff offered no evidence that the defendant knew it was violating the FLSA.

---

[209]43 F. Supp. 2d 965 (N.D. Ill. 1999).
[210]64 F. Supp. 2d 85 (N.D.N.Y. 1999).

In *Hardrick v. Airway Freight Systems, Inc.*,[211] a federal district court in Illinois held the 3-year statute of limitations appropriate where the employer had taken the position that no overtime was required of its employees, and employees were permitted to work over 40 hours in a week only on their express agreement that only straight time, and no overtime premium, would be paid for those hours. It was undisputed that the employees had worked more than 40 hours. Because the defendant employer had made no effort to investigate whether its policy of paying straight pay for overtime work was legal under the FLSA, and the employer had not consulted with an attorney to determine if its agreements with employees to avoid overtime pay were legal, the employer's actions were held to constitute a "reckless disregard" for the law, and thus were deemed "willful" for purposes of determining the appropriate statute of limitations.

In *Lockwood v. Prince George's County, Maryland*,[212] the plaintiff fire investigators sued for overtime, and a federal district court applied the 2-year statute of limitations, concluding that the employer had mistakenly believed that fire investigators were not entitled to overtime pay because they fell within the exemption for firefighters. Under those circumstances, it held that the plaintiff employees had not demonstrated that the defendant employer had acted voluntarily, deliberately, intentionally, knowingly, or recklessly in violating the statue.

In *Tran v. Tran*,[213] a federal district court in New York held that the employer's practice of hiring laborers, many of whom were immigrants and some of whom were not legally permitted to work in the United States, along with testimony that certain employees were instructed to hide when union representatives came, was evidence that the employer knew that its employment practices might have violated the laws governing payment of wages and seemed to show an intention to avoid paying proper wages. This was sufficent evidence of willfulness to make the 3-year statute of limitations applicable.

---

[211] 63 F. Supp. 2d 898 (N.D. Ill. 1999).

[212] 58 F. Supp. 2d 651 (D. Md. 1999).

[213] 2000 WL 1099906, 6 WH Cases2d 507 (S.D.N.Y. 2000).

In *Nelson v. Waste Management of Alameda County, Inc.*,[214] a federal district court in California applied the nonwillful 2-year statute of limitations based on evidence that the employer had followed the advice of counsel with respect to the payment of wages.

In *Derewiecka v. Zlored, Inc.*,[215] a federal district court in New York held that the employer's project supervisor's testimony that he consistently reviewed the employees' daily records showing regular work hours in excess of 8 hours a day and knew that no overtime was paid by employer was sufficient to permit the willfulness and 3-year statute of limitations issues to go to the jury for determination, as a reasonable juror could find that the employer acted willfully.

In *Breen v. Concrete By Wagner, Inc.*,[216] a federal district court in Illinois held that the defendant's conduct was willful when the defendant was aware of the FLSA but never investigated whether the FLSA was violated by the defendant's policies of paying travel time to a job site at a flat rate that was lower than the regular hourly rate and not including the time spent in travel as hours worked, and of not paying any compensation for return travel from a jobsite at the end of the day.

In *Heath v. Perdue Farms, Inc.*,[217] a district court in Maryland, called upon to determine whether the defendant's conduct was willful, found that prior to 1991, the company readily acknowledged that its crew leaders and chicken catchers were employees, and that although it attempted to adopt a new employment strategy in 1991 under which its work would be done by independent contractors, essentially nothing had changed from the earlier arrangement; the defendant had knowledge from a prior IRS ruling that its alleged independent contractors were employees; and once the U.S. Supreme Court had decided[218] that the "agricultural laborer" exemption could not be applied to "chicken catchers," it was clear that the payment of overtime to

[214]2000 WL 868523 (N.D. Cal. 2000).
[215]1999 WL 767203 (S.D.N.Y. 1999).
[216]1999 WL 1016267 (N.D. Ill. 1999).
[217]87 F. Supp. 2d 452, 5 WH Cases2d 1633 (D. Md. 2000).
[218]*See* Holly Farms v. NLRB, 517 U.S. 392, 152 LRRM 2001 (1996).

chicken catchers was required. The court also found that the poultry industry knew that the Department of Labor took the position that overtime was required to be paid to chicken catchers, and the defendant thus acted willfully in failing to pay overtime to its chicken catching employees.

In *Pabst v. Oklahoma Gas & Electric Co.*,[219] the Tenth Circuit affirmed the district court's refusal to extend the statute of limitations to three years, ruling that the employer was not willful in failing to pay its technicians for all their on-call time. The court deferred to the trial court's assessment that the conduct was not willful when the evidence showed that the employer had paid double time, rather than just time-and-a-half, for each hour of overtime plaintiffs actually reported, and also had permitted plaintiffs to report an hour every time they responded to an alarm, even if they actually spent as little as five minutes.

Plaintiff in *Ragnone v. Belo Corp.*,[220] was employed as the pilot of a news helicopter. His salary was set at $65,000 per annum, and he received significant additional pay for work outside his scheduled workweek. He also carried a pager and was on call while off duty, but he could and did occasionally decline to respond to calls. After the termination of his employment, plaintiff challenged his classification as an exempt employee, relying on a Labor Department decision in an unrelated case holding that the helicopter pilots there were not exempt, and seeking compensation for all his on-call time. The federal district court in Oregon found that plaintiff was not exempt, but determined that summary judgment on willfulness was not available for statute of limitations or for liquidated damages purposes. It pointed out that the person who hired plaintiff had consulted both the station's human resources manager (who had some familiarity with FLSA exemptions, although she did not follow the case law) and its general manager before initially classifying plaintiff as exempt, and that this group had considered plaintiff's training, experience, and job requirements, as

[219]228 F.3d 1128, 6 WH Cases2d 609 (10th Cir. 2000).
[220]131 F. Supp. 2d 1189, 7 WH Cases2d 30 (D. Or. 2001).

well as the practices of other stations in classifying pilots, before deciding to classify plaintiff as exempt.

6. Accrual of Limitations Period

Following the usual federal approach, the courts in both *Lipscomb v. Tucker County Commission*[221] and *Karr v. City of Beaumont, Texas,*[222] held that a separate cause of action accrues each payday when the employer wrongfully withholds overtime compensation.

In *Redman v. U.S. West Business Resources, Inc.,*[223] the plaintiffs filed suit alleging that their employer's failure to compensate them for time spent completing a mandatory job certification program violated the FLSA. The suit was filed more than 3 years after these employees had completed the certification program. The plaintiffs argued that the employer continued to violate the FLSA by failing to compensate other employees for time spent in completing the training program, and that this action constituted a continuing violation sufficient to toll the statute of limitations. The Eighth Circuit affirmed the district court's dismissal of the plaintiffs' action, focusing on the existence of a present violation of the FLSA.[224] Because the violation at issue was the employer's failure to compensate the plaintiffs for their time, the court concluded that no present violation existed and refused to toll the statute of limitations based on a continuing-violation theory.[225]

In *Higgins v. Food Lion, Inc.,*[226] a federal district court in Maryland denied the employer's motion to dismiss on the basis of the FLSA statute of limitations. The employer argued that the 3-year statute of limitations had lapsed because the employee's last day of employment had been on July 19, 1997, a Friday, and

---

[221]475 S.E.2d 84, 90–91 (W. Va. 1996) (noting and applying federal law).

[222]950 F. Supp. 1317, 1325 (E.D. Tex. 1997).

[223]153 F.3d 691, 4 WH Cases2d 1496 (8th Cir. 1998).

[224]*Id.* at 695, 4 WH Cases2d 1496 (citing United Airlines, Inc. v. Evans, 431 U.S. 553, 558 (1977) (question of whether a violation is continuing turns on the existence of a present violation)).

[225]*Id.*, 4 WH Cases2d 1496.

[226]2001 WL 77696 (D. Md. 2001).

the complaint was not filed until July 21, 2000. The court refused to use the last day of employment as the accrual date. Instead, the court adopted the general rule that a cause of action accrues on each day for which a regular paycheck is issued or due. Since at least one paycheck was due on or after July 22, the statute of limitations did not entirely preclude the suit.

In *Henchy v. City of Absecon*,[227] a federal district court in New Jersey denied the employer's summary judgment motion, which was directed toward liability for the period more than two years before the suit was filed. Plaintiff sought to include this portion of the suit either on a continuing violation theory or on the basis of estoppel. As to the continuing violation theory, the court agreed with plaintiff that most courts appear to treat discrimination claims as continuing violation claims, but pointed out that rather than discrimination, the plaintiff asserted liability for overtime, and that repeated failures to compensate properly for overtime are not treated as a continuing violation under the FLSA. It reserved for trial the disputed factual issues relating to estoppel, and thus denied the summary judgment motion.

In *Moss v. Crawford & Co.*,[228] defendant's motion for summary judgment on statute of limitations grounds was denied, the court, holding that defendant's failure to post notices as required by 29 C.F.R. §516.4, tolled the statute as a matter of law, except to the extent that individual plaintiffs' knowledge of their rights could be shown, and these issues were not suitable for determination on summary judgment.

In *Chao v. Virginia Department of Transportation*,[229] a federal district court in Virginia declined to apply either the 2- or the 3-year statute of limitations against the Secretary of Labor's claim for injunctive relief against alleged record-keeping violations, holding that the limitations period applied to claims of wages, overtime and liquidated damages, but not to record-keeping claims.

---

[227] 148 F. Supp. 2d 435, 7 WH Cases2d 183 (D. N.J. 2001).
[228] 2000 WL 33374982 (W.D. Pa. 2000).
[229] 157 F. Supp. 2d 681 (E.D. Va. 2001).

7. *Equitable Tolling and Equitable Estoppel*

The employees failed to communicate their concerns to their union representatives or legal counsel before the limitations period ended in *Redman v. U.S. West Business Resources, Inc.*,[230] and the court refused to apply the doctrine of equitable estoppel. The plaintiffs argued that the provision of their collective bargaining agreement that required the employer to pay for books and tuition associated with the mandatory certification program, but was silent on the issue of compensation for the time spent completing the program, had "'lulled' them into inaction" and should operate to toll the statute of limitations. The Eighth Circuit rejected this argument because of a lack of evidence that the employer intended to mislead the employees and the employees' own failure to complain.

One court has held that in an opt-in collective action under Section 16(b), where various circumstances resulted in lengthy delay in the defendant's responding to a request initially made by the plaintiffs at the time the complaint was filed for the names and addresses of other employees similarly situated to the named plaintiffs, the statute of limitations would be tolled with respect to the opt-in plaintiffs from the date of the filing of the complaint until the date of the defendant's response.[231]

In *Reich v. Southern New England Telecommunications Corp.*,[232] the court held that the statute of limitations was tolled from the date that defendant should have, but did not, file its response to the Secretary's request for production of documents (seeking the names, titles, and payroll records of all individuals in five job categories), so as to preclude the employer's benefiting from its delayed compliance with discovery requirements.

In *Bureerong v. Uvawas*,[233] the defendants asserted a statute of limitations defense to the plaintiffs' FLSA claims. The court said equitable tolling was appropriate in some circumstances,

[230] 153 F.3d 691, 4 WH Cases2d 1496 (8th Cir. 1998).

[231] Myers v. Copper Cellar Corp., 3 WH Cases2d 1081 (E.D. Tenn. 1996).

[232] 892 F. Supp. 389, 404 (D. Conn. 1995). A later decision on the merits in this matter was affirmed, without discussion of this issue, at 121 F.3d 58 (2d Cir. 1997).

[233] 922 F. Supp. 1450, 3 WH Cases2d 383 (C.D. Cal. 1996).

"'as in the case of inability to bring suit or exercise one's remedy.'"[234] Equitable tolling applied in this case for the time the plaintiffs were physically restrained at the defendants' facilities until they were released by California state officials.[235]

The 3-year statute of limitations was held to have been equitably tolled where the employer had previously litigated a related FLSA claim against the Secretary of Labor in federal court.[236]

A federal district court in Florida, in *Antenor v. D & S Farms*,[237] refused to toll the 2-year statute of limitations for an FLSA claim because the employer had failed or refused to display a required FLSA poster. Although plaintiffs relied on contrary precedent from other circuits, and although the district court agreed that "migrant workers [such as plaintiffs] are generally among those most unfamiliar with the complexities of the law,"[238] the court found the question of tolling had already been decided against plaintiffs by its own circuit's precedent.[239]

In *Miccoli v. Ray Communications, Inc.*,[240] the plaintiff argued that in his suit, filed more than 3 years after the claims accrued, the statute of limitations should be extended by equitable tolling because the employer had posted no notice of employee rights under the FLSA as required by 29 C.F.R. §516.4. Despite this allegation, the plaintiff had supplied no evidence to establish the truth of this claim, and, accordingly, the district court in Pennsylvania granted summary judgment to the employer on it.

In *Chao v. Virginia Department of Transportation*,[241] a federal district court in Virginia applied the equitable tolling doctrine to deny the Virginia Department of Transportation's (VDOT) motion for summary judgment on the basis of the statute of

---

[234] *Id.* at 1463, 3 WH Cases2d 383 (quoting Partlow v. Jewish Orphans' Home of S. Cal., Inc., 645 F.2d 757, 760 (9th Cir. 1981)).

[235] *Id.*, 3 WH Cases2d 383.

[236] Ahern v. State, 662 N.Y.S.2d 684, 686 (Ct. Cl. 1997).

[237] 39 F. Supp. 2d 1372 (S.D. Fla. 1999).

[238] *Id.* at 1379.

[239] McClinton v. Alabama By-Products Corp., 743 F.2d 1483 (11th Cir. 1984), and Kazanzas v. Walt Disney World Co., 704 F.2d 1527 (11th Cir.), *cert. denied*, 464 U.S. 982 (1983).

[240] 2000 WL 1006937 (E.D. Pa. 2000).

[241] 157 F. Supp. 2d 681 (E.D. Va. 2001).

limitations. In 1995, individual transportation construction inspectors filed suit against VDOT for overtime violations, alleging that they had not been properly paid for travel time between work sites. The action grew to include 352 inspectors before it was dismissed in December 1996, based on the U.S. Supreme Court's decision in *Seminole Tribe of Florida v. Florida.*[242] Two months earlier, the inspectors had filed a similar complaint in state court. The state court action was subsequently dismissed in May 2000, relying on both *Alden v. Maine,*[243] and a Virginia Supreme Court decision holding that the Commonwealth may not be sued by its employees in state court for violations of the FLSA without its consent. Two months later, the Secretary of Labor filed this suit on behalf of the inspectors. Defendant argued that the Secretary's complaint was barred by the statute of limitations. The Secretary argued that the statute of limitations was equitably tolled because VDOT had adequate notice of the claims and because the inspectors had diligently pursued their claims. The court applied the equitable tolling doctrine in this case because (1) VDOT had notice of the claims since 1995, (2) the inspectors and the Secretary had been diligent in pursuing their claims, (3) the Secretary's action serves both public and private interests, and (4) the remedial scheme of the FLSA permits the Secretary to benefit from the actions filed by the inspectors. Thus, the court tolled the statute of limitations from December 1995 (the date the inspectors filed their individual complaints) to July 2000 (the date the Secretary filed its complaint in federal court). The court also rejected VDOT's arguments that equitable tolling applies only in situations of misconduct by the defendant and that equitable tolling does not apply to states. The court concluded that a failure to apply equitable tolling here would allow VDOT to frustrate the objectives of the FLSA.

In *Baba v. Grand Central Partnership, Inc.*,[244] a federal district court in New York rejected one and accepted one of the plain-

---

[242]517 U.S. 44 (1996).
[243]527 U.S. 706 (1999).
[244]2000 WL 1808971, 142 Lab. Cas. (CCH) ¶34,181 (S.D.N.Y. 2000).

tiffs' two equitable arguments relating to the statute of limitations, estoppel and tolling. Plaintiffs had worked without pay for the Grand Central Partnership during the years 1993–1995, and filed suit only in 1999. Thus plaintiffs acknowledged that, without at least one of the equitable defenses, their claim would be entirely barred by the statute of limitations. With respect to the equitable estoppel argument, the court noted that there was not a single allegation of employer misconduct for at least three years prior to filing the complaint; and that therefore, plaintiffs could not, by the definition of the defense, prevail. With respect to the equitable tolling argument, the court noted that there was conflicting evidence concerning the facts, and preserved the equitable tolling claim pending further discovery. Thus, the court denied the employer's motion for summary judgment with leave to renew upon a fuller record.

In *Henchy v. City of Absecon*,[245] a federal district court in New Jersey denied the town's motion for summary judgment based on the 2-year statute of limitations. Plaintiff argued that the statute of limitations should be equitably tolled because the police chief repeatedly assured him that his overtime compensation was proper and because the police department had failed to post the requisite minimum wage and overtime notices required by regulation.[246] The court concluded that there were genuine issues of material fact on both issues, and thus held that summary judgment would be inappropriate. The court also rejected the town's argument that the police officer's contemporaneous suspicion as to the legality of the town's action precluded his invocation of the equitable tolling doctrine.

In *Hasken v. City of Louisville*,[247] a federal district court in Kentucky concluded that there was a genuine issue of material fact on whether the statute of limitations was tolled during the time period that the firefighters did not know how their overtime was calculated. The city argued that the statute of limitations had expired for several firefighters because the claims were

---

[245] 148 F. Supp. 2d 435, 7 WH Cases2d 183 (D. N.J. 2001).
[246] *See, e.g.*, 29 C.F.R. §516.4.
[247] 173 F. Supp. 2d 654, 6 WH Cases2d 1814 (W.D. Ky. 2001).

more than 3 years old. Plaintiffs argued that the limitations period was tolled because they did not learn about the city's improper calculation of their rate of pay until the local paper published an article on the issue. The city responded by stating that the requisite postings provided sufficient notice. The court disagreed with defendant, concluding that the postings failed to address the critical issue of the method by which the hourly rate was calculated.

C. Laches

In *Bowe v. SMC Electric Products, Inc.*,[248] the court held the defendant was not entitled to summary judgment on the basis of the doctrine of laches where it failed to show it was prejudiced by the plaintiff's delay in asserting an overtime claim.

D. Good Faith Defenses

1. *Section 10: Actions Taken in Good Faith, in Conformity With, and in Reliance on Written Rulings or Enforcement Policies of the Administrator*

a. *General Nature of the Defense*

In *Herman v. Suwannee Swifty Stores, Inc.*,[249] a federal district court in Georgia found that the employer could not establish the good faith defense under the Portal-to-Portal Act on the basis of its own interpretation of the FLSA alone. Instead, the employer was required to indicate its reliance upon some administrative regulation, order, ruling, approval, or interpretation, which it had failed to do.

The court in *Herman v. Palo Group Foster Home, Inc.*,[250] after rejecting the defendants' good faith defense under Section 10 on the merits, "note[d] in passing"[251] that the defendants were

[248]935 F. Supp. 1126, 1135 (D. Colo. 1996).
[249]19 F. Supp. 2d 1365 (M.D. Ga. 1998).
[250]976 F. Supp. 696, 5 WH Cases2d 828 (W.D. Mich. 1997).
[251]*Id.*, 5 WH Cases2d at 834.

technically barred from asserting it since they had failed to plead it affirmatively. On the merits, the court rejected the defendants' attempt to assert a good faith defense on the basis of a document from the Wage and Hour Division which stated that a certain amount of meal credit was allowed in 1985.[252] The court stated that the defendants should not have ignored the mandates of the FLSA and should have recalculated the deduction every year.[253]

d. "In Reliance On"

In *Henchy v. City of Absecon,*[254] a federal district court in New Jersey denied the town's motion for summary judgment based on good faith reliance on a Settlement Agreement between another town and the Department of Labor and on two opinion letters published by the Department of Labor. The plaintiff, a police officer seeking overtime compensation for dog-handling duties, argued that the good faith defense was not applicable because his agreement with the town did not comply with either the settlement agreement or the DOL letter rulings. Plaintiff pointed to specific differences between his agreement and the terms of the DOL-approved settlement agreement and its opinion letters. The court determined that there were genuine issues of fact as to both the actual reliance on the documents named and the conformity of defendant's practices with those documents, and thus denied summary judgment.

e. "Any Written Administrative Regulation, Order, Ruling, Approval, or Interpretation"

An employer that has relied upon its own erroneous interpretation of an administrative guideline cannot successfully assert the Section 10 good faith defense.[255]

---

[252]Herman v. Palo Group Foster Home, Inc., 976 F. Supp. 696, 704 (W.D. Mich. 1997).

[253]*Id.*

[254]148 F. Supp. 2d 435, 7 WH Cases2d 183 (D. N.J. 2001).

[255]Nelson v. Alabama Inst. for Deaf & Blind, 896 F. Supp. 1108, 1114 (N.D. Ala. 1995); L&F Distribs. v. Cruz, 941 S.W.2d 274, 3 WH Cases2d 1158 (Tex. App. 1996).

Carrasco v. Texas Transportation Institute, Texas A&M University Systems[256] held that an employer could not rely on an investigation summary by a DOL investigator to form the basis of a good faith defense under Section 10.

The Fourth Circuit has rejected a county's claim that it was immune from backpay under the Portal-to-Portal Act because it relied on the advice of its attorney who in turn had spoken with an unknown representative of the Wage and Hour Division.[257] The court also held that the district director had no authority to speak for the agency.[258]

2. *Section 11: Actions Taken in Good Faith and With Reasonable Grounds for Believing They Were Not in Violation of the Act*

a. *General Nature of the Defense*

While denying partial summary judgment because "fact issues remain" on the defense, one district court provided a detailed explanation of the employer's substantial burden of proving good faith in order to avoid or diminish an award of liquidated damages.[259]

> It is not enough, for instance, to plead and prove ignorance of the wage requirements. . . . Good faith requires some duty to investigate potential liability under the FLSA. . . . Lack of good faith is demonstrated when an employer "knows, or has reason to know, that his conduct is governed by the [FLSA]."[260]

A federal district court in South Carolina in *Carter v. City of Charleston*[261] held that the city was liable for liquidated damages

---

[256] 908 S.W.2d 575, 577 (Tex. App. 1995).

[257] Roy v. County of Lexington, 141 F.3d 533, 548–49, 4 WH Cases2d 869, 876 (4th Cir. 1998).

[258] *Id.*

[259] Karr v. City of Beaumont, 950 F. Supp. 1317, 1325–26, 133 Lab. Cas. (CCH) ¶33,511 (E.D. Tex. 1997) (citing and quoting principally Reeves v. International Tel. & Tel. Corp., 616 F.2d 1342, 1353 (5th Cir. 1980), *cert. denied,* 449 U.S. 1017 (1981), and also Mireles v. Frio Foods, Inc., 899 F.2d 1407, 1415 (5th Cir. 1990), and Cox v. Brookshire Grocery Co., 919 F.2d 354, 357 (5th Cir. 1990)).

[260] *Id.* (citations omitted).

[261] 995 F. Supp. 620, 4 WH Cases2d 453 (D.S.C. 1997).

because it failed to show both that the city's actions were in good faith and that it had reasonable grounds for believing its actions were not a violation of the FLSA.[262] On the critical issue of the length of plaintiffs' tour of duty, although the city had offered proof of a written policy that contemplated a firefighter shift schedule of 24 ¼ hours, for 12 years the city had taken no steps to implement or enforce the policy.

In *Heidtman v. County of El Paso,*[263] the Fifth Circuit held that the district court did not abuse its discretion in awarding the prevailing plaintiffs, employees of a public visitors center, liquidated damages. The plaintiffs were administrative employees of the center, and the administrative exemption had been claimed for them despite the fact that many of their duties were routine and that they did not regularly exercise discretion. The court reasoned that because the county and city suspected they were not in full compliance with the FLSA, they could not have acted in good faith and with reasonable belief that they were in compliance with the law.

The Fifth Circuit held in *Bernard v. IBP Inc.*[264] that the district court did not abuse its discretion in awarding liquidated damages against a meat processing plant that failed to pay its maintenance employees for meal breaks during which employees had significant restrictions and were often interrupted. Although the employer presented evidence that it had acted in good faith, the court said that the district court nonetheless had discretion to award liquidated damages. Given that an FLSA violation had occurred, the Fifth Circuit did not consider the award of liquidated damages to be an abuse of discretion.

---

[262]*See also* Troutt v. Stavola Bros., Inc., 905 F. Supp. 295, 302, 131 Lab. Cas. (CCH) ¶33,329, 2 WH Cases2d 1541 (M.D.N.C. 1995) ("An award of liquidated damages is mandatory, but may become discretionary if the employer can establish 'to the satisfaction of the court that the act or omission giving rise to such action was in good faith and that [the employer] had reasonable grounds for believing that his act or omission was not in violation of the [FLSA]'" (alterations in original; quoting 29 U.S.C. §260)).

[263]171 F.3d 1038, 5 WH Cases2d 385 (5th Cir. 1999).

[264]154 F.3d 259, 4 WH Cases2d 1604 (5th Cir. 1998).

In *Adkins v. Mid-American Growers, Inc.*,[265] the Seventh Circuit found that a district court's doubling of compensatory damages was proper only if the employer had no reasonable basis for believing itself completely exempt from the FLSA. The outcome of that issue would depend on a remanded question involving whether it was feasible for a greenhouse operator to separate out exempt agricultural work from nonexempt work performed by employees.

The Sixth Circuit in *Herman v. Palo Group Foster Home Inc.*[266] affirmed the decision of the District Court for the Western District of Michigan finding the defendants' violations to be willful when they had previously been investigated twice for the same kinds of activities by the Department of Labor, had previously paid back wages and been informed of the requirements of the law by the Department, and had engaged in the same or similar conduct a third time.

In *Cunningham v. Gibson Electric Co., Inc.*,[267] a federal district court awarded liquidated damages in addition to overtime pay based on the failure of the defendant to overcome its substantial burden to demonstrate a good faith basis or reasonable belief that its conduct was lawful. Consistent with the prevailing view, the court held that the use of liquidated damages to effectively award "double damages" is considered the norm, rather than the exception, for FLSA overtime violations. The court found that the defendant, an electrical construction company, had presented no evidence that it acted reasonably in requiring the plaintiff to work without overtime pay on projects it knew would require more than 40 hours a week.

In *Debejian v. Atlantic Testing Laboratories, Ltd.*,[268] a federal district court in New York held that to avoid liquidated damages, the employer must take active steps to ascertain the dictates of the FLSA and then act to comply with them, and that the employer's evidence that it had contacted counsel (identity unrecalled) and learned about "the requirements of an exempt

---

[265]167 F.3d 335, 5 WH Cases2d 129 (7th Cir. 1999).
[266]183 F.3d 468, 5 WH Cases2d 837 (6th Cir. 1999).
[267]43 F. Supp. 2d 965 (N.D. Ill. 1999).
[268]64 F. Supp. 2d 85 (N.D.N.Y. 1999).

employee," without having provided the position description or the duties of the position in question, were insufficient in this regard.

In *Taylor v. County of Fluvanna*,[269] a court awarded double damages to a county police officer who was due overtime by his employer, the county sheriff's office.[270] The court found that the sheriff, as the employer with control over his employees, did not act in good faith because he knew of the FLSA violation, knew of the increasing overtime payments owed to his employees, and had the authority to move money among budgets to satisfy these costs but did not do so.

In *Schneider v. City of Springfield*,[271] the court awarded liquidated damages in an amount less than twice the back wages due to a fire dispatcher who recovered overtime under the Act. The court held that the employer had a good faith basis —its underlying mistaken reliance on an FLSA handbook and its misreading of a DOL opinion letter—to believe that its fire dispatchers fell within the 53-hour overtime provision of Section 7(k). Noting that liquidated damages must be awarded against an employer lacking good faith and may be awarded against an employer who proves good faith, the court decided to award less-than-double damages. Specifically, the court awarded the amount equal to the prejudgment interest that would have been due on its back pay award, [272] citing the doctrine established by Sixth Circuit case law[273] to the effect that when either no liquidated damages or less-than-double liquidated damages are awarded, the plaintiff must receive, in addition to the actual back pay due, at least the equivalent of prejudgment interest.

In *Herman v. Hector I. Nieves Transport Inc.*,[274] the district court awarded double damages to the plaintiff on account of the defendant's willful violations of the FLSA. The court also ex-

---

[269]70 F. Supp. 2d 655, 5 WH Cases2d 1255 (W.D. Va. 1999).

[270]*Id.* at 662, 5 WH Cases2d 1255. *See also* 29 U.S.C. §§216(b), 260; Lyle v. Food Lion, Inc., 954 F.2d 984, 987 (4th Cir. 1992).

[271]2000 WL 988279, 140 Lab. Cas. ¶34, 064 (S.D. Ohio 2000).

[272]*See* discussion of prejudgment interest at §IV.C.3.a.

[273]McClanahan v. Matthews, 440 F.2d 320, 326 (6th Cir. 1971).

[274]91 F. Supp. 2d 435, 6 WH Cases2d 1469 (D.P.R. 2000), *aff'd on appeal of denial of exemption,* 6 WH Cases2d 1441 (1st Cir. 2001).

tended the period of wage recovery from 2 years to 3. The employer paid its truck-driver workers on a per-trip basis regardless of the amount of time for the trip or in executing other duties required by the employer, such as washing their trucks, and failed to maintain time records of any kind. The Department of Labor earlier alerted the employer about these violations of the FLSA and the appropriate statutory provision for calculating the hourly wages of his drivers. The court held that the employer willfully disregarded the warning and continued to violate the FLSA. The court awarded double damages and issued an injunction against further violations of the statutory requirements. Although the employer had argued its reliance on the motor carrier exemption under Section 13(b)(1) of the Act, the court found without discussion that the unsuccessful exemption claim did not "preclude a finding of a lack of good faith and objective reasonableness."[275]

b. Burden of Pleading and Proof

One court addressed the issue of whether the Section 11[276] defense to liquidated damages, like the defenses under Sections 9 and 10,[277] must be "pleaded and proved" by the employer despite the lack of statutory language to that effect. In *Dutcher v. Randall Foods,*[278] the court relied upon state procedural law, which required that affirmative defenses be pleaded, and determined that in the absence of a proper pleading, and without the consent of the plaintiff to trial of the issue without a pleading, the defense had been waived.[279]

In *Sanders v. Elephant Butte Irrigation District of New Mexico,*[280] the court adhered to the principle that the court's discretion extends to awarding full liquidated damages even if a defendant proves both aspects of the Section 11 defense. It noted that a

---

[275]6 WH Cases at 1480.
[276]29 U.S.C. §260.
[277]29 U.S.C. §§258, 259.
[278]546 N.W.2d 889, 892, 70 FEP Cases 1426 (Iowa 1996) (Equal Pay Act case, applying Iowa Rule of Civil Procedure 101, citing federal and state authorities).
[279]*Id.* at 893.
[280]112 F.3d 468, 3 WH Cases2d 1573 (10th Cir. 1997).

"court may refuse to award liquidated damages if the employer demonstrates both that it acted in good faith and with honest intentions to comply with the FLSA." Even if the employer makes this showing "the district court may still in its 'sound discretion' award liquidated damages up to the amount of its § 216 compensatory award."[281]

c. Judicial Findings Required; Standard of Review on Appeal

In *Arias v. United States Service Industries, Inc.*,[282] the Court of Appeals for the D.C. Circuit reversed a judgment for the employer and noted that "[if on remand] the District Court fails to find 'good faith' and 'reasonable grounds,' appellants will be entitled to both actual damages and liquidated damages (equal to actual damages)."

d. Subjective Good Faith

In *Adams v. United States,*[283] the Court of Federal Claims addressed whether certain supervisory border patrol agents were exempt under the executive exemption. The court ruled that field operations supervisors, who supervised lower-level employees, assigned them to work with supervisory Border Patrol agents, and were responsible for time and attendance, pay raises recommendations, performance evaluations as well as recommendations for bonuses, met the test for executive employees under the Act. The court ruled that the first-line supervisory border patrol agents, however, did not qualify for the executive exemption because they did not supervise a recognized organizational unit with a continuing function. Instead, each day, they were assigned a group of six to eight agents to supervise in the field. The agents whom they supervised changed day to day because the first-line supervisory agents supervised geographic areas rather than a particular group of employees.

---

[281]*Id.* at 471, 3 WH Cases2d 1573. This principle is discussed in detail and extensive authority appears at notes 460 and 469–71 in this chapter in the Treatise.

[282]80 F.3d 509, 512, 131 Lab. Cas. (CCH) ¶33,362, 3 WH Cases2d 321 (D.C. Cir. 1996).

[283]44 Fed. Cl. 772, 6 WH Cases2d 1097 (1999).

The court concluded that supervision of a recognized organizational unit with a continuing function is a requirement of the test for the executive exemption, which the supervisory agents did not meet.

Based on evidence presented in a bench trial, a federal district court in Ohio held in *Schneider v. City of Springfield*[284] that the city was entitled to the good faith defense when the fire chief relied on a Fair Labor Standards Handbook and two DOL letter rulings in making the incorrect determination that a dispatcher, who was also a trained firefighter, was subject to the Section 207(k) partial overtime exemption for firefighters and police officers. Good faith was also evidenced by the lack of union grievances and the lack of discussion of the issue during labor-management committee meetings, and by the fact that independent retained labor law counsel never informed the city of potential FLSA violations in this connection.

In *Elwell v. University Hospitals Home Health Care Services*,[285] the court declined to award liquidated damages after determining that the employer acted in the good faith belief that the plaintiff was overtime-exempt as a professional. There were no earlier indications to the employer that the employee was not exempt. The employer presented evidence of the professional status of the employee based upon a fee-based employment arrangement. While unavailing in terms of the professional exemption, the evidence was sufficient to excuse liquidated damages, according to the court.

In *Pabst v. Oklahoma Gas & Electric Co.*,[286] the Tenth Circuit affirmed the trial court's ruling that the employer's actions were reasonable and in good faith when it failed to pay its technicians for all their on-call time. The court, indicating that it might have reached a different result in the role of initial factfinder, found no abuse of the district court's discretion in its determination that the employer did not act willfully, noting that the employer had paid double time, rather than just time-and-a-half, for each

---

[284] 2000 WL 988279 (S.D. Ohio 2000).
[285] 1999 WL 1212863 (N.D. Ohio 1999).
[286] 228 F.3d 1128, 6 WH Cases2d 609 (10th Cir. 2000).

hour of overtime plaintiffs actually reported, and had permitted plaintiffs to report an hour every time they responded to an alarm, even if they actually spent as little as five minutes.

e. Objective Reasonable Belief

In *Shea v. Galaxie Lumber & Construction Co.*,[287] the employee was originally hired by an office manager and was told to keep track of her own time cards. The employee regularly worked in excess of 40 hours per week but never received compensation at one and one-half times her regular rate for those hours. When the office manager left the company, the plaintiff assumed many of her duties, including preparation of payroll, and continued to work more than 40 hours per week. As a defense to the plaintiff's claim for liquidated damages under the FLSA,[288] the employer alleged that it had acted upon a reasonable belief that its actions were in compliance with the FLSA. The district court agreed that the employer had demonstrated good faith, emphasizing that the plaintiff herself had payroll preparation duties.

On appeal, the Seventh Circuit rejected this reasoning, stating that an employer cannot satisfy its burden of demonstrating objective good faith by asserting that lower-level employees were responsible for the violations. Furthermore, although the employer might have assumed that the employee was an expert on the FLSA, there was no evidence in the record to demonstrate the reasonableness of that assumption. Finally, the court noted that the employer had done nothing to ascertain its compliance with the FLSA, in that it had not consulted with its attorney or its accountant.

In *Reich v. Southern New England Telecommunications Corp.*,[289] the court found that the employer's general inquiry to a local Wage-Hour office about the legality of its pay system was insufficient to establish a good faith defense to liquidated damages; rather, the employer must "ask the appropriate question in its inquiry."

---

[287] 152 F.3d 729, 4 WH Cases2d 1473 (7th Cir. 1998).

[288] 29 U.S.C. §216(b) (1998).

[289] 121 F.3d 58, 72, 134 Lab. Cas. (CCH) ¶33,569, 4 WH Cases2d 33 (2d Cir. 1997).

In *Holzapfel v. Town of Newburgh,*[290] the district court denied partial summary judgment on the Section 11 defense in a canine care case because the city's witness indicated that the city had no knowledge that any officer was spending more than 2 hours per week for which they were compensated in such duties. The court held that it was up to a jury to determine whether the city should have anticipated the officers' dogged determination in the performance of their work!

The following cases do not appear to be in accord with the normally heavy burden required of defendants in establishing this defense.

In *Featsent v. City of Youngstown,*[291] the court of appeals held that it was within the district court's discretion under Section 11 to award partial liquidated damages where it had found that the employer showed good faith and reasonable grounds for believing its actions were not in violation of FLSA based on the city's reliance on the implicit advice of its counsel during negotiations with its employees.

In *Sack v. Miami Helicopter Service,*[292] the district court determined that it had discretion to award partial liquidated damages in a "close case," in which the employer had demonstrated that it had "acted in good faith and that [its] decision as to applicability of the overtime pay requirements was not unreasonable."[293] The court also noted that a large liquidated damages award was inappropriate because the plaintiff knew that he had stopped receiving overtime pay, "but did not object or complain . . . about the unpaid overtime wages until after he left his employment more than a year later."[294]

The good faith defense to liquidated damages was rejected in *AFSCME v. Louisiana*[295] where, after a non-jury trial, the court found that the state acted in good faith in denying the undercover game officer's overtime claims, but was negligent (and

---

[290]935 F. Supp. 418, 424–25 (S.D.N.Y. 1996).

[291]70 F.3d 900, 907, 131 Lab. Cas. (CCH) ¶33,313, 2 WH Cases2d 1697 (6th Cir. 1995).

[292]986 F. Supp. 1456, 4 WH Cases2d 490 (S.D. Fla. 1997).

[293]*Id.* at 1473, 4 WH Cases at 502–03.

[294]*Id.,* 4 WH Cases2d at 502–03.

[295]2001 WL 29999 (E.D. La. 2001).

therefore not reasonable) in handling such claims. Supervisors were aware of the overtime worked but had not asked for any accounting of the overtime and/or comp time hours.

Plaintiff in *Ragnone v. Belo Corp.*,[296] was employed as the pilot of a news helicopter. His salary was set at $65,000 per annum, and he received significant additional pay for work outside his scheduled workweek. He also carried a pager and was on call while off duty, but he could and did occasionally decline to respond to calls. After the termination of his employment, plaintiff challenged his classification as an exempt employee, relying on a Labor Department decision in an unrelated case holding that the helicopter pilots there were not exempt, and seeking compensation for all his on-call time. The federal district court in Oregon found that plaintiff was not exempt, but determined that summary judgment on willfulness was not available for statute of limitations or for liquidated damages purposes. It pointed out that the person who hired plaintiff had consulted both the station's human resources manager (who had some familiarity with FLSA exemptions, although she did not follow the case law) and its general manager before initially classifying plaintiff as exempt, and that this group had considered plaintiff's training, experience, and job requirements, as well as the practices of other stations in classifying pilots, before deciding to classify plaintiff as exempt.

In *Bjerke v. Nash Finch Co.*,[297] after plaintiff proved violations of the Equal Pay Act (EPA) at a jury trial, the district court granted plaintiff liquidated damages on its post-trial motion. Defendant argued that it had acted in good faith, but the court found that defendant had demonstrated no action to ascertain whether its practice of paying female packing room workers less than male general warehouse workers violated the law, even though the alleged violation had been brought to its attention on a number of occasions. The court therefore found that the defendant had not met its burden of proving good faith and reasonableness.

---

[296]131 F. Supp. 2d 1189, 7 WH Cases2d 30 (D. Or. 2001).

[297]2000 U.S. Dist. LEXIS 19777, 84 FEP Cases 1350,1353 (D.N.D. 2000).

f. Effect of a Jury Verdict on Willfulness for Statute of Limitations Purposes on a Judge's Discretion Under Section 11

On motion for summary judgment, one Michigan district court found the employer's violations of the Act to be willful for statute of limitations purposes and then, following the Sixth Circuit's decision in *Equal Employment Opportunity Commission v. City of Detroit Health Department,*[298] summarily denied the employer's Section 11 defense, holding that its "previous finding of willfulness mandates an award of liquidated damages equal to the amount of back wages awarded above."[299]

The federal district court in *Theisen v. City of Maple Grove*[300] refused to award liquidated damages in a case where the jury had found no willful violation of the FLSA. The court first took that jury's determination into account, expressing the view that the same standard of willfulness applies to the question of liquidated damages as to the statute of limitations, and stating that the jury's negative determination "militates against"[301] an award of liquidated damages. It distinguished *Maple Grove* from a contrary ruling in the same district in *Rudolph v. Metropolitan Airports Commission,*[302] noting that the order of Judge Kyle in *Rudolph* cited authority from a bench trial in which there had been no findings on the subject of willfulness. The court went on to make independent findings that the defendant had acted in good faith and with reasonable grounds for believing its conduct conformed with the law.

---

[298] 920 F.2d 335, 358 (6th Cir. 1990).

[299] Herman v. Palo Group Foster Home, Inc., 976 F. Supp. 696, 706 (W.D. Mich. 1997). *See also* L & F Distribs. v. Cruz, 941 S.W.2d 274, 285, 3 WH Cases2d 1158, 132 Lab. Cases (CCH) ¶33,471 (Tex. App. 1996) (discussing circuit split as to whether jury finding of willfulness which the trial judge refused to set aside precluded consideration of Section 11 defense and observing that "we cannot say that the trial court did not consider" employer's good faith).

[300] 41 F. Supp. 2d 932 (D. Minn. 1999).

[301] *Id.* at 941.

[302] 41 F. Supp. 2d 932.

g. Amount of Liquidated Damages Awarded

In *Schneider v. City of Springfield*,[303] a federal district court in Ohio refused to award liquidated damages upon finding that the city had met its burden of proving good faith, but held that the plaintiff was entitled to prejudgment interest in lieu of liquidated damages. Specifically, the court awarded the amount equal to the prejudgment interest that would have been due on its back-pay award, [304] citing the doctrine established by Sixth Circuit case law[305] to the effect that when either no liquidated damages or less-than-double liquidated damages are awarded, the plaintiff must receive, in addition to the actual back pay due, at least the equivalent of prejudgment interest.

E. Estoppel

A federal district court in *Campbell v. HSA Managed Care Systems, Inc.*,[306] refused to apply the doctrine of equitable estoppel to an employee's FLSA claim for unpaid overtime. The employer claimed that because the plaintiff had refused to submit an "overtime correction sheet" requested by the employer and needed to compute the back pay owed, the employee's failure to cooperate should estop the claim. The court found that it was the employee's supervisor who discouraged the employee from filling out proper overtime reports and that therefore the employee's failure to cooperate with an employer's efforts to redress the violation should not bar her FLSA claim for unpaid overtime.

In *Theisen v. City of Maple Grove*,[307] a federal district court held that the accrual date for the 2-year retrospective period for nonwillful FLSA overtime violation damages is ordinarily the date the action was filed. The court rejected the plaintiffs' claim that equitable estoppel should extend the date back to the time

[303]2000 WL 988279 (S.D. Ohio 2000).
[304]*See* discussion of prejudgment interest at §IV.C.3.a.
[305]McClanahan v. Matthews, 440 F.2d 320, 326 (6th Cir. 1971).
[306]4 WH Cases2d 365 (N.D. Ill. 1997).
[307]41 F. Supp. 2d 932.

of a discussion with the police chief supervisor in which the plaintiffs first demanded overtime compensation. The plaintiffs argued that the chief's demand for subsequent meetings delayed the filing of their complaint, giving rise to an estoppel. The court held that a letter from the plaintiffs' counsel to the chief and the city administrator "suggesting and requesting" a stipulation that the accrual of the action be regarded by the parties as the date the plaintiffs first met to discuss their FLSA claims was evidence that such an agreement had not been reached at the meeting. Furthermore, the court found no grounds for estoppel in the absence of unmistakable evidence that the defendant knew its requests for subsequent meetings would delay the plaintiffs in filing their action.

1. *Regular Acceptance of Improper Wages*

In *Bowe v. SMC Electrical Products, Inc.*,[308] the court held that the defendant was not entitled to judgment as a matter of law based on the affirmative defense of equitable estoppel, even where the employee asserting an overtime claim had accepted more than 300 paychecks, because the employee raised genuine issues for trial with respect to whether he knew that the defendant would not pay overtime, whether the defendant was aware of an obligation to pay overtime, whether the employee's delay in bringing the action was intentionally misleading as the defendant claimed, and whether the defendant had relied on the plaintiff's delay to its detriment.

In *Hardrick v. Airway Freight Systems, Inc.*,[309] a federal district court in Illinois refused to allow the affirmative defense of estoppel where the plaintiff employees had agreed to work overtime at the employees' regular rate. The court stated that the FLSA does not distinguish between whether an employee was required to work overtime hours or whether such overtime hours were requested by the employee. Rather, the court held, any time a covered hourly employee works more than 40 hours, the employee must receive the overtime rate.

---

[308]935 F. Supp. 1126, 1135 (D. Colo. 1996).

[309]63 F. Supp. 2d 898 (N.D. Ill. 1999).

An employee was not estopped from asserting a wage claim because of false time records where the employer knew or had reason to know that the reported hours were not correct.[310]

2. *Failure to Demand Overtime Compensation*

In *Mcknight v. Kimberly Clark Corp.*,[311] the Tenth Circuit ruled that a failure to adequately record claimed overtime is "fatal" to a later claim for that time if the company has no reason to be aware of it. In this case, the employee admitted that he was paid for the overtime recorded on his time sheet and that the uncompensated overtime was the result of his failure to record such time.

A federal district court has denied summary judgment to both employer and employee on the issue of whether the employer had "actual or constructive knowledge" that its employee was working overtime where the court held that a general issue of material fact existed as to when the employer learned that the employee was claiming payment for overtime worked.[312]

In *Bjornson v. Daido Metal U.S.A., Inc.*,[313] the court granted summary judgment to an employer on the issue of whether an employee was owed back wages for overtime worked but not recorded. The employee had claimed and been paid for 694 hours of overtime over a 2-year period, then filed suit claiming that he had worked more overtime than he had recorded. The court held that the employee raised no genuine issue of material fact as to whether he had actually worked more hours or whether the employer had actual or constructive knowledge that he had worked more hours than he had claimed.

In *Slattery v. HCA Wesley Rehabilitation Hospital, Inc.*,[314] a federal district court in Kansas granted summary judgment in an FLSA overtime pay case in which the plaintiff failed to show that the employer had actual or constructive knowledge of the

---

[310]Cunningham v. Gibson Elec. Co., 43 F. Supp. 2d 965, 975–77 (N.D. Ill. 1999).
[311]149 F.3d 1125, 4 WH Cases2d 1297 (10th Cir. 1998).
[312]Friou v. L.E. Coppersmith Inc., 4 WH Cases2d 1422 (S.D. Tex. 1998).
[313]12 F. Supp. 2d 837, 4 WH Cases2d 1428 (N.D. Ill. 1998).
[314]83 F. Supp. 2d 1224, 5 WH Cases2d 1541 (D. Kan. 2000).

alleged overtime worked. The collective bargaining agreement provided that overtime would be paid for work over 8 hours in a day, including in the 8 hours a half-hour break. The actual practice was, however, for some employees to work through, rather than taking time off for, the break. Thus, the pay was actually less than would have been provided under the contract for 8 hours per day of actual work, but the violation, if any, was of the contractual provisions, not of the FLSA. The court noted that the defendant's policy mandated prior approval for overtime work to be performed, that working off the clock was strictly prohibited, and that the plaintiff never advised the defendant that she performed work off the clock. The court dismissed the plaintiff's allegation that she was afraid to report the overtime because the plaintiff admitted that she received appropriate overtime pay on every occasion that she had reported overtime hours.

4. *Collective Bargaining, Custom, and Practice*

In *Bernard v. IBP Inc.*,[315] the Fifth Circuit held that despite the provisions of an applicable collective bargaining agreement, the plaintiffs, maintenance employees at a meat processing plant, were not required to pursue a grievance prior to filing an FLSA suit. The court held that a plaintiff's right to pursue a suit under the FLSA is completely independent from his or her rights under the collective bargaining agreement and not "preempted" by it.

The U.S. Court of Appeals for the Seventh Circuit, in determining that the particular on-call time in question was not compensable, enforced the private contractual arrangements under which the employees had volunteered to serve as emergency medical technicians for the on-call crew, observing that "[a]lthough the FLSA overrides contracts, in close cases [where the statutory and regulatory standard is deliberately uncertain] it makes sense to let private arrangements endure."[316]

---

[315]154 F.3d 259, 4 WH Cases2d 1604 (5th Cir. 1998).

[316]Dinges v. Sacred Heart St. Mary's Hosps., Inc., 164 F.3d 1056, 1059, 5 WH Cases2d 78 (7th Cir. 1999).

When a police union negotiated a collective bargaining agreement with separate monthly stipends to compensate "K-9" officers for "off-the-clock" time they spent training, grooming, feeding, and cleaning up after their dogs and to compensate DARE (Drug Abuse Resistance Education) officers for time spent preparing and giving their drug education talks to school children, a district court[317] refused to follow relatively clear statutory[318] and DOL regulatory[319] provisions, deciding instead to exclude these monthly stipends from the regular rate and credit the stipends against the overtime owed. In the court's view, it "better serves the spirit and purpose of the FLSA" and avoids an unjust "windfall" not to give effect to the normal regular rate calculation and to permit the credit where the parties expressly agreed to the stipends in lieu of overtime payments for such work, especially when the resulting overtime owed will be doubled as liquidated damages.

As has been pointed out,[320] Section 3(o) of the FLSA provides a special rule with respect to time spent "changing clothes or washing at the beginning or end of each workday" where such time is covered by an applicable collective bargaining agreement.[321] In *Turner v. City of Philadelphia*,[322] a federal district court in Pennsylvania held that a city's policy over a 30-year period of not compensating correctional officers for time changing in and out of uniforms, which was not specified in a collective bargaining agreement, could still be excluded for FLSA purposes because this policy was a custom and practice under Section 203(o). The court held that the union's "acquiescence" over a 30-year period clearly constituted a custom and practice.

In *Nelson v. Waste Management of Alameda Co.*,[323] a federal district court in California held that a union and an employer may agree in a collective bargaining agreement to pay for lunch

[317]Albanese v. Bergen County, 991 F. Supp. 410, 423 (D.N.J. 1997).
[318]29 U.S.C. §207(e)(5), (6), and (7).
[319]29 C.F.R. §778.207.
[320]*See* Treatise at p. 471.
[321]29 U.S.C. §203(o).
[322]96 F. Supp. 2d 460 (E.D. Pa. 2000).
[323]2000 WL 868523 (N.D. Cal. 2000).

periods even when the employee is relieved of duties. However, the court held that such an agreement did not mean that a claim for overtime under the FLSA could be made for these hours if the employees were not relieved of work during the lunch periods, thus reaching the same result as in *Slattery v. HCA Wesley Rehabilitation Hospital, Inc.*[324]

The circuit courts have taken differing approaches[325] on the effect, in terms of the practical realities of various industries, of Section 3(o) on claims of unionized workers for overtime arising from matters which may or may not be covered by the section's language. Questions about the scope of "changing clothes or washing" and the meaning of "by the express terms of or by custom or practice under" a collective bargaining agreement continue to be litigated, and the effect of recent interpretations by the Department of Labor[326] has also entered the picture.

In a case brought by chicken processing workers, the district court in *Pressley v. Sanderson Farms, Inc.*[327] held that "as a matter of law the time spent by Plaintiffs walking, . . . donning, doffing, and cleaning their equipment, is not compensable work under

---

[324]83 F. Supp. 2d 1224, 5 WH Cases2d 1541 (D. Kan. 2000).

[325]Major court of appeals decisions in this area before this year were *Hoover v. Wyandotte Chemicals Corp.*, 455 F.2d 387 (5th Cir. 1972) (where a long-standing practice exists in connection with clothes changing time under a collective bargaining agreement, and in negotiations the union proposes a change to which the employer does not agree so the practice remains as before, the additional time which the unit sought to have included remains excluded from working time by custom or practice and the employees are not entitled to additional compensation); *Arcadi v. Nestle Food Corp.*, 38 F. 3d 672, 2 WH Cases2d 644 (2d Cir. 1994) *aff'g* 841 F. Supp. 477 (if parties to a contract negotiate over an issue and have an understanding that resolves it, then practice exists even in the absence of express written terms); *Leahy v. City of Chicago,* 96 F.3d 228 (7th Cir. 1996) (where provisions of a labor agreement by their terms fully protect employees' FLSA rights, the agreement is a defense to liability under the FLSA); *Bernard v. IBP, Inc. of Nebraska,* 154 F.3d 259 (5th Cir.1998) (provisions of the collective bargaining agreement did not "pre-empt" plaintiffs' claims for overtime under the FLSA; *Leahy* decision is "preposterous," and completely ignores *Barrentine v. Arkansas-Best Freight System, Inc.,* 450 U.S. 728 (1981) (defines the relationship between rights provided by collective bargaining agreements and enforceable through grievance procedures vs. rights provided by the FLSA and enforceable through the courts)).

[326]Letters by John Fraser, Acting Administrator, dated Dec. 3, 1997, WHM: 99:8107, and Michael Kerr, Acting Administrator, dated Jan. 15, 2001, 2001 WL 58864.

[327]2001 WL 850017 (S.D. Tex. 2001).

the FLSA."[328] It rejected defendant's argument under Section 3(o) that its collective bargaining agreement with plaintiff-employees completely barred plaintiffs' claims that the defendant failed to pay them for all hours worked. After noting that the defendants had failed to bring to the court's attention all the pertinent and arguably controlling circuit court case law, it rested its partial denial of defendant's summary judgment motion on the finding that a factual issue existed as to whether all plaintiffs were covered by the collective bargaining agreement.

In *Anderson v. Pilgrim's Pride Corp.*,[329] a Texas federal district court entered judgment in a chicken processing company's favor following a bench trial on the production employees' claims that the company failed to pay them for donning and doffing time. The court held that such clothes changing time was excluded from compensable work time under Section 3(o) because the collective bargaining agreements under which the employees worked did not provide payment for clothes changing time, the employees at the company never had been compensated for clothes changing time—at least for the period covered by the collective bargaining agreements—and the employees' collective bargaining agent had proposed paying employees for such time during collective bargaining negotiations, but the company had rejected the proposal.

The Third Circuit joined the Second and the Fifth Circuits[330] in taking a broad view of the phrase "custom or practice under a collective bargaining agreement" when it affirmed the district court's determination that a "custom or practice" of nonpayment for clothes changing time existed in *Turner v. City of Philadelphia*.[331] There summary judgment had been granted against the claim of plaintiff corrections officers for overtime compensation for time spent changing into and out of their uniforms. The court held that the city's 30-year policy of not

---

[328] *Id.* at *3.

[329] 147 F. Supp. 2d 556 (E.D.Tex 2001).

[330] Arcadi v. Nestle Food Corp., 38 F.3d 672, 2 WH Cases2d 644 (2d Cir. 1994); Bernard v. IBP, Inc. of Neb., 154 F.3d 259 (5th Cir. 1998).

[331] 262 F.3d 222, 225–27 (3d Cir. 2001), *aff'g* Turner v. City of Phila., 96 F. Supp. 2d 460 (E.D. Pa. 2000).

compensating the corrections officers for clothes changing time resulted in this time being excluded from work time as a "custom or practice under a bona fide collective bargaining agreement" under Section 3(o) even though this policy was neither specified in a collective bargaining agreement nor raised in contract negotiations. The court reasoned that a particular custom or practice can become an implied term of a labor agreement through a prolonged period of acquiescence.

While not relying on Section 3(o), but instead construing 29 C.F.R. §785.23, one of the regulatory provisions for special situations in which agreements between employees and employers may properly determine what is to be counted as hours worked, the Sixth Circuit, in *Brock v. City of Cincinnati*,[332] reversed the district court's entry of judgment in favor of 12 plaintiff police officers following a bench trial. The Sixth Circuit directed entry of judgment in favor of the city on the officers' claims for payment for canine-care work performed at home while off duty. The city and officers had negotiated payment of two hours per week for time spent on canine-care work. The city argued that this constituted a "reasonable agreement" under 29 C.F.R. §785.23 to determine compensable time for activities performed at home. The district court held that the agreement was not reasonable because it far underestimated the actual amount of FLSA canine-care "work" actually performed by the officers. The Sixth Circuit reversed because there was no evidence that the city knew its officers were spending far more time on canine care than the agreement covered, the officers' union agreed to the collective bargaining agreement provision at issue, and the non-monetary benefits to the officers associated with canine care. These non-monetary benefits included a police vehicle to take home for the dog, the construction of kennels by the city at the officers' homes, and the protection and affection provided by a pet. When combined with the money paid to the officers, these other factors rendered the agreement within the range of reasonableness.

---

[332] 236 F.3d 793 (6th Cir. 2001).

G. Res Judicata and Collateral Estoppel

2. *Res Judicata*

a. Final Adjudication on the Merits

In *DeBraska v. Milwaukee,*[333] a federal district court gave res judicata effect to a settlement agreement, holding that the agreement and subsequent dismissal of the action amounted to a final judgment on the merits. The court emphasized that the settlement agreement had been approved by the court and was explicitly incorporated into the dismissal order, that it appeared that the parties intended that the settlement would preclude later litigation of the issues raised in the case, and that the court dismissed the previous action "on its merits and with prejudice."

b. Identity of Parties in the First and Second Proceedings

In *Reich v. D.C. Wiring, Inc.*,[334] the defendants attempted to rely upon an earlier litigation involving the Department of Labor and another employer, in which the federal court had concluded that individuals who performed cable television installation services were independent contractors and not employees for FLSA purposes. If applied in favor of D.C. Wiring, such a finding would have precluded liability. The court concluded that the government could not be bound by a prior litigation to which the party asserting estoppel had not been a party.

In *DeBraska,*[335] the court gave res judicata effect to the resolution of a prior action in which the original complaint, filed in 1988, described the plaintiffs as "law enforcement-officers employed by the Milwaukee Police Department and as members in good standing of the MPA [Milwaukee Police Association]," and the complaint filed in the subsequent action described the nonidentical named plaintiffs using almost identical language.

---

[333]11 F. Supp. 2d 1020, 4 WH Cases2d 1377 (E.D. Wis. 1998).
[334]940 F. Supp. 105, 107-08, 3 WH Cases2d 885 (D.N.J. 1996).
[335]11 F. Supp. 2d 1020, WH Cases2d 1377.

Further, the court found it relevant that the individual plaintiffs were members of the same union, and that one of the attorneys had acted as co-counsel in the previous case. Thus, the district court concluded that there was an identity between the parties in the first and second cases.

In *Chao v. Virginia Department of Transportation*,[336] a federal district court in Virginia denied the DOT's assertion that the Secretary's claim for FLSA violations was barred as a result of res judicata, based on the predecessor suit by 40 inspectors which went to judgment on the merits. The court observed that identity of both claims and parties was necessary for res judicata, and found that neither was present in the case before it.

c. Subsequent Proceeding Must Involve the Same Claim as the First Suit

In *DeBraska*,[337] the court gave res judicata effect to the resolution of a prior compensatory overtime claim. In the first case, police officers alleged that the police department had refused to allow the plaintiffs to take time off "under circumstances where the granting of the request would not unduly disrupt the operation of the police department." The second complaint alleged that vesting approval for time off in the middle management of the police department "violates the rule that compensatory time shall be given to all if the use of compensatory time does not unduly disrupt the operations of the public agency." In concluding that the two actions presented the same underlying claim, the district court rejected the police officers' argument that the current complaint alleged only violations that occurred after the dismissal of the first complaint. Because the underlying claims were both based on the statutory "unduly disrupt" standard, claiming new damages was held insufficient to overcome the res judicata problem.

A district court held that an arbitrator's decision against an employee on the issue of his wrongful termination barred the

---

[336] 157 F. Supp. 2d 681 (E.D. Va. 2001).
[337] 11 F. Supp. 2d 1020, WH Cases2d 1377.

employee's action against his employer alleging violations of the FLSA and retaliatory discharge.[338] The court held that there was a perfect identity of things, causes, and litigants between the two cases.[339]

In *Yapp v. Excel Corp.*,[340] a divided panel of the Tenth Circuit affirmed a decision of the district court, holding that the plaintiff's suit against his employer for wrongful discharge was precluded by his prior suit for unpaid overtime compensation under the FLSA, which was dismissed with prejudice after settlement. The court relied on *Clark v. Haas Group, Inc.*[341] and the Restatement (Second) of Judgments.

In *Chao v. Virginia Department of Transportation*,[342] a federal district court in Virginia denied the DOT's assertion that the Secretary's claim for FLSA violations was barred as a result of res judicata, based on the predecessor suit. The court observed that identity of both claims and parties was necessary for res judicata, and found that neither was present in the case before it. The Secretary sought both prospective and restitutionary injunctions, and those claims, unlike the private claims previously litigated, asserted a public interest.

3. Collateral Estoppel

In *Rogers v. City of Troy*,[343] the court held that the doctrine of collateral estoppel did not preclude it from determining whether the city had violated the FLSA because there was no identity of issues between a state action, which was essentially a breach of contract action, and the present case, which was brought under the FLSA.[344]

---

[338]Ramirez de Arellano v. American Airlines, Inc., 957 F. Supp. 359 (D.P.R.), *aff'd on different reasoning*, 133 F.3d 89 (1st Cir. 1997).

[339]*Id.* at 361.

[340]186 F.3d 1222, 5 WH Cases2d 872 (10th Cir. 1999).

[341]953 F.2d 1235 (10th Cir. 1992).

[342]157 F. Supp. 2d 681 (E.D. Va. 2001).

[343]949 F. Supp. 118, 3 WH Cases2d 1105 (N.D.N.Y. 1996).

[344]*See also* Meringdo v. New York City, 3 WH Cases2d 49 (S.D.N.Y 1995); Reich v. D.C. Wiring, 940 F. Supp. 105, 107–08, 3 WH Cases2d 885 (D.N.J. 1996).

Another district court held that employees were bound by findings of fact in a second FLSA action against the state by co-employees where the parties agreed in the stipulation that the issues in the two actions were nearly identical and the second action controlled the outcome of the first action.[345]

H. Failure to Exhaust Remedies: Effect of Arbitration Awards

In *Montes v. Shearson Lehman Brothers, Inc.*,[346] the Eleventh Circuit vacated an arbitration award denying a claim for unpaid overtime because the arbitrators' decision represented a "manifest disregard of the law." The court concerned itself with distinguishing a "manifest disregard of the law" that justifies vacating an arbitration award from a misinterpretation of the law, which does not. The court explained that an arbitration panel manifestly disregards the law only when (1) the record demonstrates that the panel was "conscious" of the applicable law, "and deliberately ignore[d] it;"[347] and (2) the evidence presented does not "clearly support the award."[348] In this case, it appeared from the record that the arbitration panel had adopted the argument of the employer's counsel urging it to "not follow the FLSA" and instead to "do what is right, what is fair, and what is proper."

A state court held that an employee was not required to exhaust his administrative remedies under the applicable state statute before he could bring an action to recover overtime compensation under the FLSA.[349] To the contrary, an Oregon federal district court enforced a contractual provision requiring an employee to arbitrate his FLSA claim.[350] The court rejected the employee's argument that the arbitration clause deprived him of substantive rights under the FLSA because the clause

[345]Rudberg v. State of Nev., 896 F. Supp. 1017 (D. Nev. 1995).
[346]128 F.3d 1456, 4 WH Cases2d 385 (11th Cir. 1997).
[347]*Id.* at 1461, 4 WH Cases2d at 388.
[348]*Id.* at 1462, 4 WH Cases2d at 389.
[349]Laurence v. State of Colo., 910 P.2d 73 (Colo. Ct. App. 1995).
[350]Coughlin v. Shimizu Am. Corp., 991 F. Supp. 1226, 1231–32, 4 WH Cases2d 828, 831–32 (D. Or. 1998).

provides that the prevailing party is entitled to attorneys' fees and costs, while under the FLSA employers are not awarded attorneys' fees. The court reasoned that an employee has the same remedies irrespective of whether the FLSA claim is heard by the court or the arbitrator.[351]

While affirming on other grounds, the Court of Appeals for the First Circuit reversed a district court's determination[352] that an internal appeals procedure decision against an employee on the issue of his wrongful termination barred the employee's action against his employer alleging violations of the FLSA and retaliatory discharge. It expressed concern about the "apparently unilateral and adhesive nature of [the employer's] employee handbook" and held that there was a lack of fundamental fairness in the employer's grievance process including the absence of an impartial decisionmaker, inadequate discovery, and unfair reliance on alleged lack of timeliness to deny a hearing.

In *Albertson's v. Food Workers*,[353] the Ninth Circuit held that employees under a collective bargaining agreement may assert FLSA claims in court, even if those claims may be covered by the grievance/arbitration procedure. The court cited the Supreme Court decision in *Alexander v. Gardner-Denver*[354] that found statutory rights independent from a collective bargaining agreement and noted that most circuits had found that employees could sue under the FLSA without first resorting to the grievance procedure under the collective bargaining agreement.

The Fifth Circuit also held in *Bernard v. IBP Inc.*[355] that despite the provisions of an applicable collective bargaining agreement, the plaintiffs, maintenance employees at a meat processing plant, were not required to pursue a grievance prior to filing an FLSA suit. The court held that a plaintiff's right to pursue a suit under the FLSA is completely independent from

---

[351] *Id.*

[352] Ramirez de Arellano v. American Airlines, Inc., 133 F.3d 89, 91 (1st Cir.), *rev'g preclusion holding and aff'g on other grounds,* 957 F. Supp. 359, 361 (D.P.R. 1997).

[353] 157 F.3d 758, 4 WH Cases2d 1704 (9th Cir. 1998).

[354] 415 U.S. 36 (1974) (discussed, together with Barrantine v. Arkansas-Best Freight Sys., 450 U.S. 728, 24 WH Cases 1284 (1981), in Treatise at pp. 1303–07).

[355] 154 F.3d 259, 4 WH Cases2d 1604 (5th Cir. 1998).

his or her rights under the collective bargaining agreement and not "preempted" by it.

The same decision was reached in *Collins v. Lobdell,*[356] where the court of appeals affirmed the district court's decision that public employees challenging their employer's requirement concerning the mandatory use of comp time were not required to exhaust collective bargaining grievance procedures before suing in federal court.

In *Giles v. City of New York,*[357] the District Court for the Southern District of New York held that a labor contract providing for binding arbitration of disputes did not prevent employees from bringing an FLSA claim in federal court. FLSA claims were not specifically identified as being within the ambit of the labor agreement, and the arbitration provision also required the parties to split the costs arising from the arbitration, including the arbitrator's fees.

In *Floss v. Ryan's Family Steak Houses, Inc.*,[358] the Sixth Circuit reversed the district court and held unenforceable a particular agreement to arbitrate FLSA claims. While such agreements to arbitrate are generally enforceable, the court found that the arbitration agreement at issue in the case, which gave the arbitration provider unlimited discretion to alter the applicable rules and procedures, without any obligation to notify or receive consent of the employee, was unenforceable because the extensive reservation of the right to modify the terms of the agreement meant that the contract lacked adequate consideration. While reserving decision on and not itself deciding the question presented to the D.C. Circuit in *Cole v. Burns International Security Services*[359]—whether mandatory arbitration is to be enforced where the agreement imposes arbitral fees on employees seeking to enforce statutory rights, the Sixth Circuit seems favorably disposed toward the result reached by the D.C. Circuit in that case, declining enforcement of such an agreement.

---

[356]188 F.3d 1124, 5 WH Cases2d 929 (9th Cir. 1999).

[357]41 F. Supp. 2d 308, 5 WH Cases2d 294 (S.D.N.Y. 1999).

[358]211 F.3d 306, 6 WH Cases2d 17 (6th Cir. 2000).

[359]105 F.3d 1465, 1482 (D.C. Cir. 1997).

Local 1035, International Brotherhood of Teamsters v. Pepsi-Cola Allied Bottlers, Inc.,[360] was a suit brought by a union on behalf of its members for a declaration that a provision of the collective bargaining agreement was invalid under the FLSA and Connecticut state law. The employer argued that the employees had failed to exhaust their remedies under the collective bargaining agreement, and thus were barred from pursuing the case under Connecticut state law. The court noted that failure to pursue a collective bargaining agreement remedy does not preclude suit on the federal law claim,[361] and went on to find under applicable state law that pursuit of the state claim was also not barred.[362]

The decision of a divided Supreme Court in *Adams v. Circuit City*,[363] appears to resolve the question left at least partially open since *Gilmer* v. *Interstate/Johnson Lane Corp.*,[364] whether the language of the Federal Arbitration Act (FAA), which excludes from its coverage "contracts of employment of seamen, railroad employees, or any other class of workers engaged in foreign or interstate commerce,"[365] exempts only contracts of employment with transportation workers. Holding that the better reading of the language only exempts transportation employment contracts, the court concluded that a mandatory arbitration clause in an employment contract can preclude plaintiff's judicial challenge under the FLSA of an employment practice which

---

[360]83 F. Supp. 2d 301 (D. Conn. 1999).

[361]Citing Barrantine v. Arkansas-Best Freight Sys., 450 U.S. 728 (1981).

[362]The court found that the bar is not applicable under state law unless the remedy provided by the collective bargaining agreement is "meaningful," and that the remedy provided would not have been meaningful. The agreement provided that "[i]f any provision of the Article is invalid under [state law, it] shall be renegotiated for the purpose of adequate replacement." The court continued, saying that "[i]t is disingenuous to suggest that making the individual employees negotiate a provision of the C.B.A. with their employer is an adequate remedy for the case at hand. Forcing employees to initially negotiate individually with the employer would violate the express contractual provision of the agreement . . . [and] [m]aking the individual plaintiffs represent themselves before their employer logically defeats the purpose of [the state statute] which embodies the important public policy of ensuring that employees receive wages due them." 83 F. Supp. 2d at 306–07.

[363]532 U.S. 105 (2001).

[364]500 U.S. 20 (1991).

[365]9 U.S.C. §1.

otherwise would be covered by the arbitation agreement. At least in the case where the arbitration plan is fair to the prospective plaintiff, the arbitration agreement will be enforced. *Circuit City* does not by its terms directly address the enforcement of arbitration agreements as to FLSA claims, or the possible effect it might have on the future application of *Barrentine*[366] to FLSA cases.

In *Louis v. Geneva Enterprises, Inc.*,[367] decided before *Circuit City,* the district court denied the defendant's motion to dismiss or stay pending arbitration of the plaintiff's FLSA claim. The court held that, despite the language in the individual mandatory arbitration agreement, "a plaintiff has a right to vindicate his FLSA claim in court."[368] The court relied on *Barrentine,*[369] in which the Supreme Court created an FLSA exception to the general rule that agreements to arbitrate should be enforced.

Schwertfeger v. Village of Sauk,[370] decided March 23, 1991 without reference to *Circuit City,* holds that when an employee is not being paid for work that is clearly compensable as defined in the collective bargaining agreement, then *Barrentine* protects the employee's congressionally granted right to bring the FLSA claim to court.

In *Nur v. K.F.C., U.S.A., Inc.*,[371] decided the same day as *Circuit City,* the district court held that the arbitration agreement did encompass the claims in the plaintiff's suit, including the FLSA claim, because they all arose out of the plaintiff's employment. The plaintiff did not raise any arguments addressing an FLSA exception, but rather attacked the enforceability of the arbitration agreement as a whole.

In *Giordano v. Pep-Boys—Manny, Moe & Jack, Inc.*,[372] the defendant had filed a motion to compel arbitration and to dismiss the complaint without prejudice, based on an employ-

---

[366]450 U.S. at 739.
[367]128 F. Supp. 2d 912 (E.D.Va. 2000).
[368]*Id.* at 912.
[369]450 U.S. at 739.
[370]2001 WL 293115 (N.D. Ill. 2001).
[371]142 F. Supp. 2d 48, 51 (D. D.C. 2001).
[372]2001 U.S. Dist. LEXIS 5433 (E.D. Pa. 2001).

ment arbitration agreement under which plaintiff, who earned $400 per week, was required to pay half the arbitration costs. The court held that, because of its unreasonable terms, the agreement as written was unenforceable. While rejecting plaintiff's arguments based on *Barrentine* and *Gilmer,* the court ordered arbitration to the extent that defendant would limit plaintiff's share of the arbitration costs to the federal court filing fees, based on plaintiff's earlier offer to pay only that much of the cost.

I. Compromise, Settlement, Waiver, and Release

1. Private Settlement, Waiver, and Release

In *Kendall v. City of Chesapeake,*[373] the Fourth Circuit affirmed summary judgment for the employer as against employees on a claim for back wages brought under 42 U.S.C. §1983, which provides for a remedy for deprivations of constitutional and civil rights by anyone acting under color of state law. The district court held, and the Fourth Circuit affirmed, that the mechanisms established by the FLSA preclude private Section 1983 actions to enforce FLSA rights. The Department of Labor had investigated the city's failure to pay overtime to the workers in question. In 1995, the city agreed to pay back wages, and the employees accepted the payments, each one signing a release of any right to bring a suit for the back wages. Two years later, some of the employees filed suit alleging that the city, acting under color of state law, had deprived them of their FLSA rights by concealing the city's true liability and fraudulently inducing them to sign the releases. The court concluded that the FLSA's remedies were sufficiently comprehensive to preclude Section 1983 suits, stating that the FLSA includes criminal penalties for willful violators, private rights of action in both federal and state court, and authorization for the Secretary of Labor to supervise payments and bring actions to enforce the Act. This scheme, and particularly the individual enforcement provisions, evinces con-

[373]174 F.3d 437, 5 WH Cases2d 330 (4th Cir. 1999).

gressional intent to create a "carefully tailored" statutory scheme that exclusively limits private remedies to redress FLSA violations to those actions allowed by the terms of the FLSA itself.

In *Vento v. Versatile Logic Systems Corp.*,[374] the plaintiff sought overtime and liquidated damages under the FLSA and Oregon wage law. At a mandatory arbitration of the claim, the employer prevailed, and the plaintiff sought a trial *de novo*. In the trial court, the employer moved to dismiss, relying on an agreement signed by the plaintiff in consideration of a $1,000 postemployment payment, purporting to release the employer from all claims arising during the course of her employment. The trial court granted summary judgment for the employer. On appeal, the plaintiff relied on the invalidity of the release as applied to FLSA and Oregon wage claims. The appeals court did not reach the issue of whether the FLSA prohibits waiver of wage claims absent DOL supervision. Rather, the appeals court found that there was a genuine issue of material fact as to whether the $1,000 payment was sufficient to satisfy all of the plaintiff's potential claims under the FLSA and state law, and thus that the grant of summary judgment was erroneous.

In *O'Connor v. United States*,[375] the plaintiffs were members of a federal bargaining unit represented by a union, and in prior proceedings that union, which had a collective bargaining agreement with the government, instituted a grievance relating to the classification and pay of persons represented by the union. Under the Civil Service Reform Act of 1978, which covers federal employees represented by a union, employees were limited to the grievance procedure negotiated by their union. The grievance was eventually settled. In 1994, Congress amended the "exclusive remedy" provision of the CSRA by adding the word "administrative," making the pertinent sentence read:

> Except as provided in subsections (d), (e) and (g) of this section, the [grievance] procedures shall be the exclusive administrative procedures for resolving grievances which fall within its coverage.

[374] 3 P.3d 176 (Or. Ct. App. 2000).
[375] 50 Fed. Cl. 285, 289 (2001).

Plaintiffs in this case argued that, while they would still be limited in their potential *administrative* remedies, the amendment gave them the right to pursue their claim in the federal courts. The court found that such a reading would destroy the scheme created by Congress for enforcement of federal employees' rights, and thus held that the prior law, under which judicial attention to such claims was precluded, was not altered by the amendment. In addition, the court held that even if it had jurisdiction over the matter, the settlement reached between the union and the agency in the earlier grievance procedure operated as an "accord and satisfaction" of their claim. Thus the court granted defendant federal agency's motion to dismiss plaintiffs' complaint.

2. *DOL-Supervised Settlements*

In *Bullington v. Fayette County School District,*[376] a state appellate court in Georgia held that where the employer has achieved a settlement supervised and approved by the Department of Labor, and has sent a Form WH-58 agreement (based upon a settlement believed to be close to full payment) requesting that employees sign a release if they wish to accept the monetary payments, the employee releases FLSA claims if the employee cashes the check, after notice that doing so constitutes waiver of his right to sue, even if the employee refuses to sign the release.

The district court held in *Jackson v. Go-Tane Services, Inc.*[377] that, although some of the plaintiffs had signed and cashed the checks issued to them, the defendant had not met its burden of proving an agreement by the employees to release their claims under Section 216(c) in exchange for the payments. The mere signing and cashing of checks does not waive FLSA claims.[378]

---

[376] 2000 WL 1568726, 6 WH Cases2d 743 (Ga. Ct. App. 2000).

[377] 2001 U.S. Dist. LEXIS 10240 (N.D. Ill. 2001).

[378] *Id.*

3. Judicially Approved Consent Decrees

In *DeBraska v. Milwaukee*,[379] a federal district court gave res judicata effect to a settlement agreement, holding that the agreement and subsequent dismissal of the action amounted to a final judgment on the merits. The court emphasized that the settlement agreement had been approved by the court and was explicitly incorporated into the dismissal order, that it appeared that the parties intended that the settlement would preclude later litigation of the issues raised in the case, and that the court dismissed the previous action "on its merits and with prejudice."

VII. DEDUCTIONS, SETOFFS, AND COUNTERCLAIMS

The U.S. Court of Appeals for the First Circuit held in *Roman v. Maietta Construction*[380] that, in calculating back pay due an employee, it is permissible to deduct compensatory time payments already made, at the regular rate of pay, from the total amount of overtime due. The court found that although the FLSA does not expressly authorize such a setoff, as the Act requires all overtime payments to be made "in cash or its equivalent," it was nonetheless fair and reasonable in this case to prevent the employee from receiving a windfall. Moreover, the court found that the award of liquidated damages adequately compensated the employee for the employer's FLSA violations.

The principles noted in the Treatise[381] that preclude an employer from asserting a counterclaim in an employee's FLSA action do not preclude an employee from asserting an FLSA counterclaim when sued by an employer for breach of the employment agreement.[382]

---

[379] 11 F. Supp. 2d 1020, 4 WH Cases2d 1377 (E.D. Wis. 1998).

[380] 147 F.3d 71, 4 WH Cases2d 1293 (1st Cir. 1998).

[381] Pp. 1319–20.

[382] *See* H & R Block, Ltd. v. Housden, 24 F. Supp. 2d 703, 5 WH Cases2d 190 (E.D. Tex. 1998) (employee filed FLSA counterclaim in employer's state court action for violation of noncompetition and nonsolicitation clauses in employment agreement, which was then removed to federal court by additional parties added as counterclaim defendants).

Certain contractual overtime payments may be offset from FLSA overtime liability under 29 U.S.C. §§207(e)(5)–(7) and 207(h)(2). In *Nolan v. City of Chicago*,[383] a federal magistrate judge held, after a trial on the papers, that offsets to which the defendant is entitled under Sections 7(e)(5)–(7) should be calculated on a pay period by pay period basis.

In *Summers v. Howard University*,[384] the federal district court denied the defendant's motion for partial summary judgment on plaintiffs' claims for overtime for pre-and post-shift work and for uncompensated work during meal breaks. The defendant contended that it was entitled to a setoff against any amounts found to be due for "any overtime that a plaintiff was paid for hours worked beyond eight (8) hours per day or forty (40) hours per week."[385] The court found no basis for an offset under Section 207(h)(2) as there was no evidence of any overtime payments having been made in excess of what the FLSA required.

VIII. Evidence and Discovery

A. In General

In *Herman v. Davis Acoustical Corp.*,[386] a federal district court in New York ruled that the special master did not abuse his discretion by admitting an exhibit summarizing calculations made by plaintiff Department of Labor's expert based on the employer's payrolls. The court found that given the special master's "substantial legal experience," there was no danger that he would be confused by the summary aid. The court also upheld the special master's decision to admit summaries of the employer's payrolls into evidence, even though the summaries contained some errors, because it found the special master had considered the error rate.

---

[383] 125 F. Supp. 2d 324 (N.D. Ill. 2000).
[384] 127 F. Supp. 2d 27 (D.D.C. 2000).
[385] *Id.* at 32.
[386] 21 F. Supp. 2d 130, 4 WH Cases2d 1615 (N.D.N.Y. 1998).

One court[387] ordered an employer to pay all subpoenaed employee-witnesses for time spent testifying (less witness fees received) in a Section 16(b) action against it, holding that Section 15(a)(3)[388] and other federal statutes[389] barred the refusal of an employer-defendant to pay witnesses (whether hourly or salaried) subpoenaed by plaintiffs to testify on their behalf in their overtime and liquidated damages suit while paying other employee-witnesses testifying in its defense and paying its employees who were required to testify in all cases to which it was not a party. Furthermore, despite its order requiring their payment, the court ruled that testimony by these employees of the employer's refusal to pay the witnesses subpoenaed by the plaintiffs was relevant "to the issue of retaliation" against plaintiffs, not unduly prejudicial, and therefore admissible.

In *Wright v. Aargo Security Services, Inc.*,[390] a federal district court in New York ruled on the defendant's objections to discovery sought by the plaintiff of the records kept by the defendant with respect to hours worked by employees other than the plaintiff, and of overtime paid to other employees. The defendant argued that none of its other employees was situated similarly to the plaintiff, and that whether or not the FLSA was violated with respect to any other employee did not bear on the question of whether the defendant violated the statute in the plaintiff's case. The court overruled both objections, finding that time and wage records showing overtime worked by other employees are probative because they arguably bear on the defendant's knowledge of the FLSA's overtime requirements, and therefore on the question whether or not its conduct with respect to the plaintiff was willful. If the records showed numerous other violations, they might tend to show the defendant's

---

[387]Perdomo v. Sears, Roebuck & Co., 5 WH Cases2d 1021, 1023–24 (M.D. Fla. 1999) (witness left with impression that question of whether to pay him for work time lost while testifying for plaintiffs would be decided by employer after he testified).

[388]29 U.S.C. §215(a)(3).

[389]42 U.S.C. §1985(2) and (3) (prohibiting intimidation and retaliation against witnesses).

[390]2000 WL 264326 (S.D.N.Y. 2000).

reckless disregard of the requirements of the FLSA or, conversely, if they showed meticulous compliance in other employees' cases, they might tend to show that any violation in the plaintiff's case was not willful. Moreover, the overtime records of other employees could be helpful to the plaintiff in estimating the amount of overtime he worked if, as alleged by the plaintiff, the defendant did not keep adequate records of the plaintiff's hours of work.

B. The Informer's Privilege

In *Herman v. Lipe*,[391] a trial court issued a protective order based on the informer's privilege to preclude the employer from asking witnesses about the following subjects during depositions:

> [Whether] current or former employee[s] . . . spoke to an agent of the Department of Labor . . . whether [they] complained to DOL regarding minimum wage or overtime . . . [the] content of such complaint . . . [or] whether that witness knew of any . . . employees who complained to DOL . . . [and] the content of such speech.[392]

The district court affirmed this order over the defendant's objection.[393]

G. Employee Interviews

In *Morisky v. Public Service Electric & Gas Co.*,[394] lawyers who had been consulted about a possible FLSA case for unpaid overtime by certain potential plaintiffs who were employees of the defendants prepared a questionnaire, which they subsequently distributed for response at a meeting of approximately 40 company employees and possibly others, held at a firehouse. Blank copies of the questionnaire were distributed after the

---

[391] 4 WH Cases2d 699 (C.D. Ill. 1997).
[392] *Id.* at 699–700.
[393] *Id.* at 702.
[394] 91 F.R.D. 419, 2000 U.S. Dist. LEXIS 1916 (D.N.J. 2000).

meeting for use by other employees. Eventually, the attorneys received completed questionnaires from 141 individuals, some of whom became named plaintiffs or filed consents to join in the litigation. Defense counsel learned of the existence of the questionnaires at the deposition of one of the named plaintiffs. After having sought and been refused access to these questionnaires, except for a copy of a blank questionnaire, the defendants moved to compel their disclosure. The plaintiffs resisted on the grounds of attorney-client privilege and work-product privilege. A federal magistrate in New Jersey held that questionnaires drafted by plaintiffs' attorneys and completed by named plaintiffs and other potential claimants were not protected by the attorney-client privilege or the work-product doctrine. Because the initial meeting was held in an open forum where nonemployees could have attended and because employees who had neither met the attorneys nor sought legal representation completed the forms without attorney involvement, the attorney-client privilege did not apply. The only part of the questionnaire that was even arguably work product was the questions, and these had already been disclosed; the factual information in the completed surveys was not work product, and the defendants had a substantial need for the material.

H. Employee and Employer Admissions

In two cases[395] involving the admissibility of tax returns or related materials in which a worker has been characterized by the putative employer, the IRS or the worker himself as either an employee or an independent contractor, the question of whether such a characterization constituted an admission was not addressed. Both courts determined that the tendered evidentiary materials were not relevant to the determination to be made, referring to the governing "economic reality" tests.

---

[395] *Morrison v. Int'l Programs Consortium, Inc.*, 253 F.3d 5, 7 WH Cases2d 74 (D.C. Cir. 2001); *Johnson v. Unified Gov't of Wyandotte County/Kansas City, Kansas*, 2001 WL 699049 (D. Kan. 2001).

IX. Damages

C. Integration of State and Federal Damages

A Louisiana court determined that the amount of workers' compensation due under the Louisiana Workers' Compensation Act to an injured worker who had been paid less than he was due under the FLSA must be based on what the worker should have been paid pursuant to the federal minimum wage, not on the worker's actual wage. Thus, even where an employee is paid weekly wages that are below the federal minimum, the employee's temporary total disability benefits must nevertheless be calculated using the federal minimum wage rather than the employee's actual wages.[396] Contrary results would contradict strong public policy behind the state workers' compensation act and FLSA.

D. Integration With Other Federal Remedies [New Topic]

In *Tran v. Tran,*[397] a federal district court in New York, after a bench trial on claims under the FLSA and RICO,[398] awarded judgment for the plaintiff on the RICO claim in the amount of some $600,000. The court had also found a violation of the FLSA, on which the back pay and liquidated damages would have amounted to under $100,000. Both claims arose out of the same conduct by the defendant, except that a longer period was considered in the RICO claim, and, under RICO, the actual damages were tripled. The court did not award the plaintiff any judgment on the FLSA claim, in order to prevent the plaintiff from recovering twice for the same injury, and because the RICO damages covered the entire period of the FLSA damages. Subsequently, the plaintiff applied for attorneys' fees, as provided for under both statutes, and they were allowed in substantial part.

---

[396]Breaux v. Hoffpauir, 674 So. 2d 234, 3 WH Cases2d 569 (La. 1996). *See also* Trujillo v. Tanuz, 85 N.M. 35, 508 P.2d 1332 (1973).

[397]2000 WL 1099906, 6 WH Cases2d 507 (S.D.N.Y. 2000).

[398]Racketeer Influenced and Corrupt Organizations Act (RICO), 18 U.S.C. ch. 96.

XI. JURY INSTRUCTIONS

A. Generally

In *Holzapfel v. Town of Newburgh,*[399] the U.S. Court of Appeals for the Second Circuit held that jury instructions that varied somewhat from the language used in the statute were erroneous. The court concluded that the trial court's use of "reasonable" and "sufficiently related" to describe preparatory and conclusory work did not correspond to the statutory language defining work as "controlled or required," "necessarily and primarily," "integral and indispensable." The court believed that the difference created by the variance in the language was sufficient to prejudice the employee.

In *Baker v. Barnard Construction Co.,*[400] the plaintiffs sought compensation for certain travel time associated with their postliminary refueling and maintenance of construction machinery and equipment. As a matter of law, this time was compensable if it was "integral and indispensable" to their primary activities. The case was tried to a jury, and the court's instructions to the jury permitted them to determine, in effect, whether the plaintiffs had waived their right to compensation for the time in question. The jury found for the defendants on all claims. On the plaintiffs' appeal of the verdict as being based on erroneous instructions, the Tenth Circuit reversed and remanded. It found no merit in the contention that the jury instructions, taken as a whole, did not mislead the jury, finding that nothing in the instructions as a whole would allow the jury to disregard the erroneous instruction that in order to find for the plaintiffs, it must affirmatively find the absence of a waiver.

In *Turyna v. Martam Construction Co.,*[401] the court reversed and remanded the case for a new trial because "the verdict as returned appears to be internally inconsistent, and the form itself is hopelessly confused." On the verdict, the jury found

---

[399] 935 F. Supp. 418, 424–25 (S.D.N.Y. 1996).

[400] 146 F.3d 1214, 4 WH Cases2d 1249 (10th Cir. 1998).

[401] 83 F.3d 178, 179, 3 WH Cases2d 634 (7th Cir. 1996).

"against plaintiff" on Count II, which alleged retaliation claims under the FLSA and state law. However, the jury awarded punitive damages on Count II against one of the defendants. The court analyzed the case under Rule 49 of the Federal Rules of Civil Procedure and found that it had no option but to remand the case for a new trial on Count II.[402] The verdict form is attached to the published decision. [403]

The Tenth Circuit upheld a district court's refusal to instruct the jury that meal time to be bona fide must be "scheduled" and that it must occur "at a regular time," reasoning that such language does not appear in Section 785.19 of the regulations.[404] Similarly, the Fourth Circuit in a fluctuating-pay-plan case upheld a district court's refusal to instruct the jury that a "clear understanding" by employees that their hourly overtime premium was equal to one-half of the adjusted hourly rate was required.[405]

Where the issue was whether maintenance employees who could not leave the premises of the meat processing company during their meal break, were required to wear radios and tool belts during the break, and occasionally had to interrupt their breaks to attend to maintenance problems should be paid during these breaks because they were "on call" and were not on bona fide meal breaks, the court denied defendant's proffered instruction, and refused to permit argument to the jury, that plaintiffs were entitled to pay only for those lunch periods which were actually interrupted by problems requiring their immediate attention.[406]

---

[402]*Id.* at 180–81, 3 WH Cases2d 634.

[403]*Id.* at 183–85, 3 WH Cases2d 634.

[404]Bates v. Department of Corr., 81 F.3d 1008, 3 WH Cases2d 460 (10th Cir. 1996). These requirements appear at 29 C.F.R. §553.223(b).

[405]Bailey v. County of Georgetown, 94 F.3d 152, 3 WH Cases2d 776 (4th Cir. 1996).

[406]Bernard v. IBP, Inc., 154 F.3d 259, 265–66 (5th Cir. 1998).

APPENDICES

APPENDIX A.3 [EXPANDED AND RETITLED APPENDIX]

FLSA AND PORTAL-TO-PORTAL ACT AMENDMENTS OF 1996 AND LATER

Text of relevant sections of Pub. L. No. 106-151, approved December 9, 1999 (An Act to amend the Fair Labor Standards Act of 1938 to clarify the overtime exemption for employees engaged in fire protection activities)

"Employee in fire protection activities" means an employee, including a firefighter, paramedic, emergency medical technician, rescue worker, ambulance personnel, or hazardous materials worker, who—

1) is trained in fire suppression, has the legal authority and responsibility to engage in fire suppression, and is employed by a fire department of a municipality, county, fire district, or State; and

2) is engaged in the prevention, control, and extinguishment of fires or response to emergency situations where life, property, or the environment is at risk.

Text of relevant sections of Pub. L. No. 105-334, enacted October 31, 1998 (Drive for Teen Employment Act)

Sec. 1 Short Title.

This Act may be cited as the "Drive for Teen Employment Act".

Sec. 2. Authority for Minors to Operate Motor Vehicles.

(a) Amendment—Section 13(c) of the Fair Labor Standards Act of 1938 (29 U.S.C. 213(c)) is amended by adding at the end the following:

"(6) In the administration and enforcement of the child labor provisions of this Act, employees who are under 17 years of age may not drive automobiles or trucks on public roadways. Employees who are 17 years of age may drive automobiles or trucks on public roadways only if—

"(A) such driving is restricted to daylight hours;

"(B) the employee holds a State license valid for the type of driving

involved in the job performed and has no records of any moving violation at the time of hire;

"(C) the employee has successfully completed a State approved driver education course;

"(D) the automobile or truck is equipped with a seat belt for the driver and any passengers and the employee's employer has instructed the employee that the seat belts must be used when driving the automobile or truck;

"(E) the automobile or truck does not exceed 6,000 pounds of gross vehicle weight;

"(F) such driving does not involve—

"(i) the towing of vehicles;

"(ii) route deliveries or route sales;

"(iii) the transportation for hire of property, goods, or passengers;

"(iv) urgent, time-sensitive deliveries;

"(v) more than two trips away from the primary place of employment in any single day for the purpose of delivering goods of the employee's employer to a customer (other than urgent, time-sensitive deliveries);

"(vi) more than two trips away from the primary place of employment in any single day for the purpose of transporting passengers (other than employees of the employer);

"(vii) transporting more than three passengers (including employees of the employer); or

"(viii) driving beyond a 30 mile radius from the employee's place of employment; and

"(G) such driving is only occasional and incidental to the employee's employment. For purposes of subparagraph (G), the term 'occasional and incidental' is no more than one-third of an employee's worktime in any workday and no more than 20 percent of an employee's worktime in any workweek.".

(b) Effective Date—

(1) In General—This Act shall become effective on the date of the enactment of this Act.

(2) Exception—The amendment made by subsection (a) defining the term "occasional and incidental" shall also apply to any case, action, citation, or appeal pending on the date of the enactment of this Act unless such case, action, citation, or appeal involves property damage or personal injury.

Text of relevant sections of Pub. L. No. 105-221, enacted August 7, 1998 (Amy Somers Volunteers at Food Banks Act)

Sec. 1. Short Title.

This Act may be cited as the "Amy Somers Volunteers at Food Banks Act".

Sec. 2. Fair Labor Standards Act of 1938.

Section 3(e) of the Fair Labor Standards Act of 1938 (29 U.S.C. 203(e)) is amended by adding at the end the following:

"(5) The term 'employee' does not include individuals who volunteer their services solely for humanitarian purposes to private non-profit food banks and who receive from the food banks groceries.".

Text of relevant sections of Pub. L. No. 104-188, enacted August 20, 1996 (Small Business Job Protection Act of 1996)

Sec. 1. Short Title; Table of Contents.

(a) *Short Title.*—This Act may be cited as the "Small Business Job Protection Act of 1996".

. . .

Sec. 2101. Short Title.

This section and section 2102 and 2103 may be cited as the "Employee Commuting Flexibility Act of 1996".

Sec. 2102. Proper Compensation For Use of Employer Vehicles.

Section 4(a) of the Portal-to-Portal Act of 1947 (29 U.S.C. 254(a)) is amended by adding at the end the following: "For purposes of this subsection, the use of an employer's vehicle for travel by an employee and activities performed by an employee and activities performed by an employee which are incidental to the use of such vehicle for commuting shall not be considered part of the employee's principal activities if the use of such vehicle for travel is within the normal commuting area for the employer's business or establishment and the use of the employer's vehicle is subject to an agreement on the partof the employer and the employee or representative of such employee.".

Section 2103. Effective Date.

The amendment made by section 2101 shall take effect on the date of the enactment of this Act and shall apply in determining the application of section 4 of the Portal-to-Portal Act of 1947 to an employee in any civil action brought before such date of enactment but pending on such date.

Sec. 2104. Minimum Wage Increase.

(a) *Short Title.*—This section may be cited as the "Minimum Wage Increase Act of 1996".

(b) *Amendment.*—Paragraph (1) of section 6(a) of the Fair Labor Standards Act of 1938 (29 U.S.C. 206(a)) is amended to read as follows:

"(1) except as otherwise provided in this section, not less than $4.25 an hour during the period ending on September 30, 1996, not less than $4.75 an hor during the year beginning on October 1, 1996, and not less than $5.15 an hour beginning September 1, 1997;".

(c) *Conforming Amendment.*—Section 6 of such Act (29 U.S.C. 206) is amended by striking subsection (c).

Sec. 2105. Fair Labor Standards Act Amendments.

(a) *Computer Professionals.*—Section 13(a) of the Fair Labor Standards Act of 1938 (29 U.S.C. 213(a)) is amended by striking the period at the end of paragraph (16) and inserting "; or" and by adding after that paragraph the following:

"(17) any employee who is a computer systems analyst, computer programmer, software engineer, or other similarly skilled worker, whose primary duty is—

"(A) the application of systems analysis techniques and procedures, including consulting with users, to determine hardware, software, or system functional specifications;

"(B) the design, development, documentation, analysis, creation, testing, or modication of computer systems or programs, including prototypes, based on and related to user or system design specifications;

"(C) the design, documentation, testing, creation, or modification of computer programs related to machine operating systems; or

"(D) a combination of duties described in subparagraphs (A), (B), and (C) the performance of which requires the same level of skills, and

who, in the case of an employee who is compensated on an hourly basis, is compensated at a rate of not les than $27.63 an hour.".

(b) *Tip Credit.*—The last sentence of section 3(m) of the Fair Labor Standards Act of 1938 (29 U.S.C. 203(m)) is amended by striking "previous sentence" and inserting "preceding 2 sentences" and by striking "(1)" and "(2)" and such section is amended by striking the next to last sentence and inserting the following: "In determining the wage an employer is required to pay a tipped employee, the amount paid such employee by the employee's employer shall be an amount equal to—.

"(1) the cash wage paid such employee which for purposes of such determination shall be not less than the cash wage required to be paid such an employee on the date of the enactment of this paragraph; and

"(2) an additional amount on account of the tips received by such employee which amount is equal to the difference between the wage specified in paragraph (1) and the wage in effect under section 6(a)(1). The additional amount on account of tips may not exceed the value of the tips actually received by an employee.".

(c) *Opportunity Wage.*—Section 6 of the Fair Labor Standards Act of 1938 (29 U.S.C. 206) is amended by adding at the end the following:

"(g)(1) In lieu of the rate prescribed by subsection (a)(1), any employer may pay any employee of such employer; during the first 90 consecutive calendar days after such employee is initially employed by such employer, a wage which is not less than $4.25 an hour.

"(2) No employer may take any action to displace employees (including partial displacements such as reduction in hours, wages, or employment benefits) for purposes of hiring individuals at the wage authorized in paragraph (1).

"(3) Any employer who violates this subsection shall be considered to have violated section 15(a)(3).

"(4) This subsection shall only apply to an employee who has not attained the age of 20 years.".

Text of relevant sections of Pub. L. No. 104-174, enacted August 6, 1996 (1996 Compactors and Balers Safety Standards Modernization Act)

Sec. 1. Authority for 16- and 17-Year-Olds to Load Materials into Scrap Paper Balers and Paper Box Compactors

Section 13(c) of the Fair Labor Standards Act of 1938 (29 U.S.C. 213(c)) is amended by adding to the end thereof the following new paragraph:

"(5)(A) In the administration and enforcement of the child labor provisions of this Act, employees who are 16 and 17 years of age shall be permitted to load materials into, but not operate or unload materials from, scrap paper balers and paper box compactors—

"(i) that are safe for 16- and 17-year-old employees loading the scrap paper balers or paper box compactors; and

"(ii) that cannot be operated while being loaded.

"(B) For purposes of subparagraph (A), scrap paper balers and paper box compactors shall be considered safe for 16- or 17-year-old employees to load only if—

"(i)(I) the scrap paper balers and paper box compactors meet the American National Standards Institute's Standard ANSI Z245.5-1990 for scrap paper balers and Standard ANSI Z245.2-1992 for paper box compactors; or

"(II) the scrap paper balers and paper box compactors meet an applicable standard that is adopted by the American National Standards Institute after the date of enactment of this paragraph and that is certified by the Secretary to be at least as protective of the safety of minors as the standard described in subclause (I);

"(ii) the scrap paper balers and paper box compactors include an on-off switch incorporating a key-lock or other system and the control of the system is maintained in the custody of employees who are 18 years of age or older;

"(iii) the on-off switch of the scrap paper balers and paper box compactors is maintained in an off position when the scrap paper balers and paper box compactors are not in operation; and

"(iv) the employer of 16- and 17-year-old employees provides notice, and posts a notice, on the scrap paper balers and paper box compactors stating that—

"(I) the scrap paper balers and paper box compactors meet the applicable standard described in clause (i);

"(II) 16- and 17-year-old employees may only load the scrap paper balers and paper box compactors; and

"(III) any employee under the age of 18 may not operate or unload the scrap paper balers and paper box compactors.

The Secretary shall publish in the Federal Register a standard that is adopted by the American National Standards Institute for scrap paper balers or paper box compactors and certified by the Secretary to be protective of the safety of minors under clause (i)(II).

"(C)(i) Employers shall prepare and submit to the Secretary reports—

"(I) on any injury to an employee under the age of 18 that requires medical treatment (other than first aid) resulting from the employee's contact with a scrap paper baler or paper box compactor during the loading, operation, or unloading of the baler or compactor; and

"(II) on any fatality of an employee under the age of 18 resulting from the employee's contact with a scrap paper baler or paper box compactor during the loading, operation, or unloading of the baler or compactor.

"(ii) The reports described in clause (i) shall be used by the Secretary to determine whether or not the implementation of subparagraph (A) has had any effect on the safety of children.

"(iii) The reports described in clause (i) shall provide—

"(I) the name, telephone number, and address of the employer and the address of the place of employment where the incident occurred;

"(II) the name, telephone number, and address of the employee who suffered an injury or death as a result of the incident;

"(III) the date of the incident;

"(IV) a description of the injury and a narrative describing how the incident occurred; and

"(V) the name of the manufacturer and the model number of the scrap paper baler or paper box compactor involved in the incident.

"(iv) The reports described in clause (i) shall be submitted to the Secretary promptly, but not later than 10 days after the date on which an incident relating to an injury or death occurred.

"(v) The Secretary may not rely solely on the reports described in clause (i) as the basis for making a determination that any of the employers described in clause (i) has violated a provision of section 12 relating to oppressive child labor or a regulation or order issued pursuant to section 12. The Secretary shall, prior to making such a determination, conduct an investigation and inspection in accordance with section 12(b).

"(vi) The reporting requirements of this subparagraph shall expire 2 years after the date of enactment of this subparagraph."

Sec. 2. Civil Money Penalty

Section 16(e) of the Fair Labor Standards Act of 1938 (29 U.S.C. 216(e)) is amended in the first sentence—

(1) by striking "section 12," and inserting "section 12 or section 13(c)(5),"; and

(2) by striking "that section" and inserting "section 12 or section 13(c)(5)".

Sec. 3. Construction

Section 1 shall not be construed as affecting the exemption for apprentices and student learners published in section 570.63 of title 29, Code of Federal Regulations.

APPENDIX B.1.C [REPLACED APPENDIX]

SECRETARIES OF LABOR AND ADMINISTRATORS OF THE WAGE AND HOUR DIVISION

Suits and court decisions involving the Department of Labor usually contain the name either a) of the Secretary of Labor in office at the time the suit was filed or decided or b) of the Administrator of the Wage and Hour Division during whose term the suit was filed or decided. To help the reader identify such individuals and determine whether a case discussed in this treatise involved the Department of Labor, the names of the Secretaries of Labor and Administrators are listed in the table below alphabetically by the last name. In the "Office" column, an "S" indicates the individual was Secretary of Labor and an "A" indicates the individual was an Administrator. To help readers determine who held one of these positions at a specific time, two other tables follow, listing Secretaries and Administrators respectively in chronological order by dates of tenure in office.

In 1942 the Wage and Hour Division and the Public Contracts Division were combined into the Wage and Hour and Public Contracts Division. In 1950 the name was shortened to Wage and Hour Division. Corresponding variations in the Administrator's title are indicated by asterisk footnote.

Secretaries of Labor and Administrators of the Wage and Hour Division (Alphabetical Listing)

Name	Office	Start Date	End Date
Elmer F. Andrews	A	1939	1939
Peter J. Brennan	S	2/1973	3/1975
William E. Brock	S	4/1985	10/1987
Newell Brown	A	8/1955	10/1957
Elaine L. Chao	S	1/2001	—
James J. Davis	S	3/1921	11/1930
William N. Doak	S	12/1930	3/1933
Elizabeth Dole	S	1/1989	11/1990
Raymond J. Donovan	S	2/1981	3/1985
Maria Echaveste	A	7/1993	5/1997
Philip B. Fleming	A	1940	1941
Nancy Flynn	A	11/1989	3/1990
John R. Fraser	A	11/1990	10/1991
John R. Fraser	A	12/1991	2/1992
		6/1997	11/1999

Name	Office	Start Date	End Date
Arthur J. Goldberg	S	1/1961	9/1962
Alexis M. Herman	S	5/1997	1/2001
James D. Hodgson	S	7/1970	1/1973
Ronald J. James	A	11/1975	1/1977
Karen Keesling	A	2/1992	1/1993
T. Michael Kerr	A	11/1999	12/2001
Warren D. Landis	A	11/1973	7/1974
Warren D. Landis	A	2/1975	11/1975
Clarence T. Lundquist	A	10/1957	1/1969
Ray Marshall	S	1/1977	1/1981
Lynn M. Martin	S	2/1991	1/1993
William R. McComb	A**	1947	1949
William R. McComb	A	1950	7/1955
Tammy D. McCutchen	A	12/2001	—
Ann McLaughlin	S	12/1987	1/1989
James P. Mitchell	S	10/1953	1/1961
Horace E. Menasco	A	5/1971	11/1972
Robert D. Moran	A	5/1969	5/1971
Betty Southard Murphy	A	7/1974	2/1975
William M. Otter	A	7/1981	3/1985
Frances Perkins	S	3/1933	6/1945
Charles E. Pugh	A	1/1993	6/1993
Robert B. Reich	S	1/1993	1/1997
Ben P. Robertson	A	1/1969	5/1969
Ben P. Robertson	A	11/1972	10/1973
George P. Schultz	S	1/1969	7/1970
Lewis B. Schwellenbach	S	7/1945	6/1948
Paula Smith	A	5/1986	11/1989
Maurice B. Tobin	S	8/1948	1/1953
W. J. Usery, Jr.	S	2/1976	1/1977
Xavier M. Vela	A	6/1977	10/1979
Samuel D. Walker	A	4/1990	11/1990
Samuel D. Walker	A	10/1991	12/1991
L. Metcalfe Walling	A*	1937	1941
L. Metcalfe Walling	A**	1942	1946
William B. Wilson	S	3/1913	3/1921
W. Willard Wirtz	S	9/1962	1/1969

*Administrator, Public Contracts Division (Walling's tenure began pre-FLSA and continued until the Division was merged with the Wage and Hour Division in 1942, with Walling as Administrator of the merged Divisions.)

**Administrator, Wage and Hour and Public Contracts Division

Secretaries of Labor
(Chronological Listing)

To help the reader identify dates during which specific individuals held the office of the Secretary of Labor, a list of Secretaries is provided below in chronological order.

Start Date	End Date	Name
3/1913	3/1921	William B. Wilson
3/1921	11/1930	James J. Davis
12/1930	3/1933	William N. Doak
3/1933	6/1945	Frances Perkins
7/1945	6/1948	Lewis B. Schwellenbach
8/1948	1/1953	Maurice B. Tobin
10/1953	1/1961	James P. Mitchell
1/1961	9/1962	Arthur J. Goldberg
9/1962	1/1969	W. Willard Wirtz
1/1969	7/1970	George P. Schultz
7/1970	1/1973	James D. Hodgson
2/1973	3/1975	Peter J. Brennan
2/1976	1/1977	W. J. Usery, Jr.
1/1977	1/1981	Ray Marshall
2/1981	3/1985	Raymond J. Donovan
4/1985	10/1987	William E. Brock
12/1987	1/1989	Ann McLaughlin
1/1989	11/1990*	Elizabeth Dole
2/1991*	1/1993	Lynn M. Martin
1/1993	1/1997*	Robert B. Reich
5/1997*	1/2001	Alexis M. Herman
1/2001	—	Elaine L. Chao

*Gaps are the result of delays in nomination/confirmation

Administrators of the Wage and Hour Division
(Chronological Listing)

To help the reader identify dates during which specific individuals held the office of Administrator of the Wage and Hour Division, a list of Administrators is provided below in chronological order. In 1942 the Wage and Hour Division and the Public Contracts Division were combined into the Wage and Hour and Public Contracts Division. In 1950 the name was shortened to Wage and Hour Division.

Start Date	End Date	Name
1937	1941	L. Metcalfe Walling*
1939	1939	Elmer F. Andrews
1940	1941	Philip B. Fleming
1942	1946	L. Metcalfe Walling**
1947	1949	William R. McComb**
1950	7/1955	William R. McComb
8/1955	10/1957	Newell Brown
10/1957	1/1969	Clarence T. Lundquist
1/1969	5/1969	Ben P. Robertson
5/1969	5/1971	Robert D. Moran
5/1971	11/1972	Horace E. Menasco
11/1972	10/1973	Ben P. Robertson
11/1973	7/1974	Warren D. Landis
7/1974	2/1975	Betty Southard Murphy
2/1975	11/1975	Warren D. Landis
11/1975	1/1977	Ronald J. James
6/1977	10/1979	Xavier M. Vela
7/1981	3/1985	William M. Otter
5/1986	11/1989	Paula Smith
11/1989	3/1990	Nancy Flynn
4/1990	11/1990	Samuel D. Walker
11/1990	10/1991	John R. Fraser
10/1991	12/1991	Samuel D. Walker
12/1991	2/1992	John R. Fraser
2/1992	1/1993	Karen Keesling
1/1993	6/1993	Charles E. Pugh
7/1993	5/1997	Maria Echaveste
6/1997	11/1999	John R. Fraser (Acting Administrator)
11/1999	12/2001	T. Michael Kerr
12/2001	—	Tammy D. McCutchen

*Administrator, Public Contracts Division (Walling's tenure began pre-FLSA and continued until the Division was merged with the Wage and Hour Division in 1942, with Walling as Administrator of the merged Divisions.)

**Administrator, Wage and Hour and Public Contracts Division

APPENDIX E.3 [REPLACED APPENDIX]

INDUSTRIAL HOMEWORKERS APPLICATION FORM (WH-2)

The Industrial Homeworkers Application Form (WH-2) of July 1996, which appears in the Treatise at pp. 1454–55, was replaced as of December 1996 with the following:

Application for Special Industrial Homeworker's Certificate

U.S. Department of Labor
Employment Standards Administration

Note: Persons are not required to respond to this collection of information unless it displays a currently valid OMB control number.

OMB No.: 1215-0005
Expires: 03-31-01

INSTRUCTIONS:
Completion of Form WH-2 is necessary to obtain certificates to employ individual homeworkers in one of the restricted homework industries noted in item 1. below. The information collected is utilized by the Department to determine whether terms and conditions necessary to issue an individual certificate have been met. This is an application form only and not a certificate. Prepare three copies of this form and forward the original to this office. The duplicate is to be kept by the employer and the other copy given to the employee. All questions must be answered in full. The homeworker is to furnish information for Section I. The employer furnishes information for Section II. The signature of each is required on the application. Section III, Report of Medical Examination, should be completed by a licensed physician.

This report is authorized by Section 11(d) of the Fair Labor Standards Act. Completion of the form is voluntary. However, failure to provide the information will result in non-issuance of a homeworker certificate and such employment will be in violation of Section 11(d) of the Fair Labor Standards Act. (See 29 CFR 530)

Section I. Information To Be Furnished By Homeworker

1. Certificate is requested for employment in the industry checked below:

☐ Button & Buckle Manufacturing ☐ Gloves and Mittens ☐ Jewelry Manufacturing ☐ Women's Apparel

☐ Embroideries ☐ Handkerchief Manufacturing ☐ Knitted Outerwear

2. Name (Please print)	3. Address (Street No., Apt. No., if any)	
4. City or Town, State, ZIP Code	5. Age	6. Telephone Number (Include Area Code) ( )

7. Explain fully why you are unable to work in a factory

8a. Do you hold a State Homeworker Certificate?	b. If "Yes", name State	c. Expiration date of State Certificate

I have read the statements in this application and ask that the requested certificate be granted.
Signature of homeworker (If worker cannot write, signature may be made by mark (X) and witnessed by another person)

Signature or mark (X) of homeworker: Signature of witness (if necessary):

Public Burden Statement

Public reporting burden for this collection of information is estimated to average 30 minutes per response, including time for reviewing instructions, searching existing data sources, gathering and maintaining the data needed, and completing and reviewing the collection of information. Send comments regarding this burden estimate or any other aspect of this collection of information, including suggestions for reducing this burden, to the U.S. Department of Labor, Administrator, Wage and Hour Division, Room S-3502, 200 Constitution Avenue, N.W., Washington, D.C. 20210.

DO NOT SEND THE COMPLETED FORM TO THIS OFFICE

Form WH-2
Rev. Dec. 1996

Section II. Information to be Furnished by Employer

10. Name and Address, Including Zip Code of Employer

11. Name of State Vocational Rehabilitation Agency. If Any, Supervising Homeworker's Employment.

12. If work is to be distributed to homeworker from other than above address, enter name and address of firm or individual distributing work

I certify that the answers to the above questions are true and correct.

(Print or type name of employer or authorized representative)

(Telephone Number - Including Area Code)

(Title)

(Signature of employer or authorized representative)

(Date)

Section III. Report of Medical Examination

13. Name of person examined:

Nature of disability:

A	**Application to work at home because of inability to work in a factory due to physical disability.** How and to what extent does the disability affect the ability of the applicant to undertake work in a factory?
B	**Application to work at home due to need to care for an invalid.** Does the disability of the invalid warrant care to the extent of prohibiting employment of the applicant away from home? ☐ Yes ☐ No If "Yes", explain nature and extent of care required

14. What is the prognosis?

15. Name and address, including ZIP Code, of examining physician (Print or type).

16. Physician's signature

17. Date

APPENDIX E.6 [NEW APPENDIX]

APPLICATION TO EMPLOY STUDENTS AT SUBMINIMUM WAGES (WH-200-MIS)

This form is provided by the Wage and Hour Division for employers seeking authority to employ full-time students at subminimum wages in retail or service establishments or agriculture:

Application for Authority to Employ Full-Time Students at Subminimum Wages In Retail or Service Establishments or Agriculture

U.S. Department of Labor
Employment Standards Administration
Wage and Hour Division

Persons are not required to respond to this collection of information unless it displays a currently valid OMB control number.

OMB No: 1215-0032
Expires: 07-31-02

1. ☐ Initial application.
   ☐ Renewal application. Previous expiration date __/__/__

2. Authority requested:
   ☐ Not more than six (see definition of "employer" on reverse) (complete items 2, 3, 5, 8 and 9).
   ☐ Ten percent of the total monthly hours (complete items 1-7 and 9).
   ☐ Greater than ten percent of the total monthly hours (complete items 1-7, 9 and 10).

FOR OFFICE USE ONLY
cert no. _____
prev cert no. _____
☐ app ☐ den ☐ ho ☐ lap ☐ % ☐ miss ☐ SIC
RO _____ DO _____
print cert: ☐ yes ☐ no eff __/__/__ exp __/__/__
base year: ☐ 60/61 ☐ 66/67 ☐ 73/74 ☐ archive
remarks _____

3. Name and address (including ZIP code) of establishment at which full-time students will be employed:

   Date establishment began business:

4. Name and address to which correspondence should be mailed, other than item 3:

5. **Type of establishment (SIC)**
   ☐ 00 agriculture, specify: _____
   ☐ 53 general merchandise
   ☐ 54 grocery store
   ☐ 56 clothing/shoe store
   ☐ 58 restaurant/food store
   ☐ 59 other retail/service, specify: _____
   ☐ 70 hotel/motel
   ☐ 78 movie/theater
   ☐ 80 hospital/nursing home

6. Proposed Subminimum Wage:
   Not less than $_____ per hour

7. If this is a renewal of "ten percent" or "greater than ten percent," provide the total hours of employment under certificate during the most recent 12 months.
   Hours of all employees (including managers): _____
   Hours of full-time students at subminimum wages: _____
   (If you paid no full-time students less than the minimum wage, enter "0".)

8. If requesting authority for "not more than six" enter the name and address of any other location where students will be employed.
   1 _____
   2 _____
   3 _____
   4 _____
   5 _____

9. Signature and title of authorized representative:
   (See representations on the reverse side.)

Telephone No. (including area code):

Date:

10. THIS ITEM NEED ONLY BE COMPLETED ON INITIAL REQUEST FOR MORE THAN TEN PERCENT - **SEE INSTRUCTIONS**

A. Calendar month (or beginning date of each fiscal month and year)	B. Total hours of all employees	C. Hours of full-time students	D. Full-time student hours as percent of total hours	E. Percentage allowance requested	F. ☐ Check here if you used data from your own establishment. If you used base year data from another establishment, identify below.

COPY 1

Form WH-200-MIS
Rev. Dec. 1996

APPENDIX E.7 [NEW APPENDIX]

APPLICATION FOR AUTHORIZATION TO EMPLOY A STUDENT-LEARNER AT SUBMINIMUM WAGES (WH-205)

This form is provided by the Wage and Hour Division for employers seeking authority to employ a student-learner at subminimum wages.

Application for Authorization to Employ A Student-Learner at Subminimum Wages

U.S. Department of Labor
Employment Standards Administration
Wage and Hour Division

Note: Persons are not required to respond to this collection of information unless it displays a currently valid OMB control number.

OMB No. 1215-0005
Expires: 09-30-2000

Form WH-205 is completed by an employer to obtain certification to employ student-learners at wages lower than the Federal minimum wage to prevent curtailment of opportunities for employment. Submission of this information is voluntary, but failure to submit the information will prohibit the Wage and Hour Division from authorizing the employment of student-learners at subminimum rates. U.S.C. 201 et.seq.

The school officials' certification in Item 27 of the application provides temporary authority to employ the named student-learner under the terms proposed in the application which are in accordance with section 520.502 and 503 of the Student-Learner Regulations (29 CFR 520). The authority begins on the date the application is forwarded to the Regional Office of the Employment Standards Administration. At the end of 30 days, this authority is extended to become the approved certificate unless the Administrator or his/her authorized representative denies the application, issues a certificate with modified terms and conditions, or expressly extends the period of review. Note that the certificate is valid for no more than 1 school year and does not extend beyond the date of graduation.

OFFICIAL USE ONLY

A. Control number______
B. Effective date______
C. Expiration date______
D. Reviewing official______

READ CAREFULLY THE INSTRUCTIONS FOR COMPLETING THIS FORM. PRINT OR TYPE ALL ANSWERS

1. Name and address, including Zip Code, of Establishment making application:	3A. Name and address of Student-Learner:
2. Type of business and products manufactured, sold, or services rendered:	B: Date of Birth: (Month, day, year)
	4. Name and address, including Zip Code, of school in which Student-Learner is enrolled.
5. Proposed begining date of employment (Month, day, year)	
6. Proposed ending date of employment (Month, day, year)	
7. Proposed graduation date (Month, day, year)	17. Title of student-learner occupation:
8. Number of weeks in school year	18. Number of employees in this establishment
9. Total hours of school instruction per week	19. Number of experienced employees in Student-Learner's occupation
10. Number of school hours directly related to employment training	20. Minimum hourly wage rate of experienced workers in item 19
11. How is employment training scheduled (Weekly, alternate weeks, etc.)?	21. Subminimum wage(s) to be paid Student-Learner (if a progressive wage schedule is proposed, enter each rate and specify the period during which it will be paid):
12. Number of weeks of employment training at subminimum wages	
13. Number of hours of employment training a week	22. Is an age or Employment Certificate on file in this establishment for this Student-Learner? (If not, see instructions). ☐ Yes ☐ No
14. Are Federal Vocational Education Funds being used for this program?	
15. Was this program authorized by the State Board of Vocational Education?	
16. If the answer to item 15 is "No", give the name of the recognized educational body which approved this program:	23. Is it anticipated that the Student-Learner will be employed in the performance of a government contract subject to the Walsh-Healey Public Contracts Act or the Service Contract Act? ☐ Yes ☐ No

ATTACH SEPARATE PAGES IF NECESSARY

Form WH-205
Rev. July 1998

-2-

24. Outline the school instruction **directly** related to the employment training (list courses, etc.)

25. Outline training on-the-job (describe briefly the work process in which the student-learner will be trained and list the types of any machines used).

26. Signature of Student-Learner:

I have read the statements made above and ask that the requested certificate, authorizing my employment training at subminimum wages and under the conditions stated, be granted by the Administrator or his/her authorized representative.

Print or type name of Student

Signature of Student Date

27. CERTIFICATION BY SCHOOL OFFICIAL

I certify that the student named herein will be receiving instruction in an accredited school and will be employed pursuant to a bona fide vocational training program, and that the application is properly executed in conformance with sections 520.502 and 503 of the Student- Learner Regulation.

(Print or type name of official)

Signature of School Official Date

Title________________

Tel. No.________________
(Include Area Code)

28. CERTIFICATION BY EMPLOYER OR AUTHORIZED REPRESENTATIVE:

I certify, in applying for this certificate, that all of the foregoing statements are, to the best of my knowledge and belief, true and correct.

(Print or type name of employer or representative)

Signature of employer or representative Date

Title ________________

Tel. No.________________
(Include Area Code)

ATTACH SEPARATE SHEETS IF NECESSARY

Public Burden Statement

Public reporting burden for this collection of information is estimated to average 30 minutes per response, including time for reviewing instructions, searching existing data sources, gathering and maintaining the data needed, and completing and reviewing the collection of information. Send comments regarding this burden estimate or any other aspect of this collection of information, including suggestions for reducing this burden, to the U.S. Department of Labor, Administrator, Wage and Hour Division, Room S-3502, 200 Constitution Avenue, N.W., Washington, D.C. 20210. **DO NOT SEND THE COMPLETED FORM TO THIS OFFICE**

APPENDIX E.8 [NEW APPENDIX]

APPLICATION FOR A CERTIFICATE TO EMPLOY LEARNERS AT SUBMINIMUM WAGES (WH-209)

This form is provided by the Wage and Hour Division for employers seeking authority to employ learners at subminimum wages.

Application for a Certificate to Employ Learners at Subminimum Wages

U.S. Department of Labor
Employment Standards Administration
Wage and Hour Division

In Industries covered by supplemental industry learner regulations — OMB No. 1215-0012 Expires: 09-30-02

Prepare this form in triplicate. Send the original to the address shown below. A copy must be sent to the Employment Standards Administration Regional Office for your area. The remaining copy is for your files. Post the accompanying "Notice of Filing Application" in a conspicous place in your plant. Additional copies will be furnished at your request.

Failure to follow instructions or omission of data may cause the return of the application.

Part 1. Information Required Of All Applicants

1\. a. Name and address, including ZIP Code, of establishment for which application is made

b. Other name(s) used in past 2 years

☐ None

c. Name and address of parent company

☐ No parent company

2\. Date operations began at present location

3\. a. Is your establishment operating under a trade union agreement? ☐ Yes ☐ No

b. If yes, give name of union

4. a. **Specific Product(s) Manufactured** (See supplemental instructions)	Percentage of Total Production

b. Are learners to be employed at subminimum wages on all products listed in item 4? If "No, mark with an asterisk (*) the product(s) on which such learners are to be employed. ☐ Yes ☐ No

5. Efforts to recruit experienced workers in the occupation(s) for which learners are requested.

Indicate efforts made to recruit experienced workers in the occupation(s) **for which learners are requested.** You must submit with this application written evidence from the local public employment service office serving your locality that an order for experienced workers was placed with that office **not more than 15 days prior** to the date of this application.

Date of enclosed written evidence from the local public employment service office

Other Recruiting Efforts (Describe)	**Date**	**Number of Experienced Workers** Referred or applying	Hired

Public Burden Statement

Public reporting burden for this collection of information is estimated to average 30 minutes per response, including time for reviewing instructions, searching existing data sources, gathering and maintaining the data needed, and completing and reviewing the collection of information. Send comments regarding this burden estimate or any other aspect of this collection of information, including suggestions for reducing this burden, to the Administrator, Wage and Hour Division, U.S. Department of Labor, Room S-3502, 200 Constitution Avenue, N.W., Washington, D.C. 20210.

DO NOT SEND THE COMPLETED FORM TO THIS OFFICE

Form WH-209
Rev. Jan. 1997

6. Hiring of learners

Include only learners at subminimum wages. If no learners have been hired at subminimum wages, indicate "None" in column B.

a. Learner Occupations (List occupations in which learners have been employed at subminimum wages or for which a certificate authorizing such wages is requested.)	Learners Hired in Last 12 Months			
	b. Total number hired at subminimum wages	c. Number having completed authorized learning period	d. Number trained and still employed at the statutory minimum wage or more	e. Number still being trained at subminimum wages
1				
2				
3				
4				
5				

7. Monthly Employment.

Enter data for the payroll period including the 12th of each of the 12 most recent months for which data are available. For line (a) include working foremen and all nonsupervisory workers engaged in fabricating, processing, assembling, inspecting, receiving, packing, shipping, and other services closely associated with production operations. For line (b) show only the learners paid less than the statutory minimum wage in effect during that period.

Month (Enter Year)	Jan. 19	Feb. 19	Mar. 19	Apr 19	May 19	June 19	July 19	Aug. 19	Sept. 19	Oct. 19	Nov. 19	Dec. 19
a. Number of production and related workers (including learners)												
b. Number of learners at subminimum wages												

8. Employment of all production and related workers except learners paid subminimum wages (See supplemental instructions)

a. Occupations (List same ocupations as in item 6)	b. Number of workers on recent payroll (Do not count learners paid subminimum wages)	Average straight-time hourly earnings (Including make-up)		e. Number of workers paid make-up to statutory minimum wage on most recent payroll
		c. One Year Ago	d. Recent payroll	
1		$	$	
2				
3				
4				
5				
6 Other production and related occupations				
Total-all production and related workers		$	$	$

9. Type of application (Check the appropriate box(es))

A. ☐ Normal labor turnover purposes
If checked, what is the maximum number of learners you expect to employ at subminimum wages on any one day during the next 12 months?

B. ☐ New or expanding plant purposes
If checked, you must also complete Part II

- 3 -

Part II. Information Required For New Or Expanding Plants

This Part must be completed if you are requesting learners at subminimum wages to staff a new plant or expand existing operations. Do not complete this part if you are requesting learners at subminimum wages only for normal labor turnover purposes.

10. a. Expansion is due to:	b. Do you plan to add a new shift? ☐ Yes ☐ No	
	c. How many learners do you plan to hire immediately?	
	d. How many learners do you plan to have in your employ at subminimum wages on any one workday?	

11. Information on machines

a. Type of machine	b. Operators per machine	c. Number of machines now in use	Machines to be used by learners: d. New machines (number)	Idle machines: e. Number	Idle machines: f. Length of time idle (months)

12. Relocation of Production

Are you moving from another plant of your company (or closely related company) in another location or are you transferring production from such plant or have you recently so moved or transferred production?

☐ Yes ☐ No

If yes, attach a signed statement giving information required in section 522.3(e) of the Regulations Part 522.

Part III. Representations, Certification, And Signature Required Of All Applicants

I represent that, as set forth in the Learner Regulations (29 CFR Part 522), this plant meets the following conditions:

1. The issuance of the certificate requested is necessary to prevent a curtailment of opportunities for employment.
2. The issuance of the certificate will not tend to create unfair competitive labor cost advantages or impair or depress working standards for experienced workers for work of a like or comparable character in the industry.
3. An adequate supply of experienced workers, as defined in the regulations, is not available for employment.
4. Experienced workers presently employed in the plant are afforded an opportunity, to the fullest extent possible, for full-time employment.
5. Learners are available for employment at subminimum wage rates.
6. Learners to be trained under the certificate shall be afforded every reasonable opportunity for continued employment upon completion of the learning period.
7. Abnormal labor conditions such as a strike, lockout, or other similar condition, do not exist at this plant.
8. There are no serious outstanding violations of the provisions of a previous learner certificate issued to this plant or of other provisions of the Fair Labor Standards Act.
9. The notice of filing of application is posted.

I certify that I have read the application and that to the best of my knowledge and belief the answers and information given in this form and any additional or supplemental statements are true; that the representations set forth above in support of this application to obtain a learner certificate are true; that I am duly authorized to sign this application; and know that the certificate, if issued, is subject to withdrawal or annulment in accordance with 29 CFR, Part 528.

13. Name and title of person signing application (print or type)		Send the original application to:
14. Signature	15. Date	U.S. Department of Labor Employment Standards Administration Wage and Hour Division Washington, D.C. 20210
16. Date copy sent to regional office		A copy must be sent to the appropriate regional office.

SPACE FOR ADDITIONAL OR SUPPLEMENTAL INFORMATION
(Attach additional sheets if necessary)

Note: Persons are not required to respond to this collection of information unless it displays a currently valid OMB number.

APPENDIX E.9 [NEW APPENDIX]

APPLICATION AND SUPPLEMENTAL DATA SHEET WITH RESPECT TO EMPLOYMENT OF WORKERS WITH DISABILITIES AT SPECIAL MINIMUUM WAGES (WH-226-MIS AND WH-226A)

These forms are provided by the Wage and Hour Division for employers seeking authority to employ workers with disabilities at special minimum wages.

Application for Authority to Employ Workers with Disabilities at Special Minimum Wages

U.S. Department of Labor
Employment Standards Administration
Wage and Hour Division

NOTE: Persons are not required to respond to this collection of information unless it displays a currently valid OMB control number.

OMB No.: 1215-0005
Expires: 03-31-01

This is an application for the authority to employ workers with disabilities at special minimum wage rates under the Fair Labor Standards Act (FLSA), Walsh-Healey Public Contracts Act (PCA), or Service Contract Act (SCA). Please submit one copy of the completed form, and any attachments, to the address shown above. Retain a completed copy for your records. A certificate may not be granted unless a properly completed application has been received and approved. U.S.C. 201, et seq.

1. This is a request for authority to employ workers with disabilities for:

A. ☐ Work Center
☐ Hospital/Residential Care Facility (Patient Workers)
☐ Business Establishment (Special Worker)

B. Check One:
☐ Initial application (Complete all items)
☐ Renewal application (Please make any necessary corrections to reprinted information.)

C. ☐ Request for Temporary Authority by State Vocational Rehabilitation Agency or Veterans Administration

FOR OFFICE USE ONLY

Certificate Number ____
Effective Date __/__/__
Expiration Date __/__/__
Print Certificate: Yes ☐ No ☐
RO ____ **DO** ____
REMARKS: ____ **EMPLOYEES** ____

2. Name of Employer: ____
(Work Center, Hospital/Institution, Business, School Providing Placement)
Street Address: ____
Mailing Address (if different than street address): ____
City: ____ County: ____
State: ____ ZIP Code: ____
Telephone: ____

3. List the name and address(es) of all branch establishments, (BR) supported employment sites (SE), or school work experience program sites (SWEP) to be covered by this certificate. If you are making an initial application (no previous authority), enter the number of workers expected to be employed in each program. If you are providing renewal information, list the number of workers in the specific program areas on the last day of the most recent representative quarter.

Attach additional sheets if necessary.

(BR, SE, or SWEP)	NAME & ADDRESS OF SITE	NUMBER OF WORKERS

4. Parent Organization if different from that listed in (2).
Name: ____
Address: ____
Check here if mail is to be sent to parent organization rather than #2. ☐

5. Status: (check one)
☐ Public (State or local government) (PU)
☐ Private, For Profit (PP)
☐ Private, Not For Profit (PN)
☐ Other ____

6. Do you manufacture items for the Federal Government under PCA? ☐ Yes ☐ No

Do you perform any services for the Federal Government under SCA? ☐ Yes ☐ No

7. Primary disability group employed (check one)
☐ Mental Retardation (MR)
☐ Mental Illness (MI)
☐ Visual impairment (VI)
☐ Hearing impairment (HI)
☐ Alcoholism (AL)
☐ Drug Addiction (DA)
☐ Neuromuscular (NM)
☐ General - No primary group (GI)
☐ Age Related (AR)
☐ Developmental Disability (DD) Specify: ____
☐ Other (OT) Specify: ____

Public Burden Statement

We estimate that it will take an average of 45 minutes per response to complete this collection of information, including time for reviewing instructions, searching existing data sources, gathering and maintaining the data needed, and completing and reviewing the collection of information. If you have any comments regarding this burden estimate or any other aspect of this collection of information, including suggestions for reducing this burden, send them to the U.S. Department of Labor, Administrator, Wage and Hour Division, Room S-3502, 200 Constitution Avenue, N.W., Washington, D.C. 20210

DO NOT SEND THE COMPLETED FORM TO THIS OFFICE

Form WH-226-MIS
Rev. Dec. 1996

8. Estimated number of workers with a disability employed during the fiscal year ending (Date) ____________ under this certificate is ____________. (The number of workers should include all locations covered by this certificate.)

WAGE PAYMENT DETERMINATION

9. PREVAILING WAGE DETERMINATION

Please provide the following information on the four largest current contracts whether the workers with disabilities are paid an hourly rate or a piece rate. The prevailing rate should reflect the rate paid to experienced nondisabled workers in the vicinity for work utilizing similar methods and equipment. If more than 3 sources were used, attach an additional sheet headed "Prevailing Wage Determination" and provide the information obtained from these sources. (Section 14(c)(2)(B) and Part 525.10.)

Description of Work (e.g. collating, hand assembly, janitorial)	Sources (Name of Firm and Person Contacted)	Date of Contact	Prevailing Wage Provided by Source	Prevailing Wage Determined by Applicant
	1.			
	2.			
	3.			
	1.			
	2.			
	3.			
	1.			
	2.			
	3.			
	1.			
	2.			
	3.			

10. HOURLY RATES

a. How many workers with disabilities employed under the terms of this certificate are paid an hourly rate? ________ (If the answer is 0, go on to question 11.) How frequently do you rate/evaluate each worker's productivity? ____________

b. Attach to this application productivity rating/evaluation forms for three currently employed workers with disabilities who are paid hourly rates. Include all material relating to the evaluation which shows the disabled workers' individual productivity in proportion to the wage and productivity of experienced nondisabled workers performing essentially the same type, quality and quantity of work in the vicinity.

11. PIECE RATES

a. How many workers with disabilities employed under the terms of this certificate are paid piece rates? ________ (If the answer is 0, go on to question 12.)

b. Please provide the following information about the four largest current contracts on which workers with disabilities are paid piece rates and attach supporting time studies or work measurements.

Description of Work (e.g. delabel cones)	Prevailing Wage Determined for this Job (Expressed in a Rate Per Hour)	Standard Productivity (Units/Hour)	Piece Rate Paid to Workers (Rate Per Unit)

Form WH-226-MIS
Rev. Dec. 1996

Supplemental Data Sheet for Application for Authority to Employ Workers with Disabilities at Special Minimum Wages

U. S. Department of Labor
Employment Standards Administration
Wage and Hour Division

OMB No.: 1215-0005
Expires: 03-31-01

INSTRUCTIONS FOR COMPLETING FORM WH-226A-MIS

List only those workers with disabilities who earn less than the statutory minimum wage or SCA wage determination rate.

Item 2 — List each worker with a disability engaged in covered work in the worksite regardless of the amount of time spent in the program or the individual's earnings.

Item 3 — For workers paid hourly wage rates, list the rate or rates paid at the end of the fiscal quarter. For example: Jane Smith, quality control, $3.00.

For workers paid by piece rates, list the average earnings per hour. Average earnings are computed by dividing the total earnings of the individual worker by the number of hours worked during that fiscal quarter. For example, John Jones earned $600.00 during the quarter ending 6/30/–. He worked 300 hours. His average earnings per hour are $2.00.

Item 4 — Clearly identify the work performed by the workers with disabilities. For example, truck helper, assembler, machine operator, janitor, etc.

Important: Name and address of worksite should appear in Item 2 or Item 3 on the WH-226-MIS. When completing Items 2 through 4, please use information from your most recent representative fiscal quarter. Attach additional sheets if necessary.

1. Name and Address of Work Site: SCA work performed at this site? ☐

2. Name of workers with disabilities and primary disability (e.g., John Jones - cerebral palsey)	3. Average earnings per hour	4. Type of work

Public Burden Statement

We estimate that it will take an average of 45 minutes per response to complete this collection of information, including time for reviewing instructions, searching existing data sources, gathering and maintaining the data needed, and completing and reviewing the collection of information. If you have any comments regarding this estimate or any other aspect of this collection of information, including suggestions for reducing this burden, send them to the U.S. Department of Labor, Administrator, Wage and Hour Division, Room S-3502, 200 Constitution Avenue, N.W., Washington, D.C. 20210.

DO NOT SEND THE COMPLETED FORM TO THIS OFFICE

Form WH-226A
Rev. Dec. 1996

APPENDIX E.10 [NEW APPENDIX]

CERTIFICATE AUTHORIZING SPECIAL MINIMUM WAGE RATES UNDER SECTION 14(C) OF THE FLSA (WH-228-MIS)

This form is provided by the Wage and Hour Division for authorizing employers to employ Workers at Special Minimum Wage Rates under Section 14(c) of the FLSA.

Certificate Authorizing Special Minimum Wage Rates under Section 14(c) of the Fair Labor Standards Act

U.S. Department of Labor
Employment Standards Administration
Wage and Hour Division

This special certificate authorizes the employment of workers with disabilities in accordance with the requirements of 29 CFR Part 525, effective ____________________.

The certificate will remain in effect provided that all applicable provisions of the Fair Labor Standards Act, the Walsh-Healey Public Contracts Act, the McNamara O'Hara Service Contract Act, and the Contract Work Hours and Safety Standards Act and the regulations issued pursuant thereto are fully complied with. In addition, current information concerning the employment of workers with disabilities by this certificate holder must be furnished to the Wage and Hour Division upon request but in no event later than ____________________.

See the reverse of this certificate and the applicable regulations for further information.

NOTICE TO WORKERS WITH DISABILITIES PAID AT SPECIAL MINIMUM WAGES

The Fair Labor Standards Act (FLSA) provides that workers with disabilities whose disabilities impair their ability to perform the type of work being done in the establishment may be employed at wage rates below the minimum otherwise required in FLSA. Such employment is permitted only under certificates issued by the Department of Labor and must reflect the productivity of the individual worker as related to the productivity of a worker not disabled for the work being performed, and the wages being paid to experienced workers performing the same or similar work in the vicinity. Such wages are referred to as "commensurate wage rates." This establishment has a certificate authorizing the payment of commensurate wages to workers with disabilities. Workers not disabled for the work to be performed, including workers who may otherwise have disabilities, must receive at least the statutory minimum wage.

For purposes of the payment of commensurate wages under a certificate, a worker with a disability is defined as:

- An individual whose earning or productive capacity is impaired by a physical or mental disability, including those relating to age or injury, for the work to be performed.

Disabilities which may affect productive capacity include blindness, mental illness, mental retardation, cerebral palsy, alcoholism, and drug addiction. The following disabilities do not ordinarily affect productive capacity for purposes of paying commensurate wages: educational disabilities; chronic unemployment; receipt of welfare benefits; nonattendance at school; juvenile delinquency; and correctional parole or probation.

Each worker with a disability and, where appropriate, the parent or guardian of such worker, shall be informed orally and in writing by the employer of the terms of the certificate under which such worker is employed.

Complaints or questions regarding the terms and conditions of employment under a certificate may be directed to the Wage and Hour Division, U.S. Department of Labor. Action will be taken to address an individual's concerns, including where appropriate, a formal investigation of the employer.

Workers with disabilities paid at special minimum wages may also petition the Administrator of the Wage and Hour Division of the Department of Labor for a review of their wage rates by an Administrative Law Judge. No particular form of petition is required, except that it must be signed by the worker with a disability or his or her parent or guardian and should contain the name and address of the employer. Petitions should be mailed to: Administrator, Wage and Hour Division, U.S. Department of Labor, Room S-3502, 200 Constitution Avenue, N.W., Washington, D.C. 20210.

Wage and Hour Representative:	**Date**

1. **COMMENSURATE WAGE RATES**

   A. **PIECE RATE PAYMENTS.** Workers with disabilities (including patient workers in hospitals or institutions) employed on a piece rate basis must be paid not less than the prevailing piece rate paid experienced employees not disabled for the work to be performed engaged in essentially the same type of work in the vicinity. In the absence of established piece rates for similar work, time studies or other tests may be used to establish piece rates.

   B. **HOURLY RATE PAYMENTS.** Workers with disabilities (including patient workers in hospitals or institutions) employed on an hourly rate basis must be paid wage rates at least commensurate with the prevailing hourly wage rate paid experienced employees not disabled for the work to be performed in the vicinity for essentially the same type, quality, and quantity of work.

2. **CONTRACTS SUBJECT TO THE McNAMARA O'HARA SERVICE CONTRACT ACT**

   This certificate extends authority to pay commensurate wages to workers with disabilities performing work subject to the McNamara O'Hara Service Contract Act (SCA) but not less than the minimum wage rates specified below.

   A. **MINIMUM WAGE.** The SCA wage determination incorporated in a service contract with the Federal Government or the District of Columbia will specify the prevailing minimum wage rates and fringe benefits which are to be paid to each of the classes of service employees performing covered SCA contract work or work necessary to the performance of the contract.

   Workers with disabilities shall be paid commensurate wage rates based on the applicable SCA wage determination.

   B. **FRINGE BENEFITS.** All workers with disabilities who perform work on contracts subject to SCA or who perform work necessary to the performance of the contract shall be paid fringe benefits in **full** as stated on the applicable SCA wage determination and in accordance with the provisions of 29 CFR Part 4.

   C. **VIOLATIONS OF THESE SCA PROVISIONS.** Failure to comply with these SCA provisions may result in the withholding of funds to cover unpaid wages and debarment from future Federal service contracts.

   D. **COVERAGE OF OTHER EMPLOYEES.** If a certificate holder is providing any services (other than linen supply service), subject to SCA, those workers in the establishment in which the services are being performed who are not performing the service work must be paid in accordance with the applicable provisions of the FLSA. This holds true even where the non-service work would not otherwise be subject to the FLSA. Any questions regarding this requirements should be immediately directed to the office issuing this certificate.

3. **OVERTIME PAYMENT.**

   A. **FAIR LABOR STANDARDS ACT.** Persons covered by this Act, unless exempt, shall be paid not less than ONE AND ONE-HALF TIMES THEIR REGULAR RATES OF PAY AFTER 40 HOURS OF WORK IN A WORKWEEK.

   B. **PUBLIC CONTRACTS ACT.** Persons covered by this Act, unless exempt, shall be paid not less than ONE AND ONE-HALF TIMES THEIR REGULAR RATES OF PAY AFTER 40 HOURS OF WORK IN A WORKWEEK.

   C. **SERVICE CONTRACT ACT.** Persons covered by this Act, unless exempt, shall be paid overtime in accordance with the terms of the FLSA or the CONTRACT WORK HOURS AND SAFETY STANDARDS ACT, for all hours worked over 40 hours a workweek.

4. **RECORD KEEPING REQUIREMENTS.** In addition to the records required by Regulations 29 CFR Part 516, each certificate holder shall keep those records required by Regulation 29 CFR Part 4.6(g), 4.185, and Part 525.16, as applicable, including but not limited to:

   A. **DISABILITY** showing nature of the disability of each worker employed at a commensurate wage rate;

   B. **PRODUCTIVITY** showing the productivity of each worker with a disability or patient worker on a continuing basis or at periodic intervals (not to exceed 6 months in the case of workers paid hourly wage rates), including documents explaining how the productivity of workers with disabilities not p[illegible] a piece rate is determined;

   C. **PREVAILING** wage rates paid in the vicinity [illegible] experienced workers not disabled for the work to be performed (updated at least every 12 months);

   D. **PRODUCTION** standards and supporting d[illegible] including work measurements.

5. **Child Labor.** Minors younger than **18** years old must be employed in accordance with the child labor provisions of FLSA. No person under **16** may be employed in manufacturing or on a PCA contract

6. **COMPLIANCE WITH HIGHER STANDARDS.** No provisions of this certificate shall excuse noncompliance with any other Federal, State, or local law or ordinance establishing higher standards.

7. **REVIEW OR CANCELLATION.** This certificate is issued without prejudice to the rights of any party to petition for review as provided in Regulation 29 CFR Part 525. The terms of this certificate may be amended for cause upon the request of the certificate holder, or worker with a disability or the guardian or parent of such worker or upon the initiative of the Administrator or the Administrator's authorized representative. This certificate is revocable by the Administrator or the Administrator's authorized representative for cause.

APPENDIX J.2
[Replaced Appendix]

STATE MINIMUM WAGE TABLE

Source: State Statutes

A BNA Graphic/fl1yg1

State Minimum, Subminimum Wage Rates

(Subminimum Wage Rates Applicable in Specified Limited Situations Only)

State	Minimum Wage Rate	Subminimum Wage Rate	State	Minimum Wage Rate	Subminimum Wage Rate
Alabama	None	None	Montana	$5.15[19]	None
Alaska	$5.65	75%[1]	Nebraska	$5.15	75%[1]
Arizona	None	None	Nevada	$5.15	None
Arkansas	$5.15	None	New Hampshire	$5.15	75%[1]
California	$5.75	85%[2,3]	New Jersey	$5.15	[15]
Colorado	$5.15[3]	None	New Mexico	$4.25	None
Connecticut	$6.15	85%[4]	New York	$4.25	[15]
Delaware	$5.65	None	North Carolina	$5.15	90%[1]
District of Columbia	$6.15	$4.25[14]	North Dakota	$5.15	[9]
Florida	None	None	Ohio	$3.35[20]	[10]
Georgia	$3.25	None	Oklahoma	$5.15	None
Hawaii	$5.25	[15]	Oregon	$6.50	None
Idaho	$5.15	[16]	Pennsylvania	$5.15	85%[1]
Illinois	$5.15	70%[5]	Puerto Rico	$5.15-$6.50	[17]
Indiana	$5.15	None	Rhode Island	$5.65	[11]
Iowa	$5.15	75%[21]	South Carolina	None	None
Kansas	$2.65	[15]	South Dakota	$5.15	None
Kentucky	$5.15	None	Tennessee	None	None
Louisiana	None	None	Texas	$3.35	None
Maine	$5.15	[16]	Utah	$5.15	None
Maryland	$5.15	None	Vermont	$6.25	85%[12]
Massachusetts	$6.00	[6]	Virginia	$5.15	None
Michigan	$5.15	None	Washington	$6.50[18]	85%[1,3]
Minnesota	$5.15[7]	$4.25[8]	West Virginia	$5.15	None
Mississippi	None	None	Wisconsin	$5.15	75%[13]
Missouri	$5.15	85%[1]	Wyoming	$1.60	None

1 Percentage rate of the statutory minimum for learners and/or apprentices
2 Percentage rate, for first 160 hours of employment
3 By state wage board order(s)
4 Percentage rate, for first 200 hours of employment
5 Percentage rate, for up to six months
6 Scale of rates for specified occupations
7 $4.90 an hour, for employer whose annual gross volume is less than $500,000
8 For employees under age 20, for up to 90 days
9 Subminimum rate to certain students may be granted
10 Eighty-five percent for student learners, for period of up to 180 days
11 At rate determined by director of labor, for up to 90 days
12 Percentage rate for retail, wholesale, and service establishments by wage order, for up to 240 hours or 30 days for learners
13 Percentage rate, for student learners age 14 to 18, under wage order
14 For persons with less than 60 calendar days experience in laundry and dry cleaning occupation
15 Subminimum rate may be prescribed by rules
16 Special license or certificate may be issued authorizing subminimum rate
17 For non FLSA employees, 70% of FLSA rate ($5.15 an hour). Rates established by mandatory decrees higher than FLSA rate continue in effect.
18 $5.15 an hour, for employees of certain contractors providing services to medical care recipients
19 $4.00 an hour, for employer whose annual gross volume is $110,000 or less
20 FLSA rate for employer whose annual volume is over $500,000. $2.80 an hour, for employer whose annual gross volume is less than $150,000
21 For learners age 16; age 18 in hazardous occupations.

Source: State statutes, rules and regulations

A BNA Graphic/fl1yg2

TABLE OF CASES

*References are to footnote numbers in chapters (e.g., **8:** 39 refers to footnote 39 in chapter 8). Alphabetization is letter-by-letter (e.g., "Newspapers" precedes "New York").*

D

E

F

G

H

I

J

M

Q

R

T

U

Y

Z